The Routledge Handbook of Tourism and Hospitality Education

Tourism is much more than an economic sector, it is also a social, cultural, political and environmental force that drives societal change. Understanding, responding to and managing this change will inevitably require knowledge workers who are able to address a range of problems associated with tourism, travel, hospitality and the increasingly complex operating environment within which they exist.

The purpose of this *Handbook* is to provide an insightful and authoritative account of the various issues that are shaping the higher educational world of tourism, hospitality and events education and to highlight the creative, inventive and innovative ways that educators are responding to these issues. It takes as its central focus a dynamic curriculum space shaped by internal and external factors from global to local scales, a variety of values and perspectives contributed by a range of stakeholders, and shifting philosophies about education policy, pedagogy and teaching practice. A benchmark for future curriculum design and development, it critically reviews the development of conceptual and theoretical approaches to tourism and hospitality education. The *Handbook* is composed of contributions from specialists in the field and is interdisciplinary in coverage and international in scope through its authorship and content.

Providing a systematic guide to the current state of knowledge on tourism and hospitality education and its future direction, this is essential reading for students, researchers and academics in Tourism, Hospitality, Events, Recreation and Leisure Studies.

Dianne Dredge is Professor in the Department of Culture and Global Studies, Aalborg University, Denmark. She has 20 years' experience as a tourism and environmental planner in various locations including Australia, Canada, Mexico and China. Dianne's research focus is on tourism planning, policy and governance with a particular focus on the role of the state, relational and discursive policy development, community participation and capacity building.

David Airey is Professor Emeritus at the University of Surrey. He has been involved in tourism education for 40 years. He began his academic career at Surrey, then spent time with the UK Ministry of Education and with the European Commission before returning to academia in 1993. His research focuses on matters related to education and to tourism policy. In 2006 he received the UNWTO Ulysses Award for his services to tourism education.

Michael J. Gross is a Lecturer with the University of South Australia in Adelaide. His research and publishing focus are on hospitality management and tourism management areas, with particular interests in international education, development and internationalization of hospitality firms, China hospitality industry, destination marketing, destination image, lifestyle tourism, consumer involvement and place attachment.

The Routledge Handbook of Tourism and Hospitality Education

Edited by
Dianne Dredge, David Airey
and Michael J. Gross

Routledge
Taylor & Francis Group

LONDON AND NEW YORK

First published 2015
by Routledge
2 Park Square, Milton Park, Abingdon, Oxon OX14 4RN

and by Routledge
711 Third Avenue, New York, NY 10017

Routledge is an imprint of the Taylor & Francis Group, an informa business

British Library Cataloguing in Publication Data
A catalogue record for this book is available from the British Library

Library of Congress Cataloging in Publication Data
The Routledge handbook of tourism and hospitality education /
edited by Dianne Dredge, David Airey, Michael J. Gross.
   pages cm
   Includes bibliographical references and index.
   1. Tourism–Management. 2. Tourism–Planning. I. Dredge, Dianne.
   II. Airey, David. III. Gross, Michael J.
   G155.A1R685 2014
   910.71′1–dc23   2014008100

ISBN: 978-0-415-84205-1 (hbk)
ISBN: 978-0-203-76330-8 (ebk)

Typeset in Bembo and Stone Sans
by Florence Production Ltd, Stoodleigh, Devon, UK

Printed and bound in Great Britain by
TJ International Ltd, Padstow, Cornwall

Contents

Contents

Contents

Figures

Tables

Contributors

David Airey is Professor Emeritus at the University of Surrey. He has been involved in tourism education for 40 years. He began his academic career at Surrey, then spent time with the UK Ministry of Education and with the European Commission before returning to academia in 1993. During his time at Surrey he has been head of School and Pro-Vice Chancellor, responsible for teaching and learning. He retired from his full-time post in 2009 and now continues at Surrey on a part-time basis. He currently holds a number of visiting professorships and fellowships and is involved in a range of projects. His research focuses on matters related to education and to tourism policy. In 2006 he received the UNWTO Ulysses Award for his services to tourism education.

John S. Akama received his PhD training in geography from Southern Illinois University and he is a founder member of tourism training at Moi University, Kenya. For many years, he taught both undergraduate and postgraduate tourism courses at Moi University and also participated in curriculum review and development. Professor Akama has undertaken extensive research in tourism policy and planning, destination management, sustainable tourism and curriculum development and has widely published in a number of journals and books. In 2009, he moved to Kisii University, where he now serves as Vice-Chancellor.

Maureen Ayikoru is a Senior Lecturer in Tourism Management at Anglia Ruskin University in the UK, having previously been at Middlesex University in London. Maureen graduated with a PhD in tourism from the University of Surrey in 2008, where she researched about the ideological influences in tourism in higher education in England. Her thesis examined the role of higher education policies and other authoritative texts in constructing and reshaping institutional practices in higher education and the ensuing implications. Maureen's research interests are in sustainable development and tourism in developing countries (Sub-Saharan Africa), higher education policies and theoretical/methodological issues in social (tourism) research.

Paul Barron is Reader in the School of Marketing, Tourism and Languages, Edinburgh Napier University. After an initial career in hospitality management, Paul commenced his academic career at Glasgow Caledonian University, during which time he completed an MSc in Human Resource Management at the University of Strathclyde. Paul then spent 11 years as Senior Lecturer at the University of Queensland, Australia, and gained a PhD which examined international students' educational experiences in Australian universities. Paul has authored over 50 articles in the fields of hospitality and tourism and served as Executive Editor of the *Journal of Hospitality and Tourism Management* for six years. Paul is currently Hospitality Subject Editor for the *Journal of Hospitality, Leisure, Sport and Tourism Education*.

Pierre Benckendorff is a Senior Lecturer and social scientist in the School of Business, the University of Queensland, Australia. He has more than 10 years of experience in education and research in the tourism field in Australia and internationally. Previous and current experience includes teaching and development of undergraduate and postgraduate curricula in introductory tourism management, tourist behaviour, international tourism, tourism transportation, tourism technologies, tourism futures and tourism analysis. Pierre has received a number of teaching and learning grants, awards and commendations including a national Carrick Citation for Outstanding Contributions to Student Learning. His research interests include consumer behaviour, the impact of new technologies on tourism, tourism education and tourism scholarship and epistemology.

Mads Bødker is an Associate Professor at the Copenhagen Business School, Department of IT Management. His primary interests lie in the fields of human–computer interaction (HCI) and interaction design. Focusing on the domain of tourism, his current research challenges dominant assumptions within IT, HCI and technical work previously applied to tourism by focusing on experiential, affective and sensory perspectives. Inspired by human geography and phenomenology, his work emphasizes the understanding of tourist places as performances, and aims to inspire and derive implications for design of mobile IT services from place-oriented research methods.

Caryl Bosman is a Senior Lecturer in Urban and Environmental Planning in the Griffith School of Environment and a member of the Urban Research Program, Griffith University, Australia. She holds a PhD in Urban Planning, a Bachelor of Architecture and a National Diploma in Architecture. Caryl has worked in architectural practices in South Africa, London and Australia and taught in both architectural and planning degree programmes. Her current research interests focus on urban histories, urban design and suburban landscapes. Caryl has a special interest in studio pedagogy, planning for ideals of community, active adult lifestyle communities and placemaking discourses in tourist cities.

David Botterill is a freelance academic and higher education consultant, Visiting Research Fellow at the Centre for Tourism at the University of Westminster, London, Professor Emeritus in the Welsh Centre for Tourism Research, Cardiff Metropolitan University and Fellow of the Association for Tourism in Higher Education. He holds a Visiting Professorship at the Breda University of Applied Sciences, the Netherlands, and was a visiting scholar at James Cook University, Australia, in 2011, and the State University of Campinas (UNICAMP), Brazil, in 2012. Recent publications include: *Tourism and Crime: Key Issues* (2010) with Trevor Jones, *Key Concepts in Tourism Research* (2012) with Vincent Platenkamp and *Medical Tourism and Transnational Healthcare* (forthcoming) with Guido Pennings and Tomas Mainil.

Andrea Boyle, originally from England, gained an undergraduate award in law (LLB, Hons). She commenced a career in education as a teacher and designer of teaching material for vocational-related tourism subjects at a further education institute in northern New South Wales. For many years Andrea has been a lecturer for a range of subjects in the School of Tourism and Hospitality Management at Southern Cross University, Lismore, Australia. This included the role of unit coordinator for first-year core undergraduate units/subjects as well as Coordinator of the Work Integrated Learning final year Internship programme. Having completed the Graduate Certificate in Higher Education (Learning & Teaching) at SCU, she is now undertaking a PhD exploring education for sustainability within tourism higher education.

Noreen M. Breakey joined the University of Queensland in 2005 in the hotel/hospitality management stream. Noreen has a wealth of industry experience, having worked in hotels, resorts, tour operations, travel agencies, events, and government in Australia and overseas. Over the past nine years, Noreen has occupied various teaching-related service roles, including the First Year Experience Coordinator, and the Undergraduate Program Director, and she is currently the Acting Program Director for Postgraduate Programs. Noreen has developed an international reputation for her research on tourism and hospitality education, provides advice on Academic Boards, and has been awarded for her teaching initiatives.

Matthew L. Brenner is a Research Assistant and PhD candidate with the University of Queensland Business School, Australia. With an academic background in accounting, he completed a Master of Science in Hotel, Restaurant and Institutional Management from Pennsylvania State University, USA, where he was subsequently engaged as an Instructor with the School of Hospitality Management from 2001 to 2006. Matthew is published in the foodservice management field and has also held culinary and foodservice management positions in hotels, resorts, restaurants and private clubs throughout Australia, Canada and the United States.

Carl Cater is a Senior Lecturer in tourism at Aberystwyth University, Wales, and his research centres on the experiential turn in tourism and the subsequent growth of special interest sectors, particularly adventure tourism and ecotourism. He has undertaken field research, supervision and teaching worldwide, including Australia, China, Malta, Nepal, New Zealand, Norway, Papua New Guinea, Tibet and Vanuatu. He has worked on projects for the Great Barrier Reef Marine Park Authority, New South Wales Department of Education, the World Tourism and Travel Council, Gold Coast City Council, the Gold Coast Adventure Travel Group, Tourism Queensland and the Tourism Society. He is a fellow of the Royal Geographical Society, a qualified pilot, diver, lifesaver, mountain and tropical forest leader, and maintains an interest in both the practice and pursuit of sustainable outdoor tourism activity. He has written over 20 papers and book chapters, is co-author (with Erlet Cater) of *Marine Ecotourism: Between the Devil and the Deep Blue Sea* (2007), and is an editorial board member of *Tourism Geographies, Journal of Ecotourism and Tourism in Marine Environments*.

Kellee Caton is Associate Professor of Tourism Studies at Thompson Rivers University, Canada. She received her PhD from the University of Illinois Urbana-Champaign in 2008. Her research interests include humanism in tourism, morality and ethics, consumer culture, the role of tourism in ideological production, the lived experience of tourism and its role in human development and epistemological and pedagogical issues in tourism. She sits on the editorial board of *Annals of Tourism Research* and the executive committee of the Tourism Educational Futures Initiative, as well as the scientific committee of the Critical Tourism Studies conference series. She also serves as chair of the university-wide curriculum committee of Thompson Rivers University.

Michele Day worked at Southern Cross University, Australia, from 1995 to 2013. Before joining the School of Tourism and Hospitality Management, Michele worked as a solicitor, specializing in professional negligence. Her teaching has covered business law, industrial relations, business ethics and human resource management. Research interests include workplace issues, with an emphasis on the commitment of casual hospitality employees in the hotel industry, and teaching and learning matters including student experience and future delivery options. Michele has also held a number of administrative roles relating to teaching and learning.

Theo de Haan is interested in the playing field – destinations – where tourism business, people and tourists meet. He is course leader of NHTV's ITMC International Tourism Management Studies English-taught Bachelor course (500 students) in the Netherlands. This 'liberal' study connects reflection and knowledge with practice in one-month fieldwork exercises, placements and independent research resulting in 'understanding' destinations. He enjoys working with NHTV's international Master students TDM Tourism Destination Management in Australasia in a three-month field research project that adds to the experience and knowledge of students and lecturers and builds incomparable high value relations with the complex reality that tourism is part of.

Kay Dimmock teaches and researches within the School of Tourism and Hospitality Management at Southern Cross University, Australia. During her career Kay has taught in subject areas from business management and strategy to leisure and marine-based tourism. She has published in peer-reviewed journals, and individually and collaboratively written book chapters and contributed to technical reports. Her PhD developed a conceptual model applicable to adventure leisure and marine tourism experiences. Kay has guest edited a special edition of the journal *Tourism in Marine Environments* and supervised student research programmes on interpretive signage in national parks, and tourism managers' adaptation approaches to climate change. She has written the School's first marine-based tourism unit for undergraduate studies and works with several postgraduate students on their doctoral programmes.

Dianne Dredge is Professor in the Department of Culture and Global Studies, Aalborg University, Denmark. She has 20 years' experience as a tourism and environmental planner in various locations including Australia, Canada, Mexico and China. Dianne's research focus is on tourism planning, policy and governance with a particular focus on the role of the state, relational and discursive policy development, community participation and capacity building. She also undertakes research in higher education policy, teaching and learning. Dianne won an Australian National Carrick Citation for Outstanding Contributions to Student Learning in 2007, and was Chief Investigator on the national project 'Building a Stronger Future: balancing professional and liberal education ideals in tourism and hospitality education'.

Johan R. Edelheim is Professor and Director of the Multidimensional Tourism Institute (MTI), a position incorporating Dean for Tourism Studies at the University of Lapland, Department Head for Hospitality Studies at Rovaniemi University of Applied Sciences and Principal of Lapland Tourism College. Johan is also a visiting professor at Taylor's University in Malaysia. His working career started in the tourism and hospitality industries and evolved later to education in both vocational and higher education institutions. Johan has diplomas and degrees in such diverse disciplines as hospitality, business, education, philosophy and cultural studies. He took on his current role as director of MTI in August 2011, after 12 years at different Australian institutions. Behind most of Johan's research lies a deeply rooted belief in humanism and equality. Johan received an award for outstanding research at the Council of Australasian Tourism and Hospitality Education (CAUTHE) annual conference 2010, and has received several awards for his teaching, for example he was elected Lecturer of the Year 2011 – Australian winner.

Daniel R. Fesenmaier is Professor at the University of Florida. Also, he is Founding Director and Past Co-Chair of the Tourism Education Futures Initiative (TEFI); Fellow, the International Academy for the Study of Tourism; Visiting Fellow at the Institute for Innovation in Business and Social Research (IIBSoR) University of Wollongong, Australia, and Visiting Professor, Modul University, Vienna. Dr Fesenmaier is author of articles dealing with tourism marketing, advertising evaluation and information technology. He has co-authored a monograph and co-edited five books focusing on various aspects of tourism marketing and development and is co-founding editor of *Tourism Analysis* and was Editor-in-Chief, *Journal of Information Technology and Tourism*. Currently, he is editor of the Foundations in Tourism Research Series in the *Journal of Travel Research*.

José-Carlos García-Rosell is a researcher and educator at the University of Lapland, Multidimensional Tourism Institute (MTI). His current research and teaching interests are in the areas of sustainable business, corporate social responsibility, stakeholder theory, business ethics, tourism product development and action research. He obtained an MSc in Agricultural Economics from the University of Natural Resources and Life Sciences in Vienna, Austria, a Lic.Sc. in Marketing from the University of Oulu and a PhD in Management from the University of Lapland in Finland. His doctoral dissertation addresses the relevance of a multi-stakeholder perspective on sustainable marketing.

Donald Getz retired in July 2009 from his full-time academic position at the University of Calgary, Canada, where he remains Professor Emeritus. He held a 50 per cent position as Professor in the School of Tourism, the University of Queensland, until March 2014. He is a Visiting Professor at several other universities. Professor Getz is a leading international proponent of event studies, drawing from his extensive research, volunteering, teaching and consulting experience in many countries. His book, *Event Studies*, defines the field of study, establishes the theoretical and policy framework, and provides a detailed reference work on related research. He is also active in researching a variety of special-interest market segments, including food and wine tourism, culture and sports. His latest book, *Event Tourism*, was published in early 2013. Donald received a BES from the University of Waterloo and an MA from Carleton University, in Canada, and a PhD from the University of Edinburgh, Scotland.

Michael J. Gross is a Lecturer with the University of South Australia in Adelaide. Michael holds a Bachelor of Science in Business Administration (BSBA) with a major in Hotel and Restaurant Management from the University of Denver, USA, Masters degrees in Education (MPET) and Business (MBA) from Deakin University, Australia, and a PhD from the University of South Australia. He has an extensive professional background in international hospitality management with some of the world's leading hotel firms. He currently teaches in hospitality and tourism programmes at the undergraduate and postgraduate levels. His research and publishing focus are on hospitality management and tourism management areas, with particular interests in international education, development and internationalization of hospitality firms, China hospitality industry, destination marketing, destination image, lifestyle tourism, consumer involvement, and place attachment.

Basagaitz Guereño-Omil is a Senior Lecturer and researcher in the Tourism department at the University of Deusto in Spain. She has worked on many European-funded research projects and is currently leading the Mobility and Employability Research for Generation Erasmus (MERGE) project.

Roger Haden is an educator and author and in his role as Manager, Educational Leadership with Le Cordon Bleu, helps develop higher education programmes, including its Master of

Gastronomic Tourism. Roger spent six years teaching in and at different times managing the Graduate Program in Gastronomy at the University of Adelaide, and has an abiding research interest in gustatory taste and the aesthetics of dining. He is author of *Food Culture in the Pacific Islands* and his most recent publication is 'Lionizing Taste: Towards an Ecology of Contemporary Connoisseurship', which appears in *Educated Taste: Food Drink and Connoisseur Culture* (Jeremy Strong (ed.), 2011).

Kevin Hannam is Professor of Tourism Mobilities in the International Centre for Research in Events, Tourism & Hospitality (ICRETH), Leeds Metropolitan University, UK. He is editor (with Mimi Sheller and John Urry) of the journal *Mobilities*.

Robert J. Harrington is the 21st Century Endowed Chair in Hospitality Management at the University of Arkansas, USA. He was previously Associate Professor in the School of Hospitality & Tourism Management at the University of Guelph, Canada. His past academic responsibilities include serving as Dean and Professor at Nicholls State University, USA, and he has taught at Washington State University, the University Center César Ritz (Brig, Switzerland), and the Institut Paul Bocuse, (Lyon, France). He received the 2007 Journal of Hospitality & Tourism Research Article of the Year Award, the 2007 Champion of Education Award by the Canadian Association of Foodservice Professionals, and was the 2004 recipient of the International CHRIE Breithaupt Award for outstanding achievement. Since 2011, he has been the editor of the *Journal of Culinary Science and Technology*.

David Harrison has been Professor of Tourism in the School of Tourism and Hospitality Management at the University of the South Pacific since early 2008. A sociologist/anthropologist, he is author of *The Sociology of Modernization and Development* (1988), editor of numerous books on tourism, including *Pacific Island Tourism* (2003), and author of many journal articles. On the editorial board of several major tourism journals, he is primarily interested in the economic and socio-cultural impacts of tourism in developing societies, especially small island states, and has written on and carried out consultancy in the Caribbean, Southeast Asia, Eastern Europe, Southern Africa and the South Pacific.

Cathy H. C. Hsu is a Professor in the School of Hotel and Tourism Management at the Hong Kong Polytechnic University (PolyU). Prior to joining PolyU in July 2001, she taught in the USA for 12 years in two different state universities. She has been the Editor-in-Chief of the *Journal of Teaching in Travel and Tourism* for more than a decade and is the editor of the book, *Global Tourism Higher Education: Past, Present, and Future* (2005). She received the John Wiley & Sons Lifetime Research Achievement Award in 2009 and International Society of Travel and Tourism Educator's Martin Oppermann Memorial Award for Lifetime Contribution to Tourism Education in 2011.

Rong Huang is an Associate Professor in Tourism Marketing at Plymouth University in the UK. She is a Senior Fellow of the UK's Higher Education Academy. Her research interests focus on aspects of the tourism phenomenon, for example tourism education, international student experience, internationalization, and new academics. The subjects of her recent publications include information communication technology (ICT) and tourism curriculum, the effective use of field trips in postgraduate tourism and hospitality education, the experience of new academics, and also international experience and graduate employability.

Annica Isacsson is a Principal Lecturer at HAAGA-HELIA University of Applied Sciences, Finland. Annica has been involved in tourism for about 20 years: she has managed her own tourism company, designed, managed and implemented a tourism Bachelor-level degree curriculum, developed and managed a number of tourism-related projects and programmes, published tourism-related articles and actively integrated research and development projects into tourism implementations and teaching. Since 2013 Annica has worked as the Research Manager at HAAGA-HELIA School of Vocational Teacher Education.

Adele Ladkin is Professor of Tourism Employment in the School of Tourism, Bournemouth University, UK. She gained her PhD at the University of Surrey. Her research interests and publications are in tourism employment and education, human resources, labour migration and labour issues in the tourism, hospitality and conference industries. This includes the role of education in developing human capital for tourism workers. She was joint Editor in Chief for the *International Journal of Tourism Research* from 2003 to 2009, and she serves on the Editorial Board for a number of journals including *Annals of Tourism Research*, *Tourism Economics*, and *ACTA Turistica*.

Conrad Lashley is Lead Researcher at the School of International Hospitality Management at Stenden University of Applied Sciences, in Leeuwarden, the Netherlands. He is also Visiting Professor at Oxford Brookes University and the University of Derby in the UK as well as a host of other universities in Britain, Europe and Australia. He is editor of the Taylor and Francis list of hospitality, tourism and leisure series, and Editor Emeritus of the journal *Hospitality & Society* and a former editor of *Hospitality Review*. He has authored, co-authored, edited, or co-edited 15 books as well as many papers in journals and industry publications. His research involves several key themes including hospitality and hospitableness, empowerment and the impact of training on competitive advantage. He works closely with industry practitioners and has undertaken an array of commercial research projects.

Janne J. Liburd is Associate Professor and Director of the Centre for Tourism, Innovation and Culture at the University of Southern Denmark. She is a cultural anthropologist and her research interests are in the fields of higher education, innovation and sustainable tourism development. She has published on epistemology, open innovation and Web 2.0, tourism education, quality of life, national park development, heritage tourism, tourism crisis communication, non-governmental organizations and accountability. Dr Liburd's Doctoral Dissertation (2013) is entitled 'Towards the Collaborative University. Lessons from Tourism Education and Research'. She has conducted a number of research projects relating to competence development for tourism practitioners. She is the co-founder of the European Master in Tourism Management and the INNOTOUR platform, and serves on several editorial boards. Dr Liburd is the past Chair of the BEST Education Network (2005–10).

Robert Maitland is an urban economist whose work focuses on how tourism shapes cities and cities shape tourism. Professor Maitland's current research centres on tourism and everyday life, new tourist areas in London, tourism in world cities and national capitals, and social tourism. He is past Chair of the Association for Tourism in Higher Education, the subject association for tourism in the UK, and Co-Chair of the international ATLAS City Tourism and National Capitals Research Group. He recently led an ESRC-funded International Seminar Series on Social Tourism and Regeneration, and recent books include *World Tourism Cities*, *Tourism in National Capitals* and *Global Change and Social Tourism*.

Melphon A. Makaya is former founding Chair of the Department of Tourism Management, School of Hospitality and Tourism at Kenyatta University, Nairobi, Kenya. He has also taught at Moi University and worked in the Kenyan tourism industry. His research interests are in tourism training and education as well as tourism development in less developed countries. Currently, he is pursuing doctoral studies in Business and Economics, focusing on community involvement in tourism at Monash University, Australia.

Gianna Moscardo has qualifications in applied psychology and sociology and joined the School of Business at James Cook University, Australia, in 2002. Prior to joining JCU, Gianna was the Tourism Research project leader for the CRC Reef Research for eight years. Her research interests include understanding how consumers, especially tourists, make decisions and evaluate their experiences, and how communities and organizations perceive, plan for, and manage tourism development opportunities. She has published extensively on tourism and related areas with more than 170 refereed papers or book chapters.

Ana María Munar is Associate Professor at the Department of International Economics and Management, Copenhagen Business School, Denmark. She holds an MSc in Political Science and a PhD in Business and Economics. Her research interests are tourism and information and communication technologies, globalization processes, destination branding, and policy and trends in tourism education. Her latest work provides insights on the impact that Web 2.0 and social media technologies have on tourism. Her articles examine the role of digital mediation on cultural change and social reproduction. She is a board member of Imagine. Creative Industries Research Center and a member of the Center for Leisure and Culture Services at Copenhagen Business School.

Barry O'Mahony is Professor of Services Management and Chair of the Department of Marketing, Tourism and Social Impact at Swinburne University of Technology, Australia. Barry has taught undergraduate, postgraduate and doctoral courses in Australia, Ireland, Hong Kong, Malaysia and the United States and has developed and delivered undergraduate and postgraduate programmes in hospitality and tourism. He has served on higher education programme accreditation panels for the Victorian and New Zealand governments, is a company director of the accrediting body the International Centre of Excellence in Tourism and Hospitality Education, and a member of the academic boards of Le Cordon Bleu and William Angliss Institute.

Michael C. Ottenbacher is Professor in Hospitality Management and Marketing at Heilbronn University, Germany. Prior to joining Heilbronn University, he was teaching at San Diego State University, USA, University of Guelph, Canada, and University of Surrey, UK. In addition to academia, he has extensive business experience. He worked in senior hospitality positions in the USA, UK, France and Germany. He currently holds visiting professorships at the Institute Paul Bocuse in France and Taylor's University in Malaysia. He sits on the editorial boards of a number of journals, and has been the co-editor of the *Journal of Hospitality and Tourism Education* since August 2012.

Harald Pechlaner holds a Chair in Tourism and is Director of the Center for Entrepreneurship at the Catholic University of Eichstätt-Ingolstadt (Germany), and Scientific Director of the Institute for Regional Development and Location Management at the European Academy of Bozen/Bolzano (EURAC research), Italy. He is also a board member of AIEST (Association

Internationale d'Experts Scientifiques du Tourisme) and was president of DGT (Deutsche Gesellschaft für Tourismuswissenschaft, 2002–12) and ICRET (International Center of Research and Education in Tourism, 2000–10). His main areas of expertise include destination governance, resort and location management, as well as entrepreneurship.

Petia Petrova is Academic Practice Advisor at the University of Birmingham. She has a longstanding interest in the value of education, professional development and employability. Her past research has focused on tourism students' career expectations and aspiration, and tourism employers' perceptions of tourism degrees and graduates. She has an enduring commitment to the employability of graduates and has held an Employability Fellow role within the University of Bedfordshire, building links and supporting students in securing placements and employment opportunities.

Vincent Platenkamp is Associate Professor in the field of cross-cultural understanding and is doing research into cross-cultural competencies in the context of an international classroom, into transnational healthcare and culturalism and in the relations between politics and tourism in politically unstable regions like the Middle East. His main approach is to generate hidden knowledge, for example in international classrooms or in city districts, and to put this knowledge on the agenda of relevant discussions in the field. Apart from this, he is involved in the same type of international tourism education at NHTV as his colleagues Theo de Haan and Ariane Portegies.

Ariane Portegies is Senior Lecturer in destination development studies at NHTV University of Applied Sciences in the Netherlands. She was always involved in curriculum innovation, alongside teaching courses in the field of marketing, cross-cultural studies, and international political and economic relations. She is currently engaging in the study of imaginaries and realities through the use of visuals, arts and film, both in teaching and research.

F. Allen Powell is an Instructor in the School of Human Environmental Sciences at the University of Arkansas at Fayetteville. He holds a Master of Science in Business and Human Relations from Amberton University in Dallas, Texas. Currently, he is working on a PhD from Oklahoma State University. He is working with undergraduate honours students researching Generation Y perspectives of pricing and packaging of Arkansas wines. Other research interests include organizational behaviour in the restaurant industry, distance education, and community college curriculum design. He has over 25 years' experience in the hospitality industry and 15 years' teaching experience.

Mirian Rejowski graduated in Tourism, has a Master's degree and PhD in Communication Sciences and was a former full professor at the University of São Paulo (Brazil). She is Professor at the University Anhembi Morumbi (São Paulo) and teaches in the Tourism and Hospitality programme for undergraduate and graduate degrees. She is former editor of the *Tourism Analysis Journal* and former president of the National Association for Research and Graduate Studies in Tourism (ANPTUR). Her themes of study and research are the production and scientific communication, and higher education in Tourism and Hospitality. She leads a Research Group and is a fellow of CNPq productivity (National Research Council). She won the Tourism Researcher Award in 2010 granted by the National Association for Research and Graduate Studies in Tourism (ANPTUR).

Jarmo Ritalahti is a Principal Lecturer at HAAGA-HELIA University of Applied Sciences, Porvoo unit, Finland. He has been involved in tourism programmes for almost 20 years by designing and implementing college and Bachelor-level tourism curricula and through managing tourism educational programmes and projects in the area of sustainability, regional development, intermediation and quality of life. Jarmo is a member of many international tourism networks and is co-author of a book on development work methods.

Richard N. S. Robinson joined the University of Queensland in 2005, after an extended career as a chef, predominantly managing private club/heritage facility sector foodservice operations. Since then he has taught a suite of hospitality/tourism management classes and supervised several higher degree research students. He has coordinated and worked in research teams for funded national and international projects on tourism workforce issues and food tourism, and pursues the scholarship of teaching and learning. Richard's work in these areas is disseminated through leading academic journals, edited books, industry periodicals and conferences. He has also received university, national and international awards for his teaching and research.

Gilly Salmon is one of the world's leading thinkers in online learning. She researches and publishes widely on the themes of innovation and change in higher education and the exploitation of new technologies of all kinds in the service of learning. She is internationally renowned for her significant contributions to online education, including research, innovation, programme design, teaching methods and the use of new technologies. Currently Pro Vice-Chancellor, Learning Transformations, at Swinburne University of Technology, she was previously Executive Director and Professor (Learning Futures) at the Australian Digital Futures Institute, Australia, and Professor of E-learning and Learning Technologies, and Head of the Beyond Distance Research Alliance and the Media Zoo, at the University of Leicester in the UK.

Kurt Seemann is an Associate Professor and Director of the National Institute for Design Research (NIDR) at Swinburne University of Technology, Australia. He has contributed to the scholarship of technology and design in tourism and hospitality with work in the areas of cultural tourism, heritage tourism, tourism facility and technology management, and as Director of Research and Higher Degree Research Training in the School of Tourism and Hospitality Management at Southern Cross University, Australia. Dr Seemann was appointed as 'Thinker On-hand/Thinker Online' to the state board of the Design and Technology Teachers Association (DATTA) of Victoria. He is currently the International Representative elect on the national board of DATTA Australia.

Richard Sharpley is Professor of Tourism and Development at the University of Central Lancashire, Preston, UK. He has previously held positions at a number of other institutions, including the University of Northumbria (Reader in Tourism) and the University of Lincoln, where he was professor of Tourism and Head of Department, Tourism and Recreation Management. His principal research interests are within the fields of tourism and development, island tourism, rural tourism and the sociology of tourism. He has published numerous journal articles on these subjects and his books include *Tourism and Development in the Developing World* (2008), *Tourism, Tourists and Society* (4th edition, 2008), *Tourism, Development and Environment: Beyond Sustainability* (2009) and *The Study of Tourism: Past Trends and Future Directions* (2011).

Pauline J. Sheldon is Professor Emerita at the University of Hawaii's School of Travel Industry Management, where she served as Interim Dean, and currently specializes in corporate social responsibility, sustainable tourism, wellness tourism and knowledge management in tourism. She holds a PhD in Economics, a Master's in Business Administration, and a Bachelor's degree in Mathematics. She is Chair of the Board and Past President of the International Academy for the Study of Tourism. In 2008 she received the UNWTO Ulysses prize for her contributions to knowledge in sustainable tourism. In 2009 she was recognized with the International Travel and Tourism Research Association Lifetime Achievement Award. She co-founded the Tourism Education Futures Initiative (TEFI); and chaired the BEST Education Network. She also co-founded TRINET (Tourism Research Information Network) and has worked with the United Nations World Tourism Organization, APEC International Center for Sustainable Tourism, and the World Bank.

Marianna Sigala is Associate Professor at the University of the Aegean, Greece. Before joining the University of the Aegean, she had been lecturing at the universities of Strathclyde and Westminster in the UK. Her interests include service management, Information and Communication Technologies (ICT) in tourism and hospitality, and e-learning. She has professional experience from the Greek hospitality industry and contributed to several international research projects. Her work has been published in several academic journals, books and international conferences. She is currently the editor of the journal *Managing Service Quality* and the *Journal of Hospitality & Tourism Cases*. She is a past President of EuroCHRIE and has served on the Board of Directors of I-CHRIE, IFITT and HeAIS.

Roberta Leme Sogayar graduated in Tourism, Specialist on Environmental Education (State University of São Paulo), Master in Tourism, Parks and Recreation Administration (Western Illinois University, USA), Master in Hospitality from University Anhembi Morumbi (São Paulo). She is a full-time teacher at University Anhembi Morumbi within the programmes of Tourism, Hotel Management and Events. She has won an award of Academic Excellence from the university and the David Wilson Award on research granted from Laureate International Universities. She has also been an external consultant for the Ministry of Education since 2010, evaluating Tourism and Hospitality degrees throughout the country. She is an active member of the Tourism Education Future Initiatives (TEFI) and her main research interests are focused on tourism higher education development and the changing paradigms that affect the field.

Yahui Su is an Associate Professor at the Teacher Education Centre at the National Kaohsiung University of Hospitality and Tourism (NKUHT) in Taiwan. Her main interests include lifelong learning, tourism education and curriculum, and student employability. Yahui was the Section Chief of Curriculum at the Teacher Education Centre (2008–9) and the Section Chief of Career Placement in the Office of Research and Development (2010–12), NKUHT. She has tutored tourism students and has taught practicum courses in the Department of Travel Management. Yahui's current research project seeks to develop the competence of university students to promote their employability with the concept of self-directed and lifelong learning as a framework.

Mandy Talbot is a PhD candidate and lecturer at the School of Management and Business at Aberystwyth University in the UK. Her research interests include: farm-based tourism, livelihood diversification, international tourism development and tourism education. She is particularly interested in the use of IT and student-led learning in the classroom.

John Tribe is Head of Tourism and Professor at the University of Surrey, UK. His undergraduate, postgraduate and doctoral studies were all undertaken at the University of London, the latter at the Institute of Education. He is a Fellow of the Higher Education Academy, Fellow of the International Academy for the Study of Tourism, Fellow of the Association for Tourism in Higher Education and Academician of the Academy of the Social Sciences. His research concentrates on sustainability, epistemology and education and he has authored books on strategy, philosophy, economics, education and environmental management in tourism. He was the specialist adviser for tourism for the UK government's 2008 Research Assessment Exercise (RAE) and is a member of sub-panel 26 for the 2014 Research Excellence Framework (REF). He is editor of *Annals of Tourism Research* and the *Journal of Hospitality, Leisure Sport and Tourism Education.*

Tony S. M. Tse is Assistant Professor and Programme Director (Industry Partnerships) at the Hong Kong Polytechnic University's (PolyU) School of Hotel and Tourism Management. Tony holds a Bachelor of Social Science from the University of Hong Kong, MBA from Macquarie University and PhD from Southern Cross University, Australia. He has an extensive professional background in marketing, and currently teaches in hospitality and tourism programmes at the undergraduate and postgraduate levels. Tony has been involved in the planning and development of PolyU's teaching hotel since its inception. The hotel started operations in April 2011, and has since played a unique role in serving the educational needs of the School and its 2,200 students. Tony has a special interest in tracking the fulfilment of the hotel's educational role as part of its commitment to the community and as a laboratory for hospitality research.

Michael Volgger is a researcher at the Institute for Regional Development and Location Management at the European Academy of Bozen/Bolzano (EURAC research), Italy, and doctoral student at the Catholic University of Eichstätt-Ingolstadt, Germany. His main areas of expertise include destination governance and location management, innovation, and cooperation in tourism.

Maree Walo has been a member of the School of Tourism and Hospitality Management at Southern Cross University, Australia, since 1994. She has approximately 15 years' experience in hospitality in a variety of management positions. Maree has had key leadership roles within the School and has extensive experience with curriculum development and course coordination. As part of a teaching team, Maree was a recipient of an Australian Learning and Teaching Council Citation for Outstanding Contributions to Student Learning (2011) and has received a number of institutional teaching awards. Maree's research interests include tourism and hospitality higher education with particular focus on issues in curriculum design and development.

Paul Weeks is currently Director of Academic Studies at the Hotel School Sydney. He joined Southern Cross University's School of Tourism & Hospitality Management in 1991 after 20 years' managerial experience in hotel, motel and food service organizations. Previous and current experience includes instructional design for subjects offered through the School's distance education programmes, development of curricula for management and technology subjects, services management and information technology. He has co-authored two Australian texts: *Club Management,* and *Managing Convention Businesses.* Research interests include IT in hospitality; education (the role of feedback; technology use by students within private education providers); convention services, and club management. Paul received an inaugural Vice Chancellor's award for Teaching Excellence and two subsequent VC's Teaching Awards as a member of two teaching teams.

Paul A. Whitelaw is Associate Director of Higher Education and Quality at William Angliss Institute, Melbourne and is Immediate Past Chair of the Council of Australasian University Tourism and Hospitality Educators (CAUTHE). He received the VC's Award for Teaching Excellence in 2001. Paul co-chaired the University's Task Force into Student Transition and Attrition in 2002. Paul has been a senior investigator in several projects worth more than $250,000 in total for the Sustainable Tourism Cooperative Research Centre, and more than $600,000 in Carrick/ALTC/OLT funded projects. He has published in the areas of the development and deployment of digital supported pedagogies. In 2007 Paul led the highly successful Academic Literacy Project at VU, he also holds academic service positions, including journal editorial board membership.

Erica Wilson is Senior Lecturer in the School of Tourism and Hospitality Management at Southern Cross University in Lismore, Australia. Erica holds a PhD on women's solo travel constraints, a postgraduate diploma in Environmental Studies, and a first-class honours degree in Tourism Administration. Currently, Erica is particularly interested in critical approaches to the study and teaching of tourism/leisure. She is also the Associate Editor and Reviews Editor for the *Annals of Leisure Research*. Erica's research publications and conference papers have focused on women's travel and leisure, leisure constraints/negotiation, sustainable tourism and tourism in protected areas, critical pedagogy and reflexive/qualitative/feminist research methodologies.

Preface

There is no doubt that the global higher education sector is undergoing seismic transcendental change. Moreover, there is no blueprint for this recasting of higher education and no holy grail at the end of all this change. It's an ongoing project where globalization, neoliberal management policies and practices, increased mobility and competition mean that restructuring and reform are constant. Access to and participation in higher education are now recognized as fundamental to improving economic performance and, by corollary, community well-being. Massive investment in higher education is taking place in a range of developing countries and the hegemony of the developed countries will be increasingly challenged.

The global higher education environment, and within this tourism, hospitality and events (TH&E) education, will be remarkably different in five, 10 or 20 years' time. Although time-lines differ from nation to nation, as a relatively new area of teaching and research, TH&E education expanded rapidly in the 1980s and 1990s within the expanding higher education systems and off the back of massive growth in tourism and hospitality service sectors. Vocationalism stood at the centre of the early provision but as the subject areas expanded and matured, as new academics entered the field and as new research extended the knowledge base so other concerns of educators became more prominent, captured by Tribe's idea of the Philosophic Practitioner.

The past decade or so has witnessed something of a battle between the burgeoning neoliberalism of the higher education environment and the broader more philosophical goals of the educators for TH&E. This battle provides a kind of leitmotif for this book. In essence the book provides an account of the various ways in which the educators in TH&E have understood, responded to and dealt with the twin pressures of providing a rigorous, challenging and life-changing education for their students while at the same time dealing with an environment of institutional rivalry and competition, accountability and constant change, which are all a part of the modern university. The chapters of this *Handbook* illustrate that the environment has not stood in the way of adventurous and exciting developments in education for TH&E. Above all, the authors, all of them educators in this field, clearly show, time and again, that TH&E provides a stimulating and highly suitable setting for a twenty-first-century education. In doing so they provide examples of how to proceed in this challenging world as well as pointers to meeting the challenges that future change will bring.

We note that this *Handbook* title includes the terms 'tourism and hospitality', and was named thus for the purpose of brevity only. We acknowledge that our field includes many other areas such as events, sports, leisure, recreation, travel, and others variously labelled. Our intention in assembling this collection of chapters has been to take an inclusive and welcoming view of such variety, and we hope that readers will see and appreciate this diversity and richness expressed throughout the chapters.

Acknowledgements

We would like to thank the global community of tourism, hospitality and events educators whose support and collegiality were, and continue to be, an unending source of inspiration. In particular, we would like to acknowledge the chapter authors, unfortunately too many to list here, who demonstrate not only in the pages of this *Handbook* but also in their daily activities as educators, that passion, commitment and creativity are alive and well in the neoliberal university.

The editors would also like to thank the Australian Government Office for Learning and Teaching for their support of the project *Building a stronger future: balancing professional and liberal education ideals in tourism and hospitality education* (CG-1020), which was undertaken between 2009 and 2012. This project provided an initial opportunity for us to work together, but has inspired the deep, ongoing camaraderie and passion we share for the world-making potential of tourism, hospitality and events education.

Finally, we would also like to extend the most heartfelt thank you to Philippa Mullins and the team at Taylor and Francis. Pippa's editorial assistance and professionalism set the benchmark.

Dianne Dredge
David Airey
Michael J. Gross

Abbreviations

AGM	annual general meeting
AITO	Association of Independent Tour Operators
ALSSS	Academy of Learned Societies in the Social Sciences
ANT	actor-network theory
AONE	American Organization of Nurse Executives
APEC	Asia Pacific Economic Cooperation
AQF	Australian Qualifications Framework
AR	action research
ASPH	Association of Schools of Public Health
ATHE	Association for Tourism in Higher Education
ATLAS	Association for Tourism and Leisure Education
BESTEN	Business Enterprises for Sustainable Tourism Education Network
BMIHMS	Blue Mountains International Hotel Management School (Australia)
CAUTHE	Council for Australasian University Tourism and Hospitality Education
CEC	Career Education Corporation
CLI	Composite Learning Index
CNAA	Council for National Academic Awards
CPE	Council for Private Education
CRS	Classroom Response System
CSCW	Computer Supported Collaborative Work
CSR	corporate social responsibility
CTS	Critical Tourism Studies
D.HTM	Doctorate of Hotel and Tourism Management
DCMS	Department of Culture, Media and Sport
EC	Executive Committee
ECPH	Educated Citizen and Public Health
ECTS	European Credit Transfer and Accumulation System
EDB	Economic Development Board
EFD	Education for Sustainable Development
EfS	Education for Sustainability
EHEA	European Higher Education Area
ELLI	European Lifelong Learning Indicators
EMBOK	Event Management Body of Knowledge
EMBRATUR	Empresa Brasileira de Turismo (Brazil)
EMTM	European Master in Tourism Management

Abbreviations

EQF	European Qualifications Framework
ERASMUS	European Community Action Scheme for the Mobility of University Students
ESD	Education for Sustainable Development
ESRC	Economic and Social Research Council
EU	European Union
EURYDICE	Network on Education Systems and Policies in Europe
F&B	food and beverage
FELU	Faculty of Economics, Ljubljana University
FTMS	Financial Training and Management Services
FYE	first-year experience
GDP	gross domestic product
HCI	human–computer interaction
HE	higher education
HEA	Higher Education Academy
HEFCE	Higher Education Funding Council for England
HEI	higher education institute
HESA	Higher Education Statistics Agency
HH	HAAGA-HELIA University of Applied Sciences, Finland
HKCAAVQ	Hong Kong Council for Accreditation of Academic and Vocational Qualifications
HLST	hospitality, leisure, sport and tourism
IAST	International Academy for the Study of Tourism
IAU	International Association of Universities
IBC	International Branch Campus
IC	international classroom
ICHM	International Centre of Hospitality Management (Adelaide, S. Australia)
IIBSoR	Institute for Innovation in Business and Social Research
IOM	Institute of Medicine of the National Academy of Sciences
IPA	importance performance analysis
IT	information technology
ITMC	International Tourism Management Consultancy
IxD	interaction design
IUCN	International Union for Conservation of Nature
JAB	Joint Admissions Board
JACS	Joint Academic Coding System
KCSE	Kenya Certificate of Secondary Examination
KECTOUR	Tourism Knowledge Exchange Centre Network
KUC	Kenya Utalii College
LDB	National Law for Guidelines and Basis for Education (Brazil)
LEAP	Liberal Education and America's Promise
LTSN HLST	Learning and Teaching Subject Network for Hospitality, Leisure, Sport and Tourism
MBECS	Meeting and Business Event Competency Standards
MDG	Millennium Development Goals
MESD	major English-speaking destination
MICE	meetings, incentives, conferences and exhibitions
MIS	management information systems

MOOCs	Massive Online Open Courses
MTI	Multidimensional Tourism Institute
NACNEP	National Advisory Council on Nurse Education and Practice
NGO	non-governmental organization
NKUHT	National Kaohsiung University of Hospitality and Tourism
NLG	National Liaison Group for Tourism in Higher Education
NMIT	Northern Melbourne Institute of TAFE (Australia)
NSS	National Student Survey
OE	overseas experience
OECD	Organization for Economic Cooperation and Development
OFSTED	Office for Standards in Education
OLT	Office for Learning and Teaching
PBL	problem-based learning
PDP	personal development planning
PEI	private education institutions
PISA	Programme for International Student Assessment
PNG	Papua New Guinea
PolyU	The Hong Kong Polytechnic University
PPE	Philosophic Practitioner Education
QAA	Quality Assurance Agency for Higher Education
QF	Qualifications Framework
RAE	Research Assessment Exercise
REF	Research Excellence Framework
RIT	Research Informed Teaching
ROI	return on investment
SDL	service-dominant logic
SDU	University of Southern Denmark
SHTM	School of Hotel and Tourism Management (PolyU)
SINAES	National System of Evaluation of Higher Education (Brazil)
SNA	social network analysis
STHM	School of Tourism and Hospitality Management (USP)
T&H	tourism and hospitality
TAFE	Technical and Further Education
TDM	tourism destination management
TEFI	Tourism Education Futures Initiative
TEQSA	Tertiary Education Quality and Standards Agency
TH&E	tourism, hospitality and events
THE-ICE	The International Centre of Excellence in Tourism & Hospitality Education
TIM	Tourism Intelligence Monitor
TRG	Tomorrow's Guestroom
TRINET	Tourism Research Information Network
UAE	United Arab Emirates
UAS	universities of applied science
UGC	University Grants Committee
UK	United Kingdom
UNDESD	United Nations Decade of Education for Sustainable Development
UNDP	United Nations Development Programme

Abbreviations

UN ESCAP	United Nations Economic and Social Commission for Asia and the Pacific
UNESCO	United Nations Educational, Scientific and Cultural Organization
UNLV	University of Nevada Las Vegas
UNSW	University of New South Wales
UNWTO	United Nations World Tourism Organization
UQST	University of Queensland, School of Tourism
USA	United States of America
USP	University of South Pacific
UX	user-experience
VET	vocational education and training
WIL	work-integrated learning
WTTC	World Travel and Tourism Council

Part I
Introduction to the Handbook

1

Tourism, hospitality and events education in an age of change

David Airey

School of Hospitality and Tourism Management, University of Surrey, UK

Dianne Dredge

Department of Culture and Global Studies, Aalborg University, Denmark

Michael J. Gross

School of Management, University of South Australia, Australia

Introduction

Taken together, tourism, hospitality and events (TH&E) in university education have now had about 40 years of fairly continuous growth and development. During this time they have attracted the attention of a number of researchers and officials who have sought to explain, rationalize, theorize and draw conclusions and predictions about their development. Notably the edited work by Airey and Tribe (2005) brought together some of the thinking at least about the tourism elements of education and more recently a major study in Australia has reviewed the progress, issues and challenges for these subjects (Office for Learning and Teaching, 2012). At the same time, three journals have been established dealing with educational issues for TH&E: the *Journal of Hospitality and Tourism Education, Journal of Hospitality, Leisure, Sport and Tourism Education* and the *Journal of Teaching in Travel and Tourism*. Notwithstanding these developments, the scholarly literature examining curriculum issues or the pressures and changes affecting this important education sector remains relatively limited. At a time of significant change in higher education when the role of universities and of different subject areas is increasingly being questioned, and decisions are being taken to reshape the system of higher education, a review of the issues for TH&E education represents an important addition to the literature. This is the purpose of this book: to provide an insightful and authoritative account of the various issues that are shaping the higher educational world of TH&E.

Perhaps the most important aspect of the background to this *Handbook* is that higher education itself has now entered a period of major change. After a few decades of expansion, higher education sectors in most countries have transitioned from elite to mass providers of programmes with significant implications for the consumption of public resources. Higher education has become increasingly intertwined with national policy goals with institutions expected to deliver on a range of economic and social objectives (e.g. improved education rates, increased accessibility for socio-economic disadvantaged groups, economic innovation) whilst at the same time being increasingly burdened with regulation, static or declining public funding per student and incentive-based funding. These changes have notably prompted a shift towards user-pays funding models in which increasingly students (or their parents) rather than the taxpayer have become responsible for financing education.

Alongside this, universities operate in a much more competitive national and international environment. Here internal and external scrutiny with consequent published rankings of institutions play a pivotal role in attracting students, and new providers, both commercial and from further and vocational education, put added pressure on the existing institutions in what has now become a marketplace. The response to this more competitive environment with less guaranteed public funding and with greater transparency of performance metrics is that institutions are increasingly reviewing and adapting their positions and their provision. Within this, decisions about programmes, about the curriculum and about course delivery all become central to the success and even survival of institutions. And, as an added pressure, while this is taking place, there is evidence that student demand for TH&E programmes in some parts of the world is beginning to falter.

This background suggests it is essential for both academics and university managers to have a better understanding of what they offer and teach and how the environment within which this takes place is changing. For their part the students have the right to understand what is offered by their programmes and the subsequent TH&E career pathways, and employers also have the right to understand degree structures, content and choices, especially when they are employing graduates of these programmes or if they are providing student support and mentoring during students' study.

Aim and objectives

Against this context of rapid and sustained change, the aim of this *Handbook* is to identify and critically examine the challenges for those offering higher education programmes related to tourism, hospitality and events. In achieving this aim, the *Handbook* is guided by the following objectives:

(1) To explore the philosophical foundations of TH&E education, current debates and future directions.
(2) To review and appraise the current state of the art and future development of TH&E within the global higher education context.
(3) To explore empirical knowledge and accounts of reflective practice in TH&E education with particular focus on the curriculum space.
(4) To provide empirical knowledge and stories of reflective practice about TH&E curriculum delivery.
(5) To encourage dialogue across the disciplinary boundaries about current issues and challenges in TH&E education.
(6) To confront future challenges and discuss potential directions for TH&E education in the short, medium and long terms.

In addressing these objectives, the Handbook focuses particular attention on the development and delivery of the curriculum, which is seen here as the crucial heart of the educational endeavour. It is in shaping, forming and delivering the curriculum that the academic community meets the needs of the students and society at large, including employers. Further, in the current environment, the curriculum plays a key role in the highly international and competitive world of higher education. Particular attention is paid to the balance between professional and liberal education in the higher education environment and to the needs and expectations of educators, industry, students and university managers.

Recognizing that the TH&E curriculum does not exist in isolation, this *Handbook* also seeks to place it within its wider setting. Notably it seeks to explore the philosophic foundations of the curriculum and to examine its rapidly changing context. Here the global environment and increased competition, the opportunities and threats presented by technology, the changing needs of industry, the pressures on the academic workforce and the dynamic nature of student markets are some of the challenges currently facing worldwide TH&E education. Skills shortages are also a significant issue that affects the capacity of the tourism industry to develop and innovate. TH&E education programmes have an important role in addressing this issue, by producing graduates with the knowledge, skills, creative problem solving and adaptive capacities to operate in increasingly complex and challenging environments.

Across the world, calls have been made for a 'paradigm' shift in the TH&E education curriculum, and for greater attention to be placed on the mix between vocational skill building and 'higher order' knowledge associated with critical and reflective tourism, hospitality and event practitioners. As the editors of this *Handbook*, we appreciate and fully support this call, but we also note that this debate, if interpreted narrowly as a call to transition from one paradigm to another, has the potential to limit the scope of what TH&E education could be and the societal contributions it could make. Therefore, this *Handbook* is framed as an opportunity to identify, explore and confront multiple paradigms and values that can underpin TH&E education (Macbeth, 2005).

In doing so we critically examine and build upon the idea of the philosophic practitioner education (Tribe, 2002) and its later development applied to the curriculum space (Dredge *et al.*, 2012), conceptualizing it as socially constructed, dynamic and flexible. In these developments, the TH&E curriculum space is one in which there is commitment to the development of both graduate capabilities and knowledge to varying levels, and that institutions can occupy different positions in the curriculum space depending upon the particular sets of factors to which they are subject. These theoretical underpinnings are explored in the first chapters of the *Handbook* and provide a foundation for the chapters that follow.

The book deals with higher (university-level) education relating to tourism, hospitality and events. These are normally presented as distinct and discrete areas of study, albeit often provided in the same academic department. For this reason some of the chapters here deal with them separately. However, they often display more similarities than differences. Notably, as summarized below, all of them are relative newcomers to university education, with the implications that this has for establishing themselves in the academy, and they face similar issues, for example in the balance between their vocational and academic orientations. As a result many of the chapters have relevance to all three subject areas.

The *Handbook* draws together a range of authors from various countries and educational systems and backgrounds. Some are emerging scholars and educators and others are well established. Such an approach allows us to explore the range of influences faced by curriculum planners and designers in considering the future of TH&E education and from a range of perspectives. The *Handbook* obviously has direct relevance for such planners and designers, but it will also appeal to wider audiences including those in recreation and leisure studies, and in other professional fields.

Development of TH&E education

It is difficult to identify a precise point when the study of a particular subject begins. In the case of tourism, hospitality and events, they are all relative newcomers to university higher education as distinct subjects. For hospitality, Cornell University's School of Hotel Administration in the United States is something of an outlier with a foundation date of 1922 (McIntosh, 1992). For the most part, until at least the mid-1960s, hospitality higher education was provided mainly by vocational schools, led by the *Ecole Hôtelière de Lausanne* founded in 1893 (now a part of the University of Applied Sciences of Western Switzerland). For tourism, while elements were included in programmes in geography and trade, and there were some early tourism programmes at the University of Rome in 1925, the University of Vienna in 1936, and at the universities of St Gallen and Berne in Switzerland from 1941 (Medlik, 1965), it was not until the early 1970s that tourism began to appear more generally in the repertoire of higher education, again with a distinctly vocational orientation. As for events, these programmes are even more recent with most appearing after the turn of the twenty-first century and strongly influenced and often operated alongside programmes in hospitality and tourism.

Once established, the programmes grew massively in number and spread geographically. This was influenced in part by the growth in scale and awareness of tourism, hospitality and, more recently, events, as global activities and also by the growth of higher education itself; by the expansion of existing, and by the creation of new, universities. The latter in particular have appeared to be keen to introduce new areas of provision such as TH&E. So, for example, between 1970 and 2010 student enrolments in higher education in the UK increased from about 600,000 (Office for National Statistics, 2002) to 2.4 million (Higher Education Statistics Agency, 2011). The equivalent growth in Australia was from 161,455 in 1970 to over 1.2 million in 2011 (Department of Education, Training and Youth Affairs, 2001; Department of Industry, Innovation, Science, Research and Tertiary Education, 2012). Using tourism enrolments as an example, these grew in the UK from about 20 in 1972 (Airey, 2005) to 9,000 in 2011 (Walmsley, 2012), while in Australia, based on numbers of tourism programmes from the very first in 1978, there were 61 by 2005 (Breakey & Craig-Smith, 2008). Similar developments have now taken place elsewhere in the world, for example in China; with its first tourism programme in 1978, there were 967 degree-level institutions by 2010 recruiting 596,100 students (Xiao, 2000; Yang & Song, 2011).

Apart from growth and geographic spread the other key aspect in the development agenda for TH&E has been played out in the formation of the curriculum. Initially the programmes were distinctly vocational (Airey, 2005; Nailon, 1982). This in many ways matched the rising managerialism evident across the university system (Ayikoru *et al.*, 2009) in which the development of higher education was judged in the context of national economic competitiveness and prosperity. As TH&E grew and developed the key question revolved around the balance between a vocational and an academic orientation to the curriculum and the extent to which industry and employers on the one hand and the academy on the other should influence the curriculum. This is a theme that has appeared in a number of studies (Dredge *et al.*, 2012; Lashley & Morrison, 2000; Lynch *et al.*, 2011; Tribe, 2002). In some ways, even though the issues are the same for all the three areas of study, tourism, hospitality and events have in fact pursued rather different emphases. Hospitality has generally retained a stronger vocational orientation, witnessed particularly in the provision of training restaurants and even dedicated hotels as a part of the academic enterprise, providing the students with opportunities to develop vocational skills. Events programmes also often pick up this vocational theme in providing students with opportunities to stage and manage training events. For tourism, the vocational elements have some prominence in field trips but beyond these programmes tend to have a greater classroom focus.

These headline issues related to the curriculum have been brought into rather sharper focus by the two key changes, already noted, that are affecting higher education: the shift in university funding away from the taxpayer and toward the student; and the increased scrutiny of higher education, especially in terms of the quality and relevance of teaching and research, and the subsequent publication of league tables. In brief these have heightened the need to attract students and have provided greater comparative information both to students themselves as well as to the universities and the wider population. The result has been, on the one hand, that universities have become increasingly aware of the volume and quality of their research outputs, on which their academic reputations are forged, hence emphasizing the academic face of their work. On the other hand, the scrutiny of teaching programmes, including issues such as employment success rates, has placed greater emphasis on the student experience and student satisfaction. For TH&E subject areas that are still establishing themselves in the academy, this provides a key background tension both to prove themselves as academically respectable with obvious implications for an emphasis on research and theory as well as to maintain their apparent links with industry and employment potential. In this lie the ongoing tensions both for the curriculum and for the ways in which academics use their time. There is a danger here, noted by Airey *et al.* (2014), that unless TH&E can contribute both to reputation and to income especially from student recruitment then their positions in the academy are not secure.

One of the keenest changes for higher education has come from its increasing internationalization, ranging from the sharp competition to recruit international students and the opening of international campuses as well as efforts to introduce international standardization and recognition of qualifications. Paradoxically, at a time of increasing competition for students during which institutions seek ways to differentiate themselves, much of the international impetus seems to have prompted more standardization. The growth of programmes delivered in the English language, rather than in local tongues, in order to attract international students is one manifestation of this. But at a more profound level, in Europe, for example, the Bologna Process has sought to create a common European Higher Education Area (EHEA) with the associated Tuning Project, commencing in 2000, producing a European Qualifications Framework (EQF) that links the qualification systems of participating countries (Tuning, 2010) as well as common outcomes in a range of subject areas. Similarly, the search for international recognition and accreditation as a basis to gain international credibility in a competitive market has promoted international recognition schemes such as that of the United Nations World Tourism Organization (undated) and THE-ICE (2012) that typically provide a standardizing template to judge programmes. This standardization has also been picked up at a national level as a part of the drive to ensure that growth in higher education is not at the expense of academic standards. This is perhaps best exemplified by the Subject Benchmark exercise of the Quality Assurance Agency in the UK (Quality Assurance Agency, 2008) which now sets out the nature and characteristics of programmes in specific subjects, including TH&E, which is followed nationally. The extent to which this standardization sets boundaries in the development and delivery of the curriculum represents a new type of challenge.

After 40 or more years of development TH&E education is in an interesting and in some ways contradictory position. It has proved that it can be successful in recruiting students and indeed is now a significant part of some institutions, but there is also evidence of programme closures and mergers for lack of student demand (Fidgeon, 2010). It has established a reputation for research with, at least in tourism, some top-ranked research journals, yet the latest research evaluation exercise in the UK spoke of the long tail of mediocre outputs (Higher Education

Funding Council for England, 2009). It has a reasonably good track record for graduate employment, but it also shows some very weak links with its related industrial sector (Cooper, 2006). The curriculum has broadly become established (Airey, 2008) but the debates about the balance between capabilities and knowledge still remain (Dredge *et al.*, 2012). In short TH&E education is not one thing, there are differences between the three components and there are differences between institutions and countries. Yet in many ways the future that they are facing is common. It is one in which public funding will continue to be replaced by private funding and more private universities will be established; in which competition for students will intensify including competition from online provision; in which standardization and accreditation will become more commonplace; in which in their search for finance and reputation (and possibly for a place in the top 200) university leaders will be increasingly selective in the programmes that they retain in their institutions; and in which research outputs will continue to play the key role in reputation. In this context, for any institution or programme, understanding and agreeing the design of the curriculum and the quality of its delivery become of vital importance. It is these that lie at the heart of this book.

Approach

In many ways this *Handbook* extends the work of the 2010–12 Australian Government Office for Learning and Teaching (OLT) multi-institution research project led by Dr Dredge titled 'Building a Stronger Future: balancing professional and liberal education ideals in tourism and hospitality education'. The aim of this project was to map the Australian TH&E undergraduate curricula paying particular attention to the balance between professional/vocational education and liberal education. Its purpose was to clarify what constitutes TH&E education in the higher education environment. The project was founded on respect for the diversity of TH&E degree offerings and the independence and autonomy of higher education institutions. It was underpinned by a commitment to establishing collaborative dialogue between industry, higher education providers and the academic community about the future of TH&E education and practice. In mapping the Australian undergraduate curriculum space, the project identified strengths, weaknesses and future opportunities, and set the groundwork for a collaborative and shared vision of curriculum space. While this was an Australian-focused project, it is relevant to anyone interested in understanding more about the global context of tourism and hospitality education. The final project reports are available at: http://tourismhospitalityeducation.info

The approach of the project provides a key starting point for this *Handbook* in its goals to examine more globally the current debates, controversies and questions in the field of TH&E education. Like the project the book takes as its central focus a dynamic curriculum space shaped by internal and external factors from global to local scales, a variety of values and perspectives contributed by a range of stakeholders, and shifting philosophies about education policy, pedagogy and teaching practice. It maps out key issues in the curricula over the near, medium and long term. It is primarily aimed at academics, but will also find a market among educators and managers in further and technical education and the growing number of private education providers.

Structure of the book

This brief introductory chapter has set out some of the key issues that are shaping education for TH&E. Changes in the balance between public and private funding; increased national and international competition; the prominence of metrics and rankings in measuring institutional performances; and the continuing importance of providing a link with employment provide some of the key practical challenges facing TH&E education. At the same time the academic dimensions of these important areas of study have not been standing still. A few decades of research have massively expanded the knowledge base and have provided scope for a much deeper and richer area of study which in its turn has brought into focus the more philosophical issues associated with studying tourism, hospitality and events. This has also brought into focus the balance between the vocational and the theoretical and between teaching and research. These issues set the stage for an exciting period of change, one that will be played out in all aspects of education but especially in relation to the curriculum. This book is designed to explore how the world of TH&E education is responding to these changes. In doing so it provides the context, examines the changes and provides examples. It explores the tensions and changes in the curriculum as well as in the other elements that make up the repertoire of education. And it takes its examples from many different parts of the world.

Part II deals with some of the philosophical foundations that have been identified and are helping to guide the ways in which TH&E education is developing. Prominent among these is the balance between what Caton (Chapter 4) refers to as the 'practical' and the 'liberal'. Tribe's (2002) proposal of the 'Philosophic Practitioner' considered this more than 10 years ago. Here he revisits his earlier work (Chapter 2) to emphasize that in the contest between vocational and liberal education the crucial need is to make an informed choice about the curriculum underpinned by a carefully crafted philosophy of education. Edelheim (Chapter 3) picks up a similar theme and, after an exploration of some of the philosophical issues underlying educational decisions, he provides examples from Finland where education programmes at different levels are emphasizing different aspects of the curriculum in a common setting. Meanwhile, Caton (Chapter 4), in the same setting of the curriculum, makes the case for the inclusion of the humanities to increase 'students' capacities for success in creating a more sustainable and just tourism world'. In Chapter 5 Dredge *et al.* continue with the theme of the curriculum, setting out an approach to viewing the curriculum space that allows for the dynamic nature and overlapping of the force field of influences on the decisions about the use of the space; in doing so they provide a different view of the balance between liberal and skills-based education. Gross and Lashley (Chapter 6) examine the inclusion of liberal values in the hospitality curriculum, and review the similar experience of other occupationally oriented areas of study before going on to set out the issues for hospitality itself. Finally in this part Volgger and Pechlaner (Chapter 7), taking the curriculum space as their starting point, provide the findings of an empirical study of the ways in which the space is used in hospitality and tourism programmes in German-speaking Europe. Indeed the curriculum space and its composition, use and balance (or imbalance) is the key concept that underpins all the chapters in this part. Clearly the curriculum space is the battleground where the various forces influencing education need to be resolved.

With the title 'The changing context', Part III deals with some of these influencing forces and sets out some of the opportunities that they present for TH&E education. The part opens with Munar and Bødker (Chapter 8) considering the opportunities presented by information technologies as a means to enhance critical curriculum development. As they express it 'This chapter is a call to pursue a curricular design across and beyond disciplinary boundaries and aims to provide a more democratic and plural academic conversation.' Following this, with what is perhaps the most pervasive influence of the last 20 years, is a chapter by Ayikoru (Chapter 9) dealing with neoliberalism and managerialism. Here the author sets out the background to neoliberalism and what it has meant for higher education before going on to illustrate its implications for entrepreneurialism and the student experience. The theme of democratization linked to information technology is picked up in Chapter 10 in which O'Mahony and Salmon examine Massive Open Online Courses (MOOCs) and their potential for transforming TH&E education, including the provision of opportunities for a much wider range of potential students. Hannam and Guereño-Omil (Chapter 11) position education for tourism within the wider context of the development of mobility more generally. In this they point to the challenges and opportunities that a more mobile world presents to educators. Neoliberalism, information technologies and mobilities provide key starting points for any attempt to explain or understand what is happening in education. Here they provide important context for the subsequent parts of this book. But there are other key elements of the changing context and the remaining chapters in Part III deal with some of these. In Chapter 12, Sheldon and Fesenmaier introduce us to the Tourism Education Futures Initiative (TEFI) which is a network of international tourism scholars working towards, among other things, a values-based tourism education that is mindful of tourism's potential to create a better world. Sharpley (Chapter 13) continues this line of thought with an exploration of sustainable tourism development and how it might 'be utilized as a vehicle for encouraging students to engage with debates surrounding the concept of sustainable development and, more importantly, to reflect critically on their own role and values in achieving a more sustainable world'. The final chapter in this part by Barron (Chapter 14) explores the internationalization of education and the issues and implications for TH&E education. He reminds us that internationalization has multiple meanings and rationales, and that the values underpinning international curricula must therefore be explicitly communicated

Part IV, 'The curriculum space: from global to local', explores how the range of global forces explored in the previous parts are playing out to influence TH&E education in different countries. Hsu (Chapter 15) notes that tourism education has emerged as a result of increased recognition of the economic significance of tourism in many Asian countries. She explores how policies in a range of areas (e.g. education, workforce training, economic and industrial policy) have converged to stimulate entrepreneurial and innovative approaches to education. Sogayar and Rejowski (Chapter 16) explore the development of tourism, hospitality and events education in Brazil where massive growth in both enrolments and number of courses was experienced in the 2000s. They make a similar observation that the growth of tourism courses paralleled the rising importance of tourism as an economic sector. However, the distinguishing feature of this system for them is the large number of private institutions that offer TH&E education. The chapters by Harrison (17) and Mayaka and Akama (18) explore the challenges of globalization and increased mobility in developing country contexts (South Pacific and Sub-Saharan Africa respectively). While they are very different contexts, it is interesting that in both regions there are tensions between local demands and global influences. While budgetary constraints, lack of expertise and funding are significant issues, Mayaka and Akama call for new innovative models based on regional collaboration. Harrison highlights the challenges of developing a culturally appropriate tourism and hospitality curriculum in the South Pacific, pointing out that global discourses about the liberal/vocational balance lack relevance where the standard of English is low, the school system encourages rote learning, and many students have cultural backgrounds that 'emphasize respect for authority and discourage nonconformity, all of which make it difficult for university students to develop a genuinely critical approach to their learning and wider social environments'. In the final chapter of this part (Chapter 19), Botterill and Maitland explore why the tourism academy must proactively engage in public affairs using the case of the Association for Tourism in Higher Education (ATHE) in the UK. Drawing from 20 years of ATHE these authors highlight that the debate about tourism education should not be solely and internally focused in the academy, but that there are important benefits of engaging in broader public discussions about tourism and higher education.

Part V on 'Curriculum delivery' contains a variety of chapters that explore how innovative and creative educators in a variety of settings are responding to the global and local challenges described in previous parts. In Chapter 20 Bosman and Dredge explore how tourism's role as an agent of place change and issues of sustainability are being addressed within a post-disciplinary environmental planning project-based studio. García-Rosell (Chapter 21) explores how the use of problem-based learning (PBL) in sustainability teaching opens up opportunities for going beyond reflection to support critical reflexive practice that enables students to question assumptions embodied in both theory and professional practice. In Chapter 22, Liburd presents an approach to transforming the quality of tourism education by the use of values-based education, Web 2.0 technologies and collaboration, and illustrates that learning by making connections in different domains of life, between new concepts, things, phenomena and existing knowledge, enriches the learning experience.

Breakey, Robinson and Brenner (Chapter 23) explore the philosophical underpinnings of hospitality education. They are mindful of the challenges of producing academically prepared and professionally relevant graduates and make explicit a number of important dimensions that require consideration in curriculum design and delivery. Su (Chapter 24) addresses the development of lifelong tourism learning opportunities that equip students for future learning, employment and life in a dynamic tourism world. Isacsson and Ritalahti (Chapter 25) profile the innovative approach taken to work-integrated and service learning at HAAGA-HELIA (HH) University of Applied Sciences, Finland, an approach enhanced through the integration of pedagogy and the physical and social characteristics of the learning environment. In Chapter 26, Portegies, Platenkamp and de Haan reframe fieldwork as a conceptual space 'where people who work in and around tourism, meet those who think and learn about tourism'. In doing so they highlight the important learning possibilities and challenges of engaging students in international fieldtrips. In the final chapter in this part, Harrington, Ottenbacher and Powell (Chapter 27) address the question of whether digital technologies can be used to enhance the quality of student learning and, specifically, facilitate learning in service quality, service management and customer satisfaction. They highlight the strengths and weaknesses of using crowdsourcing as a way of solving a problem or creating a product, and digital and audio-visual technology in learning about service quality and customer satisfaction.

Part VI of the book dealing with 'Issues and challenges' is characterized by a collection of chapters representing a broad range of issues related to TH&E education. The part opens with Seemann's (Chapter 28) conceptual framework for how design may be included in the professional education of tourism graduates so they may enhance the human valued experience that people have with the made-world around them. The next three chapters concern employment, beginning with Petrova (Chapter 29), who reflects upon how government discourse and policy around employability have affected higher education (HE) practice in tourism HE. Set against a growth in the expansion of courses in TH&E fields, Ladkin's chapter (30) considers the characteristics of labour markets, and outlines the types and nature of academic jobs, and the career development of academics with specific reference to career advancement strategies and career mobility. Huang (Chapter 31) examines industry engagement with tourism and hospitality education from students' perspectives, wherein the views of students on different types of university engagement with the tourism and hospitality industry at a tourism and hospitality school in Britain are analysed.

Benckendorff and Moscardo (Chapter 32) adopt a generational perspective on the curriculum space, beginning with the premise that Generation Y represents one of the largest and most recent cohorts of students in higher education. These authors consider how the curriculum space needs to evolve in order to accommodate the values and future aspirations of Generation Y students studying tourism, hospitality and event management. This then leads into a pair of chapters that deal with new-generation technology and its relationship with higher education. Sigala (Chapter 33) critically reviews previous pedagogical approaches (e.g. constructivism and collaborative (e)-learning) and proposes conversational and connectivism learning as more effective learning theories to explain learning and knowledge development in the current environment, because they are in accordance with the tenets of cooperative education, service-dominant-logic and co-creation approaches, which are also advocated to address current transformation trends. Talbot and Cater (Chapter 34) provide a case study on the use of wikis to facilitate student-led learning on a tourism management module that highlights how students collaborated within their groups to create their wiki sites (e.g. sharing ideas and creating knowledge) and how this produced more cohesive group work.

The focus next turns to events as Getz (Chapter 35) considers the teaching of event management and event tourism, with an emphasis on curriculum design. The three dimensions of acting, knowing and being are used to put forward specific ideas on what to teach, as well as appropriate pedagogic methods within a framework for understanding and creating knowledge about planned events.

The following two chapters represent case studies on hospitality topics, as Haden (Chapter 36) presents the case study of Le Cordon Bleu to outline the cultural and educational factors that have supported the emergence of Gastronomy (also known as Food Studies, particularly in the USA) as a higher education discipline. The chapter argues for the intrinsic value and relevance of studies in gastronomy, particularly with regard to contemporary culture and the environment (sustainability), and to innovation in higher education. Tse (Chapter 37) then analyses what makes Hotel ICON in Hong Kong a teaching hotel from the perspectives of architecture, the hotel management model, engagement of staff, student internships and industry relevance. The part closes with a chapter by Boyle, Wilson and Dimmock (Chapter 38) that presents the results of a meta-level website content analysis of the presence of sustainability within the tourism higher education curriculum in Australia, with the aim of addressing the central research question driving this analysis: 'Where is sustainability in the tourism curriculum space?'

Conclusion

In sum, the *Handbook* delivers a mix of theoretical, applied, discursive and reflective chapters. Some chapters present original empirical work and others are theoretical or conceptual in nature. However, the common thread is that all chapters seek to open up new ways of reflecting on and understanding the key issues shaping TH&E education and to assist scholars, educators and higher education managers to better anticipate and respond to the challenges that lie ahead. To this end, the scope of the *Handbook* includes a variety of values and perspectives contributed by a range of stakeholders, and explorations of shifting philosophies about education policy, pedagogy and teaching practice in TH&E higher education.

Together the chapters provide the basis for the final part of the book with a chapter (39) in which the editors look forward from the current state of TH&E education toward the future. In doing so the messages of all the chapters are drawn upon to consider how TH&E education can help to create the future in a post-industrial, post-disciplinary world. As we put it:

> The path that TH&E education has taken so far, in emerging from a strictly vocational starting point and becoming a post-industrial area of study where reflexivity, critical thinking and multi-disciplinarity are now common practice, leads us to the view that we

remain well positioned to meet future challenges but as educators, we must also embrace the stewardship of our field.

And further: 'In this future, curriculum content will still matter, but the experience of learning, the deep, intimate connections between knowledge and daily life, and the capacity to develop critical, mindful and reflexive practice must be foregrounded if TH&E education is to make a difference.'

References

Airey, D. (2005). 'Growth and Development'. In D. Airey & J. Tribe (Eds.), *An International Handbook of Tourism Education* (pp. 13–24). Oxford: Elsevier.

Airey, D. (2008). 'Tourism Education: life begins at 40'. *Teoros*, 27(1), 27–32.

Airey, D., & Tribe, J. (2005). *An International Handbook of Tourism Education*. Oxford: Elsevier.

Airey, D., Tribe, J., Benckendorff, P., & Xiao, H. (2014). 'The Managerial Gaze: the long tail of tourism education and research'. *Journal of Travel Research,* in press.

Ayikoru, M., Tribe, J., & Airey, D. (2009). 'Reading Tourism Education: neoliberalism unveiled'. *Annals of Tourism Research*, 36(2), 191–221.

Breakey, N., & Craig-Smith, S. (2008). 'Trends and Issues in Tourism and Hospitality Degree Education in Australia: will the bubble burst?' Paper presented at the 18th Annual Council for Australian University Tourism and Hospitality Education (CAUTHE) Conference, Tourism and Hospitality Research, Training and Practice: 'Where the bloody hell are we?', 11–14 February, Gold Coast, Australia.

Cooper, C. (2006). 'Knowledge Management and Tourism'. *Annals of Tourism Research*, 33(1), 47–64.

Department of Education, Training and Youth Affairs. (2001). Higher Education Students Time Series Tables. Canberra: Commonwealth of Australia.

Department of Industry, Innovation, Science, Research and Tertiary Education. (2012). Higher Education Statistics. Retrieved 1 December 2012 from: http://www.innovation.gov.au/HigherEducation/ HigherEducationStatistics

Dredge, D., Benckendorff, P., Day, M., Gross, M., Walo, M., Weeks, P., & Whitelaw, P. (2012). 'The Philosophic Practitioner and the Curriculum Space'. *Annals of Tourism Research*, 39(4). 2154–76.

Fidgeon, P. (2010). 'Tourism Education and Curriculum Design: a time for consolidation and review?'. *Tourism Management*, 31(6), 699–722.

Higher Education Funding Council for England. (2009). *RAE2008 Subject Overview Reports*. Bristol: Higher Education Funding Council for England.

Higher Education Statistics Agency. (2011). *Students in Higher Education Institutions*. Available: http://www.hesa.ac.uk/index.php?option=com_datatables&Itemid=121&task=show_category&catdex= 3 (Accessed 8 February 2014).

Lashley, C., & Morrison, A. (2000). *In Search of Hospitality: theoretical perspectives and debates*. Oxford: Butterworth-Heinemann.

Lynch, P., Molz, J. M., McIntosh, A., Lugosi, P., & Lashley, C. (2011). 'Theorizing Hospitality'. *Hospitality and Society*, 1(1), 3–24.

Macbeth, J. (2005). 'Towards an Ethics Platform for Tourism'. *Annals of Tourism Research*, 32(4), 962–84.

McIntosh, R. (1992). 'Early Tourism Education in the United States'. *Journal of Tourism Studies*, 3(1), 2–7.

Medlik, S. (1965). *Higher Education and Research in Western Europe*. London: University of Surrey.

Nailon, P. (1982). 'Theory in Hospitality Management'. *Journal of Hospitality Management*, 1(3), 135–43.

Office for Learning and Teaching. (2012). *Building a Stronger Future: balancing professional and liberal education ideals in undergraduate tourism and hospitality education Final Report 2012*. Sydney: Australian Government Office for Learning and Teaching.

Office for National Statistics. (2002). 'Students in Further and Higher Education: by type of course and gender, 1970–71 to 1997/98', *Social Trends 30*. London: Office for National Statistics.

Quality Assurance Agency. (2008). *Subject Benchmark Statement, Hospitality, Leisure, Sport and Tourism*. Gloucester: QAA. Available: http://www.qaa.ac.uk/Publications/InformationAndGuidance/Pages/ Subject-benchmark-statement-Hospitality-leisure-sport-tourism-2008.aspx (Accessed 13 March 2013).

THE-ICE. (2012). *International Centre of Excellence in Tourism and Hospitality Education (THE-ICE)*. Available: http://www.the-ice.org/about-us/who-we-are (Accessed 12 September 2012).

Tribe, J. (2002). 'The Philosophic Practitioner'. *Annals of Tourism Research*, 29(2), 338–57.

Tuning. (2010). *Tuning Sectoral Framework for Social Sciences*. Bilbao: University of Duesto.

United Nations World Tourism Organization. (undated). *Tedqual*. Andorra: UNWTO.

Walmsley, A. (2012). *Tourism Intelligence Monitor: ATHE report on tourism higher education in the UK 2012*. Brighton: Association for Tourism in Higher Education.

Xiao, H. (2000). 'China's Tourism Education into the 21st Century'. *Annals of Tourism Research*, 27(4), 1052–5.

Yang, J., & Song, H. (2011). 'Tourism Education Programmes in Mainland China'. *AngloHigher, The Magazine of Global English Speaking Higher Education*, 2, 8–9.

Part II
Philosophical foundations

2

The curriculum

A philosophic practice?

John Tribe

School of Hospitality and Tourism Management, University of Surrey, UK

Introduction: a runaway, random curriculum?

I am going to take the opportunity in this chapter to revisit, juxtapose, compare, extend and apply various ideas that I have developed during my long interest in higher education – particularly as applied to tourism – and I would like to start by reference to Anthony Giddens (1999), who proposed that we live in a runaway world. This is a world that is moving fast and somehow out of our control, so that we are often behind events and rarely able to shape them. The curriculum and what to teach face this very same problem. We are often squeezing curriculum design between other activities, playing catch-up, patching, mending, but rarely do we make the time to get ahead of things, to carefully and thoughtfully plan the crucial business in higher education of what to teach. We certainly very rarely approach curriculum design afresh with a clean sheet of paper.

But more alarming is that alongside the idea of a runaway curriculum we might also note some of its random and hidden features. On what basis do we decide what to teach? For the sake of emphasis I am going to outline a range of factors which I have called the 12 Ps. They are:

- power
- pals
- patronage
- precedent
- pragmatism
- pleading
- parochialism
- parsimony
- prospects
- popularity
- politicians
- path dependency.

By doing this I wish to underline the fact that at times the curriculum can at worst be accidental, path-dependent, ill-informed and merely adequate. For example, precedent can play an important role so that in many cases custom and practice are key determinants of the curriculum. Parsimony is another important consideration so that cost considerations increasingly constrain our imaginative visions. At a more prosaic level pals and pleading reflect the messy internal politics of curriculum design. Here the curriculum may be skewed to the special interests of individual academics. For example economists are prone to claim that 'we must teach two modules of economics'. Additionally patronage and power reflect the special influence of key decision makers as well as the less visible aspects of power which permeates everyday life through taken-for-granted ideology and discourse (Ayikoru *et al.*, 2009). Politicians may frame the rules at a more general level or in some places create very tight curriculum regulations, and prospects – especially the prospect of paid work – leaves the inevitable imprint of vocationalism on curricula. Path dependency describes the tendency of the present and future curriculum to be largely determined by past decisions especially in relation to recruitment of academic specialisms, acquired resources and existing physical infrastructure.

But against this, the territory opened up so often and so eloquently by Ron Barnett alerts us to the importance of two other Ps which are often overlooked. They are:

- purposes
- philosophy.

The aim of this chapter then is to create a thinking space and to foreground purposes and philosophy as important counterbalances to the sociological observations of curriculum's runaway and random tendencies. In doing so it divides into four main sections covering rationale, analysis, the philosophic practitioner and a conclusion.

Rationale: the state we are in

If we engage in a situational analysis of the current state of the tourism curriculum a number of relevant factors present themselves for consideration. The first of these is amateurism. This chapter, and my interest in education, is inspired and guided by an early work of mine 'The Philosophic Practitioner' (Tribe, 2002), a work that I completed after my PhD study at the Institute of Education, University of London, under the guidance of Ron Barnett. Here I was subject to deep immersion in educational theory and philosophy and profited from discussions and conversations with academics with similar interests from around the world. I mention this because I am a little concerned about the proliferation of education experts in tourism. The following qualification seems plausible: because I teach I am therefore an expert in education. But the danger here can be illustrated by the proposition that someone who works in a nuclear power installation is therefore necessarily an expert in atomic physics. One result of this amateurism is that works on tourism education are often under theorized. They very rarely locate specialist literature, or position themselves within wider educational debates. Indeed one may justifiably worry about their credibility especially those that appear to be based on little more than brainstorms or the deliberations of committees.

A second observation is that we live in a world of mixed educational messages or perhaps an incompatibility between means and stated ends. To look at the various brandings and mission straplines of universities (their stated ends) we might think we lived in a new age of enlightenment. The following examples are from various parts of the world:

- To learn and to apply for the benefit of mankind (Hong Kong Polytechnic University, Hong Kong)
- To transition knowledge to the benefit of humanity (University of Surrey, UK)
- (To) reward(s) excellence and innovation and promote(s) engagement with local, national and international communities (University of Queensland, Australia)
- To develop leaders of character dedicated to serving the greater good (Texas A&M, USA)
- To be the University of choice in nurturing innovation and talent in science, technology and development (Moi University, Kenya).

But such bold, warm, idealistic statements do not always chime with the everyday management practices of education (their means). Rather it is often noted that universities have rather easily swallowed and digested the business practices of managerialism and neoliberalism (Ayikoru et al., 2009). An example of the former is the widespread use of league tables, key performance targets and management (and learning) by objectives. Neoliberal agendas similarly incite universities to be competitive, entrepreneurial, market-led and PR-proficient. So the university curriculum is caught between 'serving the greater good' and serving up roughly commodified readily marketable knowledge. Two unintended consequences arise from this: the de-professionalization of academics and the surface learning of students.

Further there is a global tendency to be sidetracked by sustainability. Of course, we all want to encourage a better understanding of the principles of sustainability and to develop ways of putting theory into practice. But sustainability, like 'security' and 'health and safety' threatens to engulf all other competeing concepts and principles as being the overriding mantra of the moment. Above all sustainability is not really an end in itself. Achieving sustainability just means that we have found a system whereby we do not destroy or undermine our development. It does not provide much insight about what kind of a world we want to create.

A fourth but related point about education results from the 2008 global financial crisis. The term global financial crisis is a widely used but inaccurate term. It is inaccurate because the crisis is not global but since the crisis severely hit Europe and North America it has assumed that role as an example of ethnocentric narrow-mindedness. However the crisis did at least cause some reflection. To what extent did the education system and especially business schools contribute to a narrowness of thinking and an education that led to widespread action seemingly devoid of ethical principles? Indeed we might ask how far short universities fell of their missions of benefiting mankind and humanity and point to a significant gap here between outcomes and stated aims.

Fifth, for the academy in general, but also for tourism specifically, we live in a world of knowledge messiness, uncertainty and proliferation so that the relationship between the world, knowledge of that world and the curriculum is not an obvious fit. In tourism this has been characterized by the expression 'The Indiscipline of Tourism' (Tribe, 1997). Here the argument goes that there are many competing knowledges about tourism – managerial knowledge, social science knowledge, disciplinary knowledge, interdisciplinary knowledge and extra-disciplinary knowledge. So the question arises about which parts of this complexity of knowing should be incorporated into the curriculum.

These points translate into a number of challenges for curriculum development in tourism. First, there is a need to reject amateurism and insist on deep theoretical and academic engagement. Second, universities themselves are not much help in steering our curriculum choices, instead exhibiting somewhat schizophrenic divisions between idealism and consumerism. Third, the global financial crisis has demonstrated systemic and substantive weaknesses in current conceptions of the curriculum. And, finally, our extent and breadth of knowledge far exceed the capacity of the curriculum to carry it all. In sum we need to make an informed choice about what to teach and why. We need a carefully crafted philosophy of tourism education.

Analysis: philosophical and sociological aspects

This section examines some important philosophical and sociological aspects of the curriculum. In terms of philosophy it considers methods, key concepts, aims and ideology. Its sociological enquiry considers the impact of academic culture and networks on curriculum.

Methods

So how should we go about designing a curriculum? Typically approaches fall into two possibilities. The first is empirical research. We collect data and ask basic questions such as: What do students want? What do employers want? What do academics want? What are job-related needs? This seems easy enough and many studies have pursued this path. But this approach only begs a further question. That question is: 'What is the curriculum for?' If it is just for employability then we can readily collect data on employer wants and job needs. But there are clearly a number of possible aims for the curriculum and so research that is to be credible about curriculum content will inevitably fall back to conceptual (Xin *et al.*, 2013) and philosophical enquiries. The following paragraphs will clarify some of the essential conceptual issues starting with meaning of the curriculum.

Curriculum

The term curriculum has taken on a variety of meanings and attention will initially be focused on clarifying its various meanings and its boundaries. A simple definition of the curriculum can be found in Taylor and Richards (1979), who define the curriculum as that which is taught. More complex definitions include that used by Kerr (1968), which embraces a much wider experience capturing all the learning which is guided by an institution. There is also a literature which unearths a hidden side to the curriculum (Cornbleth, 1984). Here the spotlight falls not just on the explicit aims and objectives of the curriculum, but also on the implicit values that accompany it. Exponents of the hidden curriculum point to the significance of what is left out of the curriculum as well as what is put in. In fact the term curriculum is more widely used and accepted in compulsory education than in higher education, and in many older universities and traditional single honours degrees it is the canon of the discipline that determines what is to be taught.

I will define the curriculum as a whole programme of educational experiences that is packaged as a degree programme. Its constituent parts are a number of modules or courses, which in turn may be specified as a series of syllabi or course contents. A core curriculum represents a compulsory element.

Curriculum space

Alongside this, I have previously proposed a wider concept of curriculum space to capture not just what is taught, but all of what might be taught. The term curriculum space is used to denote the expanse or area that contains the range of possible contents of a curriculum. It is therefore an imaginative space. Curriculum space is filled with knowledge, skills and attitudes. Students take educational journeys through different parts of curriculum space and according to the routing of their journey (i.e. the curriculum they follow) they will be exposed to different packages of knowledge and end up in different places with different perspectives, attitudes and competences. Curriculum space can be interrogated in a variety of different ways. We may ask what are the purposes of a curriculum and precisely what is it preparing students for? We may ask what values are endorsed by this or that curriculum?

The idea of framing (Bernstein, 1971) is useful to understand the point of curriculum space. Bernstein explained the term framing thus: '[referring to] the degree of control teacher and pupil possess over the selection, organization and pacing of knowledge transmitted and received in the pedagogical relationship' (p. 50). The construction of any particular curriculum will entail framing, where some areas of curriculum space will be included, and others excluded. Curriculum space represents a template against which any particular framing of the curriculum can be evaluated. When a framed curriculum is located within curriculum space, what is left outside the curriculum becomes evident. Evaluation may proceed by examination of not just what is inside the frame, but also what has been excluded. Curriculum space therefore offers ways of problematizing the curriculum planning exercise by highlighting a range of possible competing claims. Curriculum framing further illustrates the idea that a potential contest exists over the contents of the tourism curriculum.

Figure 2.1 is used to explore this idea further. The idea and diagram of the curriculum force field is introduced to illustrate the range of influences on the curriculum. Curriculum planning is subject to a number of forces which according to their relative power attract the curriculum in one or other direction. Different curriculum configurations may arise according to the relative strength of different parts of the force field.

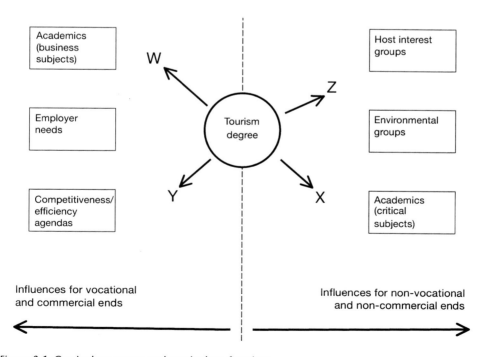

Figure 2.1 Curriculum space and curriculum framing

Assume the whole area between the squares designates possible curriculum space, that is a complete map of possible curriculum contents. It is proposed that any particular framing of a curriculum in curriculum space is affected by the power and influence of the surrounding squares, which provide in effect a force field. So, for example, academics in business subjects will lobby to include components such as demand and consumer choice for tourism services, consumer satisfaction and marketing. The square designating the needs of employers might promote personal transferable skills such as problem solving, communications and team working in their framed curriculum.

Assume that the circle towards the middle of Figure 2.1 labelled 'tourism degree' represents the frame of the curriculum. It delineates what is to be included and what is to be left out of the curriculum. What lies within the circle is the chosen curriculum, but note that there will necessarily remain a large part of possible curriculum space which is not framed by a particular curriculum. The point is that this frame may be dragged across different parts of possible curriculum space to rest for example at points X, Y, W or Z.

The eventual resting position of the framed curriculum will depend upon the influence exerted by any of the surrounding squares. Thus we might envisage a curriculum being framed around point W, where the influence of business subjects has been strong. Alternatively, assuming critical subjects to include sociology, we might expect the curriculum at point X to include an analysis of the effects of tourism on host communities. Similarly, if the framed curriculum is drawn to point Y, it will lay considerable emphasis on developing enterprise skills. Point Z would suggest a curriculum rich in the analysis of Sustainable Tourism. Indeed one can imagine less neat scenarios. It is also possible that the circle that is used to represent the curriculum might be shattered, with blobs of the curriculum scattered across curriculum space without any overall coherence.

The main purpose of Figure 2.1 is to underpin the idea that there is not one tourism curriculum that is given, or indeed obvious, or which can claim to be 'the' curriculum, but that the curriculum can be framed in a variety of ways. The fact that tourism is a 'soft' field (Biglan, 1973) permits this variety of framings. Indeed perusal of the tourism courses currently on offer demonstrates the diversity of different framings and considerable product differentiation. A less charitable interpretation would be one of curriculum chaos and anarchy.

Aims, ideology and discourse

As the curriculum is framed, by accident or design, two distinct types of curriculum emerge. A vocational curriculum for inducting students into the commercial and operational activities of tourism is framed towards the left of Figure 2.1. A non-commercial curriculum that brings awareness of a wider set of activities which constitute tourism's wider society and world is framed towards the right of the diagram. In fact there are a variety of aims that might inform the tourism curriculum including by way of examples:

- Vocational competence
- Operational competence
- Employability
- Critical analysis
- Liberal engagement
- Academic study
- Ethical management.

Of course these and other aims may be mixed and matched but the most important issue for this chapter is that without a carefully thought-out set of aims, curriculum design becomes a rudderless free-for-all, subject to the chaotic rule of the 12 Ps.

Having established the need for carefully thought-out aims, a note of caution should be introduced about ideology and discourse. Ideology (Althusser, 1984; Barnett, 2003) may be thought of as a system of beliefs that informs and directs the thinking and activities of those who subscribe to it. It frames thought and guides action and its presence may lead to the promotion of some and the suppression of other views. Ideologies are partial. Ideologies are also often unseen. Apple (2004) has explained how the curriculum is often an ideological project either knowingly or unknowingly, where it just imitates a current 'common sense' view of the world.

The Foucauldian notion of discourse (Foucault, 1971) is also useful in any critical examination of the curriculum, revealing as it does the constructive power of language. Foucault explained how language and the rules and practices that give statements meaning have the power to regulate what can be said and done. Discursive formations and practices perform a subtle selector function by legitimizing some knowledge and sidelining others. In this way discourses regulate what is sayable and what people readily do. Ayikoru et al. (2009) have exposed the quiet but extensive influence of the neoliberalist ideology on university practices in general and on the curriculum. We should therefore be aware of ideological curriculum formulations. For example courses which are located on the left in Figure 2.1 might be termed vocationalist or operationalist if their aim is focused exclusively on the needs of the industry. Courses that are located on the very right of this diagram might be termed academicist, environmentalist or idealist where they operate in a purely theoretical domain without regard to the practical needs of the business of tourism.

Further inside the black box: sociological observations

As well as the philosophical concerns about curriculum aims, it is instructive to consider the sociological aspects of how a tourism degree is constructed. A common model in the university sector is for a course committee to develop a course with a view to validation. Validation is the official stamp of approval signifying that the designated constitutional procedures of the institution have been adhered to, and that a new degree meets the institution's generic design criteria and is therefore acceptable.

During this process a number of influences can be detected at work. It is likely that the course leader will have a considerable influence, as it is he or she who will steer the course through its various stages. The course leader may also have some influence in recruiting the course team. Team members will each be socially located as part of an institution, part of a faculty, and as a member of an academic tribe (Becher & Trowler, 2001) of a particular discipline. Each of these roles will exert a particular influence and will cause different tourism puzzles, to use Kuhn's (1962) terminology, to emerge as being worthy of investigation, and differing methodologies to be appropriate to analyse these puzzles. So an academic whose home discipline is accounting is likely to promote a very different tourism degree to one whose home discipline is sociology.

The influence of individual academics is of particular significance for degree programmes in areas such as tourism which are pre-paradigmatic (Kuhn, 1962). In disciplines such as physics where there is more consensus around an agreed paradigm, such matters are of less consequence since academics will work within that paradigm. There will therefore be less debate about what the core of a physics degree should look like. Similarly, for faculties such as dentistry, I suspect we would find the process of framing in curriculum space is largely straightforward and uncontested. But tourism is much more problematic. This is first because there is no clear agreement about what constitutes tourism knowledge (Tribe, 1997). To use Kuhn's terminology, there is no single paradigm which describes the field and there is little agreement on what should be included in normal tourism studies. Second, unlike dentistry, it is less clear exactly what tourism graduates will do upon qualifying. So, for tourism the absence of an agreed paradigm and the diversity (or even lack) of employment possibilities mean that there is room for a whole variety of curriculum configurations.

As tourism as a field has expanded so has its supporting superstructure and this plays a part in curriculum development. Tribe (2010) discusses some of these; for example journal titles have proliferated. The editors and referees of such journals are important gatekeepers who determine the direction of knowledge creation and underwrite areas of importance. Networks with inner and outer circles develop. These include the International Academy for the Study of Tourism (IAST), CAUTHE (Council for Australian Tourism and Hospitality Education), ATLAS (Association for Tourism and Leisure Education), THE-ICE (The International Centre of Excellence in Tourism and Hospitality Education), TEFI (Tourism Education Futures Initiative), BESTEN (Network for Sustainable Tourism). Additionally the United Nations World Tourism Organization (UNWTO) has a Themis Foundation to 'enable Member States to devise and implement education and training policies'.

There are a variety of other factors that can influence an emerging degree. Prominent amongst these are marketing activities to understand the needs of consumers of degrees. Equally the mission of a particular university, efficiency requirements and organizational imperatives such as modularization and semesterization can be significant. Academics have to forge degrees within the resource constraints of an institution. For example efficiency requirements may dictate that some subjects are offered as a compulsory common core to a certain family of degrees so that economies of scale can be achieved by way of large lecture groups. Similarly, semesterization and modularization may dictate the size of the components of a degree and this may favour the delivery of some modules as against others, for some are more readily delivered in small discrete chunks.

Curriculum: a contested concept

This section has revealed that the curriculum – what to teach – is in fact a contested concept. It is both sociologically and philosophically contested. Philosophically it has been revealed that there is a large potential curriculum space for tourism and that framing any particular curriculum involves a knowledge choice. An informed choice requires both clarity of aims and an awareness of the existence and power of ideology and discourse. Sociologically it has been revealed that curriculum design is not just an epistemological project but a human endeavour. As such there are important considerations of academic culture and the operation of networks that impinge on curriculum design. Being mindful of this enables us to approach the next section, which discusses the philosophic practitioner curriculum for tourism education.

The philosophic practitioner: a curriculum for tourism education

It would be foolish to approach any serious consideration of the university curriculum without reference to Barnett. In this section I would like to position my work on 'The Philosophic Practitioner' in between one of his classic pieces and a more recent piece. In what must be the seminal text on the subject – *The Idea of Higher Education* – Barnett (1990: 202–3) concludes that there are six 'minimal educational conditions' that are necessary to fulfil the condition of higher education. These include:

- A deep understanding of some knowledge claims
- A radical critique of knowledge claims
- Competence to develop critique in the company of others
- Self-direction and independent inquiry
- Self-reflection
- Open dialogue and cooperation.

This is a crucial starting point since it distinguishes higher education from, say, schooling or further education. Of particular note are the needs for deep understanding of knowledge (expertise), open dialogue (disputation) and a critical evaluation of knowledge (scepticism).

Mindful of this challenge I developed the concept of 'The Philosophic Practitioner' (see Figure 2.2) (Tribe, 2002). It arose from my dissatisfaction with previous research on the tourism curriculum and was inspired by my reading of the wider literature on higher education and particularly of Schön and Barnett.

The grid in Figure 2.2 represents a fluid, four-quadrant curriculum space consisting of:

- Vocational action
- Vocational reflection
- Liberal action
- Liberal reflection

The four quadrants result from the intersection of two axes. The vertical axis is a liberal/vocational continuum representing the ends of the curriculum. The horizontal axis is a reflective/active continuum representing the stance of the learner. This imagining of curriculum space enabled me to demonstrate that a curriculum for mere vocational action was an excessively narrow framing. Philosophic Practice was offered as a more comprehensive framing. Its aims were carefully and systematically clarified building on a critique of Schön's (1991) idea of the

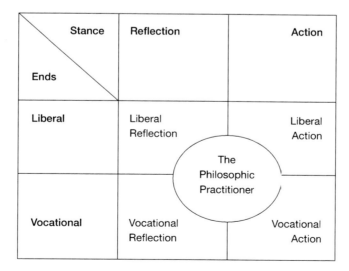

Figure 2.2 The philosophic practitioner

Source: Tribe (2002: 348). (Reproduced with permission from Elsevier.)

Reflective Practitioner. Schön stressed the importance of adding reflection in and on action to professional education in an effort to extend it from a state of passive learning of professional skills and knowledge. He advocated the cultivation of a continual dialectic between the vocational world as theorized about and the world as encountered, so as to develop what he termed professional artistry. This is clearly also an important consideration for tourism.

However, I argued that Schön's framing, though important, did not go far enough. It did not challenge the curriculum to engage with or challenge the staus quo in the wider world in which professional practice takes place. So whilst Reflective Practice focused on effective vocational action informed by continual reflection, Philosophic Practice added the new dimensions of liberal reflection and liberal action. A systematic analysis and development of the concept of liberal education (Tribe, 2000) resulted in three main objectives being set for Liberal Reflection. First it should encourage and equip professionals to be sceptical about given truths. This is an idea that I later developed in an article called 'The Truth about Tourism' (Tribe, 2006). Second, Liberal Reflection should encourage awareness of hidden ideology and power. Third, it should extend to reflection about what constitutes 'the good life' in the wider world affected by tourism. Liberal Reflection therefore entails a strong aesthetic and ethical dimension. In other words graduates should not just be educated to provide the means to achieve existing ends but should be active in setting the agenda for worthwhile aims of tourism. This might be termed Big Education.

Liberal Action responded to the critique of armchair philosophers who do not 'walk the talk'. Its objective is to develop the skills necessary to put the ideas of Liberal Reflection into practice. In this way Philosophic Practitioners should not only demonstrate professional competence in their careers in tourism but would also take responsibility for stewardship and the ethical and aesthetic development of the wider world of tourism. They would be ethical activists. The concept has become particularly relevant since the financial crisis where an excessively narrow education has proved to be dysfunctional, encouraging highly individualistic behaviour based on short-term profit-taking at the expense of the long-term well-being of society and the planet. Some critics of Philosophic Practitioners have said that the concept is too 'other worldly' and 'does not equip students for jobs'. Such critics have not read beyond the title. For it must be emphasized that Philosophic Practice entails a full four-quadrant education and that one of these is vocational action which covers the equipping of students with job-specific vocational skills and knowledge – including marketing, management, quality and leadership.

In a recent book Barnett (2013) re-examines what universities could and should become and in doing so sets out a clear blueprint for the curriculum of the future. His starting point is a twin critique of impoverished ideas and a lack of hope. His approach is to categorize universities according to three axes of endorsing/critical, deep/surface and pessimistic/optimistic, as well as to propose six criteria of adequacy for imaginative ideas. Inspired by Barnett, it is possible to summarize a number of current conceptions of the university with a view to seeing which are compatible with Philosophic Practice.

First the Entrepreneurial University. This is the university-as-business acting like a business and therefore concentrating on maximizing business opportunities and profit. In terms of the curriculum such a university would contribute to the commodification of knowledge which would be packaged and sold to attract students to generate income. This would be an agenda-following university where the curriculum is developed primarily as a means to profit. On the other hand the World-Class University might be characterized as aspirational. It aspires to be number 1 or in the top 10. In doing so it may be minded to follow and emulate the leaders. Its end is a high position in the league tables, and if it takes that too seriously or too narrowly then it will pursue any means to achieving that end. Its curriculum may therefore be designed with a strong emphasis on student satisfaction. Next there is the No-frills University. Like its namesakes in the airline industry, this is a relentlessly cost-cutting institution. Low costs offer competitive advantage and mass student enrolments. A no-frills curriculum means one that is standardized and cheap to deliver. Costly complexity is to be avoided. Further, the University-for-a-Better-World is somewhat different from the entrepreneurial or no-frills universities. Rather than cost and profit the key question is agenda setting about what is and makes a better world. Here the curriculum is likely to be idealist, academic, and exhibit strong ethical dimensions.

And it is against these that Barnett proposes the Ecological University. That is the university that understands its situation within, and charts its path through, multiple ecologies (Guattari, 2005). These include knowledge economies, ecologies of the person, economic ecologies and ecologies of the physical world. It is one that has care and concern about the world and is interested in not just sustainability but rather more general well-being. It is engaged with the world, serves the world not in a subservient way but contributes to the definition of the interests of the world.

It is interesting therefore to evaluate the Philosophic Practitioner against Barnett's schema and imagination. In terms of his three axes it is critical, deep and optimistic. Neither the Entrepreneurial University nor the No-frills University would be compatible with Philosophic Practice. Their conceptions of higher education are just too narrow. That is not to say the Philosophic Practice dismisses or is antagonistic towards enterprise. Rather to say that an ideology of entrepreneurialism would not encourage Liberal Reflection and Action. On the other hand Philosophic Practice should indeed be at the very heart of a World-Class University, but only one that wishes to be world class because of its aims rather than its league table position. It should be clear that Philosophic Practice is highly compatible with a University-for-a-Better-World but that its attention to vocational action and reflection make it more grounded and practical and indeed valuable for its graduates than a purely philosophic analysis and contemplation of 'the good life'.

However, the Philosophic Practitioner would provide a good practical curriculum framework for the Ecological University. It is concerned with similar multiple ecologies – knowledge ecologies, economic ecologies, and ecologies of the person and the physical world. Both favour the wider concept of well-being rather than sustainability. Both seek engagement with the world, hence the emphasis in the Philosophic Practitioner on action as well as reflection. Both have a strong mission to define and shape the direction of human development of and in the world. But the Ecological University does suggest an important consideration that was not made explicit in the initial conception of the Philosophic Practitioner. That is that it 'is never in a state of being; it is always in a process of becoming' (Barnett, 2013: 135). This is an important imperative to avoid ossification. Philosophic Practitioners should be pursuing creative futures, always extending the boundaries.

Conclusion

This chapter is titled 'The curriculum: a philosophic practice?'. As such it both endorses the Philosophic Practitioner curriculum and argues that curriculum design itself should be a philosophic practice. So in this conclusion I would like to briefly review not only the Philosophic Practitioner but also some other recent initiatives and writings in the area. For example TEFI (the Tourism Education Futures Initiative) has formulated TEFI values that should be incorporated into the tourism curriculum (Sheldon et al., 2011). These values are:

• Stewardship
• Knowledge

- Professionalism
- Ethics
- Mutual respect.

This initiative makes an important contribution to advocating the place of values in the curriculum. But some important philosophical and sociological questions are overlooked. Why these values? How were they arrived at? And what exactly do they mean? For example should a community show mutual respect for a developer that wishes to move their village against their wishes? (There is of course a hidden value in 'mutual respect' which is adherence to the status quo.) Next, Dredge *et al.* (2012) offer some interesting reflections on the Philosophic Practitioner and propose a new model. But similar philosophical and sociological questions remain unanswered. Why this content and model? How was it arrived at? And what exactly does it mean? In contrast Belhassen and Caton (2011) in their discussion on the need for critical pedagogy in tourism demonstrate a fuller enagement with the philosophy of knowledge and learning.

Finally the curriculum for the Philosophic Practitioner is tested against the challenges for the curriculum which were outlined at the beginning of this chapter. First, it is not a product of amateurism but of sustained theoretical and academic engagement. Second, in the face of the confusion between idealism and consumerism exhibited by many universities, the Philosophic Practitioner offers a clearly thought-out way to steer a path through these competing demands to strive for employability and practical idealism rooted in the real world. Third, the global financial crisis has caused (particularly business schools) to embark on a desperate search for the re-ethicalization of the curriculum. Practical ethics are at the heart of the Philosophic Practitioner which persistently reflects on the meaning of, and the right actions to achieve, the good life. This same broad emphasis on ethics prevents the Philosophic Practitioner from getting exclusively focused on, or sidelined by, just sustainability. Finally in our overcrowded knowledge world the Philosophic Practitioner offers a simple yet profound model to inform the choice about what to teach and why.

References

Althusser, L. (1984). *Essays on Ideology*. London: Verso.
Apple, M. W. (2004). *Ideology and Curriculum*: London: Routledge.
Ayikoru, M., Tribe, J., & Airey, D. (2009). 'Reading Tourism Education: neoliberalism unveiled'. *Annals of Tourism Research*, 36(2), 191–221.
Barnett, R. (1990). *The Idea of Higher Education*. Buckingham: Open University Press.
Barnett, R. (2003). *Beyond All Reason: living with ideology in the university*. Buckingham: Open University Press.
Barnett, R. (2013). *Imagining the University*. London: Routledge.
Becher, T., & Trowler, P. (2001). *Academic Tribes and Territories*. Buckingham: Open University Press.
Belhassen, Y., & Caton K. (2011). 'On the Need for Critical Pedagogy in Tourism Education'. *Tourism Management*, 32(6), 1389–96.
Bernstein, B. (1971). 'On the Classification and Framing of Educational Knowledge'. In M. Young (Ed.), *Knowledge and Control: new directions for the sociology of education*. (pp. 47–69). London: Collier-Macmillan.
Biglan, A. (1973). 'The Characteristics of Subject Matter in Different Academic Areas'. *Journal of Applied Psychology*, 57(3), 195–203.
Cornbleth, C. (1984). 'Beyond Hidden Curriculum?' *Journal of Curriculum Studies*, 16(1), 29–36.
Dredge, D., Benckendorff, P., Day, M., Gross, M. J., Walo, M., Weeks, P., & Whitelaw, P. (2012). 'The Philosophic Practitioner and the Curriculum Space'. *Annals of Tourism Research*, 39(4), 2154–76.
Foucault, M. (1971). *L'Ordre du Discours*. Paris: Gallimard.
Giddens, A. (1999). *Runaway World: how globalization is reshaping our lives*. London: Profile Books.
Guattari, F. (2005). *The Three Ecologies*: London: Continuum.

Kerr, J. F. (1968). *Changing the Curriculum*: London: University of London Press.

Kuhn, T. (1962). *The Structure of Scientific Revolutions*. Chicago, IL: University of Chicago Press.

Schön, D. (1991). *The Reflective Practitioner*. Aldershot: Arena.

Sheldon, P. J., Fesenmaier, D. R., & Tribe, J. (2011). 'The Tourism Education Futures Initiative (TEFI): activating change in tourism education'. *Journal of Teaching in Travel & Tourism*, 11(1), 2–23.

Taylor, P. H., & Richards, C. (1979). *An Introduction to Curriculum Studies*. Slough: NFER Publishing.

Tribe, J. (1997). 'The Indiscipline of Tourism'. *Annals of Tourism Research*, 24(3), 638–57.

Tribe, J. (2000). 'Balancing the Vocational: the theory and practice of liberal education in tourism'. *Tourism and Hospitality Research*, 2(1), 9–26.

Tribe, J. (2002). 'The Philosophic Practitioner'. *Annals of Tourism Research*, 29(2), 338–57.

Tribe, J. (2006). 'The Truth about Tourism'. *Annals of Tourism Research*, 33(2), 360–81.

Tribe, J. (2010). 'Tribes, Territories and Networks in the Tourism Academy'. *Annals of Tourism Research*, 37(1), 7–33.

Xin, S., Tribe, J., & Chambers, D. (2013). 'Conceptual Research in Tourism'. *Annals of Tourism Research*, 41, 66–88.

3

Ontological, epistemological and axiological issues

Johan R. Edelheim

Multidimensional Tourism Institute (MTI), University of Lapland,
Rovaniemi UAS, and Lapland Tourism College, Finland

Introduction

This chapter presents the foundational components of any tourism, hospitality and event (TH&E) studies curriculum, namely the ontology, epistemology and axiology of TH&E; or, in other words, how we come to understand what the fields are, what makes us accept certain matters as being truthful and constituting knowledge, and how we establish what is valuable either for its own sake, or for something else when we negotiate what to include in a curriculum.

TH&E studies as separate academic subjects, or combined as an academic branch, can act as a field that is taught to students, an academic genre to study, and more importantly as a practice aimed at enhancing and enriching the society within which TH&E takes place. I will in this chapter refer to TH&E studies, fully conscious of the fact that studies in these sub-fields take different shapes, and are taught separately from one another at some institutions. My aim in this chapter is, however, to investigate the philosophical foundations and issues of these studies, and as they have fairly similar antecedents I will disregard the diversity they take in practice. They are dealt with here together as TH&E studies.

In taking on the task to write about ontological, epistemological and axiological issues of TH&E studies I doubt whether I will be the first person to admit that the words ontology, epistemology, and axiology always initially leave him dumbfounded. Even after nearly 15 years as an academic and having taught research methodologies for several of these years, as well as supervising several honours, Master's and PhD candidates, I always have to go back to basics and remind myself what the concepts refer to. The reason for this is not that I do not know anything about the meanings behind the words, but maybe rather because none of the words is part of my daily vocabulary, or of what I think of as my reference frame in which I go about my work. I will, despite this, explain how the interpretations set by these concepts in actual fact make up the whole reference frame for my work, and that my daily vocabulary is very much what it is, due to them.

Ontology, epistemology, and axiology

Ontology, epistemology, and axiology lay the foundations for how we, as individuals, understand the world we live in, the determinations we make about issues relating to truth, and the matters we consider to be of value to us individually, and to society at large. I will initially clarify the meaning of the words jointly, and will then go on to discuss each concept, and the influence it has on the way we talk about, study, and educate for TH&E.

Ontology, or the study of being, creates the framework for how we, as individuals, connected in societies, make sense of the reality in which we live. The power of ontology is that it gives us the keys to unlock the way reality is understood, by taking as its object of study the actual being of things, matters, concepts, experiences, and words – essentially of everything. Epistemology, or the study of knowledge, receives in our rationalist society more emphasis because it sets out to explain why we jointly decide that certain things are true, and others are not. Science, and the interpretation of scientific results, changes the way society acts at all stages of life. For example, 'smoking is bad for the health', and 'burning fossil fuels changes our environment' are presented as truths based on scientific research, and accepted, or not, equally based on convincing arguments that are claimed to be representing knowledge. Axiology, or the study of value or of goodness, is definitely the philosophical strain out of these three that has received least attention, even though it is fundamentally linked to our actions in our daily lives. The value of something can be seen as having intrinsic properties, valuable in its own right, or to have extrinsic properties, valuable for the sake of something else, which in turn can have intrinsic properties. Understanding what TH&E is, how knowledge is negotiated in the field, and what makes TH&E valuable and to whom, should be the prerequisites for developing any curriculum – but how often these are frankly explored, is another matter.

Ontologies of TH&E

Ontology is, as stated above, 'the study of being', even though etymologically it should be referred to as ousiology, because the Greek word *ousia* means 'being' or 'existence' (Barnhart, 1988: 728). Ontology should literally be the study of 'a being'. But, that is how language works; certain meanings are assigned to certain words, and thereafter codified to be interpreted according to their accepted definition. Ontologies of TH&E refer to how we understand the existence of concepts, actions, theories, and words related to TH&E. Textbooks for TH&E studies generally start with an introductory chapter that sets the scene, describes the basics of the studies, potentially defines some foundational words and concepts, and thus creates the reality of TH&E studies that our students and peers accept as an authoritative one. No introductory chapter that I have come across has overtly stated that it aims at creating 'the ontology of TH&E', but that is in essence what they are doing.

Ontology is in post-positivist texts seen as describing the nature of reality (Jennings, 2010), rather than reality per se – this is to highlight that socially constructed realities can exist side by side without contradicting one another (Saukko, 2003). It is therefore important for critical theorists to ground their ontology claims in their own social reality. However, the roots of ontology reach much further back in philosophy than the modern use of it as a description of reality or realities. Aristotle referred to what we call ontology as 'first philosophy', 'The philosophical study of existence or being' (Martin, 2002: 217). The philosophical strand that has most closely taken the study of the being of things and experiences as its focus, is Phenomenology.

Central to the argument of Heidegger's interpretation of phenomenology is the concept he named Dasein or 'being-in-the-world', which has a threefold structure: understanding – and an associated meaning; mood – that is, our mood has a bearing upon how we encounter the environment; and discourse – or the fact that something that can be formulated can be understood (Stumpf, 1994: 506). In his first major work, Being and Time, Heidegger proposed that the question about Being and the meaning of Being had been investigated since the times of Plato. However, the mode of investigation had over time become confused and needed a different approach where the conventional way of addressing ontology was rejected (Heidegger, 1962). 'The fundamental nature of Dasein is always to be in a world. World here means a context, an environment, a set of references and assignments within which any meaning is located' (Moran, 2000: 233). Heidegger's famous example to illustrate Dasein is of how individuals experience 'equipment for writing, sewing, working, transportation, measurement' (1962: 97). Heidegger suggests that a pure phenomenology without any pre-cognition does not make sense, because an object, such as a piece of equipment, does not have any properties, or an essence, that would uncover its meaning in a transcendental sense. A hammer has meaning only in terms of its intended usage, and that same hammer does not contain any traces of other tools, such as stepladders, that might be necessary to perform the acts for which the hammer is used (Stumpf, 1994). The point of thinking about TH&E ontologies through the concept of Dasein is that it gives us an actual picture of their being – how is the reality of TH&E created in the world in which TH&E students study?

Franklin (2008) suggests that TH&E academics are doing themselves an injustice in accepting an ontology of TH&E that puts them at the margins of society. Living in neoliberal societies influenced by Weberian work ethics where leisure-time and pursuits are secondary in importance to work, means that TH&E is often seen as a parenthesis in society. TH&E textbooks commonly start with a phrase like 'tourism is one of the fastest growing industries in the world', or similar for hospitality and events. This is meant to lend credibility to the topic, but is in reality diminishing the topic by creating a reality where the matter is not at the centre, but rather it is just an 'industry', and not even the largest one, but rather a growing one. The first sentence of these textbooks has therefore created a reality where the being of TH&E is apologized for and subordinated to matters of higher importance such as employment, income, or whatever it is compared to. Franklin suggests that tourism should be placed at centre stage because 'tourism is not fragmented into a repetition of sites and an eternal present, but a formidable socio-technical rhizome, . . . with a series of substantial ordering effects' (2008: 32). By ordering the being of TH&E reality differently, a different ontology is born wherein other facets of society are seen through their connection to TH&E, not TH&E's connection to them.

Epistemologies of TH&E

Epistemology can etymologically be traced to the Greek word *epistēmē* – knowledge, which again comes from *epistanai* – to understand, or to know (Barnhart, 1988). Just as *Dasein* in Heidegger's terminology refers to how the individual makes sense of being and meaning through understanding, mood and discourse (Heidegger, 1962), so in epistemology lies the explanation of how knowledge is created in our minds, and accepted in our societies. What our society refers to as knowledge and truth are results of processes of negotiation carried out amongst people considered experts in their fields. New discoveries, adjustments of old information, and best practices are all ideas dressed in convincing words and backed up with either data or logic to constitute a 'correct', 'true' position about a matter.

Belhassen and Caton (2009) divide the knowledge – the epistemology – created and used in TH&E studies into three different categories based on a linguistic framework: morphology of TH&E; new interpretations of TH&E; and problem solving of practical issues of concern to TH&E stakeholders. Their framework succinctly shows how the language we use when creating TH&E knowledge is making truth claims in different ways. The first category, the morphology or lingo, refers to how terminology is introduced to TH&E studies, often from other disciplines, and given a meaning in TH&E literature. Examples of words and concepts that are part of the language TH&E academics nowadays use as part of their normal discourse are 'the tourist gaze' (Urry, 1990), or an 'experience flow' (Csikszentmihalyi, 1991) – in both cases theoretical words commonly used in other fields describing specific phenomena. By applying these words in a tourist context they are introduced to the accepted language TH&E academics use to communicate their ideas to one another.

The second category, the new interpretations of phenomena in TH&E, highlights that different researchers perceive reality in different ways and by offering explanations that in their mind portray that reality better, new knowledge is created. The academic community internally regulates which new understandings are recognized by using peer-review processes where experts in different fields evaluate whether the new interpretations reach an acceptable level. Academics also try to promote the reliability of their views of reality by, for example, creating ranking lists for publications in which new knowledge is published, citation indices, or by other means showing the impact, and thus credibility, of their findings.

The third category, in Belhassen and Caton's (2009) linguistic framework of TH&E epistemology, contains knowledge that is created by describing how the application of previously accepted theories and models of 'real life' cases enhances the operating conditions of that stakeholder's practice. These practical applications are the most common ways of furthering TH&E epistemologies. Theoreticians use words to describe how the event, business, community, non-governmental organization, destination, or whichever stakeholder acted as the practical component, changed their practices in some way and how those new ways of acting, analysing, or understanding practical matters led to, or at least could lead to, a better functioning environment.

If ontology of TH&E is metaphorically seen as the reality into which new students of the topics are thrown by definitions of standard features in the academic fields, then epistemology acts as the measurement by which that reality is accepted as a truthful description of the real world outside academia. Both are dependent on an established common language, and an understanding of set features. These matters create the basic ingredients of TH&E curricula, but the important matter from the perspective of how curricula develop is how institutions value different kinds of understandings, and that is where the axiologies of TH&E come into focus.

Axiologies of TH&E

The basic premises of both Tribe's (2002) description of Philosophic Practitioner Education (PPE), and Dredge et al.'s (2012) description of the curriculum space, lie in the balance that is needed to create a workable curriculum in TH&E, which satisfies the different learning outcomes that different stakeholders evaluate as necessary for students to have by the time they graduate. Education is generally given value for the goodness it brings to the individual who is its recipient, but even more importantly through the increased value that individual represents to the society in which they will function after the education is completed.

Different nations set different policies for how to achieve increased educational goals, and invest differently in education as a whole. Both the PPE and the curriculum space models incorporate how different stakeholders involved in the curriculum process place different values on different learning outcomes, based on what they consider being of worth to their own interest spheres. The axiology of TH&E, in terms of education, is thus created through the negotiation that takes place at the curriculum development stage. Depending on the power that stakeholders participating in the curriculum development process have in arguing for the value of specific outcomes, the curriculum space is shaped and positioned.

TH&E studies in Kittilä, Finnish Lapland

Finland is a nation-state in northern Europe that gained its independence in 1917 after having been under the rule of Russia since 1808, and before that under Swedish rule. The educational system bears influences from the Swedish system, but has also evolved on its own into a model nowadays benchmarked by many nations around the world. The reason for these benchmarking exercises in recent years is that international comparative studies have shown that students completing Finnish compulsory education achieve amongst the best results globally (Organization for Economic Cooperation and Development, undated). The reason this is noteworthy is that all education in Finland is state funded, and that very few private schools exist that would skew the results in favour of more intensive funding opportunities. Finland has always spent a comparatively large amount of its gross domestic product (GDP) on education (6.8 per cent in 2010, World Bank, 2013), and the society highly values education, and individuals' educational achievements. Many institutions of higher education offer at least bachelor degree level studies delivered fully in English, and some are also offering Master's degrees in English. Though, with education being state funded there is also a strong control by the Department of Education on student numbers enrolled.

Finland is geographically a relatively large nation in Europe with the eighth largest landmass, but with a comparatively small population, approximately 5.4 million inhabitants, making it the twenty-sixth largest nation in Europe (This is Finland, 2013). The northernmost region of Finland, Lapland, which this case will focus on, is geographically the largest part of Finland. Lapland makes up a third of the nation's area, but is the home to only 3.7 per cent of the nation's population, i.e. approximately 180,000 people. Two-thirds of Lapland's population live in the regional centres of Rovaniemi and Kemi-Tornio, with the remainder spread out in 20 local councils. One of these is located in the north-west of Lapland in the fell district called Kittilä (Lapin liitto, 2009).

Lapland's, as well as Kittilä's, modern history of employment and population change is a story of a society moving rapidly from agrarian roots to the experience society. Lapland's population grew quickly during the early 1900s, reaching 108,000 by 1940, 170,000 by 1950, and a peak of 221,000 inhabitants in 1967 (Lapin Liitto, 2009; Pennanen & Hirttiö, 1992). This growth followed the independent nation's land policies where state-owned land was put to active use through agriculture, forestry, and infrastructure projects capitalizing on water power. Societal changes in the late 1960s and early 1970s resulted in a major exodus of the younger population to the south of Finland and to Sweden to get jobs in factories (Lassila, 2001). The population remained, thanks to state investments, relatively stable at approximately 200,000 between 1970 and 1997 when, in connection with a financial slump, the Finnish state was forced to cut down on subventions to regional areas. The population in Lapland has since decreased steadily to the current 183,000, and until recently the only growing regions were the regional urban centres. Kittilä grew in a similar pattern to the rest of Lapland until the early 1970s when there were 7,200 inhabitants. The following 30 years saw that number decrease to 5,800 in 2002 (Lapin liitto, 2009). Thereafter, Kittilä has been one of the few regional councils to experience a population increase – in 2012 there were approximately 6,400 inhabitants (Kittilän kylät, 2013).

From the early 1900s to the 1980s, Kittilä's population's major sources of income were agriculture and forestry. This is reflected in the fact that as early as 1910 the state set up the first agriculture school, Kittilän maatalousoppilaitos (Arkistolaitos, 2013). Kittilä was also one of the first districts in Lapland with budding tourism and hospitality enterprises when accommodation and transport were offered to leisure travellers coming to trek and to ski in the fell-area surrounding the district's highest peak Levi (Lassila, 2001). In the reconstruction of the infrastructure after the Second World War, during which a majority of the region's buildings had been destroyed, it was decided that girls' vocational education would be separated from the agriculture school into a 'home economy' school, Kittilän kotitalouskoulu. This was active from 1947 to 1953 (Arkistolaitos, undated). A new building in the centre of the district was erected in 1954 and the school was named Kittilän emäntäkoulu – the Kittilä Matron School, which was active until 1987, after which it was renamed Kittilän kotitalousoppilaitos – Kittilä Home Economy Institute (Levi.NYT, 2009). The educational focus of the school started evolving in the early 1970s with a move away from its agricultural matron-roots towards a stronger focus on preparing students for careers in production kitchens. The school was merged with the agriculture school in 1992 and renamed Kittilän maaseutuammattien oppilaitos – Kittilä School of Agricultural Professions, but went through yet another change in 1999 when it changed its focus into hospitality and tourism, and its name to Levi-Instituutti (Levi.NYT, 2009).

The education offered in Kittilä had up to that point been focused on secondary education, but from 1999 onwards there were also opportunities for students to enrol in multimode higher education degrees through Rovaniemi University of Applied Sciences (UAS). By 2006 Levi-Instituutti was incorporated into Lapin Matkailuoppilaitos – Lapland Tourism College, with campuses in two other districts. This offered diplomas in hospitality, tourism and leisure. The most recent change occurred in 2010 when the college joined Matkailualan tutkimus- ja koulutusinstituutti – the Multidimensional Tourism Institute (MTI), which is an institute that coordinates TH&E education at all post-compulsory levels as well as TH&E research in all of Lapland. The education offered at MTI comes through its partner institutions: Lapland Tourism College, vocational secondary education; Rovaniemi UAS, applied hospitality and tourism education at bachelor and Master's levels; and University of Lapland, major in tourism studies as a part of social sciences at bachelor, Master's, and doctorate levels. Students at MTI are enrolled, and eventually graduate, from the institutions offering the separate diplomas and degrees, but have, through their studies, opportunities to select learning modules offered at the other institutions, as well as to participate in project studies where student groups from different educational modes study together. The different degrees and diplomas are not seen in a hierarchical sense as being at different levels, but rather as being different necessary dimensions of TH&E industries, which are offered at a multidimensional institute.

By looking at the development of education in Kittilä certain trends, especially in the axiologies of TH&E, can be distinguished. Nation-states fund education that is considered to be of value to the society. In the early stages of Finland's history the focus was on basic education, vocational education related to agriculture nationwide, and on university education in two cities in the south of the country. Societal changes took place in Finland during the rebuilding stage after the Second World War due to the loss of almost a full generation of men in the war. Women were needed to join the workforce to a larger extent and this led to the development of educational institutions that would prepare women to carry a larger role in managing their households, such as the Kittilä Home Economy School, founded in 1947. The impact of the post-war baby boom meant a further adjustment in society, and thus also education. A more equal number of men and women went on from compulsory education to further studies, but with conservative values still reigning, women were given alternatives that would capitalize on 'female traits'. Post-secondary education started being available more widely, with health-care schools, teachers', and technical colleges established in regional areas. An example of this was the Kittilä Matron School founded in 1954, where girls aged from 16 to 20 learned the work of an agricultural matron in charge of a farm, or later, when the society was undergoing a turn towards a stronger emphasis on industrialization in the early 1970s, focused on operational and supervisory positions in production kitchens.

The downturn in agriculture and forestry paved the way for a stronger emphasis on service professions. Vocational education in Kittilä was aimed at servicing agricultural professions, but later changed into hospitality when the community came to depend more on service industries (ELY, 2011). The 1970s and 1980s brought about further educational changes when the higher education sector expanded, with universities created in several regional capitals, and the former separate colleges being merged and centralized also to regional capitals. A reform in the post-secondary education in the late 1980s and early 1990s saw the demerger of higher education courses from vocational schools and the creation of polytechnic universities, or in Finnish terms universities of applied science (UAS) (Helakorpi, 2007). Lapland got its own university in 1979 with its home in Rovaniemi. This was the only Finnish university given the right to offer tourism as a major in their social sciences faculty (Ylä-Kotola, undated), and UAS institutions were created in both Rovaniemi and in Kemi-Tornio.

Hospitality and later tourism education at a supervisory level had from the 1960s been offered at only one institution in the south of the country (Haaga Yhtymä, 2013), but came, through the larger changes in the sector, to be part of the UAS repertoire with bachelor degrees offered at 15 different institutions, amongst them in Rovaniemi. University TH&E education is still only offered as a major at the University of Lapland, but other Finnish universities have developed a network of TH&E courses so that students at participating universities are offered a chance to choose tourism as a minor together with majors in related fields, such as geography or business.

The value given to TH&E as fields of development and employment grew in Lapland as transport links were improved and money was invested in accommodation facilities and leisure activities. Youth education was mostly offered only on campus, but together with expectations of lifelong learning, UAS adult education brought about more flexibility. Therefore, students in Kittilä could start studying bachelor programmes in hospitality management at Levi-Instituutti in combination with Rovaniemi UAS in the early 2000s. However, this option was later discontinued as a means of saving money that was spent on teachers' transport and accommodation between Rovaniemi and Kittilä (150km), leaving students from the Kittilä region again with on-campus vocational education on offer locally.

The curriculum space framework's force field(s) applied on MTI

The latest developments in TH&E education in Kittilä come through courses created through MTI's project pedagogy where student groups from vocational education, UAS degrees, and university degrees are jointly involved in events in the community. MTI participates in events at different places around Lapland, one of these being an annual theatre festival in Kittilä. During the event, students from the different study groups receive different tasks, from practical operational tasks for vocational students, supervisory tasks for UAS students, and planning and development tasks for university students. The assessable items for the projects also differ for students from the different groups so that they fulfil the expectations of set curricula at each institution. Students from the vocational group of MTI need to demonstrate skills and competences achieved, students from the UAS do reflective pieces that underline how theories have been applied, or could have been applied at the event, and students from the university write reports that evaluate the event and plan how it could be enhanced in the future.

An important part of Dredge et al.'s Curriculum Space Framework (2012) is the notion of a 'force field' in the TH&E curricula. This force field relates to the internal and external influences that shape the curricula at different institutions. By accepting that each curriculum is a negotiated compromise where a multitude of different stakeholders' perceptions of necessary learning outcomes are collected, it is easy to perceive a curriculum as having been formed by different forces. The key challenge in the Curriculum Space Framework is that institutions generally have to solve how to form their curriculum alone, and are thus forced to make strategic choices on what is included, and what is not, based on the institution's size and resources. A possible solution to this dilemma is offered to institutions that are not trying to do this on their own, but rather combine forces with likeminded institutions and together offer separate curricula to satisfy different stakeholders more broadly, whilst cooperating internally where practical.

MTI was established in 2009 through the combination of TH&E education and research from three separate educational dimensions. Educational institutions in Lapland grapple with the challenge of serving a large geographical area with few inhabitants and an active and growing TH&E sector. The institutions stay separate, each fulfilling their own role in society, and each working according to their own set of rules and laws that govern how they may act, and what they may do. The institutions offer degrees and diplomas that aim to satisfy different outcomes in society and carry out their own student recruitment and administration. By agreeing to cooperate in the fields of TH&E each is allowed to concentrate on a smaller sector of the curriculum space, and the compromises that need to be made are easier to negotiate when certain tasks and roles can be handed to another educational dimension; see Figure 3.1 for an illustration of MTI's possible force fields.

Students enrolling in the programmes offered at the institutions always concentrate on just their own award and there is no objective to reduce the administrative lines between the separate institutions. The metaphor MTI uses is that it creates a fruit salad of TH&E education, each component still clearly distinguishable in the whole, but tasting better through complementing

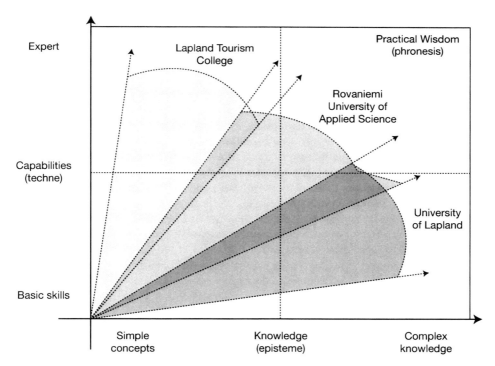

Figure 3.1 MTI's possible force fields within the curriculum space framework

Source: Adapted from Dredge *et al.* (2012: 2167).

other fruits. This is in contrast to the often used metaphor of a melting pot, because it conjures up images of distinct features being absorbed into a standardized mass where none of the initial ingredients exists in its original form.

The reason MTI wants to be seen as a fruit salad is exactly because of the forces active in the curriculum space. Students wanting, for example, to become executive chefs need to be trained in skills and competences offered by kitchen specialists, so that they can satisfy the industry they are heading to. But as no individual is exactly the same, some might want to learn about finance too, in order to know how to become a self-employed restaurateur, while others might want to learn about event catering, and so on. For students selecting courses offered at another institution credits are transferred to the diploma or degree programme that they are taking across MTI, and if they at a later stage decide to continue their education in one of the other dimensions then they will be able to get advanced standing for units already completed.

MTI was created in an environment before radical changes had started to take place in Finnish TH&E higher education, but now as those macro-changes start to make themselves known it is becoming all the more logical to carry on with the cooperation. With funding models that are encouraging shorter study times, cooperations like this would seem to be a useful way to progress.

Impacts on Finnish TH&E education from changes in the macro-environment

All education leading to an award is state funded in Finland, and thus also state regulated in terms of numbers of students being allowed to enrol in different degrees each year, and available degrees at different institutions. After having allowed the higher education field to expand rather continuously from the early 1970s until the early 2000s to provide the citizens of the nation, as well as foreign nationals, opportunities to gain higher education in fields considered necessary for society, recent years have provided quite a change. The demographics of Finland have changed with fewer children being born, and the previously decided numbers of degrees offered at different institutions are argued to be too large.

A simultaneous process has been the increased urbanization which has depleted some areas of the country of their school-aged population, and given especially the south of the country a much denser population. Beyond the nation, Finland is a member state of the European Union, and changes that have been brought about by the Bologna Process and the development of the European Higher Education Area (EHEA), as well as by the Tuning (2010) project creating a joint European Qualifications Framework (EQF) (see Chapter 1), have lately had a great impact on Finnish higher education institutions.

The legislation for universities was initially changed to assure them the same autonomy as other universities in EHEA, but in order to maintain control over the universities a new funding model was developed and implemented in 2012 (Narikka & Nurmi, 2013), and subsequently in 2014 for UAS institutions. The three cycles of higher education (bachelor, Master's, and doctorate degrees) described in the Bologna documents meant that Finnish universities and UAS institutions suddenly seemed to be on a level playing field, at least from an international perspective. The development of the dual model of higher education in Finland was aimed at providing different educational pathways for students aiming for different industries, but suddenly this dual model did not work due to changes in the macro-environment (Helakorpi, 2007). A subsequent change to the UAS sector was undertaken where available degree numbers were decreased radically, for example 38 per cent of TH&E degrees were discontinued nationally with some UAS's losing the right to offer TH&E degrees altogether.

The funding models for universities and UAS institutions differ significantly, with the former given a more expressly academic role, and the latter a stronger focus on teaching and community engagement. University funding is based on performance on a number of indicators within which average percentages of students reaching 55 credits per year, candidate, Master's and doctorate degrees completed, and other teaching-related matters carry almost similar weightings to the number of peer-reviewed publications and competitive grants and other research-related matters. By contrast, UAS funding is geared to teaching-related matters for 85 per cent with community engagement or industry-related grants making up the most of the remainder (Narikka & Nurmi, 2013).

These changes in the macro-environment have naturally also had an influence on the TH&E curricula on offer in Finland, just like in the rest of the world. Some UAS institutions have merged their former TH&E department with, for example, business studies, and continue to have some courses from the former curricula on offer, but other places have strategically decided to just teach out current students and thereafter discontinue these areas of study. The epistemology of TH&E in Finnish higher education is therefore shrinking with fewer courses on offer, fewer topic-specific academics and thus fewer industry-driven projects coordinated within the UAS by people who are familiar with the international research field. The ontology of TH&E being on the margins of society has definitely not helped TH&E academics to build a case for their courses.

But central to all of these macro-changes is what appears to be a lessening of the value given to TH&E studies in society, and through that amongst potential students. TH&E continues to be a marginal field without an overtly intrinsic value for the nation. Leisure time is valued as important to individuals, and thus indirectly to society as it provides people with opportunities to regenerate so that they can return refreshed and productive to work. TH&E is valued for providing employment opportunities, but is criticized for being full of lowly paid jobs. TH&E is valued for the positive impacts it can have on regenerating a region's culture, or for the opportunity it brings to capitalize on natural values, but is equally criticized for potential negative impacts it has on all sectors it is in contact with (Jafari, 2005). The global requirements placed on academics to produce more peer-reviewed material that seldom, if ever, is consumed by the industries to which it relates and seldom, if ever, is read by political decision makers, mean that the value of the field of TH&E academia might diminish even more. TH&E industry actors hire consultants with education in other fields to advise them on matters that TH&E academics study, and politicians listen first to experts in the fields TH&E is related to because they are seen as overarching matters in which TH&E are only components. One could claim that TH&E in academia is at a crossroads where the next actions will determine how it is valued in the future, and thus in which direction it will continue to develop.

Product life cycle of TH&E studies

One way of picturing the development of TH&E education is by analysing it through the help of a lifecycle model, such as the Destination Lifecycle model (Butler, 1980). TH&E studies in academia have over the last 40 years gone through the different stages that can be likened to a product life cycle starting with:

- 'Development' of higher education (HE) studies, based in many cases on earlier vocational studies, or as minor subjects offered in conjunction with a related major. Published research during this stage happened in journals focusing on other issues and TH&E was generally the empirical case environment in which the theories of the other discipline were applied.

- 'Introduction' of TH&E studies in select universities across the world with very few competing offerings. The degrees were often taught by academics educated in another discipline but establishing a new field based on their personal interests. The first TH&E-specific journals were established and an eclectic mix of research was accepted in them based on the disciplines in which the researchers were educated (Jafari, 2003), but from an epistemological perspective also depending on the field peer-reviewers were familiar with and thus willing to accept as truthful descriptions of reality in the new field (Belhassen & Caton, 2009).

- In the 'Growth' stage there was a flurry of new TH&E degrees established at universities, as well as a first clear diversification of TH&E into separate tourism, hospitality and, somewhat later, event degrees. Traditional universities rarely took on these new degrees, but in countries with a large component of funding coming from tuition fees, cooperations were created where private providers could offer TH&E programmes with the degrees being validated through cooperation with a university in return for royalties for all enrolled students (Jafari, 2003). The first academics educated within the field started to work at universities and teach the now more established field to growing classes of students. Research journals followed a similar growth with a multitude of ever more specific titles being published to cater for the academics active in all the new degree programmes.

- 'Maturity' is reached at the stage when no new degrees and no new research journals are being established. At the maturity stage the emphasis is placed on consolidating brand reputation, getting certificates of quality assurance, and more highlighted differentiation.

- 'Decline' or rejuvenation is the stage where some competitors start to withdraw from the field because there is not enough demand for the available products. Some try to rejuvenate their offering by rebranding it, or by consolidating several earlier separate degrees into one. TH&E academics might move on to other disciplines that are offering more secure employment and others are hedging their bets by publishing their research in several disciplines' journals to stay relevant to a larger audience.

The downfall of product lifecycle models is that they are weak tools for making predictions. It is seldom possible to forecast how long different stages will last, and proactive decisions are thus challenging. However, the model's value is in its simplicity and in the clearly developed strategies for the different stages. A manager in the TH&E academic world can estimate where their offering is on the product life cycle, and can thereafter adjust the communication with different stakeholders to maximize the achieved value.

Conclusion

This chapter has presented the being – ontology, the knowledge – epistemology, and the value – axiology, of TH&E studies by investigating the philosophical underpinnings of what these studies are: what sort of reality TH&E students and academics are thrown into; and how they understand that reality based on how it is presented to them. The way knowledge is created is also discussed and through that measurements for what the TH&E community consider to be true are established. Finally the value of TH&E is discussed and through that implications for curriculum development based on these foundations.

The empirical case of the chapter is an analysis of the development of TH&E education in Kittilä, Finnish Lapland, to highlight how curricula are shaped by factors in society. The case shows that TH&E education has followed the society's development from an agrarian economy, through industrial times towards a service, and ultimately an experience economy. The education offered has changed based on what society values, and how society sees its own reality and future. The empirical section continued by linking TH&E education in Kittilä with the Multidimensional Tourism Institute (MTI), a cooperation between three different educational dimensions: university, university of applied science, and vocational education. MTI was used to show how cooperating institutions might be able to reduce the challenge posed by the competing interests of stakeholders.

The final part of the chapter introduces macro-changes to TH&E education in Finland, though they are almost global. This section retraces the importance of paying attention to ontologies, epistemologies and axiologies of TH&E because they form the way the field is perceived, and thus also shape decisions made about education in the field. A final analysis of where TH&E education lies on a product life cycle finds that maturity might have been reached in many cases, and some signs of decline and rejuvenation are also in the air. The product lifecycle analysis is aimed at creating debate about how TH&E studies are to prepare for the future to ensure that the discipline is rejuvenated based on strong foundations, rather than allowing it to go into an uninformed decline.

References

Arkistolaitos. (2013). 'Maatalousoppilaitokset' (Schools of Agriculture). Available: *Arkistolaitos* (The National Archive in Finland): http://wiki.narc.fi/portti/index.php/Maatalousoppilaitokset (Accessed 25 August 2013).

Arkistolaitos. (undated). 'Kittilän kotitalousoppilaitos' (Kittilä School of Home Economy). Available: *Arkistolaitos* (The National Archive in Finland): http://www.narc.fi:8080/VakkaWWW/Selaus.action;jsessionid=667B8A348EA1D3DC3F9471A70C1A12BF?kuvailuTaso=AM&avain=45468.KA (Accessed 25 August 2013).

Barnhart, R. K. (Ed.). (1988). *Chambers Dictionary of Etymology*. Edinburgh: Chambers.

Belhassen, Y., & Caton, K. (2009). 'Advancing Understandings: a linguistic approach to tourism epistemology'. *Annals of Tourism Research*, 36(2), 335–52.

Butler, R.W. (1980). 'The Concept of a Tourist Area Cycle of Evolution: implications for management of resources'. *The Canadian Geographer*, 24(1), 5–12.

Csikszentmihalyi, M. (1991). *Flow – the Psychology of Optimal Experience*. New York: Harper Perennial.

Dredge, D., Benckendorff, P., Day, M., Gross, M. J., Walo, M., Weeks, P., & Whitelaw, P. (2012). 'The Philosophic Practitioner and the Curriculum Space'. *Annals of Tourism Research*, 39(4), 2154–76.

ELY (2011). 'Kulttuuri Maiseman Muotoutuminen' (The Development of a Cultural Landscape). Retrieved 20 August 2013 from Centre for Economic Development, Transport and the Environment (ELY) in Lapland. Available: http://www.ymparisto.fi/default.asp?contentid=180907 (Accessed 25 August 2013).

Franklin, A. (2008). 'The Tourism Ordering: taking tourism more seriously as a globalising ordering'. *Civilisations*, 57(1–2), 25–39.

Haaga Yhtymä. (2013) 'Haaga Yhtymän historia' (The History of Haaga Corporation). Available: *Haaga Yhtymä* from: http://www.haaga.fi/yritys/historia (Accessed 18 August 2013).

Heidegger, M. (1962). *Being and Time*, 7th edn. Translated J. Macquarrie & E. Robinson. Oxford: Basil Blackwell.

Helakorpi, S. (2007). 'Ammattikorkeakouluinstituutio – historiaa ja siitä opittavaa' (University of Applied Sciences Institutions – history and its lessons). *KeVer – Journal of Finnish Universities of Applied Sciences*, 6(4). Available: http://www.uasjournal.fi/index.php/kever/article/view/35/69 (Accessed 18 August 2013).

Jafari, J. (2003). 'Research and Scholarship – the basis of tourism education'. *Journal of Tourism Studies*, 14(1), 6–16.

Jafari, J. (2005). 'Bridging Out, Nesting Afield: powering a new platform'. *Journal of Tourism Studies*, 16(2), 1–5.

Jennings, G. (2010). *Tourism Research*, 2nd edn. Milton, Queensland: John Wiley & Sons Australia.

Kittilän kylät. (2013). *Kittilän kylät – Enämpi elämistä (The Villages of Kittilä – more fulfilling living)*. Kittilä: Kideve Elinkeinopalvelut.

Johan R. Edelheim

Lapin liitto. (2009). 'Väestö' (Population). Available: *Lapin liitto – Väestö*. Retrieved from: http://www.lapinliitto.fi/195 (Accessed 11 August 2013).

Lassila, J. (2001). *Lapin koulutushistoria – Kirkollinen alkuopetus, kansa-, perus- ja oppikoulut, osa 1* (The History of Education in Finnish Lapland – elementary education carried out by the church, primary schools, comprehensive schools and secondary schools, Part 1), Acta Univ. Oul. E 49. Oulu: University of Oulu.

Levi.NYT. (2009). 'Levi-Instituutti on jo 10-vuotias' (Levi-institute is already ten years old). Available: http://www.levinyt.fi/archive.php?id=1617 (Accessed 15 August 2013).

Martin, R. M. (2002). *The Philosopher's Dictionary*, 3rd edn. Peterborough: Broadview.

Moran, D. (2000). *Introduction to Phenomenology*. Florence, KY: Routledge.

Narikka, J., & Nurmi, E. (2013). *Uudet yliopistot ja uudistuvat ammattikorkeakoulut* (The New Universities and the Renewed Universities of Applied Sciences). Helsinki: Tietosanoma.

Organization for Economic Cooperation and Development. (undated). *OECD – Program for International Student Assessment – PISA*. Available: http://www.oecd.org/pisa/ (Accessed 15 July 2013).

Pennanen, V., & Hirttiö, H. (1992). 'Luoteis Lapin väestö ja elinkeinot' (The People and Living of North-West Lapland). Available: http://www.lapinliitto.fi/c/document_library/get_file?folderId=90644&name=DLFE-9616.pdf (Accessed 20 August 2013).

Saukko, P. (2003). *Doing Research in Cultural Studies – An Introduction to Classical and New Methodological Approaches*. London: Sage Publications.

Stumpf, S. E. (1994). *Philosophy – history and problems*, 5th edn. San Francisco, CA: McGraw-Hill.

This is Finland. (2013). *Finland in Facts*. Available: http://finland.fi/Public/default.aspx?contentid=160032&nodeid=44491&culture=en-US (Accessed 15 August 2013).

Tribe, J. (2002). 'The Philosophic Practitioner'. *Annals of Tourism Research*, 29(2), 338–57.

Tuning. (2010). *Tuning Sectoral Framework for Social Sciences*. Bilbao: University of Duesto.

Urry, J. (1990). *The Tourist Gaze*. London: Sage Publications.

World Bank. (2013). *Public Spending on Education*, total (% of GDP). Available: http://data.worldbank.org/indicator/SE.XPD.TOTL.GD.ZS (Accessed 15 August 2013).

Ylä-Kotola, M. (undated). *About us*. Available: http://www.ulapland.fi/InEnglish/About-us (Accessed 20 August 2013).

4

On the practical value of a liberal education

Kellee Caton

Tourism Management, Thompson Rivers University, Kamloops, Canada

Introduction

Among the many intellectual treasures left to the modern world by the ancient Greeks is the notion of *paideia*. In contrast to the term *banausos*, which means technical, skill-building education, *paideia* refers to the education of whole persons toward the pursuit of achieving the full development of what it means to be human (Fotopoulos, 2005). In ancient Greece, this meant a well-rounded education that included the development of the mind, body and spirit through the inclusion of diverse disciplines like mathematics, rhetoric, music and gymnastics. Today, as Cornel West (2009: 22) conveys, it means something more like 'a deep education' that connects us 'to profound issues in serious ways'. As he goes on to explain, *paideia* 'instructs us to turn our attention from the superficial to the substantial, from the frivolous to the serious. [It] concerns the cultivation of self, the ways you engage your own history, your own memories, your own mortality, your own sense of what it means to be alive as a critical, loving, aware human being'.

Contemporary higher education in TH&E generally falls far short of paideia. Indeed, it is becoming quite commonplace to hear critiques of today's curriculum as overly vocational, being bent toward the development of skills and competencies for handling TH&E as business activities, at the expense of providing students with the chance to explore their chosen field through a more liberal model of higher education – one that would allow them to better come to grips with TH&E as not simply domains of economic activity, but as phenomena of great social consequence (e.g. Tribe, 2002, 2008a; Inui *et al.*, 2006; Ring *et al.*, 2009; Belhassen & Caton, 2011). Indeed, hospitality is more than the sale of hotel rooms and restaurant meals, and tourism and events are more than the packaging for consumption of interesting sites, cultures and heritages. TH&E are activities through which people from different cultures, with different personalities and life histories, encounter one another and one another's spaces. We are speaking of a domain highly inflected by power relations, which has the capacity to engender a host of troublesome impacts, but also to serve as a profound space of possibility for positive change. This growing recognition of TH&E as worldmaking forces (Hollinshead, 2007) is indeed the driver behind calls for curriculum development beyond the narrow confines of a vocationalistic, or even a managerialistic, model.

In this chapter, I seek to make a case for the role of the liberal arts in TH&E higher education. As I hope the following pages will demonstrate, heavier inclusion of the liberal arts in the TH&E curriculum is not motivated by pie-in-the-sky idealism. Instead, a liberal curriculum has many practical benefits to offer as we seek to prepare the next generation of citizen-leaders in our field – especially if we are willing to stop and ask serious questions about what kind of tourism world we want to bring about in the future. In making this case, I in no way wish to diminish the value of vocational components within TH&E curricula. Indeed, many benefits can be reaped from vocational education. Instead, I wish to emphasize the importance of not abandoning traditional liberal education principles in constructing TH&E programmes. I also have no illusions about the very real difficulties that will accompany attempts to integrate the humanities more fully into the TH&E curriculum space (Dredge *et al.*, 2011; Ayikoru *et al.*, 2009). The pressures that create the curriculum in its current form are serious and should not be dismissed lightly. Indeed, in my own work in the near term, I am beginning to explore faculty members' and administrators' perceptions of the challenges that lie in bringing more humanities content into the TH&E classroom. Nevertheless, it is important to explore the value that does lie in liberal approaches to higher education and to keep the conversation alive, as we simultaneously struggle against the forces that make enlarging the curriculum space difficult. It is in that spirit that this chapter departs.

The humanities in TH&E education: sleeping on the porch?

In a keynote address given at the 2011 Surrey Tourism Conference, held in celebration of the twentieth anniversary of the publication of the special issue of *Annals of Tourism Research* on 'Tourism Social Science', Professor Annette Pritchard asked the audience to consider whether tourism studies has become 'a house divided'. Tourism studies has been cogently described by Tribe (1997, 2010) as a bisected field – with one portion addressing its business-oriented features and the other portion being dedicated to its analysis from a social science perspective – and Pritchard was querying the audience about the degree to which each of these sides of tourism studies genuinely respects and engages with the knowledge base of the other side, ultimately raising questions about our sustainability as a field if we carry on in our current divided manner.

Indeed, critiques of the traditional TH&E curriculum generally emphasize the importance of embracing both social science and business concerns, arguing that the latter tends to be advanced at the expense of the former (Tribe, 2002, 2008a; Inui *et al.*, 2006; Ring *et al.*, 2009). In support of a broad curriculum that transcends simply vocational concerns, Tribe's (1997) diagram of the epistemological domain of tourism nicely illustrates the idea that tourism knowledge can and should derive from a thick base of diverse disciplines, each of which can contribute in its own way to approaching the phenomenon. The diagram depicts tourism studies as a central object, surrounded by a band of disciplines – including sociology, geography, political science, law, psychology, philosophy and economics – which contribute to its development as an area of study. This ideal, however, does not necessarily reflect the reality of TH&E curricular practice. It seems rare to hear of philosophy courses in TH&E curricula. Furthermore, the arts scarcely receive any mention at all – indeed, they do not even make it by name into Tribe's abstraction (although his own work is a beautiful exception to their typical absence in tourism scholarship; see especially Tribe, 2008b). This situation is echoed in the intellectual landscape of dissertation study as well, with history, a discipline of quasi-humanities and quasi-social science pedigree, standing as the only representative of the humanities in Weiler *et al.*'s (2012) assessment of the top 14 disciplines informing tourism doctoral study in the United States, Canada, Australia and New Zealand. Tourism education may well be a house divided, with business and social science concerns tugging against each other, but the humanities – a major part of the essential foundation of a true liberal arts education – haven't even made it through the door. This represents a lost opportunity, for the humanities have a great deal to offer TH&E higher education.

The conditions of possibility

Before considering examples of potential applications of the humanities to the TH&E curriculum, it is helpful to set the stage by considering some of the key pedagogical benefits of the humanities in an abstract sense. Such benefits no doubt go beyond what can be enumerated in the space of one chapter and so I have chosen simply to highlight five, which I feel are particularly relevant to the TH&E context (as discussed later in the chapter) and which capture something of the breadth of the pedagogical value held within the humanities. After presenting these abstract benefits, I then proceed to a brief discussion on what it might mean to actualize these kinds of benefits within TH&E education. What might the future of our field look like, if steered by graduates who had developed these capacities? But first, what of practical value is generally to be gained from a liberal arts education?

Think for yourself! Building critical reasoning capacity

Although he is now revered as the father of classical philosophy, Socrates wasn't much appreciated by the authorities in his own day – and if you ask the critical theorists, the dialogical pedagogical approach he pioneered, which today bears his name as the 'Socratic method', still isn't high on the list of any powers-that-be in our own era who have a vested interest in maintaining the status quo. Socrates was a radical questioner. Never one to offer a polemic or claim to hold certain answers to life's complex problems, he instead saw himself as a gadfly, whose purpose it was to sting the sluggish horse of Athenian democracy into life by asking nettling questions that would force his interlocutors to consider the logic of their own arguments. Socratic reasoning has left a powerful mark on the discipline of philosophy and is one important reason why philosophy has been such a valued part of liberal arts education – and why it should be drawn upon more heavily in TH&E studies and management programmes.

To understand the importance of Socratic thinking, it is helpful to consider what happens without it. In her case for the vital role of the humanities in producing and maintaining democracy, philosopher Martha Nussbaum (2010) recounts a story from Socrates' own era, which I have often used in my own classroom and in other contexts in which I've written about the importance of the humanities: that of Thucydides' account of the aftermath of the Mytilene rebellion. According to Thucydides, when the colonists of Mytilene rebelled against Athens, a demagogue named Cleon gave a powerful speech about honour to the Assembly, urging Athenians to respond with violence by killing all the men in the colony and enslaving the women and children. The Assembly was persuaded by his rhetoric and dispatched a ship to carry out these orders. Next, however, another orator named Diodotus took to the podium and sought to calm the Athenians and encourage a merciful response to the rebellion. His speech was apparently even more persuasive than Cleon's had been, because the Assembly voted to change its mind and to send a second ship to stop the first one. By the luck of the fates, the second ship was able to catch the first, which was becalmed at sea. As Nussbaum notes (2012: 50), 'so many lives, and such an important policy matter, were left to chance rather than reasoned debate. If Socrates had gotten . . . people to stop, reflect, and analyze Cleon's speech, and to think critically about what he was urging, at least some would likely have resisted his powerful rhetoric and dissented from his call to violence, without needing Diodotus's calming speech'.

As this anecdote illustrates, without an awareness of the importance of deconstructing arguments and critiquing their logic, nor with a strong sense of what one's self and one's community truly value and wish to promote, people are easily swayed by forces such as authority, celebrity and peer pressure, rather than solid argumentation, in making decisions that affect their own future and the lives of others. Our TH&E students are no different and it is they who will participate in consequential decision-making about our world as future professionals in the field. The skills of logical reasoning and critical analysis, so richly imparted by philosophy, are of great practical importance for making sound decisions in the realm of public policy and in the business world. Our students must learn not to accept arguments at face value, but to think through their logic independently – to realize that they have the freedom to make up their own mind about a situation and then to use that freedom accordingly and in an informed way. Philosophy has a powerful toolkit to offer in this regard.

Deal with reality! Accepting complexity and taking responsibility in an antifoundational world

Lest we start to believe that the benefits of philosophy are limited to method – that this discipline's pedagogical value lies only in its style of engagement with the world rather than in the knowledge content it has produced – we must move beyond philosophy's noble roots in forging its classic dialogical approach and consider the field's epistemological contributions in more recent times. The history of philosophy lies in the search for universal answers to life's big questions. What does it mean to be good or just or righteous? What constitutes a life well lived? Does human life have a purpose and if so, what is it? Thinkers from antiquity to modernity have grappled with questions like these, usually with a goal of positing some finite system of logic that would produce an answer with a truth that could stand outside of time or circumstance. More recently, however, philosophy has taken a postmodern turn toward a position, alternately referred to as historical realism or pragmatism, which eschews universal answers to life's big questions, instead taking any attempts to achieve such answers as products of the values and reasoning styles of the people producing them (Rorty, 1989, 1999; West, 1991).

Inherent in the turn to postmodern ways of thinking across the academic landscape has been the risk of moral relativism (McGettigan, 2000) – that intellectual life would simply devolve into an endless series of deconstructions of the positions of various interlocutors or movements. Historical realism and pragmatism have forged a path out of this abyss, however, by accepting the reality of values and ethical norms as particular and situated, but arguing that the constant work of humanity lies precisely in recognizing morality as a negotiated human construct that we are empowered to contemplate and shape, in the quest to produce a world that better reflects humanity at our best. The goal of philosophy has thus shifted in the contemporary era beyond the search for universal answers to the examination of life's important questions within the context of a person or society's circumstances, a process that involves Socratically interrogating the assumptions behind status quo reasoning and reflecting on one's own values and those of one's social group or society. Rorty (1999) beautifully expresses this idea of the purpose of modern philosophy as the practice of coming to 'hold our time in thought' – an act that is crucial for living intentionally in our pursuits rather than being beholden to the whim of tradition or power (Belhassen & Caton, 2011). The turn away from a search for universals and toward the application of philosophy's toolkit for living intentionally within the space of our own circumstances has freed the discipline to grow in fertile new directions that have brought it closer to cultural studies, as a form of social critique engaging with the local and specific, but without abandoning its roots as a dealer in life's big questions. The scholarship that has blossomed in philosophy's postmodern turn thus holds great potential for use in the TH&E classroom because it can help students to build a bridge of thought between TH&E practice, broader social issues and forces and deeper questions of value and meaning in human life.

Use your imagination! Seeing the possible beyond the actual

In 2009, literary criticism scholar Brian Boyd made a daring move to explore the potential evolutionary origins of art and storytelling. Evolutionary psychology is currently flourishing as an academic field, having been nourished by major developments in cognitive neuroscience over the past decade; however, it continues to be an unpopular perspective in the arts and in cultural studies, which generally prefer to see human possibility as hinging on cultural factors alone, rather than being also partially undergirded by biology (a position only strengthened by the need to take a cautionary stance, given the abuses that ensued the last time evolutionary biology got tangled up in the study of human capabilities, back in the scary 'sociobiology' days of the 1970s). Without denying the central importance of culture in creating the human achievements we identify with modern civilized living, Boyd argues that art-making and storytelling go deeper than culture – that they have a biological basis that can be explained by examining their role in the evolution of our species. Boyd offers several compelling arguments to support this contention, including that art occurs universally in human societies and has persisted over thousands of generations; that it takes the same major forms in all societies (music, dance, visual representation, storytelling and poetry); that it often involves a high cost in terms of time, energy and other resources for the person making it; that it 'stirs strong emotions, which are evolved indicators that something matters to an organism'; and that it develops early, reliably and naturally (i.e. without special training) in all normally abled persons (Boyd, 2009: 73).

So, if there is an evolutionary purpose for art, then what is that purpose? According to Boyd, art can be seen as a form of cognitive play that basically hones creative capacity. It starts with the human attraction to pattern, which we seek for the purpose of making order out of chaos, for predicting what will come next. As a species uniquely inhabiting the 'cognitive niche', we gain most of our evolutionary advantage from our intelligence, and so information and the ability to process it effectively constitutes the cornerstone of our potential (Boyd, 2009: 89). Art represents a domain in which we can play with pattern and hence enrich our mental abilities to recognize it on different levels and in different forms. An analogue with physical play is illuminative here, and it is worth quoting Boyd at length:

> Evolution can install general guidelines for action—nature's factory settings—but for some behaviors fine-tuned choices and wider ranges of options that can be deployed at short and context-sensitive notice make a decisive difference. This applies particularly to the volatile sphere of social relations, and especially to the most urgent situations, flight and fight. Such behaviors can be fine-tuned by experience and the range of options extended by exploratory action. Creatures with stronger motivations to practice such behaviors and to explore new options in advance, in situations of low danger and adequate resources, will fare better than those without. The more pleasure that creatures have in play in safe contexts, the more they will happily expend energy in mastering skills needed in urgent or volatile situations, in attack, defense, and social competition and cooperation. This explains why in the human case we particularly enjoy play that develops skills needed in flight (chase, tag, running) and fight (rough-and-tumble, throwing as a form of attack at a distance), in recovery of balance (skiing, surfing, skateboarding), and in individual and team games.
>
> (Boyd, 2009: 92)

Just as physical play allows humans to hone a range of survival skills that may be needed on short notice and in highly context-dependent situations, art and the opportunity for cognitive play it provides through engagement with pattern nurtures creativity, forging new neural pathways in our brains and equipping them to imagine new options not constrained by the realities of the immediate situation. Progress in human civilization – from science and technology to peace-building and pleasure – hinges largely on this kind of creative and imaginative capacity. Universities exist, at least in large measure, to provide a space for this type of capacity development. They are places where students can 'try on' new ideas, explore new problems and subject old problems to new ways of thinking. Indeed, working through hypothetical scenarios and 'test driving' different potential solutions to problems, through case competitions and the like, is often a major component of the curriculum in applied fields, like law, business and TH&E. Less commonly, however, are the humanities seen as a resource for encouraging intellectual experimentation in applied fields. This is a shame, because the arts are so effective at catalysing growth in mental flexibility. The fictional, hypothetical spaces that are created through literature, film, the visual arts and so forth allow us to mentally step out of reality onto an alternative ontological platform, which gives us a new vantage point from which to effectively critique the real world (Barone, 1995) and a new sense of what the alternative possibilities might look like. Thus, the arts can extend philosophy's ability to unlock our capacity for independent, original thought into the realm of imagination for what possibilities might lie beyond the here and now – a hugely important capability for our TH&E students to develop, given that the future is necessarily uncertain and given the magnitude of environmental, sociocultural and economic challenges, unimaginable to earlier generations, that they will face as tomorrow's professionals in our field.

Do unto others! Cultivating empathic capacity and moral imagination

Closely related to the arts' capacity to help us imagine possibilities that aren't immediately and materially present and also to their capacity to help us deal with the reality of complexity, is their ability to catalyse our empathetic development. The arts help us grow as relational subjects, capable of putting ourselves in each others shoes and understanding the emotions that other's experience. As Nussbaum (2010), who has been a chief advocate for the humanities in higher education, explains, we are not born innately viewing others around us as being infinitely deep and complex, with their own internal worlds of emotion and their own rights to pursue their needs and desires. Instead, as she argues, as babies, our first experiences are simply of other animated shapes, which move about ministering to our own needs, and it is an act of learning – indeed, an accomplishment – to come to view these shapes as human beings like ourselves, who have needs like our own and who experience joy and pain just as we do. We are generally able to achieve this accomplishment pretty well with regard to the people we interact with most closely: our family members, our friends and maybe even members of our local or national communities. We increasingly struggle, however, to extend the status of full humanity to those more distant from us, either physically such that we never directly encounter them or socially such that we define them as differing from ourselves in key ways (e.g. with regard to religion, ethnicity) that carry a lot of weight in our contemporary social world and prevent us from relating successfully across categorical boundaries.

The arts are a primary way that we can come to better extend empathy to others (Barone, 1995; Nussbaum, 2010). As discussed above, they allow for the creation of a rich imaginative space, in which we can approach life's serious issues in a less threatening atmosphere of play and open possibilities (Boyd, 2009). They allow us to try on different identities, to experiment with what it would be like to be in another person's position, to imagine that the circumstances we find ourselves in could be different. They enable us to enter into moments of duality, in which our own identity and perspective is preserved, but in which we simultaneously imaginatively enter into the perspective of another (Verducci, 2000). Even though we can never completely apprehend another person's perspective, we are enlarged by this stretch into duality and it leaves us more aware of the reality that we indeed exist relationally with others (Noddings, 1984). Literature and drama (on page, stage or film) can be highly effective at catalysing this process because of the vivid characters created through these modes; such a plethora of characters expands the repertoire of personhoods with which we can potentially identify – but, importantly, in the safe and playful space of the fictional hypothetical.

This step toward empathy demonstrates the arts' ability to spur not only pure imagination, in terms of having the mental flexibility to conjure that life might be different from the here and now and to consider how we might act upon different potential situations, but also the capacity for moral imagination (Lederach, 2005) – a fundamental ability that human beings have to think creatively about how they can relate to one another in more just, loving and mutually fulfilling ways. The imaginative leap of empathy is one of coming to locate another person within the circle of 'we', rather than as an outsider in the structure of 'us' and 'them'. In person-oriented fields like tourism, in which communities and cultures are a central resource, both as an attraction driving tourist desire in the first place and as agents in the negotiation process that creates tourism development outcomes, interpersonal and intergroup relationship success is key, and the arts can be of great value in helping us hone our capacities for relational thinking and living.

Embrace your inner human! Remembering the person inside the student

One of the major implications that flows from Boyd's (2009) work on the evolutionary origins of art and story, as discussed above, is that art is natural and fundamental to the human experience. We need play and creativity for our normal mental and emotional development. The technocratic bent of contemporary civilization would generally have us forget this. The ideologies of capitalism, materialism and performativity (Ayikoru et al., 2009), which drive our tourism world and the larger world beyond it, give little respect to the need for creative cognitive play – despite the ironic fact that the success of products and services and the organizations purveying them often hinges somewhere down the line on the creative work of their designers and marketers. Thus, the humanities are often seen as frivolous and are dismissed as something that can be dispensed with in the ever-tighter curriculum space that the neoliberalization of higher education forces us to work within (Dredge et al., 2011; see also Chapter 1).

Is it any surprise, then, that our students can sometimes seem less-than-engaged in our classrooms, easily distracted by the lure of portable technologies that can connect them back immediately to the richly stimulating social world of their peers and families, or even simply given over to the seductions of doodling on a notebook, a mind actively emanating its creative capacity even as it tries to give attention to developing the 'competencies' it is told will lead to economic success upon leaving the safety of the university gates? Although students may indeed be greatly motivated by the fear of future unemployment and economic failure, or more positively by the desire for the material and nonmaterial rewards that come with career success in the contemporary world, there is a gap between that rational, higher-order motivation and the basic motivation of human beings for ongoing cognitive development through the nourishment of playful engagement with pattern. Surely we have nothing to lose by attending to that deeper motivation and nurturing it through classroom activities. And what we have to gain is great: more attentive students, who are more engaged and fulfilled by the classroom experience, and who are hence more relaxed and open to new ideas and more primed for cognitive growth that can serve them – and our field – better in the future. Student-centred education surely means, among other things, attending to the reality of the human being inside the learner. The humanities offer incredible resources for creating classroom environments that do this better.

The humanities also help us to attend to the deeper needs of our students in another sense. As Rosales (2012: 20) cogently notes in her campaign for contemplative education, our students' 'minds strive for knowledge, but their hearts search for meaning'. In her words:

> If we in higher education truly accept a responsibility to prepare the next generation to tackle humankind's internal and external conflicts, then we also have to recognize the internal and external landscapes in which this transformation takes place. The curriculum of most postsecondary institutions has traditionally placed the cognitive pursuits of its faculty, students and staff at the fore, while neglecting to account in any systematic way for the role that affective development plays in the formation of a responsible, educated and energized citizenry. In other words, intellect and heart live separate lives on most university campuses. . . . Neglecting to address, value and strengthen the fundamental connections between knowledge and love leads to an impoverished understanding of the world and inhibits the kind of authentic transformation that education has the power to foster.

It is in this sense that a return to paideia-oriented thinking, as expressed in this chapter's opening paragraph, is needed in higher education, especially in applied fields like TH&E, which tend to be the shortest on it. If students perceive a sense of purpose in the classroom, which goes beyond their own training as future subjects of the economic system and if not only their reasoning capacity but also their emotions are fully tuned in, then we will be much closer to recapturing higher education's original vision as an intrinsically motivating experience that leads to both individual and social good. We can better serve our learners by engaging their full personhood, and the humanities – as their name suggests – have a great way of speaking to the human in all of us.

Actualizing the possible in TH&E education

In her keynote address at the seventh annual Tourism Education Futures Initiative conference, Conscious Travel founder and social change-agent Anna Pollock spoke of the sweeping changes facing tourism practice today. Indeed, those working in the tourism industry in the mid-twentieth century, when mass tourism looked open for spectacular growth, could scarcely have imagined the social, economic and environmental realities that characterize life a mere 50 years later. Pollock's images of the realities of modern tourism – lines of exhausted travellers delayed at an airport over a terrorism alert, overcrowded beaches, swirling waste – illustrate the dystopian side of change, but she also calls attention to positive developments. In today's 'experience economy' (Pine & Gilmore, 1999), consumer values are shifting, such that people are seeking not just more stuff and more status, but 'more meaning, more deeply felt connections, more substance, more control and a greater sense of purpose' (Pollock, 2013). Consumers are also increasingly concerned with ethics in the realm of consumption, including in tourism (Weeden & Boluk, 2014). Organizations are also recognizing that approaches not in step with this changing consumer ethos and not sustainable for the planet and the people on it are also not going to be good for business over the long term (KPMG International, 2012). Today's TH&E graduates are indeed coming of age in a different kind of world.

The capacities a liberal education can foster – free thought, acceptance of responsibility, creativity and imagination, empathetic citizenship – and the enhancement of classroom engagement it can produce hold tremendous value for preparing our students for facing this new tourism world, changing it for the better and even making it more economically productive. Philosophy and the arts can be drawn upon in a variety of ways in the TH&E curriculum to encourage such outcomes, beginning quite simply with spurring students to think more deeply about their reasons and goals for undertaking a TH&E career in the first place. As it stands, our students rarely seem to reflect on why they are interested in working in the TH&E field, apart from perhaps a vague notion that they themselves find travel enjoyable. This is a shame, because our field has deep roots in the notion of hospitality, cultural sharing and care for others. It is frequently lamented that today's TH&E workers often lack a 'service or hospitality ethic', and this is surely at least partially attributable to a lack of reflection on the part of those working in the industry about the qualities of care-taking, engagement and culture-sharing that make TH&E a special and worthwhile human enterprise to begin with. A culture of hospitality cannot be created by simply ordering those on tourism's front lines to treat others with care and thoughtfulness. Instead, it must be cultivated, by nurturing a workforce of individuals who have reflected on the value of the occupation they have undertaken and have come on their own to embrace certain ideals. In a world of changing consumer values, where meaningful experiences are increasingly central to tourist desire, recovering our field's underlying ethic of hospitality will no doubt be crucial in creating the kinds of offerings tourists will value.

Lest we forget, however, despite our field's noble roots in the art of hospitality, tourism is not always virtuous. Indeed, it can be highly exploitative, to its own workers, to the environment and to the people and cultures that become its 'products'. Thus, tomorrow's TH&E leaders need to be encouraged not only to reflect Socratically on their own values and actions but also to be able to effectively take apart the arguments that support the maintenance of tourism as a largely low-wage industry with lousy benefits and job security and with work that is often uncreative, repetitive and boring (Belhassen, 2007). Similarly, they need to be able to contemplate 'big picture' issues in their field, such as resource overconsumption and waste, leakage of tourism benefits from underprivileged back to overprivileged parts of the world and issues of representation of toured people and cultures through site promotion and production.

The ability to appreciate complexity, to think critically about one's responsibility to oneself and others, and to extend empathy and full humanity to those others is also key to the future success of TH&E practice. As Higgins-Desbiolles and Blanchard (2010) argue, we often focus so much on tourism as an economic powerhouse – and hence on training students to work within tourism as an economic sphere – that we tend to forget that it also has a serious social function: tourism can bring people together across lines of difference to encounter one another and one another's cultures and spaces, and can therefore potentially foster understanding and peace. Far from being the mere fancy of idealists and romantics, this social function of tourism as a promoter of peace has been embraced by the United Nations in position statements and is receiving increasing scholarly attention (Moufakkir & Kelly, 2010). But, as we all know, this potentially productive and mutually enlightening encounter between hosts and guests often goes terribly wrong in reality. Too often, hosts feel disrespected by guests who overrun their spaces, showing little care for the environment or the local way of doing things (e.g. Wilson et al., 2008). They become frustrated by foreign-owned enterprises that profit from the use of their lands without contributing fairly to the development of their communities (e.g. Shani & Pizam,

2012). They feel shut out of their own spaces (e.g. Bruner, 2005). They feel used, as their cultures (Santos & Yan, 2008) and sometimes even their bodies (e.g. Kibicho, 2009), are offered up for consumption. Sustainable tourism development cannot occur unless hosts' feelings are taken seriously. To proceed otherwise is to engender only cynicism and resentment on the part of hosts, selfishness and entitlement on the part of guests and increased social and economic inequality and strife for humanity as a whole.

As tomorrow's TH&E leaders, our students need to learn how to take other people's feelings seriously and to treat them with respect. They must learn to imagine communities and their spaces and cultural legacies not as commodities to be exploited for profit, but as entities of great meaning to other human beings. Likewise, they must come to see the TH&E industry's employees – including their own future selves – not as disposable cogs in a corporate wheel, deserving of little in the way of pay or security, but as creative beings with something of value to contribute. Recognizing the worth of all people – tourists, locals in destinations and workers in the industry – and learning to be in touch with their perspectives, their accomplishments, their challenges and their hopes for the future can help TH&E development and practice to start in the right place, and thus can surely move us closer to the UN's vision of tourism as a special kind of economic industry, which has additional social purposes to fulfil. As such, tourism could even begin to stand as a model for other industries of what economic development could look like if it drew on human beings and their relationships with one another as its greatest resource. In short, if it is to become sustainable and serve as an exemplar of good practice to other industries, tourism needs to rediscover its humanity.

Philosophy and the arts are among the key educational resources for developing the kinds of capacities that our students will need to function in the TH&E world we find ourselves in. They will need to be able to think for themselves – out of the binds set by the reigning power structures of the day, out of the boundaries of 'the way things have always been done'. They will need creativity and flexibility to function under conditions of uncertainty, conditions which will surely change many times before they reach the end of their careers. They will need to be able to relate to and get along with people very different from themselves, in the increasingly globalized work- and life-spaces they will inhabit and in the inherently culturally complex field in which they serve. And they will need to know that they have the power – and the responsibility – to transcend the status quo and change the world for the better. Of what practical value is a life characterized by a lack of freedom, imagination, empowerment and meaningful moral engagement with others?

It is for these reasons that a return to paideia in higher education – and its infusion into applied fields like TH&E – is so desperately needed. Our students have a hunger for greater meaning in the classroom, even if it is sometimes only latent within them, even if they do not always realize it or cry out for it and let us know. An education that facilitates this engagement with greater meaning, this connection of individual learners' lives with their own histories and values and with substantive issues outside themselves, this sort of reflection and cultivation of selves and communities that sets people in touch with what it means to be alive and what it means to be human (West, 2009) is of immense practical value. It can do nothing less than reconfigure the possibilities: redefine the very terrain for a kind of new world that might one day be realized, in tourism and beyond.

References

Ayikoru, M., Tribe, J., & Airey, D. (2009). 'Reading Tourism Education: neoliberalism unveiled'. *Annals of Tourism Research*, 36, 191–221.

Barone, T. (1995). 'The Purposes of Arts-Based Educational Research'. *International Journal of Educational Research*, 23, 169–80.

Belhassen, Y. (2007). 'Inciting the Sociological Imagination'. *Annals of Tourism Research*, 34, 1078–81.

Belhassen, Y., & Caton, K. (2011). 'On the Need for Critical Pedagogy in Tourism Education'. *Tourism Management*, 32, 1389–96.

Boyd, B. (2009). *On the Origin of Stories: evolution, cognition, and fiction*. Cambridge, MA: Belknap Press.

Bruner, E. (2005). 'Slavery and the Return of the Black Diaspora'. In E. Bruner (Ed.), *Culture on Tour: ethnographies of travel* (pp. 101–25). Chicago, IL: University of Chicago Press.

Dredge, D., Beckendorff, P., Day, M., Gross, M. J., Walo, M., Weeks, P., & Whitelaw, P. (2011). 'Conceptualizing the Perfect Blend in the Tourism and Hospitality Education Curriculum Space'. In M. Gross, *Tourism: Creating a Brilliant Blend: proceedings of the 21st Annual CAUTHE Conference* (pp. 1–19). Council for Australian University Tourism and Hospitality Educators National Conference, 8–11 February, Adelaide, Australia.

Fotopoulos, T. (2005). 'From (Mis)Education to Paideia'. *International Journal of Inclusive Democracy*, 2, 1–33.

Higgins-Desbiolles, F., & Blanchard, L. (2010). 'Challenging Peace through Tourism: placing tourism in the context of human rights, justice and peace'. In O. Moufakkir & I. Kelly (Eds.), *Tourism, Progress and Peace* (pp. 35–46). Wallingford, UK: CABI.

Hollinshead, K. (2007). '"Worldmaking" and the Transformation of Place and Culture: the enlargement of Meethan's analysis of tourism and global change'. In I. Ateljevic, A. Pritchard, & N. Morgan (Eds.), *The Critical Turn in Tourism Studies: innovative research methodologies* (pp. 165–96). Amsterdam: Elsevier.

Inui, Y., Wheeler, D., & Lankford, S. (2006). 'Rethinking Tourism Education: what should schools teach?' *Journal of Hospitality, Leisure, Sport and Tourism Education*, 5, 25–35.

Kibicho, W. (2009). *Sex Tourism in Africa: Kenya's booming industry*. Farnham, UK: Ashgate.

KPMG International. (2012). 'Expect the Unexpected: building business value in a changing world'. Available: http://www.kpmg.com/dutchcaribbean/en/Documents/KPMG%20Expect_the_Unexpected_ExctveSmmry_FINAL_WebAccessible.pdf (Accessed 5 September 2013).

Lederach, J. (2005). *The Moral Imagination: the art and soul of building peace*. New York: Oxford University Press.

McGettigan, T. (2000). 'Flawed by Design: the virtues and limitations of postmodern theory'. *Theory and Science* 1(1): Available: http://theoryandscience.icaap.org/content/vo.001.001/05mcgettigan.html (Accessed 5 September 2013).

Moufakkir, O., & Kelly, I. (Eds.) (2010). *Tourism, Progress and Peace*. Wallingford, UK: CABI.

Noddings, N. (1984). *Caring: a feminine approach to ethics and moral education*. Berkeley: University of California Press.

Nussbaum, M. (2010). *Not for Profit: why democracy needs the humanities*. Princeton, NJ: Princeton University Press.

Pine, B. J., II, & Gilmore, J. (1999). *The Experience Economy: work is theatre and every business a stage*. Boston, MA: Harvard Business School Press.

Pollock, A. (2013). 'Waking Tourism up to an Uncertain Future: educating for lives of change and consequence'. Available: http://www.slideshare.net/AnnaP/tefi-2 (Accessed 5 September 2013).

Ring, A., Dickinger, A., & Wöber, K. (2009). 'Designing the Ideal Undergraduate Program in Tourism: expectations from industry and educators'. *Journal of Travel Research*, 48, 106–21.

Rorty, R. (1989). *Contingency, Irony and Solidarity*. Cambridge: Cambridge University Press.

Rorty, R. (1999). *Philosophy and Social Hope*. London: Penguin.

Rosales, J. (2012). 'Cultivating Minds and Hearts'. *University Affairs*, August, 18–24.

Santos, C., & Yan, G. (2008). 'Representational Politics in Chinatown: the ethnic Other'. *Annals of Tourism Research*, 35, 879–99.

Shani, A., & Pizam, A. (2012). 'Community Participation in Tourism Planning and Development'. In M. Uysal, R. Perdue, & M. J. Sirgy (Eds.), *Handbook of Tourism and Quality-of-Life Research: enhancing the lives of tourists and residents of host communities* (pp. 547–64). New York: Springer.

Tribe, J. (1997). 'The Indiscipline of Tourism'. *Annals of Tourism Research*, 24, 638–57.

Tribe, J. (2002). 'The Philosophic Practitioner'. *Annals of Tourism Research*, 29, 338–57.

Tribe, J. (2008a). 'Tourism: a critical business'. *Journal of Travel Research*, 46, 245–55.

Tribe, J. (2008b). 'The Art of Tourism'. *Annals of Tourism Research*, 35, 924–44.

Tribe, J. (2010). 'Tribes, Territories and Networks in the Tourism Academy'. *Annals of Tourism Research*, 37, 7–33.

Verducci, S. (2000). 'A Moral Method? Thoughts on cultivating empathy through method acting'. *Journal of Moral Education*, 29, 87–99.

Weeden, C., & Boluk, K. (Eds.) (2014). *Managing Ethical Consumption in Tourism*. London: Routledge.

Weiler, B., Moyle, B., & McLennan, C. (2012). 'Disciplines that Influence Tourism Doctoral Research: the United States, Canada, Australia and New Zealand'. *Annals of Tourism Research*, 39, 1425–45.

West, C. (1991). *The Ethical Dimensions of Marxist Thought*. New York: Monthly Review Press.

West, C. (2009). *Brother West: living and loving out loud*. New York: Smiley Books.

Wilson, J., Richards, G., & MacDonnell, I. (2008). 'Intracommunity Tensions in Backpacker Enclaves: Sydney's Bondi Beach'. In K. Hannam & I. Ateljevic (Eds.), *Backpacker Tourism: Concepts and Profiles* (pp. 199–214). Clevedon, UK: Channel View.

5

The philosophical practitioner and the curriculum space

Dianne Dredge
Department of Culture and Global Studies, Aalborg University, Denmark

Pierre Benckendorff
UQ Business School, The University of Queensland, Brisbane, Australia

Michele Day
Southern Cross University, Australia

Michael J. Gross
School of Management, University of South Australia, Australia

Maree Walo
School of Tourism and Hospitality Management, Southern Cross University, Australia

Paul Weeks
The Hotel School Sydney, Southern Cross University, Australia

Paul A. Whitelaw
College of Business, Victoria University, Australia

Introduction

The balance between liberal and vocational education within tourism and hospitality (T&H) curricula has become an increasingly noteworthy topic of discussion since Tribe (2002a), drawing from Schön's reflective practitioner (1982, 1983; Schön & Rein, 1994), argued for a curriculum that nurtures the 'philosophic practitioner'. The philosophic practitioner education (PPE) requires a curriculum that is composed of vocational, professional, social science and humanities

Reprinted from 'The Philosophic Practitioner and the Curricula Space', *Annals of Tourism Research*, 39(4): 2154–76, Dredge, D., Benckendorff, P., Day, M., Gross, M., Walo, M., Weeks, P. & Whitelaw, P., 2012, and reproduced with permission from Elsevier.

knowledge and skills that promote a balance between satisfying the demands of business and those required to operate within the wider tourism world. Several authors have been calling for this balance in education for some time (e.g. see Baum, 2005; Inui & Lankford, 2006; Lashley, 1999; McKercher, 2002), but there remain considerable challenges in terms of defining programme content, modes of delivery, appropriate pedagogies, skills and graduate capabilities (Tribe 2000). These challenges are derived from a range of internal and external factors that shape the possibilities of delivering the PPE at different institutions. This chapter argues that a more nuanced conceptualization of the PPE is required that acknowledges core principles (e.g. critical management skills and developing student reflexivity), but that also allows flexibility in the way PPE is defined and delivered at different institutions. The intention is to advance the PPE and to make it relevant to different cultural, political and educational contexts.

The aims of this chapter are to review contemporary debates about tourism and hospitality education and to present a dynamic PPE curriculum space framework that can be used to facilitate discussion, understanding and decision-making about the T&H curriculum within different higher education contexts. The conceptual framework presented is derived from discussions taking place, particularly in the professional education literature, that seek to reconcile 'knowing', 'doing' and 'being' (Barnett & Coate, 2005). In this chapter, the PPE (Tribe, 2002a) and 'education for ethical tourism action' (Tribe, 2002b), derived from the works by Schön (1983) and inspired by Aristotle, provide the basis for this development.

In addressing the above aim, the chapter is divided into four sections. The first section provides a background to the PPE. The second section briefly reviews the higher education context and the range of meta-influences shaping the T&H curriculum at the institutional level. In the third section, literature dealing with the curriculum space, and specifically the issue of balancing liberal education and vocational ideals, will be reviewed. In particular, the PPE, which has captured significant academic attention over the last 10 years, will be discussed. In the fourth section, we analyse the force field of influences that affect the T&H curriculum space. In the final section, we present a conceptual framework that acknowledges the dynamic and socially constructed nature of the T&H curriculum space, and we suggest potential applications of the framework and ideas for future research. Whilst the chapter reflects upon the global context and draws significantly from international contributions, it specifically responds to an Australian imperative to better understand the curriculum space in the face of rapid and sustained change in higher education policy.

Blending vocational and liberal education

Contemporary scholarship divides higher education as two broad categories: liberal and vocational. The distinction between liberal arts education and vocational education, and the desired balance between them, provides the basis of discussion in many areas of study, but particularly in professional education programmes such as town planning, accounting, nursing and tourism. Liberal education (*liber* = free in Latin) refers to a curriculum that develops general knowledge and fosters complex, independent thinking and transferable intellectual and practical skills. Advocates of a liberal education argue that it should be oriented towards social and political ends and in the context of the role the learner can take as a 'good citizen' into the future (Farnham & Yarmolinsky, 1996; Nussbaum, 2010). It gives the learner the capacity to confront problems, think creatively and make a contribution to society.

Liberal education has its genesis in the notion that pursuit of knowledge for its own sake, rather than for its utility, is not only a sufficient educational goal, but desirable (Blanshard, 1973). The composition of a liberal education curriculum commonly includes the study of such disciplines as arts, humanities and social sciences, and aims to develop capacity for thought, reason, pursuit of knowledge and understanding. While definitional debates abound, it is also helpful to note that liberal education can be distinguished by what it is not: vocational, exclusively scientific or specialist in any sense (Hirst, 1974). The purpose of a liberal education is to provide an enculturation process that develops an awareness and ongoing ability to critically reflect on the intellectual world (Wegener, 1978), preparing graduates for free-thinking citizenship. A liberal education experience is a dialectical one that concentrates on broadening students' understanding of the relationship between the individual and society (Taylor et al., 1985). A graduate would be equipped with qualities such as a breadth of disciplinary knowledge; the ability to distinguish among contested ideologies; an appreciation of the dialogue between knowledge and values; and an ability to connect ideas and information.

Vocational education (vocatio = 'call' in Latin) provides training and practical skills for a specific trade or occupation. Professional education represents a merging of both liberal and vocational education whereby the learner engages in specialized education and training for a particular occupation (Lum, 2009). The art of professional practice has been the subject of increasing attention in a range of fields subject to contemporary moral and practical challenges such as bioethics, education, medicine, politics, planning and, now, T&H studies. The term 'phronesis' is derived from Aristotle's Nicomachean Ethics wherein the contributions of scientific knowledge (episteme) and technical knowledge (techne) by themselves are understood to be insufficient in determining good professional action (see Flyvbjerg, 2001). For Aristotle, phronesis, defined as practical wisdom or prudence, is also necessary. In Aristotle's view, phronesis requires actors to draw not only from episteme and techne, but also from maturity and experience (i.e. prudence), to determine good and virtuous actions.

Tourism and hospitality programmes across the globe have followed different developmental paths and have engaged in the development of student understanding, criticality and reflexivity associated with the PPE in diverse ways (Lashley, 1999; Morrison & O'Mahony, 2003). However, for educators in both tourism and hospitality fields, how to foster practical wisdom or prudence is a significant common challenge. Students require learning opportunities that facilitate the development of higher order knowledge, opportunities to learn and practise skills, and opportunities to apply and reflect on practical judgement. This requires one to recognize their ethical position and values and those of others within the particular setting and to apply in situ judgement. The resultant 'good life' of actors is one that is characterized by active and virtuous public engagement by professionals in local contexts. The goal of educating T&H professionals who have the knowledge, skills and practical wisdom to act in a worldmaking capacity has been addressed by both Tribe (2002a) and Jamal (2004), and provides the foundation of the PPE.

The philosophic practitioner education

Calls for greater attention to the balance between vocational and professional skills and the broader critical thinking and analytical skills usually associated with the social sciences and humanities are becoming more frequent in the T&H education literature. Much of this literature cites the work of Tribe (2002a: 340–1), who conceptualizes the curriculum space in terms of two dimensions:

> ends and stance. The first relates to that part of the world which is the focus of the curriculum, and the second to how the curriculum promotes engagement with these ends. Ends are represented by an axis of purposes toward which the curriculum is constructed and aimed.

These include vocational ends of employability and liberal ends focused in freedom of thought about tourism. . . . The stance axis describes different modes of study and expression which promote the curriculum's ends. The alternative stances that can be adopted in tourism education are reflection and action.

Figure 5.1 illustrates the two dimensions in the PPE. In this figure, Tribe (2002a) defines the curriculum as the 'whole educational experience packaged as a degree programme' and which may include knowledge, skills, assessment, learning experiences and so on (p. 339). Students take different educational journeys through the curriculum space depending upon the way their programme of study has been framed by the institution, the lecturers who deliver the courses and what core subjects and electives they take. According to Tribe, the philosophic practitioner should have skills and knowledge in all four domains. Moreover, he observes that although the four domains are represented separately in the diagram, in practice they would be integrated in the curriculum model.

The PPE captures the ambition of T&H education to meet the demands of industry and promote employability of graduates. It also harnesses the idea of the critically engaged and mindful role of T&H graduates in society. As such, it has become an influential framework for depicting the challenges faced by curriculum planners and has received increasing critical attention and support since its publication (Ring *et al.*, 2009; Belhassen & Caton, 2011). However, it is now over 10 years since Tribe presented the PPE, and whilst the core principles of the framework remain sound, the present higher education context is significantly different. In this context a number of points are raised about the PPE.

First, despite the fact that Tribe conceptualizes the curriculum broadly to encompass 'the whole educational experience', discussions of the framework have tended to focus on a perceived trade-off between knowledge and skills in curriculum content. This discussion has taken place at the expense of considering how pedagogy, a focus on the student experience and the framing of assessment can bridge liberal and vocational education and deliver a whole

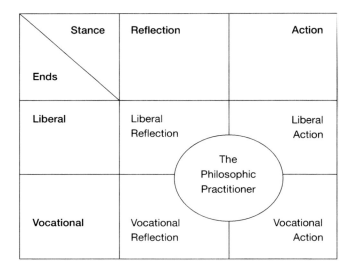

Figure 5.1 The philosophic practitioner

Source: Tribe (2002a: 348). (Reproduced with permission from Elsevier.)

education experience. For example, Work Integrated Learning (WIL), where students are required to simultaneously reflect on their engagement in work practice while considering the application and relevance of theoretical concepts and models, integrates knowledge and skills thus overcoming the need for a trade-off (Cooper et al., 2010).

Second, the framework conceptualizes 'reflection' and 'action' as alternatives placed on two axes. However, one can simultaneously exhibit the capacity to be both highly reflective and action-oriented, and presumably this position is located in the circle in the middle of Figure 5.1. However, reflexivity, or the capacity to act based on self-reflection and awareness of the impacts on others, is dynamic and developed incrementally over one's student and professional life. In a simple example, a scaffolded student assessment task might involve a student learning a skill (e.g. evaluating a tourism product), reflecting upon how they undertook the evaluation in terms of their own skills and knowledge deficits, improving the process through research and design, repeating the task, and then critically analysing and articulating the process they went through. In this instance, action and reflection are present in student reflexivity. This brings into question whether the reflection/action axis in Figure 5.1 oversimplifies the dynamic relationship between reflection and action that can be more accurately likened to a dynamic feedback loop progressing over one's professional life.

Third, the framework offers a single 'expert' position on what a good PPE in T&H education should encapsulate. Yet Wells (1996) prompts us to question who is in the best position to identify what is required to be included as part of the curriculum, and observes that academic educators have tended to dominate such discussions. Sociologists interested in the production of knowledge have observed the existence of different knowledge-oriented life worlds, wherein different stakeholder groups (e.g. academics, students, managers and industry) attribute different meanings to practical and theoretical knowledge (Knorr Cetina, 2007). From this perspective, the position of the philosophic practitioner circle in the diagram is more appropriately conceived as multiple circles defined by a wide range of stakeholders with diverse values.

Finally, the dynamic processes of learning and the development of understanding over time are not adequately represented in Figure 5.1. Human learning passes through various stages (e.g. novice, beginner, performer, competent performer, expert) and there is a developmental leap between the rule-bound knowledge and the fluid and dynamic performance of knowledge demonstrated by experts (Bordieu, 1977; Dreyfus & Dreyfus, 1986). This learning requires critical and reflective engagement with 'troublesome knowledge' and may involve lifelong learning well beyond a three-year undergraduate curriculum (Meyer & Land, 2003, 2005). The PPE in Figure 5.1 is somewhat static and does not incorporate the dynamic nature of knowledge and skill development over one's professional and personal life.

So, while the PPE is a thought-provoking abstract representation of the trade-offs made between reflection–action and vocational–liberal knowledge, since its development there have been significant advances in thinking about the social construction of knowledge and the dynamic processes associated with knowledge accumulation and lifelong and life-wide learning. To this end, it is important to rethink the debate over what constitutes a PPE in T&H education.

A reflective action-oriented practitioner

Tourism and hospitality have been described as hallmark activities of the postmodern world: they are activities that are 'worldmaking' in that they have a creative and transformative role in the making of people and places and in the production of meanings, values and understandings about the past, present and future (Hollinshead, 2009; Urry, 2003). In other words, where well managed within an integrated and sustainable approach, T&H can give meaning to places and people, add value to cultural and environmental resources, and promote peace and understanding. They can increase cultural awareness and social and cultural tolerance; address poverty, empower communities and contribute to improving economic and social well-being (e.g. Higgins-Desbiolles, 2006, 2008; Sharpley, 2009; United Nations World Tourism Organization (UNWTO), 2010). Conversely, where T&H are less well managed, or the focus is simply as a tool for economic growth and development, a range of impacts and issues can result which are well documented and extend well beyond the economic bottom line.

This expansion in the way that tourism and hospitality are conceived, and their shifting roles in society from the traditional boosterist business focus to broader roles as agents of social, political, economic and environmental change are increasingly recognized by a variety of stakeholders (Tourism Education Futures Initiative (TEFI), 2009; UNWTO, 2010; World Travel and Tourism Council (WTTC), 2010). Jamal (2004) discusses the PPE and raises questions about the ethical and value positions that underpin T&H professional practice. She calls for greater responsibilities and ethical action and argues the importance of preparing students to take on stewardship roles in the broader processes of societal change. These discussions also highlight the need for skilled tourism and hospitality management practitioners who can manage change in positive, creative worldmaking ways. Therefore, implications for the T&H curriculum to look beyond business education and embrace a broader social science education are quite clear. The tourism curriculum needs to develop a society for all stakeholders and not just a society for business (Sheldon *et al.*, 2008; Tribe, 2001).

Issues in implementing the philosophical practitioner education

T&H curricula are socially constructed from the interactions, trade-offs and choices made by a range of stakeholders including academic educators, university managers, students and industry employers (Sigala & Baum, 2003). Tribe's (2002a) conceptualization of a PPE that integrates philosophic and vocational ends to develop worldmaking, ethical professionals has received considerable backing from the academic community (Ring *et al.*, 2009; Belhassen & Caton, 2011). However, in an increasingly finite and crowded curriculum space the emphasis on applied, skills-based education that delivers job-ready graduates sits uneasily against a liberal social science education that seeks to develop the understanding, wisdom and criticality associated with the PPE (Belhassen & Caton, 2011; Dredge *et al.*, 2012). Not surprisingly, it has been difficult to ground and implement PPE in many institutions, particularly in those countries where higher education reform is constant (e.g. countries in the European Higher Education Area and Australia).

The PPE is useful in representing the various trade-offs that take place between liberal and vocational education and between vocational skills and higher order application of those skills in T&H education. Tribe's (2002b) 'education for ethical tourism action' model lays the groundwork for the philosophical practitioner education, arguing for the development of disciplinary-based and reflective learning opportunities that promote stewardship and ethical tourism within the curriculum space. The current chapter furthers this work by conceptualizing the curriculum space within an increasingly complex and dynamic higher education sector, where there are an increasing number of stakeholders, a shift towards market models of higher education and increasing pressures from neoliberal public management (Ayikoru *et al.*, 2009). In this context, there are competing demands on institutions, educators, students and industry that result in trade-offs that shape the extent to which the PPE can be delivered. These factors have become increasingly significant since Tribe's (2002a) paper and should therefore be acknowledged in any further development of the PPE framework.

This chapter argues that a more nuanced, dynamic and differentiated approach is needed in conceptualizing the PPE due to the proliferation of public and private higher education providers that are subject to different economic, social, political and education policy pressures, the complexity of the job market and employer needs. The reality of tightening fiscal resources, a blurring of vocational and higher education, and a lowering of entrance requirements in order to increase higher education participation in many countries means that not all higher education institutions have the resources or student capacity to pursue a PPE (Dredge *et al.*, 2012). Tribe (2002a: 354) calls for a 'philosophic practitioner curriculum . . . designed to satisfy the labor market, to respond to consumer wants, and to promote economic welfare', and in doing so seems to suggest that different interpretations of the PPE are necessary to suit different conditions. This dynamic aspect of PPE as originally conceived has been overlooked in subsequent discussions. This chapter asserts the importance of the PPE as described by Tribe (2002a) and the attendant arguments of Belhassen and Caton (2011) for a critical management education. However, it adds a further dimension to this discussion by presenting a framework for critically engaging with the concept in the context of the pressures faced by institutions in T&H curriculum planning.

The PPE curriculum space as conceptualized in this chapter is a dynamic construct shaped by institutional offerings and made up of all the different learning experiences a student might take through that space. The pathways that students can take through this PPE curriculum space will differ. These alternative pathways acknowledge the different drivers influencing the curriculum space and higher education institutions, and the diverse demands of industry and communities for different skill sets. Our contention here is that there are common core knowledge and skills which form the basis of academic standards for T&H education and the PPE will be developed depending upon the institution, some contexts, some industries and communities.

Whilst other authors have discussed the balance between liberal and vocational education, this chapter distinguishes itself in two ways. First, this chapter incorporates the notion of a 'force field' of influences on T&H education (see Dredge *et al.*, 2012). Many authors have tended to adopt an authoritative meta-narrative or polemic around 'what ought to be' in terms of the balance between liberal and vocational education, and have recognized somewhat unevenly the presence of different stakeholders' interests and perspectives (cf. Craig-Smith *et al.*,1994; Hobson, 1995; Wells, 1996) and different external and university-specific influences that shape the curriculum space (Tribe 2002). This chapter draws from these discourses and also incorporates the notion that there is a 'force field' of issues that exerts influence on the curriculum space and that trade-offs and satisficing decisions are made by university managers, curriculum designers and academic educators in response to these issues.

A second point of distinction between this chapter and previous research is that this chapter is situated within a much more complex environment than when the PPE was first developed. Specifically, this chapter is set against a background of continuous higher education policy reform, heightened fiscal austerity within the education sector, shifts in student demand, increasing global competition, greater attention on quality and performance measures and institutional and staff fatigue from increased expectations, reporting requirements and multiple accountabilities (Inui & Lankford, 2006; Ayikoru *et al.*, 2009). Across the globe, the tourism industry has also been subject to sustained pressure as a result of concerns over, for example, climate change, terrorism, global financial conditions, environmental crises and health alerts. The tourism industry continues to call for a better skilled and more innovative workforce. Reflecting upon these pressures, this chapter builds upon the PPE by incorporating the dynamic lifelong learning element that is inherent in professional practice (and is suggested in Tribe's text but not depicted in the PPE diagram). The conceptual model presented later in the chapter additionally incorporates the idea of a progressive learner, mindfully engaged in the stewardship of societal change over time (Tribe, 2000b; Jamal, 2004; Jamal *et al.*, 2011).

Influences on higher education

International context

The debate about T&H education takes place against a background in which there have been profound changes at an international level. Most notably, in Europe, the Bologna Process has sought to create a common European Higher Education Area, including the standardization of bachelor, Master's and doctorate cycles, the setting of minimum quality standards and European-wide recognition of qualifications. The Tuning Project, commencing in 2000, has been the vehicle to achieve these goals, producing a European Qualifications Framework that links the qualification systems of participating countries together (Tuning, 2010).

The Tuning Project has grappled with the complex overlapping of subject areas by producing outcomes (e.g. subject descriptors, knowledge, skills and competencies) in a range of subject areas, including business and management education, and it has produced a sectoral framework for the social sciences (Tuning, 2009). Recognizing that the Bologna Process will transform European education, many countries have also sought to refine and clarify degree structures, knowledge and skill development and graduate outcomes. With the Bologna Process under way for over 10 years, Australia has lagged behind in addressing such issues in a structured and strategic way.

While the Bologna Process has addressed T&H education to the extent that it is generally located within the rubric of business and/or social science, in many European countries it has stimulated discussion on key issues such as curriculum design and the balance between liberal and vocational knowledge in programme content (Ring *et al.*, 2009; Stuart-Hoyle, 2003; Tribe, 2002a); on the influence of education policy on the evolution of programme offerings (Amoah & Baum, 1997; Pearce, 2005; Spennemann & Black, 2008); and on the influence of neoliberalism, new public management and globalization (Ayikoru *et al.*, 2009; Pearce, 2005). In the face of increasing global competition and quality concerns, other countries such as the UK have developed national curriculum guidelines and benchmark statements (Airey, 2008; Botterill & Tribe, 2000; Fidgeon, 2010; Quality Assurance Agency (UK), 2009).

THE AUSTRALIAN CONTEXT

In Australia, analysis of the influences on T&H education has received uneven attention and consideration of strategic directions has been limited (Hobson, 1995; Pearce, 2005; Wang & Ryan, 2007). This lack of attention is partly due to the diversity of programmes and the variety of institutions involved, but also because over the years the drivers and educational philosophies underpinning the field have evolved significantly. As a result, underpinning rationales for programmes, curriculum content and delivery have morphed reactively rather than being informed by any strategic analysis or visioning process (Dredge *et al.*, 2012). However, the establishment of the Tertiary Education Quality and Standards Agency (TEQSA) sets the scene for the development of an Australian Qualifications Framework (AQF), the setting of minimum programme accreditation standards and discipline-based teaching and learning standards. These developments mean that an assessment of the issues and challenges faced by Australian T&H education stakeholders is a timely first step towards establishing clarity around key issues relating to academic standards, curriculum design, and relationships between the vocational education and training (VET) and higher education sectors.

The higher education sector in Australia has been in a state of continuous reform for over three decades, with the pace of change unlikely to slow (Coady, 2000; Marginson & Considine, 2000). These reforms have positioned education as a key economic activity and the sector is now ranked amongst Australia's top five export sectors (Australian Government, 2010). Despite this growth, the sector is in a considerable state of flux. The AQF, which seeks to introduce a nationally consistent, comprehensive and flexible framework of qualifications, has created considerable debate and uncertainty. The complexity of offerings and the different interests of universities and other educational institutions have meant that the debate is taking place in a complex and highly contested social space (Buchanan et al., 2010). In this context, universities and the VET sector have been engaged in a prolonged round of reviews and course restructurings in response to a framework that is changing and adapting.

Despite these achievements, a number of domestic and international factors have combined to place downward pressure on international higher education demand. The impact of a stronger Australian dollar, the impact of the global financial crisis, increased competition from other countries, reputational damage caused particularly by racial conflict, changes to student visa and skilled migration rules and the collapse of some private colleges are starting to impact on student demand (Phillimore & Koshy, 2010). Phillimore and Koshy (2010) estimate a medium-term decline in enrolments in higher education will equate to revenue losses between $2.6 and $7.0 billion AUD ($3.2 to $6.2 billion US). These predictions suggest that higher education will continue to undergo reform, with significant implications for the staffing, content and delivery of onshore and offshore programme offerings.

In addition to volatility within the higher education sector, the Australian tourism industry has also been subject to considerable pressures as a result of external factors such as global economic conditions, exchange rates, ethnic conflict, terrorism, health alerts and demographic and cultural shifts that have dampened market demand. A full explanation of these pressures is outside the scope of this chapter (cf. Commonwealth Department of Resources, Energy & Tourism, 2008; Tourism Research Australia, 2008). However recent inquiries and reports that point to a lack of innovative capacity, the difficulty of retaining good staff and poor career prospects as major impediments to the future development of an innovative tourism sector are germane to the present discussion.

While economic drivers feature prominently in discussions about the future of T&H education, T&H have also been identified as potential tools to address the United Nations millennium development goals (UNWTO, 2010), which include poverty alleviation, tolerance, social responsibility, employment and environmental conservation (Higgins-Desbiolles, 2006, 2011). Tourism changes landscapes, patterns of social and economic development, and its impacts are uneven and cumulative. This peculiarity places 'a special burden . . . on education because as economic prosperity and consumer satisfaction are generated from the development of tourism, changes to people and place also occur' (Tribe, 2002: 339). Externalities produced by an industry that is principally profit-driven need to be managed. The challenge for T&H education is to produce graduates who can rise to the challenge of providing leadership for and stewardship over tourism (Sheldon et al., 2008; Tribe, 2002a). Herein lies the challenge of conceptualizing a T&H management curriculum space that is focused enough to produce graduates who have strategic leadership and higher order thinking skills, and flexible enough to support a variety of pathways through the space to produce adaptable human capital for industry and society more generally.

Influences on the T&H curriculum space

McKercher (2002) observes that there is a remarkable consistency in the evolution of T&H management programmes in many parts of the world (see Airey & Tribe, 2005; Breakey & Craig-Smith, 2007, 2008; MacLauren, 2005; Spennemann & Black, 2008). This consistency is at least in part due to the impact of internal and external forces that interact to shape the curriculum space. By the 1980s, the rise of tourism as a global economic activity triggered calls from industry for better-qualified professionals (Fidgeon, 2010). Tourism and hospitality university degree programmes across the globe were born from pragmatic and utilitarian concerns that emphasized a need to address gaps in workforce skills and opportunities for economic development. In Australia, tourism was perceived optimistically in the 1980s as a tool to assist in the economic restructuring and diversification of regional areas. Such optimism was reinforced by reforms in the higher education sector that prompted universities to respond by forming schools of tourism and developing a range of professional degrees (Hobson, 1995). As McKercher (2002: 203) observes, 'high market demand coupled with low establishment costs and the absence of existing market leaders made tourism education an attractive proposition'. The result has been strong growth in both numbers of programmes and an expansion of degree programmes since the 1980s.

However, the failure of government funding to keep pace with the costs of education provision and the introduction of reforms that have created multiple accountabilities (e.g. to governments, student-consumers, etc.) and heightened the focus on quality assurance, reporting and governance have taken their toll (Watty, 2006). The optimism of the 1980s has given way to a very different environment where there are now few stand-alone schools of T&H and it has become harder to maintain a field-specific stance on what should and should not be included in the curriculum. New public management influences have promoted a flattening of organizational structures with many tourism schools subsumed into larger organizational units. Economic rationalism and the push for efficiencies have led to the introduction of common core first-year structures across faculties, and a crowded curriculum in later years when there is pressure to cover subject-specific content relevant to the programme of study (Marginson & Considine, 2000).

There is also evidence to suggest that student profiles have changed significantly. There is more diversity within the student body as a result of different pathways, life experience, ethnicity, location, study mode, aspirations and expectations (Benckendorff *et al.*, 2009; McKercher, 2002). There has been strong growth in articulations from post-secondary vocational courses and international institutions as a result of the government's push that 40 per cent of all Australians between 25 and 34 years will have a bachelor level or above qualification. In many programmes, domestic demand has plateaued and international student intakes have expanded. There have been significant increases in domestic off-campus and overseas/offshore delivery of programmes. This growth has been aided, up until recently, by the Government's Skills Shortage Occupation List, which included many T&H-related jobs (Australian Government, 2008). A number of tourism and hospitality providers have also been successful in boosting student numbers by introducing new programmes in allied areas such as sports and event management. These shifts in student diversity and learning styles have challenged traditional pedagogies and modes of programme delivery.

These forces interact together in complex ways to create a force field of influences on the curriculum space. Despite the magnitude of change over the last decade, T&H education has not been subjected to the same level of reflective and self-critical debate as other disciplines and fields of study characterized by crises in enrolments (e.g. humanities and social sciences) or where professional or accrediting bodies have been involved (e.g. town planning, psychology and accounting). Instead, much of the research in T&H education has focused on the building blocks of the educational experience, such as student retention and experience, assessment, flexible learning and graduate attributes or competencies (Benckendorff, 2007, 2009; Benckendorff *et al.*, 2009; Braun & Hollick, 2006; Dimmock *et al.*, 2003). There has been less attention devoted to innovative and creative pedagogies, curricula or assessment that blends both higher order subject matter and reflective skill development.

A conceptual framework of the curriculum space

Advancing a curriculum space framework

This discussion reveals a complex force field of influences that shape and change the curriculum space. Together these factors create a curriculum space where the different values of stakeholder groups and competing pressures combine to create a complicated decision-making environment for curriculum content, graduate capabilities, modes of delivery and staffing issues. Efforts to better understand and conceptualize the curriculum space become increasingly important in the context of balancing liberal and vocational education within an increasingly crowded curriculum space under pressure from a variety of macro, meso and micro influences. Taking as a starting point Tribe's PPE and the critique and the influences discussed above, we reconceptualize the T&H management curricula space in Figure 5.2.

In this framework, the curriculum space is bounded by points I, II and III. The size, shape and location of the space reflect the force field of influences as well as the institutional history and future ambitions of the institution. There are seven key points on Figure 5.2 that warrant explanation:

A. This is the base point of an institution's student intake. It can be located anywhere within the space. Importantly, its location says a lot about how the institution views the quality

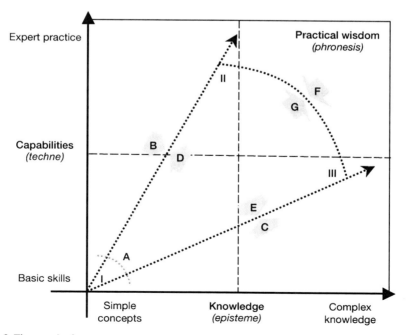

Figure 5.2 The curriculum space

and nature of its incoming cohort. The closer to the origin, the less 'equipped' the students are in terms of graduate capabilities and knowledge – the further out from the origin, the more 'equipped' the incoming students are with graduate capabilities and knowledge. The location of A can also indicate the balance of graduate capabilities versus knowledge amongst the incoming students. The longer the trajectory from A to the outer perimeters (II and III) the more ambitious the institution's 'transformation' agenda; the shorter the trajectory, the less ambitious.

B. External pressure driving knowledge at the expense of skills and capabilities. The external pressure on this arc is forcing the curriculum away from higher graduate capabilities to the pursuit of liberal knowledge. For example, it may be that the position of this arc is driven by government policy requiring learners to have a higher level of theoretical knowledge.

C. External pressure driving graduate capabilities at the expense of knowledge. The external pressure on this arc is forcing the curriculum away from knowledge to pursue a stronger focus on capabilities. It may be that this is driven by industry demands for job-ready graduates who know how to work.

D. Internal pressure driving a stronger focus on capabilities. This is where the institution is seeking to place stronger emphasis on and evidence of the acquisition of graduate skills, attributes and capabilities.

E. Internal pressure driving a stronger focus on knowledge. This is where the institution seeks to place stronger emphasis on research and the acquisition of knowledge. For example, this may be the result of institutional branding and positioning to differentiate an institution from vocationally based competitors.

F. Pressure reducing the use of innovative pedagogy and expansive technologies. Of all of the pressures, it is most likely that this is driven by short-term financial pressure. However, it could also be driven by academics seeking to return to didactic pedagogies (e.g. Socratic traditions).

G. Pressure driving more efficient teaching approaches and technologies to enlarge the curriculum. This is where the institution is seeking to expand innovative pedagogies to cover more in the curriculum without additional cost.

The framework highlights two important observations. Pressures B, C and F are 'shrinking' the curriculum space whilst D, E and G are seeking to expand it. However, the coordinated application of pressure in two or more places (e.g. C and D) may result in 'moving' the curriculum without necessarily shrinking or expanding it. It is proposed that pressures B and C come from stakeholders outside the academy, such as government and industry funding sources that may be keen to control costs whilst pressures D and E are driven by sympathetic stakeholders such as educators who are seeking to expand the curriculum. That said, there is still scope for the academy to work in concert with industry and government to fund a shifting of the curriculum space as noted above. Ultimately, these perspectives can incorporate and frame resource decisions as not merely financial decisions to reduce costs, but also as political decisions to reshape and/or relocate the curriculum.

This framework builds upon the PPE by incorporating the following advances. First, the axes have been reconceptualized to incorporate the idea that knowledge *and* capabilities are developed in educational pathways through the curriculum space. In replacing Tribe's 'reflective–action stance', we do not seek to conflate skills with capabilities, but rather capture a depth and richness of understanding that are not immediately present in the notion of skills. Second, the use of 'capabilities' (y-axis) moves us away from the idea that reflection and action need to be traded off; depending upon students' educational pathways, they can develop in both areas. Third, the use of 'knowledge' (x-axis) seeks to reflect the idea that vocational and liberal education are not alternatives but can coexist. Moreover, knowledge is accumulated; simple concepts, practical knowledge of cause and effect relationships learned early in the curriculum pathway, are practised, reflected upon, enhanced through the development of interdisciplinary understandings to the point where complex reasoning, based on accumulated practical and theoretical knowledge, emerges. Here phronesis or practical wisdom, as described at the beginning of this chapter, is approximated. Fourth, knowledge and skill development is a dynamic process. The use of vectors to delineate the curriculum space incorporates the idea that graduates, employing the skills and reflective practices learned during their programme of study (and regardless of whether the programme emphasizes vocational or social science education), continue lifelong and life-wide learning beyond the curriculum space. To this end, over time and beyond graduating, an individual moves towards the upper right-hand point on Figure 5.2 to reach a phronetic practice.

Figure 5.3 takes this diagram further to illustrate the different curriculum spaces that institutions may adopt based on the influences upon programme and subject offerings, educator expertise and student values and preferences amongst other factors. In this figure the curriculum space 'A' suggests an institution that is committed to higher order social science and humanities knowledge and teaching and learning practices, seeking to deliver graduate capabilities within this focus. In curriculum space 'B' an institution may be primarily committed to graduates' capabilities and will deliver social science and humanities knowledge to the extent that it supports graduates' capabilities. Further, 'A' and 'B' may represent different programmes offered by the same institution. In other words, the diagram is a useful tool at a variety of scales that can conceptualize the distinction between higher education providers, between programmes, and between subjects.

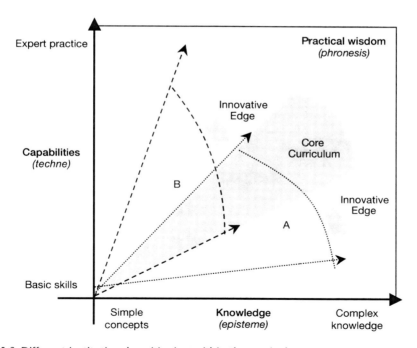

Figure 5.3 Different institutional positioning within the curriculum space

Figure 5.3 incorporates the idea that there is no ideal position in the diagram (i.e. the philosophic practitioner circle in the middle of Tribe's framework shown in Figure 5.1 suggests there is an 'ideal' balance, although in the text of his paper, Tribe distances himself from such a position). Rather, education providers can identify a competitive or desired position within the curriculum space which represents their aspirations and choices about programme offerings, content, modes of delivery, pedagogy and so on. Different institutions will have different positions in the framework and there will be different resourcing implications from their positioning. Furthermore, in curriculum design and renewal, curriculum planners may seek to enhance this positioning, by pushing to explore the possibilities at the edge of the curriculum space.

Figure 5.3 suggests the potential for movement in the positioning of an institution through time. The 'innovative edge', representing the institution's frontiers in the curriculum space, will shift in anticipation of, and reaction to, opportunities presented by the various internal and external environmental forces. An institution engaging in a reflexive approach to analysis of positioning options within a dynamic environment will develop a better understanding of environmental forces, better conceive viable strategic and tactical options, and thus enhance prospects for competitive advantage. For example, Positions 'A' and 'B' may represent institutions that aspire to maintain their respective balances of graduate capabilities and knowledge while progressively extending their curriculum orientation towards the expert stage.

Possible uses of the curriculum space framework

Several useful applications of the conceptual curriculum space framework for T&H education come to mind. First, at a conceptual level the framework indicates the general location of a minimum core curriculum for T&H education. The extension of this minimum core curriculum space is depicted as pushing out from the innovative edge, capturing the notion that the curriculum space is dynamic and needs to continually question the boundaries of orthodox curriculum content, design and delivery practices with a view to addressing the needs of society into the future. Identifying this minimum core curriculum is useful for industry because it assures industry stakeholders that graduates have the same foundational skills and understandings, regardless of the emphasis of their higher education provider and programme choice. The use of the framework to identify a common core is not intended to detract from the need to maintain a diverse range of T&H programmes in the education space.

Second, the conceptual framework is a reflective tool that helps curriculum planners and designers position their own (and other) degree programmes within the curriculum space. The framework can help to identify programme differences, core strengths and unique selling points of their programmes. From a strategic perspective, the framework could be used as a market analysis tool to identify areas where training gaps exist in the market or, conversely, areas of the curriculum space that are crowded by many competitors. In this context, the level of comparative analysis can range from an individual unit or subject level to entire programmes. Mapping individual subjects onto the curriculum space would allow an institution to determine whether its curriculum is broad or narrowly focused and whether the emphasis is on capabilities or knowledge (or both). Mapping entire programmes provides an opportunity to examine the portfolio of degrees and qualifications offered by an institution and this information can be compared with other institutions for benchmarking purposes.

Third, the framework can be used for decision-making about a school or department's staffing profile. For example, heads of schools or deans may use the framework to evaluate the spread or concentration of staff expertise in terms of knowledge and capabilities and plan accordingly to address gaps. Using the framework as a reflective tool can highlight areas where staff recruitment is necessary.

Finally, in an effort to encourage student reflection and engagement in their own learning opportunities, processes and choices, the framework can be used as a meta-cognition tool to explain the manner in which the skills and knowledge content develops within a programme and in their future professional development. Such reflective engagement is a first step in encouraging students to appreciate the role of T&H management in worldmaking.

The framework is conceptual and helps to build understandings between the knowledge and skill development of students as they progress through their undergraduate degrees and beyond. However, there is also considerable scope for the model to be operationalized through the collection and analysis of information about individual units and whole programmes and the types of skills and knowledge these deliver. Of course, such a data collection and analysis exercise is made difficult by the diversity of units, the availability of unit and programme information and the diversity of teaching methods and approaches. Nevertheless, for those wishing to pursue such a task, the clarity in terms of the curriculum space, identification or the core curriculum and the diversity and differentiation of programmes across the spectrum of offerings, would be rewarding from a managerial perspective.

Conclusions

The aims of this chapter were to review contemporary debates about tourism and hospitality education and to present a dynamic PPE curriculum space framework that can be used to facilitate discussion, understanding and decision-making about the T&H curriculum within different higher education contexts. In addressing the first aim, it became clear that the influences and pressures on higher education today are quite different to those 10 years ago when Tribe's (2000, 2002a, 2002b) PPE was first published. There is no doubt that PPE and Education for Ethical Tourism Action models (Tribe, 2002a, 2002b) remain highly relevant in the development of T&H curricula to produce ethical, reflexive, worldmaking tourism professionals.

However, in an increasingly competitive global context, where the influences of and demands upon university managers, educators, students and industry are diverse, we see the PPE and Education for Ethical Tourism Action as dialogic concepts – their application is dependent upon and subject to the internal and external influences shaping particular higher education contexts and institutions. Whilst Tribe probably intended this, our contribution has been to bring a fuller understanding of these pressures and implications. Specifically, the framework presented makes three important points: First, it supports and builds upon the PPE framework and argues that a better understanding of the pressures on the dynamic curriculum space in different political, economic, social, policy and institutional contexts is needed. The positioning of the PPE in the curriculum space in each institution should uphold core values including understanding, criticality and reflection (Belhassen & Caton, 2011) but it should also be attentive to the pressures upon the curriculum space.

Second, and following from the previous point, the chapter and attendant framework clarifies that the PPE should not be viewed as an overarching fixed approach. Instead, the PPE in the curriculum space of each institution is dynamic and will take on a slightly different form. So, while the PPE remains valid and useful for thinking about the T&H curriculum in each institution, interpretation is necessary.

Third, the framework incorporates the lifelong learning goal of practical wisdom (phronesis) and the cumulative reflection and development of knowledge and skills over time as individuals progress through their undergraduate programmes into professional practice and beyond. To date discussion of the PPE has not acknowledged the dynamic, iterative and future orientation of education and its role in professional practice over time

Finally, however, a word of caution is necessary. The conceptualization of the curriculum space in this chapter is a tool, and like all models, frameworks and metaphors they are abstractions of reality that tend to magnify some aspects and relationships and marginalize others. In other words, they simplify complex relationships and provide a graphic tool to provoke further thought and understanding. The work presented in this chapter is further shaped by the Australian context and it is acknowledged that while there are many similarities with developments elsewhere a number of endemic developments have created some idiosyncrasies. Further work, particularly application through the analysis of subjects and programmes, is needed to test whether these conceptualizations are useful, and whether this framework has a role to play in curriculum planning activities of programme leaders, university managers and academic educators.

Acknowledgement

Support from the Australian Government Office for Learning and Teaching (CG-1020) for the project 'Building a Stronger Future: balancing professional and liberal education ideals in tourism and hospitality education' is gratefully acknowledged.

References

Airey, D. (2008). 'In Search of a Mature Subject?' *Journal of Hospitality, Leisure, Sports and Tourism Education*, 7(2), 101.

Airey, D., & Tribe, J. (Eds.). (2005). *An International Handbook of Tourism Education. Advances in tourism research.* San Diego, CA: Elsevier.

Amoah, V., & Baum, T. (1997). 'Tourism Education: policy versus practice'. *International Journal of Contemporary Hospitality Management*, 9(1), 5–12.

Australian Government. (2008). *Skilled Occupation List (SOL) and Employer Nomination Scheme Occupation List (ENSOL).* Canberra: Commonwealth of Australia.

Australian Government. (2010). *Trade at a Glance 2010.* Canberra: Commonwealth of Australia.

Ayikoru, M., Tribe, J., & Airey, D. (2009). 'Reading Tourism Education: neoliberalism unveiled'. *Annals of Tourism Research*, 36(2), 191–221.

Barnett, R., & Coate, K. (2005). *Engaging the Curriculum in Higher Education.* London: McGraw-Hill.

Baum, T. (2005). 'Global Tourism Higher Education: the British Isles experience'. *Journal of Teaching in Travel & Tourism*, 5(1/2), 27–38.

Belhassen, Y., & Caton, K. (2011). 'On the Need for Critical Pedagogy in Tourism Education'. *Tourism Management*, 32(6), 1389–96.

Benckendorff, P. (2007). 'Exploring the Flexible Learning Preferences of Tourism and Hospitality Management Students'. Paper presented at the 17th Annual CAUTHE Conference, Tourism: past achievements, future challenges, 11–14 February, Manly, Sydney, Australia.

Benckendorff, P. (2009). 'Evaluating Wikis as an Assessment Tool for Developing Collaboration and Knowledge Management Skills'. *Journal of Hospitality and Tourism Management*, 16(1), 102–12.

Benckendorff, P., Ruhanen, L., & Scott, N. (2009). 'Deconstructing the Student Experience: a conceptual framework'. *Journal of Hospitality and Tourism Management*, 84(1), 84–93.

Blanshard, B. (1973). *The Uses of a Liberal Education.* La Salle, IL: Open Court Publishing.

Bordieu, P. (1977). *Outline of a Theory of Practice.* Cambridge: Cambridge University Press.

Botterill, D., & Tribe, J. (2000). 'Benchmarking and the Higher Education Curriculum'. Retrieved 15 March 2009 from: http://www.athe.org.uk/publications/

Braun, P., & Hollick, M. (2006). 'Tourism Skills Delivery: sharing tourism knowledge online'. *Education and Training*, 48(8/9), 693–703.

Breakey, N., & Craig-Smith, S. (2007). 'Hospitality Degree Programs in Australia: a continuing evolution'. *Journal of Hospitality and Tourism Management*, 14(2), 102–19.

Breakey, N., & Craig-Smith, S. (2008). 'Trends and Issues in Tourism and Hospitality Degree Education in Australia: will the bubble burst?' Paper presented at the 18th Annual CAUTHE Conference, 11–14 February, Gold Coast, Australia.

Buchanan, J., Yu, S., Wheelahan, L., Keating, J., & Marginson, S. (2010). *Impact Analysis of the Proposed Strengthened Australian Qualifications Framework*. Sydney: Workplace Research Centre, University of Sydney.

Coady, C. A. J. (2000). *Why Universities Matter: a conversation about values, means and directions*. Sydney: Allen & Unwin.

Commonwealth Department of Resources, Energy and Tourism. (2008). *National Long Term Tourism Strategy Discussion Paper*. Canberra: Australian Government Department of Resources, Energy and Tourism.

Cooper, L., Orrell, J., & Bowden, M. (2010). *Work Integrated Learning: a guide to effective practice*. Abingdon: Routledge.

Craig-Smith, S. J., Davidson, M., & French, C. N. (1994). 'Hospitality and Tourism Education in Australia: challenges and opportunities'. Paper presented at the Tourism Research and Education in Australia Conference, Canberra.

Dimmock, K., Breen, H., & Walo, M. (2003). 'Management Competencies: an Australian assessment of tourism and hospitality students'. *Journal of the Australian and New Zealand Academy of Management*, 9(1), 12–26.

Dredge, D., Benckendorff, P., Day, M., Gross, M. J., Walo, M., Weeks, P., & Whitelaw, P. (2012). 'Drivers of Change in Tourism, Hospitality and Event Management Education: an Australian perspective'. *Journal of Hospitality and Tourism Education*, 25: 89–102.

Dreyfus, H., & Dreyfus, S. (1986). *Mind over Machine: the power of human intuition and expertise in the area of the computer*. New York: Free Press.

Farnham, N., & Yarmolinsky, A. (1996). *Rethinking Liberal Education*. Oxford: Oxford University Press.

Fidgeon, P. R. (2010). 'Tourism Education and Curriculum Design: a time for consolidation and review?' *Tourism Management*, 31(6), 699–723.

Flyvbjerg, B. (2001). *Making Social Science Matter: why social inquiry fails and how it can succeed again*. Cambridge: Cambridge University Press.

Higgins-Desbiolles, F. (2006). 'More than an "Industry": the forgotten power of tourism as a social force'. *Tourism Management*, 27, 1192–208.

Higgins-Desbiolles, F. (2008). 'Justice Tourism and Alternative Globalisation'. *Journal of Sustainable Tourism*, 16(3), 345–64.

Higgins-Desbiolles, F. (2011). 'Resisting the Hegemony of the Market: reclaiming the social capacities of tourism'. In S. McCabe, L. Minnaert, & A. Diekmann (Eds.), *Social Tourism in Europe: theory and practice* (pp. 53–68). Bristol: Channel View.

Hirst, P. H. (1974). *Knowledge and the Curriculum: a collection of philosophical papers*. London: Routledge & Kegan Paul.

Hobson, P. (1995). 'The Development of Hospitality and Tourism Education in Australia'. *Hospitality and Tourism Education*, 7(4), 25–9.

Hollinshead, K. (2009). 'The "Worldmaking" Prodigy of Tourism: the reach and power of tourism in the dynamics of change and transformation'. *Tourism Analysis*, 14(1), 139–52.

Inui, Y., & Lankford, S. (2006). 'Rethinking Tourism Education: what should schools teach?' *Journal of Hospitality, Leisure, Sport and Tourism Education*, 5(2), 25–35.

Jamal, T. (2004). 'Virtue Ethics and Sustainable Tourism Pedagogy: phronesis, principles and practice'. *Journal of Sustainable Tourism*, 12(6): 530–45.

Jamal, T., Taillon, J., & Dredge, D. (2011). 'Sustainable Tourism Pedagogy and Academic–Community Collaboration: a progressive service-learning approach'. *Journal of Tourism and Hospitality Research*, 11(2): 133–47.

Knorr Cetina, K. (2007). 'Culture in Global Knowledge Societies: knowledge cultures and epistemic cultures'. *Interdisciplinary Science Reviews*, 32(4), 361–75.

Lashley, C. (1999). 'On Making Silk Purses: developing reflective practitioners in hospitality management education'. *International Journal of Contemporary Hospitality Management*, 11(4), 180–5.

Lum, G. (2009). *Vocational and Professional Education*. London: Continuum International.

McKercher, B. (2002). 'The Future of Tourism Education: an Australian scenario?' *Tourism and Hospitality Research*, 3(3), 199–210.

MacLauren, D. (2005). 'Tourism Education in Canada: past, present and future directions'. *Journal of Teaching in Travel and Tourism*, 5(1/2), 1–25.

Marginson, S., & Considine, M. (2000). *The Enterprise University: power governance and reinvention in Australia*. Cambridge: Cambridge University Press.

Morrison, A., & O'Mahony, G. B. (2003). 'The Liberation of Hospitality Management Education'. *International Journal of Contemporary Hospitality Management*, 15(1), 38–44.

Meyer, J. H. F., & Land, R. (2003). *Threshold Concepts and Troublesome Knowledge: linkages to ways of thinking and practising within the disciplines.* Coventry: University of Edinburgh.

Meyer, J. H. F., & Land, R. (2005). 'Threshold Concepts and Troublesome Knowledge (2): epistemological considerations and a conceptual framework for teaching and learning'. *Higher Education,* 49, 375–88.

Nussbaum, M. (2010). *Not for Profit: why democracy needs the humanities.* Princeton, NJ: Princeton University Press.

Pearce, P. (2005). 'Australian Tourism Education: the quest for status'. In C. H. Hsu (Ed.), *Global Tourism Higher Education: past present and future* (pp. 251–67). Binghamton, NY: Haworth Information Press.

Phillimore, J., & Koshy, P. (2010). *The Economic Implications of Fewer International High Education Students in Australia.* Perth: John Curtin Institute of Public Policy.

Quality Assurance Agency (UK). (2009). *Subject Benchmark Statements – Hospitality, Leisure, Sport and Tourism.* Retrieved 15 October 2011 from: http://www.qaa.ac.uk/Publications/InformationAndGuidance/Pages/Subject-benchmark-statement-Hospitality-leisure-sport-tourism-2008.aspx

Ring, A., Dickinger, A., & Wöber, K. (2009). 'Designing the Ideal Undergraduate Program in Tourism: expectations from industry and educators'. *Journal of Travel Research,* 48, 106–21.

Schön, D. (1982). 'Some of What a Planner Knows'. *APA Journal,* 48, 351–64.

Schön, D. (1983). *The Reflective Practitioner.* New York: Basic Books.

Schön, D. A., & Rein, M. (1994). *Frame Reflection: towards the resolution of intractable policy controversies.* New York: Basic Books.

Sharpley, R. (2009). *Tourism Development and the Environment: beyond sustainability.* London: Earthscan.

Sheldon, P., Fesenmaier, D., Wöber, K., Cooper, C., & Antolioli, M. (2008). 'Tourism Education Futures – 2010–2030: building the capacity to lead'. *Journal of Teaching in Travel & Tourism,* 7(3), 61–8.

Sigala, M., & Baum, T. (2003). 'Trends and Issues in Tourism and Hospitality Higher Education: visioning the future'. *Tourism and Hospitality Research,* 4(4), 367.

Spennemann, D., & Black, R. (2008). 'Chasing the "Fat" – Chasing a "Fad"? The waxing and waning of tourism and tourism related programmes in Australian higher education'. *Journal of Hospitality, Leisure, Sport and Tourism Education,* 7(1), 55–69.

Stuart-Hoyle, M. (2003). 'The Purpose of Undergraduate Tourism Programmes in the United Kingdom'. *Journal of Hospitality, Leisure, Sport and Tourism Education,* 2(1), 49–74.

Taylor, R., Rockhill, K., & Fieldhouse, R. (1985). *University Adult Education in England and the USA: a reappraisal of the liberal tradition.* London: Croom Helm.

Tourism Education Futures Initiative (TEFI). (2009). *A Values-Based Framework for Tourism: building the capacity to lead.* TEFI.

Tourism Research Australia. (2008). *Through the Looking Glass: the future of domestic tourism in Australia.* Canberra: Commonwealth Department of Resources, Energy and Tourism.

Tribe, J. (2000). 'Balancing the Vocational: the theory and practice of liberal education in tourism'. *Tourism and Hospitality Research,* 2(1), 9–26.

Tribe, J. (2001). 'Research Paradigms and the Tourism Curriculum'. *Journal of Travel Research,* 39(4), 442–8.

Tribe, J. (2002a). 'The Philosophic Practitioner'. *Annals of Tourism Research,* 29(2), 238–57.

Tribe, J. (2002b). 'Education for Ethical Tourism Action'. *Journal of Sustainable Tourism,* 10(4), 309–24.

Tuning. (2009). *Reference Points for the Design and Delivery of Degree Programmes in Business.* Bilbao: University of Duesto.

Tuning. (2010). *Tuning Sectoral Framework for Social Sciences.* Bilbao: University of Duesto.

United Nations World Tourism Organization (UNWTO). (2010). *Tourism and the Millenium Development Goals.* Madrid: UNWTO. Retrieved 15 October 2011 from: http://www.unwto.org/tourism&mdgsezine/

Urry, J. (2003). 'Globalising the Tourist Gaze'. Retrieved 15 October 2011 from: http://www.comp.lancs.ac.uk/sociology/papers/Urry-Globalising-the-tourist-gaze.pdf

Wang, Z., & Ryan, C. (2007). 'Tourism Curriculum in the University Sector: does it meet future requirements? Evidence from Australia'. *Tourism Recreation Research,* 32(2), 29–40.

Watty, K. (2006). 'Addressing the Basics: academics' view of the purpose of higher education'. *Australian Educational Researcher,* 33(1), 23–39.

Wegener, C. (1978). *Liberal Education and the Modern University.* Chicago, IL: University of Chicago Press.

Wells, J. (1996). 'The Tourism Curriculum in Higher Education in Australia: 1989–1995'. *Journal of Tourism Studies,* 7(1), 20–30.

World Travel and Tourism Council (WTTC). (2010). *Progress and Priorities 2009–2010.* New York: WTTC.

6

Hospitality higher education

A multidisciplinary approach to liberal values, hospitality, and hospitableness

Michael J. Gross

School of Management, University cf South Australia, Australia

Conrad Lashley

School of International Hospitality Management,
Stenden University of Applied Sciences, Leeuwarden, the Netherlands

Introduction

The balance between liberal and vocational values in hospitality higher education studies has long been a space within which education stakeholders have contested the rationales and merits of particular conceptual emphases. The ideological hegemony of the vocationalist agenda in the hospitality higher education curriculum has been well documented (Foucar-Szocki & Bolsing, 1999; Lashley, 2009; McCabe *et al.*, 2008; Mulcahy, 1999). Hospitality scholars have spent the last decades chronicling and lamenting the steady and seemingly irreversibly hopeless decline of hospitality studies into the abyss of instrumental commercialism. Appeals for more attention to the balance between vocational and professional skills and the broader critical thinking and analytical skills usually associated with the social sciences and humanities are becoming more frequent in the tourism and hospitality education literature (Jamal, 2004; Jamal & Menzel, 2009; Munar, 2007; Ring *et al.*, 2009). There has been a steady and growing stream of literature calling for the need to revitalize hospitality education and to incorporate liberal educational ideals and reflexive learning practices (Airey & Tribe, 2000; Inui & Lankford, 2006; Lashley, 1999, 2000, 2007; Morrison & O'Mahony, 2003).

What the hospitality literature to date has yet to integrate is an understanding of the place of hospitality studies in a wider struggle encompassing and experienced by professional and business studies generally. Extant hospitality literature has lacked a broader historical perspective through which to understand the context of such debates. The lens applied to analysis of literature in this area has tended toward the self-referential, drawing predominantly from tourism, hospitality and events (TH&E) literature, and containing the analysis within the community of TH&E scholars (Airey & Tribe, 2005; Barrows & Bosselman, 1999; Lashley & Morrison, 2000). This chapter takes a broader approach, expanding the focus to include literature from a range of disciplines in order to examine the premise that hospitality studies is not the sole discipline where vocational curriculum hegemony exists, but rather that it is one of many disciplines in which this phenomenon occurs.

Far from being another arcane academic argument of little value or little importance to the hospitality industry or to management practice, the study of hospitality from these more tangential perspectives is essential for future academic understandings and the building of competitive strategy within commercial organizations. Through a better understanding of the provision of hospitality and acts of hospitableness, commercial organizations are better able to recognize the emotional experiences involved and ensure that management practice focuses on their production. Hospitality involves more than a service encounter (Lashley *et al.*, 2005) and concepts of hospitality can be used to build loyal customers as 'commercial friends' (Lashley & Morrison, 2003). It is crucial for understanding the anxieties, concerns and sources of satisfaction for guests.

Such an analysis will help us to better understand the contemporary intellectual terrain within which hospitality studies presently reside, and to conceive a future that is equipped with stronger tools to redress the vocational/liberal imbalance that currently predominates. This conceptual chapter uses a multidisciplinary approach to examine the consequences and future prospects of liberal values in hospitality higher education studies. The purpose of this chapter is therefore to explore the potential that a multidisciplinary approach that envisions a wide social nature of hospitality and hospitableness has to contribute to the discourse of liberal values in hospitality higher education.

Multidisciplinary perspectives of liberal values

Liberal values, by their necessarily evolutionary, subjective, and contestable nature, are not usually accorded universally accepted definitions. There are, however, certain qualities that are typically ascribed to them in an education context such as capacity for thought, reason, pursuit of knowledge, and understanding (Hirst, 1974). Liberal education pursues knowledge for its own sake rather than for its utility, and aims to produce whole citizens (Blanshard, 1973).

The year 1959 was a defining moment for the critical assessment of American business schools delivered by two key reports: Higher Education for Business (Gordon & Howell, 1959), and The Education of American Businessmen: a study of university-college programs in business administration (Pierson, 1959). Both reports disparaged business schools' curricula as too narrowly vocational, and in need of recognizing their obligation to produce responsible citizens. Since then, business scholars have produced an ongoing stream of criticism which has had as its core tenet that graduates from business curricula lack skills and knowledge of cultural awareness, leadership skills, creativity and critical thinking, and global perspectives (Colby *et al.*, 2011; Datar *et al.*, 2010; Drucker, 1969; Hogarth, 1979; Khurana, 2007; Mintzberg, 2004; Morsing & Rovira, 2011; Petit, 1967; Porter & McKibbin, 1988). No doubt some of the concerns and catalysts for change relate to periodic shocks inflicted on the world that are attributed in large part to professional moral and ethical shortcomings (Klein, 2007).

Consistent with this chapter's purpose, we now review a number of other disciplines that have had similar experience to hospitality's effort to integrate liberal values in the curriculum, in order to examine commonalities and distinctions experienced among them. For our analysis we chose evidence from four disciplines that share hospitality's occupational orientation in the higher education curriculum: accounting, engineering, health, and law. All of these example disciplines have active voices advocating a greater appreciation and inclusion of liberal values.

Accounting

Accounting scholars' awareness of and concern about the field's relationship with liberal arts has deep historical roots (Hanslein, 1930; Howard, 1930, 1936; Larimore, 1937; Murphy, 1952). Kohl (1961) characterized accounting as one of the practically oriented useful arts, and argued for a rapprochement with the theoretically oriented liberal arts, in effect calling for each to compromise to achieve a stronger whole. The desired outcomes would be a concomitant raising of consciousness of business and the necessities of life, as well as enhanced intellectualism in accounting practice. Liberal themes that have been emphasized as particularly significant for this field include the need for ethical development (Jeffrey, 1993; Ponemon & Glazer, 1990), and recognition of social and environmental needs (Palliam, 2010). These themes acknowledge accounting's role as scorekeeper to enterprise, and the duty that the profession bears for honest and reliable reporting and interpretation of economic transactions according to regulatory standards. Other authors have suggested that institutional structures are inadequate, and may be remedied by identifying and integrating essential liberal arts skills such as writing, communication, personal intelligence, critical thinking, and problem solving into curricula (Fogarty, 2010; Willits, 2010), or by developing capstone courses incorporating a liberal learning philosophy designed to equip graduates with the ability to better adapt to environmental changes as well as to changes in the profession itself (Ahlawat et al., 2012).

Engineering

Prominent among the pressures exerted on the engineering profession to vocationalize its curriculum are advances in science and technology. Graduates' skills and knowledge must be up to date; however, graduates must also be able to communicate. This example illustrates the dilemma faced by the field as it wrestles with the stereotype of the inarticulate technocrat (Newman, 1957). Liberal themes that have been emphasized as particularly significant for this field include the need to overcome gender discrimination (Rotter, 1982), and elitism whereby engineering students perceive liberal arts students as 'majoring in unemployment' (Patnaik, 2012: 31). Some authors have advocated along similar lines to other professions in a general call for greater inclusion of liberal values in engineering curricula (Badawy, 1982; Bakilapadavu & Shekhavat, 2013; Lata & Devika, 2013). Prescriptions to remedy the divide have included adopting an existential approach that conceives technology and humanism as a shared experience (Bella, 1990), designing courses such as robot design that emphasize artistic expression and social relevance (Turbak & Berg, 2002), and converging technology and literacy, with the aim of producing graduates who both understand the technological world in which they live and understand the implications of those technologies (Klein & Balmer, 2007). Eppes et al. (2012) proposed an assessment regime incorporating five 'intellectual and practical skills' of critical and creative thinking, enquiry/analysis, problem solving, and information literacy. Vaz (2012) advocated a similar approach based on 10 interdisciplinary learning outcomes.

Health

Among the disciplines reviewed in this section, health is perhaps the most closely analogous to hospitality in its attention to the physiological aspects of human life. This may be reflected in the aspects of emotional service labour inherent in the hospitable caring for others. Health's approach to greater liberal values has relied in large part on a merging of liberal and professional education, organized through the conduits of professional associations such as the American

Organization of Nurse Executives (AONE), Association of Schools of Public Health (ASPH), Institute of Medicine of the National Academy of Sciences (IOM), National Advisory Council on Nurse Education and Practice (NACNEP), and collective initiatives such as Educated Citizen and Public Health (ECPH) and Liberal Education and America's Promise (LEAP) (Albertine *et al.*, 2012; Fleeger & Connelly, 2012; Fox, 2008; Hovland *et al.*, 2009; Rospond, 2012). Remedies suggested to address the divide have come from Riegelman (2012) for evidence-based problem solving; unifying liberal arts values under the umbrella of global public health (Hill *et al.*, 2012); and valuing philosophy's role in advancing health outcomes (Sankowski, 2009).

Law

The evolution of society continually produces new challenges for how to conceive systems of rules in such diverse areas as human rights, labour, civil and criminal procedure, and international commerce. Law is fertile territory for the debate about liberal values, as legal structures serve as mediators of social relations, and an understanding of law is central to the notion of democratic citizenship (Collier, 2005). Kirkpatrick illustrated the symbiotic nature of this relationship in his 1965 paper that examined the need for lawyers to develop judgment, but that only through the practice of law can judgement be truly developed. The collection of papers in Sarat's 2002 edited book made a powerful case for the duality of law's place in the liberal arts as well as liberal arts' place in law curricula. Remedies suggested to address the divide include greater use of research and writing (Parker, 2002; Walter, 2002); using a blending instead of bridging strategic curriculum approach (MacDonald & Ramaglia, 2004); and providing an action framework for lifelong learning to sustain professional values (Conison, 2006).

Against the above background and prelude, we now examine the potential for integration of a multidisciplinary approach with hospitality and hospitableness, concepts that occupy the heart of the hospitality education curriculum.

Searching for hospitality and hospitableness

British hospitality academics have taken up some of these ideas about the wider social nature of hospitality and hospitableness. Two edited books and a research journal have invited the publication of pieces that explored the wider meanings of hospitality and acts of hospitality and hospitableness in society. *In Search of Hospitality: theoretical perspectives and debates* (Lashley & Morrison, 2000) and *Hospitality: a social lens* (Lashley *et al.*, 2007) contain chapters written from various social science perspectives. More recently a new journal, *Hospitality & Society* (Lynch *et al.*, 2011), has provided a forum for research into hospitality as a human phenomenon. In addition, non-hospitality academics, writing from an array of social science disciplines, have contributed chapters to *Mobilizing Hospitality: the ethics of social relations in a mobile world* (Molz & Gibson, 2007). This contains a number of interesting perspectives including the use of hospitality as a metaphor to explore the absorption or rejection of out-group members by in-group members.

Reactions to the direction of discussions and debates opened up in these publications have been interesting if somewhat diverse. For many academics in the hospitality management field across the globe, the impact of the first of these books was described as being like having 'a light bulb switched on', as it was for the editors once they began to think this way (Bell, 2005, 2007a, b; Lashley *et al.*, 2007). For others, the reaction was either 'So what?', or downright hostile (Slattery, 2002). To some extent, the different reactions to the book are a by-product of perceptions, political stances, and philosophical positions adopted by the commentators. Some are clearly locked into traditional models of hospitality management education, concerned with immediate relevance to the industry. These commentators reflect the closed system of thinking and discourse observed by Botterill (2000). Others, however, recognize the value of developing a theoretical underpinning to the field which moves away from mere applied management studies. The development of reflective practitioners (Schön, 1983) or even 'philosophic practitioners' (Tribe, 2002) requires a more rounded appreciation of the field than merely developing the skills to manage.

The work of Derrida (1998; 2000a, b) has been influential on a range of social science academics, and many of the contributions to *Mobilizing Hospitality: the ethics of social relations in a mobile world* (Molz & Gibson, 2007) were informed by Derrida's writings on hospitality. In addition, historians (Walton, 1998, 2000a, b, 2005), philosophers (Telfer, 1996, 2000), and those writing on comparative literature (Rosello, 2001; Tresidder, 2011) write about hospitality, some using Derrida's work, others building on it. Although the guest–host relationship, central to the study of hospitality, also overlaps with tourism, social science studies have used hospitality concepts to explore the relationship between host communities and their relationships with non-hosts such as immigrants, asylum seekers and refugees (Garcia & Crang, 2005; Hage, 2005; Molz, 2005). Gibson's (2003, 2006) work used hospitality as a way of exploring relationships between guards and inmates in a prison context. Robinson *et al.* (2005) provided some interesting insights into hospitality by the use of literary criticism to analyse two poems. The key point is that there has been a growing interest in hospitality as an academic subject from a wide range of academic disciplines and academics in both the hospitality management and social science fields have engaged with these.

Earlier observations (Lashley, 2000) suggest that hospitality could be conceived of and studied in three domains which are independent of each other but which overlap, shown visually as a Venn diagram. Admittedly, this was a somewhat crude and oversimplistic representation, but the three domains do provide a framework for analysis and discussion of current work as well as future directions for research. In other words, the study of hospitality can encompass the social cultural contexts of hospitality, the practice of hospitality in private domestic settings, and the commercial setting of hospitality. The benefit of the Venn image is that these three settings are not hermetically sealed but overlap and inform each other, and that studies can focus on any one of a range of overlapping relationships.

Although the notion of the social or cultural domain have caused some commentators difficulty (Brotherton, 2002), the study of the responsibilities associated with being a good host are a feature of social constructs which are rooted in a society's culture. In so-called modern societies the duty to protect guests, to provide succour, to take in the poor and share food and drink and provide secure accommodation to guests are much less explicitly pronounced than in pre-industrial societies. The strength of these obligations are, however, still relevant today in many parts of the world. During the US-led war with Iraq the person responsible for betraying Saddam Hussein's sons to US forces in Iraq was himself a fugitive, because his tribe claimed that he dishonoured them by betraying his two guests to their enemy. He broke the tribe's sacred code of hospitality, to provide protection to those who were guests in his own home. In this case the two sons were killed during the attack by US troops on the house in which they were sheltering.

The changing nature of perceptions of guests and the rigidity of obligations for hosts to meet socially defined standards of hospitality is an important issue for future research in host and guest relations. Evidence from British history suggests that social and cultural obligations to be hospitable lasted into the medieval period but began to break down in the sixteenth and seventeenth centuries. One half of Shakespeare's plays use the dishonouring of the laws of hospitality as a device to increase the villainy of a character's actions – the killing of the king, Duncan, whilst a guest in Macbeth's house is a famous example. In the play *King Lear*, Gloucester is blinded by King Lear's sons-in law and he cries out, 'But you are my guests'. Contemporary audiences would have understood that these acts were breaking the laws of both hosts to protect their guests, and of guests to act honourably to their hosts. Obligations in Western societies to behave honourably as guest or host have nothing like the same cultural sanction that they once had: a situation perhaps intensified by the advent of mass travel and tourism.

To some extent these obligations to be hospitable have changed as a result of increased travel, and as the emergence of commercial provision to support travellers has developed. Certainly, there are important lessons to be learnt from the study of the social and cultural domain of hospitality. First, different societies will have degrees of culturally defined obligations to be hospitable. Some cultures will require individuals to meet certain levels of expectation to offer hospitality to strangers. Thus different societies will be more or less predisposed to be hospitable to the stranger/tourist. Second, obligations to offer hospitality to strangers change over time. Increased contact with visitors seems, particularly in commercial hospitality contexts, also to reduce these obligations to be hospitable. Familiarity, it seems, can breed contempt. Third, it is possible to reintroduce frontline hospitality and tourist staff to these obligations to be hospitable through training and management practice. Walton's (1998, 2000a) various works on the history of British seaside resorts confirms the reluctance of sections of the seaside host community to accept visitors. For example he reports that local populations made up of large numbers of retirees often acted as a brake on the ability of the local tourism industry to adapt and change with changes in consumer demands. Retirees, making up a ratepayer lobby, would actively limit tourism industry attempts to attract more tourists to the town.

The private domain of hospitality has recently provided the source for some interesting studies. On one level, the domestic context has been identified as an important arena for learning about receiving guests and the obligations of the host. In one study half the accounts of 'special meal occasions' (Lashley *et al.*, 2005) were located in domestic settings, and the language of domestic hospitality was used to evaluate hospitality in commercial settings, 'they made me feel at home' for example. O'Mahony's (2003) profile of five leading restaurateurs in Australia suggested that learning about food and dining, and hospitality in the home was a common source of inspiration. In some cases, learning to cook with a mother or grandmother was an important source of skill. In other cases, the experience of food and drink, and hosting, provided a source of inspiration that became invaluable when they entered the restaurant business (O'Mahony, 2007).

On another level, many hospitality businesses are themselves 'commercial homes' (Lynch & MacWhannell, 2000). Commercial homes (Lynch, 2005) in guest houses, bed and breakfast establishments, farm-stay properties, and small hotels in particular involve guests staying in the same dwelling as the host (Lashley & Rowson, 2010). Lynch and MacWhannell (2000) provide a useful model for understanding the relationships between paying guests and hosts depending on the degree to which they share domestic private space. Although the interface between resident guest and host are at their sharpest in the accommodation sector, pubs, inns and bars, and some restaurant and café businesses have close links between the home and the commercial activity.

The challenge of linking hospitality domains/industry and curriculum

Internationally it is a truism to say that micro-firms dominate hospitality provision. Despite the rapid growth of large firms with major market shares in all sectors, over 70 per cent of the firms in accommodation, food and drink provision typically employ ten or fewer employees (Lashley & Rowson, 2010). Very substantial numbers of these firms employ no staff outside the immediate family and friends (Getz *et al.*, 2004). Most importantly, few have classically entrepreneurial business motives. In their study of 1,396 micro-firms in hospitality and tourism in the UK, Thomas *et al.* (2000) found that fewer than one in eight registered 'to make a lot of money' as one of their main reasons for being in business. They are 'lifestyle' firms who want to have more control of their lives, or who 'like the life', and 'make a reasonable' living. Often the domestic setting is seen as 'not having to work' or presents a business opportunity where their life skills, learnt in the home, provide them with an opportunity to 'work at home' (Lashley & Rowson, 2005). In their exploration of one hundred-plus couples buying small hotels in Blackpool, Lashley and Rowson (2010) found that the majority had sold a domestic property, typically a three- or four-bedroom house, to buy the Blackpool hotel. For many, owning a seaside hotel had been a lifelong dream. The overlaps between the commercial provisions within a domestic setting, being paid to provide hospitality, are at the heart of these dreams (Lashley & Rowson, 2010).

These linkages between domestic and commercial domains in micro-firms in hospitality and tourism have important implications for those attempting to provide assistance to small firms in the sector, or to improve the quality of services experienced by visitors. The business motives of lifestyle firms are more closely associated with a personal and domestic agenda, and do not readily recognize the need for formal management practices. In many cases, high levels of business failure and churn in ownership have a negative effect on overall business development for the tourism profile of the destination. For example, estimates of the change in ownership of Blackpool hotels was conservatively estimated at 20 per cent per year, though some professionals suggested it could be as high as 50 per cent (Lashley & Rowson, 2005), whilst estimates of changes in pub tenancies in the UK were thought to be in the region of 30 per cent per year (Lashley & Rowson, 2002).

There has been ongoing debate, in particular, about the extent to which commercial hospitality can be authentic when compared with private hospitality. Warde and Martens (2001), for example, in their interviews covering dining experiences, said that interviewees tended to regard commercial dining experiences as being less authentic than those in domestic settings. Certainly, the philosophy of hospitableness suggests that the ulterior motives associated with commercial hospitality might reduce the genuine quality of hospitableness. Whilst recognizing this as a potential tendency, Telfer (2000) suggests that it is not inevitable that commercial hospitality is inhospitable. She suggests that individuals who are naturally hospitable may be attracted to work in the sector and provide hospitable behaviour. She also points out that many small firms may be operated for other than commercial reasons and these may offer genuinely hospitable experiences. Lashley *et al.* (2005) found that interviewees were able to recognize hospitality experiences as being genuine in both commercial and domestic settings. When asked to recount their most memorable meal experiences about half the occasions were in domestic settings, whilst the other half were in commercial settings. Interestingly both appeared to be recognized as having authenticity, though the language of domestic hospitality was used to evaluate experiences in commercial settings. Emotional requirements to feel safe and secure, welcome and genuinely valued dominate the assessment of authenticity in both settings. Ritzer (2001, 2007) suggests that there are McDonaldizing and globalizing tendencies, particularly in corporate hospitality provision, which will create increased inhospitable hospitality in the commercial sector. The relationship, therefore, between private and commercial settings of hospitality provides some interesting insights into hospitality and some exciting avenues for research.

The commercial domain is clearly influenced by these social and cultural, and domestic domains of hospitality. It is important that those studying hospitality recognize the interplay of both the cultural and domestic on the commercial provision of hospitality. It is also important that commercial providers develop a more subtle understanding of hospitality so as to focus on building long-term customer relationships. Successful hosts are able to engage customers on an emotional and personal level, which creates feelings of friendship and loyalty amongst guests. Telfer (2000) is correct in saying that commercial hospitality need not be inevitably inhospitable; there are many examples of those managing hotels, pubs and restaurants that provide generous and warm feelings amongst their clients because they recognize the key importance of customer experiences, and the need for these to be genuinely felt. On the other hand, Ritzer (2007) makes a powerful criticism of corporate providers that ultimately prioritize shareholder interests above those of guests/customers, employees, and other stakeholders.

Conclusions – learning from other disciplines

We have argued in this chapter that a multidisciplinary approach to the discourse of liberal values in hospitality education will become progressively more consequential as our understanding and appreciation of the wider social nature of hospitality and hospitableness increase. Our analysis demonstrates that hospitality higher education shares common characteristics with other professional disciplines from which we may derive parallel but also discipline-specific future directions for hospitality higher education.

A common denominator among the other four discipline examples and hospitality is that all provide essential services in society. However, the four disciplines are all considered 'professional' services while hospitality practitioners are not accorded the same status as lawyers and doctors, for example. The reasons for this may be manifold, such as the perception of rigour required for a professional degree, the professional standards to which their practices are held, or the degree of regulatory governance to which they are subjected, all of which are not as apparent in the hospitality trade. This does not make hospitality's aspiration to liberal values any less worthy, as the role that hospitality and hospitableness play in society is as vital as in any profession.

Industrial and commercial definitions such as those articulated by various industry and trade bodies are useful in that they describe a cluster of services provided by a variety of organizations in different sectors of the industry. These definitions are essentially economic in that they describe hospitality through the supply of goods and services. They help establish an understanding of the similarities and differences between hospitality provision in different sectors through hotels, bars, restaurants, etc., and encourage the consideration of the service context in which hospitality takes place. That said, these economic definitions are essentially limited and flawed by their preoccupation with the here and now.

A wider understanding of hospitality suggests first that hospitality is essentially a relationship based on host and guest. To be effective, hospitality requires the guest to feel that the host is being hospitable through feelings of generosity, a desire to please, and a genuine regard for the guest as an individual. Consequently, calculative hosting where the guest senses an ulterior motive can be counterproductive, because the commercial intent cuts across the experiences of hospitableness.

A second point flowing from this wider understanding is that commercial provision of hospitality suggests but one avenue for the exploration of hospitality. The social domain assists in setting the study of hospitality and the component elements in a wider social context. The value placed on being hospitable, caring for strangers, assisting the poor and providing hospitality to those in need, within a society's value system is an additional and fruitful line of enquiry. Similarly, the relationship between guest and host still takes place in private settings. These private domestic settings can be revealing because many of the commercial operations have grown from early domestic settings; the private domain of hospitality continues to be an important forum for establishing commonality, mutuality, and reciprocity between host and guest.

A third reason for developing this wider understanding of hospitality activities flows from this second point, namely, current expressions of hospitality in Western industrial societies represent but one of a number of possibilities. The wider study of hospitality in both contemporary pre-industrial settings and earlier historical periods could reveal much to better understand current hospitality activities. This chapter has attempted to indicate how the study of hospitality in a wider context could enrich and enhance the study of commercial applications of hospitality activities. There may be those in the practitioner community who regard these discussions as arcane and somewhat sterile. Hopefully, there will be others, however, who see the potential benefits of academics following lines of enquiry which establish hospitality as a robust academic discipline. Bringing together academics from both the hospitality management field and the broader social sciences represents an important step towards establishing a theoretical framework for the study of hospitality in all its domains.

References

Ahlawat, S., Miller, G., & Shahid, A. (2012). 'Promoting Liberal Learning in a Capstone Accounting Course'. *American Journal of Business Education*, 5(1), 11–24.

Airey, D., & Tribe, J. (2000). 'Education for Hospitality'. In C. Lashley & A. Morrison (Eds.), *In Search of Hospitality: theoretical perspectives and debates* (pp. 277–92). Oxford: Butterworth Heinemann.

Airey, D., & Tribe, J. (Eds.). (2005). *An International Handbook of Tourism Education*. Oxford: Elsevier.

Albertine, S., Petersen, D. J., & Plepys, C. (2012). 'For the Profession and For All: toward liberal education in public health'. *Peer Review*, 14(2), 24–7.

Badawy, M. K. (1982). *Developing Managerial Skills in Engineers and Scientists: succeeding as a technical manager*. New York: Van Nostrand Reinhold.

Bakilapadavu, G., & Shekhavat, S. (2013). 'Integrating Humanities and Liberal Arts in Engineering Curriculum: need, experiences and new directions'. *Social Sciences & Humanities*, 21(1), 373–82.

Barrows, C. W., & Bosselman, R. H. (Eds.). (1999). *Hospitality Management Education*. New York: Haworth Hospitality Press.

Bell, D. (2005). 'Moments of Hospitality'. In J. G. Molz & S. Gibson (Eds.), *Mobilizing Hospitality: the ethics of social relations in a mobile world* (pp. 29–44). Aldershot: Ashgate Publishing.

Bell, D. (2007a). 'Hospitality and Urban Generation'. In C. Lashley, P. Lynch, & A. Morrison (Eds.), *Hospitality: a social lens* (pp. 89–99). Oxford: Elsevier.

Bell, D. (2007b). 'The Hospitable City: social relations in commercial spaces'. *Progress in Human Geography*, 31(7), 7–22.

Bella, D. A. (1990). 'Existentialism, Engineering, and Liberal Arts'. *Journal of Professional Issues in Engineering*, 116(3), 309–21.

Blanshard, B. (1973). *The Uses of a Liberal Education*. La Salle, IL: Open Court Publishing.

Botterill, D. (2000). 'Social Scientific Ways of Knowing Hospitality'. In C. Lashley & A. Morrison (Eds.), *In Search of Hospitality: theoretical perspectives and debates* (pp. 177–97). Oxford: Butterworth Heinemann.

Brotherton, B. (2002). 'Finding the Hospitality Industry (a response to Paul Slattery)'. *Journal of Hospitality, Leisure, Sport and Tourism Education*, 1(2), 75–7.

Colby, A., Ehrlich, T., Sullivan, W. M., & Dolle, J. R. (2011). *Rethinking Undergraduate Business Education: liberal learning for the profession*. San Francisco, CA: Jossey-Bass.

Collier, R. (2005). 'The Liberal Law School, the Restructured University and the Paradox of Socio-Legal Studies'. *Modern Law Review*, 68(3), 475–94.

Conison, J. (2006). 'Law School Education and Liberal CLE'. *Valparaiso University Law Review*, 40(2), 325–44.

Datar, S., Garvin, D. A., & Cullen, P. G. (2010). *Rethinking the MBA: business education at a crossroads*. Boston, MA: Harvard Business Review Press.

Derrida, J. (1998). 'Hospitality Justice and Responsibility: a dialogue with Jacques Derrida'. In R. Kearney & M. Dooley (Eds.), *Questioning Ethics: contemporary debates in philosophy* (pp. 65–83). London: Routledge.

Derrida, J. (2000a). *Of Hospitality: Anne Dufourmantelle invites Jacques Derrida to respond* (translated by R. Bowlby). Stanford, CA: Stanford University Press.

Derrida, J. (2000b). 'Hospitality'. *Angelaki: Journal of the Theoretical Humanities*, 5(3), 3–18.

Drucker, P. (1969). 'Summing Up: preparing tomorrow's business leaders today'. *Preparing Tomorrow's Business Leaders Today* (pp. 280–90). Englewood Cliffs, NJ: Prentice Hall.

Eppes, T. A., Milanovic, I., & Sweitzer, F. (2012). 'Towards Liberal Education Assessment in Engineering and Technology Programs'. *Journal of College Teaching & Learning*, 9(3), 171–7.

Fleeger, M. E., & Connelly, T. W. (2012). 'Navigating the Perfect Storm: nursing and liberal education'. *Peer Review*, 14(2), 16–19.

Fogarty, T. J. (2010). 'Revitalizing Accounting Education: a highly applied liberal arts approach'. *Accounting Education: An International Journal*, 19(4), 403–19.

Foucar-Szocki, R., & Bolsing, C. (1999). 'Linking Hospitality Management Programs to Industry'. In C. W. Barrows & R. H. Bosselman (Eds.), *Hospitality Management Education* (pp. 37–65). New York: Haworth Hospitality Press.

Fox, C. R. (2008). 'Considering Liberal Learning and Health Professions'. *Journal of Physical Therapy Education*, 22(2), 12–15.

Garcia, F., & Crang, P. (2005). Hospitality, the City, and Cafe Culture: cosmopolitanism, conviviality and contemplation in Chueca, Madrid. Paper presented at the 'Mobilising Hospitality: the ethics of social relations in a mobile world' Conference, 26–27 September, Lancaster: Lancaster University.

Getz, D., Carlsen, J., & Morrison, A. (2004). *The Family Business in Tourism and Hospitality*. Wallingford: CABI Publishing.

Gibson, S. (2003). 'Accommodating Strangers: British hospitality and the Asylum Hotel debate'. *Journal of Cultural Research*, 7(4), 367–86.

Gibson, S. (2006). 'Border Politics and Hospitable Spaces in Stephen Frears's "Dirty Pretty Things"', *Third Text*, 20(6), 693–701.

Gordon, R. A., & Howell, J. E. (1959). *Higher Education for Business*. New York: Columbia University Press.

Hage, G. (2005). Nomadic Hospitality and the Gift of Rest. Paper presented at the 'Mobilising Hospitality: the ethics of social relations in a mobile world' Conference. 26–27 September, Lancaster: Lancaster University.

Hanslein, J. D. (1930). 'The Position of Accounting in the Small Liberal Arts College'. *Accounting Review*, 5(2), 150–2.

Hill, D. R., Ainsworth, R. M., & Partap, U. (2012). 'Teaching Global Public Health in the Undergraduate Liberal Arts: a survey of 50 colleges'. *American Journal of Tropical Medicine and Hygiene*, 87(1), 11–15.

Hirst, P. H. (1974). *Knowledge and the Curriculum: a collection of philosophical papers*. London: Routledge & Kegan Paul.

Hogarth, R. M. (1979). *Evaluating Management Education*. Chichester: John Wiley.

Hovland, K., Kirkwood, B. A., Ward, C., Osterweis, M., & Silver, G. B. (2009). 'Liberal Education and Public Health: surveying the landscape'. *Peer Review*, 11(3), 5–8.

Howard, S. E. (1930). 'Accounting Instruction in the Liberal Arts Curriculum'. *Accounting Review*, 5(2), 146–9.

Howard, S. E. (1936). 'Accounting in a Liberal Arts Curriculum'. *Accounting Review*, 11(2), 149–57.

Inui, Y., & Lankford, S. (2006). 'Rethinking Tourism Education: what should schools teach?' *Journal of Hospitality, Leisure, Sport and Tourism Education*, 5(2), 25–35.

Jamal, T. (2004). 'Virtue Ethics and Sustainable Tourism Pedagogy: phronesis, principles and practice'. *Journal of Sustainable Tourism*, 12(6), 530–45.

Jamal, T., & Menzel, C. (2009). 'Good Actions in Tourism'. In J. Tribe (Ed.), *Philosophical Issues in Tourism* (pp. 227–43). Bristol: Channel View Publications.

Jeffrey, C. (1993). 'Ethical Development of Accounting Students, Non-Accounting Business Students, and Liberal Arts Students'. *Issues in Accounting Education*, 8(1), 86–96.

Khurana, R. (2007). *From Higher Aims to Hired Hands: the social transformation of American business schools and the unfulfilled promise of management as a profession*. Princeton, NJ: Princeton University Press.

Kirkpatrick, B. F. (1965). 'Law and the Liberal Education'. *American Business Law Journal*, 3(3), 363–71.

Klein, J. D., & Balmer, R. (2007). 'Engineering, Liberal Arts, and Technological Literacy in Higher Education'. *IEEE Technology and Society*, 26(4), 23–8.

Klein, N. (2007). *The Shock Doctrine: the rise of disaster capitalism*. London: Penguin Books.

Kohl, M. (1961). 'Objectives of Accounting Education in the Liberal Arts College'. *Accounting Review*, 36(4), 631–4.

Larimore, T. R. (1937). 'Accounting in the Small Liberal Arts College'. *Accounting Review*, 12(2), 180–3.

Lashley, C. (1999). 'On Making Silk Purses: developing reflective practitioners in hospitality management education'. *International Journal of Contemporary Hospitality Management*, 11(4), 180–5.

Lashley, C. (2000). 'Towards a Theoretical Understanding'. In C. Lashley & A. Morrison (Eds.), *In Search of Hospitality: theoretical perspectives and debates* (pp. 1–17). Oxford: Butterworth Heinemann.

Lashley, C. (2007). 'Discovering Hospitality: observations from recent research'. *International Journal of Culture, Tourism and Hospitality Research*, 1(3), 214–26.

Lashley, C. (2009). 'The Right Answers to the Wrong Questions? Observations on skill development and training in the United Kingdom's hospitality sector'. *Tourism and Hospitality Research*, 9(4), 340–52.

Lashley, C., & Morrison, A. (Eds.). (2000). *In Search of Hospitality: theoretical perspectives and debates*. Oxford: Butterworth Heinemann.

Lashley, C., & Rowson, W. (2002). 'A Big Firm Waiting to Grow? Franchisees in the pub sector. *Strategic Change*, 11(4), 56–74.

Lashley, C., & Morrison, A. (2003). 'Hospitality as a Commercial Friendship'. *Hospitality Review*, 6(3), 31–6.

Lashley, C., & Rowson, B. (2005). *Developing Management Skills in Blackpool's Small Hotel Sector: a research report for England's North West Tourism Skills Network*. Nottingham: Nottingham Trent University.

Lashley, C., & Rowson, B. (2010). 'Lifestyle Businesses: insights into Blackpool's hotel sector'. *International Journal of Hospitality Management*, 29(3), 511–19.

Lashley, C., Morrison, A., & Randall, S. (2005). 'More than a Service Encounter? Insights into the emotions of hospitality through special meal occasions'. *Journal of Hospitality and Tourism Management*, 12(1), 80–92.

Lashley, C., Lynch, P., & Morrison, A. (Eds.). (2007). *Hospitality: a social lens*. Oxford: Elsevier.

Lata, P., & Devika. (2013). 'Instilling Creativity, Critical Thinking and Values for Holistic Development through Humanities and Liberal Arts Courses among Engineering Students'. *Social Sciences & Humanities*, 21(1), 329–40.

Lynch, P. (2005). 'Reflections on the Home Setting in Hospitality'. *Journal of Hospitality and Tourism Management*, 12(1), 37–49.

Lynch, P., & MacWhannell, D. (2000). 'Home and Commercialized Hospitality'. In C. Lashley & A. Morrison (Eds.), *In Search of Hospitality: theoretical perspectives and debates* (pp. 100–17). Oxford: Butterworth Heinemann.

Lynch, P., Molz, J. G., McIntosh, A., Lugosi, P., & Lashley, C. (2011). 'Theorising Hospitality'. *Hospitality & Society*, 1(1), 3–24.

McCabe, V. S., Gross, M. J., & Reynolds, P. (2008). 'Toward the Development of Best Practice in a Postgraduate International Hospitality Management Program'. *Journal of Teaching in Travel & Tourism*, 8(2/3), 283–304.

MacDonald, D. B., & Ramaglia, J. A. (2004). 'Teaching International Business Law: a liberal arts perspective'. *Journal of Legal Studies Education*, 22(1), 39–64.

Mintzberg, H. (2004). *Managers not MBAs: a hard look at the soft practice of managing and management development*. San Francisco, CA: Berrett-Koehler Publishers.

Molz, J. G. (2005). Cosmopolitans on the Couch: mobilising hospitality and the internet. Paper presented at the 'Mobilising Hospitality: the ethics of social relations in a mobile world' Conference. 26–27 September, Lancaster: Lancaster University.

Molz, J. G., & Gibson, S. (Eds.). (2007). *Mobilizing Hospitality: the ethics of social relations in a mobile world*. Aldershot: Ashgate Publishing.

Morrison, A., & O'Mahony, G. B. (2003). 'The Liberation of Hospitality Management Education'. *International Journal of Contemporary Hospitality Management*, 15(1), 38–44.

Morsing, M., & Rovira, A. S. (2011). *Business Schools and their Contribution to Society*. London: Sage.

Mulcahy, J. D. (1999). 'Vocational Work Experience in the Hospitality Industry: characteristics and strategies'. *Education + Training*, 41(4), 164–74.

Munar, A. M. (2007). 'Is the Bologna Process Globalizing Tourism Education?' *Journal of Hospitality, Leisure, Sport and Tourism Education*, 6(2), 68–82.

Murphy, M. E. (1952). 'Accounting in the Liberal Arts College'. *Accounting Review*, 27(4), 517–22.

Newman, R. P. (1957). 'A Comparison of the Speaking Ability of Liberal Arts and Engineering Upperclassmen'. *Speech Monographs*, 24(3), 227–31.

O'Mahony, B. (2003). 'Social and Domestic Forces in Commercial Hospitality Provision: a view from Australia'. *Hospitality Review*, 5(4), 37–41.

O'Mahony, B. (2007). 'The Role of the Hospitality Industry in Cultural Assimilation: a case study from colonial Australia'. In C. Lashley, P. Lynch, & A. Morrison (Eds.), *Hospitality: a social lens* (pp. 73–87). Oxford: Elsevier.

Palliam, R. (2010). 'Identity, Variety and Destiny in Accounting Education for a Social–Environmental and Liberal Arts Tradition'. *Issues in Social and Environmental Accounting*, 4(2), 149–67.

Parker, C. M. (2002). 'A Liberal Education in Law: engaging the legal imagination through research and writing beyond the curriculum'. *Journal of the Association of Legal Writing Directors*, 1(Fall), 130–43.

Patnaik, R. (2012). 'Liberal Education Complements Engineering'. *Peer Review*, 14(2), 31.

Petit, T. A. (1967). *The Moral Crisis in Management*. New York: McGraw-Hill.

Pierson, F. C. (1959). *The Education of American Businessmen: a study of university-college programs in business administration*. New York: McGraw-Hill.

Ponemon, L., & Glazer, A. (1990). 'Accounting Education and Ethical Development: the influence of liberal learning on students and alumni in accounting practice'. *Issues in Accounting Education*, 5(2), 195–208.

Porter, L. W., & McKibbin, L. E. (1988). *Management Education and Development: drift or thrust into the 21st century?* New York: McGraw-Hill.

Riegelman, R. (2012). 'Liberal Education and Preparation for the Health Professions'. *Liberal Education*, 98(2), 54–9.

Ring, A., Dickinger, A., & Wöber, K. (2009). 'Designing the Ideal Undergraduate Program in Tourism: expectations from industry and educators'. *Journal of Travel Research*, 48(1), 106–21.

Ritzer, G. (2001). *The McDonaldization of Society*. Thousand Oaks, CA: Pine Forge.

Ritzer, G. (2007). 'Inhospitable Hospitality?' In C. Lashley, P. Lynch, & A. Morrison (Eds.), *Hospitality: a social lens* (pp. 129–39). Oxford: Elsevier.

Robinson, M., Lynch, P., & Conn, S. (2005). Hospitality Through Poetry: control, fake solidarity and breakdown. Paper presented at the 14th CHME Research Conference. 13–15 May, Bournemouth: Bournemouth University.

Rosello, M. (2001). *Postcolonial Hospitality: the immigrant as guest*. Stanford, CA: Stanford University Press.

Rospond, R. M. (2012). 'Integrating Pharmacy and the Health Sciences with a Liberal Education'. *Peer Review*, 14(2), 20–3.

Rotter, N. G. (1982). 'Images of Engineering and Liberal Arts Majors'. *Journal of Vocational Behaviour*, 20(2), 193–202.

Sankowski, E. (2009). 'Philosophy, Public Health, and Liberal Education'. *Peer Review*, 11(3), 9–11.

Sarat, A. (Ed.). (2002). *Law in the Liberal Arts*. Ithaca, NY: Cornell University Press.

Schön, D. A. (1983). *The Reflective Practitioner: how professionals think in action*. London: Temple Smith.

Slattery, P. (2002). 'Finding the Hospitality Industry'. *Journal of Hospitality, Leisure, Sport and Tourism Education*, 1(1), 19–28.

Telfer, E. (1996). *Food for Thought*. London: Routledge.

Telfer, E. (2000). 'The Philosophy of Hospitableness'. In C. Lashley & A. Morrison (Eds.), *In Search of Hospitality: theoretical perspectives and debates* (pp. 38–55). Oxford: Butterworth Heinemann.

Thomas, R., Lashley, C., Rowson, B., Xie, Y., Jameson, S., Eaglen, A., Lincoln, G., & Parsons, D. (2000). *The National Survey of Small Tourism and Hospitality Firms 2000: skills demands and training practices*. Leeds: Leeds Metropolitan University.

Tresidder, R. (2011). 'Reading Hospitality: the semiotics of Le Manoir aux Quat'Saisons'. *Hospitality & Society*, 1(1), 67–84.

Tribe, J. (2002). 'The Philosophic Practitioner'. *Annals of Tourism Research*, 29(2), 338–57.

Turbak, F., & Berg, R. (2002). 'Robotic Design Studio: exploring the big ideas of engineering in a liberal arts environment'. *Journal of Science Education and Technology*, 11(3), 237–53.

Vaz, R. F. (2012). 'Designing the Liberally Educated Engineer'. *Peer Review*, 14(2), 8–11.

Walter, M. R. (2002). 'Erasing the Lines between Law School and the Liberal Arts Curricula'. *Journal of the Association of Legal Writing Directors*, 1(Fall), 153–7.

Walton, J. K. (1998). *Blackpool*. Manchester: Keele and Edinburgh University Press.

Walton, J. K. (2000a). *The British Seaside: holidays and resorts in the twentieth century*. Manchester: Manchester University Press.

Walton, J. K. (2000b). 'The Hospitality Trades: a social history'. In C. Lashley & A. Morrison (Eds.), *In Search of Hospitality: theoretical perspectives and debates* (pp. 56–76). Oxford: Butterworth Heinemann.

Walton, J. K. (2005). *Histories of Tourism*. Clevedon: Channel View Publications.

Warde, A., & Martens, L. (2001). *Dining Out*. London: Sage.

Willits, S. D. (2010). 'Will more Liberal Arts Courses Fix the Accounting Curriculum?' *Journal of Accounting Education*, 28(1), 13–25.

7

Interdisciplinarity, transdisciplinarity and postdisciplinarity in tourism and hospitality education

Michael Volgger

Institute for Regional Development and Location Management,
European Academy Bozen/Bolzano (EURAC research), Italy

Harald Pechlaner

Institute for Regional Development and Location Management,
European Academy Bozen/Bolzano (EURAC research), Italy, and Chair in Tourism,
Centre for Entrepreneurship, Catholic University of Eichstätt-Ingolstadt, Germany

Introduction

Although tourism may have reached its maturity (Airey, 2008), the disciplinary status of tourism is a topic of ongoing discussion. Some see tourism as having already matured into a discipline (Goeldner, 1988; Leiper, 2000), whereas others argue that tourism is still pre-paradigmatic in the Kuhnian sense (Kuhn, 1970; Tribe, 2005). The latter position understands tourism as a field of study that crosses disciplinary boundaries (Jafari & Ritchie, 1981; Tribe, 1997).

This chapter aims to inform this discussion by scrutinizing the disciplinary understanding of tourism as reflected in curricula for a Master's degree in Tourism, Hospitality and Events (TH&E) in German-speaking countries. Although knowledge generation is different from knowledge delivery, analysing the modes of packaging tourism knowledge for education, i.e. curricula (Tribe, 2000; 2002), may also provide indications towards better understanding the frontiers of TH&E knowledge (Tribe & Xiao, 2011).

The focus of this chapter lies on curricula in general, and the curriculum space (Dredge et al., 2012; Tribe, 2002) in particular. We propose a comparative and circular reading of TH&E curricula by distinguishing two dimensions in the curriculum space – the origin of the knowledge taught and its structure – and by highlighting one perspective – cores and peripheries. The first dimension refers to the tangible locus of knowledge, i.e. the institutional dimension of the curriculum space (academia vs. applied field) (Gibbons et al., 1994; Nowotny et al., 2001; Spode, 1998; Tribe, 1997). The second dimension refers to the primarily intangible, but equally influential, knowledge structure, i.e. the metaphorical dimension of the curriculum space (disciplines, fields and other compartments of knowledge) (Echtner & Jamal, 1997; Spode 1998).

Disciplines and the curriculum space

Disciplines are probably the most important structuring principle in academic knowledge generation and delivery. They are related to a division of labour within academia, and different institutions of higher education (faculties or institutes), and resulting from a history of increasing specialization, or, as some would argue, harmful fragmentation, that accelerated significantly in the twentieth century. A discipline can be defined as 'a distinctive body of knowledge and an organized set of rules and conceptual structure for advancing knowledge' (Tribe, 2000: 810).

A discipline can be characterized by the following criteria (Hirst, 1974): (1) a web of interrelated concepts; (2) a particular logical structure that binds the concepts; (3) testability within this web using its particular criteria and logical structure; and (4) irreducibility to other disciplines. According to similar approaches, disciplines consist of webs of constructs (theories), methods (ways of producing and testing knowledge) and aims or application domains (Donald, 1986; Toulmin, 1972). Some authors additionally request the existence of a dedicated community, means of communication (such as journals), tradition and a set of values (King & Brownell, 1966).

Disciplines do not coincide with curricula; however they are intertwined. Curricula are both more and less than disciplines. They are less inclusive, because they comprise only the teaching aspect of disciplines: 'A curriculum is the organization of knowledge for transmission in education' (Tribe, 2000: 810). However, they are also broader than disciplines, meaning that curricula may also exist for fields of study that do not qualify under strict criteria as disciplines. The relevant point is that notions of compartmentalization of knowledge (disciplines, but not only) may also express themselves in curricula – potentially providing insights not only into the teaching, but also into the disciplinary status of the subject.

Within the scope of this chapter, a TH&E curriculum is understood as what is taught and also what is omitted in a TH&E-related programme, packaged in courses and modules (Tribe, 2002, 2005). Applying a spatial notion to this education package (see Abbott, 1995; Becher & Trowler, 2001; Dogan, 1997), one can speak of a curriculum space (Dredge et al., 2012; Tribe, 2002, 2010). Various perspectives can be distinguished in the curriculum space. For instance, commentators propose educational ends (vocational vs. liberal education, or skills vs. knowledge), giving rise to the balancing ideal of the philosophic practitioner (Dredge et al., 2012; Schön, 1983; Tribe, 2002). As another perspective, Dredge et al. (2012) suggest total size (amount of content) of the curriculum space. We depart slightly from these valuable ideas and apply the two dimensions of origin of knowledge and compartmentalization of its delivery. However, we focus primarily on the second aspect: the perspectives of disciplinarity in TH&E curricula. By applying a core–periphery scheme (e.g. Dredge et al., 2012), we investigate the disciplinary understanding of TH&E that may underpin the curriculum space.

Structuring TH&E knowledge: the disciplinary status of tourism

Discussion of the disciplinary status of tourism is ongoing and highly controversial (Benckendorff & Zehrer, 2013; Darbellay & Stock, 2012). Those who deny the disciplinary status refer mainly to tourism's missing distinctive body of knowledge and its reliance on other disciplines (Tribe, 1997), to which the predominance of mainly multidisciplinary and less interdisciplinary approaches seems to testify (Airey, 2008; Jafari & Ritchie, 1981). The conclusion drawn within this perspective is that tourism is 'an object of study (field) rather than a way of studying (discipline)' (Tribe, 1997: 653). Cooper et al. (1998) hold similar positions.

In contrast, Leiper (2000) and Goeldner (1988) are major exponents of the 'tourism as a discipline' view; especially Leiper (1981) who sees a need for developing interdisciplinary accounts into a general and systematic discipline of tourism ('tourology'). Finally, a third group of authors maintains a more prudent position. For instance, Echtner & Jamal (1997: 880) argue that 'while tourism studies could potentially develop into a discipline, it is concluded that there are many practical and philosophical reasons that hamper its evolution'.

The present chapter takes a similarly prudent stance in a two-fold manner. First, while the disciplinary status of tourism is an ongoing and contested issue, there seems to be a degree of consensus that the object of tourism should not be limited to one particular 'traditional' discipline (Coles et al., 2006; Darbellay & Stock, 2012). Second, a more dynamic view of disciplinarity might appropriately reduce tension between the two aforementioned positions (Beier & Arnold, 2005). In this context, we consider it more appropriate to discuss the dynamic status of TH&E research and education, i.e. the question of whether tourism is a mature/maturing field (Ryan, 1997; Sheldon, 1991; Xiao & Smith, 2006) or is still in its infancy (Belhassen & Caton, 2009). Therefore, this chapter tries to capture potential structuring forms of TH&E education in a dynamic manner by alluding to potential oscillating movements within the curriculum space (see Figure 7.1).

Multi-, inter-, trans- and postdisciplinarity: definition of the concepts

Tourism 'does not recognize disciplinary demarcations, no matter how distinct the disciplinary boundaries might seem to be. Its concerns, more often than not, cross disciplinary boundaries and find themselves at home' (Jafari & Ritchie, 1981: 22). Starting from the assumed consensus that TH&E research and education require combining a range of traditional disciplines, the question that arises is how to combine them. We discuss four main approaches to such disciplinary combinations below.

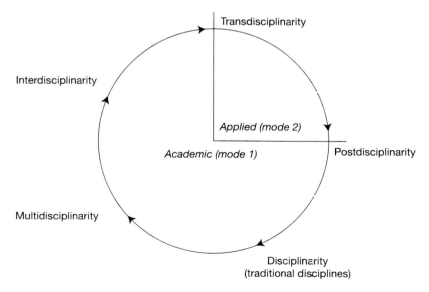

Figure 7.1 The dynamics of disciplinary approaches to TH&E education (and research)

Multidisciplinarity

Whereas so-called cross-disciplinary research tries to understand specific disciplinary issues from the perspective of another discipline (Jafari & Ritchie, 1981), multidisciplinarity draws upon different disciplinary specializations to understand one phenomenon better, without merging their views (Pechlaner & Reuter, 2012). Distinct disciplinary approaches, with their own methodologies, are applied to a field or a common theme in parallel: 'Multidisciplinarity draws on knowledge from different disciplines but stays within their boundaries' (Choi & Pak, 2006: 351). Thus, the different points of view observe the same object but remain separate (Darbellay & Stock, 2012).

This multidisciplinary understanding in TH&E is represented for instance in the approach offered in Jafari & Ritchie (1981), who identify economics, sociology, psychology, geography and anthropology as main contributing disciplines. Darbellay & Stock (2012: 452) hold that so far multidisciplinarity has dominated in tourism studies, where 'the research object is decomposed into multiple dimensions and perspectives, yet juxtaposed without interaction'. Thus, the weakness of multidisciplinary approaches might lie in the fragmented nature of knowledge that lacks the glue sticking the various aspects together (Bodewes, 1981).

Interdisciplinarity

Interdisciplinarity strives for research findings 'between disciplines' (Beier & Arnold, 2005; Leiper, 1981) to solve common research goals through dynamic interactions across disciplinary boundaries (Darbellay & Stock, 2012). Thus, it is based on the cooperative development of synthetic terminology and methods (Pechlaner & Reuter, 2012; Tress et al., 2005). Interdisciplinarity is 'characterized by the explicit formulation of a uniform, discipline-transcending terminology or a common methodology' (Gibbons et al., 1994: 29). The most distinctive element of interdisciplinarity is the creation or delivery of new knowledge that is not reducible to established disciplines due to profound integration of disciplinary concepts and/or methodologies (see Braun & Schubert, 2003; Pechlaner & Reuter, 2012; Tribe, 1997).

Based on a network analysis of the research space of tourism, with its tribes, colleges and territories, Benckendorff & Zehrer (2013: 141) conclude that 'tourism research continues to be inter-disciplinary'. However, interdisciplinarity is a challenging endeavour (Darbellay & Stock, 2012) and is, according to Tribe (1997), mainly concentrated within the sub-area of tourism business studies (business interdisciplinarity).

Transdisciplinarity

Transdisciplinarity refers to the explicit abandonment of disciplinary boundaries. Indeed, Tribe (1997) collates the term extradisciplinary to transdisciplinary in order to denote the creation of knowledge outside existing disciplines, by resorting to practical sources. Transdisciplinarity involves contesting established places (institutions) of knowledge production, thus replacing the knowledge privilege of science with a more heterarchic open space of knowledge production. Nowotny et al. (2001) refer to this space with the metaphor of the ancient agora.

Transdisciplinary approaches start with problems (Jafari & Ritchie, 1981) and develop specific theoretical bases, methods and implementations that are not reducible to an already existing discipline (see Gibbons et al., 1994).

> [T]ransdisciplinarity contributes to a joint problem solving that it is more than juxtaposition; more than laying one discipline alongside another. . . . If joint problem solving is the aim,

then the means must provide for an integration of perspectives in the identification, formulation and resolution of what has to become a shared problem.

(Nowotny, 2003: 1)

It is questionable whether transdisciplinarity leads to establishing a new discipline or goes beyond disciplines (see Buckler, 2004). Preferring the second option, some argue that it is mainly the closeness to practice that distinguishes transdisciplinary approaches (see Tress *et al.*, 2005; Tribe, 1997).

Postdisciplinarity

Other authors have raised a similar discussion about the abandonment of disciplinary boundaries by calling it 'postdisciplinarity'. We hold that the main difference between both discussions refers to their main point of reference, for transdisciplinarity this means practice ('mode 2' in Tribe, 1997, and Nowotny *et al.*, 2001) and for postdisciplinarity the academic context ('mode 1' in Tribe, 1997, and Nowotny *et al.*, 2001) (see Figure 7.1).

Postdisciplinarity (or supradisciplinarity) is described as a perspective that contests disciplines and other academic demarcations by questioning their content, nature and exclusiveness (Beier & Arnold, 2005). In concrete terms, this might go as far as doubting the qualification of TH&E as relevant units for structuring academic inquiry and teaching. Suggested alternatives refer to mobility (Hannam, 2009) or customer value (as prominent in an analysed curriculum in the context of this study). Buckler (2004: 2) writes: 'The term "postdisciplinarity" evokes an intellectual universe in which we inhabit the ruins of outmoded disciplinary structures, mediating between our nostalgia for this lost unity and our excitement at the intellectual freedom its demise can offer us'. In other words: whereas transdisciplinarity challenges established 'real' places of knowledge production (academia), postdisciplinarity rather questions the 'metaphorical' spatialization of knowledge production and delivery (division of knowledge in disciplines, etc.).

Postdisciplinary positions contest the epistemological unit of 'disciplines' as such, and look for radically alternative ways of organizing heterogeneous knowledge (Coles *et al.*, 2006; Law, 2004; Ren *et al.*, 2010; Ritchie, 2008). In particular, they contest the utility of disciplines when the majority of (research) problems are not territorialized (Hellström *et al.*, 2003). Second homes, crisis/security, identity and the various instances of health tourism are sometimes proposed as candidates for postdisciplinary accounts (Beier & Arnold, 2005; Coles *et al.*, 2006; Hollinshead, 2010; Ritchie, 2008).

Postdisciplinary knowledge production rejects the 'parochialism and policing' of disciplines (Coles *et al.*, 2006: 305) as well as the 'artificial division of academic labour' (Goodwin, 2004: 65). However, postdisciplinarity does not mean that traditional disciplines have disappeared, it simply wants purposely to acknowledge diversity by adding a flexible, network and problem-centred approach to existing epistemologies and ontologies (Coles *et al.*, 2006; Hollinshead, 2010; Ren *et al.*, 2010; Ritchie, 2008; Visnovsky & Bianchi, 2005). Briefly, postdisciplinarity wants to (re-)assemble very different kinds of knowledge and modes of knowledge production (see Ren *et al.*, 2010).

Core–periphery approach to TH&E disciplinarity and education

A core–periphery structure is evident in various contexts, including regional development (Krugman, 1991), social network analysis (SNA) (Borgatti & Everett, 1991) or tourist destination image (Lai & Li, 2012). Furthering previous reflections of Airey & Johnson (1999), we argue that it could also provide a valuable lens to judge the disciplinary (or if required, extradisciplinary or indisciplinary) approach evident in TH&E curricula. Subsequently we first discuss the usefulness of a core–periphery approach to TH&E knowledge production and delivery, and then apply this core–periphery thinking to graduate-level programme curricula in TH&E education in German-speaking countries.

Core–periphery reflections have an established tradition in depicting the tourism field (often and not coincidentally illustrated as a circle). Early on, Jafari & Ritchie (1981) acknowledged the need to develop a common body of knowledge in tourism. More than 20 years later, Airey & Johnson (1999) and Airey (2005) could report that this objective had at least been partly achieved, and that tourism programmes are becoming increasingly similar. Such convergence of curricula might be taken as an indicator of an increasingly stabilized knowledge core of TH&E in general. '[T]he fears about fragmentation appear to have been unfounded. Most tourism programmes are basically very similar' (Airey, 2005: 21).

Besides identifying core–periphery structures among publications in the TH&E field (Benckendorff & Zehrer, 2013), core–periphery descriptions proposed both single concepts (theory) lying at the core of tourism knowledge production and delivery, as well as broader ranging conceptualization of knowledge generation in tourism (epistemology). Concerning core concepts, previous commentators (Airey, 2005, 2008; Tribe, 1997; Tribe & Xiao, 2011) have suggested 'tourism gaze' (Urry, 1990), 'tourism multiplier' (Archer, 1977), 'host and guest' (Smith, 1977) or 'Tourism Area Life Cycle' (Butler, 1980). A further candidate might be 'tourist destination'.

Concerning epistemology, building on prior reflections of Jafari & Ritchie (1981), Tribe (1997) presented a model of tourism studies, to be precise, actually distinguishing two quite separate fields of tourism studies: tourism business studies and non-business tourism studies (tourism social science) (see also Tribe, 2010). According to Tribe, these two fields build a medium layer of tourism knowledge creation, encompassed by established disciplines (philosophy, geography, economics, sociology, etc.). In this context, Tribe implicitly identified two cores of tourism knowledge production: a so-called 'band k' characterized by 'mode 1' (academic knowledge production), and a 'mode 2', which covers tourism knowledge production taking place in tourism practice, mainly in the business of tourism (see also Gibbons et al., 1994; Nowotny et al., 2001).

In the first core, 'band k', the study of tourism interacts with traditional disciplines. It is here 'where tourism theories and concepts are distilled' and 'where tourism knowledge is created' (Tribe, 1997: 650). In particular, Tribe (1997) describes the nature of knowledge production in this first core as often being multidisciplinary and interdisciplinary, the latter being true especially for the subfield of tourism business studies ('business interdisciplinarity'). In contrast, so-called 'mode 2' knowledge production takes place outside the disciplines in the practical world. Therefore, according to Tribe it could be called transdisciplinary or extradisciplinary knowledge production.

The core–periphery concept has the advantage of shifting attention slightly away from the contested, fuzzy and partly politicized question of the disciplinary status of TH&E. First, it offers an opportunity to focus on the more basic question – that can also be empirically studied (see Airey & Middleton, 1984; Stuart-Hoyle, 2003) – of what forms the core of TH&E research and education. Second, having scrutinized the core (the 'what'), one might reflect on where this knowledge comes from and how it is compartmentalized (role of disciplines, role of practice and industry). Third, this information could help to locate TH&E on the dynamic continuum of maturity between field and discipline, and thus promote a procedural understanding of its (in-)disciplinarity (see Beier & Arnold, 2005).

Such core–periphery considerations might be applied to both TH&E knowledge production and TH&E education, with for instance Dredge *et al.* (2012) speaking of a core curriculum. Assuming that the areas of producing and teaching knowledge overlap to a certain extent (Tribe, 2005), and by identifying some core–periphery models found empirically in TH&E graduate programmes, this present chapter contributes to the stepwise procedure of better capturing and monitoring 'the indiscipline of tourism' (Tribe, 1997).

Inter-, trans- and postdisciplinarity: evidence from TH&E curricula

Applying the different disciplinary-crossing approaches to education raises one interesting question of where their integration is accomplished. In multidisciplinary approaches, different disciplines are integrated by the students themselves, whereas in interdisciplinary teaching approaches, the integration is an explicit part of the curriculum (Jafari & Ritchie, 1981). Trans- and postdisciplinary teaching goes beyond disciplines. Their integration happens prior to teaching, or is omnipresent in the teaching approach through a specific formulation of the aims: 'Whereas inter-disciplinary programs start with the discipline, trans-disciplinary programs start with the issue or problem and through the processes of problem solving, bring to bear the knowledge of those disciplines that contribute to a solution or resolution' (Jafari & Ritchie, 1981: 24).

Based on these reflections, the purpose of our study was to identify the disciplinary (and disciplinary-crossing or indisciplinary) approaches found in TH&E graduate programme curricula in German-speaking countries (Germany, Austria and parts of Switzerland; also including, however, programmes taught in English). For the context of this study, TH&E graduate programmes were defined as having either TH&E items in their title, or offering at least five ECTS-credits (European Credit Transfer and Accumulation System, with about 25 to 30 hours per credit point) to be gained in individual courses (compulsory or optional) that satisfy these criteria. Almost 90 per cent of the programmes considered mentioned 'tourism', 'hospitality' or 'events' in the programme title. In Germany, Austria and the German-speaking parts of Switzerland, about 35 universities or universities of applied sciences were offering some form of TH&E education in Master's programmes (the imprecision stems from some marginal forms, such as private business schools not accredited by the state, or study programmes where tourism subjects play only a very limited role). The weight of the tourism part, its structural integration and the contents delivered varied quite extensively. Similar variation was also encountered in earlier studies in other countries (Airey & Middleton, 1984).

From initially screening the collected curricula, we identified six prototypes of curricula structure and depicted them as both modularized intersection models and core–periphery models (see Figure 7.2, which builds on the different approaches introduced in Figure 7.1). Next, mainly based on their graphical representations, we allocated the collected curricula to the relevant set of the six prototypical categories. In the presented six intersection models in Figure 7.2, the vertical rectangles represent the ordering mechanism that explicitly dominates the curriculum structure and that often functions as a guiding principle for identifying the programme modules. In contrast, the horizontal rectangles represent (partly implicit) areas, to which the structuring principles of the vertical rectangles are applied. The same distinction sits at the heart of the six core–periphery models also shown in Figure 7.2. The core comprises the sources of the knowledge that is delivered (or the underlying structuring principle), whereas the outer layers indicate areas of application of the so structured knowledge.

Regarding the terminology used in Figure 7.2, discipline stands for a 'distinctive body of knowledge' (Tribe, 2000: 810), that has matured to a significant degree and is well established

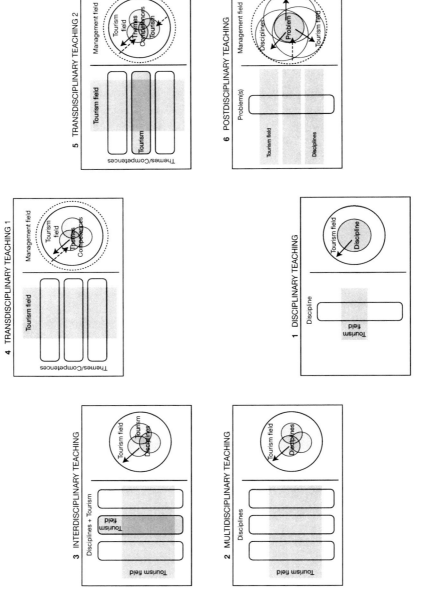

Figure 7.2 A core–periphery perspective of the disciplinary approaches to TH&E education

and recognized in academia. Mainly for simplicity, we treat business/management as a discipline. However, we acknowledge that some have doubts about this, and see business/management as a mature field (see Tribe, 1997). A field is rather 'an object of study' (Tribe, 1997: 653). We use theme as a unifying line of thought within a 'context of application' (Gibbons et al., 1994: 168), which is however less circumscribed and less established than a field. A competence is an 'ability to solve a problem' (Tribe, 1997: 654) and a problem is 'a concern of people' (Cohen et al., 1972: 3).

Type 1 – disciplinary teaching

In Type 1, a single traditional discipline dominates and provides the framework within which (normally to a minor degree) TH&E aspects are covered. In all of the identified cases this single discipline is business/management, meaning that what is taught is essentially the business of tourism. The curriculum is similar to a standard curriculum in business/management with some dedicated courses that discuss specific features of TH&E as a field of application. Thus, paralleling Tribe's (1997) terminology, we could call this approach the business disciplinarity of tourism.

Type 2 – multidisciplinary teaching

Multidisciplinary teaching combines knowledge and approaches of different disciplines to deliver a better understanding of the TH&E field ('band k' in Tribe, 1997). In this case we would mainly find instances of TH&E-oriented lectures with different, but clear and explicit, disciplinary backgrounds, without providing dedicated courses that help the student integrate the delivered disciplinary knowledge. In other words, the teaching core consists exclusively of the disciplines, and this knowledge core is applied to the field of TH&E. Typically, various faculties at an institute of higher education contribute to such a TH&E programme.

Type 3 – interdisciplinary teaching

What distinguishes Type 3 from Type 2 is mostly the attempt to integrate the different disciplinary approaches to TH&E into one or more comprehensive courses. These integrating courses also tend to present TH&E concepts that express a profound integration of disciplinary knowledge. TH&E is not only present as a latent field of application within the taught disciplinary knowledge, but is considered part of the teaching core. Therefore, integrating lectures typically accompany the parallel teaching of disciplinary strands.

Although specific TH&E knowledge moves into the core, these programmes remain strongly rooted in specific disciplines, with a strong role of business/management and less prominent roles for geography, cultural studies and economics. Therefore, this parallels what Tribe (1997) called business interdisciplinarity (mainly residing within 'band k').

Type 4 and Type 5 – transdisciplinary teaching 1 and 2

What seems characteristic of transdisciplinary TH&E programmes is the fact that the applied world of TH&E (external to academia) with its practical issues becomes the main structuring principle of the curriculum. Neither the academic organization of knowledge (e.g. disciplines) nor academia as an autonomous place of knowledge production exerts a particular influence on the curriculum. The role of disciplines becomes minor, although there is strong conceptual borrowing from business/management. Positioned at the core of the curriculum are different themes or competencies considered important for mastering the business practice of TH&E 'out there'. Examples of such competencies and themes are sustainable development, family businesses, innovation in TH&E, intercultural competencies, competencies in social responsibility and environmental ethics, mastering future issues, and competencies in information and communication technology.

The main distinction between Type 4 and Type 5 resembles that between Type 2 and Type 3, and concerns the role of the field of TH&E as a potential source of knowledge generation. Whereas Type 4 (transdisciplinarity teaching 1) derives the main competencies/themes to be taught from the business field in general, Type 5 seems to assume a certain kind of specific TH&E competence (inspired by the practical world of TH&E), which becomes part of the curriculum core. These latter modules could be called 'TH&E focus courses'.

However, in both Type 4 and Type 5 cases, we may note a clear switch into what Tribe (1997) called delivering 'mode 2' (practice-driven) knowledge.

Type 6 – postdisciplinary teaching

Postdisciplinary teaching shares its ambition with transdisciplinary teaching to transcend disciplinary structures. However, it seems to display a stronger relation to the traditional academic area of knowledge production ('mode 1'). In sourcing from the academic area, it retains – somewhat paradoxically – a role for disciplines. Therefore, we may interpret postdisciplinarity as closing the circle towards disciplinary approaches to tourism education. However, disciplines do not appear as a core of teaching, but rather as peripheral areas with some bidirectional exchange of ideas with the core. The latter comprises a central problem that is deemed detrimental based on experiences from both management fields and theoretical reflections. For instance, such a problem might be the 'creation of customer value', the 'role of the customer in society' or 'problem solving' (as a methodological competence). These problems provide the basis for arranging the curriculum and the backbone for exchange with different related fields (e.g. tourism) and disciplines within it. Often, the curriculum distinguishes between core lectures delivering the theoretical toolset and courses covering application and so-called contextual areas.

This approach is guided by a very pragmatic and eclectic exchange between the different modes and areas of knowledge production (mode 1 and mode 2, theoretical and practical), which is unified by a common problem. It seems also characterized by increasing difficulties in distinguishing between areas of knowledge application (fields) and knowledge sources. Finally, compared to other disciplinary approaches, not only the role of disciplines but also the role of an established field such as TH&E seem to have less impact on the structuring of postdisciplinary curricula.

Allocation to prototypes

The next step in the analysis involved assigning the different TH&E master programmes in German-speaking countries to the six prototypes discussed previously (see Table 7.1). What becomes apparent is that Type 5 (transdisciplinary 2) dominates in TH&E Master's curricula in German-speaking areas, followed by Type 1 curricula (disciplinary) and Type 3 curricula (interdisciplinary). Interestingly, we found no Type 2 curriculum (multidisciplinary). The biggest difficulties in assigning curricula appear between curriculum Type 4 (transdisciplinary 1), Type 5 (transdisciplinary 2) and Type 1 (disciplinary). This may be due to the fact that most transdisciplinary approaches have strong conceptual relationships with more traditional

Table 7.1 The distribution of higher education types among universities and universities of applied sciences in German-speaking countries

Teaching approach	Type 1	Type 2	Type 3	Type 4	Type 5	Type 6
Universities	1	0	2	1	2	2
Universities of applied sciences	6	0	2	1	16	1
Total number of educational organizations	7	0	4	2	18	3

disciplinary approaches of business/management. This observation agrees with the findings of Airey & Johnson (1999).

Further patterns appear when distinguishing between universities and universities of applied sciences, the latter having by definition a strong vocational orientation. Universities of applied sciences, which today account for the greater part of higher education in TH&E in German-speaking countries, demonstrate two peaks in their curriculum design, namely a lower peak in Type 1 disciplinary approaches and a higher peak in transdisciplinary approaches of Type 5. This underscores their dedication to approaches of either business disciplinarity of TH&E or to practice-oriented, transdisciplinary teaching.

In contrast, academic universities are more evenly distributed among the different curriculum orientations and do not show a marked peak. However, as far as the transdisciplinary curriculum in universities is concerned, they remain closer to the disciplinary side of the continuum (see also the discussion above). Figure 7.3 highlights these differences in disciplinary approaches to curriculum design between the two major categories of TH&E higher education in German-speaking countries.

Inter-, trans- and postdisciplinarity: evidence from T&H programme descriptions

To increase the validity and depth of our findings, we added an analysis of self-description of disciplinary approaches to curricula design and teaching. The rest of this chapter, therefore, reports on findings from a content analysis (Krippendorff, 2012; Ring *et al.*, 2009) of brief descriptions of study programmes found on university websites that accompany the respective curriculum and are intended to give interested students an initial overview. The studied descriptions include text found directly on the websites or in attached digital brochures. We excluded single course descriptions and graphical or tabular representation of the curriculum itself (with the course titles) from the analysis.

The results of the content analysis arranged by identified disciplinary approach (Types 1 to 6) are listed in Table 7.2. The first column of Table 7.1 represents keywords or themes either covered literally in the analysed graduate programme descriptions (the first five) or represented by a predefined list of synonyms. The two rather descriptive categories included in the column are given in italics. The percentages reported are based on a comparison within each type of curriculum.

As illustrated in Table 7.2, in 62 per cent of all descriptions of tourism graduate programmes we find reference to TH&E teaching approaches that are not confined to (traditional) disciplines (cross-disciplinarity, interdisciplinarity and multidisciplinarity). This percentage is paralleled by about 53 per cent of descriptions mentioning the necessity of a holistic approach to TH&E education based on the reported complexity of the tourism phenomenon (44 per cent). Sustainability (present in 35 per cent of descriptions) seems to be an important driver towards

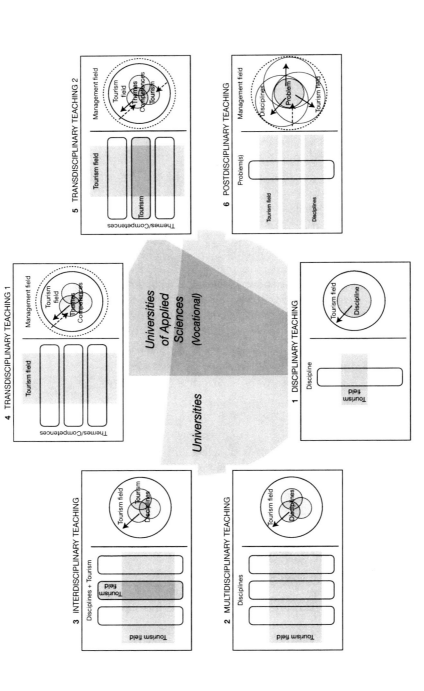

Figure 7.3 The distribution of disciplinary approaches among higher education types

Table 7.2 The distribution of keywords in programme descriptions among higher education types

Keywords/themes	Type 1 (%)	Type 2 (%)	Type 3 (%)	Type 4 (%)	Type 5 (%)	Type 6 (%)	All types (%)
Cross-disciplinarity	14	–	0	0	11	0	9
Interdisciplinarity	14	–	100	50	33	33	38
Multidisciplinarity	0	–	50	0	11	33	15
Transdisciplinarity	0	–	0	0	0	0	0
Postdisciplinarity	0	–	0	0	0	0	0
Explicit reference to one traditional discipline	57	–	25	50	44	0	41
Explicit reference to more traditional disciplines	0	–	75	0	17	67	24
Competencies	57	–	50	50	50	100	56
Skills	43	–	25	0	56	0	41
Practice	71	–	100	100	89	100	88
Theory	71	–	100	50	72	100	76
Holism/systems approach	29	–	75	50	56	67	53
Complexity	57	–	50	50	44	0	44
Current aspects	0	–	25	50	44	33	32
Internationality	86	–	75	100	89	33	82
Dynamic aspects	57	–	25	50	78	67	65
Interculturality	43	–	75	0	50	0	44
Regional development	0	–	50	0	11	33	15
Sustainability	14	–	50	0	50	0	35
Health	0	–	0	0	11	0	6
Entrepreneurship	0	–	0	50	17	0	12
Economic aspects	71	–	100	0	67	67	68
Socio-cultural aspects	14	–	100	50	56	33	50
Ecological aspects	14	–	50	0	28	0	24
Tourism	71	–	100	100	100	67	91
Hospitality	43	–	25	0	17	0	21
Leisure	0	–	25	50	28	0	21

Note: The percentages reported are based on a comparison within each type of curriculum.

transcending disciplinary structures in TH&E teaching, followed by references to regional development (15 per cent), entrepreneurship (12 per cent) and health (6 per cent). However, when comparing the three pillars of sustainability, economic aspects (68 per cent) are more often alluded to than socio-cultural (50 per cent) or ecological elements (24 per cent).

The numbers compiled in Table 7.2 reveal that when programme descriptions refer to teaching approaches that span traditional disciplinary boundaries, they most often use the keyword interdisciplinarity (38 per cent of all cases). Trans- and postdisciplinarity are not mentioned in any of these descriptions, which indicates that they might still be less widespread in their use, making them less attractive in study programme advertisements. Some 41 per cent of descriptions explicitly mention one traditional discipline, 24 per cent more than one. Astonishingly, more texts refer to TH&E practice (88 per cent) than to TH&E theory (76 per cent). This seems to point towards the profound vocational orientation in TH&E education in the German-speaking countries surveyed. Another keyword alluded to by a vast majority (82 per cent) of programme descriptions concerns the international dimension. In contrast to other countries (Middleton & Ladkin, 1996), hospitality (21 per cent) and leisure (21 per cent) play a minor role in TH&E graduate programmes in German-speaking countries.

Type 1 (disciplinary teaching)

In programme descriptions related to Type 1 curricula, those keywords indicating boundary crossing are least prominent: 28 per cent of descriptions refer to either cross-disciplinarity (14 per cent) or interdisciplinarity (14 per cent), whereas 57 per cent of descriptions explicitly refer to one traditional discipline. Economic and business-oriented keywords dominate the descriptions; discipline-crossing fields such as sustainability (14 per cent) are less common. Compared to the other types, hospitality (43 per cent) has a relatively important role. Thus, as far as Type 1 curricula are concerned, the offered (self-) descriptions coincide with our expectations and match quite well with our external classification based on the curricula.

Type 3 (interdisciplinary teaching)

Within this category, all of the assigned curricula were accompanied by programme descriptions referring to interdisciplinarity (100 per cent). According to our expectations, explicit reference is also made to at least two traditional disciplines, which is common (75 per cent) in descriptions of Type 3 curricula. This is accompanied by widespread indication of fields such as sustainability (50 per cent) and regional development (50 per cent), as well as a rather even distribution of references to the three pillars of sustainability.

The numerous references to multidisciplinarity are surprising. The most likely explanation relates to the fact that both multidisciplinarity and interdisciplinarity are referred to within the same texts, meaning that both approaches are probably contemporaneous in the same curriculum.

Types 4 and 5 (transdisciplinary teaching 1 and 2)

Compared to all other types, the descriptions accompanying curricula of Type 4 and Type 5 seem to have reduced the very concept of disciplines to a minor role. Only 50 per cent or 61 per cent of the programme descriptions explicitly refer to one or more traditional disciplines, the lowest percentage among all types. This low profile of disciplines even extends to the low presence of keywords that indicate discipline-crossing teaching: interdisciplinarity is mentioned in 50 per cent or 33 per cent of the descriptions, multidisciplinarity in 0 per cent or 11 per cent. What characterizes Types 4 and 5, according to the assumptions, is a strong emphasis on practice (100 per cent or 89 per cent) over theory (50 per cent or 72 per cent). Not accidentally, the field of entrepreneurship is more common (50 per cent or 17 per cent) than in descriptions referring to other curriculum types.

Type 6 (postdisciplinary teaching)

What is striking about descriptions relating to postdisciplinary curricula in TH&E graduate programmes are three things that also in this case concur with our expectations and the external analysis. First, we found no explicit reference to just one traditional discipline. If disciplinary references are present, they mention multiple disciplines. However, the concept of disciplines seems slightly more important than in transdisciplinary approaches. Second, practice (100 per cent) and theory (100 per cent) were again mentioned with equal frequency. Third – and probably most remarkably – the area of tourism was mentioned in only 67 per cent of postdisciplinary approaches, which is the lowest percentage among all types of curricula.

Conclusion

Combining an external analysis of curricula with a content analysis of the self-descriptions provided by the institutions of higher education, this chapter has examined the curriculum space of TH&E graduate programmes in German-speaking countries. By applying a core–periphery lens, we have paid attention to two dimensions of spatiality in curricula: the institutional dimension of spatiality (academia vs. applied field) and the metaphorical dimension (compartmentalization of knowledge in disciplines, fields, etc.). In this context, however, the chapter's focus has mainly been on the disciplinary understanding of tourism that is apparent from the surveyed TH&E curricula. We have identified interdisciplinary, transdisciplinary and postdisciplinary approaches to TH&E curricula, as well as approaches that teach tourism encapsulated within a single traditional discipline. Based on analyses of the German-speaking programmes presented, six broader conclusions may be drawn.

First, approaches to TH&E teaching that are not confined to traditional disciplines predominate. In particular, connecting TH&E with other discipline-crossing fields such as sustainability and regional development appears to promote interdisciplinary teaching of TH&E. Discipline-crossing approaches may have several advantages. However, due to the necessity to integrate different kinds of knowledge, they may also face a latent risk of superficiality.

Second, the analysed curricula and their presentation are apparently not underpinned by an understanding of 'tourism as a discipline'. If nevertheless one needs to take a closer look, transdisciplinary curricula seem to come closest to such an interpretation of tourism studies. However, such curricula are mostly practice-oriented, indicating that (if ever) the drive towards a stronger disciplinary status might come from the applied world of the business of tourism. This finding is in accordance with the thoughts of Tribe (1997).

Third, and related to point two, our analysis further confirms that the two discussed dimensions of the curriculum space, i.e. the institutional dimension of the locus of knowledge production/delivery, and the metaphorical dimension of its compartmentalization, are highly related. In concrete terms: the disciplinary understanding of TH&E revealed in the examined curricula seems to greatly depend on their respective orientation towards the two modes of knowledge production (mode 1 and mode 2, academic and practice-based). Furthermore, a quite sharply distinguished pattern of distribution in terms of different types of disciplinary understanding appears to exist between the two major types of institutions for TH&E education in German-speaking countries (universities and universities of applied sciences). With few exceptions, graduate programmes in the vocationally oriented universities of applied sciences show either a transdisciplinary orientation or teach TH&E as a field of application within a traditional business and management curriculum. Universities are more diverse and balanced in their orientation, also giving relatively stronger attention to interdisciplinary and postdisciplinary TH&E curricula.

Fourth, as reported for other countries (Airey & Johnson, 1999; Belhassen & Caton, 2009), business and industry issues as well as vocational orientation remain important pillars of TH&E teaching. Whereas a lasting influence of the social sciences is evident in tourism knowledge production (Benckendorff & Zehrer, 2013), the predominance of business and management in TH&E teaching seems to be particularly profound (at least as far as German-speaking countries are concerned). Postdisciplinary curricula might come near to what Tribe (2002) called 'vocational reflection'.

Fifth, the curricula have been ordered into a kind of circular relationship to try to demonstrate that while transdisciplinary approaches are indeed the most extradisciplinary (i.e. practice-oriented), postdisciplinary approaches seem to contain a force back towards academia in general and – ironically – towards disciplines in particular. Indeed, postdisciplinary curricula seem to be characterized by a decreasing understanding of TH&E as a field that requires specialized kinds of knowledge. Thus, contrary to what some might expect, postdisciplinarity might lessen the weight of TH&E as a relevant category in knowledge compartmentalization.

Sixth, the analysis allowed us to identify different cores and peripheries of TH&E curricula. Tourism appears both as a core and a periphery. Other cores found range from traditional disciplines to themes and problems. Overall, this core–periphery lens was deemed useful to classify the different types. Further studies could use it to identify missing elements in curricula, for instance the relative absence of a core – a core theme or core problem – in the context of non-business oriented TH&E education (and research).

References

Abbott, A. (1995). 'Things of Boundaries'. *Social Research*, 62(4), 857–82.

Airey, D. (2005). 'Growth and Development'. In D. Airey & J. Tribe (Eds.), *An International Handbook of Tourism Education* (pp. 13–24). Amsterdam: Elsevier.

Airey, D. (2008). 'In Search of a Mature Subject'. *Journal of Hospitality, Leisure, Sport and Tourism Education*, 7(2), 101–3.

Airey, D., & Middleton, V. T. C. (1984). 'Course Syllabi in the UK: a review'. *Tourism Management*, 5(1), 57–62.

Airey, D., & Johnson, S. (1999). 'The Content of Degree Courses in the UK'. *Tourism Management*, 20(2), 229–35.

Archer, B. H. (1977). *Tourism Multipliers: the state of the art*. Cardiff: University of Wales Press.

Becher, T., & Trowler, P. (2001). *Academic Tribes and Territories*, 2nd edn. Buckingham: Open University Press.

Beier, M. J., & Arnold, S. L. (2005). 'Becoming Undisciplined: toward the supradisciplinary study of security'. *International Studies Review*, 7(1), 41–61.

Belhassen, Y., & Caton, K. (2009). 'Advancing Understandings: a linguistic approach to tourism epistemology'. *Annals of Tourism Research*, 36(2), 335–52.

Benckendorff, P., & Zehrer, A. (2013). 'A Network Analysis of Tourism Research'. *Annals of Tourism Research*, 43, 121–49.

Bodewes, T. (1981). 'Development of Advanced Tourism Studies in Holland'. *Annals of Tourism Research*, 8, 35–51.

Borgatti, S. P., & Everett, M. G. (1999). 'Models of Core/Periphery Structures'. *Social Networks*, 21(4), 375–95.

Braun, T., & Schubert, A. (2003). 'A Quantitative View on the Coming of Age of Interdisciplinarity in the Sciences 1980–1999'. *Scientometrics*, 58(1), 183–9.

Buckler, J. A. (2004). 'Towards a New Model of General Education at Harvard College'. Discussion paper. Online. Available HTTP: <http://www.lancs.ac.uk/ias/events/general07/docs/interdisc/Interdisc-Buckler-Harvard.pdf> (accessed 5 May 2013).

Butler, R. W. (1980). 'The Concept of a Tourism Area Cycle of Evolution: implications for management and resources'. *Canadian Geographer*, 24(1), 5–12.

Choi, B. C., & Pak, A. W. (2006). 'Multidisciplinarity, Interdisciplinarity and Transdisciplinarity in Health Research, Services, Education and Policy: definitions, objectives and evidence of effectiveness'. *Clinical and Investigative Medicine*, 29(6), 351–64.

Cohen, M. D., March, J. G., & Olsen, J. P. (1972). 'A Garbage Can Model of Organizational Choice'. *Administrative Science Quarterly*, 17(1), 1–25.

Coles, T., Hall, C. M., & Duval, D. T. (2006) 'Tourism and Post-Disciplinary Enquiry'. *Current Issues in Tourism*, 9(4/5), 293–319.

Cooper, C., Fletcher, J., Gilbert, D., Shepherd, R., & Wanhill, S. (1998). *Tourism: principles and practices*. London: Pitman.

Darbellay, F., & Stock, M. (2012). 'Tourism as Complex Interdisciplinary Research Object'. *Annals of Tourism Research*, 39(1), 441–58.

Dogan, M. (1997). 'The New Social Sciences: cracks in the walls'. *International Social Science Journal*, 49(3), 429–43.

Donald, J. (1986). 'Knowledge and the University Curriculum'. *Higher Education*, 15, 267–82.

Dredge, D., Benckendorff, P., Day, M., Gross, M. J., Walo, M., Weeks, P., & Whitelaw, P. (2012). 'The Philosophic Practitioner and the Curriculum Space'. *Annals of Tourism Research*, 39(4), 2154–76.

Echtner, C., & Jamal, T. (1997). 'The Disciplinary Dilemma of Tourism Studies'. *Annals of Tourism Research*, 24(4), 869–83.

Gibbons, M., Limoges, C., Nowotny, H., Schwartzman, S., Scott, P., & Trow, M. (1994). *The New Production of Knowledge*. London: Sage.

Goeldner, C. R. (1988) 'The Evaluation of Tourism as an Industry and a Discipline'. Paper presented at the First International Conference for Tourism Educators. Mimeo. Surrey.

Goodwin, M. (2004). 'Recovering the Future: a post-disciplinary perspective on geography and political economy'. In P. Cloke, M. Goodwin, & P. Crang (Eds.), *Envisioning Human Geography* (pp. 65–80). London: Arnold.

Hannam, K. (2009). 'The End of Tourism? Nomadology and the mobilities paradigm'. In J. Tribe (Ed.), *Philosophical Issues in Tourism* (pp. 55–70). Bristol: Channel View.

Hellström, T., Jacob, M., & Wenneberg, S. (2003). 'The "Discipline" of Post-Academic Science: reconstructing paradigmatic foundations of a virtual research institute'. *Science and Public Policy*, 30(4), 251–60.

Hirst, P. (1974). *Knowledge and the Curriculum*. London: Routledge.

Hollinshead, K. (2010). 'Tourism Studies and Confined Understanding: the call for a "new sense" postdisciplinary imaginary'. *Tourism Analysis*, 15(4), 499–512.

Jafari, J., & Ritchie, J. R. B. (1981). 'Towards a Framework for Tourism Education'. *Annals of Tourism Research*, 8, 13–33.

King, A. R., & Brownell, J. (1966). *The Curriculum and the Disciplines of Knowledge*. New York: Wiley.

Krippendorff, K. H. (2012). *Content Analysis: an introduction to its methodology*, 3rd edn. Thousand Oaks, CA: Sage.

Krugman, P. (1991). 'Increasing Returns and Economic Geography'. *Journal of Political Economy*, 99(3), 483–99.

Kuhn, T. S. (1970). *The Structure of Scientific Revolutions*. Chicago, IL: University of Chicago Press.

Lai, K., & Li, Y. (2012). 'Core–Periphery Structure of Destination Image'. *Annals of Tourism Research*, 39(3), 1359–79.

Law, J. (2004). *After Method: mess in social science research*. London: Routledge.

Leiper, N. (1981). 'Towards a Cohesive Curriculum in Tourism: the case for a distinct discipline'. *Annals of Tourism Research*, 8, 69–84.

Leiper, N. (2000). 'An Emerging Discipline'. *Annals of Tourism Research*, 27(3), 805–9.

Middleton, V. T. C., & Ladkin, A. (1996). *The Profile of Tourism Studies Degree Courses in the UK: 1995/6*. London: National Liaison Group.

Nowotny, H. (2003). 'The Potential of Transdisciplinarity'. Discussion paper. Online. Available HTTP: <http://helga-nowotny.eu/downloads/helga_nowotny_b59.pdf> (accessed 10 May 2013).

Nowotny, H., Scott, P., & Gibbons, M. (2001). *Re-thinking Science: knowledge and the public in an age of uncertainty*. Cambridge: Polity Press.

Pechlaner, H., & Reuter, C. (2012). 'Multidisziplinarität, Interdisziplinarität, Transdisziplinarität: perspektiven für den tourismus?'. In A. Zehrer & A. Grabmüller (Eds.), *Tourismus 2020+ interdisziplinär: Herausforderungen für Wirtschaft, Umwelt und Gesellschaft* (pp. 13–22). Berlin: ESV.

Ren, C., Pritchard, A., & Morgan, N. (2010). 'Constructing Tourism Research: a critical inquiry'. *Annals of Tourism Research*, 37(4), 885–904.

Ring, A., Dickinger, A., & Wöber, K. (2009). 'Designing the Ideal Undergraduate Program in Tourism'. *Journal of Travel Research*, 48(1), 106–21.

Ritchie, B. (2008). 'Tourism Disaster Planning and Management: from response and recovery to reduction and readiness'. *Current Issues in Tourism*, 11(4), 315–48.

Ryan, C. (1997). 'Tourism: a mature discipline?'. *Pacific Tourism Review*, 1(1), 3–5.

Schön, D. A. (1983). *The Reflective Practitioner*. London: Temple Smith.

Sheldon, P. J. (1991). 'An Authorship Analysis of Tourism Research'. *Annals of Tourism Research*, 18(3), 473–84.

Smith, V. (Ed.). (1977). *Hosts and Guests: the anthropology of tourism.* Philadelphia: University of Pennsylvania Press.

Spode, H. (1998). 'Grau, Teurer Freund . . . was ist und wozu dient Theorie?'. In H. P. Burmeister (Ed.), *Auf dem Weg zu einer Theorie des Tourismus* (pp. 21–40). Rehburg: Evangelische Akademie.

Stuart-Hoyle, M. (2003). 'The Purpose of Undergraduate Tourism Programmes in the UK'. *Journal of Hospitality, Leisure, Sport and Tourism Education.* 2(1), 49–74.

Toulmin, S. (1972). *Human Understanding (Vol. l).* Oxford: Clarendon Press.

Tress, G., Tress, B., & Fry, G. (2005). 'Clarifying Integrative Research Concepts in Landscape Ecology'. *Landscape Ecology,* 20(4), 479–93.

Tribe, J. (1997). 'The Indiscipline of Tourism'. *Annals of Tourism Research,* 24(3), 638–57.

Tribe, J. (2000). 'Indisciplined and Unsubstantiated'. *Annals of Tourism Research,* 27(3), 809–13.

Tribe, J. (2002). 'The Philosophic Practitioner'. *Annals of Tourism Research,* 29(2), 338–57.

Tribe, J. (2005). 'Tourism, Knowledge and the Curriculum'. In D. Airey & J. Tribe (Eds.), *An International Handbook of Tourism Education* (pp. 47–60). Amsterdam: Elsevier.

Tribe, J. (2010). 'Tribes, Territories and Networks in the Tourism Academy'. *Annals of Tourism Research,* 37(1), 7–33.

Tribe, J., & Xiao, H. (2011). 'Developments in Tourism Social Science'. *Annals of Tourism Research,* 38(1), 7–26.

Urry, J. (1990). *The Tourist Gaze,* London: Sage.

Visnovsky, E., & Bianchi, G. (2005). 'Editorial'. *Human Affairs,* 15. Online. Available HTTP: <http://humanaffairs.sk/editorial.htm> (accessed 5 May 2013).

Xiao, H., & Smith, S. (2006). 'The Maturation of Tourism Research: evidence from a content analysis'. *Tourism Analysis,* 10(4), 335–48.

Part III

The changing context

8

Information technologies and tourism

The critical turn in curriculum development

Ana María Munar

Department of International Economics and Management,
Copenhagen Business School, Frederiksberg, Denmark

Mads Bødker

Department of IT Management, Copenhagen Business School,
Frederiksberg, Denmark

Introduction

Scholars concerned with epistemological enquiry and advancements of knowledge production in tourism (Coles *et al.*, 2006; Tribe, 2006; Belhassen & Caton, 2009; Darbellay & Stock, 2012) differentiate between the phenomenological world of tourism, the world of knowledge production (i.e. the intellectual endeavours to comprehend tourism), and the world of tourism education or tourism as a subject matter. Belhassen and Caton (2009) conceptualize tourism education as an application of scholarship that represents particular dimensions of tourism knowledge progression. While acknowledging the usability of such a division, the metaphorical three worlds proposal offers a limited theoretical framework. Tourism education as a research object comprehends two other worlds: (1) its own phenomenological world, i.e. activities and relationships that take place in the real world (e.g. the social relations established among scholars and students, the ideological positions of those with managerial responsibilities, or the large and complex web of stakeholders of the institution where tourism education takes place); and (2) the epistemological world of tourism education as a field of intellectual production, this knowledge being different from the scholarly knowledge produced by studying the phenomenon of 'tourism', i.e. the tourism industry, tourists' behaviour, etc. (e.g. research articles that aim to understand how virtual learning environments impact students' learning abilities). The importance and specific identity of the epistemology of tourism education becomes apparent when looking at journals such as the *Journal of Hospitality, Leisure, Sport and Tourism Education* or at academic conferences and networks such as the Tourism Education Futures Initiative and the Association for Tourism in Higher Education. These media and networks are arenas of knowledge production where academic 'conversations' (Belhassen & Caton, 2009) about tourism education's 'plural knowledgabilities' (Hollinshead, 2013) take place. This *Handbook* is an example of such a world. It can also be argued that tourism education knowledge production finds its applicability both in the phenomenological world of tourism, for example through graduates applying their knowledge in their daily work, and in that of education, for example when researchers apply innovative methodological tools or design new courses. Tourism education is therefore a highly complex relational scientific object, similar to other post-disciplinary scientific objects with specific distinct qualities that cannot be comprehended by one or a few traditional disciplines (Darbellay & Stock, 2012).

This complex object of research evolves by way of three major dimensions of influence: (1) the materialities dimension – an existing body of research and scholarly production of knowledge, which comprises materialities such as scholarly texts (articles, books, etc.), learning materials and technical tools which are increasingly digital; (2) the social dimension – the academic practices, pedagogical traditions, power and ideological dominance, as well as disciplinary hegemonies of established research and scholarly 'tribes' in this research field; (3) the institutional dimension – the systems and structures resulting from the politics, market conditions and legal norms that embed higher education institutions in which tourism programmes are offered; these institutional structures have different spatial levels of influence, from global standards of quality metrics (e.g. the journal citation index, international rankings systems, quality accreditation agencies, etc.) to national and local rules and procedures. The way in which these three dimensions evolve and interrelate shapes the opportunities and limitations of information technologies (IT) education in tourism programmes. While acknowledging the relevance of an institutional dimension, the analysis of this chapter focuses on the other two, i.e. materialities and social dimensions.

This chapter deals with a crucial question that affects the worlds of tourism education and lies at the intersection of multiple fields of knowledge. What should a tourism curriculum that aims to provide knowledge on information technologies look like? While pedagogical dimensions such as the evolution of virtual learning environments and the increased use of IT in multiple aspects of learning and teaching practices have received increased attention by tourism scholars (see, for example, the special issue on the topic of IT and education published in 2006 by the *Journal of Hospitality and Tourism Education,* and other papers such as Haven and Botterill, 2003; Dale and Lane, 2007; Beard *et al.*, 2007; and Cantoni *et al.*, 2009), very few contributions discuss the curricular dimensions of this topic (Munar & Gyimóthy, 2013). This is surprising considering that the issue of curriculum design is a crucial one and that IT plays a key role in the evolution of tourism (Poon, 1993).

Curriculum design is often the product of ideological hegemonies in a specific field of knowledge. Tribe provides examples of how, in the case of tourism, this design could be seen as a result of the ideological dominance of a scientific–positivist paradigm that prioritizes 'the efficient management of tourism' and 'nurtures a vocationalist perspective based on technique and means rather than ends' (2001: 444). Inspired by Habermas's (1978) theory of knowledge-constitutive interests, he advocates the need to approach curriculum design from alternative paradigmatic positions such as interpretivism and critical theory which aim towards enlightenment, understanding and emancipation. It is our hypothesis that while 'the knowledge progression' (Belhassen & Caton, 2009: 335) experienced in the field of tourism studies has resulted in the advancement of a post-foundational situation with representation of multiple paradigms or 'epistemes' (Darbellay & Stock, 2012) expanding and improving curricular design in tourism studies, the sub-field of IT studies in tourism is at a very preliminary stage characterized by a scientific–positivistic and technopian (Kozinets, 2008) ideological dominance. This is a situation similar to the one criticized by Tribe more than a decade ago for tourism education as a whole. This chapter examines the consequences that such a narrow curriculum implies for tourism education and analyses the question of information technologies as research object. It presents a series of alternative epistemological traditions, proposes the incorporation of principles from design as a way to enhance critical curriculum development, and finally aims to provide a more democratic and plural academic conversation that may help to rethink IT in the tourism curriculum.

Information technologies and the tourism curriculum

Limited territory of knowledge production and ideological dominance

There is an established research field attempting to describe the technological landscape of tourism and an eagerness to understand new technology. However, and despite the profound impact that technological innovation, adoption and use has on tourism, most of the papers studying IT 'deal with single empirical studies while conceptual papers driving theory development and critique are rare' (Gretzel, 2011: 758). A majority of the research enquiry in this field focuses on 'The Business of Tourism' (Tribe, 2010: 30); it is highly driven by an applied business research agenda and appears dominated by a (post) positivistic methodological approach (for a critical review of this research field see e.g. Gretzel, 2011; Munar et al., 2013; Bødker & Munar, 2014) with weak influence from other disciplinary fields of the social sciences or humanities such as tourism sociology, anthropology, geography or philosophy. This epistemic dominance perpetuates one particular ontological view where the tourist is conceptualized as the utility-maximizing consumer.

This limited territory of knowledge production is mirrored in the curriculum of tourism. Usually the linkage between digital technology and tourism, both at undergraduate and graduate levels, takes place in marketing and managerial courses introducing the development of e-tourism and the impacts of IT on tourism production and consumption. Eventually, specific courses on e-tourism with a major focus on e-business and managerial and strategic aspects of technology are offered. The complex epistemological world of digital technologies is reduced to the Business of Technology and conceptualized as being a subsection of other fields such as economics or management. Furthermore, as a reminder of traditional disciplinary divisions established between engineering/technical studies and social sciences or humanities, knowledge on the making and designing of digital systems, including coding and programming, is rarely part of the tourism curriculum. Also it is infrequent to see teams of social science or humanities scholars working collaboratively with IT researchers to develop educational activities aiming to address the production and implementation of high-end technologies in tourism processes. The result is that the study of technological change is conceptualized and taught as a silo in tourism education or reduced to a few chapters in a textbook.

Dominant research discourses and territories act as gatekeepers and represent 'taken-for-granted' assumptions (Tribe, 2006; Belhassen & Caton, 2009). As knowledge is historically rooted and interest bound (Habermas, 1987), our ideologies play an active role in the shaping of academic knowledge and result in academic curricula with specific ideological frameworks. From an ideological perspective, the dominance of the Business of Tourism promotes technological change as a utopia with technopian and work-machine features. In technopian (Kozinets, 2008) accounts, technology appears as a supreme good, central to the enhancement of communities and society. The tourism experience can be brought to a perfected state thanks to the proper utilization of IT. It is a morally optimistic scenario where human kind achieves increased benefits through technology adoption and where the tourist reaches its ultimate potential, thanks to technology. The work-machine (Kozinets, 2008) perspective sees technology as the way to achieve economic prosperity, growth and efficiency. According to these accounts, IT increases productivity and wealth in tourism destinations and helps tourists to achieve 'successful' lifestyles and gain benefits with a minimum investment of time and money. Both technopian and the work-machine ideological views concur and support a curriculum design that places the needs of the tourism industry, growth, profitability and the market at the centre, the result being 'a tourism curriculum for the efficient management of tourism' (Tribe, 2001: 444). This situation may help to produce graduates with good applied business skills. However, it leaves crucial aspects of the relationship between technology and tourism unexplored.

Arguably, contemporary IT studies in tourism are still at a stage similar to the first, advocacy phase of tourism research in general (Jafari, 1990). This stage is characterized by a methodological hegemony and an overall 'optimistic' discourse on the relationship between technology and social change. In this case we can talk about tourism IT education still largely remaining in the advocacy phase. The absence of critical and interpretivist traditions, and the poor presence of other disciplines in this field of research have some crucial consequences for the way in which IT and tourism curricula have been designed and implemented in tourism programmes. The rigidity of the epistemic field of IT tourism research is mirrored in a tourism curriculum that often follows course structures that in many cases mimic traditional management education, with divisions, such as marketing, strategy and the like, that are unable to grasp the inter- and postdisciplinarity (Coles et al., 2006; Darbellay & Stock, 2012) of the technical–societal–individual tourism phenomenon. Gretzel also advocates a turn in technology research and proposes that future agendas should focus on the socio-technical system as a unit of analysis, a 'co-evolution triangle of users, knowledge and technology' (2011: 762). As mentioned by Munar and Gyimóthy (2013: 262) the task ahead in IT tourism research lies in

> revealing the complex relationship of technological change with power relations, justice, and the establishment and transformation of norms, values, and beliefs; the impacts of technological change in human cognition; digital mediation of humor, love, and emotion; the complex interrelationship of technology with nature and environment; and how all these different phenomena are embedded in and transformed through tourism.

The IT tourism curriculum today is limited and should be expanded, however there is a difficult road ahead as this is dependent on the expansion of this territory of knowledge production and an increased diversity of the established networks and dominant scholarly traditions.

A direct consequence of this narrow understanding of the relationship between technology and tourism is that knowledge production on digital technologies is mostly absent in relevant areas where tourism is understood as a broader social phenomenon; for example in sustainability and cultural studies, and surprisingly also in media studies in tourism which tend to focus on art and culture, examining films, literature, music and other cultural productions without paying much attention to digital media. Often conferences focusing on IT knowledge production such as the ENTER series show a high dominance of a research enquiry conducted under the scientific–positivistic paradigm and a hegemony of managerial and marketing approaches (Munar et al., 2013) (see the published conference proceedings of ENTER for details), while the Critical Tourism Studies (CTS) conference series, a key contributor to the advancement of interpretivist and critical epistemological approaches in tourism (Pritchard et al., 2011), generally shows a very modest representation of IT studies. Also, there is a factual separation between those who are trained to achieve competences in the development of technological solutions (often graduated from computer science, engineering or IT design programmes) and those who are taught to analyse and reflect on what tourism is and what it could become.

Despite this isolation, the use and development of technology is a crucial, embedded element of late-modern tourism in its multiple and complex dimensions. Darbellay and Stock (2012: 444) provide a relevant conceptualization of tourism as a mode of engagement with the world:

> we can define the touristic, or society's touristic dimensions, as a relationship to people, objects, practices, and self in which re-creation occurs (i.e. practices of controlled de-controlling of self-control in the sense of Elias and Dunning (1986)), which is combined with bodily dis-placement and inhabiting a place of otherness.

We propose that this relationship to the world enacted through mobility and recreation is (and has always been) technology mediated and enabled. From the transformation of the ways in which the movement of people in space takes place, to the ways in which individuals can dream and fantasize about travel, technical tools have the capacity to catalyse exponential change in social, political, cultural, or economic processes. As Lash indicates, our societies are: 'regulated by an extraordinarily powerful interlacing of social and technical systems: by precisely, socio-technical systems. . . . The individual in the second modernity is profoundly a socio-technical subject' (2002: xiii). Technology enabled transformations are at the core of the evolution of humanity (Hayles, 2012). Where tourism IT was typically built to support traditional business motives in tourism as well as planning, and branding efforts, requiring complex and state-of-the-art computational equipment, IT is now a fundamental aspect of everyday experiences (Yoo, 2010). The social use of technologies in tourism is shaped as a result of a complex interrelation between technologies and their affordances – the social capabilities enabled by technological tools – and the way in which people and institutions make use of those affordances (Baym, 2010).

A variety of media and information technologies increasingly constitute the interface of tourism. Farman (2012) has noted how the term interface is not merely an indication of use affordances of a technology (such as buttons, widgets, levers or visual representations of action-taking possibilities), but represents the way technologies allow the world to appear to us. Using the example of increasingly smart and ubiquitous mobile devices, Farman proposes an understanding of life in an IT-saturated world as an assembly of different spatial forms where the physical and virtual multiply to become sites of social and cultural production. Similarly, in his early edited work on the discipline of interaction design, Winograd suggests: 'People are thought of as *inhabitants* rather than as *users* of buildings . . . we approach software users as inhabitants, focusing on how they live in the spaces that designers create'. (1996: xvii, italics in original). With the introduction of mobile and ubiquitous computing and pervasive data infrastructures, the idea that people live their life 'through' technology, or that technology plays a significant role in the way lives are experienced and practised, is unavoidable. It may not be particularly true for tourism (compared to other types of practices) but it seems particularly poignant, arguably since tourism is thought of as a non-technological practice, almost literally far removed from the technologies that dominate the working life. However, digital mobile guides, maps, cameras, social networks, music players, ebooks, phones, and other digital devices are progressively becoming an integral part of the tourism experience. Tourism is technological and a range of technologies shape behaviours and performances (social, embodied and cultural).

It is a rather commonplace observation that mobile phones, tablets and portable computers combined with high-speed data networks are increasingly in the hands of the individual consumer, but how do we educate tourism and hospitality students to take an active part in an ongoing (re)construction of touristic places and performances that such tools afford? Our stand is that IT plays a key role in the phenomenological world of tourism and that the epistemological world of tourism lags behind in the understanding of this complex object of research. Furthermore, we argue that this has negative consequences for the quality of tourism education. The challenge for our academic community is to design a curriculum that acknowledges the complexities of ubiquitous IT and provides students with cognitive and practical tools to understand and further develop the interrelations and complexities that arise.

Expanding the territory, expanding the curriculum

Our proposal is therefore a call for an expansion of the territory of knowledge production in this field and a change towards a curriculum that reflects multiple and diverse ontologies, methodologies, scholarly traditions and ideological narratives of the phenomenon of tourism and technologies. This section presents three theoretical frameworks grounded in different epistemological traditions that examine how human cognition is altered and expanded thanks to its relationship to technology: situated action and ethnomethodology, actor–network theory and embedded cognition. These theoretical frameworks present novel epistemological proposals and methodological avenues to understand the implications that IT has for tourism and that tourism has for IT. What these proposals have in common is that they transgress the hegemonic conceptualization of technology as a tool or system of tools for control and management purposes or as representing a technical knowledge-constitutive interest (Habermas, 1978). They posit a relational definition of technology as research object. Humans make sense of themselves and their social and natural environments by establishing and enacting a relationship with the world which is essentially technology-mediated and embedded.

The theoretical approach of ethnomethodology and situated action underscores the view that human action depends in essential ways on its material and social circumstances. As explained by Suchman 'the significance of actions and their intelligibility resides neither in what is strictly observable about behaviour, nor in a prior mental state of the actor, but in a contingently constructed relationship among observable behaviour, embedded circumstances and intent' (2007: 125). The main thesis of this approach is that human action cannot be reduced to bodily movements or to the workings of the mind; the significance of action is fundamentally embedded in the social and physical worlds and mutual intelligibility is achieved with reference to the particulars of every situation. Therefore, the study of humans and technologies needs to consider that cognitive processes occur in a relationship between individuals and the world of artefacts and technics, and that any meaning derived from this relationship takes place in specific circumstances.

Actor–network theory (ANT) also provides a complementary research avenue to study the relevance of non-human as well as human influences in the analysis of social change. ANT aims to bypass a traditional methodological division between subjects (people) and objects (artefacts) (Latour, 1999). Technology is not 'a distinct set of materiality, machines, and artifacts that can be isolated methodologically as an object of research' instead, technological materialities and objects are actors in constantly evolving constellations of networks (Ek, 2013: 21). ANT is increasingly being applied in tourism social science studies (e.g. Tribe, 2010; Ren, 2011; van der Duim, 2007) but it is still seldom in technology research enquiry (Ek, 2013).

Challenging a conceptual division between mind and body as separate entities, the idea of embedded cognition claims that human language and actions are bodily embedded and enacted, and that the affordances and attributes of objects in the environment support and extend memory, idea production and complex thinking (Hayles, 2012). Additionally, embedded cognition acknowledges that a large part of the process of thinking does not take place at the level of the conscious mind (or self-awareness) but at the level of the non-conscious and unconscious (Hayles, 2012). Similarly in tourism education there is a need for studies and narratives 'which locate the situated particularity of "body" and "emotion"' (Jamal & Hollinshead, 2001: 67). The theory of embedded cognition is closely related to contemporary technogenesis. Technogenesis relates to the 'dynamic interplay between the kinds of environmental stimuli created in information-intensive environments and the adaptative potential of cognitive faculties in concert with them' (Hayles, 2012: 97). Thanks to this dynamic interplay, late-modern societies are experiencing changes in cognitive modes. The implications of these changes are first the transformation of teaching and learning processes and second the evolution of the way in which our intellectual endeavours take place, now in a close relationship with the development of digital technologies.

At the heart of this interplay lies the transformation of selective attention from traditional deep attention to an increased relevance of hyper attention (Hayles, 2012). Deep attention is needed when coping with complex cultural or scientific works. Hyper attention is characteristic of someone scanning webpages and associated with hyper reading; on the other hand, deep attention is a human capacity cultivated through centuries and correlated to deep reading. Hyper attention is fast, flexible and useful in switching between textual and visual data materials, to quickly provide an overview of digital spaces, as in the case of tourists surfing review sites and looking for hotels. 'Surfing,' a metaphor popularly used when referring to Web usage, reflects the speed and the lightness of this attentive mode, but also its shallowness and lack of attention to detail. The increased importance of hyper attention has radical consequences for tourism education and scholarship.

The theories of embedded cognition, situated action and ANT transcend traditional disciplinary boundaries. They provide a new morphology (Belhassen & Caton, 2009), a landscape of new theoretical terms, that expands the possibilities of discussing and talking about technology in tourism and moves beyond managerialism.

IT design as a vehicle of critique

In the previous section we argued that the engagement in technology within the field of tourism education has primarily involved a strict managerial and business-oriented epistemology. This means that technologies are usually understood as productivity tools that increase the effectiveness of tourism as a business or the effectiveness of touristic users as they go about their planning of experiences or their other experiential agendas such as wayfinding or gleaning information from mobile technologies.

The aim of this section is to provide a further expansion of the morphology of the field of tourism studies by showing how a deeper engagement with technology in tourism education can be facilitated. A central argument is that a tourism technology curriculum must necessarily navigate in a space between practice and theory/methodology. Second, we advocate that design practices in the field of IT can also afford a more critical sensibility to the subject of tourism – an ability to imagine tourism differently through design. Knowledge of design can contribute to the embedment of emancipatory knowledge-constitutive interest (Habermas, 1978) in the curriculum and enhance critical-thinking abilities allowing not only the management of tourism but the imagining of and the making/becoming of tourism. Design bridges instrumental rationality that aims to dominate and control the environment, and communicative rationality that is essentially reflective criticism (Habermas, 1978, 1987). Design is inscribed with social norms. Typically the functionality of a design follows the societal, cultural or situated norms.

As indicated previously, an underlying premise of our argument is that tourism and the touristic as a special way of relating to the world is fundamentally technological, i.e. it requires particular technologies (ranging from planes to smartphones and data infrastructures) to be realized. Other technological fields of education (e.g. computer science or engineering) have a prominent focus on practice and doing design that work in the real world, and even if they may not typically engage critically in design work, they retain an indispensable practice of technology where students need to understand how technologies work and how technologies impact upon people and practices. In the next section we emphasize perspectives that stage practical design work as a particular form of enquiry, perspectives that are as good as absent from the current mainstream tourism curriculum.

Design as a practice

Simon famously argued that design means to devise 'courses of action aimed at changing existing situations into preferred ones' (1981: 129). The interrelation between design and the worldmaking capacity of knowledge production advocated by critical theory is evident in this definition. From Simon's rather expansive notion of design it would seem that all kinds of intervention using IT in tourism would be a form of design, since the drive for implementation is some form of change. In this chapter we suggest a somewhat narrower definition of design that focuses on design as a particular mode of enquiry that rests on the dialogics of frames, materials and situations (Schön, 1983).

A design enquiry typically begins by framing a problem or a set of challenges. Design as a particular form of problem solving relies on generative metaphors that frame a domain. Metaphors both conceal and privilege certain aspects of a thing. To say, for example, that 'X is like Y' entails filtering out specific dimensions of the phenomenon under scrutiny. Theories, in this sense, are a means to guide the framing of a question or a design problem – they allow design practitioners to go back and forth between different perspectives in a disciplined way, whilst retaining a richness and a complexity of the field in which one is aiming to intervene. When a designer makes things, the material used to explore ways of doing (paper, sketching, mock-ups, prototypes, etc.) talks back to the designer, allowing a variety of insights and learning to appear. These can be surprising and lead to new frames within which a design project is couched. This in turn leads to new dialogues with the material and so on. Finally, a design is evaluated under certain conditions that lead to new insights and potentially reframe the original questions asked of the design.

To give a simple example of an approach to design, Rogers *et al.* (2011) (see Figure 8.1) have suggested an interaction design (IxD) lifecycle model that indicates the iterative nature of design work in the field of IT. Crucially, the model highlights the dialogical relationship between the identification of needs and requirements and (re-)design (left). For a design project to progress, representations and artefacts that aid designers in traversing a space of opportunities are needed. These typically come in the shape of rough sketches (Buxton, 2007), sequential depictions (e.g. storyboards of use, Carroll, 1995; Bødker, 1999) or other types of representations. Such initial work can be based on both everyday experiences or might be the product of more disciplined interventions in the field. Early ideas and suggestions are gradually filtered through a prototype with varying levels of detail, evaluated, and new iterations of problem formulation or new sets of ideas might emerge from the process.

In the tourism curriculum, and drawing largely on our own experiences and academic networks, we have not found that the dialogical and practical work of design play any significant role.

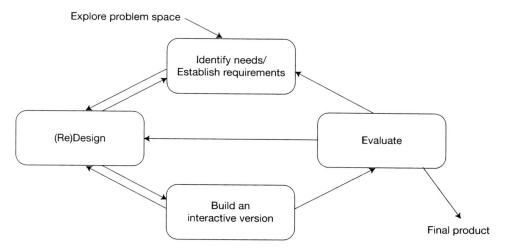

Figure 8.1 Simple interaction design lifecycle model
Source: Rogers *et al.* (2011: 332).

There are many obvious benefits of a significant design component to tourism education. It provides a solid understanding of user needs and requirements, how to model them (i.e. how to produce representations of the context and actors one wants to design for), and how to create artefacts (or prototypes) that explore and elicit how needs might be met. Typically, a design education includes a strong focus on developing students' ability to traverse a design space using both formal and informal methods and tools. It includes skills in sketching as well as other forms of representations that aid in the material engagement with a problem. It might also include skills in various forms of user and stakeholder involvement, ethnography, or ethno-methodological approaches to gathering insights on the context, the people or the particular communities who will use a design. Whilst graphical or product design skills are not the first priority in any tourism or hospitality curriculum, the field of IT presents a number of challenges and opportunities for tourism to which we see design as a useful approach. As it is, the set of IT skills that tourism education focuses on converges with the focus on managerial issues to produce candidates with an understanding of management information systems (MIS) and the use of IT products in tourism marketing efforts rather than IT design and innovation skills.

The move towards design, however, requires a mindset that is foreign to the traditional skills taught in the academy. The marriage of classical design skills and IT is of relatively recent date. Winograd's edited volume on Bringing Design to Software (1996) was one of the early works that staged design as a central practice in software development, a practice that was then typically understood as situated well within the engineering tradition. Following this work and a plethora of related work, Interaction Design has evolved as a cross-disciplinary practice that to some extent bridges academia and industry (see e.g. Fallman, 2003; Rogers *et al.*, 2011). Interaction Design is situated alongside other academic fields such as Human–Computer Interaction (HCI), Human Factors (or Ergonomics) and Computer Supported Collaborative Work (CSCW), drawing on the insights that these fields have generated in the academic space for several decades. Whilst using analytical approaches, it has been argued that interaction design goes beyond the typical ideals of knowledge as either inductive or deductive. 'Knowing' in the context of interaction design entails what is often described as abductive reasoning.

Abductive reasoning allows for subjective intuition and experience to be active forms of problem solving, and typically understanding seems to appear as flashes of insight (Kolko, 2009). As such, it generally goes against the grain of traditional academic upbringing. Based on our own experience it might even be anxiety-provoking to many students who fear plunging into the unknown, but as a form of reasoning it resonates deeply with the kinds of problem solving in which designers are typically engaged. The iterative shaping of a design space through the production and recombination of artefacts and representations combined with a general knowledge of how things work as well as empirical knowledge and analytical tools are joined together in the practice of abductive reasoning in design work.

Critical design

While it would be impracticable to suggest that tourism and hospitality students should also be trained as fully fledged interaction designers, we propose that interaction design also entails a possible critical design component that might be brought to the tourism curriculum. Importantly, this also opens up the practice of IxD as a powerful means to 'imagine tourism differently' and also a way to include value and moral dimensions by envisioning what tourism should be or what tourism could become. Designers such as Dunne and Raby (2001) as well as design and HCI researchers such as Sengers et al. (2005), McCarthy and Wright (2005), Gaver et al. (2003) or Agre (1997) have argued in different ways for design as a vehicle of critique. Dunne and Raby suggest that critical design is 'design that asks carefully crafted questions and makes us think . . . [it] pushes the cultural and aesthetic potential and role of electronic products and services to its limits' (2001: 58). Galloway et al. propose a number of insights from tactical design interventions aimed at 'design concept generation, and prototyping to generate two novel, if highly-situated forms of technologically-mediated city tourism' (2003: 1). All interventions were staged in Rome, Italy, and included situationist-inspired algorithmic walks to encourage other ways of walking and serendipitous discovery at the margins of traditional touristic sites as well as socially awkward reversals of the traditional host–visitor relations through 'renting out' tourists to perform everyday chores for locals. While some interventions were not necessarily successful in terms of prescribing a particular design, they were part of a tapestry of knowledge that led to the production of prototypes that played with the notions of being or becoming local and visitor.

More recent work has similarly explored the space of urban experiences and tourism. The iPhone and Android smartphone app 'Indeterminate Hikes+' (IH+, see http://ecoarttech.org/projects/indeterminate-hike) is, according to the designers (description of app, available on Google Play store), a

> tool for environmental imagination and meditative wonder, renewing awareness of biological, cultural, and media ecologies and slowing participants down at the same time. The app works by importing the rhetoric of wilderness into virtually any place accessible by Google Maps and encouraging its users to treat these locales as spaces worthy of the attention accorded to sublime landscapes, such as canyons and waterfalls.

Tourism technology scenarios are often used as rather unreflective test beds for a variety of technical work on ubiquitous and mobile computing. Bødker and Browning (2012) have argued that typical metaphors for such scenarios rely on readily recognizable metaphors such as mobile guidebooks, wayfinding devices or devices that aid visitor interpretation of sights. Galloway et al. (2003) and others have pointed to a very different way of applying design in the space of tourism technologies. Rather than limiting their imaginative technologies to the realm of marketing, visitor information systems or management technologies, they use technologies to reimagine how urban tourism can be performed and the IH+ app aims to incorporate a wider range of senses in the experience of the city. A critical application of design research acknowledges that technologies shape experiences and the ways in which we conduct our lives. Importantly, it also acknowledges that these effects are contingent on conscious choice and not inevitably determined by the technical artefact in and of itself. The possibility to reimagine how technologies affect our cultural practices and experiences is always there.

Conclusion

This chapter presents a proposal to transform the discursive arena in which the IT tourism curriculum is developed. It is a call to pursue a curricular design across and beyond disciplinary boundaries because both the complexity of technology and tourism as objects of research exceed the mastery of any disciplinary field. As indicated by Coles *et al.*, knowledge should account for the 'complexity, messiness, unpredictability, hybridity of the contemporary world' (2006: 313).

We believe that curriculum expansion in this field demands first a conceptualization of IT as a complex and relational object of research and second an understanding of the relationship between human and techniques as presented by the theoretical frameworks of embedded cognition, situated action, ANT and critical design. Technologies and their ways of shaping touristic performances may be included as objects for reflection-in-action. To understand how such reflection might take place, this chapter has outlined how design as a particular practice works to create dialogical spaces in the interstices between materials and humans. We have argued that taking an interaction design component seriously in tourism education entails a turn towards combining abductive reasoning and practical experimentation with the analytical forms (user insights, viability, integration into business objectives. etc).

This chapter follows the strategy of introducing novel theoretical perspectives as a means to foster curricular innovation. This strategic choice has a long tradition in tourism research and it is similar to the process of knowledge progress in tourism studies (Belhassen & Caton, 2009) that consists of advancing the dynamic of incorporating academic metaphors (as the concepts and definitions represented by the theories here presented) and relating these to the epistemic development of tourism. Tribe (1997) visually describes this process in his model of the creation of tourism knowledge as an imagined area nurtured by the knowledge of multiple disciplines where tourism scholarship is advanced and created (called band k in his model).

The future of tourism education depends on the academic community looking abroad and benefiting from the brilliant expansion that takes place in other knowledge fields, such as the evolution in digital humanities, (critical) design or philosophy, but also to nurture a better and deeper dialogue among its own research tribes and academic traditions as those represented by the ENTER and the CTS conferences. We need to dismantle a situation of 'wars of position' (Gramsci, cited in Belhassen & Caton, 2009) where academic networks and specific epistemologies work to maintain hegemonic positions and act as gatekeepers of the right truth. IT research in tourism needs a democratic revolution, a move beyond managerialism and technopian/work-machine ideologies towards a post-foundational arena of multiple truths. We have emphasized the potential of playful and visionary/critical designerly practices to accentuate the deep connections between practical making, critical imagination, and innovations in the field of tourism IT. We believe that there is hope for both tourism education and tourism knowledge production in promoting dialogue and plurality in academic scholarship, as beautifully indicated by Belhassen and Caton (2009: 348):

The discursive nature of knowledge production can function to improve society by inducing a sense of reflexivity in those who recognize such characterizations of power, language, knowledge, and truth operating in everyday practice.

Hopefully this critical account of the situation of IT in the curriculum of tourism education will help to increase both diversity and reflection in this field.

References

Agre, P. (1997). 'Toward a Critical Technical Practice: lessons learned in trying to reform AI'. In G. Bowker, S. L. Star, & W. Turner (Eds.), *Social Science, Technical Systems, and Cooperative Work: beyond the great divide* (pp. 131–57). Mahwah, NJ: Lawrence Erlbaum.

Baym, N. K. (2010). *Personal Connections in the Digital Age*. Cambridge: Polity Press.

Beard, C., Wilson, J. P., & McCarter, R. (2007). 'Towards a Theory of e-Learning: experiential e-learning'. *Journal of Hospitality, Leisure, Sport and Tourism Education*, 6(2), 3–15.

Belhassen, Y., & Caton, K., (2009). 'Advancing Understandings: a linguistic approach to tourism epistemology'. *Annals of Tourism Research*, 36(2), 335–52.

Bødker, S. (1999). 'Scenarios in User-Centered Design – Setting the Stage for Reflection and Action'. In *Proceedings of the Thirty-Second Annual Hawaii International Conference on System Sciences* (HICSS '99), Vol. 3. IEEE Computer Society, Washington, DC. Available: http://dx.doi.org/10.1016/S0953-5438(00)00024-2 (Accessed 5 August 2013).

Bødker, M., & Browning, D. (2012). 'Beyond Destinations: exploring tourist technology design spaces through local-tourist interactions'. *Digital Creativity*, 23, 204–24.

Bødker, M., & Munar, A. M. (2014). 'New Territories in Information Technologies and Tourism Research'. In A. A. Lew, M. C. Hall, & A. M.Williams (Eds.), *The Wiley-Blackwell Companion to Tourism*. Oxford: Blackwell.

Buxton, B. (2007). *Sketching User Experiences – getting the design right and the right design*. San Francisco, CA: Morgan Kaufmann.

Cantoni, L., Kalbaska, N., & Inversini, A. (2009). 'E-learning in Tourism and Hospitality: a map', *Journal of Hospitality, Leisure, Sport and Tourism Education*, 8(2), 148–56.

Carroll, J. M., (Ed.). (1995). *Scenario-based Design: envisioning work and technology in system development*, New York: John Wiley.

Coles, T., Hall, M. C., & Duval, D. T. (2006). 'Tourism and Post-disciplinary Enquiry'. *Current Issues in Tourism*, 9(4–5), 293–319.

Dale, C., & Lane, A. (2007). 'A Wolf in Sheep's Clothing? An analysis of student's engagement with virtual learning environments'. *Journal of Hospitality, Leisure, Sport and Tourism Education*, 6(2), 100–8.

Darbellay, F., & Stock, M. (2012). 'Tourism as Complex Interdisciplinary Research Object'. *Annals of Tourism Research*, 39(1), 441–58.

Dunne, A., & Raby, F. (2001). *Design Noir: the secret life of electronic objects*. Basel: Birkhäuser.

Ek, R. (2013). 'Tourism Social Media as a Fire Object'. In A. M. Munar, S. Gyimóthy, & L. Cai, (Eds.), *Tourism Social Media: transformations in identity, community and culture* (pp. 19–34). Bingley: Emerald.

Fallman, D. (2003). 'Design-Oriented Human–Computer Interaction'. In *Proceedings of the SIGCHI Conference on Human Factors in Computing Systems* (CHI '03) (pp. 225–32). New York: ACM.

Farman, J. (2012). *Mobile Interface Theory: embodied space and locative media*. New York: Routledge.

Galloway, A., Sundholm, H., Ludvigsen, M., & Munro, A. (2003). 'From Bovine Horde to Urban Players: multidisciplinary interaction design for alternative city tourisms'. Workshop paper for Designing for Ubicomp in the Wild Workshop at MUM, 10–12 December, Norrköping, Sweden. Available: http://people.dsv.su.se/~hillevi/publications/MUM2003workshop_final.pdf (Accessed 5 August 2013).

Gaver, W. W., Beaver, J., & Benford, S. (2003). 'Ambiguity as a Resource for Design'. In *Proceedings of the SIGCHI Conference on Human Factors in Computing Systems* (CHI '03) (pp. 233–40). New York: ACM.

Gretzel, U. (2011). 'Intelligent Systems in Tourism'. *Annals of Tourism Research* 38, 757–79.

Habermas, J. (1978). *Knowledge and Human Interests*. London: Heinemann.

Habermas, J. (1987). *Theory of Communicative Action*, Vol. 2. Boston, MA: Beacon Press.

Haven, C., & Botterill, D. (2003). 'Virtual Learning Environments in Hospitality, Leisure, Tourism and Sport: a review'. *Journal of Hospitality, Leisure, Sport and Tourism Education*, 2(1), 75–92.

Hayles, N. K. (2012). *How We Think: digital media and contemporary technogenesis.* Chicago, IL: University of Chicago Press.

Hollinshead, K. (2013). "Postdisciplinarity and the Rise of Intellectual Openness: the necessity for plural knowability." Keynote speech presented at the conference Welcoming Encounters: Tourism research in a postdisciplinary era, 19 June. Neuchatel, Switzerland.

Jafari, J. (1990). 'Research and Scholarship: the basis of tourism education'. *Journal of Tourism Studies,* 1(1), 33–41.

Jamal, T., & Hollinshead, K. (2001). 'Tourism and the Forbidden Zone: the underserved power of qualitative inquiry'. *Tourism Management,* 22, 63–82.

Kolko, J (2009) 'Abductive Thinking and Sensemaking: the drivers of design synthesis'. *Design Issues,* 26(1), 15–28.

Kozinets, R. (2008). 'Technology/Ideology: how ideological fields influence consumers' technology narratives'. *Journal of Consumer Research,* 34, 865–81.

Lash, S. (2002). 'Foreword: individualization in a non-linear mode'. In U. Beck & E. Beck-Gernsheim (Eds.), *Individualization* (pp. vi–xix). London: Sage.

Latour, B. (1999). *Pandora's Hope: essays on the reality of science studies.* Cambridge, MA: Harvard University Press.

McCarthy, J., & Wright, P. (2005). 'Putting 'Felt-life' at the Centre of Human–Computer Interaction (HCI)'. *Cognition, Technology and Work,* 7, 262–71.

Munar, A. M., & Gyimóthy, S. (2013). 'Critical Digital Tourism Studies'. In A. M. Munar, S. Gyimóthy, & L. Cai (Eds.), *Tourism Social Media: transformations in identity, community and culture* (pp. 245–62). Bingley: Emerald.

Munar, A. M., Gyimóthy, S., & Cai, L. (2013). 'Tourism Social Media: a new research agenda'. In A. M. Munar, S. Gyimóthy, & L. Cai (Eds.), *Tourism Social Media: transformations in identity, community and culture* (pp. 1–18). Bingley: Emerald.

Poon, A. (1993). *Tourism, Technology and Competitive Strategies.* Oxford: CABI.

Pritchard, A., Morgan, N., & Ateljevic, I. (2011). 'Hopeful Tourism: a new transformative perspective'. *Annals of Tourism Research,* 38(3), 941–63.

Ren, C. (2011). 'Non-Human Agency, Radical Ontology and Tourism Realities'. *Annals of Tourism Research,* 38(3), 858–81.

Rogers, Y., Preece, J., & Sharp, H. (2011). *Interaction Design: beyond human–computer interaction,* 3rd edn. Chichester, West Sussex: John Wiley.

Schön, D. (1983). *The Reflective Practitioner: how professionals think in action.* New York: Basic Books.

Sengers, P., Boehner, K., David, S., & Kaye, J. (2005). 'Reflective Design' In O. W. Bertelsen, N. O. Bouvin, P. G. Krogh, & M. Kyng (Eds.), *Proceedings of the 4th Decennial Conference on Critical Computing: between sense and sensibility (CC '05)* (pp. 49–58)., New York: ACM.

Simon, H. A. (1981). *The Sciences of the Artificial,* 2nd edn. Cambridge, MA: MIT Press.

Suchman, L. (2007). *Human–Machine Reconfigurations: plans and situated actions.* Cambridge: Cambridge University Press.

Tribe, J. (1997). 'The Indiscipline of Tourism'. *Annals of Tourism Research,* 24(3), 638–57.

Tribe, J. (2001). 'Research Paradigms and the Tourism Curriculum'. *Journal of Travel Research,* 39, 442–8.

Tribe, J. (2006). 'The Truth about Tourism'. *Annals of Tourism Research,* 33(2), 360–81.

Tribe, J. (2010). 'Tribes, Territories and Networks in the Tourism Academy'. *Annals of Tourism Research* 37(1), 7–33.

Van der Duim, R. (2007). 'Tourismscapes: an actor–network perspective'. *Annals of Tourism Research,* 34(4), 961–76.

Winograd, T. (Ed.). (1996). *Bringing Design to Software.* New York: ACM.

Yoo, Y. (2010). 'Computing in Everyday Life: a call for research on experiential computing'. *MIS Quarterly,* 34, 213–31.

9

Neoliberalism and the new managerialism in tourism and hospitality education

Maureen Ayikoru

Senior Lecturer, Anglia Ruskin University, UK

Introduction

This chapter reviews ongoing debates on neoliberalism and their implications for public sector management, contextualized in terms of higher education (HE) policies and practices in tourism and hospitality from across the globe. It posits neoliberalism as a hierarchical discourse that can be examined at three interrelated levels, macro, meso and micro levels, but where the boundaries are fluid rather than discrete. The perception and presentation of universities and other higher education institutions (HEIs) as 'the guardians and creators of knowledge produced for the greater good of humanity', and for which these institutions are perceived and project themselves as 'the watchdogs for the free interchange of ideas . . . including freedom to dissent from prevailing orthodoxies' (Lynch, 2006: 3) is put to scrutiny. The chapter aims to demonstrate how neoliberalism has concomitantly ushered in a shift in the power balance in HE, making it possible to identify the key beneficiaries. In so doing, the chapter unveils what are thought to be logical ambiguities in the new, if not constantly evolving, discourses in HE, centred on such notions as 'student experience' and 'research excellence' in order to pinpoint the ensuing ironies and implications of neoliberalism and the new managerialism in tourism and hospitality education. The chapter mulls over questions such as 'Is excellence in student experience and research possible in the presence of limited or non-excellent experiences for those who serve the students (academics, student support services as exemplars)?' Or a borrowed but more discerning thought by the Roman poet Juvenal VI who posed the question '*quis custodiet ipsos custodes?*' The chapter seeks to demonstrate that there are possible emotional and logical limits to the extent to which neoliberalism and the new managerialism can contribute to the attainment of the contemporary goals of tourism and hospitality in HE.

Neoliberalism: an overview

The term 'neoliberalism' used in most academic and policy discourses entails a variety of economic, social and political ideas, policies and practices that operate at both individual and institutional levels (McCarthy & Prudham, 2004; Saad-Filho & Johnston, 2005). It may be defined as 'a theory of political economic practices which proposes that human well-being can best be advanced by the maximization of entrepreneurial freedoms within an institutional framework characterized by private property rights, individual liberty, free markets and free trade' (Harvey, 2006: 145).

In one of the most enriching accounts of the history of neoliberalism, Harvey (2005) traces its origins to a wave of macroeconomic and political changes in the 1970s and 1980s. The changes were notably reflected in the first ever liberalization of the Chinese economy under its communist leader Deng Xiaoping in 1978 and the drastic changes to US monetary policy under Paul Volcker as chairman of the Federal Reserve from 1979. These macroeconomic changes were closely followed and reinforced by parallel political developments and the ensuing policies, that is the election into political office of Margaret Thatcher in the UK in 1979 and Ronald Reagan in the USA in 1980. What seemed to be common to these four individuals (Volcker, Reagan, Thatcher and Xiaoping), according to Harvey, was that they unveiled what were then 'minority arguments that had long been in circulation' and ensured through several struggles (e.g. undermining the power of the trade unions and hence the relationship between organized labour and wage structure, fusion of ownership and management of capital enterprises that privileged stock values over production as the yardstick for measuring economic activity) that 'these became majoritarian', with 'Volcker and Thatcher subsequently transforming neoliberalism [that was once an] obscure economic doctrine into the central guiding principle of economic thought and management' (Harvey, 2005: 2).

Similarly, some researchers contend that neoliberalism is merely an extension of the laissez-faire economic theories and practices that were prevalent during and up to the 1930s (prior to the Great Depression), and ones that had been anticipated by classical economists and were readapted in the 1970s (to the present) to deal with stagnations in economic growth, unprecedented levels of inflation (stagflation) and the ensuing economic recession (e.g. Chomsky, 2012; Turner, 2008). Reflecting mostly on the US situation, Chomsky (2012) further intimates that the 1970s had seen sudden and sharp changes in economic strategy manifested in 'a significant shift of the economy from productive enterprise that produced things people needed or could use to financial manipulation', coupled with 'de-industrialization, off-shoring of production' (2012: 3–4) that culminated into the 'concentration of wealth in the hands of the financial [and corporate] sector' (p. 5) without necessarily benefiting the economy and society.

The neoliberal turn thus entails at least three central features, namely, deregulation, privatization and the reduced role of the state from many areas of social provision (e.g. healthcare and education) and the firm entrenchment of the economic logic of efficiency and performativity in socio-cultural and political spheres, operationalized through a 'free' market environment (Beckham et al., 2009; Grummell et al., 2009; Harvey, 2005; Holborow, 2012; Rhoades & Slaughter, 2004). The market in a neoliberal sense represents the ideological platform that catalyses competition and innovation (Harvey, 2005). The 'free' market is considered fundamental to the successful operation of the neoliberal ideals as it supposedly represents a natural and ineluctable concept around which all economic, social and cultural issues can be organized and evaluated independently in order to ensure that economic growth, wealth and prosperity can be attained by various entities for their own benefits (cf. Chomsky, 2012; Harvey, 2005; Holborow, 2012; O'Flynn, 2007).

The view that the markets may not be as perfect and efficient as proclaimed by neoliberal enthusiasts/apologists (cf. Davies et al., 2006) is overridden with counterarguments that attribute any imperfections or unrealized potential to unnatural interferences by the state, trade unions or indeed the implementation of social welfare programmes (Friedman, 1962; Hayek, 1982; O'Flynn, 2007). It follows that all entities engaged in this 'free' market environment should, within the limits of their own abilities, succeed (in generating wealth, being competitive or what have you), providing there are no artificial interferences with the markets. Failure to succeed in such circumstances can be explained in terms of the inability to recognize the opportunities available in the market or to take an innovative approach to engaging with competitors in the market or, well, simply not being naturally talented. In other words, the failure can only be attributed to the entity concerned and not the markets themselves.

Although neoliberalism emphasizes deregulation and a reduced role of the state in favour of a 'free' market environment, the combination of corporate and financial power/capital and the desire to enhance and consolidate these necessitates the involvement of the state as a legitimizing entity. The state creates and defines favourable macroeconomic policies and an enabling environment at the macro level and facilitates institutions at the meso level in their implementation (cf. Harvey, 2005; Holborow, 2012; Rhoades & Slaughter, 2004). In this sense, Harvey asserts that 'the advocates of the neoliberal way now occupy positions of considerable influence in education (universities and many "think tanks"), in the media, in corporate boardrooms and financial institutions, in key state institutions (treasury departments, the central banks), and also in those international institutions . . . that regulate global finance and trade' (2005: iii). Subsequently, argues Harvey (2005), neoliberalism has, to some extent, facilitated the restoration or reconstruction of the power of economic elites and (upper) classes in a way that makes it possible to identify its main beneficiaries in different parts of the world, namely, the brash entrepreneurs and the new rich as well as some traditional upper classes that have succeeded in hanging onto a consistent power base.

What has been presented up to this point is a brief introduction to neoliberalism, one that does not do justice to such a complex, multifaceted and necessarily controversial contemporary ideology. What is however clear from this snapshot is that neoliberalism has, for many observers, become the most dominant idea or hegemony that defines and reconstitutes the way in which different entities (individuals, organizations, states, markets, etc.) interact with one another, although of course with some notable variations (Chomsky, 2012; Harvey, 2005; Zajda, 2005). The dominance associated with neoliberalism as an idea has often attracted a political economy approach to the topic in various contexts but strongly rooted in ideology critique. A similar approach is taken here, but one in which the critique focuses on tourism and hospitality in HE. It must however be noted from the outset that it can be misleading to focus on tourism and hospitality in HE, when the managerialist strategies and practices at subject or department levels and their implications for individuals therein (i.e. at the micro level) draw directly from and mirror those of the host institution (meso level) and by extension the broader HE and the macroeconomic and political environment (within a country, regionally or even globally).

Neoliberalism, higher education, tourism and hospitality in higher education

Neoliberalism remains one of the most debated contemporary ideologies from a political economy and educational perspective (e.g. Apple 2001; Grummell et al., 2009; Harvey 2005, 2006; Holborrow, 2012, Lynch, 2006, 2010; Torres & Schugurensky, 2002) and one whose ideological character and manifestation in and through tourism in HE has been dealt with elsewhere (e.g. Ayikoru et al., 2009). The chapter focuses on managerialism as manifested in and through the discourse on student experience and entrepreneurialism (or academic capitalism) and their implications for HEIs, thereby taking a qualitative shift from the previous work. These two discourses are not only interrelated, but they have also been identified in the literature as some of the key features of neoliberalism in (tourism and hospitality) HE during the past two decades (cf. Holmwood, 2012; Lynch, 2010; Sabri, 2011).

Neoliberalism in an educational context is normally rationalized in terms of the need to increase international competitiveness, profitability and discipline within the sector and, by extension, in the host economy (cf. Apple, 2001; Grummell et al., 2009). The education sector, with HEIs as focal points, is regarded as a site where a (pseudo) 'free' market environment is viable, one that can be operationalized through the adoption of new forms of management which act as the organizational correlates of neoliberalism in various contexts (Grummell et al., 2009; Lynch, 2010). As a management perspective, neoliberal ideals in HEIs can best be understood in terms of how the issues identified and defined at the macro level (e.g. the global macroeconomic climate, supra national, regional or national policy levels) penetrate through varied and different layers of an institution (the meso level) and crucially to the individuals involved in them (micro level) (cf. Ayikoru et al., 2009; Holborrow, 2012, Lynch, 2010; Rhoades & Slaughter, 2004). The adoption of such a perspective in managing the affairs of, and the people in, public sector organizations such as those of HEIs is what is commonly referred to as managerialism. According to Newson (1994), it entails (cf. Lynch, 2006; Rhoades & Slaughter, 2004):

The shift from collegial self-governance to managerialism as the dominant mode of institutional decision-making, one which links the programmatic activities of the university more directly to the control and influence of external constituencies like governments, the business community, funding agencies and the like . . . a shift in the primary objectives of the universities from the creation, preservation and dissemination of social knowledge to the production, and distribution of market knowledge.

(Newson 1994: 152)

In this sense, managerialism repositions HEIs directly or indirectly, as consumer-oriented corporate entities but not, as it were, into sites of autonomous knowledge creation and dissemination (Davies et al., 2006; Deem et al., 2007; Grummell et al., 2009; Holborow, 2012; O'Flynn, 2007; Rhoades & Slaughter, 2004). The arguments adduced for this paradigmatic shift encompass inter alia the need to increase the efficiency of these institutions, hold them more accountable to all the relevant publics (taxpayers, funding agencies, the industry, students, etc.) and to ensure that they deliver research, scholarship and education that is relevant to the needs of the industry and the economy at large (Apple, 2001; Barnett, 1990, 1997; Grummell et al., 2009; Holborow, 2012; Holmwood, 2012; Rhoades & Slaughter, 2004).

In the past few decades, like much of the public sector in most parts of the world, the HE sector has begun to reform itself by adopting management strategies that resemble business-like practices, e.g. fierce competition for students, funding, well-accomplished academics, etc. (Ayikoru et al., 2009; Lynch, 2010; O'Flynn, 2007; Rhoades & Slaughter, 2004; Torres & Schugurensky, 2002; Zajda, 2005). These reforms occur with some notable variations in different parts of the world and within countries and regions and also depending on the nature of the institutions involved (cf. Kipnis, 2007; Morshidi, 2010; Sancar & Sancar, 2012). In some cases, these reforms are clearly embedded in the mission statements of the institutions, sometimes unpretentiously described as 'corporate plans or strategic corporate plans' (cf. Barnett, 1997, 2003). There is a compulsion to blow one's own trumpet in all of those things that one does excellently or for which there is a desire to be perceived as being excellent, leading HEIs and their ethos to adopt several strategies that allow them to attract and enhance favourable perceptions from the relevant publics. Entrepreneurialism constitutes one such strategy.

Entrepreneurialism, tourism and hospitality in higher education

Entrepreneurialism or academic capitalism is a term used by Rhoades & Slaughter (2004) to describe the perceived engagement of colleges and universities in market and market-like behaviours whose nature and scope transcend what such institutions used to do in the past, i.e. operating book stores, selling tee shirts and mugs, and where professors published textbooks and engaged in consulting for profit. They argue that publicly owned colleges and universities, which have lost most of the public sector funding, now sell a wide range of products commercially as a basic source of income. They emphasize that 'today, higher education institutions are seeking to generate revenue from their core educational, research and service functions, ranging from the production of knowledge created by the faculty to the faculty's curriculum and instruction (teaching materials that can be copy-righted and marketed)' (2004: 37). Academic capitalism or entrepreneurialism in this sense closely reflects some of the key features of neoliberalism inasmuch as it is a direct implication of the same. It is introduced here to emphasize the view that a series of processes are reshaping HE and the way in which any one ethos may interact with others and the outside world of society (cf. Barnett 1997, 2003; Giroux, 2005; Grummell *et al.*, 2009; Holborow, 2012; Lynch, 2010; Rhoades & Slaughter, 2004). Barnett (2003: 65, 67, 68, 71) describes entrepreneurialism in the following manner:

> Entrepreneurialism invites . . . deep levels of change [where] universities add to their repertoire of undertakings and undergo fairly visible performative change. . . . Ever reaching out for new markets, new forms of collaboration, new pedagogies, new client groups and new frontline activities. . . . The test of the validity of the ventures . . . is that which the market will bear. [Entrepreneurialism is] an ideology that comes from outwith the university, but . . . one that is being increasingly accepted and endorsed by the university, at least in its managerial domain.

The reference made to 'visible performative change', 'new client groups' and the 'market' points to a link between the defining characteristics of entrepreneurialism, neoliberalism and managerialism, making it possible to explicate entrepreneurialism's manifestation in tourism and hospitality in HE. Contemporary HE in general and tourism and hospitality education in particular are familiar with one or more of the defining characteristics of entrepreneurialism quoted here from Barnett (2003). However, it must not be forgotten that entrepreneurs recognize opportunities and reposition themselves through creative innovations, to provide products and services for which there is a gap in the market. Taken in this context, and within the historical evolution of tourism and hospitality in HE in different parts of the world (cf. Airey & Tribe, 2005), these interrelated fields are, in a sense, a success story of what may light-heartedly be described as entrepreneurial ventures in the global HEIs. Subsequently, the most common feature that closely mirrors the neoliberal logic in entrepreneurial tourism and hospitality in HE entails the vocational foundation of these courses in HE, which were and continue to declare their commitments to prepare students for the world of work, sometimes to the exclusion of other values associated with HE (e.g. Ayikoru *et al.*, 2009; Barnett, 1990; Lynch, 2006).

A cursory investigation into the course aims and objectives of tourism and hospitality in HE (cf. Airey & Johnson, 1998) from across the globe should make this vocational situatedness, to varying degrees, more less self-evident. Paradoxically, employers in the industry still find it difficult to see where all the emphases on vocationalism in the tourism and hospitality courses and increasingly in the entire HE benefit them (e.g. Baum, 2006; Evans, 2001; MacLaurin, 2005; Reichel, 2005). An interesting case in point that is relevant to the entire global HE fraternity emanates from the McKinsey Report on *Education to Employment* published in 2013. The McKinsey Center for Government in the USA is a management consultancy firm that prides itself on 'advising and counseling many of the most influential businesses and institutions in the world' (www.mcKinsey.com/about_us/our_people). The 2013 report, written against the backdrop of the increasing levels of global youth unemployment and drawing to some extent on the findings of the Programme for International Student Assessment (PISA) implemented by the Organization for Economic Cooperation and Development (OECD) since 2000, focuses on nine countries (Brazil, Germany, India, Mexico, Morocco, Turkey, Saudi Arabia, the UK and the USA). It claims as one of its key highlights, which is worth quoting at length here, that:

> employers, education providers, and youth live in parallel universes. . . . Fewer than half of youth and employers, for example, believe that new graduates are adequately prepared for entry-level positions. Education providers, however, are much more optimistic: 72 per cent of them believe new graduates are ready to work. . . . In large part, the three major stakeholders are not seeing the same thing because they are not engaged with each other. . . . Meanwhile, more than a third of education providers report that they are unable to estimate the job-placement rates of their graduates. Of those who say they can, 20 per cent overestimated this rate compared with what was reported by youth themselves.
>
> (McKinsey & Company, 2013, Executive Summary: 18)

Whilst a typical academic reaction to such a report might be a critique based on one or more parameters, the report raises an important issue nevertheless. That is, the efficacy of the entrepreneurial logic adopted by the education providers with the rich allure that almost guarantees employability prospects in the industry (cf. Pearce, 2005) in an employment environment that is suffused with several unknown variables in the post-2008 financial crisis (cf. Holborow, 2012). HEIs continue to maintain the basic division between education and training (cf. Zais, 1976) where they provide education and employers are expected to induct graduates into their organizations' ethos through in-house training. It is considered here that as long as this division persists, whilst at the same time HEIs elect to position themselves as academic capitalists (cf. Rhoades & Slaughter, 2004), HEIs will increase their vulnerability to managerialist pressures aimed at meeting graduate employability expectations. In other words, academics will be pressurized to deliver that which seems impossible to deliver to the level of exactitude expected by employers, graduates or even the academic management hierarchy, simply because they, like the employers themselves, do not have control over the unknown variables that affect the employment environment (cf. Holborow, 2012; Lynch, 2010; Rhoades & Slaughter, 2004). But how do these constantly evolving entrepreneurial discourses influence the student–HEI relationship? A discussion on the student experience presents an interesting perspective from which to analyse this important relationship.

The student experience

The student experience, which means different things to different people in an HE context, can be cited as one of the interesting and sometimes intriguing manifestations of neoliberalism in HE in general (cf. Sabri, 2011). The interest in students' overall well-being during their HE studies is not an entirely new concept, nor one that can be attributed exclusively to the neoliberal turn explained in the preceding sections. Rather, it is something that can be traced to the idea of HE that aimed to inculcate a special level of personal development in the student, one that has conventionally taken the form not only of such things as pastoral care, lectures and tutorials, but also an interest in developing critical thought in the learners (cf. Barnett, 1990, 2003). Writing specifically about 'the expence of the institutions for the education of youth', Adam Smith made some interesting observations in the *Wealth of Nations* (1776, Book V, article II) which resonate rather well with some of the contemporary moralization discourses on student experience in HE. Smith notes that:

> the institutions for the education of the youth may . . . furnish a revenue sufficient for defraying their own expence. The fee or honorary that the scholar pays to the master naturally constitutes a revenue of this kind. (V.1.130)
>
> In other universities, the teacher is prohibited from receiving any honorary or fee from his pupils, and his salary constitutes the whole of the revenue which derives from his office. His interest is, in this case, set directly in opposition to his duty as it is possible to set it . . . and if his emoluments are to be precisely the same, whether he does or does not perform some very laborious duty, it is certainly his interest . . . either to neglect it altogether, or . . . to perform it in as careless and slovenly a manner as that authority will permit. (V.1.136)
>
> In the University of Oxford, the greater part of the public professors have, for these many years, given up altogether even the pretence of teaching. (V.1.137)

Whilst the context in which Smith explicated the issue of youth education, the nature of payment for this education and the role of the teacher or professor may have been very different (i.e. an attempt at deriving logical, scientific and philosophical arguments for laying the foundations of capitalist economics), they resonate peculiarly well with some of the varied issues about students' experiences in HEIs with regard to learning, teaching, tuition fees, etc. But just how relevant are these thoughts to tourism and hospitality in HE in the twenty-first century? Commenting on trends in learning and teaching within a UK (but possibly international) tourism education context, Wheeller (2005) raises an important point about the valorization of research-led teaching whereby institutions reward research-active lecturers and are themselves rewarded through funding (quotas), noting, interestingly, that

> the 'accepted' approach seems to be that research-led teaching is the panacea to stimulating, up-to-date teaching. . . . This, however, not only assumes that researchers do introduce their research material into their lectures. But, fundamentally, that they do, in fact (willingly and enthusiastically), actually embrace classes, and students, in the first place.
>
> (Wheeller, 2005: 311)

The ironies encapsulating the role of research and teaching in this tourism perspective do seem partly to be what Adam Smith was implying as quoted above (V.1.136–7), but for which ongoing moralization of the student experience discourse in HEIs based on learning and teaching can be recontextualized. In other words, while a prestigious academic career is mostly associated with accomplishments in research, the relationship between research and teaching which has been artificially separated in HE, but where teaching is perhaps of more immediate value to the (increasingly tuition-fees paying) student than research, may be cited as one justification for the renewed interest in student experience (cf. Lynch, 2010; Sabri, 2011). Given its significance to students' learning experience and the career prospects of academics, it would be interesting to know just how much support individual academics receive from their HEIs or specific departments in pursuit of research.

Subsequently, student experience to varying degrees has come to symbolize and represent the neoliberal turn in HE (cf. Sabri, 2011; Lynch, 2012). HE institutions have, as a matter of necessity for some but a routine obligation for others, implemented several performative measures to ensure students have the best experiences in their chosen institutions, but also to position themselves as competitive providers of the services students are purchasing, for which HEIs need to bid for most of the funding (cf. Gibb *et al.*, 2013). The renewed interest in the student experience is thus closely linked to the changing relationship between the students and the HEIs (cf. Barnett, 1997), where students have, for some HEIs, unmistakably become customers and are no longer the conventional learners they once were thought to be (cf. Barnett, 1990; Giroux, 2005; Rhoades & Slaughter, 2004). This in turn is associated with the changes in HE funding, from the time when there was an almost universal reliance on public sector funding (excepting private institutions) to the present when students and HEIs account for a reasonable amount of the funding through tuition fees and other income-generating activities (Gibb *et al.*, 2013; Rhoades & Slaughter, 2004).

In these changing circumstances, argue Gibb *et al.* (2013), the pursuit of individualistic research and teaching becomes unwarranted as a greater proportion of the funding comes in from other sources. Meanwhile academics that manifest strong entrepreneurial tendencies and are willing to engage closely with the relevant publics are better placed to attain full actualization and recognition of their work (Gibb *et al.*, 2013). It is perhaps unsurprising to see the emerging trends in strategic collaborations amongst on the one hand tourism and hospitality academics in terms of research and scholarship and on the other HEIs in developed and emerging nations, in Asia in particular. The latter can be seen in franchised course delivery, 'offshoring' of course provision, virtual campuses, student recruitment, consultancies, to mention but a few. In times such as these, it would certainly be 'unwise' to fail to collaborate in one or more of these ways; after all, survival in the marketplace depends increasingly on such strategic alliances.

The unprecedented interest in obtaining student feedback and improving all aspects of provision based on such feedback is thus consistent with the idea of 'excellence in customer service' (Anderson & Zemke, 1991; Hudson & Hudson, 2013) that requires an unambiguous knowledge of who the customer is, what their needs are and how best to meet those needs from their perspective rather than that of the service provider. These views are summed up into 'commandments and principles' of excellent customer service (Anderson & Zemke, 1991) that operate on the simple logic that any organization (regardless of its nature and scope) that understands these principles well and implements them robustly will, *ceteris paribus,* be able to deliver excellent customer service and gain, in return, customer loyalty and hence competitive advantage. Academics in the hospitality field as well as tourism marketing will perhaps be more familiar with these views than for example their tourism social sciences counterparts. What remains unknown, however, is the extent to which academics in these fields have or would consider applying these customer service principles directly to their students-turned-customers as is increasingly expected by their managers and what the long-term implications might be for all parties involved.

Consequently, these reforms in HEIs and the ensuing competitive pressures have, in unexpected ways, enabled students-cum-customers to be taken far more seriously than they ever were under full state-sponsored HE, hence making them, alongside entrepreneurial academics, one of the key beneficiaries of the neoliberal turn in HE. However, this 'power-to-the-consumer' discourse, rather than being a sudden reactivation of a genuine interest in the student experience, is based on a narrow and instrumental view of that experience which mostly only adds to the increased performative regimes in HE, of which tourism and hospitality are a part (cf. Holborow, 2012; Lynch, 2012; Sabri, 2011). Subsequently, there is emerging research in HE that points to the rise in gender-based emotional labour required for effectively dealing with the strategic shift in student experience as well as the many variants of the neoliberal project in this sector (e.g. Acker, 2006; Grummell *et al.*, 2009; Henkel, 2000; Lynch, 2010; G. Lynch 2012).

HEIs that traditionally are hierarchical and patriarchal in most parts of the world (Lynch, 2010), have, prior to the strong influences of neoliberalism, mostly been replete with all sorts of inequality found in their host societies (cf. Bourdieu, 1993; Giroux, 2005). A well-documented aspect of this problem, aside from the social stratification or class issues in different types of HEIs (cf. Bourdieu & Passeron, 1977), has been the low levels of representation of women in professorial and higher level management hierarchies (cf. Acker, 2006; Knights & Richards, 2003). Although the neoliberal project with its emphasis on the market forces and the role of competition should have in principle addressed some of the inequalities, they seemed to have catalysed contextually different but inequality-reinforcing managerialist performative regimes in HEIs (cf. Holborow, 2012; Lynch, 2010).

For instance, the renewed interest in student experience calls for high levels of emotional engagement required for providing 'customer service' to the students and, as noted by Lynch (2010), this type of work fits rather well with the care duties that in most societies are undertaken by women. Women's predisposition to embrace their emotions and sometimes use this as a strategy to cope with work–life balance or lack thereof (cf. Small *et al.*, 2011), makes them 'ideal' candidates in providing care-related work both at home and at work (Lynch, 2010). In this sense, 'women are . . . disproportionately encouraged to do the "domestic" work of the organization, and/or, the care work (e.g. running courses, teaching, thesis supervision, pastoral care), neither of which count much for individual career advancement even though they are valuable to the students and the reputation of the university' (Lynch, 2010: 56; cf. Grummell *et al.*, 2009; Henkel, 2000; Husu, 2000). Further, success in academic careers and the ensuing prestige lies mostly in quality research outputs, including scholarly (intellectual) public engagement and not, as it were, in the excellent performance of 'care-duties' (cf. Henkel, 2000). Besides, depending on the intensity of the neoliberal managerialist project and the ensuing performative targets, research and teaching may not be pursued simultaneously in tourism and hospitality in HEIs, or even if this was attempted, the powerful role of the gatekeepers to the various publication outlets would constitute another layer of artificial barricade for those who attempt both.

For now, there are relatively few publications that highlight the gendered implication of the neoliberal project in tourism and hospitality education. The work by a number of academics in tourism (e.g. Aitchison, 2001; Pritchard & Morgan 2007; Small *et al.*, 2011) has attempted to break the silence over the gendered implications of tourism knowledge production that has hitherto closely mirrored the highly institutionalized and masculinized trends in mainstream HE. Attempts have also been made to explicate the challenges of dealing with work–life balance that in a neoliberal HE has weighed heavily on women. Given the implicit geographical and contextual boundaries in these cited works and the limited reflection on the voices of related fields of hospitality as well as male academics who most likely perform the care roles in their respective HEIs, it is clear that more research is needed in this area to reflexively understand the wider implications of these gendered neoliberal and managerialist projects in tourism and hospitality education.

Conclusion

This chapter explicates some of the ongoing debates on the neoliberal turn in tourism and hospitality in HE, manifested in and through the discourses of entrepreneurialism and student experience. It demonstrates that the neoliberal project that traces its origins to a complex range of macroeconomic and political issues and that for some time was a subjugated discourse (cf. Chomsky, 2012) has not only reshaped HE in most parts of the world, but also is closely associated with a strategic repositioning of HEIs with several implications for individuals (students, academics, etc.). The main features of neoliberalism discussed in the chapter encompass entrepreneurialism (or academic capitalism, after Rhoades and Slaughter, 2004) and the renewed interest in the student experience (cf. Sabri, 2011). Neoliberalism and its many variants are regarded as hierarchical discourses whose influences on HEIs can be examined at three interrelated levels, namely, the macro, meso and micro levels, each with contextually different manifestations and implications. In its current manifestation in HEIs, students and entrepreneurial academics can be cited as key beneficiaries of the neoliberal project in HE (cf. Gibb et al., 2013; Holborow, 2012; Sabri 2011).

The chapter argues that there is a serious problem with academic capitalism manifested through curriculum reforms that are supposed to reflect what is valuable in an employment or labour market (cf. Holborow, 2012; Rhoades & Slaughter, 2004). It asserts that there are no guarantees that such reforms are able to yield the desired results, particularly for the prospective graduates whose 'investment' the HEIs are competing to attract. So that with regard to 'academic capitalism' (Rhoades & Slaughter, 2004), a potentially intriguing situation that requires serious reflection from academic managers is this, what if, one day, students who are increasingly being treated as 'customers' realized after graduation that employers are, after all, not interested in their qualifications that had been marketed to them as having clear employability features and prospects (cf. McKinsey & Company, 2013). In a typical customer environment in some parts of the world, an unsatisfied customer can return the product that fails to meet their needs or, better still, in tourism and hospitality experiences, good will gestures may be extended to the customers hopefully to make good out of unmet expectations. But how would the academic capitalists manage such bizarre situations, if a student body, largely turned into customers, were to exercise their full powers and demand answers? Whilst this may be a hypothetical scenario today, a close reflection on the very idea of perceiving students as customers, or market forces as trendsetters in social and political decisions, or deregulation of all kinds as evidenced in the contemporary neoliberal world was, according to Giroux (2005) and Chomsky (2012), unimaginable in the 1940s or 1950s.

The chapter also contemplates the possibility that the neoliberal project has facilitated and enhanced gendered inequalities in supposedly inclusive areas such as tourism and hospitality, despite the recent aspirational research advocating an agenda for a 'hopeful' tourism (cf. Pritchard et al., 2011). These issues are already receiving due attention in the mainstream HE literature that implicates the different categories of gatekeepers and their varied and carefully structured responsibilities in determining and enforcing the criteria of excellence (in research and student experience) without the slightest reflection on the implications for various groups and individuals therein (cf. Acker, 2006; Grummell et al., 2009; Henkel, 2000; Husu, 2000; Knights & Richards, 2003; Lynch, 2010). Future research in tourism and hospitality in HE will do well to empirically examine these issues, with particular reference to the balance between research and teaching, tenure and prestige.

References

Acker, J. (2006). 'Inequality Regimes: gender, class and race in organisations'. *Gender and Society*, 22(4),139–58.

Airey, D., & Johnson, S. (1998) *The Profile of Tourism Studies Degree Courses in the UK: 1997/98, Guideline 7*. London: National Liaison Group for Higher Education in Tourism.

Airey, D., & Tribe, J. (Eds.). (2005). *An International Handbook of Tourism Education*. London: Elsevier.

Aitchison, C. (2001). 'Gender and Leisure Research: the codification of knowledge'. *Leisure Sciences*, 23(1),1–19.

Anderson, K. & Zemke, R. (1991). *Delivering Knock Your Socks Off Service*, revised edn. New York: Amacom.

Apple, M. W. (2001). 'Comparing Neo-Liberal Projects and Inequality in Education'. *Comparative Education*, 37(4), 409–23.

Ayikoru, M., Tribe, J., & Airey, D. (2009). 'Reading Tourism Education: neoliberalism unveiled'. *Annals of Tourism Research*, 36(2), 191–221.

Barnett, R. (1990). *The Idea of Higher Education*. Buckingham: Open University Press.

Barnett, R. (1997). *Higher Education: a critical business*. Buckingham: Open University Press.

Barnett, R. (2003). *Beyond All Reason: living with ideology in the university*. London: Open University Press.

Baum, T. (2006). *Human Resource Management for Tourism, Hospitality, and Leisure: an international perspective*. London: Thomson.

Beckham, A., Cooper, C., & Hill, D. (2009). 'Neoliberalisation and Managerialisation of Education in England and Wales – a case for reconstructing education'. *Journal of Critical Education Policy Studies*, 7(2), 311–45.

Bourdieu, P. (1993). *Sociology in Question*, trans. R. Nice. London: Sage.

Bourdieu, P., & Passeron, J. (1977). *Reproduction in Education, Society and Culture*, trans. R. Nice. London: Sage.

Chomsky, N. (2012). *Occupy*. New York: Penguin.

Davies, B., Gottsche, M., & Bansel, P. (2006). 'The Rise and Fall of the Neoliberal University'. *European Journal of Education*, 41(2), 305–19.

Deem, R., Hillyard, S., & Reed, M. (2007). *Knowledge, Higher Education and the New Managerialism*. Oxford: Oxford University Press.

Evans, N. (2001). 'The Development and Positioning of Business Related University Tourism Education: a UK perspective'. *Journal of Teaching in Travel & Tourism*, 1(1), 17–36.

Friedman, M. (1962). *Capitalism and Freedom*. Chicago, IL: University of Chicago Press.

Gibb, A., Haskins, G., & Robertson, I. (2013). 'Leading the Entrepreneurial University: meeting the entrepreneurial development needs of higher education institutions'. In A. Altmann & B. Ebersberger (Eds.), *Universities in Change, Innovation, Technology, and Knowledge Management* (pp. 9–45). New York: Springer Science and Business Media.

Giroux, H. (2005). 'The Terror of Neoliberalism: rethinking the significance of cultural politics'. *College Literature*, 32(1), 1–19.

Grummell, B., Devine, D., & Lynch, K. (2009). 'The Care-less Manager: gender, care and new managerialism in higher education'. *Gender and Education*, 21(2), 191–208.

Harvey, D. (2005). *A Brief History of Neoliberalism*. Oxford: Oxford University Press.

Harvey, D. (2006). 'Neoliberalism as Creative Destruction'. *Geografiska Annaler, Series B: Human Geography*, 88(2),145.

Hayek, F. A. (1982). *New Studies in Philosophy, Politics, Economics and the History of Ideas*. London: Routledge and Kegan Paul.

Henkel, M. (2000). *Academic Identities and Policy Changes in Higher Education*. London: Jessica Kingsley.

Holborow, M. (2012). 'Neoliberalism, Human Capital and the Skills in Higher Education – the Irish case'. *Journal of Critical Education Policy Studies*, 10(1), 93–111.

Holmwood, J. (2012). 'Markets *versus* Publics: the new battleground of higher education'. *Harvard International Review*, (Fall), 12–15.

Hudson, S., & Hudson, L. (2013). *Customer Service for Hospitality and Tourism*. Oxford: Goodfellow Publishers.

Husu, L. (2000). 'Gender Discrimination in the Promised Land of Gender Equality'. *Higher Education in Europe*, 25(1), 221–8.

Kipnis, A. (2007). 'Neoliberalism Reified: *Suzhi* discourse and the tropes of neoliberalism in the People's Republic of China'. *Journal of the Royal Anthropological Institute*, 13, 383–400.

Knights, D., & Richards, W. (2003). 'Sex Discrimination in UK Academia'. *Gender, Work and Organisation*, 10(2), 213–38.

Lynch, G. A. (2012). *The Sacred in the Modern World: a cultural sociological approach*. Oxford: Oxford University Press.

Lynch, K. (2006). 'Neoliberalism and Marketisation: the implications for higher education'. *European Educational Research Journal*, 5(1), 1–17.

Lynch, K. (2010). 'Carelessness: a hidden doxa of higher education'. *Arts and Humanities in Higher Education*, 9(1), 54–67.

McCarthy, J., & Prudham, S. (2004). 'Neoliberal Nature and the Nature of Neoliberalism'. *Geoforum*, 35, 275–83.

McKinsey & Company (2013). Education to Employment: designing a system that works. Available: http://mckinseyonsociety.com/downloads/reports/Education/Education-to-Employment_FINAL.pdf (Accessed 10 July 2013).

MacLaurin, D. (2005). 'Tourism Education in China: past, present and future directions', in C. Hsu (Ed.), *Global Tourism Higher Education: Past, Present and Future* (pp. 1–25). New York: Haworth Hospitality Press.

Morshidi, S. (2010). 'Strategic Planning Directions of Malaysia's Higher Education: university autonomy in the midst of political uncertainties'. *Higher Education*, 59(4), 461–73.

Newson, A. J. (1994). 'Subordinating Democracy: the effects of fiscal retrenchment and university–business partnerships on knowledge creation and knowledge dissemination in universities'. *Higher Education*, 27(2), 141–61.

O'Flynn, J. (2007). 'From New Public Management to Public Value: paradigmatic change and managerial implications'. *Australian Journal of Public Administration*, 66(3), 353–66.

Pearce, P. (2005). 'Australian Tourism Education: the quest for status', in C. Hsu (Ed.), *Global Tourism Higher Education: Past, Present and Future* (pp. 251–67). New York: Haworth Hospitality Press.

Pritchard, A., & Morgan, N. (2007). 'De-centring Tourism's Intellectual Universe, or Traversing the Dialogue between Change and Tradition'. In I. Ateljevic, A. Pritchard, & N. Morgan (Eds.), *The Critical Turn in Tourism Studies: innovative research methodologies* (pp. 11–28). Oxford: Elsevier.

Pritchard, A., Morgan, N., & Ateljevic, I. (2011) 'Hopeful Tourism: a new transformative perspective'. *Annals of Tourism Research*, 38(3), 941–63.

Reichel, A. (2005). 'Tourism and Hospitality Higher Education in Israel'. In C. Hsu (Ed.), *Global Tourism Higher Education: Past, Present and Future* (pp. 61–88). New York: Haworth Hospitality Press.

Rhoades, G., & Slaughter, S. (2004). 'Academic Capitalism in the New Economy: challenges and choices'. *American Academic*, 1(1), 37–60.

Saad-Filho, A., & Johnston, D. (Eds.). (2005). *Neoliberalism: a critical reader*. Ann Arbor, MI: Pluto Press.

Sabri, D. (2011). 'What's Wrong with "the Student Experience"?'. *Discourse: Studies in the Cultural Politics of Education*, 32(5), 657–67.

Sancar, C., & Sancar, M. (2012). 'Neoliberal Mechanisation of Education'. *Turkish Journal of Educational Technology*, 11(3), 246–54.

Small, J., Harris, C., Wilson, E., & Ateljevic, I. (2011). 'Voices of Women: a memory-work reflection on work–life dis/harmony in tourism academia'. *Journal of Hospitality, Leisure, Sport and Tourism Education*, 10(1), 23–36.

Smith, A. (1776). *An Inquiry into the Wealth of the Nations*. London: Methuen & Co.

Torres, C. A., & Schugurensky, D. (2002). 'The Political Economy of Higher Education in the Era of Neoliberal Globalisation: Latin America in comparative perspective'. *Higher Education*, 43(4), 429–55.

Turner, R. (2008). *Neoliberal Ideology: history, concepts and politics*. Edinburgh: Edinburgh University Press.

Wheeller, B. (2005). 'Issues in Teaching and Learning'. In D. Airey & J. Tribe (Eds.), *An International Handbook of Tourism Education* (pp. 309–18). Oxford: Elsevier.

Zais, R. (1976). *Curriculum: principles and foundations*. New York: Thomas Crowell.

Zajda, J. (Ed.). (2005). *International Handbook on Globalisation, Education and Policy Research: global pedagogies and policies*. Dordrecht: Springer.

10

The role of Massive Open Online Courses (MOOCs) in the democratization of tourism and hospitality education

Barry O'Mahony

Faculty of Business and Enterprise, Swinburne University of Technology, Australia

Gilly Salmon

Learning Transformations, Swinburne University of Technology, Australia

Introduction

Early educational theorists have commonly expounded the link between philosophy and education, positioning education as a moral, social imperative and public good (Peters, 1966). By contrast, hospitality and tourism education evolved from an operational context (Airey, 2005; Morrison & O'Mahony, 2003) and the vocational ethos permeating the curriculum has focused, in the main, on extrinsic goals. The advent of degree-level studies, however, prompted the development of a holistic body of knowledge (Airey, 2005) which has allowed tourism to gain 'recognition as a separate area of study in its own right' (Fidgeon, 2010: 700). While the higher education tourism curriculum has incorporated liberal studies such as geography and sociology and included social goals such as poverty alleviation, the hospitality curriculum has, for the most part, remained true to its vocational roots (Lashley, 2013).

Arguments for the inclusion of a more liberal hospitality framework in the mid-to-late 1990s have led to the recognition of two curriculum streams within hospitality programmes. These are: hospitality studies – informed by a range of disciplines; and hospitality management education – aimed at the development of managerial competencies (Lashley & Morrison, 2000; Morrison & O'Mahony, 2003; Wood, 2013). However, the potential of the hospitality studies stream has yet to be fully realized. There are a number of reasons for this. One is that the emphasis on the development of managerial competencies has aligned well with employment outcomes and the needs of the industry (Slattery, 2002). Another is that there has been an increasing reliance on education as an export industry in many countries. Both of these issues support a government focus on improving efficiency in what has been described as a 'neoliberal' funding environment (Ayikoru *et al.*, 2009; Marginson & Considine, 2000; O'Mahony, 2009).

Ayikoru *et al.* (2009) explain the rationale behind these changing funding conditions advising that there has been a push to reduce the emphasis on the consumption of public resources in higher education. With education in most countries acknowledged as a basic human right, however, the numbers of citizens seeking a university degree have increased significantly. Access to higher education has been improved with the upgrading of many Colleges of Advanced Education and Polytechnics but this has placed an increasing financial burden on state resources. This has prompted governments to seek ways to reduce costs and improve efficiency within higher education systems. Private education providers have also been encouraged in many countries in a move towards a 'user pays' system. As a result, hospitality higher education has remained a competency-oriented discipline that is underpinned by market rather than social imperatives.

As noted in Chapter 1, higher education has entered an era of significant change in which the role of universities is being questioned. This represents an opportunity to re-examine the philosophy underpinning educational goals and within this environment Massive Open Online Courses (MOOCs) can play a significant role in helping to restore the social and moral underpinnings of education, particularly within developing countries. Indeed, MOOCs have the potential to contribute to education's fundamental role as a public good and lead to the democratization of education, particularly within the tourism and hospitality sector. This chapter explores this potential and reflects on how these higher goals might be realized.

The aims of this chapter are to locate MOOCs in the current hospitality and tourism milieu and to reflect on the role of MOOCs in the democratization of tourism and hospitality education. The chapter has the following objectives:

(7) To explore the drivers in the development of global tourism and hospitality education.
(8) To reflect on the rise of MOOCs, their philosophical underpinnings and potential future directions.
(9) To examine the potential of MOOCs in the democratization of tourism and hospitality education.
(10) To present a model tourism and hospitality curriculum that positions MOOCs to play a key role in the democratization of tourism and hospitality education.

Drivers in the development of global tourism and hospitality education

As noted by Airey *et al.* in Chapter 1, hospitality, tourism and events have been relatively recent additions to higher education. Previously most formal tourism and hospitality programmes were provided within the vocational sector and were generally aligned with catering and hotel management programmes. In the case of hospitality, the curriculum has traditionally included an amalgam of craft, ritual and inherited practice with little agreement on what constitutes the core body of knowledge (Nailon, 1982). For the most part, the transition from vocational to higher education has reduced the emphasis on traditional practice and increased the focus on customer satisfaction. However, this has not always been the case. Moreover, the move towards a more liberal orientation that emerged in the late 1990s and early 2000s has yet to permeate the hospitality curriculum (Lashley & Morrison, 2000; Morrison & O'Mahony, 2003) and this has meant that the vocational elements of hospitality education, when transferred to a university environment, have added significantly to the institution's average cost of programme delivery. This is particularly evident in the food and beverage area where operational kitchens and restaurants have eroded returns with implications for the viability of many hospitality programmes (O'Mahony, 2009).

Tourism programmes have also faced a series of challenges. For example diversity in tourism education has been a longstanding issue (Theuns & Rasheed, 1983), not only in relation to programme and course content but also in relation to the duration of programmes and the faculties, departments, schools or colleges in which they are offered. For instance, some programmes have been offered within business schools and others within agricultural colleges. There are also 'basic differences in the structure of the education system of the various countries which results in variations in duration and content of equivalent programs' (Theuns & Rasheed, 1983: 42). One reason for this is that tourism has been considered as both an economic phenomenon as well as a social and human one and this has led to different approaches to tourism education (Fidgeon, 2010).

Consequently, research in tourism and hospitality higher education reflects a continuous search to provide a model university curriculum (McIntosh, 1983; Lashley & Morrison, 2000). There has, for example, been a consistent quest to develop programmes with the best combination of subjects that prepare students for careers in business. McIntosh (1983: 134) advises that 'when the schools design a curriculum, they start with the needs of the likely employer of the graduate four years hence – a business employer orientation to the entire curriculum'. For tourism, Fidgeon (2010) concludes that this has occurred to meet the needs of the growing tourism market indicating that, as is the case in hospitality higher education, it is the employment outcomes that are driving demand for tourism programmes. Nevertheless, he recognizes that while 'pedagogic research has centred on the vocational origins of tourism in higher education; [there is also] the need to broaden the curriculum from its essentially business orientated origins and the appearance of tourism as a subject of study within further education' (Fidgeon, 2010: 700). This move away from a managerial focus has been criticized in the mass media on the basis that tourism content lacks academic rigour and does not provide sufficient skills training for tourism graduates (Fidgeon, 2010). Thus, while the development of tourism as an academic discipline has, for the most part, been successful, the development of tourism graduates for industry positions has been questioned. At the same time hospitality higher education programmes have been criticized, particularly in relation to their ability to prepare graduates to think outside existing practices and to develop what Airey and Tribe (2000: 290) refer to as the tradition of developing the 'powers of the mind'.

Tribe (2002) sought to address these apparent contradictions by proposing a balance between liberal and vocational education to develop both the knowledge and skills required for the vocational ends of employment. In so doing, he highlights the difference between liberal education and skills-based or vocational education defining the tourism and hospitality curriculum as a holistic educational experience in what he refers to as the 'Philosophic Practitioner Education' (PPE). Dredge et al. (2012: 2156) explain that liberal education 'refers to a curriculum that develops general knowledge and fosters complex, independent thinking and transferable intellectual and practical skills'. Dredge et al. (2012) contend that liberal education can develop reflection and independent thinking and should therefore be valued for its own sake rather than just for its utility. Like Tribe (2002), Dredge et al. (2012) conceptualize curriculum space in two dimensions. These are vocational outcomes, that is those that are needed to succeed in tourism and hospitality employment, and liberal outcomes which focus on reflection and freedom of thought. They also propose 'a balance between vocational and professional skills and the broader critical thinking and analytical skills' (Dredge et al., 2012: 2157).

At the same time, research into tourism higher education has emphasized a more rounded curriculum that features the socio-cultural and psychological issues of tourism. This has included the need to consider the place of global issues such as sustainability and poverty alleviation within the curriculum (Ateljevic, 2009; Caton, 2012). Caton (2012), for example, argues for a more philosophical direction in tourism and asserts that moral philosophy should be given a more prominent place in tourism scholarship. She believes that the economic perspective that currently permeates tourism education should be underpinned by an ideology that moves away from the notion of generating more output from less input. She advocates a moral and ethical focus in tourism development and tourism education along with the development of ethics in tourism service noting that 'traditionally, higher education was envisaged as a truly public good, in the economic sense of the term' (Caton, 2012: 1922). Moreover, knowledge created within the university environment was shared within society by graduates thereby contributing to the enlightenment of others within the community. Education therefore had utility and contributed beyond individual students, thus having a public benefit. In today's neoliberal world, however, education is considered a private good, that is a saleable product of commercial value.

It should be noted, however, that Tribe (2002) does not consider a purely philosophic, liberal approach to tourism and hospitality education as adequate for university graduates. Instead he seeks to develop a curriculum that includes a liberal framework that can be adapted to vocational action. In simple terms, this translates into the development of a curriculum that provides graduates with the ability to reflect on the liberal elements of their studies and to be capable of integrating that knowledge and understanding within industry practice. This standpoint can, therefore, allow tourism and hospitality programmes to be tailored to the needs of graduates and industry. This could include customizing all of the critical dimensions of educational provision including delivery type, mode and style, as well as assessment and progression. For example programmes could be delivered in face-to-face, blended or online mode (thus providing a place for MOOCs within the curriculum space), in a unit or modular format and progression from one unit or module to the next may or may not be dependent on the successful completion of a prerequisite unit or module.

The rise of MOOCs and their philosophical underpinnings

The term MOOCs is reported to have been first coined in Canada in 2008 when free, open access to a course was granted to the general public and attracted over 2,000 participants (Downes, 2009). The details of this event are corroborated by Daniel (2012), who alerts us to a variety of definitions of MOOCs, the majority of which describe them as open, online courses delivered via the Web to large groups of participants who typically do not receive credit for participation. Initially MOOCs were facilitated by open access materials delivered through a variety of digital technologies that took advantage of the availability of information on the World Wide Web. As such, they were informal programmes that brought together readily available information in a relatively loosely structured format. These early MOOCs were based on a philosophy that valued participation and engagement with educational materials and with other participants in the programme. As such, they were in keeping with Illich's (1971) contention that education should be self-directed and empower all who wish to learn by providing access to learning resources using new technologies. In his pioneering work, Illich advocated the notion of a peer network that used computers to match those who wished to learn with those who wished to share or teach in what he described as learning webs. To Illich, learning webs were an answer to what he termed a huge 'professional apparatus' consisting of educators and buildings that are supported by regressive taxation. In other words, learning webs could potentially provide the benefits and efficiencies envisaged by the neoliberal policies noted earlier in this chapter.

MOOCs also provide a number of other benefits including the development of independent learning skills, access to community programmes and opportunities for lifelong learning. However, MOOCs have now moved in two directions in what are classified as cMOOCs and xMOOCs (Daniel, 2012). cMOOCs, are those that provide free and open access and encourage participants to network and share information through high levels of group interaction. These MOOCs have become known as connectivist MOOCs, where the pedagogy is based on the sharing of knowledge across the group or network (Siemens, 2006; Teplechuk, 2013). In contrast, xMOOCs are those MOOCs that rely on a professor or teacher to deliver information or content in a more traditional approach using various web-based platforms for delivery. These MOOCs work on a large scale often using technology to automate assessment (Brown, 2013; Teplechuk, 2013). While considered by many to be another form of distance education, xMOOCs are positioned in the market as a type of 'disruptive technology' or its more apt revised term a 'disruptive innovation' (Bower & Christensen, 1995).

A disruptive innovation is so called because it represents a product or service innovation that disrupts the existing market in unexpected ways. This generally occurs by first improving a product or service, often extending it to a new consumer segment and later lowering prices within that market (Christensen, 1997). These innovations are frequently associated with start-up firms that promote disruptive innovations with a market strategy designed to capture the market by catching competitors off-guard, gaining a foothold in the market and then displacing competitors. Disruptive innovation companies use off-the-shelf, often cheap, components or technology in simple product architecture that appeals to consumers (Christensen, 1997).

Many of these elements can be identified within xMOOCs such as Coursera, EdEx, Udacity and a number of emerging conglomerates. These entities control the platforms through which courses are accessed; although courses are provided by a number of top-tier institutions through these platforms, the distinction between ownership of the platform and ownership of the course is sometimes unclear. There is some clarity in regard to Coursera, which now has 62 partner universities, and Udacity in that Coursera is reported to have been financed to the tune of at least US$22 million and the founders of Udacity have received venture capital of over US$21 million since its inception (Lewin, 2012). Since venture capitalists do not invest in non-profit making ventures, it can be concluded that xMOOCs will seek a significant return on investment at some point in the future. This is likely to include some form of payment from xMOOC participants which may include charges for tuition, assessment, certification, additional tutorial support and credit for entry into formal degree programmes as well as revenues from advertising. As a result, xMOOCs may be seen to be currently testing a business proposition with a view to future, long-term business sustainability, while their university partners could be seen to be buying a market position for their institutions in case MOOCs leave traditional universities behind by becoming true disruptive innovations.

In one sense xMOOCs are innovative in that they represent the ultimate form of market-oriented educational production, shifting education to corporate entities, increasing competition and developing virtual brands that blur the lines between domestic and international students. At another level, however, they are far from cutting edge in that the technology, delivery and support provided differ little from existing online courses. Moreover, the concept of open, mass education is not new, for example the establishment of the Open University in the UK shares a number of similarities with today's MOOCs. The initial vision for the Open University was of an accessible third-level institution that was open to all. Access was provided using what was then a relatively new technology, that is the broadcast medium of television. This allowed university lecturers to present their lectures on television and it wasn't unusual for one to turn on one's TV in the middle of an academic lecture or to witness a major medical procedure taking place in one's living room, as it were. This was a significant leap forward in the democratization of education in the UK and was a true liberation of education for its time. It was available to all who owned a TV set in the UK and could be accessed from the home regardless of whether one was formally enrolled at the Open University or not. For those who were enrolled, however, credit was granted and successful completion of courses resulted in the granting of degrees. Thus MOOCs do not represent a paradigm shift in education, at least in the manner envisaged by Kuhn (1962). That is, MOOCs do not open up new approaches or understandings supported by the consensus of the scientific or, in this case, the academic, community. Fast forward to 2014 and MOOCs provide similar access to education using what is now relatively cheap access through the World Wide Web, enabled by a variety of electronic devices. The platforms that present these courses can also be accessed from anywhere in the world. Thus, in the case of MOOCs, the reach is wider and they are accessible to all who wish to participate anywhere in the world. As a result, the potential role of MOOCs in the democratization of education is immense.

However, MOOCs also face a number of challenges. With no barriers to entry MOOCs are accessible to a wider audience than their more select university counterparts thereby extending consumer segments (Christensen, 1997). However, open entry for students who have not yet developed the requisite background knowledge can be a barrier to success for many participants (O'Mahony & Sillitoe, 2001). Universities that have enabled access to non-traditional, on-campus students in the past have grappled with this issue and have found that significant additional support needs to be provided to assist these students to develop the required learning skills to successfully complete university programmes. In many countries entry requirements are also controlled by various educational bodies and based on achieved knowledge levels, for example the Australian Qualification Framework in Australia and similar bodies in the UK and elsewhere. Thus, while MOOCs can achieve economies of scale based on large numbers of students, successful completion of courses and programmes will be an ongoing challenge. This is already becoming evident in the attrition rates of many MOOCs (Brown, 2013; Daniel, 2012) and is likely to become a major issue for xMOOCs if participant fees are introduced.

Providing and maintaining quality in the online environment is another issue. As noted in Chapter 1, quality in higher education is generally linked with research outputs and universities develop their brands on the basis of research reputation. In the online learning space, however, quality is more difficult to measure. Moreover, some universities offering MOOCs are not as well known in the global market and, as a result, quality of MOOC courses will be based solely on participants' perceptions of pedagogy, curriculum design, delivery and assessment as well as the delivery platform. While quality has frequently been an issue in early online education, online learning has come a long way since it was first introduced. Extensive research and improved delivery platforms have greatly improved provision and empirically tested, pedagogically sound models and frameworks have been developed to support online education (Shaughnessy & Fulgham, 2011).

These models, and the studies that support them, show that for online learning to be successful and productive, participants need to be supported through a structured developmental process. A structured learning scaffold implies prior design providing a familiar and sequenced routine leading to increasing control by the learners and promoting peer engagement. The Salmon (2011) five-stage model provides this framework and scaffold. The model shows how participants can benefit from increasing skill and comfort in working, networking and learning online, and what the person or people providing the human support need to do at each stage to help students to achieve this success. The model also shows how to motivate online participants, to build their learning through appropriate online activities and tasks (called e-tivities) and to pace them through programmes of education and development. Nearly all participants will progress through the five stages, provided that they are given good instructions (invitations) on how to work together, appropriate e-tivities to promote action and interaction, motivation through both purpose and feedback and the necessary technical support. Stages 3–5 are the more productive and constructive stages, but to get to these levels participants should have first taken part in e-tivities pitched at Stages 1 and 2.

For learners at Stage 1 individual access and purposeful reasons to go online frequently and repeatedly are essential prerequisites for full participation and engagement. Stage 2 involves individual participants establishing their online identities and then finding others with whom to interact. They start to understand the benefits and requirements of working with others in their online environments. At Stage 3, participants engage in mutual exchange of information and make learning-related contributions. Up to and including Stage 3, a form of cooperation occurs whereby each person supports the other participants' goals. At Stage 4, course-related group discussions and activities develop and the interaction becomes collaborative, more team-oriented and more complex. Knowledge construction begins at Stage 5, when participants are comfortable working together online and develop an ability to exploit fully the benefits for their learning. They are free, active and confident in further pursuing ideas and goals, discovering, reflecting and presenting for assessment.

Most importantly, however, each stage requires participants to have the minimum capability to exploit the e-learning platform or environment in use. Each stage calls for different human support skills and engagement. Participants will differ in the amount of time each will need at every stage before progressing. For example the model applies to all online learning software, but if experienced participants are introduced to online learning platforms that are new to them, they will tend to linger for a while at Stages 1 or 2 but then move on quite rapidly through the stages. People are likely to cycle through the model many times as they increase their knowledge and explore their learning in different domains. More experienced participants will move more rapidly towards Stages 4 and 5, often helping those less experienced online. E-tivities must be designed for each stage in sequence.

Clearly then online learning is different, perhaps even more complex than traditional classroom delivery. It is not a 'one size fits all' environment and online teachers need to be aware of both the learning skills and technological capability of their students. They need to build a programme of e-tivities for online learning in a manner that anticipates how individuals are likely to exploit the system at each stage. The e-tivities need to be appropriate to the skill levels of the majority of students in order to achieve active online learning, good contributions, interaction between participants and increased student satisfaction. Those that teach into online programmes (known as e-moderators) should understand the model and, if properly applied, they are likely to spend less time trying to recruit recalcitrant participants and more time supporting creative e-tivities.

Thus online teachers, particularly those who engage in high enrolment MOOCs, need certain skills beyond those that are traditionally found within universities. Moreover, MOOCs encourage teachers at all levels of education to review and reinvigorate their learning designs and teaching skills. However, while professional development programmes are available for e-moderators and such development is considered to be the key to successful high quality online learning, it has been curiously difficult to scale, especially in higher education (Gregory & Salmon, 2013). As a result, those responsible for the teaching of academic knowledge, of assessment and of quality, need to form teams with other professionals to develop skills to design and prepare for learning in the digital environment (Salmon, 2013). In addition, new approaches to enable staff to understand the social and emotional nature of working in groups online, as well as to develop key skills in facilitation (usually called 'e-moderating) are also essential (Salmon, 2011).

Salmon's research has developed since the first grounded research in the 1990s at the Open University in the UK. She introduced and then refined the structure of the five-stage model so that the framework could act as both a design tool and a guide for students to enable them to share knowledge and engage with others in the online environment. One of the most important issues in the design of high quality, engaging online learning is to enable both learners and their tutors to get used to being in the digital environment, building trust and effective learning teams. Salmon argues that MOOCs plus a scaffold are the key to heading towards creating quality with volume. As a result, it is possible to provide a quality online educational experience and to achieve predetermined learning outcomes by systematically ensuring that quality permeates curriculum development, design, delivery, assessment and validation.

In summary, then, quality online education is multifarious, complex and relatively expensive. Moreover, many of the other important elements of the educational experience do not enjoy the same economies of scale as the online delivery component. This is one reason why mass education seeks to use automated assessment and grading which is often seen as a trade-off between access and quality (Teplechuk, 2013). Teplechuk's (2013) recent research into the launch of MOOCs at the University of Edinburgh estimated the typical costs of launching these courses at £250,000. The exercise was also described as a 'black hole for academic staff time' (Teplechuk, 2013: 45) with the only notable return on investment being an increase in publicity for the university. As a result, MOOCs can represent a significant financial burden to universities in the start-up phase and while broadening a university brand to a global audience is achievable, this also means engaging with new competitors in an environment where expertise at one level or another may be lacking. As well as platform designers and technology experts, MOOCs are reliant on capable online teachers and this capability may or may not be readily available within the current academic fraternity.

Given these conditions, it is unclear whether MOOCs can fulfil Christensen's (1997) requirement that a disruptive innovation must first improve a product or service before lowering prices. Indeed, Brown (2013: 243) asserts that: 'MOOCs are not filling a significant gap in the undergraduate education market' mainly because they provide minimal support which requires participants to have developed their learning skills elsewhere. While this may account for some attrition, it is proposed that another factor for the failure of MOOCs to attract undergraduate students is a lack of credibility with employers, based on perceptions of low quality, the absence of formal credit and many of the issues related to graduate outcomes noted earlier. This would also suggest that MOOC participants do not see the courses as a credible alternative to campus-based education. Instead, they may simply be viewed as a fun way to participate in education for self-development and social interaction rather than an opportunity to gain employment or career advancement skills. As a result, MOOCs are unlikely to provide all of the benefits associated with traditional universities and are an unproven entity in the workplace because their value has yet to be established. Indeed, John Tammy of Forbes.com questions the value of all forms of online education describing it as a bubble waiting to burst. He points out that students enrol in traditional universities to access the brand and network rather than actual educational content. He cites Princeton as an example asserting that neither employers nor students care about what is learned there. Rather it is about buying status and the 'right' friends (Tammy, 2013).

While xMOOCs are still in an experimental phase with some significant investments yet to yield a return, Georgia Institute of Technology is about to test this proposition by offering a new Master's level computer science degree where all units that make up that programme will be delivered as MOOCs. A traditional Master's degree in computer science at this institution currently costs in excess of US$43,000 but this programme is to be offered for US$6,600 (Kahn,

2013). Consequently, the programme will provide additional insights into the potential of MOOCs to deliver a full credit-bearing programme at a price point that relies on economies of scale to provide a reasonable return on investment. At the same time this trial will show whether a new consumer segment can be accessed and whether lowering prices for this programme will allow the institution to create a sustainable business. Thus we are likely to see whether xMOOCs do indeed fit with Christensen's (1997) definition of a disruptive innovation.

The potential of MOOCs in the democratization of tourism and hospitality education

From a tourism and hospitality education perspective xMOOCs could play a vital capacity-building role. For example the United Nations World Tourism Organization (UNWTO) has singled out tourism higher education as a means to improve the competitiveness of tourism businesses and the regions in which those businesses are located (Ayikoru et al., 2009). As a result, localized tourism education can deliver significant employment opportunities as well as economic benefits for developing countries.

Moreover, skill shortages have become a major challenge within the industry in many countries. For example a recent report into the tourism and hospitality labour force in Australia found that 35,800 jobs in the sector remained unfilled in 2011 (DeLoitte Access Economics, 2011) and there are also shortages in many developing countries. This is becoming a critical issue in those countries where tourism is a major contributor to GDP because it has a detrimental impact on the capacity of these countries to achieve international standards and therefore to develop as world-class destinations. In Malaysia, for example, the hospitality and tourism sector was ranked second after manufacturing in terms of its overall economic contribution in 2011 and is critical to that country's aspirations to be a fully developed country by 2020 (Hassan, 2008; O'Mahony et al., 2011; Tourism Malaysia, 2012).

As noted in Chapter 1, there has been a global call for a paradigm shift in hospitality and tourism education and for the balance of higher order knowledge and vocational skills within hospitality and tourism programmes to be re-examined to better reflect the challenges faced by practitioners. The general view is that the curriculum within higher education institutions should provide a more holistic experience while at the same time being cognizant of industry needs. It is possible to design a programme where MOOCs develop the higher order knowledge required by reflective industry practitioners. For example Tribe's (2002) philosophical practitioner education (PPE) provides a useful structure to capitalize on the benefits of MOOCs. This PPE framework shows how both liberal and vocational elements can coexist within the curriculum and how the tourism and hospitality curriculum can be constructed with various ends in mind, for example employability outcomes versus freedom of thought. Tourism and hospitality higher education programmes, however, are diverse and often contextualized based on their main discipline area, for example arts, science or business. As a result, students must tackle a core group of subjects within the main discipline which are sometimes only tangentially linked to the study of tourism or hospitality, such as a series of science subjects combined with a major in hospitality or tourism. It is proposed that this requirement to provide coverage in discipline areas that are often unrelated to tourism and hospitality is crowding curriculum space, diluting the curriculum and may indeed be negatively impacting tourism programme demand. Moreover, the development of vocational skills within a higher educational environment is often unrealistic, poorly taught and lacks industry relevance. For example the author has observed instances within on-campus training restaurants where 15 students were endeavouring to develop waiting skills with four or five customers, which is hardly a realistic experience.

Using Tribe's (2002) PPE as a framework guided by Dredge *et al.*'s (2012) prescription that includes knowledge, skills, sense of being and practical wisdom, universities could employ MOOCs to develop a curriculum that progressively builds the liberal, reflective skills required to provide the critical, inquiring mindset that would allow graduates to engage effectively within the tourism and hospitality industry. Broad-based liberal studies that stimulate reflection on the 'social, cultural and psychological effects at the point of destination'(Theuns & Rasheed 1983: 45) should be included, so that graduates understand the wider community benefits of tourism (Ateljevic, 2009; Caton, 2012; Dredge *et al.*, 2012; Higgins-Desbiolles, 2006). As the programme progresses, the occupational skills noted by Lashley (2013), such as human resource management, finance and operations management, along with consumer behaviour. service quality, customer satisfaction and research methods could be introduced using real-world problems, case studies and industry projects to focus and refine critical thinking skills. These would add to the social and communication skills that are developed in those online learning environments that employ Salmon's (2011) five-stage model and thus empower students to tackle specific emerging challenges in tourism and hospitality.

As noted by Tribe (2002) and Dredge *et al.* (2012), the optimum hospitality and tourism curriculum should also include a variety of elements that are located within the vocational domain and generally comprise industry-related competencies. Universities rely on practical training, often in simulated environments such as training restaurants, to develop a number of these competencies. However, many of these types of skills are dependent on repetition in order to develop proficiency. Examples include checking guests in via a front of house computer package or carrying three or more plates to a table. It is arguable whether non-contextual exposure to short stints of vocational training in a simulated educational environment can provide these skills and, if so, whether those skills can be retained until after graduation when students enter the workplace.

There are more efficacious ways to develop reflective, philosophic practitioners (Schön, 1983; Tribe, 2002). For example vocational competencies could simply be learned within industry where continual exposure to best practice will ensure their proper embedding. Practical industry experience in the form of work placements or internships is a key component of many hospitality and tourism higher education programmes and previous studies have shown that these placements are considered to be vital to students' overall educational development (O'Mahony *et al.*, 2001). These work placements involve coordination between universities and industry partners and it is proposed that this existing framework could be extended. That is, the theoretically based, liberal studies curriculum outlined above could be supported by a university-supervised cadetship or apprenticeship model designed to supplement the cognitive, higher order skills developed using MOOCs. This concept could also be implemented under existing university structures in tourism and hospitality education and would answer the consistent calls for curriculum relevance related to the graduate outcomes that are designed to prepare graduates to work in the industry (Lashley, 2013). It could be further developed along the lines of teacher training models where teachers are placed within schools as part of their educational studies and these placements could be supported by integrative online assessment.

There are also a number of other benefits that would accrue from this type of programme. First, there are benefits to working while studying. That is this mode of study can provide immediacy in terms of integrating the theory learned in the MOOC programme within the workplace. It can provide a capacity-building role within developing countries by having available workers progressively increasing their skills within the industry supported by an internationally oriented programme of study that assists the industry to achieve international standards. It can assist employers to develop realistic career paths based on progression within the programme and thereby reduce skill shortages. At the same time students would save on the costs of overseas travel and accommodation as well as the opportunity costs of leaving their communities for several years to achieve their educational goals. Difficulties with obtaining student visas would be overcome and the loss of knowledge that occurs when some students choose to remain overseas after their studies would be stemmed.

It would also have benefits for universities. For example declining government revenue in many western countries has led to the introduction of, or increase in, university fees for local students. In the UK this has led to a 13 per cent decline in enrolment numbers between 2012 and 2013 (Brown, 2013). While there is an established link between education and economic performance (OECD, 2012) at present increasing enrolments are reported to be associated with emerging economies where rising populations and economic growth have increased demand for education (Brown, 2013). The model curriculum presented here seeks to capitalize on this demand while presenting a holistic educational experience in a curriculum that 'acknowledge[s] the different drivers influencing the curriculum space and higher education institutions, and the diverse demands of industry and communities for different skills sets' (Dredge et al., 2012: 2161). In this way the values and input of a wide range of stakeholders can be more fully reflected in the tourism and hospitality curriculum.

Conclusion

Within the current neoliberal, managerial approach to public sector spending (Marginson & Considine, 2000; Ayikoru et al., 2009) rationalization has increased the need for industry relevance within tourism and hospitality programmes. At the same time there have been consistent calls for the inclusion of a liberal studies framework in both tourism and hospitality curricula with a strong socio-cultural, ethical emphasis (Ateljevic, 2009; Caton 2012; Lashley & Morrison, 2000; Morrison & O'Mahony, 2003).

This chapter proposes a model curriculum that employs MOOCs as a key component in achieving a balanced curriculum that distinguishes between liberal and vocational ends (Tribe, 2002). More specifically, it is proposed that theoretical, liberal studies should be provided by universities using MOOCs to improve access for students with an emphasis on students from developing countries. In this scenario MOOCs provide the educational architecture to support a developmental curriculum that, when coupled with the vocational elements of industry-based training, can provide a holistic and rounded education. In the proposed model, liberal and vocational learning outcomes could be achieved, while the needs of employers and communities could be incorporated into curriculum design. In this way MOOCs can have a deep and meaningful impact on poverty alleviation within developing countries and the broader benefits to society noted earlier can be realized.

While xMOOCs currently provide the most appropriate platform to achieve these goals, it is suggested that if financial gain were sublimated in favour of the dissemination of knowledge in a free and open manner, then MOOCs could indeed become emancipatory and provide a valuable and effective pathway towards the democratization of tourism and hospitality education. Within this framework MOOCs have the potential to restore education to its position as a moral, social imperative and a public good.

References

Airey, D. (2005). 'Growth and Development'. In D. Airey & J. Tribe (Eds.). *An International Handbook of Tourism Education* (pp. 13–24). Oxford: Elsevier.

Airey, D., & Tribe, J. (2000). 'Education for Hospitality'. In C. Lashley & A. Morrison (Eds.), *In Search of Hospitality: theoretical perspectives and debates* (pp. 276–91). Oxford: Butterworth-Heinemann.

Ateljevic, I. (2009). 'Transmodernity: remaking our (tourism) world?'. In J. Tribe (Ed.), *Philosophical Issues in Tourism* (pp. 278–300). Bristol: Channel View.

Ayikoru, M., Tribe, J., & Airey, D. (2009). 'Reading Tourism Education: neoliberalism unveiled'. *Annals of Tourism Research*, 36(2), 191–221.

Bower, J. L., & Christensen, C. M. (1995). 'Disruptive Technologies: catching the wave'. *Harvard Business Review* (January–February). Available: http://hbr.org/1995/01/disruptive-technologies-catching-the-wave/ (Accessed 13 September 2013).

Brown, S. (2013). 'Back to the Future with MOOCs?'. *Proceedings of the ICICTE Conference*. Available: http://www.icicte.org/Proceedings2013/Papers%202013/06-3-Brown.pdf (Accessed 13 September 2013).

Caton, K. (2012). 'Taking the Moral Turn in Tourism'. *Annals of Tourism Research*, 39(4), 1906–28.

Christensen, C. M. (1997). *The Innovator's Dilemma: when new technologies cause great firms to fail*. Cambridge, MA: Harvard Business Press.

Daniel, J. (2012). 'Making Sense of MOOCs: musings in a maze of myth, paradox and possibility'. *Journal of Interactive Media in Education*, Single paper issue, 1–22.

DeLoitte Access Economics. (2011). *Australian Tourism Labour Force*, Canberra: Australian Government Publishing Service.

Downes, S. (2009). *New Technology Supporting Informal Learning*. Available: http://halfanhour.blogspot.com/2009/04/ (Accessed 12 July 2013).

Dredge, D., Benckendorff, P., Day, M., Gross, M. J., Walo, M., Weeks, P., & Whitelaw, P. (2012). 'The Philosophic Practitioner and the Curriculum Space'. *Annals of Tourism Research*, 39(4), 2154–76.

Fidgeon, P. R. (2010). 'Tourism Education and Curriculum Design: a time for consolidation and review?'. *Tourism Management*, 31(6), 699–723.

Gregory, J., & Salmon, G. (2013). 'Professional Development for Online University Teaching'. *Distance Education,* 34(3), 256–70.

Hassan, A. M. (2008). *To Build and to Demolish Malaysia. Strategic Information and Research Development Centre (SIRD)*. Selangor: Vinlin Press.

Higgins-Desbiolles, F. (2006). 'More than an "Industry": the forgotten power of tourism as a social force'. *Tourism Management*, 27, 1192–208.

Illich, I. (1971). *Deschooling Society*, New York: Harper & Row.

Kahn, G. (2013). 'The MOOC that Roared: how Georgia Tech's new, super-cheap online Master's degree could radically change American higher education'. Available: http://www.slate.com/articles/technology/technology/2013/07/georgia_tech_s_computer_science_mooc_the_super_cheap_master_s_degree_that.html (Accessed 25 July 2013).

Kuhn, T.S. (1962). *The Structure of Scientific Revolutions*. Chicago, IL: University of Chicago Press.

Lashley, C. (2013). 'Managing the Tyranny of Relevance: linking with industry but not too much! *Worldwide Hospitality and Tourism Themes,* 5(3), 283–95.

Lashley, C., & Morrison, A. (2000). *In Search of Hospitality: theoretical perspectives and debates*. Oxford: Butterworth-Heinemann.

Lewin, W. (2012). 'Universities Reshaping Education on the Web'. *New York Times,* 17 July.

McIntosh, W. (1983). 'Tourism Education: a model university curriculum in tourism'. *Tourism Management*, June, 135–7.

Marginson, S., & Considine, M. (2000). *The Enterprise University: power governance and reinvention in Australia*. Cambridge: Cambridge University Press.

Morrison, A., & O'Mahony, G. B. (2003). 'The Liberation of Hospitality Management Education'. *International Journal of Contemporary Hospitality Management*, 15(1), 38–44.

Nailon, P. (1982). 'Theory in Hospitality Management'. *Journal of Hospitality Management*, 1(3), 135–43.

O'Mahony, B. (2009). 'University Kitchen Nightmares Enter a New ERA'. *Hospitality Review*, 11(4), 5–8.

O'Mahony, B., Lahap, J., & Sillitoe, J. (2011). 'The Development of a Service Delivery Model for the Malaysian Hotel Sector: a focus on developing, formulating, synthesising and refining a new model'. *Journal of Tourism, Hospitality and Culinary Arts*, 3(1), 1–24.

O'Mahony, G. B., & Sillitoe, J. F. (2001). 'Identifying the Perceived Barriers to Participation in Tertiary Courses among Hospitality Employees'. *International Journal of Contemporary Hospitality Management*, 13(1), 21–9.

O'Mahony, G. B., McWilliams, A., & Whitelaw, P. (2001). 'Why Students Choose a Hospitality-Degree Program: an Australian case study'. *Cornell Hotel Restaurant and Administration Quarterly,* 42(1), 92–6.

Organization for Economic Cooperation and Development (OECD) (2012). *Education at a Glance 2012: highlights,* OECD Publishing. Available: *http://dx.doi.org/10.1787/eag_highlights-2012-en* (Accessed 4 July 2014).

Peters, R. S. (1966). *Ethics and Education,* 5th edn. London: George Allen & Unwin.

Salmon, G. (2011). *E-moderating: the key to teaching and learning online,* 3rd edn. London: Routledge.

Salmon, G. (2013). *E-tivities: the key to active online learning,* 2nd edn. London: Routledge.

Schön, D. (1983). *The Reflective Practitioner.* New York: Basic Books.

Shaughnessy, M. F., & Fulgham, S. (2011). *Pedagogical Models: the discipline of teaching online.* New York: Nova Science.

Siemens, G. (2006). 'Connectivism: learning theory or pastime of the self amused?'. Available: http://www.elearnspace.org/Articles/connectivism_self-amused.htm (Accessed 4 July 2013).

Slattery, P. (2002). 'Finding the Hospitality Industry'. *Journal of Hospitality, Leisure, Sport and Tourism Education,* 1(1), 6–12.

Tammy, J. (2013). *Sorry Left and Right, No Job Requires a College Degree.* Available: http://www.forbes.com/sites/johntamny/2013/02/10/sorry-left-and-right-no-job-requires-a-college-degree/ (Accessed 7 June 2013).

Teplechuk, E. (2013). 'Emergent Models of Massive Open Online Courses: an exploration of sustainable practices for MOOC institutions in the context of the launch of MOOCs at the University of Edinburgh'. Unpublished MBA Thesis, University of Edinburgh.

Theuns, H. L., & Rasheed, A. (1983). 'Alternative Approaches to Tourism Education with Special Reference to Developing Countries'. *Tourism Management,* March, 42–51.

Tourism Malaysia (2012*). Tourism Report. Malaysian Tourism Promotion Board.* Available: http://corporate.tourism.gov.my/ (Accessed 16 January 2013).

Tribe, J. (2002). 'The Philosophic Practitioner'. *Annals of Tourism Research,* 29(2), 338–57.

Wood, R.W. (2013). 'Hospitality Management Education: themes, trends and issues'. In R. Wood (Ed.), *Key Concepts in Hospitality Management* (pp. 127–32). Thousand Oaks, CA: Sage.

11

Educational mobilities
Mobile students, mobile knowledge

Kevin Hannam
International Centre for Research in Events, Tourism &
Hospitality (ICRETH), Leeds Metropolitan University, UK

Basagaitz Guereño-Omil
Department of Tourism, University of Deusto, Bilbao, Spain

Introduction

Students travel. As part of their curriculum they frequently go on field trips to a broad range of international destinations. They travel on gap years as backpackers and they travel in search of, and to develop, their identities as volunteers. Students are thus a very mobile section of society (Duke-Williams, 2009). Be it emigrating to another country for an entire course, a shorter period abroad as a segment of their studies, a gap year travelling or working abroad, studying within a different region within their own country or studying locally within their country of origin and having to tackle the daily mobilities this entails, all contribute to the growing complexities of student life (Bhandari & Laughlin, 2009; Duke-Williams, 2009; Holdsworth, 2009). Holdsworth (2009: 1852) adds that '[s]tudents are constantly on the move: between halls; from place of residence (which may be halls of residence, privately rented accommodation, or parental home) to campus; as well as from "home" to university'. She goes on to argue that local students' mobility patterns are much more extreme than those who move region or country and that they are often trivialized by policy makers who state that 'going to HE [Higher Education] was . . . the same as going to school or college, all that was different was that they caught a different bus' (Holdsworth, 2009: 1860).

To travel as part of education has been recognized by most cultures around the world and was an integral part of the Grand Tour. Brodsky-Porges (1981) noted that the French writer Montaigne in the 1500s argued that students needed 'some direct adventuring with the world, a steady and lively interplay with common folk, supplemented and fortified with trips abroad'. Tourism students tend to travel more than most as it is frequently an integral part of their curriculum, on modules or to conduct research for a dissertation. They are also encouraged to take part in wider tours to enrich their experiences so as to become more employable – with some extreme cases such as Arizona State University owning cruise ships to take their students around the world. This chapter thus examines this phenomenon from a mobilities perspective, as these educational 'tours' and exchanges cannot be simply seen as a form of tourism but are intimately related to wider forces of international mobility in the twenty-first century.

The chapter outlines the significance of the mobilities paradigm as a framework for understanding both students' movements across international borders in search of innovative educational experiences and the internationalization of the tourism and hospitality curriculum through international exchange programmes. It thus analyses the movement of students in terms of linkages with other forms of mobility such as migration as well as the movement of ideas across international borders. It is widely assumed that these forms of international mobility are a 'passport' to mobility capital and enhanced employability prospects as demonstrated by numerous universities' marketing initiatives (Holdsworth, 2009). Nevertheless, through a discussion of the experiences of Erasmus exchanges from a UK perspective, it is argued that student educational travel experiences remain a valuable source of mobility capital. It is concluded that greater research into the lifestyle mobilities of students are needed as well as evaluations of international curricula as the structures of knowledge become more mobile. Moreover, developments in social media may enhance and replace some but not all of contemporary students' international educational mobilities in the future.

Tourism and educational mobilities

The study of tourism has often been seen as on the periphery of the social sciences, but the mobilities paradigm arguably allows us to place travel and tourism at the core of social and cultural life rather than at the margins (Franklin & Crang, 2001; Coles & Hall, 2006). From this perspective, tourism mobilities are viewed as being bound up with both everyday and mundane journeys as well as with the more exotic encounters that have been the mainstay of much analysis in contemporary tourism. From a mobilities perspective, tourism is seen as integral to wider processes of economic and political development processes and even constitutive of everyday life (Franklin & Crang, 2001; Coles & Hall, 2006; Edensor, 2007; Hannam & Knox, 2010).

It is not just that tourism is a form of mobility like other forms of mobility such as commuting or migration but that different mobilities inform and are informed by tourism (Sheller & Urry, 2004). Thus we need to continually examine the multiple mobilities in any situation: mobilities involve the movement of people but also the movement of a whole range of material things as well as the movement of thoughts and ideas – including educational ones (see Williams, 2006; Allen-Robertson & Beer, 2010). In short, proponents of the mobilities paradigm argue that the concept of mobilities is concerned with mapping and understanding both the large-scale movements of people, objects, capital and information across the world, as well as the more local processes of daily transportation, movement through public space, and the travel of tangible and intangible things within everyday life simultaneously (Sheller & Urry, 2006; Hannam et al., 2006).

A great deal of mobilities research has analysed forms and experiences of so-called 'corporeal' travel. This involves the travel of people for work, leisure, family life, migration and, indeed, education, organized in terms of contrasting time–space modalities (ranging from daily commuting to attend university or a once-in-a-lifetime round-the-world trip). For example Colin Symes (2007) has examined the corporeal choreographies of students' commuting practices in Sydney, Australia, while Holly Thorpe (2012) has researched the transnational mobilities of students involved in the global snowboarding industry. Other recent work has also considered how the technologies of travel have led to new cultural forms, including new cultural identities and subjectivities as students travel as part of the New Zealand overseas experience (OE) (Conradson & Latham, 2007; Haverig, 2011).

Political, technological, financial and transportational changes have been critical in significantly lowering the mobility barriers for many but not for all – as contemporary work on social tourism has shown (McCabe, 2009). Indeed many students face problems of immobility – Christopher Harker's (2009) research with students at the Birzeit University in Palestine examines how their experiences of university are shaped by a range of im/mobilities. In particular he shows how students who rent accommodation in Birzeit experience a range of im/mobilities that are heavily impacted by technologies and practices of the Israeli Occupation Forces that are designed to render Palestinians less mobile in the West Bank. Waters (2012: 123) furthermore has suggested that: 'international education entrenches (and in some cases, within emerging economies, actively creates) social inequalities' thus reinforcing immobilities.

Barker *et al.* (2009) meanwhile make a call for more research which examines younger people's mobilities. This call has been taken up in the UK educational context, in particular by Brooks and Waters (2010, 2011). They argue that 'while internationally mobile students are clearly only a subset of the broader category of transnational migrants, they nevertheless demonstrate important ways in which mobility is often socially-embedded, grounded within networks of both family and friends' (Brooks and Waters, 2010: 143). This is illustrated in the following discussion through an examination of student mobility in terms of the Erasmus mobility programme.

Mobile students in Europe

Although there is still a plurality of national higher education systems across Europe, since 1999 the Bologna Process has endorsed the concept of creating a more coherent and transparent European approach to higher education development, making the 'university qualifications more easily comparable' (Keeling, 2006: 207) and becoming jointly more globally competitive and attractive for students and scholars worldwide. By creating a European Higher Education Area (EHEA) the Bologna Process makes operative the academic mobility of students and staff at a transnational level (Eurydice, 2010), mainly since it fosters the European Credit Transfer and Accumulation System (ECTS), the same credit system used in the Erasmus exchange scheme (Bologna Declaration, 1999), whereby the European Commission 'specifically promotes European curricular dimensions' (Barkholt, 2006: 26).

Erasmus mobilities

Erasmus is the European Union's (EU) flagship mobility programme in education and training and one of the best-known EU-level actions. The programme is named after the philosopher, theologian and humanist Erasmus of Rotterdam (1465–1536), known as an opponent of dogmatism. The acronym Erasmus may also be read as EuRopean Community Action Scheme for the Mobility of University Students. It was established in 1987 and since then has enabled more than two million students from across Europe to pursue learning experiences in other countries.

Erasmus partnerships generally involve two European universities signing a collaboration agreement to send and receive staff and students of the partner university, and, more recently, also to offer the opportunity for students to train in enterprises. Student mobility tends to be for a semester while staff mobility tends to be for rather shorter periods such as a few days. There are of course variations on this. Encouraging such mobility has been a core aim of the EU since its inception and has been an integral part of fostering its ideology of European-ness. The Green Paper published by the European Commission (2009: 2) lies within this framework;

its title *Promoting the Learning Mobility of Young People* highlights the growing importance of mobility in learning both for students, 'as students access new knowledge and develop new linguistic skills and intercultural competences', and for educational establishments, as they make them 'more open, more European and international, more accessible and efficient'.

The aim is to promote a type of mobility that we might characterize as:

- Organized: 'mobility should be linked to specific learning outcomes and lead to the attainment of qualifications, credits and/or professional qualifications'.
- European: 'deals with mobility between the countries currently participating in EU programmes'.
- Transnational: 'on the basis that a move to another country is likely to be more challenging and enriching'.
- Within sectors: 'from the world of education to the world of business and vice-versa; from education to voluntary action; from vocational training to academia, from public research bodies to business'.
- Physical: 'while recognizing also the value of virtual mobility'.
- Young people: 'the main cohort envisaged would be 16–35 year olds'.

For the individual, however, it has long been assumed that such educational travel adds critical social and economic value and thus enhances social mobility, mobility capital and employability (Brooks & Waters, 2010). From the EHEA perspective, mobility is widely being perceived 'in terms of a voluntary decision, of a horizontal basis and of cultural, social and economic enhancement both for the individual and for society' (Teichler & Jahr, 2001: 444). Studies have demonstrated that students who have benefited from the Erasmus programme are more likely to move after their studies (Teichler, 1996) and highlighted a rapid expansion in measures of formal standardization for facilitating recognition of academic mobility (Teichler, 2004). In terms of the consequences of the Erasmus grant on future mobility and job prospects, it has also been argued that the experience brings the opportunity of gaining better skills, both study-related and interpersonal-related skills (Teichler, 1996; Bracht *et al.*, 2006). Bracht *et al.* (2006: 16) argue that:

> The university leaders rate the former ERASMUS students' career opportunities most favourably, and most of them expect that their career advantage will increase in the future. Four fifth[s] believe that a study abroad often increases the chance of getting a reasonable job. More than half expect that ERASMUS students more often than non-mobile students get a position appropriate to their level of educational attainment, and one quarter that ERASMUS has a more positive impact on the employability of graduates than any other type of study abroad.

However, it has not been clear what the impact of Erasmus has had on the students' later careers. If you do an Erasmus exchange it is widely assumed that you become more European, gain more mobility capital and become more employable. But whether this is actually true has yet to be really verified: 'academics, students, and parents take mobility for granted rather than question the validity of the assumption on which it is based' (Holdsworth, 2009: 1861). The identification of whether Erasmus has really enhanced the employability of the students after Erasmus has become a priority in the current economic climate of Europe.

From a mobilities perspective, while 'brain drain' and 'brain gain' are well-known concepts, research is showing a more complex picture (Rivza & Teichler, 2007). Some students and researchers are increasingly interested in earning multiple degrees in multiple countries, before perhaps returning to their home countries after 8–12 years of international study and work experience; hence, the emergence of the mobility terms 'brain trair.' and 'brain circulation'. These concepts present benefits, risks and new challenges for both sending and receiving countries (Knight, 2011: 237).

There are also economic constraints to the sending and receiving of Erasmus students as many university heads in the UK bemoan the fact that the UK is a net receiver of students. In terms of Erasmus mobility, the latest data from the European Commission show that Spain is the most popular country in terms of both destination and origin of students (Education and Culture DG, 2011). The top countries sending students within the programme in 2009/10 were Spain (31,158 students, taking the top of the ranking over France), followed by France, Germany, Italy and Poland. The picture is quite similar in terms of destinations, which is Spain (receiving 35,386 students), followed again by France, the UK, Germany and Italy. The main difference is the place of the UK, which although it does not have a relevant space in terms of outgoing students, it does constitute a main receiving country, at third place in 2010/11 as Figure 11.1 shows.

Erasmus exchanges are also about leisure opportunities and there are many examples of students engaging in the programme to have what has been called in the USA a 'Spring Break experience' – visiting another European destination for a couple of months to engage in hedonistic consumption. Prague even has its own Erasmus theme nights (see Figure 11.2).

The UK context

Starting with student mobility more generally within the UK itself, it has long been the tradition within the UK that students moving into higher education leave the region of their parental

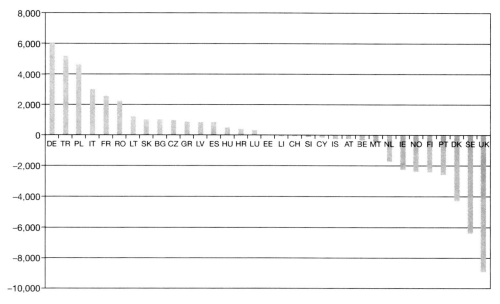

Figure 11.1 Net result of Erasmus student mobility for studies by country (2010/11)
Source: Authors, based upon European Commission data.

Figure 11.2 Erasmus socialization

Source: http://metropartyprague.com/event/mad-mad-erasmus-mondays/ (Reproduced with permission).

home and study at a higher education institution (HEI) elsewhere – 'going away to uni'. In recent years, while there is evidence of a shift to more students studying locally, nevertheless, there are still significant numbers of students choosing HEI's in other regions of the UK (Holdsworth, 2009; Patiniotis & Holdsworth, 2005). This form of localism versus mobility has strengthened and increased the two-tier system within HEIs (Holdsworth, 2009) between 'the "affluent movers" and the "disadvantaged stayers"' (Smith, 2009: 1801). Indeed, some universities are working hard to remove the barriers to student mobility and it is apparent that students wish to study away from their region of origin; however, 'it is also apparent that financial considerations will be the number one factor limiting student mobility' (Bhandari and Laughlin, 2009: ix). This issue was also identified by other researchers who concluded that students are worried about their levels of debt and how they are going to make the repayments.

There are many incentives to studying at a HEI away from home. However, many argue that these incentives are merely perceived, rather than actually being realized (Holdsworth, 2009). Despite this, Holdsworth (2009: 1862) has argued that, 'whether or not students actually benefit from moving away in the ways that are popularly portrayed, the fact that these assumptions are so credible means that students who move away can rely on promoting personal qualities that are assumed to derive from their particular mobility experiences'. Popular discourse about going to university epitomizes the preconceived notion that all students have a choice of which HEI they wish to attend, with university promotional material being a huge factor: 'University prospectuses promote their locality as well as the institution, thus incorporating the assumption that mobile undergraduates have a choice about location' and 'as such, the experiences of students taking different paths to university, which do not involve mobility, are excluded from popular images of going to university' (Holdsworth, 2009: 1849).

Duke-Williams (2009: 1827) further argues that 'students who remain at their parental home during the course of their studies may have different future mobility propensities to those who have moved away from home'. Due to the increased financial burden of studying, more and more students are having to undertake paid employment with 'more than half . . . working more than the guideline set by most universities of 15 hours a week', and unsurprisingly, 'students from poorer backgrounds are much more likely to work than are those from middle-class households' (Munro et al., 2009: 1815). Therefore, local students are doubly disadvantaged over their more mobile counterparts.

As universities are becoming more diversified in their student population, many first-generation students from disadvantaged backgrounds are beginning to attend HE. Their 'daily mobility of travelling to university represents a more radical displacement than students travelling daily from "studentland" or halls of residence, (or moving on a termly basis between "home" and university)' (Holdsworth, 2009: 1860). After graduating from university, students who are not returning to HE for a higher level degree face a number of options, including returning to their 'home' town or country (if they moved in the first place), staying in the locality where they studied, or moving to find an altogether new location (Duke-Williams, 2009: 1826).

As far as Erasmus is concerned, although UK universities tend to have a policy of one student out, one student in, in practice overall this relation is approximately one outgoing student to two incoming students. In terms of evolution in the last decade, the Erasmus outgoing number has increased by 157 per cent with a total of 11,724 Erasmus students recorded in the 2009/10 academic year (British Council, 2011). Figure 11.3 shows that the relation between outgoing and incoming students is not balanced currently, although while the trend shows an increase in both cases, between 2004/5 and 2009/10 the outgoing figure increased just over 50 per cent while between 2004/5 and 2008/9 the number of incoming students increased by 29 per cent.

Data gathered by the British Council shows that for UK Erasmus students France is the most popular destination, constituting the country of destination of almost 33 per cent of the students. Spain constitutes the second destination country, with almost 23 per cent (which contradicts the general picture of mobility, Spain followed by France), followed by Germany, Italy and the Netherlands. In terms of subject areas, Erasmus mobility in the UK is led mainly by language students, which constitute more than half of total Erasmus students (3,079 out of 7,437 to study and 2,161 out of 3,406 for work placements in the study period 2008/2009). Language and Philology is the subject which, not surprisingly, also sent most students abroad.

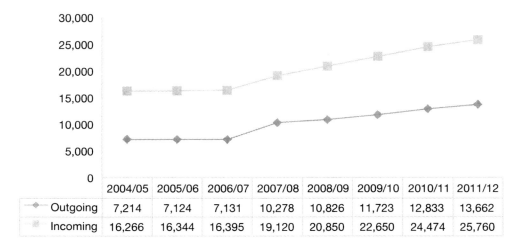

	2004/05	2005/06	2006/07	2007/08	2008/09	2009/10	2010/11	2011/12
Outgoing	7,214	7,124	7,131	10,278	10,826	11,723	12,833	13,662
Incoming	16,266	16,344	16,395	19,120	20,850	22,650	24,474	25,760

Figure 11.3 Erasmus mobility for the UK (2004–12)
Source: Authors, created from European Commission data.

This is followed (although not closely) by Business Studies and Management Sciences (977 students in 2008/2009), Law (705), Social Sciences (700) and Art and Design (517). In terms of the geographical distribution, London is one of the most popular destinations for EU students who chose the UK as an Erasmus destination, with other locations such as Glasgow, Leeds, Manchester, Nottingham and Sheffield following. Places matter, as the students on these exchanges seek destinations with significant leisure provision. Nevertheless, increasingly it is not just students who are on the move as we shall see below in our discussion of the mobile curricula.

Mobile knowledge

We began this chapter by stating that students travel, although not all students travel due to a range of financial and political constraints. At the same time, education and knowledge themselves are also travelling. Ideas and educational curricula are all on the move, as we see by the growth in international and transnational educational developments. This has led to the building of new physical infrastructure such as campuses by universities from one country in another country, the transfer of staff from one country to another for short and longer periods of time, developments in terms of an internationalization of curricula with programmes being transferred from one place to another, the forging of numerous public–private partnerships following neoliberal economic models and the increasing use of new technologies to maintain these partnerships and allow the movement of ideas.

From a mobilities perspective it is significant to consider this in terms of the mobility of ideas: 'By looking at the mobility of ideas we are, as Tarde has put it, focusing upon the movement of the "flickering flame" of the single mind to a more "brilliant illumination" (Tarde, 1899/2000: 86) as ideas spread across a contemporary mediascape' (Allen-Robertson & Beer, 2010: 530). They go on to argue that 'new media resources . . . have remediated the flow of ideas leading to new possibilities, ranges and accumulations' (2010: 530). The movement of ideas has also been facilitated by processes of digitalization and archiving. The movement of ideas in terms of knowledge per se has long been divided between tacit and explicit knowledge (Polanyi, 1966). Tacit knowledge is seen as being person- and context-specific: more than can be expressed in words; while explicit knowledge is that which is transmittable in formal and systematic ways (via curricula for example).

Williams (2006) develops this further by building on Blackler's (2002) knowledge typology: embrained knowledge, dependent on conceptual skills and cognitive abilities; embodied knowledge, resulting from experiences of physical presence; encultured knowledge, emphasizing shared meanings arising from socialization and acculturation; embedded knowledge, in different language systems (organizational) cultures and (work) groups; and encoded knowledge in the signs and symbols to be found in traditional forms such as books, manuals, as well as new forms such as websites:

> Encoded knowledge is the most mobile form. In contrast, tacit knowledge is inherently less mobile because it cannot be fully articulated through documented (i.e., codified), and possibly even through verbal, forms, but is learned through experience. . . . Embrained and embodied knowledge are necessarily indivisible from the individual, and so are fully transferable via corporeal mobility. . . . In contrast, encultured and embedded knowledge represent relational knowledge, grounded in the institutionally specific relationships between individuals . . . [and are] only partly transferable through corporeal mobility.
>
> (Williams, 2006: 591)

Such movement of knowledge is increasingly significant but also place-dependent and requires physical infrastructure to become embedded. As a result many universities have been building new International Branch Campuses (IBCs) in other countries. IBCs evidence the increasing use of public–private partnerships in the service of neoliberal economic development goals (see Ayikoru, Chapter 9 in this volume). Countries such as Malaysia and the United Arab Emirates (UAE) are increasingly importing 'well-established institutions [from] countries that attract a large number of international students . . . to aid in improving the host government's education-related reputation and signalling to the world that it is modernizing its economy and its desire to be a regional education hub' (Lane, 2011: 367).

Jane Knight (2010) explains that in many countries that are undergoing economic transition the demand for higher education is increasing due to changing demographics, the shift to lifelong learning, the growth of the knowledge economy and the need for highly skilled workers. While this demand is increasing, the ability of local public higher education providers to supply this education is limited due to resource constraints and is being increasingly satisfied by the incoming IBCs to the extent that it is estimated that by 2025 there will be 7.2 million international students studying at IBCs (Bohm et al., 2002). However, not all IBCs have been successful and a number of major universities have had to withdraw from significant overseas investments. Nevertheless, there has been a shift away from encouraging student mobility, towards programme and provider mobility as well as the increasing use of new technologies to create 'virtual' campuses.

Virtual campuses have become common with many universities opening up virtual branches on sites such as Second Life, but much of the initial hype surrounding virtual learning was unrealistic and led to some high-profile failures. As Cartelli et al. (2008: 122–3) argue: 'If eLearning and virtual campus initiatives are to be sustainable then it is vital that stakeholders understand how new models of teaching and learning transform the institution and how they can be used to enhance knowledge construction, flexibility, and inclusiveness.' A major recent development in this have been Massive Open Online Courses (MOOCs), which provide informal higher education learning experiences without the formal accreditation of a degree programme (see

O'Mahony and Salmon, Chapter 10 in this volume). A key aim of these online courses, however, is to inspire many more students to seek the accreditation of a formal degree.

Moreover, the integration of Web 2.0 has transformed the online learning experience for many students. Key elements in a Web 2.0 educational design are interaction, joint creation of content, critical thinking and collaboration between students and teachers both face to face and online via social media such as discussion forums, blogs and wikis. Liburd and Christensen (2013) provide examples of Web 2.0 learning activities from the INNOTOUR platform, which is a joint platform for students, teachers, businesses and researchers of tourism (see also Liburd, Chapter 22 in this volume).

Conclusion

The chapter has outlined the significance of the mobilities paradigm as a framework for understanding both students' movements across international borders in search of innovative educational experiences and the internationalization of education through the development of partnerships. It thus places the analysis of the movement of students in terms of linkages with other forms of mobility such as migration as well as the movement of ideas across international borders. It is widely assumed that these forms of international mobility are a 'passport' to mobility capital and enhanced employability prospects as demonstrated by numerous universities' marketing initiatives (Holdsworth, 2009). Nevertheless, through a discussion of the experiences of Erasmus exchanges from a UK perspective it has been argued that student educational travel experiences remain a valuable source of mobility capital. It is concluded that greater research into the lifestyle mobilities of students is needed as well as further evaluations of international curricula as the structures of knowledge become more mobile. Developments in social media may enhance and replace some but not all of contemporary students' international educational mobilities in the future.

Acknowledgements

This chapter has benefited from the MERGE collaborative project funded by the European Commission – Grant 518352 –LLP-1-2011-1-UK-ERASMUS-ESMO. Thanks go to the Partners in the MERGE consortium: Itziar Elexpuru, Arantza Arruti, Lourdes Villardón and Alvaro Moro (University of Deusto, Spain), Ala Al-Harmarneh and Felix Schubert (University of Mainz, Germany), Wolfgang Arlt (Internal evaluator, West Coast University, Germany), Pavel Bryla, Tomasz Domanski and Agnieszka Brzękowska (University of Lodz, Poland), Margari León-Guereño and Josu Aranberri (i2basque) and Bob Brown (External evaluator, UK).

References

Allen-Robertson, J., & Beer, D. (2010). 'Mobile Ideas: tracking a concept through time and space'. *Mobilities*, 5(4), 529–45.

Barker, J., Kraftl, P., Horton, J., & Tucker, F. (2009). 'The Road Less Travelled – new directions in children's and young people's mobility'. *Mobilities*, 4(1), 1–10.

Barkholt, K. (2006). 'The Bologna Process and Integration. Theory: convergence and autonomy'. *Higher Education in Europe*, 30(1), 23–9.

Bhandari, R. & Laughlin, S. (Eds.). (2009) *Higher Education on the Move: New Developments in Global Mobility*. New York: Institute for International Education.

Blackler, F. (2002). 'Knowledge, Knowledge Work and Organizations'. In C. W. Choo, & N. Bontis (Eds.), *The Strategic Management of Intellectual Capital and Organizational Knowledge* (pp. 47–62). New York: Oxford University Press.

Bohm, A., Davis, D., Meares, D., & Pearce, B. (2002). *Global Student Mobility 2025: forecasts of the global demand for international higher education.* Tasmania: Media Briefing, IDP Education Australia.

Bologna Declaration. (1999). *The European Higher Education Area: joint declaration of European Ministers of Education convened in Bologna,* 19 June.

Brodsky-Porges, E. (1981). 'The Grand Tour: travel as an educational device, 1500–1800'. *Annals of Tourism Research,* 8(2), 171–86.

Bracht, O., Engel, C., Janson, K., Over, A., Schomburg, H., & Teichler, U. (2006). *The Professional Value of ERASMUS Mobility.* Final Report presented to the European Commission – DG Education and Culture. Brussels: European Commission.

British Council (2011). *British Council Learning.* Available: http://www.britishcouncil.org/erasmus-facts-and-figures.htm (Accessed 31 August 2013).

Brooks, R., & Waters, J. (2010). 'Social Networks and Educational Mobility: the experiences of UK students'. *Globalisation, Societies and Education,* 8(1), 143–57.

Brooks, R., & Waters, J. (2011). *Student Mobilities, Migration and the Internationalization of Higher Education.* New York: Palgrave.

Cartelli, A., Stansfield, M., Connolly, T., Jimoyiannis, A., Magalhães, H., & Maillet, K. (2008). 'Towards the Development of a New Model for Best Practice and Knowledge Construction in Virtual Campuses'. *Journal of Information Technology Education,* 7, 121–34.

Coles, T., & Hall, C. M. (2006). 'Editorial: the geography of tourism is dead. Long live geographies of tourism and mobility', *Current Issues in Tourism,* 9(4–5), 289–92.

Conradson, D., & Latham, A. (2007). 'The Affective Possibilities of London: Antipodean transnationals and the overseas experience', *Mobilities,* 2(2), 231–54.

Duke-Williams, O. (2009). 'The Geographies of Student Migration in the UK'. *Environment and Planning A,* 41(8), 1826–48.

Edensor, T. (2007). 'Mundane Mobilities, performances and spaces of tourism'. *Social & Cultural Geography,* 8(2), 199–215.

Education and Culture DG. (2011). *Erasmus – Facts, Figures & Trends. European Union support of student and staff exchanges and university cooperation in 2009/2010.* Luxembourg: Publications Office of the European Union.

European Commission. (2009). *Green Paper: promoting the learning mobility of young people.* COM 329. Brussels: European Commission.

Eurydice. (2010). *Focus on Higher Education in Europe 2010: the impact of the Bologna Process.* Brussels: European Education, Audiovisual and Culture Executive Agency.

Franklin, A., & Crang, M. (2001). 'The Trouble with Tourism and Travel Theory?'. *Tourist Studies,* 1(1), 5–22.

Hannam, K., & Knox, D. (2010). *Understanding Tourism.* London: Sage.

Hannam, K., Sheller, M., & Urry, J. (2006). 'Editorial: mobilities, immobilities and moorings'. *Mobilities,* 1(1), 1–22.

Harker, C. (2009). 'Student Im/mobility in Birzeit, Palestine'. *Mobilities,* 4(1), 11–35.

Haverig, A. (2011) 'Constructing Global/Local Subjectivities – The New Zealand OE as governance through freedom'. *Mobilities* 6(1), 102–23.

Holdsworth, C. (2009). '"Going Away to Uni": mobility, modernity, and independence of English higher education students'. *Environment and Planning A,* 41(8), 1849–64.

Keeling, R. (2006). 'The Bologna Process and the Lisbon Research Agenda: the European Commission's expanding role in higher education discourse'. *European Journal of Education,* 41(2), 203–23.

Knight, J. (2010). 'Higher Education Crossing Borders: programs and providers on the move'. In D. Johnstone, M. D'Ambrosio, & P. Yakoboski (Eds.), *Higher Education in a Global Society* (pp. 42–69). Cheltenham: Edward Elgar.

Knight, J. (2011). 'Education Hubs: a fad, a brand, an innovation?'. *Journal of Studies in International Education.* 15(3), 221–40.

Lane, J. (2011). 'Importing Private Higher Education: international branch campuses'. *Journal of Comparative Policy Analysis,* 13(4), 367–81.

Liburd, J., & Christensen, I.-M. (2013). 'Using Web 2.0 in Higher Tourism Education'. *Journal of Hospitality, Leisure, Sport & Tourism Education,* 12(1), 99–108.

McCabe, S. (2009). 'Who Needs a Holiday? evaluating social tourism'. *Annals of Tourism Research,* 36(4), 667–88.

Munro, M., Turok, I., & Livingston, M. (2009). 'Students in Cities: a preliminary analysis of their patterns and effects'. *Environment and Planning A*, 41, 1805–25.

Patiniotis, J., & Holdsworth, C. (2005). 'Seize that Chance! Leaving home and transitions to higher education'. *Journal of Youth Studies*, 8(1), 81–95.

Polanyi, M. (1966). *The Tacit Dimension*. London: Routledge and Kegan Paul.

Rivza, B., & Teichler, U. (2007). *The Changing Role of Student Mobility*. UNESCO Forum Occasional Paper Series Paper no. 16. Paris: UNESCO.

Sheller, M., & Urry, J. (Eds.). (2004) *Tourism Mobilities: places to play, places in play*. London: Routledge.

Sheller, M., & Urry, J. (2006). 'The New Mobilities Paradigm'. *Environment and Planning A*, 38(2), 207–26.

Smith, D. (2009). 'Student Geographies, Urban Restructuring, and the Expansion of Higher Education'. *Environment and Planning A*, 41, 1795–804.

Symes, C. (2007). 'Coaching and Training: an ethnography of student commuting on Sydney's suburban trains', *Mobilities*, 2(3), 443–61.

Teichler, U. (1996). 'Student Mobility in the Framework of ERASMUS: findings of an evaluation study'. *European Journal of Education*, 31(2), 153–79.

Teichler, U. (2004). 'The Changing Debate on Internationalisation of Higher Education'. *Higher Education*, 48(1), 5–26.

Teichler, U., & Jahr, V. (2001). 'Mobility during the Course of Study and After Graduation'. *European Journal of Education*, 36(4), 443–58.

Thorpe, H. (2012). 'Transnational Mobilities in Snowboarding Culture: travel, tourism and lifestyle migration'. *Mobilities* 7(2), 317–45.

Waters, J. (2012). 'Geographies of International Education: mobilities and the reproduction of social (dis)advantage'. *Geography Compass*, 6(3), 123–36.

Williams, A. (2006). 'Lost in Translation? International migration, learning and knowledge'. *Progress in Human Geography* 30(5), 588–607.

12

Tourism Education Futures Initiative

Current and future curriculum influences

Pauline J. Sheldon
School of Travel Industry Management, University of Hawaii

Daniel R. Fesenmaier
School of Tourism and Hospitality Management, Temple University, USA

Introduction

Students entering the uncertain world of the future and, in particular, the vulnerable tourism sector, need different skills, aptitudes and knowledge to succeed; and to achieve this goal, educational systems need radical change (Wallis & Steptoe, 2006). A fundamental re-tool and redesign is necessary. No incremental change, but rather change in the nature of what is taught and how it is taught. Skills and knowledge sets must be redefined, structures and assumptions need to be questioned, and the old ways of doing things must be replaced with a programme that actually enables our children to be prepared for a century of challenges. In tourism, employment in the coming decades must have a very different profile than it does today. In 2020 students will be applying for jobs that do not even exist today, and much of what we teach our students is obsolete by the time they graduate. These pressures and the increasing need for responsible stewardship of tourism destinations call out for a new paradigm of values-based tourism education. This chapter will describe the work of the Tourism Education Futures Initiative (TEFI) community. In particular, examples of how the TEFI values have been incorporated into tourism curricula will be described.

TEFI values and principles

The Tourism Education Futures Initiative (TEFI) was established in 2006 by a few concerned tourism educators (Sheldon *et al.*, 2008). They inquired into the need for change and recommended diverse approaches that constitute a framework for a new tourism curriculum. The vision of TEFI is to not only to work to reshape tourism education worldwide, but to

155

help the leaders of the tourism industry follow practices that are rooted in five basic values. For an introduction to TEFI, please see our website: www.tourismeducationfutures.org. The first TEFI meeting was held in 2007 at Modul University Vienna, Austria, to discuss the status of tourism education and to assess whether there was consensus on the need to develop alternative models for tourism education. During this meeting, a process emerged that is both proactive and action-oriented to create a fundamental change in tourism education. The TEFI process includes an annual conference and working groups, which move the TEFI agenda forward between conferences. Importantly, the working groups provide essential energy and direction resulting in the development of concrete action-oriented tools that can be used by tourism educators. For example, one working group conducted a pre-meeting survey of participants regarding key knowledge and skill sets needed for the tourism graduate of the future while another group developed a 'values inventory' which may be used as a basis for programme assessment.

The first TEFI Conference at Modul University Vienna explored various futuristic scenarios of society to which tourism education programmes would need to adapt. Modifying tourism education programmes to fit a multitude of possible world scenarios, or even a single preferred scenario, was found to be a task fraught with too much specificity and uncertainty. Instead, TEFI participants concluded that whatever world scenario emerges in the future, certain core values were needed to provide students with the foundation to meet the multitude of uncertainties presented by that future. Given this consensus, TEFI moved to define these value sets. At the second TEFI Conference at the University of Hawaii, USA, five values-based principles were defined so that they can be fully integrated into tourism education programmes so as to ensure that students become responsible leaders and stewards for destinations (see Figure 12.1).

The five values identified during this conference are: Ethics; Stewardship; Knowledge; Professionalism; and Mutuality. They are conceptually portrayed as interlocking value principles demonstrating their interconnectedness and permeability. TEFI members envisioned that

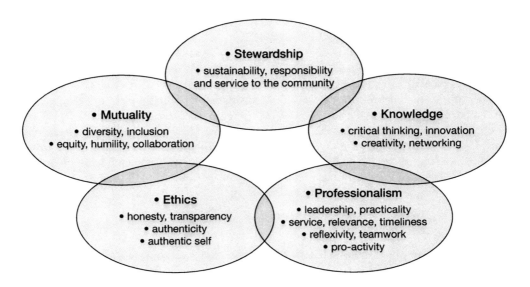

Figure 12.1 Tourism Education Futures Initiative (TEFI) values

educators can use subsets of the five value principles to integrate into their courses as appropriate. The following provides a detailed description of these values and how they can be incorporated into the learning experience. (This section is based on the work of many TEFI members as reported in the TEFI White Paper *A Values-Based Framework for Tourism Education: building the capacity to lead* (TEFI, 2010).)

TEFI values in the tourism curriculum

Each of the five TEFI values-based principles is discussed below with an emphasis on how that concept can be incorporated into the tourism student learning process. For each principle we provide a definition and then identify the content that should be included in the learning experience along with specific learning objectives.

Ethics

Definition

Ethics distinguishes between behaviour that is right and behaviour that is wrong. It is the basis for good action and provides a framework for judging actions that are questionable. Ethical behaviour means striving for actions that are deemed 'good' based on principles and values. It also involves making such principles and values explicit and rendering processes that lead to transparent decisions. Recognizing that good actions do not occur in a vacuum but are derived from specific value systems, ethical behaviour further requires an understanding and respect for actions based on different systems.

Content

Teaching ethics involves:

1   *Introducing students to Ethics as a field of study with practical importance*
This includes the definition of Ethics; encouraging reflexivity and decolonization of the self; recognizing diversity; outlining the practical importance of ethical behaviour; discussing the specific issues and challenges in the context of tourism; exemplifying the implications of unethical behaviour; and identifying the stakeholders in certain ethical dilemmas.

2   *Exposing students to different ethical traditions and principles*
This includes helping students understand what traditions and principles exist (e.g. Utilitarianism, Kantian ethic of respect for others, Aristotelian virtue ethics, Religion, Principles of benevolence, honesty, autonomy, justice, etc.). It also includes the explanation of these traditions, and illustrates how they influence actions. Highlighting differences and potential areas of conflict between them is also an important part of the curriculum. Students also need to be equipped with the means to achieve reconciliation, by engaging in the principles of negotiation, and learning how conflicts can be resolved and compromises reached.

3   *Drawing connections to issues of power and politics*
Students need to be able to identify sources of power, discuss the importance and principles of the legitimization of power, and to emphasize the role of existing power structures in determining ethical outcomes.

4   *Evoking actions*

To assist students in acting ethically, ensuring they are exposed to sources which can guide their actions, encouraging them to develop their own Codes of Conduct, and having students identify and implement good actions.

Specific student learning objectives in the tourism context

Students who study Ethics in the tourism context should be able to:

- Recognize its importance in general and specifically for tourism.
- Judge their own and others' actions.
- Value transparency.
- Respect different ethical traditions/approaches.
- Identify potential and actual conflicts and set actions in place to mitigate them.
- Know which resources are available when dealing with ethical concerns.
- Provide ethical leadership and initiate changes for the better.

Knowledge

Definition

Knowledge can be described as: (1) expertise and skills acquired by a person through experience or education; (2) the theoretical or practical understanding of a subject; (3) facts and information about a field; or (4) awareness or familiarity gained by experience of a fact or situation. This implies that knowledge is more than data (summary descriptions of parts of the world around us) and more than information (data put into a context). Knowledge comes in both explicit and tacit formats. In most instances, it is not possible to have an exhaustive understanding of an information domain so knowledge is ceaselessly incomplete. Knowledge is created through processes of selecting, connecting and reflecting. Knowledge is always already predicated by existing knowledge, which means that knowledge involves interpretation and contextualization and existing knowledge should be challenged.

Content

The knowledge creation process should address *creativity, critical thinking*, and *networking* for change and innovation through complex cognitive processes of perception, reasoning, learning, communication, association and application.

Creativity

Creativity has been identified as a key factor to adequately address the seismic changes facing contemporary society and as a driving force towards knowledge creation and socio-economic advancements. It is often useful to explicitly distinguish between creativity and innovation. Creativity is typically used to refer to the act of producing new ideas, approaches or actions that are appropriate to the problem at hand, while innovation often begins with creative ideas and involves a process of both generating *and applying* such creative ideas in a specific context for human, cultural or economic purposes. The ethical dimension of creativity and creative knowledge should be addressed. Dealing with future insecurity and uncertainty requires 'thinking outside the box', looking at existing domains and problems from a new angle. Promoting such a culture of creativity that acknowledges and seeks to learn from failure encourages students to move from hypothesis and conventional knowledge towards new possibilities and originality. Creativity and knowledge formation take place in an organizational set-up, for example, but not exclusively, in the format of educational institutions or business organizations. It is essential to envisage outcomes consisting of both factual and procedural knowledge, and finding a balance between the two is essential for the comprehension and application of knowledge.

Critical thinking

Critical thinking calls for an unrelenting examination of any form of knowledge and the knowledge-creation process to recognize the existence (or non-existence) of the use and power that supports it and the further conclusions to which it tends. It is important that knowledge is contextualized in order to recognize unstated assumptions and values. Critical thinking is not only about criticizing but being critical of the constitution of knowledge and underlying dogmas. Students should therefore be encouraged to make the implicit explicit, and identify ethnocentric bias and prejudice whenever deciding upon or solving a problem. Embodying an ethical dimension in mainstream disciplines in social sciences can enrich the thinking and add relevant dimensions of critical thinking, not only for the critique as an academic exercise, but critique as part of a constructive pursuit. Responsible citizenship evolves through knowledge-enhancing critical thinking.

Networking

The dissemination and development of knowledge take place in social environments. Social networks can create or assist in refining the use of knowledge. Bridging social networks can link different repositories of knowledge with the potential innovation effects. Networks and knowledge repositories are becoming more open as a consequence of the development of technical and institutional remedies connected to social media. Hereby, the identification and solving of problems increasingly take place through sharing and cooperation in open knowledge systems, where providers and users of knowledge meet and exchange information. Students and higher education institutions must understand and address the issues of open knowledge sources and open innovation, which are in contrast to issues of knowledge hoarding, protection and monopolizing in closed learning environments. New ways of thinking about the professions are essential. Higher educational institutions must prepare students to become practitioners, researchers, philosophical scholars and knowledge brokers throughout their studies and in their subsequent careers.

Specific student learning objectives in the tourism context

As a phenomenon, industry, career and lifestyle, tourism constitutes exceptional learning opportunities. The specific student learning objectives in the tourism context are:

- Understanding the value and power of knowledge rather than data or information.
- The art and skill of sharing knowledge, including new codes of conduct.
- Harvesting from new knowledge intermediaries.
- Developing equitable ways of communication with industry and community – across national borders and disciplines.
- Humility and courage in the fields of data creation and management, information management and knowledge creation and management.
- The art of questioning the answer – challenge what is taken for granted.
- Letting go – risking the adventure of creative journeys, using creativity tools and new ways of collaboration.

- Strengthening students' critical thinking skills through interactive teaching processes.
- Shifting from solely valuing and rewarding individual achievement toward collective action, participation and contribution.

Stewardship

Definition

Stewardship implies the responsibility to care for something, or someone, and the accountability to exercise responsibility. The value of stewardship is deeply rooted in the notion that the Earth is a divine gift, which we are permitted to use and take care of for the benefit of future generations. Importantly, stewardship provides the foundation for the basic concepts in sustainable development. This definition also suggests that tourism faculty and students should learn to take leadership in three distinct aspects of stewardship:

- Sustainability
- Responsibility
- Service to the community.

Further, it assumes that all stakeholders have responsibility for the environment and that they, along with all members of society, should exercise responsibility. Responsibility also implies the existence of rights. If all stakeholders are to take responsibility for the future of the planet in tourism, empowerment of those who are currently in a position of powerlessness is called for, just as the restraint of power of others may be necessary. Whereas local communities may help facilitate liaison-building based on a shared sense of contextual responsibility, it is important to recognize that communities are not homogenous units that easily reach consensus. Service to the community is one way that stakeholders can demonstrate their commitment to taking responsibility.

Content

A frequent claim is that sustainable tourism development can be achieved. Arguing that sustainability is achievable over a period of time fails to understand that change is the norm rather than the exception. Choice in lifestyle, cultural preferences and patterns of consumption and communication are not the same between generations and these are rather unpredictable. Similarly, it is not feasible to assume that a destination (or attraction, etc.) that 'stays the same' will go on forever (Hall & Butler, 1995: 102). These arguments indicate that the very idea of striking a balance in which the environment, economy and social and cultural elements are in equilibrium can be seen as an oxymoron. Appreciating the complexities of socio-cultural values, quality of life aspirations, and the biophysical and economic systems in which tourism takes place over time, an integrated approach to stewardship and, therefore, a process-oriented and holistic understanding of sustainable development is essential.

Stewardship also implies that individuals and organizations acknowledge their responsibilities and act accordingly. All stakeholders have responsibility for the environment and the society, requiring the use of influence or power. Responsibility and stewardship also imply the existence of rights. If all stakeholders take responsibility for the future of the planet in tourism, empowerment of those who are currently powerless is necessary, as is the restraint of power of other groups. The stakeholders with responsibilities include destination governments, generating country governments, tourism industry firms and organizations, employees, tourists, host communities, media and investors.

Finally, stewardship includes service to the destination community, allowing stakeholders to take responsibility. In the context of tourism education, in addition to the destination host community other communities worthy of consideration are: students, graduates, and the global tourism academic community. Volunteer tourism is an example of implementing service to the destination community. Whilst the motives for this activity are undoubtedly good, there are questions as to whether this is an appropriate way of achieving a more sustainable world. In order to implement knowledge of stewardship in the tourism curriculum, students should be exposed to debates which challenge conventional ideas and taken-for-granted discourses, and educators must consider how they address the nature and sense of responsibility in the students.

Professionalism

Definition

Professionalism is a rather nebulous term as it implies not only a profession and the skills, competencies or standards associated with it, but also an attitude and behaviour that reflect these. It has also been defined as the ability to align personal and organizational conduct with ethical and professional standards that include a responsibility to the customer or guest and community, a service orientation, and a commitment to lifelong learning and improvement. Professionalism is defined as incorporating leadership, a practical approach (practicality), attention to services, concern for the relevance and timeliness of evidence, reflexivity, teamwork and partnership-building skills, and proactivity. Proactivity involves taking the initiative to address problems in one's service domain and a commitment to excellence in one's domain of expertise. According to Bateman and Crant (1993: 105): 'Proactive people scan for opportunities, show initiative, take action, and persevere until they reach closure by bringing about change. They are pathfinders (Levitt & March, 1988) who change their organization's mission or find and solve problems.' This is in keeping with the notion of leadership, which is the ability to inspire individual and organizational excellence, to create and attain a shared vision, and to successfully manage change to attain the organization's strategic ends and successful performance.

Content

The core values of professionalism are a requirement for all tourism and hospitality academic programmes. It is educators' responsibility to expose students to high-quality and appropriate professionalism. The term 'new professionalism' is used by Sachs (2003) to distinguish between 'old' forms of professionalism which debate characteristics of professions and the extent to which occupational groups might be acknowledged as professions, and 'new' forms which, claims Sachs, assume a 'changed analytical perspective' and are seen to be more 'positive, principled and postmodern' (p. 182). The distinction between old and new forms of professionalism is useful, although the notion that new forms of professionalism are necessarily 'positive' and 'principled' should be considered with caution, as there is also evidence of a less 'principled' discourse in action.

While there is no overall agreement as to what constitutes a profession, certain key aspects are commonly cited that seek claim to professional status. These generally include reference to specialist knowledge, autonomy and responsibility (Hoyle & John, 1995). Professionalism, therefore, implies that such characteristics are evident in an individual's work. It is also linked to ethics or ethical behaviour. Some refer to it as an emotion, or a feeling of being professional. TEFI appears to include some of both, where professionalism is a series of behaviours and beliefs. To achieve success in the behaviour of professionalism requires an attitude (ethical belief) of what makes a true professional. It also seems that leadership is key, because the professional that exhibits positive leadership often displays other components in a positive manner. The learning process should include the following content:

Relevance, reflexivity, timeliness

The learning process for professionalism should include a focus on the relevance of information for industry situations. It should also provide mechanisms for students to be reflexive as they progress in their learning. This could include journaling about their experiences, discussing with colleagues or supervisors about their learning. Professionalism also requires a sense of timeliness with regard to meetings, classes, projects, etc. It also requires a level of respect for others' time.

Practicality, partnership, leadership

Practicality is an important element in tourism studies, and it is advisable that students learn about the practical implications of their studies by discussing and solving cases, engaging in internships, service learning, mentoring programmes and other modalities. This may involve students working with other stakeholders during their studies, and developing partnerships with them. The interpersonal skills necessary to develop successful partnerships should be an essential part of the curriculum in this area. Last but not least, leadership skills need to be developed in our students. Students should be cognizant of the different leadership styles, and of their own propensity to a particular style. Cultural contexts for leadership need also to be discussed as leadership varies from culture to culture.

Student learning objectives

Using Bloom's Taxonomy to determine learning objectives with respect to professionalism, the first step to implementation is to define the basic concepts underpinning professionalism, which include: list, define, describe, identify, show, label, collect, examine, summarize, describe, interpret, contrast, differentiate and discuss. The second stage involves application and analysis and, therefore, the learning objectives should include: apply, demonstrate, calculate, illustrate, show, solve, examine, classify, experiment, discover, analyse, separate, order, explain, connect, compare and select. The third stage includes synthesis and evaluation: combine, integrate, modify, plan, create, design, invent, compose, prepare, generalize, rewrite, assess, decide, grade, test, measure, recommend, convince, judge, explain, discriminate, support, conclude and summarize. Finally, it is suggested that students could either be exposed to a case study or an actual experiential learning environment (e.g. internship) where the assessment criteria would be incorporated into the learning objectives and assignments.

The specific learning objectives for professionalism are:

- To define professionalism and its components.
- To be able to decide what is relevant to a given situation.
- To learn the skills of reflexivity.
- To understand timeliness and all the ways it influences the work life.
- To know how to make knowledge practical.
- To acquire the skills to develop successful partnerships with other stakeholders.
- To understand different leadership styles in tourism contexts – and their own.

Mutual respect

Definition

Within the TEFI framework mutual respect has been initially defined as diversity, inclusion, equity, humility, collaboration. However, during the TEFI III summit in 2009 the meaning of this value was refined and extended by the participants. Mutual respect is seen as a value grounded in human relationships that requires attitudinal developments that are evolving, dynamic and involve acceptance, self-awareness of structural inequalities, open-mindedness, empowerment, and ability to revisit one's cultural understanding of the world.

Content

Several important elements of the mutuality value are highlighted:

1   Mutuality is a 'process' that is evolving and dynamic, emphasizing that achieving mutual respect is a long-term and even lifelong learning process that can be developed at different levels, starting from the individual to the society and global levels. It also can apply to human–animal relationships particularly in the context of how animals are used in tourism. This development from survival values of one's own isolated existence to relational/global consciousness of mutuality has been researched for the last 25 years by eminent sociologist Ronald Inglehart (1990). In his longitudinal World Values Survey covering two-thirds of the world population he has been capturing global evolution of the personal, social, public and cultural values which he conceptualizes under a theory of a 'Spiral of Values' (see also Webster, 2001).

2   Mutuality starts with 'self-awareness' and understanding of one's own identity, values, cultural drivers and behavioural patterns. Engaging in philosophy of self, and understanding self-identity, is a prerequisite to understanding the values and beliefs of other people, and developing positive attitudes to diverse identities. It is important to recognize that structural inequalities exist, including race, sex, gender and religion, and acknowledge these inequalities to eliminate the bias. Self-awareness also helps to question the 'I versus Them' attitude and moves from comparing and contrasting to accepting and sharing. Self-awareness also helps to perceive self as a positive change agent.

3   Mutual respect is about 'behaviours and attitudes'. Respect of self and others is an attitude which involves recognition and acknowledgement of other peoples' views. It goes beyond formal structures and legal frameworks for social inclusion and diversity, and it is grounded into early age education; and,

4   Mutuality is grounded in 'human relationships'. Respect of self and others is developed through open interactions, through constructive communication and discussions, conflict avoidance and management, empathy and acceptance. Mutuality is about developing respectful relationships between self and people through sharing and understanding values and attitudes. Mutuality starts with changing our own mindset and the way of constructing and perceiving reality. It involves open discussions and appreciation of diverse opinions.

Tourism education is a medium through which mutual respect can be promoted. However, we believe that mutuality is a process that starts from self and, therefore, cannot be taught directly as a subject but rather facilitated through the whole variety of general self-awareness and conflict resolution courses which would need to be a compulsory part of the whole tourism programme (undergraduate and postgraduate). Another way of incorporating mutual respect into the tourism curricula is to ensure that students are exposed to diverse social and cultural values and behaviours, and to encourage positive attitudes towards diversity.

Specific student learning objectives

The specific learning objectives for mutuality are:

- The promotion of respect and the feeling of recognition.
- Innovative thinking and learning methods.
- Closer cooperation with 'real life' through joint development projects with the industry.
- Students as active participants and decision makers, creating an atmosphere of mutual respect and support.
- The role of teachers should change from 'fact tellers' to facilitators of a student's own development.
- A learning environment that is inclusive, safe and dynamic, where students are not afraid to take the initiative, should be created.
- Self-awareness as a prerequisite to mutual respect should involve faculty, because teachers should understand their role as positive change agents to promote mutuality.
- Continuous training is needed for all staff members to build an understanding of diverse cultural backgrounds and value systems.
- Teachers should be able to recognize their own values and be open to question and revisit these values.
- Mutual respect should be promoted between staff members as well as between teachers and students.

Mutual respect is a process of self-development and thus is unique for every individual. Therefore, mutuality cannot be measured and assessed as a learning outcome in the curriculum. However, it is vital to incorporate mutuality elements and principles into study modules. Tourism curricula should be based on a variety of approaches, experiences and knowledge. They should incorporate courses related to professional and personal development, sociology, theology and cultural studies to facilitate students' understanding of drivers for change. Critical thinking skills should be emphasized in the curricula, and students' ability to initiate open dialogue, manage conflicts and reach mutually beneficial agreements should be rewarded. Subjects promoting cooperation, inclusion and diversity should be included in tourism studies.

Case studies of implementing value-based principles into a tourism curriculum

The ideas presented above are meant to be used creatively by educators in their course materials. The specifics of how to incorporate them are left to the educator. However, a number of programmes around the world have successfully implemented them. Two such programmes and the steps they have taken to incorporate TEFI values are described below.

Case 1: MODUL University Vienna, Austria

Background

MODUL University Vienna is an internationally-oriented organization for research and education on tourism, sustainable development, new media technology and public governance.

It was established by the Vienna Chamber of Commerce with a commitment to sustainability and innovation as the key drivers of long-term success. It aims to foster independent and original research and bring the benefits of innovation to the research community and the general public. In pursuit of its mission, the university supports internationalization, lifelong learning, equity and social justice and applies rigorous standards of scholarship and it promotes the principles of freedom of scientific thought and teaching as well as equal opportunity. Sustainability and environmental protection are key principles wherein it embraces the need for development strategies that meet the needs of the present without compromising the welfare of future generations. Sustainability represents an integral part of the curriculum and research agenda, where the university operates in a manner that minimizes environmental risks and adverse effects on the environment. The research and educational programmes at MODUL University Vienna focus on future-oriented strategies that provide answers to economic, environmental and social questions in conjunction with the demand for sustainable economic development and corresponding strategies. As such, the TEFI values lay the basis and direction for the education offered by MODUL University Vienna, which is committed to innovation and sustainability as key drivers of success in a dynamic and knowledge-based society.

Graduates of MODUL University Vienna value peoples' ideas and creativity, and are prepared to:

- Deal with complexity (Progress and Innovation)
- Challenge what the society takes for granted and embrace change (Knowledge)
- Support the principles of equity and justice (Ethics)
- Value diversity and humanity (Mutual Respect)
- Serve as ambassadors of sustainable and responsible living (Stewardship).

Implementation of TEFI values

MODUL University Vienna has actively integrated the five TEFI values into many of its programmes starting with the design of its faculties and extending to the day the students graduate. The following list briefly outlines some of the key activities implemented by the university.

- MODUL University Vienna follows an integrated sustainability approach and therefore tries to balance the economic, the social and the environmental dimension of sustainable development. Environmental and social sustainability is a key principle of MODUL University Vienna, acknowledging and embracing the urgent need for development strategies that meet the needs of the present and improve the welfare of future generations.
- Sustainability represents an integral part of the curriculum and research agenda, and is also reflected in the daily workflow. The university operates in a manner that minimizes environmental risk and adverse effects on the environment.
- All incoming students are informed of TEFI values which guide the operation of the university. In particular, students of MODUL University Vienna are encouraged to develop the following traits: interpersonal skills, perseverance, originality, future-mindedness, high talent, aesthetic sensibility and wisdom. In addition to these individual traits, responsibility, nurture, altruism, civility, moderation, tolerance and work ethic will be fostered amongst the university staff and the students (e.g. the university has a pellet heating system and solar panels; electricity is bought from a renewable energy provider; a group of faculty, staff and students ('Sustainability Committee') are permanently working on suggestions about how to further develop the university's key principle).

- The university funds 'The Scholarship of Hope' which supports students with innovative ideas in the area of sustainability. The ideas should be able to be implemented at MODUL University Vienna in order to continue and support its ongoing goal of becoming one of the world's most sustainable universities.
- Each graduating student is invited to sign a 'pledge' which essentially commits them to following TEFI values throughout their life.
- Besides actively implementing the principles of social and environmental sustainability at the university itself the committee also seeks to share the knowledge gained. Publishing knowledge first serves to transfer insight to other institutions and is, second, a benchmark of the quality of its own efforts. Thus, the Sustainability Committee has submitted several projects to the Austrian Sustainability Award and has been very successful so far. It won first place in the 'Structural Foundation' category and third place in the 'Curriculum Development and Teaching Approach' category in 2012, and second place in the 'Structural Foundations' category in 2010.
- Sustainability Week is a periodic week of interesting activities and events, each time focusing on a different sustainability-related theme. The goal is to raise awareness on a specific topic, foster students' participation and ultimately help students to critically reflect on their own behaviours. The extracurricular activities are wide-ranging (presentations, conferences, film screenings, visits, competitions, etc.), and take place in a convivial and thought-sharing atmosphere.

In summary, MODUL University Vienna is a significant exemplar of how a whole campus can embrace the TEFI values.

Case 2: European Master in Tourism Management (EMTM)

Background

The European Master in Tourism Management (EMTM) is a university Master's programme certified by Erasmus Mundus quality brand from the European Union. It is offered on three different European campuses: Kolding in Denmark, Ljubljana in Slovenia and Girona in Spain. The programme has been in operation since 2006, and under the Erasmus Mundus brand since 2009. The EMTM is a fully integrated two-year joint European programme promoted and tailor-made by three university partners: The University of Girona (Spain), known for its research and pursuit of teaching excellence in tourism product innovation and destination management; the University of Southern Denmark (Denmark), internationally recognized for its research and education in the field of sustainable tourism development; and the University of Ljubljana (Slovenia), renowned for its excellence in tourism policy design and tourism environmental management and economics. The medium of instruction is English.

Students follow a mandatory mobility scheme, starting the first semester in Kolding, Denmark, where they are introduced, at an advanced level, to the conceptualization of tourism development with particular attention to sustainability, strategic communication and economics. Moving next to Ljubljana, Slovenia, for the second semester, students learn about policy instruments, indicators and management tools available for tourism policy and strategy design, with emphasis on environmental issues in tourism development. Spending the third semester in Girona, Spain, students become competent in effectively implementing tourism with particular emphasis on the effective management of organizational networks, consumers, innovation processes and new tourism products. The fourth semester is exclusively devoted to the completion of the Master's thesis. After a successful and timely completion of all four semesters, students are awarded a joint diploma (degree) of Master of Science in Tourism Management. EMTM's three main objectives are to:

(a) prepare future professionals to strategically manage and make sustainable and effective decisions in placements of high responsibility in tourism institutions;
(b) provide future professionals with an integrated knowledge of the dynamics of tourism development, the principles of sustainable management, environmental issues, the role of cultural diversity and creativity for innovation and the governance of tourism networks, the quality management of customer services; and
(c) train future researchers in the field of tourism management.

Implementation of TEFI values

In the design of the programme, the EMTM academic board chose to include the TEFI values into the programme's learning objectives together with those defined by the Erasmus Mundus programme. Each learning objective is matched with a point of assessment throughout the programme – this could be a particular exam or project. Students are evaluated on their demonstration of the values.

Students begin their studies with the first semester at the University of Southern Denmark (SDU). Here they are introduced to the TEFI values via a study book, group projects and lectures. Instructors use the values to engage in critical thinking, specifically by challenging students to critically reflect upon these in contexts of sustainable tourism development.

Through the INNOTOUR platform, EMTM students are exposed to the TEFI values in a Web 2.0 learning environment. Students explore the meaning of the values through exchange with blogs and wikis in a multicultural and global context (Liburd and Christensen, 2013).

During the second semester at the Faculty of Economics, Ljubljana University (FELU), the values are integrated into teaching and also into the assessment and evaluation of students. The three-level assessment system is used, as demonstrated in Table 12.1.

The inherently blended learning environment beacons the students to reflect, interact and gain new understandings of real and complex issues in tourism (Liburd and Christensen, 2013). In summary, the EMTM programme is a unique multicultural programme with mandatory mobility in a values-infused, transnational learning environment.

The way forward

With the goal to fundamentally transform tourism education, TEFI will move forward by engaging all stakeholders in adopting a new vision statement where TEFI 'seeks to be the leading,

Table 12.1 Three-level assessment system

Evaluation scale	Able to define a value in tourism
Exceeds expectations (3)	Student shows good standard to define and explain the concept/value.
Meets expectations (2)	Student shows reasonable standard to define and explain the concept/value.
Fails to meet expectations (1)	Student fails to define and explain the concept/value.

forward-looking network that inspires, informs and supports tourism educators and students to passionately and courageously transform the world for the better'. In order to meet this vision, we will work within the academic community to encourage a critical examination of tourism education wherein programmes consider all aspects of the education process and include the basic values underlying curriculum and coursework, potential redesign of coursework including the integration of proven technologies, the metrics used to evaluate the success of the coursework as well as the success of the educators. In addition, TEFI will work directly with students to reflect their unique understanding and perspective to the redesign of education. TEFI will also engage with university administrators including deans, rectors, chancellors and provosts with the goal of identifying and implementing programmatic review policies including faculty evaluations which will encourage improved means for evaluation. Finally, we will invite leading industry thinkers to define a new model for tourism education, and the tourism industry itself, to reflect the important role that tourism plays in society.

As such, there are several steps that TEFI will take to make a difference in the years ahead including:

1   *Fostering innovative learning experiences for students at all levels.*
2   *Developing new tools and methods for teaching and evaluating tourism education.*
3   *Re-visioning tourism scholarship and the metrics for faculty success.*
4   *Advocacy for tourism as a field of study and employment.*
5   *To be a place where future issues related to tourism education are debated.*

At TEFI 7 (sponsored by Oxford Brookes University, UK, in 2013) the theme was 'Tourism Education for Global Citizenship: Educating for Lives of Consequence' and it focused on issues related to the design of learning experiences for tourism and social entrepreneurship. The meeting followed the Skoll World Forum on Social Entrepreneurship, and drawing inspiration from this, three of the TEFI keynote speakers spoke to the need to 'wake up' tourism to a new paradigm, and to recognize the significant policy shifts that are occurring at the international level. Delegates were also challenged to re-examine their understanding of global citizenship and discover ways to include new dimensions of contribution in the classroom. In response to these challenges, TEFI has agreed to adopt a number of new initiatives within the five-point programme described in this chapter, including creating a new setting for tourism education and social entrepreneurship: the TEFI Change Walking Workshop. Importantly, the programme will be designed with an experiential format that inspires faculty learning and social entrepreneurship by embedding tourism education in a tourism setting (the initial project will be held in Nepal in 2014) where faculty will be required to work with local entrepreneurs and conduct daily lectures where the overall goal is to integrate their experiences into course materials at their home university.

Beyond developing a new school of thought for tourism education, TEFI will continue to provide leadership by supporting alternative approaches to the creating and sharing of knowledge. The Internet and social media have transformed the creation, transmission and consumption of knowledge by creating an inexpensive and easily accessible framework within which scholars can share knowledge; the results of which have led to a complete transformation of books and journals whereby publishers struggle to maintain control over access to this material. Indeed, the development of social systems such Wikipedia, YouTube, Blogs, Facebook, Twitter, and Google's effort to digitize 15 million books, offers society the opportunity to create, transform and store knowledge, which, in turn, can lead to significant changes in our understanding of ourselves and the world around us. As such, the publishing world is beginning to change by modifying their business models whereby they struggle to maintain control over material they seek to lock behind login platforms while creating new streams of revenue. TEFI will partner with the International Academy for the Study of Tourism (IAST) to consider an online journal of tourism research with open and free access in keeping with initiatives in other fields (such as Economics), where the goal is to transform the processes of review and production such that they are transparent, interactive and supportive of critical review, idea creation and they recognize the contribution by the various stakeholders of the journal. The benefits of such a journal would be to give scholars worldwide free access to quality tourism research. As the project progresses, online knowledge sharing and creation will become a vital part of the platform moving towards a liquid journal where scholars debate online. It is anticipated that this new 'social model' of publication within tourism will encourage scholars to 'socialize' the knowledge transfer process so as to lead to higher quality articles, further and faster growth in idea generation and transmission, and therefore provide an important framework for knowledge creation in the field of tourism. Scholars and practitioners in tourism and elsewhere should benefit as research in tourism becomes more transparent, more understandable and more dynamic. Also, the experiences gained by this effort in building the journal should provide for a better understanding of how to support knowledge creation and learning within the classroom.

Finally, TEFI will support the tourism industry through partnerships with other like-minded organizations such as the Business Enterprises for Sustainable Tourism Education Network (BESTEN), the Critical Tourism Studies group (CTS), United Nations World Tourism Organization (UNWTO) and the Organization for Economic Cooperation and Development (OECD). In particular through OECD, TEFI will cooperate on a series of policy reports focusing on the role of education in tourism development. It is hoped that this partnership will lead to a better understanding and appreciation of the role of tourism in society, especially within the context of new strategies for sustainable tourism development.

These forward-looking activities represent only some of the many activities in which the TEFI community will continue to meet its goal of addressing the huge challenges facing tourism education and the tourism industry. It is hoped that you find this material useful as you consider your role in tourism education and fostering the leaders of tomorrow. Also, it is hoped that you are (or become) a member of the TEFI community and a forceful advocate for tourism futures where TEFI values form the foundations of your curriculum and your relationship with the leaders of the tourism industry.

Acknowledgments

The authors would like to acknowledge the many tourism academics at the various TEFI conferences that significantly contributed to the TEFI White Paper, entitled *A Values-Based Framework for Tourism Education: building the capacity to lead,* from which much of this chapter is drawn. We would also like to acknowledge Karl Woeber, President of Modul University Vienna, and Tanja Mihalic and Janne Liburd, Directors of the EMTM programme, for their assistance in writing the two cases.

References

Bateman, T. S., & Crant, J. (1993). 'The Proactive Component of Organizational Behavior: a measure and correlates'. *Journal of Organizational Behavior,* 14, 103–18.
Hall, M., & Butler, R. (1995). 'In Search of Common Ground: reflections on sustainability: complexity and process in the tourism system: a discussion'. *Journal of Sustainable Tourism,* 3(2), 99–105.
Hoyle, E., & John, P. D. (1995). *Professional Knowledge and Professional Practice.* London: Cassell.

Ingelhart, R. (1990). *Culture Shift in Advanced Industrial Societies*, Princeton, NJ: Princeton University Press.

Levitt, B., & March, J. (1988). 'Organizational Learning'. *Annual Review of Sociology,* 14, 319–40.

Liburd, J., & Christensen, I. (2013). 'Using Web 2.0 in Higher Tourism Education'. *Journal of Hospitality, Leisure, Sport and Tourism Education,* 12, 99–108.

Sachs, J. (2003). 'Teacher Professional Standards: controlling or developing teaching'. *Teachers and Teaching: theory and practice,* 9 (2), 175–86.

Sheldon, P., Fesenmaier, D., Woeber, K., Cooper, C., & Antonioli, M. (2008). 'Tourism Education Futures 2010–2030: building the capacity to lead', *Journal of Teaching in Tourism and Travel,* 7(3), 61–8.

Tourism Education Futures Initiative (TEFI). (2010). White Paper. *A Values-Based Framework for Tourism Education: building the capacity to lead.* Available: http://www.tourismeducationfutures.org/ (Accessed 3 October 2013).

Wallis, C., & Steptoe, S. (2006). 'How to Bring our Schools out of the 20th Century'. *Time,* Sunday, 10 December. Available: http://content.time.com/time/magazine/article/0,9171,1568480,00.html (Accessed 3 October 2013).

Webster, A. (2001). *Spiral of Values: the flow from survival values to global consciousness in New Zealand.* Hawera, NZ: Alpha Publications.

13

Teaching responsible tourism

Responsibility through tourism?

Richard Sharpley
University of Central Lancashire, UK

Introduction

The fundamental benefit of studying tourism lies not in what we can learn about the phenomenon of tourism itself. Rather, it is what can be learnt through the study of tourism that is arguably of most value (Sharpley, 2011). Putting it another way, the purpose of tourism education, reflecting its roots in hospitality and catering management programmes, has long been to meet the employment needs of a burgeoning economic sector. That is, its explicit aim has been and, in many instances, continues to be the provision of practical knowledge and skills relevant to a career in tourism. Indeed, an analysis of tourism curricula around the world would reveal a predominance of business- and management-related modules, often complemented by practical field visits and industry placements or internships.

Such a vocational focus is, in many respects, both logical and justifiable. As the demand for tourism continues its inexorable growth, there is of course an increasing need across the entire spectrum of the so-called tourism 'industry' for employees with appropriate knowledge and skills to meet the needs of present and future tourists. At the same time, however, the study of tourism, particularly within the higher education context in which many programmes or courses are located, is (or should be) about more than simply 'teaching' students a prescribed set of knowledge and skills. Not only has it entered what Airey (2008) refers to as a 'mature stage' manifested in a more critical approach within a socio-cultural framework, but also recent years have witnessed an interrogation of tourism education with respect to its form, content and output. Specifically, the debate has focused on both how to inculcate students with a set of values appropriate to leading the development and practice of tourism in the twenty-first century in particular (TEFI, 2013) and how tourism education might meet or reflect the purposes of university/higher education more generally – that is to create informed, critical, creative and free-thinking individuals.

Of course, these arguments are well rehearsed (for example, Jamal & Robinson, 2009; Tribe, 2002). The point is, however, that the study of tourism is uniquely placed to fulfil both of these roles. Tourism is intimately and irrevocably interconnected with the world within which it occurs; it has evolved into a de-differentiated socio-economic phenomenon. Consequently, the study of tourism offers the opportunity not only to explore the relationship that people, tourists, have with the physical, social, cultural, political and technological world but also, through an analysis of these relationships, to develop our knowledge and understanding of our world. In short, tourism acts as a lens on our social world, a lens through which transformations and challenges can be identified, understood and critically analysed.

In some respects, this is not a new idea; others having referred previously to tourism as a metaphor for the contemporary social world (Dann, 2002). However, it provides an additional dimension to tourism education; tourism is no longer studied for its own sake (as fascinating as that might be) but as a medium for exploring and potentially enhancing students' understanding and critical appreciation of contemporary trends, issues and challenges such as globalization, consumption, international political economy, technology and communication, or the environment and development. Indeed, it is in the context of the last of these, the global project of development (sustainable or otherwise), that tourism arguably represents a most powerful lens for not only identifying contemporary development processes and challenges but also encouraging critical reflection on the part of students.

More specifically, the potential contribution of tourism to the economic and social development of destinations has long been recognized and promoted. Since the World Tourism Organization asserted more than 30 years ago that 'world tourism can . . . help eliminate the widening economic gap between developed and developing countries and ensure the steady acceleration of economic and social development and progress' (WTO, 1980: 1), not only has tourism become embedded in the development policies of many nations but also, of course, the role of tourism in development has long been a fundamental element (albeit in different guises) of taught tourism programmes. Indeed, it is likely that the concept of sustainable tourism development (that is the contribution of tourism to sustainable development, as opposed to the more parochial focus on the sustainability of tourism itself) in particular features in some form or another in most, if not all, tourism programmes. The opportunity exists, therefore, both to address critically the global challenges of development and sustainability through the lens of tourism and, perhaps more importantly, to stimulate engagement with those challenges amongst students. In other words, the opportunity exists to encourage students to reflect upon their own values with respect to the environment and (sustainable) development.

The purpose of this chapter, therefore, is to explore how the study of tourism or, more specifically, the study of sustainable tourism development may be utilized as a vehicle for encouraging students not only to engage with debates surrounding the concept of sustainable development as the contemporary yet widely contested paradigm of global development, but also and, perhaps, more importantly, to reflect critically on their own role and values in achieving a more sustainable world. In particular, it explores how responsibility, in an environmental and developmental sense, may be 'taught' through the study of tourism. The first task, then, is to consider why it may be thought necessary to focus on responsibility as a value to be encouraged through tourism in higher education and, indeed, what 'responsibility' is.

Why teach 'responsibility'?

The notion of responsibility has been implicit and, in some respects, explicit within the study of tourism for more than two decades, albeit primarily as an approach to tourism and its development and management. Since the early 1970s, of course, there had been growing concern over the negative consequences of tourism with a number of now widely cited commentators questioning the wisdom of promoting its rapid and unfettered growth (for example, de Kadt,

1979; Turner & Ash, 1975; Young, 1973). By the mid-1980s, responses to the alleged impacts of tourism had coalesced into what became known as alternative tourism, a concept that even at that time attracted criticism (Cohen, 1987), yet still nowadays continues to be referred to frequently in tourism development discourse. Implicit within the principles of alternative (to mass) tourism was the requirement for a more responsible approach to tourism development giving precedence to the environmental, social and economic needs of the destination. It is not surprising, therefore, that the term 'responsible tourism' soon entered the tourism lexicon. For example, Haywood (1988) pursued the idea of 'responsible and responsive tourism planning' whilst Richter (1989: viii), in the preface to a book on the politics of tourism in Asia, made reference to a 'Centre for Responsible Tourism'. By the early 1990s, responsible tourism had become synonymous with environmentally and socially appropriate tourism development and, in particular, was a term employed by both proponents and critics as a collective descriptor of alternative forms of tourism (Cooper & Ozdil, 1992; Harrison & Husbands, 1996; Wheeller, 1991). In short, responsibility had become explicit within tourism studies, though not as a social value but as a prescriptive set of rules for environmentally and socially appropriate tourism development.

Soon, the original concept of responsible tourism was superseded, of course, by that of sustainable tourism development, a broader approach that, since the mid-1990s, has dominated the study of tourism (and, indeed, the national and international tourism policy agenda) from a development perspective. However, not only has sustainable tourism development remained a contested and frequently misunderstood concept, but also its viability as an objective of tourism development has in recent years become increasingly challenged (Mundt, 2011; Sharpley, 2009). Perhaps as a consequence, responsible tourism has re-emerged or, more precisely, returned to the fore as an allegedly more appropriate approach to tourism. Sharing more generally the objectives of sustainable tourism development, it places the emphasis on the need of all stakeholders, including tourism businesses and tourists themselves, to take responsibility for their roles and actions in tourism (Goodwin, 2011), although it should be noted that responsible tourist behaviour is not a new idea. Some 20 years ago, for example, Wood and House (1991) exhorted people to be 'good' tourists, the baton more recently being taken up by Popescu (2008).

Interestingly, responsible tourism has also evolved as a tourism product or, more precisely, as a brand, albeit in explicit opposition to mass tourism products. In 2001, for example, responsibletravel.com was launched as the world's first dedicated online travel agent specializing in responsible holidays and now claims to offer 'the largest selection of responsible holidays anywhere on the web' (responsibletravel.com, 2013). In addition, responsible business practice has also become an objective for many tourism businesses, primarily in the UK but also elsewhere. Not only has the UK's Association of Independent Tour Operators (AITO) since 2000 been committed to promoting responsible tourism amongst its members but also many tour operators, both independent and mainstream, have adopted the principles of responsible tourism. In short, responsible tourism has evolved into a tourism-specific manifestation of what is more broadly referred to as corporate social responsibility.

There is, then, strong justification for including responsible tourism (and sustainable tourism development) in tourism curricula; long epitomizing the alternative tourism school, it demands critical analysis as a specific perspective on tourism development and management. However, this does not explain why responsibility more generally should be considered and encouraged through the study of tourism, nor indeed does it define what responsibility is. To do so, it is necessary to return to the concept of sustainable development and, in particular, to the fundamental role of the individual in its potential realization.

What is 'responsibility'?

In his recent book, *Taking Responsibility for Tourism*, Goodwin (2011) identifies three components of responsibility that he suggests are of particular relevance to tourism but which also provide a useful starting point for considering what responsibility means within the context of this chapter. According to Goodwin (2011: 32–3), these three components are:

i.   Accountability: in this widely used sense, to be responsible is to be held accountable (or, in more common parlance, to blame) for something, whether an action or inaction. In other words, if one is responsible for something happening (or not happening), it is one's 'fault'.

ii. Capability/capacity: responsibility is taken on because the individual, group or organization is both willing and able to act, to do something that makes a difference. This is similar to the idea of responsibility being the opportunity or ability to act proactively and independently, without guidance or authorization. Hence, Goodwin (2011: 33) refers to 'respons-ability'; that is having the opportunity and capacity to act in response to something.

iii. Being responsive: simply, to be expected to respond to a need or situation.

Interestingly, Goodwin does not refer to the alternative, widely understood notion of responsibility as the duty or moral obligation to do something or to behave in a particular way. Rather, in the specific context of responsible tourism, he views responsibility as informing and persuasion. That is, having raised the issues or challenges with all stakeholders, 'we must focus on demanding action from those who have the ability to make a difference' (p. 34). In adopting this position, he neatly sidesteps the rather thorny question of whether stakeholders in tourism, specifically tourism businesses and tourists themselves, have a moral duty to behave in a particular 'responsible' manner, though this of course would provide the focus for an interesting debate amongst students of tourism. It is not, however, the intention of this chapter to critique the concept of responsible tourism as proposed by Goodwin and others; again, this is something that could or should take place in the classroom (but, see Sharpley, 2012). Suffice to say that, in considering responsibility as a social value of particular relevance to environment, development and sustainability debates, viewing it as a duty or moral obligation (which may be internalized as a value) is both logical and necessary. But why should this be so?

It has long been recognized, of course, that human activity frequently impacts negatively, and sometimes disastrously, on the world's natural environment and resources. Indeed, throughout history there is ample evidence of humankind's over-exploitation or mismanagement of natural resources. As a simple example, the world's forests have always been (and continue to be) susceptible to human intervention (Williams, 2000), whether through more general clearance for habitation or agriculture or in response to specific demands. By the late fifteenth century, for instance, Mediterranean oak forests had been severely depleted by the demands of shipbuilders, as later had the oak forests of Britain, particularly between the sixteenth and eighteenth centuries. In other words, as Ludwig *et al.* (1993) succinctly observe, 'resource problems are not really environmental problems; they are human problems'. Whether the extinction of the legendary dodo in the late 1600s in previously uninhabited Mauritius or the more contemporary challenge of oil depletion, human activity 'uses up' the natural environment and resources.

Although the need for appropriate responses to resource depletion has been equally long recognized – sustainable forestry, for example, is not a recent phenomenon, there being evidence of schemes from the sixteenth century onwards to replace the forests exploited for shipbuilding – it is only recently that the intimate and interdependent relationship between the environment and development has been brought more acutely into focus. Specifically, the emergence of the sustainable development paradigm since the late 1980s has not only highlighted that development depends on a healthy environment but also that sustainability, or the 'capacity for continuance' as the objective of sustainable development (Porritt, 2007: 33), implicitly demands a moral obligation for responsible behaviour on the part of the individual. Indeed, it is this requirement that arguably distinguishes sustainable development, in conceptual terms at least, from previous policies and processes for environmental protection and management.

Certainly, from the mid-nineteenth century there existed a discernible conservation movement, the objective of which was primarily to protect natural landscapes and species from a variety of threats, from creeping industrialization and urbanization to excessive hunting and collection of species, but also to sustain particular landscapes for access and recreation. However, such protection was achieved primarily through 'top-down' processes, such as national park legislation and designation, which imposed controls over resource use. In short, conservation and environmental protection were considered to be the responsibility of government. It was only from the 1960s and the emergence of what may be described as environmentalism that an important transformation occurred, inasmuch as attention shifted from protecting natural resources through reactive management policies towards the economic, political and social causes of resource degradation and depletion. In other words, environmentalism became concerned with the processes rather than the outcomes of contemporary modernization, development and economic growth, of which tourism is of course a part. Moreover, it was also the emergence of environmentalism that underpinned the concept of sustainable development.

Sustainable development

To define sustainable development is an impossible task. Nevertheless, numerous attempts have been made to do so, although the Brundtland Commission's definition, 'development that meets the needs of the present without compromising the ability of future generations to meet their own needs' (WCED, 1987: 48), remains the most widely cited and adopted. Whilst politically attractive, however, this definition is rather meaningless, reflecting not only the vagueness and ambiguity of the concept of sustainable development (Robinson, 2004), but also the continuing controversy surrounding it. Indeed, despite the countless books and articles devoted to the topic, consensus over the meaning, objectives and viability of sustainable development remains elusive, whilst the great conundrum first identified by Redclift (1987) – that sustainable development is fundamentally oxymoronic – has yet to be resolved.

However, for the purposes of this chapter, two points demand emphasis. First, an important distinction exists between *sustainable development* and *sustainability*. As noted above, it has been argued that sustainability, or the global eco-system's capacity for continuance, is the outcome of sustainable development (Porritt, 2007); in other words, sustainable development is a process by which sustainability may be achieved. Second, not only does sustainable development remain the dominant global development paradigm and the framework within which, according to the UNWTO, all tourism should be developed, but its potential outcome, sustainability, is a necessary and logical objective for humanity. In other words, the need for sustainability is inarguable. Therefore, not only is it necessary to understand what sustainable development is, particularly as an objective of tourism development, but also the prerequisites for its achievement.

It has long been accepted that sustainable development demands a holistic and long-term approach to global development with a specific focus on inter- and intra-generational equity. In other words, the objective of sustainable development is a fairer, more equitable global society that can be sustained indefinitely. This suggests, at some risk of oversimplification, that there are two elements to sustainable development, namely, 'development' and 'sustainability' (Lélé, 1991); moreover, it is within the development context that the controversy surrounding sustainable development as a whole predominantly lies. On the one hand, not only is (environmental) sustainability a necessary objective but also there is consensus over the broad principles for its achievement: balancing the use of non-renewable resources with the development of renewable resources; balancing the rate at which waste is deposited in the ecosystem with the assimilative capacity of the environment; and a global population and capital levels of consumption that remain within the Earth's capacity (Goodland, 1992).

On the other hand, both the processes and objectives of development remain contested. For example, one of the principal criticisms of the Brundtland Report is that it espouses, albeit somewhat surreptitiously, a traditional economic growth-based approach to (sustainable) development following an implicitly techno-centric philosophy – in a sense, business as usual. Conversely, the eco-centric approach, giving primacy to resource protection and conservation, would advocate a no-growth or steady-state economic approach to development. At the same time, the notion of development itself remains contested, although contemporary understandings of the concept are perhaps best summarized by the United Nations Development Programme (UNDP). In its 2010 Human Development Report (UNDP 2010: 22), it states that development is:

> the expansion of people's freedoms to live long, healthy and creative lives; to advance goals they have reason to value; and to engage actively in shaping development equitably and sustainably on a shared planet. People are both the beneficiaries and drivers of human development, as individuals and in groups.

Thus stated, human development has three components:

- *Well-being*: expanding people's real freedoms—so that people can flourish.
- *Empowerment and agency:* enabling people and groups to act—to drive valuable outcomes.
- *Justice:* expanding equity, sustaining outcomes over time and respecting human rights and other goals of society.

It is immediately questionable to what extent tourism may contribute to this broad concept of development as opposed to the more restricted goal of economic growth, there being no inevitability that the former will follow the latter. Indeed, this is again an important topic for discussion within the tourism studies classroom. However, despite the debates surrounding sustainable development – its viability as a global development project and the means of its implantation and achievement in particular – there is the inescapable conclusion that sustainability, as the ultimate and necessary outcome of sustainable development (however conceived) requires two things: sustainable forms and levels of production and sustainable forms and levels of consumption. Moreover, and as the particular point that this chapter is attempting to make, both sustainable production and consumption require responsibility (that is a moral responsibility to contribute to sustainability) on the part of the individual. In other words, in a world increasingly defined by democratic governance and market-led economies and, hence, defined by the opportunity for individuals to make choices, it is only through the widespread adoption of responsibility – or responsible environmental values – that sustainability can be achieved.

Such an argument is not of course new. In its report *Caring for the Earth*, for example, the IUCN (1991: 43) noted that 'More affluent groups and countries live unsustainably because of ignorance, lack of concern, or incentives to wasteful consumption. For them particularly, the need is to change attitudes and practices, not only so that communities use resources more sustainably but also to bring about alterations in international economic, trade and aid policies'. Consequently, the adoption of a new social paradigm relevant to sustainable living was proposed. Equally, it is recognized that such a fundamental shift in social values remains the greatest challenge to sustainability, leading one commentator to suggest that sustainable development could only be implemented successfully when there is no opportunity for individual choice – that is, under dictatorship (Dresner, 2002). Either way, however, the importance of encouraging students to appraise critically their own sense of responsibility and/or environmental values, whether as tourists, future tourism business leaders or consumers more generally, becomes evident. And, as suggested in the introduction to this chapter, the teaching of sustainable tourism development, whether generally in the specific context of responsible tourism, provides a valuable opportunity for doing just that.

Teaching responsibility through tourism

Since the early 1990s, the concept of alternative/responsible/sustainable tourism has been an explicit element of most taught tourism programmes, whether as an identifiable module or course in its own right or within other modules such as 'Tourism and the Environment' or 'Impacts of Tourism'. Indeed, it is right and proper that it should be included in the study of tourism given not only the increasing knowledge and awareness of the consequences of the development of tourism in general but also the need to align tourism (and its officially sanctioned role as a vehicle of development) with the contemporary global development paradigm, namely, sustainable development.

In many cases, however, the teaching of sustainable tourism suffers from two related limitations. First, the focus tends to be primarily tourism-centric, reflecting the parochial conceptualization of sustainable tourism that was criticized by Hunter (1995) some two decades ago. In other words, the emphasis tends to be on exploring or proposing how tourism, as a discrete economic and social activity, may be developed and managed more sustainably or, in short, on how tourism itself may be sustained. Such an emphasis is not surprising inasmuch as the notion of alternative, responsible or sustainable tourism evolved, at least within tourism studies, as a direct response to the increasing concerns with respect to the so-called impacts of tourism. Thus, sustainable tourism development was and often still is seen primarily as a means of mitigating the negative impacts of tourism. Nor is this emphasis unjustified; future tourism employees/managers need to be aware of the resource implications of tourism development, to be able to make decisions that contribute to the effective stewardship of tourism's physical, social and cultural resources. Moreover, the focus on the sustainable management of tourism is perhaps inevitable given that the concept of sustainable tourism development is frequently manifested in the literature – and particularly in introductory textbooks – as a list of principles and practices necessary for its achievement. In other words, it is often presented as a set of management tools. However, this tourism-centric focus serves to divorce the study of sustainable tourism from the very *raison d'être* of tourism – its potential contribution to the (sustainable) development of destination areas. As Cronin (1990) suggested, tourism should be considered alongside other viable options in sustainable development policies, but the tourism-centric approach does not permit this.

Second, and consequently, the study of sustainable tourism development is frequently uncritical. Not only is sustainable tourism development often presented unquestioningly as a viable approach to the development and management of tourism but also sustainable development itself is accepted uncritically as the objective of tourism development. Yet tourism's contribution to development (sustainable or otherwise) cannot be accepted uncritically. Development itself as a global project has long been subjected to scrutiny (Rahnema & Bawtree, 1997) whilst there is no inevitability about tourism's contribution to development. Moreover, sustainable development remains a highly and increasingly contested concept. Thus, there is a need to question the validity of the concept of sustainable tourism both in its own right and as the desired outcome of tourism development. In so doing, not only will students have the opportunity to reflect upon the challenges of achieving sustainability more generally, but also their individual role and responsibility in this process will become more evident.

The starting point for a more critical and reflective approach to the study of sustainable tourism is to address the concept of development itself; if tourism is promoted primarily as a vehicle of development, it is only logical that development, both as a process and goal, should be interrogated. Though something that most people understand intuitively, development remains difficult to define and explain. Therefore, providing students with the appropriate conceptual frameworks and knowledge to reflect critically on development, the indicators and challenges of underdevelopment (a comparison between, for example, the average per capita income in a less developed country and the cost of a two-week holiday in that country usually serves as stark evidence of global inequality) and, in particular, the mechanisms and processes through which development (including sustainable development) may be supported will enable or encourage them to consider not only their own values with respect to development in general, but the potential of tourism to contribute to development in particular.

More specifically, with a foundational knowledge of the characteristics and indicators of development and underdevelopment, a broad understanding of the factors that inhibit development, from poverty to government failure, and a clear grasp of the prerequisites for sustainable development as summarized briefly earlier in this chapter, students will be in a position, through the lens of tourism, to reflect on development and sustainability and, in particular, the extent to which they recognize or experience a sense of moral responsibility towards contributing towards sustainability. Indeed, an informed assessment of the relationship between tourism and sustainable development reveals the inherent challenges of achieving sustainable tourism development or, more precisely, the difficulty in mapping tourism, as a specific social and economic activity, onto the principles and prerequisites of sustainable development. As considered elsewhere (Sharpley, 2000, 2009), not only does the structure and nature of the tourism industry militate against sustainable production, but also the significance of tourism as a form of consumption suggests that responsible tourist behaviour (or a willingness to adopt a more responsible stance towards consuming tourism) may not be as widespread as some would claim.

And it is in this latter context that the real potential of encouraging critical reflection on the part of students lies. That is, students of tourism can be encouraged to reflect on their own personal behaviour as tourists, their amenability to the notion of responsible consumer behaviour, however defined, and, as a consequence, to consider the extent to which their responses to the concept of responsible tourism mirror their response to the longer term need for a new social paradigm for sustainable lifestyles.

Of course, responsibility as defined in the context of this chapter cannot, in a traditional sense, be 'taught'; it is not the role of higher education institutions to prescribe students' values and behaviour. However, it is their role to inspire critical and independent thought, to provide a knowledge base that supports and encourages reflection and the development of values and attitudes relevant to contemporary life. As this chapter has attempted to demonstrate, the study of the relationship between tourism, development and sustainability is not only an effective vehicle for highlighting the challenges of development and sustainability more generally (challenges which, arguably, will become more acute as the twenty-first century progresses), but also offers the opportunity to encourage reflection on the role of the individual in achieving a more sustainable world. That is, it may at least stimulate contemplation of the concept of responsibility.

References

Airey, D. (2008). 'Tourism Education: life begins at 40'. *Teoros*, 27(1), 27–32. Available: http://epubs.surrey. ac.uk/tourism/40 (Accessed 11 March 2013).

Cohen, E. (1987). 'Alternative Tourism: a critique'. *Tourism Recreation Research*, 12(2), 13–18.

Cooper, C., & Ozdil, I. (1992). 'From Mass to "Responsible" Tourism: the Turkish experience'. *Tourism Management*, 13(4), 377–86.

Cronin, L. (1990). 'A Strategy for Tourism and Sustainable Developments'. *World Leisure and Recreation*, 32(3), 12–18.

Dann, G. (Ed.). (2002). *The Tourist as a Metaphor of the Social World*. Wallingford: CABI Publishing.

de Kadt, E. (1979). *Tourism: passport to development?* New York: Oxford University Press.

Dresner, S. (2002). *The Principles of Sustainability*. London: Earthscan.

Goodland, R. (1992). 'The Case that the World has Reached its Limits'. In R. Goodland, H. Daly, S. Serafy, & B. von Droste (Eds.), *Environmentally Sustainable Economic Development: Building on Brundtland* (pp. 15–27). Paris: UNESCO.

Goodwin, H. (2011). *Taking Responsibility for Tourism*. Oxford: Goodfellow Publishers.

Harrison, L., & Husbands, W. (1996). *Practising Responsible Tourism: international case studies in tourism planning, policy and development*. Chichester: John Wiley.

Haywood, K. (1988). 'Responsible and Responsive Tourism Planning in the Community'. *Tourism Management*, 9(2), 105–18.

Hunter, C. (1995). 'On the Need to Re-conceptualise Sustainable Tourism Development'. *Journal of Sustainable Tourism*, 3(3), 155–65.

International Union for Conservation of Nature (IUCN) (1991). *Caring for the Earth: a strategy for sustainable living*. Gland, Switzerland: IUCN, UNEP and WWF.

Jamal, T., & Robinson, M. (2009). 'Introduction: the evolution and contemporary positioning of tourism as a focus of study'. In T. Jamal & M. Robinson (Eds.), *The Sage Handbook of Tourism Studies* (pp. 1–16). London: Sage Publications.

Lélé, S. (1991). 'Sustainable Development: a critical review'. *World Development*, 19(1), 607–21.

Ludwig, D., Hilborn, R., & Walters, C. (1993), 'Uncertainty, Resource Exploitation, and Conservation: lessons from history'. *Science*, 269(5104), 17–36.

Mundt, J. (2011). *Tourism and Sustainable Development: reconsidering a concept of vague policies*. Berlin: Erich Schmidt.

Popescu, L. (2008). *The Good Tourist: an ethical traveller's guide*. London: Arcadia Books.

Porritt, J. (2007). *Capitalism as if the World Matters*. London: Earthscan.

Rahnema, M., & Bawtree, V. (1997). *The Post Development Reader*. London: Zed Books.

Redclift, M. (1987). *Sustainable Development: exploring the contradictions*. London: Routledge.

Responsibletravel.com (2013). *About Us*. Available: http://www.responsibletravel.com/Copy/Copy100427. htm (Accessed 26 March 2013).Richter, L .(Ed.). (1989). *The Politics of Tourism in Asia*. Honolulu: University of Hawaii Press.

Robinson, J. (2004). 'Squaring the Circle? Some thoughts on the idea of sustainable development'. *Ecological Economics*, 48(4), 369–84.

Sharpley, R. (2000). 'Tourism and Sustainable Development: exploring the theoretical divide'. *Journal of Sustainable Tourism*, 8(1), 1–19.

Sharpley, R. (2009). *Tourism Development and the Environment: beyond sustainability?* London: Earthscan.

Sharpley, R. (2011). *The Study of Tourism: past trends and future directions*. Abingdon: Routledge.

Sharpley, R. (2012). 'Responsible Tourism: whose responsibility?' In A. Holden & D. Fennel (Eds.), *Handbook of Tourism and the Environment* (pp. 382–91). Abingdon: Routledge.

Tourism Education Futures Initiative (TEFI). (2013). Tourism Education Futures Initiative. Available: http://tourismeducationfutures.org (Accessed 11 January 2014).

Tribe, J. (2002). 'The Philosophic Practitioner'. *Annals of Tourism Research*, 29(2), 338–57.

Turner, L. & Ash, J. (1975). *The Golden Hordes: international tourism and the pleasure periphery*. London: Constable.

United Nations Development Programme (2010) *Human Development Report 2010: The Real Wealth of Nations: pathways to human development*. New York: Palgrave Macmillan.

Wheeller, B. (1991). 'Tourism's Troubled Times: responsible tourism is not the answer'. *Tourism Management*, 12(2), 91–6.

Williams, M. (2000). 'Dark Ages and Dark Areas: global deforestation in the deep past'. *Journal of Historical Geography*, 26(1), 28–46.

Wood, K., & House, S. (1991). *The Good Tourist: a worldwide guide for the green traveller*. London: Mandarin.

World Commission on Environment and Development (WCED). (1987). *Our Common Future*. Oxford: Oxford University Press.

World Tourism Organization (WTO). (1980). *Manila Declaration on World Tourism*. Madrid: WTO.

Young, G. (1973). *Tourism: blessing or blight?* Penguin: Harmondsworth.

14

International issues in curriculum design and delivery in tourism and hospitality education

Paul Barron

School of Marketing, Tourism and Languages, Edinburgh Napier University, Scotland

Introduction: the internationalization landscape

Whilst the concept of internationalization has recently become a key strategic element for many universities around the world (Ayoubi & Massoud, 2007; Maringe, 2009), it might be argued that universities are, by their very nature, viewed as places where universal knowledge was sought and developed. Indeed Maringe (2009) suggests that the very first university teachers (in medieval times) were known for their travels between nations to disseminate knowledge and seek new forms of understanding from other places. In addition to the international nature of universities and the international activities of staff, the activity of providing international students with the opportunity to study overseas is not a new concept. This element of internationalization traditionally took the form of students from Asia travelling to study at universities in western countries. Indeed it has been reported that international students, particularly those from China, but also from Hong Kong, Malaysia and Singapore have been arriving in western higher education institutions for education since the latter half of the nineteenth century (Chan, 1999). Indeed, McNair (1933) noted that by 1916, some 300 Chinese students were reported in the UK studying mainly medicine, economics and engineering. The internationalization of higher education has developed from these early occurrences and a significant number of universities in the major English-speaking destinations (MESDs) of the USA, UK, Australia, Canada and New Zealand have recognized the potential benefits of this element of internationalization, and consequently have adopted various initiatives that encourage students from overseas to study for one of their qualifications (Jiang & Carpenter, 2013). Several reasons have been identified which are seen to drive contemporary university institutions towards the concept of internationalization. Maringe and Gibbs (2008), for example, identified a range of motives and rationales including:

- generating money from high international students' fees;
- enriching the experience of students and staff through a variety of models of cross-border educational experiences;

181

- incorporating an international dimension into teaching and research;
- raising the status and international standing of the institution;
- improving the overall quality of educational provision and experience of students;
- preparing graduates for global employment careers;
- exporting educational services and products; and
- achieving international standards.

In parallel to the points listed above, there continues to exist a demand for international education. Taking Chinese students who study for an overseas qualification as an example, it has been suggested that a graduate with a foreign degree is classified as having better skills and being more employable in the marketplace of industry (Fam & Gray, 2000; Gareth, 2005; Zhang, 2001) and that such students will bring home knowledge that will assist in building a strong country (Hui, 2005; Wang, 2002). The recent economic growth in the People's Republic of China has resulted in more families being able to afford to send their children to other countries for education (Chinaview, 2006; Chinaorg, 2002). There is also evidence that studying overseas has become a trend in Chinese society with Chinese parents perceiving an overseas education as having several advantages for their children such as getting direct exposure to foreign languages and culture, accessing a better education and building better skills for future competition in the job market after graduation (Yang, 2007). Finally, there continues to be an inadequate supply of university places in China's higher education with approximately 8 per cent of high school graduates able to gain a place in local universities (Li & Bray, 2007). Consequently a combination of economic growth in the region, a continued view that an overseas education is perceived as better than studying locally, and inadequate supply of local university places has resulted in a continued demand for international education. Whilst generalizations are rarely accurate, it might be suggested that this situation is reflected in many other countries and the overall demand for international education has continued to rise (Jiang & Carpenter, 2013).

This combination of supply and demand issues has resulted in a range of strategies that have been introduced and rigorously pursued by universities aimed at attracting and securing the international student market. These strategies have met with some success. With regard to attracting international students to study overseas, UK universities in session 2011/12 attracted some 435,235 non-UK students (comprising 132,550 European Union (EU) students and 302,680 non-European students) studying in higher education institutions in the UK (HESA, 2013). For session 2011/12, the number of non-EU students rose 1.6 per cent over previous session figures and continue to originate from the traditional source markets of China, Hong Kong and Singapore, which have shown continued growth despite global financial issues. A selection of emerging source countries (see for example a year-on-year increase of 18 per cent in the number of Vietnamese students deciding to undertake their studies in the UK in session 2011/12) have presented UK universities with a range of alternative horizons for their international activities. Whilst forecasts are rarely accurate and often overtaken by global occurrences, future demand for international education appears robust with, for example, a forecast 30 per cent increase in the number of international students studying in Australia by 2020 (Hurst, 2013) and a doubling of international students globally by 2025 (Maslen, 2012).

The international curricula

Thus far, discussion has focused on international students studying overseas. Whilst the importance of international students to the financial well-being of higher education institutions (HEIs) in MESDs has been argued (see for example Altbach & Knight, 2007), internationalization in higher education is considered a wider concept and has been defined as: 'the process of integrating an international perspective in the teaching/learning, research and service functions of higher education institutions' (Knight, 2001: 229).

It might therefore be suggested that internationalization comprises the processes by which HEIs compete for students globally and prepare graduates for careers in a globalized world (Hanson, 2010). Whilst these two issues are, of course, connected, it is the curriculum that is key to the preparation of graduates. Maringe and Gibbs (2008) argue that there is very little or no mention of the curriculum in the internationalization discourses of university staff. However, as Beyer and Liston (1996) argue, the curriculum is the centrepiece of university activity. How, therefore, has the move toward internationalization affected the curriculum of contemporary universities? Luong et al. (1996: 1) defined an internationalized curriculum as one that,

> values empathy and intellectual curiosity through which . . . learners participate in a mutually beneficial, internationally and multi-culturally aware learning process, engaging with and constructing global state of the art knowledge, developing understanding and useful skills, and preparing themselves to continue learning throughout personally and vocationally fulfilling lives.

It might be suggested that this definition focuses internationalization of the curriculum on the learning process and on the development of skills and attitudes within students (including the development of international and cross-cultural understanding and empathy) as much as on curriculum content and the development of knowledge in students. However, internationalization of the curriculum has been much discussed and diversely interpreted in the scholarly literature. Over the previous two decades, various definitions have evolved in attempts to provide a basis for shared understanding and the provision of information that universities can utilize as a means of developing aims and objects that will allow the achievement of their overall strategy. Yet successive global surveys of universities conducted by the International Association of Universities have indicated ongoing confusion over what internationalization of the curriculum means in practice – a situation that has hindered universities in achieving their internationalization objectives, whatever they may be (Egron-Polak & Hudson, 2010; Knight, 2006).

Whilst there are a number of studies of the higher education curriculum (Barnett & Coate, 2005), studies of internationalization of the curriculum in higher education are scarce. Such studies tend to focus on a single institution and/or a single discipline and, consequently, Barnett and Coate (2005) suggest that approaches have been piecemeal and reactive. However, it is common for higher education institutions to make specific statements regarding the skills, knowledge and attitudes their graduates will possess that will allow them to work in a globalized, interconnected world through internationalization of the curriculum. As a result, Leask (2013) argues that knowledge of, and impact on, the internationalization of the curriculum in various disciplines is poorly understood.

Turner and Robson (2008) argue that each degree programme should incorporate an international dimension and that universities have used graduate attributes as one of the drivers of internationalization of the curriculum. The notion of developing graduates who have 'global souls' (Bennet, 2008: 13) is, itself, international and the aim of most universities is to produce graduates who see themselves not only as being connected with their local communities but also as members of world communities (Rhoads & Szelényi, 2011). Most institutions now have statements of graduate qualities or attributes focused on the development of global perspectives, cross-cultural communication skills, intercultural competence and world knowledge (Jones & Killick, 2013). For example explicit in the Edinburgh Napier University Business School brochure

(2013: 6) is the statement that: 'The importance of the global business environment is reflected in our course design and enhanced through our study abroad opportunities and the collective sharing of experiences within our multi-cultural student community.'

Prior to examining the impact on the curricula that has occurred as a consequence of internationalization, it is important to consider the various formats that this educational provision takes. Linked to Maringe and Gibbs's (2008) range of motives and rationales detailed above, the move toward internationalization of education tends to focus on three issues. First, on economic issues, for example where universities generate income through attracting international students to study for their qualification (Altbach & Knight, 2007). Second, on experience issues where it is argued that both staff and students somehow benefit from international exposure (Spencer-Oatey, 2013). Finally, on opportunity or career issues where it is argued that graduates from an institution that has embraced internationalization will be better prepared for careers in the global marketplace (Laughton & Ottewill, (2000).

This provision of education can take several forms. First, international students travel to the host university campus in the host university home location, join with other home and overseas students and follow timetabled classes (Smith & Rae, 2006). An alternative to this approach is where the host university partners with an overseas institution and either provides the host university qualification in that location, or develops a partnership with the overseas institution with the aim of providing one or more joint programmes. In this instance, students are normally entirely drawn from the local population (Brookes & Becket, 2010). A further strategy that universities in the UK, the USA and Australia have adopted is the creation of a branch campus in an overseas location by a host university (see for example Nottingham University's (2013a, b) campuses in Malaysia and China). This approach aims to provide the host university educational experience within a controlled environment to local students (Wilkins et al., 2012) and whilst this approach represents a significant resource investment, the experiences of students studying in this manner have been found to be positive (Sid Nair et al., 2011). Students, wherever they may be, also have the opportunity to study via a distance mode. Whilst distance education has been available for some time, advances in information technology have improved the overall education experience and increasingly include virtual instances of traditional educational experiences (Larreamendy-Joerns & Leinhardt, 2006). In addition, internationalization can also occur through periods of study abroad or student exchange where students take the opportunity to spend one or two semesters in an overseas institution and receive cross–credit for studies undertaken during the period (Wynveen et al., 2012).

Increasingly, there are calls for these skills and perspectives to focus less on the instrumental, economic outcomes or competencies required for individuals to succeed in a globalized economy and more on ethical and responsible learning outcomes that recognize that 'human beings are social and cultural beings as well as economic ones' who need to 'think locally, nationally and globally' (Rizvi & Lingard, 2010: 201). Leask (2013) considers that educators need to take a more holistic approach and suggests that this might be achieved through the provision of structural options and pathways for course design; developing international perspectives in students, and the development and introduction of teaching and learning strategies for internationalization.

One strategy for developing an international curriculum is to introduce content that aims to prepare local students to become competent intercultural communicators (Laughton & Ottewill, 2000). While this proposal is not the only alternative for fostering multicultural education, it has considerable practical value. However, it has been suggested an understanding of the varying dimensional approaches does not necessarily equip a person with the capabilities or the competence to manage effectively in an international or multicultural context (Gannon,

2000). It is suggested, therefore, that the curriculum must encourage the development of cultural awareness and cultural sensitivity; a situation that Barron and Dasli (2010) found to be only partly achieved amongst a group of undergraduate Business Studies students. It may be suggested that educators in the Business Studies general area and in subject areas such as hospitality and tourism in particular are well placed to focus on the development of the student who possesses not only an international perspective, but also a degree of intercultural sensitivity. Indeed the use of international placements, work-based learning and the encouragement of local students to undertake a period of study abroad are all considered effective means of breaking down barriers and assisting students to enter the workforce with an open mind and without the baggage of prejudicial ignorance. Contemporary curricula can support these initiatives through discussion, analysis and reflective learning prior to and following international opportunities (Hearns *et al.*, 2007a).

Internationalizing the hospitality and tourism curricula

Recent years have seen an increase in the number of international hospitality management degree programmes (Jayawardena, 2001; Jordan, 2008) and the demand for graduates for the industry has been recognized by academics, employers and graduates (Brookes & Beckett, 2011: Hearns *et al.*, 2007a; Maher, 2004). However, Jayawardena (2001) suggests that much hospitality education is international in name only and it has been suggested that hospitality graduates have developed only moderate global perspectives (Lunn, 2006). Whilst there are few studies concerning international students studying hospitality and/or tourism management overseas, hospitality management appears attractive to international students and attracts higher than average numbers of such students (Brookes & Becket, 2011; Malfroy & Daruwalla, 2000). In her study Hsu (1996) suggested that globally the undergraduate student population studying hospitality management and/or hospitality and tourism management was becoming more diverse. This diversity appears to have continued with the Travel and Tourism subject area remaining popular amongst non-UK students. For example, the Higher Education Statistics Agency (HESA) provides useful figures regarding the diversity within the Travel and Tourism subject area that give an indication not only of students enrolled on such programmes (4,200 students in session 2011/12) (HESA, 2013) but also the continued growth in the popularity of such programmes during a difficult economic period (+2 per cent year on year from session 2005/6 to session 2011/12) (HESA, 2006, 2013). However, the international nature of such provision has been criticized by Jayawardena (2001: 310), who suggested that whilst much hospitality education is international in name, it remains local in 'design, delivery and deliberations'. Two empirical studies that included UK hospitality management degrees in their sample report that hospitality graduates have developed only moderate global perspectives (Lunn, 2006; Maher, 2004). Hearns *et al.* (2007b) argued that multiculturalism may need to be understood not only as training for competencies geared towards managing diversity, but rather as a process of educating students and staff for integration in an intercultural working environment. It is believed colleges and universities offering hospitality and tourism programmes can readily support learning in these areas by providing greater focus within their curricula on legal and other aspects of multiculturalism and multi-ethnicity.

There are few studies that have examined the internationalization of the curricula of hospitality and tourism programmes. Hsu (1996) found that whilst international hospitality students considered that there were elements of internationalization within the curricula, they felt that academic staff did not fully recognize their experiences in either classroom discussion or assessment opportunities. Diaz and Krauss (1996) argued the requirement for academic staff to develop an understanding regarding the cultural differences between international and domestic hospitality management students and provide curricula that are not only international in content, but also culturally sensitive. Barron (2002) reported on research that examined the learning issues and problems experienced by mainly Chinese students studying hospitality management at university in Australia. The problems identified were very similar in nature to common problems associated with international students studying overseas and it was concluded that in addition to language issues and experiencing feelings of dislocation and homesickness, this study also identified a range of curricular issues, such as content, delivery and assessment, that international students considered very local in focus. Barron (2003) suggested that universities make little or no effort to adjust the curricula to take into consideration the different approaches that international students prefer when learning and that international students are required to adapt to the host university curricula and adopt a range of styles that may be at odds with their preferences. In addition to issues with curricula content that was considered too 'western centric' the assessment of curricula content presented problems for these students with concerns regarding case studies, peer assessment and presentations. It has been argued that an output of an international curriculum is the need to prepare students for the world of international business through developing capability and effectiveness within the context of international operations and environment, and specifically the ability to function in a cross-cultural or multicultural context (Laughton & Ottewill, 2000).

This chapter has, thus far, attempted an overview of internationalization of higher education and highlighted a number of studies that have examined the development and impact of internationalization of the tourism and hospitality subject area. The next section of this chapter presents the findings of a case study that examines the international curricula from the perspectives of local students, international students and academic staff at a UK university as a means of developing an understanding of internationalized curriculum.

Research approach

As a means of developing an understanding of the practical impact of the extent of the internationalization of the curriculum, a brief research project was undertaken. Given the exploratory nature of this study research, a case study strategy was adopted (Yin, 2009). A single case study approach was used, so no claim is made regarding the generalizability of this study (Yin, 2009). The study sample comprised one post-92 UK university where a range of unstructured interviews were undertaken during 2013 with academic staff teaching on hospitality and tourism programmes and current students studying an undergraduate degree in hospitality and tourism management. A total of nine interviews were conducted – three with hospitality and tourism academic staff, three with local students in their final year of their undergraduate programme and three with international students (i.e. non-UK or EU students) also in their final year. Participants were contacted to request an interview and supplied with a participant information form that addressed anonymity and confidentiality. Appointments were then made to conduct an unstructured interview at the participants' convenience. The unstructured nature of the interviews encouraged a more naturalistic and conversational environment. This study recognized that the concept of internationalization is wide-ranging and a key construct of the interviews was to ascertain individual thoughts concerning the scope of internationalization in higher education. Consequently, the interview commenced by asking participants to construct their definition of internationalization. Thereafter, questions were divided into three broad sections. First, participants were asked their opinions on the relative importance of the concept of internationalization in higher education and thereafter describe how they considered that the design of the curriculum and the subsequent content of modules had been affected or influenced by internationalization. Second, participants were asked to reflect on how internationalization had affected or influenced the delivery of modules. Finally, participants were asked their opinions on how internationalization might be further used in higher education programmes as a means of best preparing hospitality graduates for careers in the global environment. Interviews lasted, on average, 25 minutes and were recorded and transcribed. Data were analysed according to the three broad areas identified above and results are discussed in the next section.

The case study university

Prior to any discussion of results, this study should be placed in context through a brief discussion of the university in question. Based in Edinburgh, this post-92 university has enrolments of over 17,000 students, with around 30 per cent of the total student body classed as international and originating from over 110 countries. The university also provides education in a number of overseas locations and currently approximately 3,500 students are taught overseas. Located within the Business School faculty, the School of Marketing, Tourism and Languages provides a range of undergraduate and postgraduate programmes in tourism and hospitality management. Reflecting the overall university profile, the School of Marketing, Tourism and Languages attracts students of all nationalities to study on campus, but also provides a range of programmes in overseas locations – most notably India and Hong Kong. This delivery is undertaken in partnership with institutions in the overseas location whereby lectures are delivered in intensive face-to-face mode by the UK university staff who are thereafter supported by local staff who provide tutorials.

Discussion of results

Local student perspectives

Local students considered internationalization as being mainly concerned with the attracting of overseas students to study on campus. This was considered by respondents to have both positive and negative consequences with one respondent neatly summarizing the general feeling by stating that:

> My experience (of internationalization of higher education) has been sharing my education with people from all over the world. I've made lots of friends and can now better understand different viewpoints, but at the same time sometimes I felt that I was the minority in the classroom.
>
> (Student A)

When asked about the importance of studying an international curriculum, all local students considered it to be an important focus of any programme of study. However, these respondents found it difficult to provide examples of how they considered the curriculum had been influenced by internationalization. Interestingly, this group of students did not really initially consider that internationalization had significantly influenced the design of the curriculum. When pressed on this matter, these students felt that other than inserting the word 'international' into several module titles, there was little evidence of internationalization within the module or programme content; this statement is in line with Jayawardena's (2001) and Lunn's (2006) findings that hospitality and tourism curricula are international in name only. However, further discussion revealed that this group of students considered that, within the proviso of the comment above, an international cohort improved the overall experience that these local students had enjoyed during their time at university through, for example, discussion of personal experiences. It was also determined that academic staff attempted to utilize a range of international examples when delivering curricula and that there was opportunity through assessment to discuss, evaluate and analyse international examples, which links closely to Maringe and Gibbs's (2008) motives and rationales for internationalization. This group of students did, however, feel that there were a range of negative consequences for delivering the international curricula. Students considered that curricula had been influenced and, indeed, designed not as a means of developing the international graduate, but agreed with Barron's (2006) assertions that international student needs and concerns were its focus. From a practical perspective, participants considered that curricula delivery had been adjusted to take into account international students' language capabilities and that there was evidence of curricula being assessed by methods that favoured the international cohort. It is suggested that these comments accord well with Barron and Dasli's (2010) study that concluded that local students displayed limited levels of intercultural sensitivity.

International student perspectives

This group of students had a very different view of the concept of internationalization. Their view of internationalization appeared generally positive and was neatly summarized by one student who stated that, in the context of her experience, internationalization was,

> evident throughout the programme. The modules I studied were international in focus and my fellow students came from a variety of backgrounds and cultures which added to the international feel of my time at university.
>
> (Student B)

The very fact of studying overseas was, naturally, an international experience for this group of students and it was considered that all elements of their educational experience had been influenced by internationalization. These students stated that the design of the overall programme and the individual module contained therein had an international dimension and that lecturing staff used a variety of international examples throughout the teaching of the modules. Students gave the example of international module titles, and module content that presented information from a variety of perspectives. Assessment was also mentioned as a key contributor to the overall internationalization of the individual modules and overall programme and students explained that, individually, they had the opportunity to influence internationalization through their choice of international examples used in assessments.

Concerning the delivery of modules, this group of students recognized internationalization from several perspectives. Students considered that the academic staff significantly contributed to the international feel of modules. This was achieved in two ways. First, this group of students recognized that the academic staff teaching on the programme were from a diverse range of nationalities and thus brought an international perspective to their approach to teaching. In addition, it was understood that lecturing staff had gained experience of teaching in an international environment through frequent overseas teaching episodes. It was generally felt that the combination of the variety of cultures and nationalities combined with international teaching experience influenced the approach to teaching modules in the home campus and that a natural international perspective was provided as a result.

Students also felt that the concept of internationalization had affected the delivery of individual modules, especially in tutorials or seminars where international examples and case studies were a regular feature. It was found that students of all nationalities were encouraged to discuss issues from their perspective and this group of students considered that this added to the international focus of the module and enriched the overall experience. Whilst it was generally found that internationalization had positively contributed to the curricula as experienced by this group of students, they also identified several disadvantages. First, this group of students recognized that due to the diverse nature of the student body in the classroom, especially the case in large lecture situations, cultural sensitivity was often either lacking or forgotten about altogether and academic staff tended to revert back to a default position and treat all students the same. Second, the advantage of academic staff teaching overseas was, simultaneously, viewed as a potential issue as occasionally academic staff would be absent for periods of time and be replaced by other, often less experienced, staff.

The above findings link neatly to Maringe and Gibb's (2008) study that highlighted the range of motives and rationales for universities becoming involved in internationalization activities and it might be suggested that the case university is achieving some success in providing these participants with an internationalized experience.

Academic staff perspectives

The academic staff who took part in this small study adopted a broader view of internationalization and considered that internationalization was not only a pragmatic, and indeed necessary, strategy that the university was required to follow, but also an overarching philosophy that permeated their entire activity as university academics. One staff member considered that internationalization was:

> something that *had* to be done as a means of ensuring the viability of the organization, but also something that *should* be done to ensure our modules and programmes are attractive to students wherever they come from
>
> (Staff Member A, my italics)

These participants considered that internationalization was a key feature of all modules and commented that curricula were directly influenced by internationalization as there is a requirement to provide a statement on how a module has been internationalized on all module descriptors. Internationalization was, however, viewed from both a positive and negative perspective by these members of staff. The positive feelings concerned four broad areas. First, the participants in this study were fully cognizant of the fact that attracting international students, whether they study on the home campus or in overseas locations, was critical to not only the financial well-being of the university, but also to its very survival. Internationalization was thus seen as a crucial and central aspect to the activities of the university. The second positive perspective concerned the student experience. This group of staff felt that a focus on internationalization as a core element of the curricula improved and enhanced the overall student experience. Examples of how this occurred included benefits associated with the multicultural classroom where the learning experience of all students was influenced by a range of perspectives and the incorporation of international examples as a means of improving teaching materials. The third positive influence was the notion that internationalization in general had provided personal benefits to the academic staff who took part in this study. It was considered that internationalizing the curriculum had required staff to think more widely when developing modules and constructing individual classes. Consequently it was felt that this had contributed to improving them as academic members of staff who provided a better teaching experience to their students. The reality of teaching in a multicultural classroom, whether at the home campus or overseas, had also improved staff knowledge regarding different cultures and boosted their confidence as an academic staff member. One participant considered that the drive toward internationalization in its broadest sense and specifically the internationalization of the curriculum had instilled an increased level of pride in the status of the university. It was felt that the university was well regarded in the international arena for both its overall provision and the appropriateness of the modules and programmes provided. The final positive influence considered by academic staff concerned graduate careers. It was felt that the international curricula, as contained within modules and programmes, were essential in providing graduates with the best opportunities to secure careers in the contemporary job market. The location of the student was irrelevant, rather it was felt that an international perspective, as provided by the internationalization of the curricula, was crucial in providing graduates with a world view that encouraged the adoption of a balanced perspective. Again, it is worth noting that the motives and rationales (Maringe & Gibbs, 2008) discussed above appear to be evident in the findings of this study.

Not all comments from academic staff were positive. The number of international students, their language ability and the varying learning styles presented challenges both at home and abroad. Participants highlighted that the number and variety of international students limited the opportunity to deliver all but the basic requirements of the curricula and it was felt that a broader, more international, view of a topic might be able to be delivered to smaller classes. Whilst not specifically related to curricula, the varying levels of English-language proficiency were highlighted by all participants as having an impact on the delivery and assessment of the curricula. Finally, staff members highlighted the variety of learning styles evident amongst such a large group of international students impacted on the delivery of the curricula.

Conclusion

This chapter has sought to provide an overview of the impact of international issues in the areas of curriculum design and development and the consequent impact on module and programme delivery in tourism and hospitality education. Using a single case study, this chapter has highlighted what internationalization of the curriculum means to local students, international students and academic staff studying on, or associated with, hospitality and tourism programmes. Whilst no claim is made of generalization of the findings of this study, it is contended that research such as this contributes to an understanding of the practical implications of the increasingly common practice of internationalization.

Whilst it might have been presumed that students and academic staff would view internationalization very differently, it was interesting to note the significant difference of opinions between local and international students. Perhaps not surprisingly, international students were better able to recognize the nature of internationalization and could not only easily identify specific examples of how the curricula had been internationalized but also understood the benefits of studying a curriculum that was international in nature. Local students were narrower in their views and internationalization of the curricula was not an obvious concept. Local participants in this study did, however, comment on the (sometimes negative) consequences of an internationalization strategy and the results of this study would indicate that effort is required on the part of the university to more effectively communicate the benefits and advantages of internationalization in general and delivering international curricula in particular.

This study found that academic staff viewed internationalization from both a positive and negative perspective. Internationalization of hospitality and tourism degrees, and therein the hospitality and tourism curricula, was a fact of contemporary university life. Whilst there were identified a number of more negative consequences of internationalization and its impact on the curricula, this study found that there was a general positive feeling about internationalization in general and its effects on the curricula. It could be argued that there was a requirement to incorporate internationalization into the curricula, and it was recognized as the result of the university's internationalization strategy. For example the multicultural classroom and a requirement to teach overseas had added to the content of the curricula being taught and developed personal confidence and teaching skills which, in turn, improved the curricula development and delivery. The cycle of the benefits of internationalization (i.e. to academic staff) is a key conclusion of this research and it is recommended that further research into the link between internationalization activities and the personal development of academic staff be undertaken.

In addition to the numerical and geographical limitations of this study, it is also recognized that several groups of key informants were not included. The introduction of restrictions for student visas (for example, Tier 4 visa regulations in the UK) will encourage MESD universities to offer their programmes overseas and it is suggested that there will be an increase in the number of students attracted to this type of educational experience. This approach will present the host university with a range of academic and curricula-based issues that would require focus on the particular content of programmes being offered. For example, is it appropriate to merely transfer a programme offered in the host location regardless of the demands of the international student? Students who take the opportunity to study an element of their programme overseas were another important omission from this study. Whilst these students have formed the focus of much previous research, it is suggested that this activity has not figured highly in the internationalization strategy of many universities, at least in the UK.

This study has highlighted that international curricula have different meanings for different groups in the higher education sphere. Internationalization is implicit in many universities' operations and hospitality and tourism schools and departments are well placed to continue to provide an internationalized experience. There is, however, a need to more explicitly communicate the rationale for and benefits of an international curriculum to students regardless of their origin or location of study.

References

Altbach, P., & Knight, J. (2007). 'The Internationalisation of Higher Education: motivations and realities'. *Journal of Studies in International Education*, 11(3/4), 290–305.

Ayoubi, R. M., & Massoud, H. K. (2007). 'The Strategy of Internationalisation in Universities', *International Journal of Educational Management*, 21(4), 329–49.

Barnett, R., & Coate, K. (2005). *Engaging the Curriculum in Higher Education*. Maidenhead: McGraw-Hill.

Barron, P. E. (2002). 'Providing a More Successful Education Experience for Asian Hospitality Management Students Studying in Australia: a focus on teaching and learning styles'. *Journal of Teaching in Travel and Tourism*, 2(2), 63–88.

Barron, P. E., (2003). 'Issues Surrounding Asian Students Studying Hospitality Management in Australia: a literature review regarding the paradox of the Asian learner'. *Journal of Teaching in Travel and Tourism*, 3(1), 23–45.

Barron, P. E., (2006). 'Stormy Outlook? domestic students' impressions of international students at an Australian university'. *Journal of Teaching in Travel and Tourism*, 6(2), 1–18.

Barron, P. E. & Dasli, M. (2010). 'Toward an Understanding of Integration amongst Hospitality and Tourism Students using Bennett's Developmental Model of Intercultural Sensitivity'. *Journal of Hospitality, Leisure, Sport & Tourism Education*, 7(1), 4–17.

Bennet, J. (2008). 'On Becoming a Global Soul: a path to engagement during study abroad'. In V. Savicki (Ed.), *Developing Intercultural Competence and Transformation* (pp. 13–31). Sterling, VA: Stylus.

Beyer, L. E., & Liston, D. P. (1996). *Curriculum in Conflict: social visions, educational agendas and progressive school reform*. New York: Teachers College Press.

Brookes, M., & Becket, N. (2010). 'Developing Global Perspectives through International Management Degrees'. *Journal of Studies in International Education*, 15(4), 374–94.

Brookes, M., & Becket, N. (2011). 'Internationalising Hospitality Management Degree Programmes'. *International Journal of Contemporary Hospitality Management*, 23(2), 241–60.

Chan, S. (1999). 'The Chinese Learner: a question of style'. *Education and Training*, 41(6/7), 294–304.

Chinaorg. (2002). More Go Abroad, But Ready to Come Back. Released 11 July. Available: http://english.peopledaily.com.cn/200207/11/eng20020711_99526.shtml (Accessed 10 June 2013).

Chinaview. (2006). More Chinese Students Studying Overseas. Released 16 October. Available: http://english.people.com.cn/200610/16/eng20061016_312044.html (Accessed 10 June 2013).

Diaz, P. E., & Krauss, J. L. (1996). 'A Needs Analysis of an Expanding Hospitality Market – Asian students'. *Hospitality Research Journal*, 20(1), 15–26.

Edinburgh Napier University (2013). *Business School Brochure*. Edinburgh: Edinburgh Napier University Press.

Egron-Polak, E. & Hudson, R. (2010). *Internationalisation of Higher Education: global trends, regional perspectives*. IAU 3rd Global Survey Report. Paris: International Association of Universities.

Fam, K. S., & Gray, B. (2000). 'Asian Values and Education Promotion: an empirical study'. Paper presented at the American Marketing Association Conference, 28 June–1 July, Buenos Aires, Argentina.

Gannon, M. (2000). *Understanding Global Cultures: metaphorical journeys through 23 nations*. Thousand Oaks, CA: Sage.

Gareth, D. (2005). 'Chinese Students' Motivations for Studying Abroad'. *International Journal of Private Higher Education*, 2, 16–21.

Hanson, L. (2010). 'Global Citizenship, Global Health, and the Internationalisation of Curriculum: a study of transformational potential'. *Journal of Studies in International Education*, 14(1), 70–88.

Hearns, N., Devine, F., & Baum, T. (2007a). 'The Implications of Contemporary Cultural Diversity for the Hospitality Curriculum'. *International Journal of Contemporary Hospitality Management*, 49(5), 350–63.

Hearns, N., Devine, F., & Baum, T. (2007b). 'The Implications of Contemporary Cultural Diversity for the Hospitality Curriculum'. *Education and Training*, 49(5), 350–63.

Higher Education Statistics Agency (HESA). (2006). Students in Higher Education Institutions, 2005/06. *HESA Publications*. Available: http://www.hesa.ac.uk/index.php/content/view/1973/239/ (Accessed 10 June 2013).

Higher Education Statistics Agency (HESA). (2013). Students in Higher Education Institutions, 2011/12. *HESA Publications*. Available: http://www.hesa.ac.uk/index.php?option=com_content&task=view&id=2663&Itemid=161 (Accessed 10 June 2013).

Hsu, C. H. C. (1996). 'Needs and Concerns of International Students: what can educators do?' *Hospitality and Tourism Educator*, 8(2/3), 68–75.

Hui, L. (2005). 'Chinese Cultural Schema of Education: implications for communication between Chinese students and Australian educators'. *Issues in Educational Research*, 15(1), 17–36.

Hurst, D. (2013). 'More International Students to Head Down Under', *Sydney Morning Herald*, 27 February. Available: http://www.smh.com.au/federal-politics/political-news/more-international-students-to-head-down-under-report-20130227-2f51p.html (Accessed 11 June 2013).

Jayawardena, C. (2001). 'Challenges in International Hospitality Management Education'. *International Journal of Contemporary Hospitality Management*, 13(6), 310–15.

Jiang, N., & Carpenter, V. (2013), 'Faculty-Specific Factors of Degree of HE Internationalisation: an evaluation of four faculties of a post-1992 university in the United Kingdom'. *International Journal of Educational Management*, 27(3), 242–59.

Jones, E., & Killick, D. (2013). 'Graduate Attributes and the Internationalized Curriculum: embedding a global outlook in disciplinary learning outcomes'. *Journal of Studies in International Education*, 17(2), 165–82.

Jordan, F. (2008), 'Internationalisation in Hospitality, Leisure, Sport and Tourism Higher Education: a call for further reflexivity in curriculum development'. *Journal of Hospitality, Leisure, Sport and Tourism Education*, 7(1), 99–103.

Knight, J. (2001). 'Monitoring the Quality and Progress of Internationalisation'. *Journal of Studies in International Education*, 5, 228–43.

Knight, J. (2006). 'Internationalisation of Higher Education: new directions, new challenges'. *2005 IAU Global Survey Report*. Paris: International Association of Universities.

Larreamendy-Joerns, J., & Leinhardt, G. (2006). 'Going the Distance with Online Education'. *Review of Educational Research*, 76, 567.

Laughton, D., & Ottewill, R. (2000). 'Developing Cross-Cultural Capability in Undergraduate Business Education: implications for the student experience'. *Education and Training*, 42(6), 378–86.

Leask, B. (2013). 'Internationalizing the Curriculum in the Disciplines – imagining new possibilities'. *Journal of Studies in International Education*, 17(2), 103–18.

Li, M., & Bray, M. (2007). 'Cross-Border Flows of Students for Higher Education: push–pull factors and motivations of mainland Chinese students in Hong Kong and Macau'. *Higher Education*, 53, 791–818.

Lunn, J. (2006). *Global Perspectives in Higher Education Subject Analysis: tourism and hospitality*. London: Royal Geographical Society with IBG.

Luong, L., Crockett, K., Lundberg, D., & Scarino, A. (1996). *Report on Internationalisation of the Curriculum July 1996*. Adelaide: University of South Australia.

McNair, H. F. (1933). *The Chinese Abroad – their position and protection – a study in international law and relations*. Shanghai: Commercial Press.

Maher, A. (2004). *Oven Ready and Self Basting? Taking stock of employability skills*. Available: www.heacademy. ac.uk/assets/hlst/documents/LINK_Newsletter/link11.pdf (Accessed 13 June 2013).

Malfroy, J., & Daruwalla, P. (2000). 'Culture and Communication in a Postgraduate Hospitality Program'. *Australian Journal of Hospitality Management*, 7(1), 27–34.

Maringe, F. (2009). 'Strategies and Challenges of Internationalisation in HE: an exploratory study of UK universities'. *International Journal of Educational Management*, 23(7), 553–63.

Maringe, F., & Gibbs, P. (2008). *Higher Education Marketing*, London: Sage.

Maslen, G. (2012). 'Worldwide Student Numbers Forecast to Double by 2025'. *University World News*, 19 February, 209.

Rhoads, R., & Szelényi, K. (2011). *Global Citizenship and the University: advancing social life and relations in an interdependent world*. Stanford, CA: Stanford University Press.

Rizvi, F. & Lingard, B. (2010). *Globalising Education Policy*, Abingdon: Routledge.

Sid Nair, C., Murdoch, N., & Mertova, P. (2011). 'Benchmarking the Student Experience: the offshore campus experience'. *Total Quality Management Journal*, 23(6), 585–97.

Smith, L., & Rae, A. (2006). 'Coping with Demand: managing international student numbers at New Zealand universities'. *Journal of Studies in International Education*, 10(1), 27–45.

Spencer-Oatey, H. (2013). 'Maximizing the Benefits of International Education Collaborations: managing interaction processes'. *Journal of Studies in International Education*, 17(3), 244–61.

Turner, Y., & Robson, S. (2008*). Internationalising the University*. London: Continuum.

University of Nottingham (2013a). *The University of Nottingham Malaysia Campus*. Available: http://www.nottingham.edu.my/index.aspx (Accessed 13 June 2013).

University of Nottingham (2013b). *The University of Nottingham Ningbo, China Campus*. Available: http://www.nottingham.edu.cn/en/index.aspx (Accessed 13 June 2013).

Wang, X. F. (2002). *Education in China since 1976*. Jefferson, NC: McFarland.

Wilkins, S., Balakrishnan, M., & Huisman, J. (2012). 'Student Choice in Higher Education: motivations for choosing to study at an international branch campus'. *Journal of Studies in International Education*, 16(5), 413–33.

Wynveen, C., Kyle, G., & Tarrant, T. (2012). 'Study Abroad Experiences and Global Citizenship: fostering proenvironmental behaviour'. *Journal of Studies in International Education*, 16(4), 334–43. Yang, M. (2007). 'What Attracts Mainland Chinese Students to Australian Higher Education?'. *Studies in Learning Evaluation*, 4(2), 1–12.

Yin, R. (2009). *Case Study Research Design and Methods*, 4th edn. Thousand Oaks, CA: Sage.

Zhang, X. (2001). *China Today: Chinese families spend heavily on children's education*. Released 23 November. Available: http://www.china.org.cn/english/2001/Nov/22548.htm (Accessed 13 June 2013).

Part IV

The curriculum space
From global to local

15

Tourism and hospitality education in Asia

Cathy H. C. Hsu

School of Hotel and Tourism Management, The Hong Kong
Polytechnic University, China

Introduction

Over the past decade (2000–2010), international tourist arrivals increased by 38 per cent from 686 million to 946 million. Much of that growth was contributed by the Asia Pacific region, which saw inbound arrivals climbing steadily from 141 million to 258 million (+83 per cent), outshining Europe (+18 per cent) and North America (7 per cent) (UN ESCAP, 2012). Within the Asia Pacific region, Southeast Asia has been the key driver for the tourism boom in recent years; inbound arrivals to this sub-region almost doubled from 36.6 million in 2000 to 69.9 million in 2010 (UN ESCAP, 2012; UNTWO, 2013a).

The year 2012 marked a new milestone for international tourism with more than one billion tourist arrivals globally (UNTWO, 2013a). Despite recent economic challenges globally, Asian countries and regions continue to see positive tourism performances. Half-year data released by the United Nations World Tourism Organization (UNTWO, 2013b) suggests that Asia Pacific was again the fastest growing tourism market in terms of arrivals (+6 per cent year-on-year), followed by Europe (+5 per cent) and Africa (+4 per cent). By absolute number of arrivals, East and Northeast Asia have been dominating in the Asia Pacific region (UN ESCAP, 2012). The best performers in this sub-region, China and Hong Kong, welcomed a total of 81.49 million overnight visitors (34.8 per cent of the regional aggregate) in 2012 (National Bureau of Statistics of China, 2013; Hong Kong Tourism Board, 2013), of which around 75 per cent and 90 per cent respectively were from short-haul markets (National Tourism Administration of the People's Republic of China, 2013a; Hong Kong Tourism Board, 2013). These figures support the forecast by Euromonitor International that intra-regional/short-haul tourism will remain as the mainstream for Asia due to factors such as price and cultural familiarity (EyeforTravel, 2007).

Tourism education often emerges as a result of the increased recognition of the economic significance of the tourism industry by the public and private sectors (Liu, 2005). This is certainly the case in most Asian countries. Due to the rapid growth of the tourism industry and governments' wish to transform from a natural resources or manufacturing economy to one of knowledge and services, governments have recognized the manpower demand and need to upgrade human capital. Thus, education is considered as a tool for economic development, but at the same time governments declare education as a segment of the economy.

Edu-tourism and edu-nomics became a high priority for Singapore, a country that does not have many natural resources or a vibrant manufacturing sector. The Global Schoolhouse initiative in 2002 is a key education policy platform that aims to transform Singapore into a knowledge and innovation hub by establishing networks and collaborations with foreign universities. It is estimated that by 2015, education will contribute to 5 per cent of Singapore's GDP, increasing from 2 per cent in 2008 (Knight, 2011). Tourism and education are also two of the 12 national key economic areas in Malaysia (Prime Minister's Department, 2012). Tourism and hospitality higher education have been highlighted as an area that has had clear signs of progress. In addition to Singapore and Malaysia, the Hong Kong government released its action agenda on China's 11th five-year plan supporting tourism growth and recommending the development of Hong Kong as a regional education hub (Hong Kong Government, 2006). In 2009, education services had been earmarked as one of the six major areas of economic development (Task Force on Economic Challenges, 2009).

Besides these three locations, tourism education, and higher education in general, also witnessed significant growth in other Asian countries. The number of tertiary students in Asia grew more than 2.5 times from 1999 to 2011 (UNESCO, 2013). Previous literature has documented the growth, current status, and challenges of hospitality and tourism education in various Asian countries (e.g. Hou, 2011; Hsu, 2005; Kim et al., 2008; Lee & Jennings, 2010; Sangpikul, 2009; Zhong et al., 2013). Generally speaking, in less developed Asian countries tourism education is struggling because of limited educational resources, including teaching facilities, qualified faculty, updated teaching materials, and expertise in curriculum development. These issues are not unique to Asia, but are common for all undeveloped and developing countries. This chapter will focus on the three economies that have the ambition to become regional education hubs – Singapore, Malaysia, and Hong Kong.

Higher education policies

A variety of factors are driving efforts to establish a nation as an education hub, including income generation, modernization of the domestic tertiary education sector, economic competitiveness, need for a trained workforce, building regional profile, soft power, and a desire to move to a knowledge- and service-based economy. As analysed by Knight and Morshidi (2011), the primary reason for Singapore, Malaysia, and Hong Kong to establish themselves as education hubs is to gain regional status and competitiveness. For Singapore, the need for a skilled workforce is also equally important. These governments have liberalized their education, particularly the private sector, to attract foreign universities to offer programmes in their jurisdiction. This is coupled with the liberalization of immigration policies to attract international students and retain these talented and skilled individuals to live and work there after graduation.

In Singapore, university education is elite, well-resourced, regarded as an investment, clearly aligned to the needs of the economy, and directed and managed by the state. Higher education is used instrumentally as a tool of economic development. Singapore's national policy is focused on improving the quality and capacity of the higher education sector by focusing on: (1) inviting and providing financial support for 'world class universities' to establish programmes and branch campuses, (2) recruiting 150,000 international students by 2015, and (3) modernizing domestic higher education institutions through international partnerships with elite universities. Reputable universities from many countries have been invited to offer niche programmes (Knight, 2011), including Cornell University and the University of Nevada Las Vegas for their hospitality programmes. It is believed that through collaborations and alliances with overseas university partners and international expertise, Singapore's vocational and higher education institutions would be able to better build Singapore's industry talent, knowledge and capacity.

The government allowed its publicly funded universities to be corporatized as private companies, which provides these universities with greater flexibilities and autonomy to recruit outstanding academics and students, and reward staff according to performance in terms of productivity and quality. This was to foster a vibrant entrepreneurial climate within the institutions.

Similarly, Malaysia's 2007 National Higher Education Strategic Plan focused on transforming its higher educational institutions into world-class universities. The Malaysian government realized in the 1980s that it would be unable to educate more than 6 per cent of its population through its own institutions, and thus began to partner with international education service providers to supplement its system of higher education (Lenn, 2000). Vision 2020 was initiated in 1991 with a policy target of having 40 per cent of youth aged 19–24 admitted into tertiary education; of which, 60 per cent would go into public universities, and the rest into private colleges (Mok, 2011). In 2007, Malaysia officially announced the launch of the Malaysian Qualifications Agency (Bernama, 2007) giving the private education sector equivalent treatment to the public universities in terms of academic standards. Public universities began to franchise their programmes to private colleges (Mok, 2011) and become more entrepreneurial.

Similar to Singapore, Malaysia's Universities and University Colleges Act 1996 enabled public institutions of higher learning to be incorporated. This provides them with greater autonomy to manage and operate their affairs in a more dynamic and proactive manner. These universities are given more administrative and financial autonomy to enter into business ventures, establish companies and consultancy firms, commercialize research findings, and recruit and remunerate teaching staff (Lee, 1999).

Despite intense competition from other Asian countries like Singapore and Malaysia, Hong Kong is determined to position itself as the regional education hub, along with its vision to become Asia's world city (UGC, 2004). Much of the government's emphasis has been on increasing tertiary education participation (from 33 per cent to 60 per cent within a decade) and the provision of diversified pathways (such as local/non-local, degree/sub-degree as well as articulation programmes) for the young generation (UGC, 2010). To retain Hong Kong's competitiveness and to differentiate it from other Asian countries/cities, a recent higher education review released by the University Grants Committee (UGC) advocates further internationalization and collaboration with the Chinese mainland for Hong Kong's higher education in areas of recruitment of non-local students, internationalization of faculty, and offering of overseas exchange opportunities, among other initiatives (UGC, 2010).

To alleviate the pressure on the UGC-funded sector and deliver additional higher education opportunities, in 2000, an initiative that encourages the establishment of private universities by means of upgrading existing post-secondary colleges and/or attracting eminent overseas universities to set up private universities in Hong Kong was proposed by the Education Commission (2000). The government resolved to provide continuous support, such as land at reduced premium and one-off grants, for the development of local private universities in the future (Hong Kong Legislative Council, 2007).

Internationalization efforts

A common focus of Asian governments is to encourage higher educational institutions to internationalize their education as a way to upgrade the quality of education and skills of graduates, including English-language competency, and thus achieve internationally recognized standards of higher education. Many students from non-English-speaking nations want to acquire English and degrees from English-speaking systems because English is the premier language of business and the profession. Singapore and Hong Kong, which were colonized by English-speaking countries, and Malaysia, which reintroduced English as the language of instruction in the schools and as the dominant language in the growing private tertiary colleges (Marginson, 2010), have the language advantage in their internationalization efforts. Many other countries in Asia have now moved to offer English-medium programmes, especially at the graduate level. These could be offered by local private universities that hire international faculty members, managed by local universities in collaboration with Western institutions, or managed by Western institutions with minimal local participation. Many governments offer incentives to attract world-class educational institutions to establish themselves in the territories through various forms of collaboration with local institutions.

According to De Myer *et al.* (2004), internationalization strategies can be categorized into the import model, export model, partnership model, and network model. Under the import model, universities draw in foreign students and faculty members. Having non-local students and faculty on campus is the most basic form of internationalization. However, the level of internationalization is associated with the relative proportions of non-local students and faculty on campus. Most Asian universities nowadays are actively engaged in international recruitment activities. Franchised programmes can be considered as an extension of the import model. The local institutions pay for the right to use the imported curriculum. Students of these programmes may or may not be issued a parchment that bears the name of the foreign university that developed the curriculum.

Under the export model, the programme-offering university flies faculty overseas to teach, or use distance-learning technologies, often supplemented by local tutors. Many Western universities have offered overseas programmes in developing markets, such as China and other Asian countries. In fact, the top three importing nations/region of foreign degrees were Hong Kong, Singapore, and Malaysia (Department of Education, Science and Training, 2005; McBurnie, n.d.; Garrett & Verbik, 2004). The drivers of hosting offshore programmes in Singapore and Hong Kong were to attract international students and supplement the capacities of local public universities that were unable to fulfil the demand for higher education among high school graduates (Lim, 2009) as the student intake of public universities is capped by the governments. Education providers see these arrangements as commercial opportunities; and students find it attractive and cheaper to study at home with a foreign provider than to go abroad. After the 1997 Asian financial crisis and devaluation of some Asian currencies, many students in Asian countries chose to study offshore programmes at home rather than going abroad to reduce costs.

The partnership model can be operated with student and faculty exchange, or joint operation of programmes. Having exchange partnership agreements would provide local students and faculty with the opportunity to study and work abroad. Those who cannot participate in study/work abroad programmes will be exposed to international students/faculty who are exchanged for a period of time. Joint operation of programmes requires a much higher level of commitment from both the foreign and local universities. For example, Cornell University's School of Hotel Administration in collaboration with Nanyang Technological University's Nanyang Business School established the Cornell Nanyang Institute of Hospitality Management in 2003 and offered a joint Master of Management in Hospitality programme. Students graduating from this programme receive a parchment that has both institutions' names listed. Such an arrangement gives local universities the opportunity to be associated with international brand name institutions. However, partnership in the form of joint operation of programmes could have the most complication in terms of curriculum design, compared to the import, export, or branch campuses models. Potential conflicts could arise due to differences in quality or philosophies of the partnering institutions. These can undermine the long-term sustainability of institutional relationships and programmes.

The network model is based on the establishment of a branch campus or a network of branch campuses in other countries. The parent university needs to station faculty members abroad on a permanent basis, which can be arranged based on internal rotation. This requires significant up-front resources and is the most risky of all internationalization models. Understanding the resources required and the potential barriers for foreign universities, Singapore Education, a multi-government agency initiative was launched in 2003. This was led by the Economic Development Board (EDB) and supported by the Tourism Board, among other agencies. EDB is responsible for attracting internationally renowned educational institutions to set up campuses in Singapore, whereas the Tourism Board is tasked with overseas promotion and marketing of Singapore education (Mok, 2011). An example of the network model is the establishment of a private campus in 2005 by the University of Nevada Las Vegas (UNLV) which worked with the Singapore Institute of Technology, offering a BSc in Hospitality Management.

The Malaysian government introduced several initiatives, including the Educity in Iskandar, Kuala Lumpur Education City, and an international student recruitment plan. The Educity project involves having eight international universities offering programmes in selected fields including hospitality management in Malaysia (Knight, 2011). Foreign universities can establish campuses only by invitation from the Ministry of Higher Education and with majority Malaysian ownership. The Ministry of Higher Education has imposed stringent standards to attract only the top-tier foreign institutions to establish campuses in Malaysia. There have been four brand campuses of foreign universities, Monash University and Curtin University of Technology from Australia, and University of Nottingham and FTMS-De Monfort University from the UK.

These models may be clearly defined on paper; however, the variety of programmes available on the market are not easily identifiable as to which model they belong to. For example, Malaysia has more than 3,000 foreign programmes being offered in its tertiary education sector, Singapore has about 1,120, and Hong Kong has 1,120 foreign programmes and five teaching centres of offshore universities (Knight, 2011). It is unclear how many of these belong to each of the different models proposed by De Meyer et al. (2004). Government policies also do not always differentiate the various models and tend to treat them all as foreign programmes when it comes to regulation. Nevertheless, the classification provides a framework for university administrators to identify the most suitable form(s) of internationalization initiatives.

Challenges of transnational offerings

The opening of the University of New South Wales (UNSW) campus in Singapore in 2007 and its closure three months later has triggered much discussion about the possible reasons for the failure, although no definitive answer was made public (Lim, 2009). Swinburne University of Technology in Thailand was also wrapped up four years after the first operation. In hospitality and tourism, both the Cornell–Nanyang and UNLV programmes in Singapore have retreated from the market. Many foreign hospitality and tourism degree and Master's programmes began to appear in the late 1990s and early 2000s in Hong Kong. These foreign universities, such as Victoria University Australia, Sheffield Hallam University, Edinburgh Napier University, and Curtin University of Technology, all collaborated with private education providers or the continuing education arm of the public universities. The majority of these programmes had left Hong Kong by the early 2010s. For example, the tourism and hospitality management top-up degree programme offered by University of South Australia in collaboration with Hong Kong Baptist University's School of Continuing Education started in 2005 and ended in 2011. Hospitality and tourism programmes by the University of Northumbria, Sheffield Hallam University, Curtin University of Technology, and University of Strathclyde have also left the Hong Kong market. In the past few years, many other hospitality and tourism programmes at the undergraduate and graduate levels have announced their entry into the Asian market; however, their programmes never got off the ground.

Western universities often are attracted by the huge market potential of offering transnational programmes and become overly optimistic. The market could well be there, but the demand is not for various reasons, including time commitment required for working adult students, tuition fees, and English-proficiency requirements. Thus, the initial decision to offer programmes was made based on miscalculated demand. The foreign universities could also have used an inadequate financial model where the full cost of programme offering was not included. As a result, the home campus actually subsidizes a large portion of the invisible costs, such as faculty members' fringe benefits, insurance, and time for research and travel. Besides, research-active faculty members may not be willing to travel long distances for such teaching assignments.

For universities that set up branch campuses overseas, if the faculty and staff were hired locally then how to instil them with the main campus culture, make them fully understand and embrace the curriculum design philosophy, and build their sense of affiliation are challenges. If the faculty were appointed from the main campus then how well they understand the local culture and how to maintain their connection with the main campus are issues to be addressed. Even for the most basic student exchange agreements, partnering schools are not always of the same quality or curriculum content and this can lead to difficulties in credit transfers. Thus, challenges abound for international activities.

Of the four internationalization models, export, partnership, and network all involve transnational offerings. Although programmes under each model may experience unique issues and concerns, there are commonalities in their transnational nature. In terms of the complexity of transnational education programmes, Eldridge and Cranston (2009) identified three types of potential problems: the lack of experience in local policies and procedure, the paradox of commercialization and education value of the programmes, and cross-cultural learning and management. While Hong Kong, Malaysia, and Singapore have relatively transparent policies and regulations, the same cannot be said about other countries where the offering of a foreign programme or the establishment of a branch campus could be very cumbersome with many issues requiring creative interpretation and negotiation. Different partners in different locations of the same country may interpret government regulations quite differently, and this leads to different actions. Without a thorough understanding of the local culture and a well-connected network, the offering of transnational programmes is extremely difficult.

Massification and privatization/commercialization of higher education brought benefits as well as some risks related to quality (Knight, 2011). The incentives for universities to offer offshore programmes include that they could reach some of the best and brightest students who do not have the means or willingness to relocate for their studies, while the school keeps its investment costs relatively low. The majority of foreign programmes offered in Asia were established in collaboration with private institutions. While few of these institutions are of high quality, the majority of them belong to the long 'tail' of lesser quality private institutions (Marginson, 2011). If the offering university depends on the local partner in performing some of the quality assurance or teaching activities, the issue could become more serious.

Quite often, students who fail to gain entry into public universities in Asia become the target market for private institutions' local or offshore programmes. This adds to the complication of the quality issue, especially if the offering university sees the offshore programme as a potential source of income, which further blurs the line between students and paying customers. If the balance between quality standard and student attrition rate is not well managed, students' perception of quality and value may be reduced. As the competition becomes more intense, other than the few top-tier institutions, overseas universities may have difficulties in defending their market positions as these markets become more sophisticated and transparent.

In Singapore, of the 3,300 post-secondary courses offered by private education institutions (PEIs), 21 per cent are hospitality personal services related; and there are varying rigour and standards among these programmes offered. Contact hours for diploma programmes in hospitality ranged from just over 100 hours to more than 600 hours. The volume of complaints remains significant, of which 40 per cent are fee-related disputes. About two-thirds of PEI teachers had not received any form of pedagogical training (CPE, 2013). To properly monitor private higher educational institutions' quality, various governments have set up regulations and agencies to oversee this growing segment of the education sector.

For Singapore, while publicly funded educational institutions are governed by the policies and regulations under the purview of the Ministry of Education, the private education sector had in the past no central governing authority under which standards and quality control were administered. In 2009, the Council for Private Education (CPE) was established, gradually improving the quality standards and profile of the private education sector through strict procedural guidelines, monitoring, and enforcement. The CPE implements two schemes: the mandatory Enhanced Registration Framework (in the areas of corporate governance, academic rigour, student protection, and information transparency) and the voluntary QA EduTrust certification (CPE, 2010, 2013).

Facing similar situations, the Malaysian Qualifications Agency was established in 2007. The Agency developed a document to serve as a guide for national standards of hospitality and tourism education for certificate, diploma, degree, all the way to doctoral degree programmes. The document includes suggestions on programme aims, learning outcomes, curriculum design, student selection, assessment, and programme administration (Malaysian Qualifications Agency, 2012). A Qualifications Framework (QF) covering a comprehensive network of academic, vocational, and continuing education programmes/qualifications, together with associated quality assurance mechanisms, was also launched in Hong Kong in 2008. The aim of establishing the QF is to clearly define the standards of different qualifications, ensure their quality, and indicate the articulation ladders between different levels of qualifications. The Hong Kong Council for Accreditation of Academic and Vocational Qualifications (HKCAAVQ) is specified as the Accreditation Authority and the Qualifications Register Authority (Education Bureau, 2008), and was tasked with assessing programmes offered by non-self-accrediting establishments, which include all private tertiary institutions and members of the Vocational Training Council.

The third area of challenge identified by Eldridge and Cranston (2009) relates to cross-cultural issues. Whether the foreign university administrators have appropriate cultural sensitivity to the local requirements; whether the methods of teaching are appropriate for achieving the objectives of the course and taking account of local cultures; and whether the physical, administrative, communication, and other resources are adequate to support successful learning (Pimpa, 2009) all determine the extent of the success of transnational programmes.

Barron and Arcodia (2002) researched Confucian Heritage Culture students who studied hospitality and tourism management in Australia. Results showed that when studying in a Western environment, students adopted learning preferences similar to their Western peers. However, when teaching and learning take place in Asia, it is more likely that the lecturers will need to adapt to Asian students' learning styles rather than the other way around because in constructing, acquiring, and transforming knowledge in different cultural settings, local culture plays different roles in learning and teaching (Lattuca, 2002).

The suitability of the Western curriculum content in an Asian context is another issue that may undermine the value of transnational programmes, especially for part-time or graduate programmes whose target audience consists of working professionals. A 'canned' curriculum that primarily focuses on Western perspectives and practices may not be perceived as high in relevancy and currency. The adaptation of the curriculum to local needs often requires long debates and approval processes from the home institution. To maintain the same learning outcomes as the programmes offered at home, Western universities may not be willing to modify their curriculum for quality assurance reasons. Any customization of the curriculum would also reduce the efficiency and economies-of-scale benefits in mass curriculum development and delivery. In addition, they may not be able to customize the curriculum due to a lack of understanding of the Asian culture and industry practices.

Many scholars have also questioned the applicability of theories developed in the West in the Asian hospitality and tourism context (e.g. Huang, 2011; Tse & Ho, 2009; Winter, 2009). Before these theories are modified to fit the Asian phenomena or new theories are developed based on Asian perspectives, current theories should be interpreted with an understanding of the Asian cultures and characteristics. This could be a challenge for faculty members from Western universities who are sent to Asia on short assignments.

Educational and instructional infrastructure in Hong Kong, Malaysia, and Singapore are on par, or even better, than those in Western countries. However, the same cannot be said for other developing Asian countries. Assumptions and expectations of Western universities and faculty are often incorrect and thus cannot be met. Simple terms such as multimedia teaching rooms, teaching materials, and refreshment break could have very different understandings between the partners. If assumptions were made and communications were not explicit, frustrations and damaged relationships could be the result. Students are the ones who eventually pay for these misgivings.

Future development of hospitality and tourism education in Asia

The proliferation of higher education providers, coupled with the global trends of marketization and privatization of higher education, has subsequently created a much diversified ecology of higher education. With the growing influence of market forces in shaping educational development in Asian societies, they are far more responsive to the market signals when developing new academic programmes, compared to their Western counterparts (Mok, 2011). The sheer number of new programmes and innovative initiatives supports this observation.

The government in Taiwan recognized the demand for a skilled hospitality and tourism workforce and founded the first hospitality-focused higher education academy in 1995. The academy was upgraded to college status in 2000 and became the National Kaohsiung University of Hospitality and Tourism in 2010 (National Kaohsiung University of Hospitality and Tourism, 2013). Today, with a population of 23 million, Taiwan has over 130 departments in higher educational institutions that offer hotel and tourism-related programmes (Hou, 2011). Malaysia has also witnessed a rapid increase in the number of public and private higher educational institutions offering hospitality and tourism programmes. Based on primary data, the number of such institutions has grown to over 40. Taylor's University, a member of the Taylor's Education Group, is one of the thriving institutions in Malaysia that have expanded quickly in hospitality and tourism. The institution was awarded university college status in 2006, and university status in 2010. The School of Hospitality, Tourism and Culinary Arts has become the largest hospitality and tourism management school in Southeast Asia. Tourism development in China had a late start; however, growth has been astronomical. By the end of 2012, there were 2,236 schools offering tourism and hospitality-related programmes: 1,097 of them were institutions of higher education and the rest (1,139) were secondary vocational schools (National Tourism Administration of the People's Republic of China, 2013b).

The curricula in Asian hospitality and tourism programmes have also evolved in the past decades from a straight copy of the Western curriculum to more of a custom-made design, or at least a localized version of the imported curriculum. The early versions of the direct copies were mostly brought back by returning young faculty members from their alma maters in the West. The evolution has been cultivated by experience accumulation and the need to differentiate their programmes from other local programmes that adapted Western curricula and overseas offshore programmes operating in the same market. Many of these programmes differentiate their offerings based on their understanding of the local culture. Terms such as Asian paradigm and Asian-based content appear in many course or subject titles. Culture-based content is also prevalent in teaching materials to help students apply Western theories and systems in a local context.

As the number of hospitality and tourism programmes expands in tertiary education, the demand for qualified faculty members continues to grow. A significant portion of those teaching in these programmes have no prior formal education in hospitality or tourism. Many of them migrated from the disciplines of language, foods and nutrition, and physical education, among others. Another trend in Asian countries is the 'upgrading' of programmes, where diploma granting institutions are upgraded to offer higher diplomas and higher diploma granting institutions are upgraded to offer degrees. As a result, faculty members now teach at an academic level higher than what they were hired to do. If they have not acquired higher academic qualifications to achieve at least one or two levels above the students, the assurance of academic rigour of those programmes would be a challenge.

The fast-paced development of the tourism and hospitality industry in Asia also creates the demand for seasoned professionals who can lead the industry forward. As the tourism industry matures, becomes more specialized, experiences more intense competition, and operates in uncertain environments, industry practitioners need to be better prepared and continue to engage in professional development activities to keep themselves competitive and to lead their organizations forward. Therefore, the demand for advanced education is tremendous.

An initiative to meet the education demand from faculty members and industry professionals was the development of the Doctor of Hotel and Tourism Management (D.HTM) programme by the School of Hotel and Tourism Management (SHTM) at The Hong Kong Polytechnic University (PolyU). The programme is designed to cater for the needs of senior industry executives, senior staff in governmental and non-governmental tourism organizations, and academics who are seeking a doctorate in hotel and tourism management. The programme in Hong Kong draws students from primarily Asian countries, but has also attracted students from North and South America as well as Europe. The offering of this programme in mainland China has also been well received by both educators and industry practitioners.

In consumer behaviour studies, country of origin has been found to be more critical when consumers are evaluating high involvement, high status, or highly specialized items (e.g. Ahmed & d'Astous, 2004). Education services certainly fall within this category. Sharma (2011) suggested that consumers in emerging markets, when compared with those from developed markets, have more favourable evaluations of and behavioural intention for products imported from developed markets. However, there is growing evidence to suggest that foreign brands are not necessarily preferred (Cui & Liu, 2001), and Western products have declined in symbolic value (Zhou &

Hui, 2003). Laforet and Chen's (2012) study also indicated a decline in preference for Western brands in China, with the country-of-origin not affecting Chinese consumers' brand choice. As higher education quality in Asia increases and the country-of-origin effect decreases, the perceived value by Asian students of education provided by Asian educational institutions will continue to increase.

The number of non-Asian students enrolling in Asian hospitality and tourism programmes has also increased in the past few years. As stated earlier, the D.HTM programme at PolyU has attracted students from the Americas and Europe. SHTM's BSc, MSc, and PhD programmes have also had many students from Western countries. Exchange programmes at the undergraduate level are also popular, with more Western students wanting to spend a semester in Hong Kong than the university can accommodate. The same is happening in other Asian countries where English is the language of instruction. This is a reflection of the quality of education provided by Asian universities and the success of various Asian hospitality and tourism industry brands. Asia has gradually gained the reputation of being the centre of excellence and future growth potential of hospitality and tourism, with top-rated airports, airlines, and hotels. Western students with a global outlook are eager to learn from Asia in an Asian environment.

Asian students represent the majority of enrolments in hospitality and tourism doctoral programmes in Western countries. Ayoun and Palakurthi (2008) surveyed US hospitality PhD programmes and reported that 49.3 per cent of the students were international, among which 75.8 per cent were Asian. The top two native languages listed by international students were Chinese (25.8 per cent) and Korean (16.1 per cent). While a large portion of these students still have the desire to stay in the West after graduation, an increasing number of them are looking for teaching opportunities in Asian universities. Many Western doctoral holders are also eager to teach in Asian hospitality and tourism programmes, whether through full-time employment, visiting appointments, or faculty exchanges. For example, in SHTM at PolyU, the 65 full-time faculty members come from 20 different countries and regions, with approximately 25 per cent coming from Western countries (SHTM, 2013). In addition to the factors of quality of programmes, success of the industry, and growth potential that draw international students, faculty members are attracted by the dynamic academic environment, excellent support for scholarly activities, attractive remuneration packages, and low income tax rates. As quality students and faculty members are two of the major pillars of quality education (Hsu, 2003), Asian universities are on their way to excellence.

Parallel to the growth of travel in Asia coming from mostly intra-regional visitors, Asian universities have begun to offer transnational programmes in other Asian jurisdictions. For example, PolyU's SHTM has begun to offer the D.HTM in 2013 and has offered the MSc in Hotel and Tourism Management programme since 2000 in Hangzhou, China, in collaboration with Zhejiang University; and a BA in Hotel and Catering Management programme in Xian, China, in collaboration with Xian Jiaotong University since 2005. Discussions are under way to offer MSc and BSc top-up programmes in other Asian countries in collaboration with local institutions. There is also the plan to franchise the BSc top-up programmes to a local college. These collaborations have historically been implemented by Asian higher educational institutions with Western partners.

Furthermore, several global programmes are under discussion with collaboration among universities from Asia, North America, and Europe. Students enrolled in those programmes will spend a portion of their study in each location. Programmes of this nature will be a departure from the past when one party is considered superior to the other(s). Partners of these new global programmes will be on equal grounds in terms of course offering, credit transfer, teaching assignments, and other related matters.

Asian universities, especially those in Hong Kong, Malaysia, and Singapore, have demonstrated more entrepreneurial approaches of education management and they are quick in responding to market demands. Although there are challenges and risks involved in such approaches, the return to success is high. As Asian universities engage in transnational programme offerings, they need to learn from the experiences of their Western counterparts that ventured into Asian markets in the past two decades. With an understanding of the causes and circumstances of failures and successes, supports from the governments, and innovative spirits, the twenty-first century will be the Asian century for hospitality and tourism education.

References

Ahmed, S. A., & d'Astous, A. (2004). 'Perceptions of Countries as Producers of Consumer Goods: a T-shirt study in China'. *Journal of Fashion Marketing and Management*, 8(2), 187–200.

Ayoun, B., & Palakurthi, R. (2008). 'Doctoral Students in the U.S. Hospitality Programs: a survey of their demographic, academic and professional characteristics'. *Journal of Hospitality and Tourism Education*, 20(4), 6–17.

Barron, P., & Arcodia, C. (2002). 'Linking Learning Style Preferences and Ethnicity: international students studying hospitality and tourism management in Australia'. *Journal of Hospitality, Leisure Sport and Tourism Education*, 1(2), 15–27.

Bernama (National News Agency of Malaysia). (2007). *MQA Launched Officially, Chairman Named.* 2 November. Available: http://www.bernama.com/bernama/v3/news_lite.php?id=293810 (Accessed 27 October 2013).

Council for Private Education (CPE). (2010). *Handbook: Enhanced Registration Framework.* Singapore: CPE.

Council for Private Education (CPE). (2013). 'Raising The Bar for Private Education'. Press release. Singapore: CPE.

Cui, G., & Liu, Q. (2001). 'Executive Insights: emerging market segments in a transitional economy: a study of urban consumers in China'. *Journal of International Marketing*, 9(1), 84–106.

De Meyer, A., Harker, P., & Hawawini, G. (2004). 'The Globalization of Business Education'. In H. Gatignon, & J. Kimberly (Eds.), *The INSEAD–Wharton Alliance on Globalizing: strategies for building successful global businesses* (pp. 104–28). Cambridge: Cambridge University Press.

Department of Education, Science and Training. (2005). 'A National Quality Strategy for Australian Transnational Education and Training: a discussion paper'. April. Canberra: Department of Education, Science and Training.

Education Bureau. (2008). *Qualifications Framework.* Retrieved October 27 2013, from: http://www.hkqf.gov.hk/guie/home.asp

Education Commission. (2000). *Learning for Life, Learning through Life: reform proposals for the education system in Hong Kong.* September. Hong Kong: Education Commission.

Eldridge, K., & Cranston, N. (2009). 'Managing Transnational Education: does national culture really matter?' *Journal of Higher Education Policy and Management*, 31(1), 67–79.

EyeforTravel. (2007). *Short-Haul Travel Will Continue to Dominate Tourism in Asia for the Next 10 Years.* 12 March. Available: http://www.eyefortravel.com/archive/short-haul-travel-will-continue-dominate-tourism-asia-next-10-years/ (Accessed 28 October 2013).

Garrett, R., & Verbik, L. (2004). *Transnational Delivery by UK Higher Education, part 1: Data & missing data.* Available: http://www.obhe.ac.uk/documents/search?region_id=&theme_id=&year=All+Years&keywords=&author=&document_type_id=1&search=Search&pageID=4 (Accessed 20 October 2013).

Hong Kong Government. (2006). *Economic Summit on "China's 11th Five-Year Plan and the Development of Hong Kong": the opportunities and challenges presented by the 11th Five-Year Plan and the outlook for Hong Kong.* Available: http://www.info.gov.hk/info/econ_summit/eng/pdf/paper_1.pdf (Accessed 26 October 2013).

Hong Kong Legislative Council. (2007). *Legislative Council Brief: developing Hong Kong as a regional education hub.* October. Hong Kong: Legislative Council.

Hong Kong Tourism Board. (2013). *Overnight Visitors to Hong Kong up 6.5% in 2012.* 28 January. Available: http://partnernet.hktb.com/filemanager/intranet/PRESS/EnglishPress/CA2013-E/Dec2012E1_1.html (Accessed 20 October 2013).

Hou, H. I. (2011). 'Policies and Strategies in Internationalizing the Hospitality Education in Taiwan'. *International Journal of Education,* 3(2), E17. Available: http://www.macrothink.org/journal/index.php/ije/article/viewFile/1075/972 (Accessed 20 October 2013).

Hsu, C. H. C. (2003). 'Hospitality and Tourism Education in the United States and Hong Kong: opportunities and challenges'. Keynote speech presented at the Second Asia Pacific Forum for Graduate Students Research in Tourism, October, Busan, Korea.

Hsu, C. H. C. (Ed.). (2005). *Global Tourism Higher Education: past, present, and future.* New York: Haworth Hospitality Press.

Huang, S. (2011). '"China, Forever": Orientalism revisited'. *Annals of Tourism Research,* 38(3), 1188–92.

Kim, Y. S., Moreo, P. J., & Raab, C. (2008). 'Hospitality Programs at Four-Year Universities in South Korea'. *Journal of Hospitality & Tourism Education,* 20(2), 34–43.

Knight, J. (2011). 'Education Hubs: a fad, a brand, an innovation?' *Journal of Studies in International Education,* 15(3), 221–40.

Knight, J., & Morshidi, S. (2011). 'The Complexities and Challenges of Regional Education Hubs: focus on Malaysia'. *Journal of Higher Education,* 62(5), 593–606.

Laforet, S., & Chen, J. (2012). 'Chinese and British Consumers' Evaluation of Chinese and International Brands and Factors Affecting their Choice'. *Journal of World Business,* 47(1), 54–63.

Lattuca, L. (2002). 'Learning Interdisciplinarity: sociocultural perspectives on academic work'. *Journal of Higher Education,* 73(6), 711–39.

Lee, M. N. N. (1999). *Private Higher Education in Malaysia.* Penang: School of Educational Studies, Universiti Sains Malaysia.

Lee, Y. S., & Jennings, G. (2010). 'The Development of "Leiports" (leisure and sports) Studies and Programs in Tertiary Education in South Korea'. *Journal of Teaching in Travel & Tourism,* 10(2), 125–42.

Lenn, M. P. (2000). 'Higher Education and the Global Marketplace: a practical guide to sustaining quality'. *On the Horizon,* 8(5), 7–10.

Lim, F. C. B. (2009). 'Education Hub at a Crossroad'. *Quality Assurance in Education,* 17(1), 79–94.

Liu, A. (2005). 'Development of Tourism Education and Training in China: progress and limitation'. *Tourism Management Research,* 5(1), 99–124.

McBurnie, G. (n.d.). *Different Perspectives on Programme and Institution Mobility.* Available: http://www.oecd.org/dataoecd/51/8/37477665.pdf (Accessed 26 October 2013).

Malaysian Qualifications Agency. (2012). *Program Standards: hospitality and tourism.* Available: http://www.mqa.gov.my/portal2012/garispanduan/PS%20Hospitality%20and%20Tourism%20(Eng).pdf (Accessed 22 October 2013).

Marginson, S. (2010). 'Higher Education in the Global Knowledge Economy'. *Procedia: Social and Behavioral Sciences,* 2(5), 6962–80.

Marginson, S. (2011). 'Higher Education in East Asia and Singapore: rise of the Confucian Model'. *Higher Education,* 61(5), 587–611.

Mok, K. H. (2011). 'The Quest for Regional Hub of Education: growing heterarchies, organizational hybridization, and new governance in Singapore and Malaysia'. *Journal of Education Policy,* 26(1), 61–81.

National Bureau of Statistics of China. (2013). *Statistical Communique of the People's Republic of China on the 2012 National Economic and Social Development.* 22 February. Available: http://www.stats.gov.cn/english/newsandcomingevents/t20130222_402874607.htm (Accessed 26 October 2013).

National Kaohsiung University of Hospitality and Tourism. (2013). *About KNUHT.* http://www.nkuht.edu.tw/intro/super_pages.php?ID=intro1&Sn=1 (Accessed 22 October 2013).

National Tourism Administration of the People's Republic of China. (2013a). *Inbound Tourists to Mainland China 2012.* 17 January. Available: http://www.cnta.gov.cn/html/2013-1/2013-1-17-17-10-20496.html (Accessed 25 October 2013).

National Tourism Administration of the People's Republic of China. (2013b). *National Tourism Education and Training Statistics 2012.* 25 March. Available: http://www.cnta.gov.cn/html/2013-3/2013-3-25-14-14-81891.html (Accessed 25 October 2013).

Pimpa, N. (2009). 'Learning Problem in Transnational Business Education and Training: the case of the MBA in Thailand'. *International Journal of Training and Development,* 13(4), 262–79.

Prime Minister's Department. (2012). *Economic Transformation Programme Annual Report 2012.* Putrajaya: Performance Management and Delivery Unit (Pemandu), Prime Minister's Department. Malaysia.

Sangpikul, A. (2009). 'Internationalization of Hospitality and Tourism Higher Education: a perspective from Thailand'. *Journal of Teaching in Travel and Tourism,* 9(1/2), 2–20.

School of Hotel and Tourism Management (SHTM). (2013). *Academic Staff*. Retrieved October 28 2013, from: http://hotelschool.shtm.polyu.edu.hk/eng/faculty/staff.jsp

Sharma, P. (2011). 'Country of Origin Effects on Developed and Emerging Markets: exploring the contrasting roles of materialism and value consciousness'. *Journal of International Business Studies*, 42(2), 285–306.

Task Force on Economic Challenges. (2009). *Recommendations from the Task Force on Economic Challenges for Promoting the Development of the Six Economic Areas*. 22 June. Available: http://www.fso.gov.hk/tfec/eng/doc/TFEC%20-%20final%20Recommendations%20_TFEC-INFO-13_%20_Eng_.pdf (Accessed 26 October 2013).

Tse, E. C. Y., & Ho, S. C. (2009). 'Service Quality in the Hotel Industry: when cultural contexts matter'. *Cornell Hospitality Quarterly*, 50(4), 460–74.

United Nations Economic and Social Commission for Asia and the Pacific (UN ESCAP). (2012). *Statistical yearbook for Asia and the Pacific 2012*. 6 November. Available: http://www.unescap.org/stat/data/syb2012/index.asp (Accessed 24 October 2013).

United Nations Educational, Scientific and Cultural Organization (UNESCO). (2013). *UIS Statistics*. Available: http://data.uis.unesco.org/?lang=en (Accessed 22 October 2013).

United Nations World Tourism Organization (UNWTO). (2013a). *UNWTO Annual Report 2012*. Madrid: UNWTO.

United Nations World Tourism Organization (UNWTO). (2013b). *International Tourism Demand Exceeds Expectations in the First Half of 2013*. 26 August. Available: http://media.unwto.org/en/press-release/2013-08-25/international-tourism-demand-exceeds-expectations-first-half-2013 (Accessed 22 October 2013).

University Grants Committee (UGC). (2004). *Hong Kong Higher Education, to Make a Difference, To Move With The Times*. January. Available: http://www.ugc.edu.hk/eng/doc/ugc/publication/report/policy_document_e.pdf (Accessed 28 October 2013).

University Grants Committee (UGC). (2010). *Aspirations for the Higher Education System in Hong Kong: report of the University Grants Committee*. December. Available: http://www.ugc.edu.hk/eng/ugc/publication/report/her2010/her2010.htm (Accessed 27 October 2013).

Winter, T. (2009). 'Asian Tourism and the Retreat of Anglo-Western Centrism in Tourism Theory'. *Current Issues in Tourism*, 12(1), 21–31.

Zhong, L., Qi, J., & Tang, C. (2013). 'Status and Prospect of Tourism Education in China'. In Z. Zhang, R. Zhang, & J. Zhang (Eds.), *LISS 2012: Proceedings of 2nd International Conference on Logistics, Informatics and Service Science* (pp. 1245–51). Berlin: Springer.

Zhou, L., & Hui, M. K. (2003). 'Symbolic Value of Foreign Products in the People's Republic of China'. *Journal of International Marketing*, 11(2), 36–58.

16

Tourism, hospitality and events curriculum in higher education in Brazil

Reality and challenges

Roberta Leme Sogayar and Mirian Rejowski
School of Tourism and Hospitality, Anhembi Morumbi
University, São Paulo, Brazil

Introduction

This chapter discusses tourism and hospitality higher education in Brazil identifying distinct phases of development and future challenges. However, prior to undertaking this analysis it is appropriate to briefly discuss the history of higher education in Brazil and the historical influences that have shaped its development. Until the early nineteenth century, the young elite of Brazil had sought European university education. The first Brazilian universities were created after 1808, when Brazil became the headquarters of the Portuguese Kingdom. The creation of the Continental Blockade imposed by Napoleon Bonaparte prevented the universities of Coimbra, Bologna, and Paris amongst others from accepting Brazilian students. These first Brazilian universities were created within priority areas of study in a colony that up until then had depended totally upon Portugal for its supply of higher education graduates. Initially medical courses emerged (1808), then Arts (1820) and Legal Sciences or Law (1827). The universities, or institutes, were isolated from their professional nature and had an elitist character that served the children of colonial aristocracy. At the time of the Brazilian Republic (1889) 14 such institutions had been created.

Modern Brazilian universities only emerged in the early twentieth century. The first one to be consolidated was the University of Rio de Janeiro in 1920, upon the gathering of programmes from both public and private institutions. The programmes continued to operate separately, but with integrated services and a Rector as their administrative superior. This model of Brazilian universities was based on a union of institutes or specific colleges and this historical fragmentation gave rise to certain frailties in higher education. The exceptions to this model were the University of São Paulo (1934) and Brasilia (1965), which were created from university projects.

From a chronological point of view, Brazilian universities are newer than those of other countries in Latin America (Leal *et al.*, 2012). They do not align with the paths of higher education in Europe or the United States, although in distinct moments they have been influenced by both systems. During the 1950s to 1970s, several federal universities were created in the Brazilian states, and state, municipal and private universities were also established. The first Law of National Guidelines and Basis for Education (LDB) in 1961 advocated for the decentralization of higher education, but kept the system of *cathedras,* a European tradition from which emanated university authority and power. It was only in 1968, with the University Reform Movement (Ministério da Educação, 1968) that the *cathedras* system was extinguished and gave way to departmentalization inspired by the American tradition (Vehine, 2008). This organization has led universities to have more administrative autonomy and promoted the consequent expansion of faculty and student representation in collegiate bodies.

An explosion in higher education took place in the 1970s driven in part by the depletion of public resources and growing private sector interest in opening new courses to meet increasing higher education demand. Under these circumstances there was a commercialization of higher education, with many programmes of questionable quality emerging during this time.

A further change occurred in the 1990s, when younger students for whom college became a basic condition for success in professional life started to drive demand. The demand for better quality higher education grew, Master's programmes proliferated, and the government was then prompted to develop regulatory standards and undertake quality assessments.

The 2000s was marked by the implementation of various assessment tools in higher education and also greater flexibility and openness to new and alternative pedagogical approaches and delivery methods. The pressures arising from societal issues such as sustainability, globalization, ethics and social inclusion meant that these issues were incorporated into curricula; there was an increasingly younger student body; increased access to a range of teaching and learning technologies; and a student body which was less willing to engage in traditional teaching ('sage on the stage') settings.

In 2003, there was a renewed expansion of the federal system of higher education with the opening of new universities, increased enrolment and the creation of new courses that were aligned with government policies for the social inclusion of disadvantaged populations. In this context, a system of quotas in universities and federal institutes was also established by Law No. 12.711, of 29 August 2012 (Ministério da Educação, 2012). This law guaranteed that 50 per cent of enrolments per course be directed towards students from public schools and low-income groups, in addition to setting a minimum percentage of minority ethnic students proportional to the latest state census data.

This brief introduction to higher education in Brazil sets the scene for this chapter which deals specifically with tourism, hospitality and events education from the 1970s. The chapter's primary objective is to understand the evolutionary and normative characteristics of course supply in these areas and to analyse their curricular configuration and reconfiguration amidst environmental changes as well as new ways of teaching.

To begin this analysis, a description of the higher education system in Brazil, including types of higher education institutions, types of courses, regulations for the evaluation of students and programmes, and national, general and specific curricular guidelines for courses of study is presented. Following this, a mapping of graduate programme supply is undertaken, which identifies the various shifts and changes taking place between 1971 and 2012. These shifts are then discussed drawing upon the perspectives of scholars who have undertaken research on the curricular development of undergraduate programmes in tourism, hotel management and events in Brazil. Finally, the chapter identifies the contributions of this study and highlights the need for a new higher education paradigm in tourism and hospitality education.

Higher education in Brazil

Structure and evaluation system

The National Law for Guidelines and Basis (LDB), Law No. 9.394, of 20 December 1996, reorders higher education and the respective qualifications of its services, highlighting within this scenario a group of public and private institutions known as 'islands of excellence' in undergraduate and graduate education (Ministério da Educação, 1996). There are three types of higher education institutions:

a. Universities
b. University centres
c. Federation of colleges, or isolated colleges or institutes.

According to data from the Ministry of Education, in September 2013 Brazil had 2,678 higher education institutes, made up of 193 universities, 40 federal institutes of education, 180 university centres and 2,265 colleges. It is noted here that the majority of higher education institutions in Brazil are colleges, which, according to regulation, are focused primarily on the teaching of professional competences, and are rarely devoted to research and extension activities, unlike universities.

In general, private institutions hire their teachers based on an hourly teaching basis, that is there is no stimulus to be involved in activities besides teaching, except for teachers linked to Master's and doctorate programmes, or teachers undertaking management activities. In public universities, however, teachers are hired on a salary and their time is divided into activities of teaching, research and extension/management.

According to the LDB, types of higher education (or modalities) include the following: technological courses, sequential courses, bachelor programmes, post-graduation programmes *lato sensu* (specialization) and *stricto sensu* (Master's and doctoral degrees) and extension programmes. Both the bachelor and the technological programmes are considered undergraduate degrees.

To ensure the quality of the system itself, higher education programmes and institutions are evaluated by the National System of Evaluation of Higher Education (SINAES), which was created by Law No. 10.861, of 14 April 2013. Under this requirement, evaluations have three main components: an evaluation of the institution; an evaluation of the programme; and an evaluation of student performance. The evaluation process analyses teaching, research, extension programmes, social responsibility, students' performance, institution management, faculty and facilities among several other criteria (Ministério de Educação, 2004).

The evaluation framework has a series of additional tools such as self-evaluation, external evaluation and a national exam of students' performance. The results of the evaluation allow the Ministry of Education to trace a panorama of quality in programmes and institutions of higher education within the country. The evaluation processes are coordinated and supervised by the National Commission of Evaluation of Higher Education.

The information obtained from SINAES is used by institutions as an administrative tool to measure institutional efficiency and academic and social effectiveness. This information is also used by government bodies to orient public policies, and by students, their families and the general public to become familiar with programmes and institutions and to help their programme selection.

The National Exam of Students' Performance is done by students who are in the final year of their degree. It is a test on subjects of general education and specific content. Its objective is to evaluate student performance based on the national curriculum guidelines for each area. Both students of hospitality and events take the test based on the National Tourism Guideline. It also evaluates the development of competencies and abilities that are necessary to deepen students' general and professional education/training as well as providing an indicator regarding Brazilian higher education in an international context. This evaluation process is integrated with the institutional evaluation and the evaluation of each programme that the institution undertakes.

According to SINAES, programmes should be evaluated periodically. There are three types of evaluations: authorization of new programmes (when a new programme is launched), recognition of a programme (after two years of completion) and renewal of recognition (programmes that have grades 1 and 2 in the National Exam of Performance).

Tourism, hospitality and events curriculum guidelines

The National Curriculum Guidelines are a set of definitions and principles, benchmarks and procedures that guide basic and higher education in terms of organization, articulation and evaluation of their pedagogical approaches. At the time of the creation of the guidelines for tourism, hospitality and events, the main objectives were: (1) to facilitate the process of transferring between institutions; (2) to offer a professional diploma ensuring the exercise of the profession as guaranteed by law; (3) to ensure minimum uniformity to the curriculum; (4) to ensure that the curriculum would have a minimum and a maximum time for degree completion; (5) to observe general rules that are valid for the country, so that students are assured equal opportunity within the same field of study in terms of content, duration and degree title.

The National Curriculum Guidelines are applied only to bachelor degrees. The guidelines allow more autonomy in defining the curriculum based on the competencies and abilities to be developed, and through the organization of a pedagogical model that is able to be adapted to the demands of society. The guidelines indicate the profile of the graduate, the skills and abilities that are expected to be developed by the completion of the degree, curriculum components, guidelines about internship, complementary activities, evaluation systems, undergraduate dissertation and characteristics of a research programme for undergraduates.

For the technological programmes, there are also guidelines that indicate the profile of graduates, minimum number of hours for the programme, specific library material, and the professional laboratories that the institution should have in order to develop students' practical experience. Table 16.1 presents the main skills and abilities, the aims of the professional profile, the suggested curriculum content as well as a minimum number of hours for the completion of tourism, hospitality and events programmes.

The suggested competencies noted in Table 16.1 are broad in nature and are aligned to the necessities and perspectives of professional education in a constantly changing global world. The technological competences contemplate an operational approach without curriculum content guidance, which promotes more flexibility in the pedagogical approach. The bachelor degree competencies present a more humanistic approach and embed a complex, interdisciplinary view, incorporating the values suggested by Tribe (2002), Sheldon et al. (2008), Morgan et al. (2011) and Dredge et al. (2012). It also points out curricular content blocks that promote integration between the theoretical and practical knowledge distributed amongst general and specific disciplines.

Table 16.1 Tourism, hospitality and events programme characteristics in Brazil

TOURISM BACHELOR PROGRAMME

Profile: Ability to understand the scientific, technical, social, economic and cultural aspects of tourism markets, their expansion and management. To observe stages in decision-making processes, present flexibility and adaptability in contextualized scenarios when dealing with different problems – current or future – in various segments of the professional field.

Main competences: Interpersonal and intercultural communication; integration within interdisciplinary teams; use of creativity within different organizational scenarios; understanding of the complexity of the globalized world; deep experience and knowledge about human relations; adequate technical performance, professional humanism, simplicity, self-assurance, empathy and ethics.

Content curriculum:
- *Basic content*: Studies related to sociological, anthropological, geographical, cultural and artistic aspects that form societies and their cultures.
- *Specific content*: Studies related to the general theory of tourism, communication and information theories, establishing further relationship with tourism administration, law, economics, statistics and accounting, and the domain in at least one foreign language.
- *Theoretical and practical content*: Studies located in the spaces of tourist flow, comprising technical visitation, tourism inventory, learning laboratories and internship.

Minimum number of hours: 2,400 (for face-to-face training programme).

HOSPITALITY BACHELOR PROGRAMME

Profile: To operate in a highly competitive and constantly changing market, with periodic and seasonal impacts, according to changes in social, economic, political, business and organizational sectors. It should also emphasize hotel management with important structural, infrastructural and its effective functioning and quality, according to the various cultural segments of hotel demand.

Main competence: To be able to integrate within a hotel group and within the unit he/she runs, contributing to the performance of interdisciplinary teams and to interact creatively within different organizational and social contexts as well as to solve situations with flexibility and adaptability in the face of organizational problems and challenges.

Content curriculum:
- *Basic content*: Studies related to humanities with emphasis on psychology, sociology and physical geography, human, economic and politics and communication sciences and arts.
- *Specific content*: Studies related to administration, economics and law applied to the Hospitality industry, interlinked with tourism, as well as studies on communication systems and computing, including mastery of at least one foreign language.
- *Theoretical and practical content*: Obtained by computer systems, including specific laboratories that will permeate the peculiarities of the hotel industry. Supervised and integrated internship, extracurricular activities, research activities and scientific initiation.

Minimum number of hours: 2,400 (for face-to-face training programme).

EVENTS TECHNOLOGICAL PROGRAMME

Profile: To operate in events, tourism and hospitality institutions offering specialized services within the activities of planning, organizing and executing social, sports, cultural, scientific, artistic, leisure among other events. The graduate should have a domain of the functional codes and of the process of dynamic interaction with all the integrated agents of tourism and the various cultural, economic, and social aspects of the region where he/she operates, with critical awareness of ethical orientations, legal and environmental issues that are crucial for his/her professional performance.

Main competence: There aren't skills and abilities listed.

Content curriculum: Not specified.

Minimum number of hours: 1,600 hours (for face-to-face training programme).

Sources: National Catalogue of Technological Programs, Ministério da Educação (2010); Tourism National Curriculum Guidelines (Ministério da Educação, 2006).

Brazilian tourism, hospitality and events undergraduate programmes

Mapping of undergraduate degrees

In Brazil, technical courses in tourism and hotel management have existed since the 1950s, with the first training programmes oriented to waiters and chambermaids (Campos, 2000). However, tourism higher education appeared two decades later, in a moment when the country was seeking to address a lack of supply of professionals, and thus a number of tourism courses emerged (Matias, 2012).

The first undergraduate course in tourism started in 1971 (bachelor) and the first course in hospitality (technological) in 1978, both in private institutions. In 1973, Universidade de São Paulo launched the first tourism degree (bachelor) in a public university. These two tourism bachelor programmes became models of vocational training and have been respectively adopted by private colleges orienting their students towards a professional approach to the market. On the other hand, public or confessional universities[1] are oriented to a professional training with a more humanistic and academic perspective.

During the 1970s, an initial phase of growth in tourism and hospitality programmes resulted from government policies that encouraged the privatization of higher education and from the belief that tourism was an important development tool. Public discourses about tourism pointed to it as an 'industry without chimneys', emphasizing its positive economic impacts (e.g. generation of income and employment, increased tax collection, foreign exchange earnings, etc.), but also acknowledged the social and cultural benefits of tourism (e.g. peace promotion, culture revival, etc.) (Jafari, 1994, 2005). However, this favourable discourse did not endure beyond the 1970s according to Solha (2002: 137):

> the expectation of a promising labor market in the 70s was limited to the triad of travel agencies–hospitality–transportation that depended on the expansion and consolidation of the market, which ended up not occurring. However, that decade was very productive as far as discussions on the subject are concerned. During that time, the first scientific events in this area took place, discussing Brazilian touristic reality, the labor market and the needs of the sector.

In the 1980s a worldwide economic crisis resulted in the stagnation of the Brazilian economy. Tourism was not valued in higher education and many undergraduate courses were closed. However, this scenario changed during the 1990s, and particularly from 1995 onwards as a result of government tourism policies,[2] together with the country's political stabilization and economic growth. During this time, Brazil experienced an increase in both international arrivals and domestic tourism. In 1999 there were 5,107 million international arrivals together with 26.7 million domestic tourists (EMBRATUR, 1990, 2000; Rabahy, 2003). In response to this growth in tourism activity, there was also an increase in the number and diversity of tourism programmes. This increase in number of tourism degrees during the late 1990s was also mirrored in a large increase in the number of higher education courses in general (Ansarah, 2002; Rejowski, 2002). Several administration programmes focused on tourism management, hotel management, events and/or leisure. In 1999 there were a total of 142 tourism programmes together with 15 hospitality programmes in the country. Figure 16.1 shows the evolution of the tourism and hospitality undergraduate programmes in Brazil from 1991 to 1999.

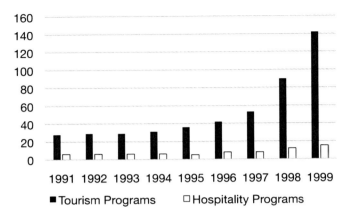

Figure 16.1 Growth of the tourism and hospitality undergraduate programmes in Brazil (1991–99)

Source: Ministério da Educação (2013).

From this time, tourism was seen as an economic activity with a promising future and higher education institutions realized the potential of this niche market segment in which there was strong growth. As a result, there was an explosion of tourism courses during the 2000s which in turn led teachers and scholars of tourism to raise concerns over the quality of several programmes (Barretto *et al.*, 2004).

This evolution of tourism higher education courses was also influenced by the development of other courses in the area of hospitality, such as hotel management, events and, more recently, gastronomy. Analysing historical data from these four courses together shows the growth of these courses from the year 2000 onwards (Figure 16.2).

Growth in the number of tourism programmes continued until 2006 (562 courses), with different additions or emphasis, such as tourism and leisure, tourism and hotel management, tourism and events, planning and organization of tourism, and recreation and leisure. From 2007 the number of programmes started to decline, and in 2012 a total of 357 courses were on offer. Hospitality programmes followed the same trend. In 2007 there were 86 courses, but in 2012 there were 77 courses on offer within the country.

As for undergraduate degrees in events and gastronomy, growth in courses commenced in 2002 and 2000 respectively. These courses evolved largely as a result of the magnitude of events and tourism business sectors, and the food and beverage sectors in large cities like São Paulo, Rio de Janeiro and others in the country.[3] Programmes in events grew steadily until 2008 (43 courses) when rationalization started to take place. In 2012 there were 39 courses on offer.

However, for a deeper analysis, it is useful to examine the number of students enrolled in and graduating from these courses from the year of 2000, when the first gastronomy courses started in the country. Table 16. 2 shows that the relation between enrolled and graduating students was relatively stable with approximately 20 per cent of all enrolled students graduating each year from tourism and hospitality courses. Also interesting to note is that the number of enrolled students in 2012 in gastronomy courses represents around 66.8 per cent of total students enrolled in tourism courses, well above the number of students enrolled in hotel management and events courses.

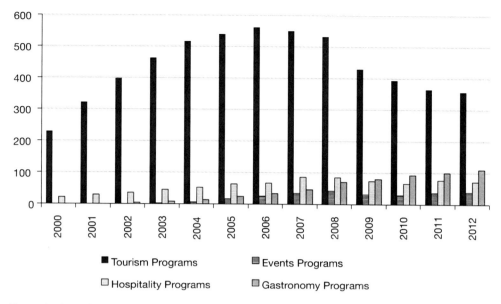

Figure 16.2 Evolution of higher education courses of tourism, hotel management and events in Brazil (2000–12)

Source: Ministério da Educação (2013).

Table 16.2 Enrolled and graduating students in tourism, hospitality, events and gastronomy undergraduate degrees in Brazil (2001–12)

Year	Tourism		Hospitality		Events		Gastronomy	
	Enrolled	Graduating	Enrolled	Graduating	Enrolled	Graduating	Enrolled	Graduating
2001	53,537	2,915	4,557	424	0	0	199	0
2002	69,455	7,343	6,037	1,015	94	3	353	15
2003	76,218	10,217	6,423	1,213	82	11	858	58
2004	76,021	12,727	6,539	1,405	145	0	1,976	254
2005	72,245	14,708	6,994	1,700	561	55	3,310	740
2006	64,892	12,900	6,476	1,438	1,222	167	4,674	1,082
2007	56,829	11,567	7,272	1,424	2,117	353	6,401	1,309
2008	49,911	9,898	8,111	1,523	2,306	400	9,721	2,137
2009	35,800	8,301	6,331	1,449	2,500	516	13,012	2,579
2010	33,392	6,902	5,944	1,312	2,772	651	15,575	3,488
2011	32,446	5,743	6,738	1,273	2,898	666	17,071	4,051
2012	29,620	5,029	6,732	1,134	3,254	708	19,771	4,384

Source: Ministério da Educação (2013).

In order to understand the evolution of courses and the number of enrolled students, their respective annual growth rates have been analysed. From the data shown in Table 16.2 and Figure 16.3, the following is observed:

a) Tourism courses have the largest number of enrolled students when compared to hospitality, events and gastronomy. However, in real terms, enrolments have been steadily decreasing since 2005. Over the last eight years, the annual rate of tourism course growth has been negative. The number of enrolled students fell as much as 28 per cent between 2008 and 2009. In 2012, the number of enrolled students was 57 per cent less than in 2002.
b) Hospitality course enrolments have been relatively stable, presenting around 6,000 to 7,000 enrolled students per year. These courses, which were developed after the initial growth in tourism courses, rank third in terms of the number of enrolments at the time of writing.
c) Events courses have the smallest number of enrolments among the four types of courses analysed with just over 3,000 enrolled students in 2012. Events courses have been characterized by high growth rates in the past, particularly between 2003 and 2007. However, since 2007 growth rates remain lower at around 10 per cent per year.
d) Enrolments in gastronomy courses have continued to increase over the period 2000 to 2012. Although the growth rate has slowed since 2008, gastronomy courses have been increasing at a rate of over 10 per cent per year. This growth has meant that the number of enrolled students in gastronomy courses now surpasses the number of students in hotel management and events.

In 2012 there were 578 higher education courses in tourism and hospitality in Brazil: 61.8 per cent of these were in tourism; 19 per cent in gastronomy; 14.3 per cent in hotel management;

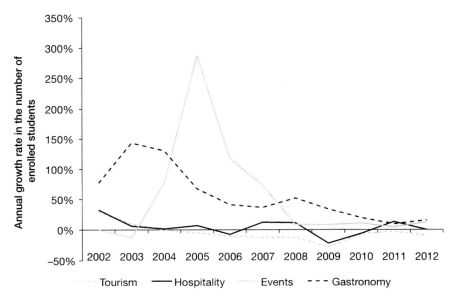

Figure 16.3 Annual growth rate of enrolled students in tourism, hospitality, events and gastronomy courses in Brazil (2000–12)

Source: Ministério da Educação (2013).

and 6.8 per cent in events. As for the type of course, in tourism the majority were bachelor degrees (around 80 per cent), and in events, they are usually technological courses. Data from the Ministry of Education about these courses present the data in two groups – one related to sectors of hotel management, restaurants and food services which includes gastronomy and hotel management courses, and the other group related to travelling, tourism and leisure, which includes courses in tourism and events.

Online courses have also been implemented within the higher education context in tourism, hotel management and events. According to the Ministry of Education in 2013 there were 24 higher education e-learning courses subdivided as follows:

- 18 in Tourism (14 technological, 4 bachelor degree and 2 licentiate[4])
- 4 in hotel management (all technological)
- 2 in events (all technological).

(Ministério de Educação, 2013)

These offerings were concentrated mostly in private institutions with only undergraduate courses in tourism and one technological course in hotel management from public institutions in the State of Rio de Janeiro. Compared with the nine e-learning courses in tourism and hotel management offered in 2009 (Matias, 2012), the growth detailed above confirms the expansion of this delivery format.

In this study, it has not been possible to examine e-learning options in traditional classroom-style courses, which, anecdotally, have also been expanding. For example, disciplines like anthropology and sociology are implementing new learning formats and systems with the use of information technologies. These courses may also be associated with a perceived decrease in delivery costs and, by corollary, a focus on increased profitability of courses in private institutions.

Contemporary concerns of curriculum building

There are many studies of tourism and hospitality undergraduate programmes in Brazil and few studies about events undergraduate programmes. In a study of scholarship in tourism higher education in Brazil, Ribeiro and Rejowski (2011) found 40 Master's dissertations and five doctoral theses produced in the period 2000–9 that examined tourism education and public higher education policy. Out of this total, the majority (37) examined undergraduate courses in tourism and two called for new paradigms of higher education. In a thematic analysis, these studies focused on training proposals (Meirelles, 2002), public policy (Teixeira, 2007), undergraduate profiles (Mota, 2007), professional skills (Fornari, 2006) and curriculum components (Onzi, 2004).

Other studies identified by Ribeiro and Rejowski (2011) addressed innovative issues such as interdisciplinarity (Dencker, 2000; Margoni, 2006), the knowledge economy (Degrazia, 2006), social inclusion and exclusion (Carneiro, 2008) and sustainability (Silva, 2005). There were six additional unclassified studies: Schulze (2006) examined ethics and aesthetics in the learning process; Dencker and Barbosa (2006), Sogayar (2010) and Sogayar and Rejowski (2011) examined hospitality[5] in higher education; Leal (2010) examined undergraduate students' perceptions of tourism higher education; and Keller-Franco and Massetto (2012) examined the construction of the curriculum. Some of these studies show current and innovative concerns for a new paradigm of undergraduate courses.

A study by Silva (2005) analysed sustainability in higher education. Based on examples of sustainability in tourism courses in other countries, particularly New Zealand, this study proposed a set of sustainability indicators for higher education institution management in three key areas: (a) managerial – style of educational management and physical environment; (b) pedagogical – pedagogic project, teaching–learning orientation and pedagogic approach; (c) social–formative – knowledge acquired by the graduate and their professional participation in the labour market. Silva applied this sustainability indicators framework in four higher education institutions and noted that none of them complied with indicators and, therefore, did not offer an education for sustainability that included, among other aspects, citizenship and joint action.

Within the context of sustainable and responsible tourism there is other research that evaluates to what extent tourism higher education programmes further the professional development of graduates focused on social inclusion. Carneiro (2008) argues that students should experience a curriculum where the central axis would be based upon social inclusion and ethics as a theoretical, conceptual and procedural justification of the programme. This proposal should be aligned with public policies for tourism development to protect these same interests. Therefore, there should be a more humanistic and inclusive curriculum focused on the needs of local communities, and on the social inclusion of indigenous inhabitants and residents of tourism regions in Brazil.

This research analyses nine programmes offered by private institutions following the National Curricular Guidelines of Tourism. In general, curricular organization promotes generalist training, followed by specific disciplinary knowledge. Programmes at different institutions are reasonably similar as far as they comply with indicators of content presented in the national guidelines. However, Carneiro (2008) considers that such a situation is not the best way to form professional identity, as the curriculum encourages moving away from particular characteristics of the region and from the potential regional or market niche that each course could potentially contribute to.

Carneiro (2008) evaluates curricular activities and points out that institutions offer disciplines that promote holistic and humanistic formation but without clarifying their political and social positioning. Thus, although many institutions still present a pedagogic proposal that reflects values and humanistic formation, it is only in daily practice that this will be perceived, through a work that is coherent and politically, technically and culturally positioned (Carneiro, 2008). The study concludes that there are contradictions between student training focused on the needs of the labour market and the prescriptions of a critical and socially responsible humanistic training. The concepts of identity, social function and social quality should work as a 'supporting tripod' for a course interested in contributing to the formation of professionals who have as a focus their personal development linked to social progress.

Dencker and Barbosa (2006), Sogayar (2010) and Sogayar and Rejowski (2011) deal with the notion of hospitality in higher education. Hospitality is seen in these studies as a new perspective to recover a humanistic vision, both for the process of professional formation and for the sector more generally.

Hospitality courses are based on a set of behaviours drawn from the basis of society and it is suggested by Dencker & Barbosa (2006) that social and humanistic values are becoming fragile as they face new technologies and globalization. They argue for the inclusion of hospitality in hotel management courses as a way of establishing a link between human and market values. They propose the inclusion of the concept of 'welcomeness' and contemplation of the dimensions of hospitality from a social–anthropological perspective (Dencker and Barbosa, 2006:76–7).

These authors suggest that the curricular basis of hospitality is made up of four thematic axes that encompass market, managerial, operational and social–anthropological dimensions: (1) assumptions and foundations of hospitality;[6] (2) analysis and development of business systems; (3) behaviour; and (4) operational strategy. In this study, the authors value the process of interaction and exchange, in which the teaching of hospitality enables one to reflect on a set of principles and values.

The presence of hospitality is also present in work undertaken by the Tourism Education Futures Initiatives (TEFI) (Sogayar, 2010). TEFI is a futures-oriented network of tourism educators that has developed, among other work, a values-based approach to tourism education. Sogayar's (2010) study examined the construction of new paradigms for higher education in tourism. The study analysed the inclusion of hospitality, explicit or implicit, in the TEFI values: ethics, knowledge, professionalism, stewardship and mutual respect. In this study, the authors argue that hospitality contributes to a new model of professional training focused on community, and to more democratized processes of service delivery, where power relations are questioned in pursuit of a more humanistic society. They further argue that hospitality should be included in tourism programmes, in the process of appointing teachers in tourism, and even in the physical environment where learning takes place.

The last study to be mentioned analyses a project-based tourism curriculum (Keller-Franco & Massetto, 2012). The project aims to address local needs for sustainable development through an education that brings better quality of life for its population and aims to achieve human dignity and social justice. The region of the subject of the study has faced many economic, social, environmental and educational challenges related to unplanned development. The authors' pedagogical political project aims at developing a project-based education, where education and sustainable development are integrated with community action and the holistic development of the individual. As a goal of this project, the authors want to develop critical thinking and proactivity through formative actions, opening a space for the construction of utopias, and respect for human limits through an education-based teaching mediation. The process of teaching mediation is done through a system of continuing teacher education (Keller-Franco & Massetto, 2012).

The proposed curriculum in this study is flexible in order to harmonize assessment activities. It adopts a participative, reflexive project-based assessment including engagement with community and other actors. Within this approach, the curriculum overcomes traditional disciplinary boundaries with the curriculum space constituted in three areas: the project, theoretical–practical nexus and the cultural and humanistic interactions. Each of these is described below:

- *Projects*: should extend the learning experience aligning personal interests alongside community needs, oriented by teachers who can bring the stimulus and challenges to construct autonomous learning processes.
- *Theoretical–practical nexus*: subjects are selected, based both on the national curriculum guidelines of the programme and the necessary knowledge to develop the learning projects. They are organized into modules that contemplate a knowledge-integrated and contextualized approach.
- *Cultural and humanistic interactions*: aim to raise awareness and comprehension and, consequently, the valuation of the local culture and the ability to articulate different knowledge areas (e.g. scientific, cultural and personal).

According to the university implementation report, this type of curriculum is considered as a 'curriculum in motion' due to its constant collective process of construction and reframing.

These above studies reflect a number of concerns mirrored in the international literature on tourism and hospitality higher education that raise awareness of the challenges associated with balancing a deeper philosophic approach to tourism education with vocational skill development.

Interestingly, studies focusing on such themes in events education have not been forthcoming, which perhaps reflects that the subject area is less mature at this present time.

Conclusions

The Brazilian higher education system is characterized by features that distinguish it from Anglo-Saxon countries as far as the supply of tourism, hospitality and events courses are concerned. The openness to private institutions has allowed uncontrolled expansion of the sector, and the growth of the tourism industry, especially over the last four decades, has added further impetus. Another important observation is that the higher education sector has been highly regulated by the government, which should, to a certain extent, be a positive factor contributing to the quality of higher education. However, this regulation may have inhibited innovative curriculum processes, centralized decision making by the institutions, and hindered the development of course identity and differentiation.

When the Brazilian system is analysed it is possible to see that the strengths and weaknesses identified in this chapter do not originate exclusively from one stakeholder, but are derived from the actions and values of a wide range of stakeholders working within a highly complex system. It is this larger system that will set the tone for tourism and hospitality education structures, curricular guidelines and universities' evaluative systems in the future. The analysis of the supply of courses in tourism, hospitality and events identified different drivers for the sector's development in the 1990s and 2000s. That said, the development of tourism, hospitality and events education in Brazil has been strongly influenced by the growth of private institutions dedicated to training professionals to meet market demands. This observation highlights the rise and recalibration of tourism programmes and the instability of hospitality and events courses influenced by the growth trajectory of gastronomy courses.

A 'crisis' situation in tourism, hospitality and events higher education has also been foreshadowed, indicated by high dropout rates and the ratio of enrolled students versus graduates. In particular, the profile of graduates in travel and tourism itself is compromised by the numerous competencies incorporated in courses, but without a clearly defined focus, image and identity.

The studies of tourism and hospitality education by Brazilian scholars outlined in this chapter point to a search for referential models that include a more humanistic grounding for students, one that is focused on values that will form differentiated professionals with analytical competences and a strong commitment towards their role as change agents. It is noteworthy that these studies are aligned with a call for a new values-based model of higher education advocated by researchers since the early 2000s. Furthermore, among these studies, it should be highlighted that a proposed project-based curriculum is being applied as a new training model, while other studies have pointed to the need to rethink components included in the curriculum. In the course evaluation process it is also vital to consider the social function of courses so that there is a clear link between curricula, what sort of graduate is being produced (i.e. knowledge, competencies, values, ethics, etc.) and what role they may take in creating a better future. These considerations will promote more informed decisions in the curriculum where humanistic and technological training will be aligned.

Acknowledgements

This chapter is part of research sponsored by the National Council of Scientific and Technological Development – CNPQ (Project CNPQ No.307386/2012-0).

Notes

1 'Confessional' universities have a religious credo or set of values and principles based on religion.
2 National Policy of Tourism (EMBRATUR, 1995) and Programme of Municipalization of Tourism implemented from 1995 to 2001 are mentioned.
3 According to data from the Ministry of Education in the website eMec (http://emec.mec.gov.br), in November 2013 there were 56 technological courses in events management, an increase of 43.5 per cent compared to the total number of courses in the previous year.
4 In Brazil, the *licenciate* is a degree between three and five years of study. The *licenciate* is different from a bachelor degree, in that the *licenciate* includes subjects related to education and therefore also qualifies the degree holder to teach in primary and secondary education.
5 The term 'hospitality' in the context of these studies conveys a philosophical and anthropological orientation to mean 'the welcoming' of a tourist or guest, and the relationships established between human beings in this process.
6 'Hospitality' would be inserted in contents of the following disciplines: Sociology of Hospitality, Applied Philosophy, History of Hotel Management and Tourism, Ceremonial and Etiquette, Leisure and Entertainment, Commensality, and Culture and Arts.

References

Ansarah, M. (2002). *Formação e Capacitação do Profissional em Turismo e Hotelaria: reflexões e cadastro das instituições educacionais no Brasil*. São Paulo: Aleph.
Barretto, M., Tamanini, E., & Silva, M. I. P. (2004). *Discutindo o Ensino Universitário de Turismo*. Campinas: Papirus.
Campos, J. R. V. (2000). 'A Eolução da Educação Profissional em Hotelaria no Brasil: o caso Senac de São Paulo como referência na área'. Dissertação de Mestrado. Escola de Comunicações e Artes, Universidade de São Paulo, Brazil.
Carneiro, A. L. M. (2008). 'A Formação Acadêmico-Professional Para a Inclusão Social nos Cursos de Turismo: dos aspectos socioeconômicos à discussão curricular'. Tese de doutorado. Pontifícia Universidade Católica de Campinas, São Paulo, Brazil.
Degrazia, C. F. (2006). 'Cursos Superiores de Turismo na Economia do Conhecimento: posicionamento estratégico de um curso de turismo no Rio Grande do Sul'. Dissertação de Mestrado. Universidade de Caxias do Sul, Brazil.
Dencker, A. F. M. (2000). 'A Pesquisa e a Interdisciplinaridade no Ensino Superior – uma experiência no curso de turismo'. Tese de doutorado. Universidade de São Paulo, Brazil.
Dencker, A. F. M., & Barbosa, C. R. (2006). 'A Introdução da Hospitalidade nos Cursos de Hotelaria'. *Turismo Visão e Ação*, 8(1), 75–89.
Dredge, D., Benckendorff, P., Day, M., Gross, M., Walo, M., Weeks, P., & Whitelaw, P. (2012). 'The Philosophic Practitioner and the Curriculum Space'. *Annals of Tourism Research*, 39(4), 2154–76.
EMBRATUR (Empresa Brasileira de Turismo). (1990). *Anuário Estatístico 1989*. Rio de Janeiro: Embratur.
EMBRATUR (Empresa Brasileira de Turismo). (1995). Programa Nacional de Municipalização do Turismo – Procedimentos, versão II. Brasília: Embratur.
EMBRATUR (Empresa Brasileira de Turismo). (2000). *Anuário Estatístico 1989*. Rio de Janeiro: Embratur.
Fornari, I. S. (2006). 'Educação Superior em Turismo: o profissional de turismo frente às competências exigidas pelo mercado de trabalho do setor hoteleiro em Natal'. Dissertação de Mestrado. Universidade Federal do Rio Grande do Norte, Natal, Brazil.
Jafari, J. (1994). 'La Cientifización del Turismo'. *Estudios y Perspectivas en Turismo*, 3(1), 7–36.
Jafari, J. (2005). 'Bridging Out, Nesting Afield: powering a new platform'. *Journal of Tourism Studies*, 16(2), 1–5.
Keller-Franco, E., & Massetto, M. T. (2012). 'Currículo por Projetos no Ensino Superior: desdobramentos para a inovação e qualidade da docência'. *Revista Triangulo*, 5(2), 3–21.
Leal, S. R. (2010). *Quality in Tourism Higher Education: the voices of undergraduate students*. Saarbrücken: Lambert Academic Publishing.
Leal, S. R., Panosso, A. N. & Trigo, L. G. G. (2012). 'Tourism Education and Research in Brazil'. In G. Lohmann & D. Dredge (Eds.), *Tourism in Brazil: environment, management and segments* (pp. 199–214). Abingdon: Routledge.

Margoni, C. C. (2006). 'Reflexões Sobre a Aplicação da Interdisciplinaridade em Cursos de Turismo'. Dissertação de Mestrado. Universidade Anhembi Morumbi, São Paulo, Brazil.

Matias, M. (2012). 'Turismo: ensino de graduação no Brasil'. *Turismo & Sociedade*, 5(1), 58–81.

Ministério da Educação. (1968) Decreto n° 5.540, de 28 de novembro. Fixa normas de organização e funcionamento do ensino superior e sua articulação com a escola média, e dá outras providências. Brasília. Available: http://www.planalto.gov.br/ccivil_03/leis/l5540.htm (Accessed 3 February 2014).

Ministério da Educação. (1996). Decreto lei n° 9.394 de 20 de Decembro. Ministério da Educação. Brazil. Available: http://www.planalto.gov.br/ccivil_03/leis/l9394.htm (Accessed 3 February 2014).

Ministério da Educação. (2004). Decreto n° 2.051, de 09 de julho. Regulamenta os procedimentos de avaliação do Sistema Nacional de Avaliação da Educação Superior (SINAES). Available: http://portal.mec.gov.br/arquivos/pdf/PORTARIA_2051.pdf (Accessed 20 January 2014).

Ministério da Educação (2006). Resolução n° 13, de 24 de novembro. Institui as diretrizes curriculares nacionais do curso de graduação em Turismo e dá outras providências. Available: http://portal.mec.gov.br/cne/arquivos/pdf/rces13_06.pdf (Accessed 6 January 2014).

Ministério da Educação (2010). Secretaria de Educação Profissional e Tecnológica. *Catálogo Nacional de Cursos Superiores de Tecnologia*. Brasília: MEC.

Ministério da Educação. (2012). Decreto lei n° 12.711 de 29 de Agosto. Brazil. Lei de Cotas: dispõe sobre o ingresso nas universidades federais e nas instituições federais de ensino técnico de nível médio. Available: http://www.planalto.gov.br/ccivil_03/_ato2011-2014/2012/lei/l12711.htm (Accessed 20 January 2014).

Ministério de Educação. (2013) *Sinopses Estatísticas da Educação Superior* – Graduação. Instituto Nacional de Estudos e Pesquisas Educacionais. Brasília. Available: http://portal.inep.gov.br/superior-censosuperior-sinopse (Accessed 20 January 2014).

Meirelles, Leila Glória do Colto Gurjão de Freitas. (2002). 'O trabalho de conclusão de curso como possibilidade de produção do conhecimento no ensino superior: curso de turismo da Universidade Federal do Pará'. Dissertação (Mestrado em Educação), Campinas, SP: PUC – Campinas.

Morgan, N., Pritchard, A., & Ateljevic, I. (2011). 'Hopeful Tourism: a new transformative perspective'. *Annals of Tourism Research*, 38(3), 941–63.

Mota, K. M. (2007). 'Formação superior em turismo da Unifor (CE): Proposta, realidade e reflexões'. Dissertação de Mestrado. Universidade de Caxias do Sul, Brazil.

Onzi, L. (2004). 'Comportamentos Profissionais como Objetivos de Aprendizagem para o Ensino de Graduação de Turismo'. Dissertação de Mestrado. Universidade Federal de Santa Catarina, Brazil.

Rabahy, W. A. (2003). *Turismo e Desenvolvimento*. Estudos Econômicos e Estatísticos no Planejamento. Barueri: Manole.

Rejowski, M. (2002). 'Enseñanza y Investigación en Turismo: revelación inicial de estudios sobre la producción científica en Brazil'. In A. N. Panosso & N. M. Castillo (Eds.), *Epistemología del Turismo: estudios críticos*. México: Trillas, 2010, pp. 113–28.

Ribeiro, J. R. & Rejowski, M. (2011). 'Ensino Superior em Turismo no Brasil: a produção acadêmica de dissertações e teses (2000–2009)'. *Revista Brasileira de Pesquisa em Turismo*, 5(3), 406–32.

Schulze, T. R. (2006). 'A Etica e a Estética como Princípios Norteadores da Aprendizagem de um Curso de Turismo'. Dissertação de Mestrado. Pontifícia Universidade Católica de São Paulo, Brazil.

Sheldon, P., Fesenmaier, D., Woeber, K., Cooper, C., & Antonioli, M. (2008). 'Tourism Education Futures, 2010–2030: building the capacity to lead'. *Journal of Teaching in Travel & Tourism*, 7(3), 61–8.

Silva, F. P. S. (2005). 'Educação Superior Sustentável. Uma análise dos cursos de turismo'. Tese de doutorado. Universidade Federal da Bahia, Salvador, Brazil.

Sogayar, R. L. (2010). 'Hospitalidade no Ensino Superior: estudo de caso do programa Tourism Education Future Initiatives'. Dissertação de Mestrado. Universidade Anhembi Morumbi, São Paulo, Brazil.

Sogayar, R. L., & Rejowski, M. (2011). 'Ensino Superior em Turismo: em busca de novos paradigmas educacionais: problemas, desafios e forças de pressão'. *Visão e Ação*, 13(3), 282–98.

Solha, K. T. (2002). 'Evolução do Turismo no Brasil'. In M. Rejowski (Ed.), *Turismo no percurso do tempo* (pp. 117–52). São Paulo: Aleph.

Teixeira, S. H. A. (2007). 'Cursos Superiores de Turismo. Condicionantes Sociais de sua Implantação: uma abordagem histórica (1968/1976)'. Dissertação de Mestrado. Universidade São Francisco, Itatiba, Brazil.

Tribe, J. (2002). 'The Philosophical Practitioner', *Annals of Tourism Research*, 29(2), 338–57.

Vehine, R. E. (2008). 'Pós-Graduação no Brasil e nos Estados Unidos: uma análise comparativa'. *Educação*, 31(2), 166–72.

17

Educating tourism students in the South Pacific

Changing cultures, changing economies

David Harrison

School of Tourism and Hospitality Management,
The University of the South Pacific, Fiji

Introduction

Unsurprisingly, over the last two decades, there has been pressure on educational and training institutions in the South Pacific to 'meet the needs' of the hospitality sector. Indeed, some such institutions already train workers for entry into the sub-supervisory level of the hospitality sector.[1] However, despite these developments, and in-house training schemes, the tourism industry, in particular, remains dissatisfied. In Fiji, clarion calls for education and training institutions to meet the needs of the country's hotel sector have been made at the annual National Tourism Forums, and Fiji's *Tourism Development Plan, 2007–2016*, recommended 'major investment and infrastructural development' for 'public sector providers . . . to meet these vocational level needs' (Sustainable Development Consortium, 2007: 126).

More widely, the Pacific Islands Forum, in its Pacific Plan, noted the need to expand regional education and training programmes in tourism and hospitality (Pacific Islands Forum Secretariat, 2005: 12), while the Asian Development Bank suggests:

> growth in the mining sector (PNG [Papua New Guinea]) and tourism (Cook Islands, Fiji Islands, Samoa, Tonga and Vanuatu) has created a rising demand for skilled labour, especially in hospitality and construction. These countries lack sufficient people with the skills in management/supervision and trades occupations capable of working to international standards.
>
> (ADB, 2008: 11)

Similarly, in Fiji, there was a request for:

> more industry specific, and industry focused education *at the degree level*. Given the urgent need for large numbers of employees with vocational skills, degree level education should remain the focus of USP [the University of the South Pacific]. USP should continue to develop a dedicated hotel management programme.
>
> (Sustainable Development Consortium, 2007: 126; emphasis added)

In fact, USP was already responding to the stated need for more involvement in tourism, albeit more slowly than some would have liked. The university was founded in 1968 (McCall, 1984), and during the 1980s it was evident that tourism was increasingly important economically. Nevertheless, Tourism Studies did not appear on the university's curriculum until the early 1990s (King, 1994; Harrison, 1998). Initially, tourism was taught as a somewhat peripheral programme, with courses contributing to other majors. At the end of the 1990s, Tourism Studies was offered as a joint major and the programme became a Department, and soon afterwards a single degree in Tourism and Hospitality was added to the curriculum. In 2008, there was a renewed commitment by the university management to support and develop tourism and, in 2009, the Department became the School of Tourism and Hospitality Management (STHM). Soon after this, a B.Com in Hotel Management was introduced, much along the lines sought by many in the tourism industry and by regional and international institutions. This is a four-year programme, with the third year spent on placement in hotels of international standard, mainly in Fiji but also in other Pacific Islands and further afield.

All this indicates that USP, one of only two regional (cross-country) universities in the world (the other is the University of the West Indies), is responding to the oft-stated need for more involvement in the tourism sector. Indeed, at the end of 2012 some 350 students, spread equally across the three degree programmes, were enrolled in the STHM, with the newest and most vocationally oriented, the B.Com in Hotel Management, proving popular, especially to workers already in the hospitality sector.

However, introducing tourism education in the region is no mere technical exercise, and several sets of tensions are involved in developing tourism education in the South Pacific context. Some are found elsewhere, while others are more specific to the region.

General issues emerging in tourism education at USP

Several issues arising from the development of tourism education at USP have long been known more generally. In particular, they concern the relationship of the tourism curriculum to the economic context, most especially the demand for tourism graduates by sectors of the tourism industry.

The most general issue is perhaps the relationship of the university as an institution to the employment 'needs' of the economy. As long ago as 1976, Dore criticized 'new states' for succumbing to the 'diploma disease' by mimicking Western educational programmes and creating courses and paper qualifications that were inappropriate in developing countries. Instead, he suggested, it would be more appropriate for them to educate and train students to take their place in the workforce (Dore, 1976).

With the development of specialist travel and tourism courses in developed and developing countries, Dore's criticisms might be less relevant. However, at the international level, debates are still ongoing as to how far tourism courses generally are able to satisfy the needs of the tourism sector in developing countries. In 1993, for instance, it was noted that the UK had an over-supply of tourism graduates, prompting the recommendation that the number of travel and tourism courses should be reduced, as should the numbers of students in courses that were retained (Evans, 1993: 245–6). Many years later, when comparing tourism courses in Australia with those in other English-speaking countries, Wang and Ryan (2007) noted a wide range of syllabuses within and across countries and suggested that:

- employers tended to focus on transferable skills, problem-solving and work experience rather than the mere award of a degree in travel and tourism;

Table 17.1 Vocational versus liberal curricula

Vocational tourism studies		Liberal tourism studies
Aim	To produce an effective labour force	Understanding tourism
Research methods	Positivist	Interpretive Critical
Values	Tourism for profit	Search for competing values Public interest
Approaches	Functional modules Transferable skills	Disciplinary approach Critical module Research methods and project Complementary studies Great books
Research	Industry-led	Issue-led Search for hidden issues
Evaluation	Performativity	Better understanding

Source: Adapted from Tribe (2002).

- student expectations were most centred on positions in management and marketing, as well as tour operations and possessing travel agencies, and were largely geared to possibilities for overseas travel; and
- tourism academics complained tourism courses were 'a-theoretical with a lack of conceptual context and links to both industry and disciplines from which the theories have been developed' (Wang & Ryan, 2007: 36) and they also felt there was a mismatch of university courses with tourism industry expectations.

Others have concentrated less on how far university tourism and travel courses meet the needs of the industry and more on whether or not they *should* aim to do so. In a paper focused largely on tourism higher education in the UK, for instance, Tribe (2002) contrasted vocational tourism studies with liberal tourism studies, and noted how they differ in their underlying aims, methods and purposes of research (Table 17.1). He recommends a balanced approach, where students are encouraged to reflect on wider issues even in 'vocational' modules and to develop 'knowledge scepticism' through working on research projects based on different paradigms. He also advocates exposure of students to holistic and critical approaches to tourism through 'great books' in the literature of tourism and courses expressly designed to subject the processes of tourism development to critical analysis (Tribe, 2002).

Another expression of this tension (albeit with notable exceptions) is that in many institutions of higher education offering courses in tourism and hospitality – often in the same schools or departments – there is a divide *between* tourism as an area of academic and critical study and hospitality which has commonly been offered as a vocational programme. Indeed, the tendency for tourism education to be increasingly influenced by neoliberal, market-led approaches has been noted by several writers (Ayikoru et al., 2009). Holden and Wickens (2007) are especially critical of this trend, which results in tourism courses becoming more vocationally and business oriented, and increasingly being considered 'a means of supporting industry and commerce'. For these authors, this is a 'myopic view' which:

risks producing a reductionist model of higher education. If courses are skewed to the needs of business, module content decided on the rationale of what is useful to business, where is the space to produce analytical, free-thinking and orthodox-challenging citizens of the future?

(Holden & Wickens, 2007: 46)

Clearly, the content of travel and tourism courses remains a topic of considerable debate, with academics tending to regret the introduction of more work-oriented 'transferable skills', and a corresponding decline in what might be described as theoretical perspectives. Indeed, among academics there is a related debate, one not discussed in detail here, as to how far 'Tourism Studies', in developed or developing countries, can be regarded a specific discipline, rather than a *field* of study (Echtner & Jamal, 1997; Tribe, 1997, 2002, 2005; Leiper, 2000; Holden & Wickens, 2007).

It is perhaps inevitable that mission statements are usually aspirational, but the tensions outlined above are evident in the stated missions of USP and of STHM. The most recent mission statement of USP (2013: 18), for instance, includes:

- providing a 'comprehensive range of excellent and relevant tertiary qualifications';
- delivering 'the benefits of advanced research and its applications';
- providing 'communities and countries in the Pacific region with relevant, cost effective and sustainable solutions, including entrepreneurship, to their main challenges'; and
- being 'an exemplar of tertiary education for the Pacific Islands in quality, governance, application of technology and collaboration with national institutions'.

Unlike a previous version, this mission statement makes no distinction between 'education' and 'training' or to the 'needs of communities' (USP, 1994). However, hostages to fortune are evident. It is a moot point as to who decides the relevance of a qualification or the problems requiring solutions. Furthermore, the links between scholarship (which is barely mentioned) and entrepreneurship and transferable *skills*, which figure prominently among the desired 'graduate attributes' (USP, 2013: 19), are not specified. In practice, though, USP authorities – for understandable financial reasons – have accepted that a major brief is to train young people from the region in subjects that are clearly vocational rather than academic, most notably including accountancy and management, two of the most popular subjects of study at USP. The current support for the development of more tourism and hospitality courses is clearly part of this trend, and is predicated on the recognition of tourism's importance in the region's economy and on the perceived validity of calls from the tourism sector for courses considered (by the industry) to be more relevant to the requirements of the tourism sector.

Similar tensions are evident in the mission of STHM, which is:

to help students develop a critical understanding and in-depth scholarly analyses of tourism and its impacts in the region and to carry out research on tourism which will enable them to take their place in the wider academic community and, more generally, to work towards recognition as a centre of excellence in education and research in tourism and hospitality for the twelve member nations that comprise the South Pacific region, and to foster knowledge and skills that will enable tourism to be a tool for the region's development.

Again, such aims and objectives are not easily reconcilable, combining as they do vocational and academic objectives, as well as tacitly embodying the aim of providing critical support for tourism in the region. Indeed, the STHM makes a major effort to cultivate good relations with other tourism stakeholders, especially through its Programme Advisory Committee and its annual Careers Fair, where it arranges interviews for graduating students with representatives of the tourism industry. However, by focusing on tourism as a development tool, it is also prepared to question how far 'the needs of the tourism industry', which is often wrongly assumed to speak with a single voice, can be equated with the development needs of Pacific Island states. Just as what is good for General Motors is not necessarily in the interest of the USA, what tourism's spokespersons require for tourism is not necessarily good for South Pacific Island states.[2]

The nature of South Pacific states: a necessary digression

If the nature of the tourism curriculum, and its relationship to the 'needs' of the economy, is a major issue, so too is the role of Western education more generally, and assessments of this depend, to a considerable extent, on how the socio-cultural and political structures of the region's island states are viewed. In this respect, the concept of a 'plural society' is relevant. The term, initially coined by Furnivall (1948) to denote societies where ethnic factions coexist economically but do not combine socially, was later developed by Smith (1975) and Harrison (1988), and has been much debated with reference to Fiji (Lawson, 1996; Harrison, 1997; Norton, 1997). However, other Pacific Island states also experience continued hierarchy and division, which are often justified in the name of 'tradition' (Lawson, 1996), and in Papua New Guinea and Solomon Islands, especially, continued conflict has had a strong ethnic component.

Plural societies were defined by Furnivall, the instigator of this model of (then) colonial societies, as follows:

> Each group holds by its own religion, its own culture and language, its own ideas and ways. As individuals they meet, but only in the market place, in buying and selling. There is a plural society, with different sections of the community living side by side, but separately, within the same political unit.
>
> (Furnivall, 1948: 304)

It can thus be argued that relations of i-Taukei (indigenous Fijians) and Fijians of Indian descent have been overwhelmingly characterized by social and cultural pluralism, where different ethnic groups adhere to different social institutions, religions and languages. Indeed, until recently, successive constitutions have ensured that political power has remained with the i-Taukei through an ethnically weighted system of communal voting. The (non-elected) Bainamarama government, which took power in a 2006 coup, suspended the 1997 constitution and, in September 2013, replaced it with a new one; but economic inequalities continue in the denial to Indo-Fijians of equal access to land.[3]

Norton has suggested that considering Fiji a plural society 'overstates the ethnic division' of Fijian society and ignores the 'convergence of the groups in respect of their values, interests and aspirations' (1997: 3–5), though events of the last two decades give scant support for this optimistic assessment. By contrast, Lawson (1996) has some sympathy with a plural society perspective, but she also notes there are clear linguistic and cultural divisions among the i-Taukei, adding that, elsewhere in the South Pacific, 'tradition' has often been used to justify the continuance of chiefly dominance (Lawson, 1996).

Despite all these differences, colonialism (including formal education) can be seen (to use a geological analogy) to have been an intrusion into the region. A very specific example of this process is the establishment of English as the language of administration throughout the South Pacific and of instruction at USP, in a context where – in most of the Pacific Island countries that constitute USP – English remains the second or even the third language of most students and many members of the academic staff. This key feature distinguishes USP, its students and syllabus, from universities in other parts of Australasia, notably Australia and New Zealand, and from the University of the West Indies, whose constituent countries all have English as their first language. A major consequence of this situation is a continuing and unresolved debate at USP concerning the extent to which the limited skills in oral and written English of many students and academic staff are reflected in academic standards, and how far the latter are compromised by the former.

Depending on what perspective is adopted, the Western education system can be seen as a threat or an opportunity in the South Pacific. For Konai Thaman, a USP professor of Tongan descent, it is undoubtedly problematic. In a series of keynote addresses, she continually contrasts a (Parsonian) Western educational system which (for her) focuses on inculcating students with values of achievement, individualism and universalism, with traditional, communal, socially oriented values that characterize the South Pacific Island societies from which they have come. The former system, she argues:

> helps create a single measure of personal success for individualistic industrialized societies, namely the attainment of wealth and status by promotion to professional and senior management positions within corporate public bureaucracies. However . . . Pacific societies are not individualist nor industrialized and Pacific peoples are proud of their various cultural heritages which have different measures according to different cultural contexts. Perhaps there is something in this discrepancy that can help explain why so many of our students do not do well in school.
>
> (Thaman, 2001: 5)

To counter this tendency, Thaman advocates 'a culturally inclusive curriculum through the incorporation of local and cultural knowledge in the curriculum of all subjects' (2001: 9) and the inclusion of indigenous worldviews, that are:

> inclusive, holistic, and champion stewarding nature, participating in community and valuing interpersonal relationships; they compliment [sic] rational objective thinking, suspicion of emotions and material productivity. Finally, indigenous perspectives are about learning to know, to do, to live together and to be.
>
> (Thaman, 2001: 11)

There is a case to be made for focusing on local cultures and customs in tourism education in the South Pacific, and for the industry to incorporate specific cultural features that enhance the 'customer experience', but it is also arguable that Thaman's position is less of a pedagogical philosophy and more of a somewhat defensive romanticization of cultures that (at least in the Fijian context) are more heterogeneous than she suggests and, throughout much of the South Pacific, are frequently rigidly hierarchical. By contrast, a quite different approach is taken by Subramani, who advocates a reformed Fijian educational system which places less stress on examinations than on a 'multicultural world' (1998: 8–9), and an end of 'theories of exclusiveness, theories that argue, for instance, that only Fijians can understand their ethos and aspirations, and that only women can have inwardness with female experience' (1998: 10).

These differing approaches to Western education reflect quite different perspectives on the nature of South Pacific societies. Whereas Thaman sees the prevailing education system as a threat to what is unique and valuable in South Pacific cultures, Subramani focuses on its potential to change an existing, plural and ethnically based economic and socio-cultural structure, facilitating the demystification of culture, ending the 'myth of ethnic superiority', and unveiling 'class interests in cultural formations' (1998: 11).

Other general issues relating to tourism education in the South Pacific can be stated quite briefly. As indicated earlier, English is unlikely to be the first language of most students. This creates real problems for lecturers and students, in that the expectations of the former are frequently frustrated, while the latter come under continuous pressure to perform at a higher standard than their ability in English allows. Second, students in secondary education throughout the South Pacific are encouraged to repeat and regurgitate information handed down by teachers, and are rarely encouraged to develop critical thinking. These two factors – the pressure to perform and to reproduce teaching material – frequently result in a tendency to plagiarize, which is hardly unique to Pacific Island education but which, in the local context, is notoriously difficult to eradicate. Indeed, the problem is compounded by the third factor, which is the paucity of resources in many schools, especially in rural areas. Finally, the home backgrounds of most students are characterized by hierarchy and a respect for elders and, among the i-Taukei, the chiefs. Together, these factors make it difficult for university students to challenge information from and/or attitudes of academic staff, and to develop the kind of critical approach to the social structures, norms and values of their own societies that is encouraged in most subjects based on Western social science.

Tourism-specific issues emerging in tourism education at USP

In addition to these general features, quite specific implications arise from the emergence of international tourism as a major development tool in the region, and the subsequent introduction of education and training geared to further developing the tourism industry.

First, most undergraduates studying tourism and hospitality at USP have had little or no direct experience of tourists. In a third-year tourism class of about 90, for example, only six indicated they had ever spoken to a tourist. On reflection, this is not surprising, for tourism in Fiji and other islands tends to be highly concentrated, and tourist accommodation and other facilities are usually some distance from residential areas. The lack of contact is reinforced because access to indigenous Fijian villages is normally obtained only by special arrangement.

Second, unlike students in more affluent societies, most South Pacific students are not accustomed to taking regular holidays away from home. They may visit friends and relatives in other regions, and a small minority have been overseas, mainly to Australia or New Zealand, but there is no tradition of holiday taking and thus little possibility of developing empathy with international visitors. Indeed, many students have never visited the main tourist destinations in their own countries. Students going on field trips, especially for the first time, tend to be overwhelmed by the experience. For example, when visiting the Yasawa islands to the north-west of Viti Levu, popular among tourists for their beaches and marine activities, a common student reaction is to exclaim that they never knew Fiji was like this. And after visiting a cruise ship in Suva, students explained their excitement and their focus on being photographed, all the time ignoring the talk from the ship's crew about the nature of the tourist experience, by saying 'but sir: it was a once in a lifetime experience'. The idea that possibilities might exist for them actually to work on the ship had simply not registered!

Third, and allied to the above, South Pacific students have little knowledge of the geography of the rest of the world, including countries of tourists' origin. Despite (sometimes desperate) attempts during the second year of tourism and hospitality courses to remedy this deficiency, knowledge of the world outside the South Pacific Islands, and the role of international tourism in it, remains limited.

As a consequence, when USP students from Fiji or from any other Pacific Island states enrol on tourism and hospitality courses, they inevitably begin a process in which they are not only expected to learn about the international tourism system and develop 'transferable skills, but where they must also absorb and understand what is, in effect, for most of them, a foreign culture' (Harrison and Lugosi, 2013). Methodists who are (at least nominally) and Hindus who are (normally) teetotal, must prepare to work with tourists who, for the most part, have a totally different orientation to alcohol. Mostly unaccustomed to Western table etiquette and Western cuisine, students are also expected to prepare themselves for participating in Departments of Food and Beverage Management, to assist in providing accommodation of an international standard, to cater for the expectations of guests whose norms and values might appear to them (especially if they have never left the family home) not only different from their own, but also outrageously so, and even to interact conversationally with their guests on a regular basis.

Irrespective of which island state they are from, the home backgrounds of most students are so far removed from that of most tourists that an apparently straightforward educational and training programme in tourism and hospitality becomes a massive task of wholesale cultural change. In a very real sense, they are being asked to participate in the global processes involved in international tourism which, for them, are now on their own doorsteps. In short, they are being globalized.

If the above assessment is valid, students graduating with a level of professional competence appropriate for entry level in management in various sectors of the tourism industry have made considerable progress. Ideally, however, a degree in tourism studies (especially in such developing societies as South Pacific Island states) should also promote among students a genuinely critical awareness of the role of international tourism and its impacts in Pacific Island countries, and this is doubly difficult to achieve. In so far as the degree is based on Western social science, successful students must develop an awareness of the nature of their own societies, their structures and cultures, and the numerous external economic, social and cultural changes to which they are subjected, as well as understanding the internal processes which condition and shape the reactions to such pressures.

Conclusions

This chapter has focused on the general and specific issues arising from the introduction and development of tourism education at USP. In a regional context where tourism is increasingly seen as a vital (and sometimes the only) force for economic development, a balance has to be struck between vocational and academic emphases on tourism and hospitality courses, and important questions are raised as to how far the expressed 'needs' of the tourism industry should be considered paramount, especially at university level.

Within USP, general conditioning factors include the relatively low standard of English of most students, for whom it is a second (or even third) language, a school system that emphasizes rote learning, and cultural backgrounds of most students where there is a heavy emphasis on respect for authority and a discouragement of nonconformity, all of which make it difficult for university students to develop a genuinely critical approach to their learning and to their wider social environments.

More specifically, tourism and hospitality students have rarely had any prior experience of tourists and the destinations they visit, of what might be described as tourism culture, or of the societies from which tourists come. And their knowledge of such societies is decidedly flimsy.

All these issues have implications for the development of a tourist studies curriculum. How academic should it be? It can be argued that debates over the role of tourism in development, and such topics as the Fordism of modern tourism, the nature of tourism destination cycles and irritation indices, the 'tourist gaze' and the characteristics of postmodern tourism, are at least as relevant to Pacific Island states as more developed societies, but there is no consensus as to how far they are necessary when preparing students for entry at supervisory or managerial level in the region's hotels. Certainly, many self-made hoteliers in the islands are likely to exhibit a degree of scepticism with respect to such theoretical content!

At a slightly different level, decisions need to be made as to how far course content in tourism and hospitality degrees should be generic, enabling graduates to work anywhere in the world – a stipulation often made by human resource managers in transnationally managed hotels – and the extent it should incorporate special consideration of tourism development in the South Pacific, both in understanding its historical development and in focusing on any perceived need to tailor the syllabus and the provision of hospitality to accommodate local needs and cultural sensitivities (for example rights to land and marine environments).

Finally, wider issues are involved. Critics of tourism in developing countries might simply dismiss advocacy of tourism as a 'development tool' as another example of colonialism, while others might follow Dore (1976) in asking what functions universities should serve in developing societies. Such questions remain highly pertinent and contentious and are likely to remain so for the foreseeable future.

Notes

1   In Fiji, these include the National Training and Productivity Centre (NTPC) and the School of Hospitality and Tourism at the Fiji National University, as well as franchised activities of such overseas-based institutions as the Australia-Pacific Technical College (APTC). Elsewhere, training in tourism and hospitality is provided at the Vanuatu Institute of Technology and at the Hospitality and Tourism Training Centre in the Cook Islands, and there are also short sub-degree level courses at the Department of Tourism, University of Papua New Guinea, and at the Department of Tourism and Hospitality at the Divine Word University, Papua New Guinea.

2   Such a dilemma is possibly less evident in national universities in the region. At USP, for example, even Assistant Lecturers in the STHM (and other parts of the university) are expected to have at least a Master's qualification and an interest in research. By contrast, travel and tourism departments in national universities in most Pacific Island countries focus almost entirely on hospitality-based vocational skills and place relatively little emphasis on postgraduate qualifications. It is a division which, again, is of much wider international proportions.

3   At the time of writing, elections under the new constitution are scheduled for 2014 and are to be held under a system of 'one person, one vote'. In this sense, *legal* discrimination on ethnic grounds is decreasing. However, attempts to *enforce* ethnic equality are unlikely to succeed. Members of the police and armed forces are overwhelmingly *i-Taukei* (indigenous Fijian), religious differences follow ethnic lines, and Christians of Indian origin even continue to worship in different churches from Methodists who are *i-Taukei*. Teachers from different ethnic groups tend to be represented by different trades unions, Fijian dialects and Hindi are largely restricted to their specific ethnic groups, and marriage across the ethnic divide separating the *i-Taukei* from Fijians of Indian descent is highly unusual. Clearly, there are exceptions, but while ethnic relations seem harmonious enough in the marketplace and at work, they generally end at the front door.

David Harrison

References

Asian Development Bank (ADB). (2008). *Skilling the Pacific: technical and vocational education and training in the Pacific.* Executive Summary. Manila: ADB.

Ayikoru, M., Tribe, J., & Airey, D. (2009). 'Reading Tourism Education: neoliberalism unveiled'. *Annals of Tourism Research*, 36(2), 191–221.

Dore, R. (1976). *The Diploma Disease: education, qualifications and development.* Berkeley: University of California Press.

Echtner, C., & Jamal, T. (1997). 'The Disciplinary Dilemma of Tourism Studies'. *Annals of Tourism Research*, 24(4), 868–83.

Evans, J. (1993). 'Tourism Graduates: a case of over-production'. *Tourism Management*, 14(4), 243–6.

Furnivall, J. S. (1948). *Netherlands Antilles.* London: Cambridge University Press.

Harrison, D. (1988). *The Sociology of Modernization and Development.* London: Routledge.

Harrison, D. (1997). 'Globalization and Tourism: some themes from Fiji'. In M. Oppermann (Ed.), *Pacific Rim Tourism* (pp. 167–83). Wallingford: CAB International.

Harrison, D. (1998). 'Aid, Government and Tourism Studies in Less Developed Countries: the route from muddle to co-operation in Fiji'. In W. F. Theobald (Ed.), *Global Tourism,* 2nd edn. (pp. 476–92). Oxford: Butterworth Heinemann.

Harrison, D., & Lugosi, P. (2013) 'Tourism Culture(s): the hospitality dimension'. *Tourism Recreation Research*, 38(3), 269–81.

Holden, A. & Wickens, E. (2007). '"Citizen of the World" or "Management Puppet"? The place of tourism studies in higher education'. *Tourism Recreation Research*, 32 (2), 41–7.

King, B. (1994). 'Tourism Higher Education in Island Microstates: the case of the South Pacific'. *Tourism Management*, 15(4), 267–72.

Lawson, S. (1996). *Tradition Versus Democracy in the South Pacific: Fiji, Tonga and Western Samoa.* Cambridge: Cambridge University Press.

Leiper, N. (2000). 'An Emerging Discipline'. *Annals of Tourism Research*, 27(3), 805–8.

McCall, G. (1984). 'The University of the South Pacific: context, purpose and prospect'. *Vestes*, 27(2), 55064.

Norton, R. (1997). *Race and Politics in Fiji,* 2nd edn. Brisbane: University of Queensland Press.

Pacific Islands Forum Secretariat. (2005). *Forum Communiqué.* Thirty-sixth Pacific Islands Forum, Papua New Guinea, 25–27 October. Suva: Pacific Islands Forum.

Pacific Islands Forum Secretariat. (2007). *2007 Pacific Plan Annual Progress Report.* Suva: Pacific Islands Forum.

Smith, M. G. (1975). *Corporations and Society.* London: Duckworth.

Subramani (1998). Developing an Alternative Pedagogy. Conference on Curriculum Development for the 21st Century, 17–18 August. CDU, Fiji.

Sustainable Tourism Development Consortium. (2007). *Fiji's Tourism Development Plan, 2007–2016.* Department of Tourism, Ministry of Tourism and Environment, Suva.

Thaman, K. H. (2001). 'Towards a Pacific Philosophy of Education: the role of teachers'. Keynote address to Fijian Teachers' Association, Women's AGM section, 11 January, Suva.

Tribe, J. (1997). 'The Indiscipline of Tourism'. *Annals of Tourism Research*, 24(3), 638–57.

Tribe, J. (2002). 'The Philosophic Practitioner'. *Annals of Tourism Research*, 29(2), 338–57.

Tribe, J. (2005). 'The Truth about Tourism'. *Annals of Tourism Research*, 33(2), 360–81.

University of the South Pacific. (1994). Mission Statement. Planning and Development Office, Suva: University of the South Pacific.

University of the South Pacific. (2013). *Strategic Plan: 2013–2018.* Suva: University of the South Pacific.

Wang, Z. H., & Ryan, C. (2007). 'Tourism Curriculum in the University Sector: does it meet future requirements? Evidence from Australia'. *Tourism Recreation Research*, 32(2), 29–40.

18

Challenges for the tourism, hospitality and events higher education curricula in Sub-Saharan Africa

The case of Kenya

Melphon A. Mayaka
School of Business and Economics, Monash University, Australia

John S. Akama
Kisii University, Kenya

Introduction

Tourism, hospitality and events (TH&E) education particularly in Sub-Saharan Africa confronts daunting problems and challenges that call for innovative approaches and inventions. The societal environment under which TH&E university education has to survive in the current period of unprecedented regional and global change and uncertainty is extremely diverse and complex. The main aim of this chapter, therefore, is to examine the challenges confronting TH&E higher education curriculum development and implementation in Africa with particular reference to Kenya.

The chapter commences with an outline of key issues in the global context of TH&E education followed by an overview of current TH&E education in Kenya. The critical issues confronting tourism education are analysed from a historical viewpoint. This historical overview is followed by an exploration of some of the key challenges of the African university education system and how these challenges impinge on TH&E provision in general, and the curriculum space in particular. The exposition of key issues provides a justification for proposals on future directions in TH&E curriculum development in Kenya. A model for the TH&E curriculum space is proposed that takes cognizance of the tensions between professional vocational skill requirements of the TH&E sector and broader liberal education provision.

An outcome-driven approach to TH&E education presupposes that a blend of theory and practice is possible within the curriculum space. Further, institutions can occupy different positions within this local and global curriculum space. Engagement of various stakeholders such as students and parents, educators, industry, and university management, that takes into consideration the diverse needs and expectations of each stakeholder group, is paramount. The view that curriculum space is socially constructed is upheld, hence the criticality of socio-cultural contexts in the TH&E curriculum space. The global context is the focus of the section that follows.

Global context

The earlier chapters of the book have provided in-depth elucidation on fundamental issues and/or challenges confronting TH&E higher education within the global context. In this regard, only key observations that are relevant in any discourse on the Sub-Saharan African context are going to be highlighted (also see Airey, 2004; Dredge et al., 2012; Lynch et al., 2011; Sigala & Baum, 2003; Xiao & Smith, 2008).

First, one of the most debated issues is the orientation towards either vocational or liberal outcomes of TH&E education. Tribe's (2002) articulation of the need to produce the 'philosophic practitioner', described as a practical individual but also one who is a good steward of the world (Tribe, 2002) reconciles these divergent perspectives. Dredge et al. (2012) build upon the philosophic practitioner arguing that it is not a static concept able to be achieved in a single programme of study. Rather, there is a balance of skills and knowledge that is needed, and there should be the possibility of varied outcomes and different types of tourism and hospitality professionals within the curriculum space. Moreover, this balance of skills and knowledge could only be interpreted within the context of its application.

Second, the body of tourism knowledge itself continues to be a key subject of discussion. Over the years, an entirely market-driven focus has been adopted in most programmes. In some instances, this consumption–production focus seems to sideline fundamental human values such as self-determination and social improvement as valuable curricula outcomes (Belhassen & Caton, 2011). Arguably, building and communicating the corpus of tourism knowledge ought to be the aspiration of TH&E curriculum design processes. The aim of such processes is to produce individuals with the capability to enhance the depth and breadth of the tourism knowledge through further scholarly engagements (Xiao & Smith, 2008). The need to balance the market demands of TH&E higher education and its contributions to knowledge is being presented here as a key curriculum development challenge.

Third, in the last two decades commentators have seen the need for strategic and systematic approaches to addressing TH&E education. Mayaka and King (2002), for example, observed that there was a need for development of integrated national strategic tourism training and education plans. A systems approach to tourism education has also been proposed (Mayaka & Akama, 2007). Regional and national systems based on various qualifications frameworks were either being formulated or proposed (Amoah & Baum, 1997; Ayikoru et al., 2009). An international framework for tourism education quality was also provided (WTO, 1997). Understandably, such frameworks are supposed to provide some form of stability and establish clear links between national or regional goals and TH&E education in a strategic manner. However, these calls for systematic and strategic approaches have largely been ignored. Evidently, even where such frameworks exist, there are difficulties in implementation (Mayaka & Prasad, 2012).

Fourth, on a rather different note, the significance of the Internet and information technology in TH&E education is an important subject in the global arena. The influence of information technology is widely discussed in relation to curricula (Buhalis, 1998; Lashley & Rowson, 2005); the impact of information technology on the future of tourism intermediaries (Buhalis & Licata, 2002); information technology's contribution to competitiveness (Law et al., 2009); and the effect of information technology on content and delivery (Busby & Huang, 2012). The full effect of information technology and its significance in curriculum content and design is far from being apprehended. One area that warrants particular attention is the influence of technological advances on the provision of and access to TH&E education. Access to information about TH&E curricula through search engines such as Google, for example, provides inspiration and avenues for institutions to understand standards in other parts of the world and learn from them. This trend and the increasing mobility of TH&E educators have resulted in the emergence of globally homogenous curricula (Hjalager, 2007).

Fifth, also notable is the increased supply of and demand for distance-learning opportunities. Distance learning is a double-edged sword. On one hand, it allows institutions to offer their programmes to a larger pool of prospective students worldwide. On the other hand, it exposes institutions and their programmes to global competition. Programmes from outside national and regional boundaries have become more easily available to students in many localities. Notably, such offerings through distance-learning mode tend to reduce time and, in some instances, cost constraints for students. The effect on local TH&E programme offerings is to undermine the value of local programmes as demonstrated in the statement by an industry executive in Kenya: 'we have so many online and distance universities that are accepting [our employees] into MBA classes. Sad that unnecessary barriers are forcing us to send our hard earned money to some foreign universities' (Mohamed, 2010). This quote refers to stricture and inflexibility in areas such as modes of provision and entry criteria which mature prospective students see as 'barriers' to enrolling in local programmes (Mayaka & Prasad, 2012). In response these students enrol into programmes outside national boundaries. In addition, while the full impact of the global online learning phenomenon on local programmes is not understood and represents an important area of further investigation, online programmes seem to present a viable route to higher education for some. Moreover, establishing vital links between TH&E education and context envisioned in previous discussions may prove more and more elusive (Mayaka & Akama, 2007; Mayaka & King, 2002).

The foregoing discussion underscores the fact that TH&E education has to survive in a complex global environment. While the relevance of global issues may vary from region to region, country to country or even among institutions, recognizing global influences and the challenges they present ought to form an important input into TH&E curricula development. This calls for broad engagement across regions, nations and between private and public organizations. Key stakeholders will need to progressively engage each other as partners, rather than competitors, in the curriculum space. This chapter proposes that while a focus on the local and national contexts of TH&E education is necessary, these local issues and challenges have to be carefully framed within a broader global context. Attention will now turn to local issues and challenges.

The local higher education context

The idea of the curriculum space being socially constructed is vital as we consider the issues and challenges facing TH&E curriculum development and implementation (Tribe, 2002). TH&E institutions and stakeholders exist within a socio-cultural environment; institutions shape the environment and the environment shapes institutions in an iterative process. This section, therefore, seeks to examine the context of the post-independence African university education system as it relates to tourism and hospitality education in Kenya and other African countries.

The first university-level education institution in Kenya, the Royal Technical College, was established in Nairobi in 1956 under the tutorage of Makerere University (Uganda). Eventually the college was upgraded to a fully-fledged university in 1970 and was renamed the University of Nairobi. It should be noted that all other universities in Kenya, with the exception of Moi University, are either second-generation or third-generation offspring of the former college. The University of Nairobi, like most other African universities created immediately after independence, was meant to be a vehicle for providing highly skilled human resource in the era of centralized manpower planning and economic development (Agbo, 2005; Eshiwani, 1999; Samoff & Carrol, 2003; Sawyerr, 2004). The World Bank and other bilateral and multilateral funding agency policies were geared toward this objective.

These higher education institutions in Africa were also supposed to follow established university models and traditions in searching for universal knowledge and truth, as well as to respond to the needs of newly created nations. In particular, because the institutions were deemed to be the means for economic development and societal reconstruction after colonization (Agbo, 2005), government commitment to university education all over Africa was, and remains, very strong. However, these aspirations have hardly been met, instead 'the university strives to remain protected from external interference from the local community and it is unwilling to break the cultural mystique and behavioural codes built over time' (Agbo, 2005: 49).

Arguably, socio-cultural contextual values were ignored in the formulation of African higher education systems. Consequently, over the years there has been a hegemonic interface between local and external cultures. A system was created through which indigenous and distinctive socio-economic and cultural contexts and local knowledge were ignored and indigenous education patterns destroyed (Watson, 1994). A view that certain forms of localized contextually relevant learning and knowledge acquisition couched in African traditions and values were not recognized is being advanced. Inevitably, forms of social exclusion and a loss of focus of higher education institutions as a public good are some indictments levelled against the public university system in Africa (Sawyerr, 2004). Seemingly, to a great extent, the university has been reduced to producing graduates to meet market demands. It is not hard to imagine that the greater mission of serving humanity is lost in such narrow consumption–production-driven pursuits.

This scenario of the African university system presents a challenge for how to develop balanced curricula that may ultimately address such ideals and, in a way, correct apparent historical asymmetries. Such propositions are however not oblivious of the criticisms levelled against most tourism and hospitality education programmes, in particular, as being place-specific and lacking in broader contextual understanding (Xiao & Smith, 2008). Instead the propositions emerge from the notion that truth and reality exist in social contexts. It is important therefore that locally derived curricula aspire for greater reflexivity, enabling learners to engage better with their own understanding and others' understanding of the world.

Due to the aforementioned historical foundations, an uneasy relationship between higher education institutions and citizens persists in TH&E education in particular. Although certain positive reforms in some universities have been observed, new forms of exclusion have also emerged (Sawyerr, 2004). The following excerpt from discussions with industry players highlights the disconnect in TH&E curricula in Kenya:

> Why would I enrol in a 3 year Bachelor's degree programme with my many years working experience? How does it feel sitting in a class with a 20 year old for 3 years? I hope you realize that all your students will still come to hotels run by Kunde College graduates. Maybe it's time Kubwa [University] and many other local universities chose only hotels and resorts led by managers with degrees.

> (Mohamed, 2010)

These sentiments reflect an uneasy relationship between industry and university educators in the design, development and implementation of TH&E curricula. The tone seems to be indicative of a common perception of the university as an exclusive institution.

The observation above also highlights another challenge TH&E curricula must address. Kenyan public universities are only just emerging from a linear system to entry, where the only path to university was through high school. Thus, although pathways for mature holders of certificates and diplomas into university programmes in TH&E educations currently exist, they are only a recent phenomenon. It seems, too, that TH&E education offerings are still entirely geared to direct entrants from school and somewhat irresponsive to needs of mature professionals. Consequently, mature students (often industry executives with reasonable financial backing) end up seeking other higher education alternatives outside the local university system.

The concerns of potential students go beyond programme content (Dredge et al., 2012). It would appear from the previous paragraphs that the physical spaces and places (classes where people go to school and with whom they learn) are an important element. Holistically, curriculum design and development should encompass various components including the educational experience, learner interactions, as well as where and when delivery is taking place. The existing contextual socio-cultural and economic issues call for context-related approaches to curriculum design and development (Mayaka & King 2002).

Other than the fundamental objective of creating a pool of necessary manpower and enhancing universal knowledge as societal truth, the other underpinning aspiration of African universities is that they were expected to be key drivers of economic growth and development in their respective countries. One would not hesitate to say that the first objective of supplying skilled labour has been met with varying levels of success in many African countries. However, as to whether the university as an institution has played a key role in meeting socio-economic demands is contestable. First, many high-ranking scholars migrated from Africa (Kenya has been significantly affected by this phenomenon) to other parts of the world in the face of economic hardships and civil unrest in many African countries from the 1970s to the 1990s (Mutula, 2002). Second, for varying reasons, such as lack of research funds and institutional limitations, inefficient leadership and administration, the contribution of university education to economic development in most African countries is still, at best, debatable, and, at worst, non-existent (Sawyerr, 2004). In this regard, there are ever-increasing levels of poverty and standards of living remain low. These are the very crucial societal challenges and problems that African university education was supposed to tackle on a priority basis.

Notwithstanding the above observations, many countries in Africa still perceive universities as being important avenues in fostering national development by way of enhancing productivity, competitiveness and economic growth. Thus, stated country objectives and education national policy frameworks are vital elements when considering the current status of TH&E education and the existing curriculum space. The Kenya government's stated objectives of university education are:

- Imparting hands-on skills and the capacity to perform multiple and specific national and international tasks.
- Creation of a dependable and sustainable workforce in the form of human resource capital for national growth and development.
- Creation of entrepreneurial capacity for empowering individuals to create self-employment and employment for others.
- Offering opportunities for advancement of learning beyond basic education with a strong leaning towards scholarship and research.

- Creation of a strong national research base at various sectors of economic and national development.
- Bridging the gap between theory and practice in various disciplines of education and training.
- Creation of a strong sense of nationalistic and global development.
- Inculcation of a culture of precision, moral discipline and work ethic which are necessary in a modern industrial and technological world (Gudo et al., 2011b).

These guidelines provide the national policy goals within which universities are supposed to deliver education, training, research and innovation. However, in practice, expanding student enrolment and enhancing the number of academic programmes continues to be the strategic thrust of university education in Kenya. For example in 1994, the annual university student enrolment admitted through the Joint Admissions Board (JAB) (a national body entrusted with student admissions into public universities) was only 10,000 compared to over 50,000 in the current intake (Jomo Kenyatta University of Agriculture and Technology, 2013). This number represents only government-sponsored students. Fees for these students are substantially subsidized by the government where students pay as little as one-tenth of the total tuition. Access to this government subsidy is through performance in the national secondary-level Kenya Certificate of Secondary Examination (KCSE). Those who don't meet minimum funding requirements but qualify for enrolment have the option of enrolling on private full-fee paying basis bringing total annual enrolment to about 100,000. In addition, a number of students are admitted to private universities.

The exponential increase in university student enrolment is contextualized against national objectives to raise educational attainment as a mechanism for economic development. Empirical evidence suggests that rapid growth in student enrolments has stretched physical infrastructure capacity and available human resources in both public and private universities (Gudo et al., 2011a; Gudo et al., 2011b). It appears then that increasing access to higher education is compromising the quality of teaching and research.

The number of public and private universities in the country has increased significantly. In 1994 there were only five public universities; today there are a total of 22 universities. Although the increase in the number of student places seeks to address equity and accessibility, the funding available to universities has not grown commensurate with this expansion. Worse still, almost every year, Kenyan universities experience shrinkage in public funding (Wangenge-Ouma, 2008; Wangenge-Ouma & Nafukho, 2011). For example there was a reduction in higher education funding in the national budget from an average of 0.94 per cent of GDP in the period 1996–2000 to 0.74 per cent in 2001–5. In response, public universities have emphasized marketing approaches that are aimed at attracting full-fee paying students over and above government-sponsored student places.

The full-fee paying students enter into programmes known by a variety of terminologies: 'parallel programmes', 'module II', 'income-generating academic programmes', 'alternative degree programmes', 'self-sponsored programmes' and 'special entry programmes' (Wagenge-Ouma, 2008: 460). This dual-track university education policy introduced in 1998 has had the effect of institutions deliberately reducing government-subsidized student places in favour of full-fee paying student places. Such a tendency disadvantages students from less-privileged socio-economic backgrounds in which case merit is compromised.

Another rarely discussed issue with regard to the dual-track system in Kenya's university student admission system is the fact that since the government fees subsidization strategy is merit-based, student admission is usually very competitive. Thus, in many instances, through this selection process administered by a centralized admission system, students end up being admitted to courses that lead to careers that are not, in the first place, their preferred choice. Consequently, in an environment of limited career opportunity, some students end up taking careers they are neither interested in nor suited to. An extreme example is where a student who wanted to do engineering gets admitted into a hospitality management degree as the only way of getting publicly funded university education.

New fields of study are seen by university managers as possible sources of revenue generation. These new fields such as TH&E and information technology are increasingly attractive amongst most universities in Kenya. In a production–consumption-driven system, there will also be pressure to increase enrolments of fee-paying students in these new areas. Programmes are therefore quickly designed with little regard to pedagogical concerns, student experience and academic resources (Wangenge-Ouma, 2008).Class sizes are larger than the capacity of facilities such as kitchens and computer laboratories, and large numbers of graduates are churned into the industry every year. Complaints about graduates have emerged:

> Hoteliers in Maasai Mara Game Reserve have an unsavoury verdict on most universities and colleges offering hospitality courses. They pointed an accusing finger at them for producing unqualified graduates. The hoteliers' spokesperson Francis Musengeti said the industry was chocked with graduates who were not up to task. The graduates are a disgrace to the hotel industry and should be taken back for further training. Clients have raised the issue of poor quality of service and food offered by them. Colleges and universities should also revise the [curricula] to conform to the changing needs in the industry.
>
> (Kemei, 2013)

Such complaints from industry are not peculiar to the Kenyan situation and are often a reflection of inadequate meaningful interaction between academia and practitioners (Lynch et al., 2011). However the voice of the industry as a key stakeholder cannot be ignored in the discussion on TH&E curriculum.

On another level, it is difficult for higher education institutions to enhance scholarship and research in tourism with the limited master and PhD supervision capacity available in most TH&E departments. This means that teaching and curricula are not constantly being fed by adequate research and contemporary professional practices. It follows then that this period of expansion has also been a period of deterioration of quality in university education in Kenya and other African countries (Oketch, 2004). Diminished quality of learning and scholarship, poor working and living conditions of faculty and students, and other constraints are ultimately the result of rapid expansion of university education coupled with restricted funding.

Some universities have come up with the so-called 'third stream' funding initiatives. These include business enterprises ranging from livestock farming to running hotels and conference facilities. While these income-generating initiatives can be important, the dangers they pose are many. A key issue is the limited ability of universities to manage enterprises and compete effectively against established private businesses. There is also the danger that university efforts and resources are often devoted to running businesses at the expense of teaching, research, scholarship and service to humanity.

The above scenario paints a gloomy picture within the local context of TH&E. However, there are also opportunities that have emerged in recent years. One such opportunity is the increasing interest of foreign investors in the local tourism and hospitality sector. These new investors such as international hotel chains, airlines and tour operators will provide much-needed employment for students. This in turn has the potential to generate full-fee paying student demand and support the development of higher level executive programmes in universities. The potential also exists for partnerships with international and multinational enterprises to enhance research and scholarship in TH&E education.

Historical perspectives of TH&E education in Kenya

Tourism and hospitality programmes were first introduced in Kenya in the present Technical University of Kenya (previously known as Kenya Polytechnic) in 1969. The initial programme was aimed at providing practical skills and competencies mainly in hotel operations management. However, a recognized need to provide specialized and more practically oriented tourism and hospitality training resulted in the establishment of the Kenya Utalii College (KUC) by the Kenyan government with financial and technical support from the Swiss government in 1975. The hotel management programme at the Kenya Polytechnic was moved to the newly established institution in the same year.

Kenya Utalii College continued to offer a diploma in hotel management and certificate courses in hotel operation areas such as food production, front office operations, housekeeping and laundry as well as food and beverage sales and services. Later inclusions in the repertoire of programme offerings were travel and tour operations, tour guiding, and tour management, albeit at certificate, associate diploma or diploma levels. It is notable that KUC took an early lead in tourism education in a way that has made a significant contribution to the industry. Certain aspects of the training offered in this institution were viewed as a good model for tourism education for developing countries (Blanton, 1992). However, changing times stimulated more innovation. For instance, KUC, having realized limitations in its original training-focused model, has sought to partner with other institutions of higher learning to strengthen its programmes.

The need for higher learning in tourism and hospitality was recognized in the early 1990s. The first tourism degree programme was offered at Moi University in 1991. Before then, those seeking degrees in TH&E went to universities abroad. Kenya Utalii College, for example, through its staff development programme, facilitated education of its staff mainly in America and Europe. These pioneer faculty members provided the first pool of degree holders in TH&E in Kenya and indeed in the entire East Africa region. Notably, this early acquisition of higher level skills in TH&E was purposefully tailored to be in sync with the need to deliver skills and competencies that were perceived to be necessary for Kenya's tourism and hospitality sector or the sponsoring institution. While the orientation of such education toward vocational or liberal ends may be a subject of discussion, it mattered less in the earlier days as focus was on skills upgrade.

A more important observation is that the deficiency of qualified TH&E educators attracted scholars from other disciplines such as geography, economics and sociology. With the diverse academic orientation of the tourism educators, quite often tourism and hospitality research was undertaken within the academic and disciplinary boundaries of the researchers; and was driven by diverse paradigm orientations and sometimes diametrically opposed philosophical values and academic viewpoints. As Airey (2004) has noted, this disciplinarity, although it adds richness to tourism knowledge, has had the unintended consequence of complicating matters in the quest for a coherent body of TH&E knowledge. Faced with new frontiers of knowledge, for example, researchers often tend to retreat into their disciplinary comfort zones frustrating this search for coherence.

Currently, several Kenyan universities offer undergraduate TH&E education (see Table 18.1). In addition, Kenya Utalii College began to offer degree programmes in tourism and hospitality in collaboration with the University of Nairobi in 2008, perhaps marking a shift in KUC's overall orientation from a pragmatic and utilitarian skills-gap filling approach to more theoretical and conceptual approaches. It can be argued that while debates about the need to balance between liberal and vocational orientations of TH&E curricula are valid and the tensions understandable, desired outcomes of curricula are a more relevant consideration (Mayaka & King, 2002). In addition, as Dredge et al. (2012) have argued, tourism and hospitality curricula and pedagogies are socially constructed. Therefore, the need to accommodate various stakeholder perspectives including those of academics, university managers, students and industry practitioners is more critical (Sigala & Baum, 2003). Such a framework can facilitate the flexibility and adaptability that allows the emergence of curricula that are relevant and embedded in their socio-cultural and economic contexts.

An initial glance at the TH&E programmes offered in Kenya (Table 18.1) does not conceal the fact that most of the programmes are business-related.

Table 18.1 University TH&E programmes in Kenya

University	Department	Programme
Public		
Moi	Tourism Management	**Bachelor of Tourism and Management (BTM)**
		Bachelor of Travel and Tour Operation Management (BTTM)
	Hospitality Management	Bachelor of Hospitality Management (BHM)
Kenyatta	Hospitality Management	Bachelor of Science in Hospitality (BSc)
		Bachelor of Science in Hospitality and Tourism Management (BSc)
	Tourism Management	Bachelor of Philosophy in Hospitality &Tourism Management (BPhil)
		Bachelor of Science Tourism Management (BSc)
Maseno	Ecotourism and Institutional Management	Bachelor of Science (Ecotourism, Hotel And Institution Management with IT) (BSc)
Nairobi	History	Bachelor of Arts Tourism (BA)
Chuka	School Agriculture Environmental Studies	Bachelor of Science (Ecotourism and Hospitality) (BSc)
Pwani	Hospitality and Tourism Management	Hospitality and Tourism Management (BSc)
Technical University of Kenya	Tourism and Travel Management	Bachelor of Technology in Tourism and Travel Management (BTech)
	Hotel and Restaurant Management	Bachelor of Technology in Hotel and Restaurant Management (BTech)
		Bachelor of Technology Hospitality Management (BTech)
	Event and Convention Management	Bachelor of Technology in Event and Convention Management
Kisii University	Business and Management	Bachelor of Tourism and Hospitality Management
Private		
USIU	School of Business	Hotel and Restaurant Management (BSc)
		Tourism Management (BSc)
Strathmore	Centre for Tourism and Hospitality	Bachelor of Science Tourism Management (BSc)
		Bachelor of Science Hospitality Management (BSc)

It is also important to note that the variety of programmes being offered to students are, at least in the short-term, intended to provide human resource to the same Kenyan job market. Given the shortage of faculty as already noted, the distinctions in the degree offerings may only be limited to labelling of the programmes rather than in approaches in pedagogy, student experience and course content. In an environment where TH&E higher education is relatively new, the apparent diversity of programmes (at least in the labels) may be confusing to parents, students and the industry. Such an observation raises a number of critical issues in the current regime of TH&E education in Kenya and, by extension, the knowledge and skills of the curricula on offer (Manono et al., 2013; Mayaka & King, 2002).

First, the increasing number of undergraduate tourism and hospitality programmes takes place against a dearth of qualified faculty. This leads to the second issue: an apparent inability to enhance research and scholarship and to build the body of relevant contextual knowledge. Consequently, as has been observed elsewhere, a pool of limited sessional teachers (with very limited reading resources) move from one university to another teaching the same material to students (Gudo et al., 2011a). Consequently, teaching in general, and TH&E research output in particular, is limited in terms of quality and usefulness in addressing relevant and pertinent socio-cultural and economic challenges in the Sub-Saharan African context.

The inadequacy of research output has been noted as characteristic of the higher education sector in Kenya and other African countries (Bloom et al., 2006). In the Kenyan case, the situation presents a significant challenge when seen in the context of the role tourism is expected to play in regional, national and international socio-economic development, and in cultural and political transformation. For instance, the tourism industry is supposed to be a major socio-economic pillar in the realization of Vision 2030, which is the Kenya government's blueprint for the country's socio-economic transformation in the coming two decades (Mayaka & Prasad, 2012). In addition, tourism is expected to be a key sector in a reformed political dispensation where there are 47 devolved (county) governments that are positioned to exercise partial autonomy in the use and management of local and regional resources.

Third, the above scenario is compounded by existing disparity of academic viewpoints and the fragmented nature of the diverse approaches and modalities that various stakeholders adopt in addressing higher education needs in the tourism and hospitality sector (Mayaka & Akama 2007; Mayaka & Prasad, 2012). The chasm between industry and academic institutions is illustrated by confusion over the names of degrees and what the differences are between them in the following quote from a senior industry executive:

> I have equally taken the liberty to Google Bachelor of Philosophy in Hospitality Management and it is only Kubwa University that offers [it]. I also find that strange. It is either a neat bachelor or masters' programme, etc. On your (Kubwa University) website you also have a straight Bachelor of Science in Hospitality Management and I wonder what is the difference?
>
> (Mohamed, 2010)

The industry executive was responding to communication from one of the authors about a Bachelor of Philosophy programme designed for and targeted at diploma holders. This programme, understandably, had a cold reception from prospective students, most of whom hold key positions in the industry. This triggered an interesting conversation between the author and the industry players. One key issue was the naming of the degree as reflected in the quote. The conversation also illustrated the divergence of views of industry and academic departments on development of curricula. While it is true that education programmes are often created without consideration of the needs of various stakeholders, it is also possible that there is failure on the part of industry, in particular, to meaningfully engage and interact with education institutions. It has been observed, for example, that while industry recognizes the need for staff to upgrade skills, support to allow time for staff to upgrade these skills is in most instances not forthcoming (Mayaka & Prasad, 2012).

Fourth, a disparity of viewpoints and fragmented nature of the approaches that various stakeholders have adopted in addressing TH&E education issues have been highlighted (Mayaka & Akama 2007; Mayaka & Prasad, 2012). One such disparity is the highly contested ongoing standardization of tourism education programmes. Although Mayaka and Akama (2007) propose a systems approach to TH&E education, the situation has become increasingly more complex with the multiplicity of stakeholder interests and, perhaps, a lack of visionary direction both in the education and tourism industry sectors.

Furthermore, a disconnect between the industry and TH&E educators exists on what constitutes quality provision of skills and competences in TH&E curricula (Mayaka & King 2002). While debates on this subject often end up in persistent blame games, there is need to focus on more important aspects such as the end results of the curriculum and the purposes for which the curriculum is created such as employability and relevance which is contextual and socially constructed (Tribe, 2002). This calls for greater engagement with key stakeholders, particularly universities and industry. Such an approach is pertinent in the Kenyan situation where industry players are also most likely to be consumers of TH&E education given the historical context of tourism and hospitality programmes in the country.

In this regard, while there is no doubt that matching TH&E education with industry and other stakeholder expectations is a complex process, the strategic significance of this in terms of destination competitiveness and broader societal considerations cannot be overemphasized. A continuous search of appropriate models of stakeholder engagement is necessary. TH&E academics and industry players need to consider each other as collaborators in the TH&E curriculum space.

Of special interest are discussions and debates concerning what is to form core TH&E curricula especially in light of the multiplicity and variability in TH&E programmes both in the local and global contexts (Airey, 2004). In the context of Sub-Saharan Africa, for instance, the early calls for standardized curricula (Mayaka, 2005) and recent standardization initiatives (Mayaka & Prasad, 2012) continue to elicit mixed responses from various stakeholders (Kamau & Waudo, 2012). However, it is important to note that the standardization path has to be trod carefully.

Whereas it is reasonable to justify standardization in view of the need for localized (institutional, regional) approaches within an overall quality assurance framework, the argument that standardization bridles innovation and creativity is also valid. Thus, broad-based consultative approaches are vital components of curriculum design. Another related issue concerns the level and scope of current TH&E curricula models in Kenya and other African countries (Mayaka 2005; Sindiga, 1994). Sindiga (1994) decries the lack of higher level thinking especially in management and pedagogical theory. Change has been slow in this dimension (Ombongi, 2010). In an era characterized by uncertainty and rapid change, TH&E curricula will need to be adaptive and responsive to changing societal and industry needs.

The need for appropriate modes of delivery to make the TH&E education programmes more convenient for working executives is quite crucial. This is especially critical in view of the working hours of industry staff and the fact that some of them work in remote areas, such as lodges and community-based tourism enterprises in rural parts of the country. Some universities have responded by offering distance-learning modules. However, one of the major challenges of distance learning is the quality of learning materials and poor Internet and other communication services in many parts of rural Kenya. Besides, the running and daily management of such courses is difficult. In many instances, daunting challenges including administering of course materials, the delivery of exams and other logistical inhibitions are common occurrences.

Since the introduction of higher education in TH&E in Kenya in 1975, the number of TH&E programmes has increased to now over 26 programmes across 11 universities. While the need to provide higher learning in tourism and hospitality (Mayaka, 2005; Sindiga, 1994) was fulfilled with the commencement of undergraduate education programmes, the existence of a variety of programmes and a multiplicity of stakeholders calls for concerted collaborative efforts in the TH&E curriculum space. Such a collaborative approach requires conscientious strategic visioning and inclusive engagement. However, as already elucidated, apart from collaborative efforts, critical issues such as developing the body of knowledge and curriculum content, curriculum outcomes, and learner pedagogical experiences are important considerations.

Theoretical model

The above discussion provides the grounds for a holistic conceptualization of the TH&E curriculum space. Figure 18.1 draws inspiration from Schuler *et al.*'s (1993) integrated model for international human resource management and relies on Haywood and Maki's (1992) model of the employment/education interface. It also borrows from Mayaka and Akama's (2007) systems framework for tourism education. In addition, the model takes into account Tribe's (2002) philosophic practitioner model and its attendant developments (Dredge *et al.*, 2012). As articulated by Dredge *et al.* (2012) a broader consideration of curriculum goes beyond a focus on content. To this end, a curriculum should contribute to knowledge production and meanings in contextual lived worlds (Cetina, 2007). The inclusion of different stakeholder values is an important element of a holistic approach to TH&E curriculum space.

Figure 18.1 recognizes the TH&E curriculum space as a flexible and adaptable initiative with many possible outcomes which may include but are not limited to employability, the individual's ambition and lifelong learning and broader societal aspirations. The curriculum space is a product of exogenous factors, i.e. economic, socio-cultural and technological factors, and endogenous

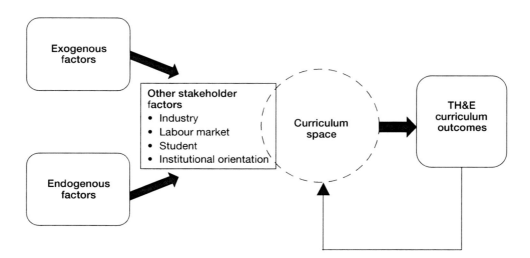

Figure 18.1 Curriculum space model

factors that relate to the internal capabilities and constraints of the institutions of higher learning. A multiplicity of stakeholders is recognized within this thinking. However, although stakeholders will have varied interests, within this space they are also collaborators. The curriculum space produces different outcomes that may impact upon the various stakeholders and the labour market, and hence a feedback loop emerges from outcomes back into the curriculum space. Overall, these outcomes are 'predicated on what students are able to experience in their learning and/or do as a result of such learning' (Priestley, 2011: 223) and the learning outcomes are lifelong rather than merely short-term behavioural ones. In this sense, outcomes are not merely stated instrumental goals such as key competences, but those that enable the learners to critically engage with their environments.

The curriculum space and curriculum development processes are hence reconstituted as socially constructed, institutions are deeply embedded and boundaries between the institutions as social systems and their contexts are blurred. Thus, Priestley (2011) underscores the need for curriculum designers to maintain a clear picture of existing contextual factors. In this regard, the model provides a framework for curricula that not only imparts knowledge and skills to learners, but also provides deeper learning experiences and meanings in different life worlds.

Conclusions and recommendations: the way forward

The societal environment in which TH&E university education has to survive in times of unprecedented uncertainty is complex. In this super-complex world, 'new frames of understanding' are necessary to make sense of the complexity and to enable institutions to have their place and exert their impact on society (Barnett, 2000: 209). This chapter provides a critical analysis of the complex environment within which TH&E education takes place, with specific reference to the Kenyan situation. Particularly, the chapter examines curriculum challenges within the broader global context as well as those challenges that are specific to the Kenya situation. The impact of global issues may vary across countries and continents, but it ought to form a critical component of TH&E curriculum discussions. As Barnett (2000) observes, the search for universal knowledge or truth may have to be abandoned. However universities and university departments have to find their space for survival in such complexity.

In the TH&E curriculum space there are tensions between local demands and global influences as well as competing values and interests. The curriculum model that is being proposed anticipates involvement of stakeholders as collaborators rather than competitors both at institutional and at macro (national) levels. Emphases shift to relating curriculum to context and outcomes rather than attempting to balance between liberal and vocational ends (Airey, 2004). Such a proposition calls for approaches that are constantly evolving in light of changing external environments in a way that enhances institutional relevance in society. The issues of funding and managing budgetary constraints cannot be ignored. In this area, there is a need for a constant search for what works. This calls for creativity and innovativeness in the design and management of TH&E education programmes (Johnstone, 2004). A carefully considered one-track funding model which invites partnerships is a good example of one such creative and innovative survival strategy for TH&E education (Johnstone, 2004). Universities and TH&E departments will therefore need greater levels of engagement with other players.

References

Agbo, S. A. (2005). 'Myths and Realities of Higher Education as a Vehicle for Nation Building in Developing Countries: the culture of the university and the new African diaspora'. In D.S. Preston (Ed.), *Contemporary Issues in Education* (pp. 49–70). Amsterdam: Editions Rodopi.

Airey, D. (2004). 'From Here to Uncertainty'. Paper presented at the Critical Issues in Tourism Education Conference, 1–3 December, Buckinghamshire, UK.

Amoah, V. A., & Baum, T. (1997). 'Tourism Education: policy versus practice'. *International Journal of Contemporary Hospitality Management*, 9(1), 5–12.

Ayikoru, M., Tribe, J., & Airey, D. (2009). 'Reading Tourism Education: neoliberalism unveiled'. *Annals of Tourism Research*, 36(2), 191–221.

Barnett, R. (2000). 'University Knowledge in an Age of Supercomplexity'. *Higher Education*, 40(4), 409–22.

Belhassen, Y., & Caton, K. (2011). 'On the Need for Critical Pedagogy in Tourism Education'. *Tourism Management*, 32(6), 1389–96.

Blanton, D. (1992). 'Tourism Education in Developing Countries'. *Practicing Anthropology*, 14(2), 5–9.

Bloom, D., Canning, D., & Chan, K. (2006). 'Higher Education and Economic Development in Africa'. Human Development Sector Africa Region, World Bank.

Buhalis, D. (1998). 'Information Technologies in Tourism: implications for the tourism curriculum'. In D. Buhalis, A. M. Tjoa, & J. Jafari (Eds.), *Information and Communication Technologies in Tourism 1998* (pp. 289–97). Vienna: Springer.

Buhalis, D., & Licata, M. C. (2002). 'The Future eTourism Intermediaries'. *Tourism Management*, 23(3), 207–20.

Busby, G., & Huang, R. (2012). 'Integration, Intermediation and Tourism Higher Education: conceptual understanding in the curriculum'. *Tourism Management*, 33(1), 108–15.

Cetina, K. K. (2007). 'Culture in Global Knowledge Societies: knowledge cultures and epistemic cultures'. *Interdisciplinary Science Reviews*, 32(4), 362–75.

Dredge, D., Benckendorff, P., Day, M., Gross, M. J., Walo, M., Weeks, P., & Whitelaw, P. (2012). 'The Philosophic Practitioner and the Curriculum Space'. *Annals of Tourism Research*, 39(4), 2154–76.

Eshiwani, G. S. (1999). 'Higher Education in Africa: challenges and strategies for the 21st century'. In P. G. Altbach & P. M. Peterson (Eds.), *Higher Education in the 21st Century: global challenge and national response* (pp. 31–8). Washington, DC: Institute of International Education.

Gudo, C. O., Oanda, I. O., & Olel, M. A. (2011a). 'Role of Institutional Managers in Quality Assurance: reflections on Kenya's university education'. *Australian Journal of Business and Management Research*, 1(2), 115–24.

Gudo, C. O., Olel, M. A., & Oanda, I. O. (2011b). 'University Expansion in Kenya and Issues of Quality Education: challenges and opportunities'. *International Journal of Business and Social Science*, 2(20), 203–14.

Haywood, K., & Maki, M. (1992). A Conceptual Model of the Education/Employment Interface for the Tourism Industry'. In J. R. B. Brent Ritchie & D. Hawkins (Eds.), *World Travel and Tourism Review* (pp. 237–48). Oxford: CAB International.

Hjalager, A.M. (2007). 'Stages in the Economic Globalization of Tourism'. *Annals of Tourism Research*, 34(2), 437–57.

Johnstone, D. B. (2004). 'Higher Education Finance and Accessibility: tuition fees and student loans in Sub-Saharan Africa'. *JHEA/RESA*, 2(2), 11–36.

Jomo Kenyatta University of Agriculture and Technology. (2013). Joint Admissions Board Admits 53,010 Candidates to Public Universities. Available: http://www.jkuat.ac.ke (Accessed 25 June 2013).

Kamau, S. W., & Waudo, J. (2012). 'Hospitality Industry Employer's Expectation of Employees' Competences in Nairobi Hotels'. *Journal of Hospitality Management and Tourism*, 3(4), 55–63.

Kemei, K. (2013). 'Hoteliers Decry Half-Baked Graduates', *Standard Digital*. Available: http://www.standardmedia.co.ke (Accessed 24 June 2013).

Lashley, C., & Rowson, B. (2005). 'Getting IT right: exploring information technology in the hospitality curriculum'. *International Journal of Contemporary Hospitality Management*, 17(1), 94–105.

Law, R., Leung, R., & Buhalis, D. (2009). 'Information Technology Applications in Hospitality and Tourism: a review of publications from 2005 to 2007'. *Journal of Travel & Tourism Marketing*, 26(5–6), 599–623.

Lynch, P., Germann Molz., J., McIntosh, A., Lugosi, P., & Lashley, C. (2011). 'Theorising Hospitality'. *Hospitality & Society*, 1(1), 3–24.

Manono, G., Kieti, D., & Momanyi, S. (2013). 'Mushrooming of Middle Level Tourism and Hospitality Training Colleges and Quality of Higher Education: a case study of Eldoret town, Kenya'. *Journal of Education and Practice*, 4(2), 57–65.

Mayaka, M. (2005). 'East Africa'. In D. Airey & J. Tribe (Eds.), *An International Handbook of Tourism Education* (pp. 161–71). Chicago, IL: Elsevier.

Mayaka, M., & King, B. (2002). 'A Quality Assessment of Education and for Kenya's Tour-operating Sector'. *Current Issues in Tourism*, 5(2), 112–33.

Mayaka, M., & Akama, J. S. (2007). 'Systems Approach to Tourism Training and Education: the Kenyan case study'. *Tourism Management*, 28(1), 298–306.

Mayaka, M. A., & Prasad, H. (2012). 'Tourism in Kenya: an analysis of strategic issues and challenges'. *Tourism Management Perspectives*, 1(0), 48–56.

Mohamed, H. (2010). Email conversation on BPhil programme.

Mutula, S. M. (2002). 'University Education in Kenya: current developments and future outlook'. *International Journal of Education Management*, 16(3), 109–19.

Oketch, M. O. (2004). 'The Emergence of Private University Education in Kenya: trends, prospects, and challenges'. *International Journal of Educational Development*, 24(2), 119–36.

Ombongi, K. (2010). Personal Conversation.

Priestley, M. (2011). 'Whatever Happened to Curriculum Theory? Critical realism and curriculum change'. *Pedagogy, Culture & Society*, 19(2), 221–37.

Samoff, J., & Carrol, B. (2003). *From Manpower Planning to the Knowledge Era: World Bank policies on higher education in Africa*. Paris: UNESCO.

Sawyerr, A. (2004). 'Challenges Facing African Universities: selected issues'. *African Studies Review*, 47(1), 1–59.

Schuler, R. S., Dowling, P. J., & De Cieri, H. (1993). 'An Integrative Framework of Strategic International Human Resource Management'. *Journal of Management*, 19(2), 419.

Sigala, M., & Baum, T. (2003). 'Trends and Issues in Tourism and Hospitality Higher Education: visioning the future'. *Tourism & Hospitality Research*, 4(4), 367.

Sindiga, S. (1994). 'Employment and Training in Tourism in Kenya'. *Journal of Tourism Studies*, 5(2), 45–52.

Tribe, J. (2002). 'The Philosophic Practitioner'. *Annals of Tourism Research*, 29(2), 338–57.

Wangenge-Ouma, G. (2008). 'Higher Education Marketisation and its Discontents: the case of quality in Kenya'. *Higher Education*, 56(4), 457–71.

Wangenge-Ouma, G., & Nafukho, F. M. (2011). 'Responses to Conditions of Decline: the case of Kenya's public universities'. *Africa Education Review*, 8(1), 169–88.

Watson, K. (1994). 'Technical and Vocational Education in Developing Countries: western paradigms and comparative methodology'. *Comparative Education*, 30(2), 85–97.

World Tourism Organization (WTO). (1997). *An Introduction to TEDQUAL: a methodology for Quality in Tourism Education*. Madrid: UNWTO.

Xiao, H., & Smith, S. L. J. (2008). 'Knowledge Impact: an appraisal of tourism scholarship'. *Annals of Tourism Research*, 35(1), 62–83.

19

Making the case for tourism in UK universities

David Botterill

Oxford School of Hospitality Management, Oxford Brookes University, UK

Robert Maitland

Centre for Tourism Research, University of Westminster, UK

Introduction

In this chapter we will present the evidence for a necessary engagement by the tourism academy with public affairs work. This will be achieved by describing the activities of the subject association for tourism in UK universities, the Association for Tourism in Higher Education (ATHE). Formed as the National Liaison Group for Tourism in Higher Education (NLG) in 1993, primarily to promote industry/university collaboration, the ATHE now provides a context-specific case study of the impacts of changes in a higher education system upon a maturing academic community. We will explore the ATHE's responses to policy and market changes and its more recent attempts to shape the agenda surrounding tourism higher education in partnership with an increasingly diverse array of academic organizations that have also set out to 'make the case' for their own subjects and activities. Drawing on the archives of the ATHE, we will identify several phases of public affairs and pressure group work over the past 20 years arguing that the ATHE has emerged from an outsider, low-profile, position to become an insider pressure group that is now embarking on more proactive, profile-raising initiatives. We conclude with a review of the lessons learnt by the ATHE and the future challenges facing tourism higher education in the UK.

This discussion represents a first attempt to review the development of the ATHE and its engagement with public affairs. It draws on documentary sources: NLG/ATHE publications, minutes of meetings of the Executive Committee, and minutes of the Annual General Meetings (AGMs). Both authors were members of the Executive Committee of NLG/ATHE for a number of years, and have chaired the organization. We draw on personal recollections and notes in developing this account, supplementing inevitable gaps in the written record.

Historical context for establishing the National Liaison Group for Tourism in Higher Education

The NLG was formed in 1993 as 'an independent body to bring together, facilitate, and forge partnerships between higher education interests and employers concerned with the UK tourism industry' (Airey & Middleton 1995: 1). From the outset, its members were not individuals but organizations: higher education institutions and companies or other bodies in the tourism industry. The formation of the NLG was a response to major changes in the UK system of higher education, and to developments in the tourism industry, affecting the industry's staffing requirements and the careers it offered. British higher education underwent a series of changes in the early 1990s that reformed its funding arrangements, and replaced a binary system with a unitary system within which institutional 'diversity' was encouraged (Filippakou et al., 2012). In 1965 a public higher education sector – predominantly polytechnics – had been added to existing universities. This created an explicitly binary model with varying funding arrangements and powers; notably polytechnics did not award their own degrees but those of the Council for National Academic Awards (CNAA). The CNAA as an awarding body sought to ensure parity among all degrees in the UK, and through its subject panels approved, evaluated and quality assured degree programmes in polytechnics and other higher education institutions (HEIs). The Further and Higher Education Funding Act 1992 changed funding arrangements, allowed polytechnics and HEIs to apply for the university title, and with it the power to award their own degrees.

Although this new system was unitary, diversity was encouraged and innovation sought as emphasis on competition and student choice developed (for example, HEFCE 2000; Department for Education and Skills 2003; Department of Business Innovation and Skills 2011: cited in Filippakou et al., 2012). Self-accreditation meant that the new universities had far greater flexibility to develop new programmes than had existed under CNAA, and subjects that were cost-effective and popular with students were favoured. At the same time, student numbers were expanding, and 'widening participation' became an important component of education policy, the post-1997 Labour governments eventually setting a target of 50 per cent participation by 2010. All this made possible a rapid growth in tourism programmes, discussed below, that would have been unlikely under previous structures. Whilst freedom from CNAA control and the prospects of new approaches could be welcomed by academics, other features of the new regime were more problematic. In both old and new universities 'the new public management' model of governance became the norm. This made universities more amenable to central government policy pressure (Filippakou et al., 2012: 325); saw the adoption within universities of governance by executive vice-chancellors and central management teams, rather than by academic senates and elected deans; and went along with the need to adapt to a state-regulated market for research and teaching funding. For individual academics and departments, the outcome was increased opportunities for growth and innovation, accompanied by a reduction in autonomy – and that inevitably fostered defensiveness and suspicion of change.

Creation and establishment of the NLG

The NLG was founded in 1993, following the abolition of the CNAA and as self-accreditation took effect. Tourism is a comparatively new subject in UK higher education. The first postgraduate programmes began in 1972 (at the universities of Surrey and Strathclyde) and the first undergraduate degrees were offered, by HEIs, in the late 1980s. Expansion in the 1990s was rapid. One of the NLG's initial priorities was to try to get a clearer picture of this rapid change. Table 19.1 shows its estimates, based on surveys of universities and HEIs in 1996 and 1998.

As Middleton and Ladkin (1996) say 'by any consideration the growth in course provision has been remarkable'. They account for it in terms of changes in public policy for higher education ('government encouragement for the provision of additional places in higher education and a

Table 19.1 NLG estimate of trends in tourism course provision 1991–98

	1991/92	*1993/94*	*1995/96*	*1997/98*
Institutions	15	36	43	50
New enrolments	1,000	2,500	4,415	not known

Sources: Middleton and Ladkin (1996); Airey and Johnson (1998).

growing emphasis on vocational courses since the 1987 White Paper on Higher Education'); expectations of continued growth in the tourism industry, its appeal as a career ('strong demand from students . . . a belief in the growth potential of the tourism industry as an employer'), and eagerness of universities to offer courses in a subject area where increasing provision seemed easy and cheap ('modularity of courses, and the relative ease (and low cost) with which tourism courses can be mounted compared with courses in science subjects and the traditional academic disciplines') (Middleton & Ladkin 1996: 3). The same survey showed that tourism teaching groups were small, averaging eight full-time staff, and that the growth of modularization meant that dedicated courses with their own staff teams were no longer the norm. These developments gave rise to a series of concerns that underlay the preoccupations of the NLG as it developed. They revolved around debates about course content, course quality, and course control, and meant that the NLG needed to find ways to influence the institutional and policy environment in which it operated.

The foundation and name of the NLG emphasized its original core purpose of improving links and fostering discussion between academics and the tourism industry. These links already existed for the small number of institutions that originated undergraduate- and postgraduate-level programmes, most active links being at local and regional level; rapid expansion meant that more formal and national collaboration was required. The tensions between what employers and academics sought in the content of tourism programmes was summarized in an early NLG paper: 'employers will wish to find that new graduate entrants to the industry are ready and able to make an immediate, as well as ongoing, contribution in the work place and will, therefore, expect a practical/specialist content in the curriculum; on the other, educators will seek to prioritize analytical, communicative and problem solving attributes' (Botterill 1996: 1). Employers' concerns with ensuring suitably qualified graduates were understandable – and presumably stronger in the 1990s before large numbers of well-qualified graduates from an expanded EU became available.

However it is not clear that such concerns translated into widespread active support for the NLG and its activities by the industry as a whole, as opposed to a number of concerned individuals. As with other archival material, information on membership is patchy, but in 1995 the NLG had 47 members, of which 12 were industry companies or associations and 35 universities. By 1999, academic membership had fallen a little to 31, but industry membership was down to 5. Broadly, industry at best accounted for 1 in 4 members, but dropped to 1 in 8. There is other evidence of limited industry involvement. The Executive Committee was from the outset chaired by an academic, and never by an industry member, and there are frequent references to the need to increase the number of industry representatives on the Executive Committee (EC meeting 1, November 1993), and to increase the number of industry members of the NLG (for example EC meetings 17, 18, 20, in 1997). Available membership lists show that key industry players – the national tourist boards, major tour operators, major airlines, major hotel groups, and travel agents – did not join, though the minutes recall attempts to recruit some of them, making use of personal contacts.

This perhaps reflects more on the nature of the 'tourism industry' than on the NLG. Though it is convenient to talk of 'the tourism industry' (as we do in this chapter) to describe a set of activities fond of describing themselves as 'the largest industry in the world', it is more accurate to see tourism as consumption that takes place in a series of sets of sectors (transport, hotels, museums, retail for example) and places (destinations). These sectors and places have very variable self-identification with tourism, and many people who work in 'the industry' will self-identify with a particular functional occupation – marketing, or finance for example – rather than with tourism. The difficulty of engaging with 'the industry' in the UK is considerable and longstanding. Indeed it was only in 2001 that the Tourism Alliance ('the voice of tourism' and intended to represent the whole industry) was formed (Tourism Alliance, 2013). It was set up after a catastrophic outbreak of foot and mouth disease that resulted in the slaughter of farm animals and the closure of large parts of the countryside to visitors. Although the economic impacts on tourism were considerably greater than on agriculture, well-organized farming lobbies gained government attention and policy priorities, whilst the poorly organized tourism industry had difficulty in making its voice heard. It was government that subsequently fostered the creation of the Tourism Alliance as a channel for industry representation. It is in retrospect unsurprising that the NLG found it difficult to liaise with this disparate 'industry' that itself lacked public affairs representation.

Despite these difficulties, the NLG succeeded in engaging with some elements of practice, and early work included advice and guidelines to support the involvement of practitioners in courses as external examiners (Roberts, 1995) and making connections between industry and higher education, including advice on placements, research, recruitment, and so on (Botterill, 1996). However the most obvious point of interest to the industry was content of programmes: what their potential recruits were taught and learnt. The need to set out the content that any programme describing itself as a tourism course should include – to define a core curriculum – was at the heart of the NLG's purpose, in the context of the loss of the CNAA and its coordinating role on curricula; the rapid growth of courses in institutions with little or no track record in tourism provision; emerging new concerns like sustainability; and curriculum impact of modularization and internationalization. The core curriculum was NLG's priority, as its first guideline publication made clear:

> It is for these reasons that the NLG devoted so much of its time in its first year to examining the need for a common core in tourism studies, talking with educationalists and employers alike in an effort to achieve the basis of a curriculum that will satisfy the employers, while maintaining academic rigour and meeting student needs for a programme of studies that will be both enriching and relevant to their long-term future careers in the travel and tourism industry. . . . The objective has been to find a common core for which broad agreement can be reached, which will at the same time provide institutions with the scope and flexibility to employ diverse approaches in the design of individual syllabi.
>
> (Holloway, 1995: 1)

The NLG proposed a core curriculum that drew on the CNAA's earlier work (CNAA, 1993) covering seven areas of knowledge that should be included in 'courses which refer to employment opportunities in tourism in the prospectuses they issue for prospective students' (Holloway, 1995: 3). These were discussed at a national conference that brought together academics and members of the tourism industry in December 1994, where they were endorsed and adopted (Holloway, 1995). Given the disparate nature of the tourism employers and indeed the institutions offering tourism courses, this was a considerable achievement. The agreed core curriculum had a strong business and vocational focus and omitted ethical concerns and non-business approaches (Botterill & Tribe, 2000). The liaison with industry delivered a curriculum that accorded with industry concerns. Three years later in 1997 Airey and Johnson (1998) in their survey of tourism degree courses ranked the top twenty aims and objectives. All the top five aims linked to preparation for careers, industry and vocation: a broader aim – 'sound education/academic understanding' – was an explicit aim in only 25 per cent of courses. How far this was driven by the core curriculum, or how far the agreed curriculum reflected an existing preference in universities is difficult to judge.

In any event whilst content was of most interest to the industry, from the academic viewpoint the curriculum had other purposes that revolved around control of knowledge and course design, and the related matter of quality assurance. The early NLG papers show concerns about what will happen to the subject in the face of rapid expansion predominantly in new universities with executive governance (for example Holloway 1995; Airey & Middleton 1995). This is understandable. Tourism as an economic activity struggled to be taken seriously, and its incorporation as a significant part of urban policy in the 1980s was beset by accusations that it was a candyfloss activity, without real worth or real jobs (Beioley et al., 1990). Tourism had emerged only recently as an academic subject, and debate about whether it was or could become a discipline in its own right was fierce amongst scholars (for example Tribe, 1997). Most tourism academics came to the subject from established disciplines (geography or economics, for example) or from the established field of business and management and the subject was institutionally rooted in newer universities. Most courses were in former polytechnics or HEIs, and the pioneer providers of postgraduate programmes, Strathclyde and Surrey, were themselves recent creations of the 1960s. Tourism was not taught at Oxbridge, London or the long-established civic universities. In these circumstances, tourism academics struggled to establish the respectability of their subjects, and feared that progress could be undermined by rapid expansion that drew in lecturers who were not subject specialists, and that was driven by university management seeking additional revenues with few added costs.

In these circumstances, the core curriculum can be seen both as an icon of subject respectability, ensuring academic rigour, and a means by which control could be wrested from executive senior management and returned to academics through taking ownership of what is to be taught as 'tourism'. Whilst the development of the core curriculum can be seen as having straightforward practical value, gaining agreement between industry and academics about what might be expected in a tourism programme, it can also be seen as part of a struggle for academic respectability and to retain or reclaim academic autonomy in a fast-changing higher education landscape. Power and symbolism proved to be important, and were thus emerging as key aspects of NLG activities. This developed further in the late 1990s and early 2000s as central government-led interventions increased with the advent of research assessment, subject benchmarking, and Teaching Quality Assurance.

From liaison to lobbying: becoming the Association for Tourism in Higher Education

The changes of the early 1990s devolved some power to universities and reduced control over courses offered, what was taught, and how. The late 1990s saw a re-centralization, of which one consequence was that the Quality Assurance Agency for Higher Education (QAA) took over the teaching quality assurance role in 1997. It mandated that each subject should have a benchmark statement, setting out expectations about standards of degrees; this included the curriculum. It also set up a process of subject review, to assess the quality of teaching provision on a subject-by-subject basis; all tourism centres were visited and reviewed between 2000 and 2002. Separately, there was a strengthening of evaluation of the quality of research, with Research Assessment Exercises (RAE) in 1996 and 2001 (Filippakou *et al.*, 2012; Martin, 2012). The NLG had completed the groundwork rapidly in its early years, and by 1996 had adopted the core curriculum, mapped provision of tourism courses, and published a series of advice notes and guidelines. The mid- and late 1990s saw the end of the period of rapid growth in courses and applicants (applicant numbers stabilized then declined a little), but a continuing growth in academic publishing, journals and PhD completions. The NLG had to engage with the new and emerging quality assurance and assessment processes, including those concerned with research.

During 1997 and 1998, the NLG was focused on its original purpose of liaison with the industry. The need to recruit new industry members was discussed at Executive Committee meetings 17 and 18 (March and May 1997), though initiatives seemed to have been unsuccessful; by October there were only five industry members and recruiting more was a priority (EC meeting 20, October 1997). The theme for 1998 and that year's conference was 'recruiting quality graduates' (EC meeting 21, January 1998) and in March it was decided to make a recruitment pitch to large employers, including an offer of one year's free membership (EC meeting 22, March 1998). These energetic efforts seem to have had at best only limited success. Meanwhile, agendas were filling with items linked to the changing higher education landscape. Responses to the Dearing Report (formally, the National Committee of Inquiry into Higher Education, chaired by Sir Ron Dearing (Dearing, 1997)) and liaison with the body responsible for standards in school education, the Office for Standards in Education (OFSTED) appeared in 1997, and in 1998 representations about the RAE were made, a letter was sent to funding councils, representations were made to HEFCE requesting a tourism sub-panel and subject representatives in the RAE. Industry liaison was limited to attempting to recruit more members and organizing the industry-related conference ('Recruiting and Retaining Quality Graduates in the Tourism Industry', Birmingham, December 1998).

It is unsurprising that the first meeting of the Executive Committee in 1999 (EC meeting 25, January 1999) agreed to consider the strategic direction of the NLG, although this was couched in terms of education and industry learning from one another. Meeting 26 in March seems to have been pivotal. The strategic direction of NLG was discussed and revised objectives were agreed for discussion at the next AGM. These envisaged that the NLG would be the subject association for tourism – the first time that 'subject association' is mentioned in minutes – and promote development and high standards 'to the mutual benefit of industry and education'. The agreed annual conference theme was strongly educationally focused and linked to changes in the education landscape ('Shaping the Tourism Curriculum in the 21st Century'; EC Meeting 26, March 1999). Subsequent meetings illustrate the pressures leading to a change in strategic direction. Major items were nominations for RAE 2001, nominations for QAA, Learning and Teaching Support Networks, a discussion with a QAA representative on the scope for NLG involvement (EC meeting 27, May 1999) and establishing a group on benchmarking for tourism, with member consultations to be organized across the country (EC meeting 28, September 1999). The transition was not smooth. At EC meeting 27, the Chair expressed concern that the agenda was 'becoming increasingly educationally orientated and stressed the need for the NLG to become more involved with industry', and at the following meeting the familiar topic of how to attract new industry members was once again addressed. However on this occasion the discussion centred on 'how to attract new [industry] members and whether they were actually needed' (emphasis added). At the 1999 AGM in December, the Executive Committee was asked to discuss 'how the organization needs to change to develop into a mature subject association' and a possible name change. At the same time one of the founding industry members of the Executive Committee resigned (amicably and with thanks for her contribution). She had provided support and meeting facilities on industry premises. The shift in the NLG's role was now clear, and the first Executive Committee meeting of 2000 took place at a university with only one industry representative. From then on, all Executive Committee meetings took place at universities. Meetings in 2000 were dominated by formalizing the change in focus and in responding to educational pressures. At EC meeting 32 (May 2000), it was agreed that a subject association was needed and decided that NLG should join the Academy of Learned Societies in the Social Sciences (ALSSS). At the AGM in November 2000 a series of changes to the constitution were proposed to change the name of the NLG to ATHE, and to revise its objectives to those of a subject association. The proposer said that 'whilst NLG had performed adequately in many of its objectives, some had been unsuccessful. Much time and effort had been used in trying to liaise and maintain links with the industry, but this did not happen as was intended'. The NLG had increasingly become a subject association and its name and constitutional changes were required to reflect that. The changes were agreed unanimously.

The early enthusiasm for education and industry liaison seems to have arisen as changes in higher education structures facilitated the rapid development of new programmes in a novel subject area that allowed expanding institutions to 'sell the dream' (Fidgeon, 2010) of exciting and exotic careers to potential students. At least some elements of the tourism industry shared concerns that this might lead to growing numbers of courses with tourism in the title but little consistency of content. They had a shared interest with academics in a core curriculum that reflected industry interests and provided a focus for quality assurance and tourism scholars' claims to ownership of the subject. Once that had been achieved with an agreed core curriculum, the scope for liaison seems in practice to have been limited. There is very little evidence of interest by key industry players, and Executive Committee discussions frequently return to the problem of how to recruit new industry members (to an organization with a modest membership fee – £350 pa – that would presumably not in itself represent a barrier to large corporations like BA, Marriott or Thomson). It is hard to avoid concluding that the interest in liaison came not so much from 'the industry' but from a limited number of key individuals within it, and it was difficult to maintain after an initial burst of enthusiasm. From an academic viewpoint, government became increasingly proactive as the 1990s wore on, and the need to maintain and improve tourism's status as a subject focused more and more on positioning within these new initiatives rather than positioning with the industry. Responding and lobbying came to the forefront of NLG's concerns, and it was developing the character and role of a subject association before it formally discussed changing its name and objectives. Had there not been a need for the NLG to transform into a subject association, it would almost certainly simply have been wound up.

ATHE the early years: finding a voice and reacting to change

The period between 2001 and 2008 (EC meetings 36–79) saw the membership rise to between 35 and 38 UK university members, peaking at 39 (EC meeting 70, February 2007). This reflected the continuing growth of new providers of tourism higher education that was fuelled by the popularity of the subject and by the public policy climate of expansion in higher education. Executive Committee minutes convey both the confidence afforded by the growth in membership and report the successes of well-attended annual conferences, but also reflect some trepidation about the capacity of ATHE to respond to the flood of public policy initiatives and changes in the higher education environment. As just one example, minutes of a discussion in early 2003 (EC meeting 50) report 16 potential policy areas for the annual conference. The working title of the conference, 'SURVIVAL – is your institution tough enough to survive the tourism jungle?' reflects the sense of unease on both collective, and individual institution, levels.

In part, the unease conveyed in the EC minutes reflected the consequence of the ambition to become a subject association combined with the inexperience of many of the EC members in public affairs work. As a new subject association the ATHE was very much an 'outsider' defined both by its lack of identity in higher education policy communities and its meagre level of resourcing. Our analysis is that during this seven-year period the ATHE matured as a public affairs organization from an 'outsider by necessity' (Grant, 1999) status to one approaching an insider status in some particular terrains of higher education policy and practice. This was achieved by collaboration with other subject associations and particularly by the emergence of the Learning and Teaching Subject Network for Hospitality, Leisure, Sport and Tourism (LTSN HLST) and its incorporation into the Higher Education Academy in 2004 (EC meeting 57).

EC meeting minutes in 2002 suggest the EC was, at best, finding its way in public affairs work. Conversations were opened with the Leisure Studies Association and an EC member attended the early meetings of the ALSSS (subsequently to become the Academy for the Social Sciences). Annual conferences reflected a general desire to engage in lobbying but the choice of which specific issues to focus on was driven mainly by the interests of individual EC members. For example, the outcomes of the RAE 2001 prompted analysis of the invisibility of tourism research and drove up attempts to influence the ensuing debates about subsequent research quality exercises (HEFCE, 2003). Collaboration among member institutions was sought to promote the idea of a tourism Knowledge Exchange Centre Network (KECTOUR) in response to a national knowledge transfer initiative. Despite these activities, the scale of the challenge facing the ATHE, at least in the area of research policy and practice, was cruelly exposed when five years later the funding councils' joint consultation on the RAE 2008 failed again to take account of tourism as a research topic save for a single reference within the small print of the Planning panel descriptor. Likewise, the KECTOUR bid was adjudged unviable given the reworking of the policy initiative to favour science and technology (EC meeting 52). Finding a voice in central government policy on tourism was also proving difficult. Plans to establish a multi-sector, public affairs voice for tourism in the wake of the foot and mouth crisis of 2002 – the Tourism Alliance – initially did not include higher education representation, although the ATHE did eventually become a subscribing member on a one-year trial basis (EC meeting 51).

Between 2002 and 2008, most progress was made in teaching and learning. The growing influence of the QAA and its regimens of external, subject and institutional, review heightened the significance of the ATHE's role as a both a way for the QAA to communicate with the subject community and a way for the subject community to share peer experiences of the processes and to provide feedback to the QAA. The Learning and Teaching Subject Network for Hospitality, Leisure, Sport and Tourism made strenuous efforts to coalesce the efforts of the several subject associations active in its subject domain (EC meetings 47, 48, 49) particularly around lobbying to improve data capture on HLST subject enrolments through the Joint Academic Coding System (JACS) (EC meeting 58). It also sought to adopt the subject associations as conduits for communicating its increasing array of activities and opportunities for pedagogic research within the HLST academic communities.

In 2005 the work of the EC took a significant turn when it engaged in the production of a strategic plan (EC meeting 55). This process signalled a growing confidence in ATHE's capacity to engage with public affairs work and simultaneously suggested a more balanced approach to lobbying not quite so dependent on the individual enthusiasms of EC members. These early signs of maturity proved influential in expanding the repertoire of lobbying activity in subsequent years. A review of the strategic plan at EC meeting 65 (March 2006) particularly seems to have triggered more proactive engagement and EC meetings 69–79 reflect a wide range of public affairs activity including: evidence to a select committee, engagement with the Economic and Social Research Council (ESRC) on the nomination of specialist tourism reviewers, an invitation to participate in planning of a diploma for 14–19-year-old high school pupils, attempts to engage regional development associations, and high-profile involvement with the Tourism Alliance and the opportunity to lobby UK government ministers on international student visa regulations and the availability of knowledge exchange funding for applied industry/academic research partnerships.

Towards a professional and proactive subject association

Whilst these activities had meant that tourism had gained a voice in the changes that were taking place in UK higher education, it was becoming clear that ATHE's lobbying stance needed to be more than reactive. The landscape of UK higher education was becoming more diverse and turbulence was a permanent feature. The number of institutions achieving university status continued to increase, and more tourism courses were established. Higher education had become a quasi-market, with tuition fees raised to £3,000 in 2004 (in England) and university and subject league tables proliferating and perceived as of critical importance by institutions and academics. From 2005, the Higher Education Funding Council for England (HEFCE) introduced the National Student Survey (NSS) – in England, Wales, and Northern Ireland – assessing final year students' satisfaction with their programmes. The Executive Committee felt there were more tourism courses in more institutions, although demand may have peaked, that the various guides and NSS gave varying ranking results – but lacked hard data. Inaccurate information about tourism was common in the public domain and was a particular concern. Like the tourism industry, tourism education was frequently seen as 'candyfloss', and, along with media studies, the default illustration for those who argued that the quality and rigour of university education was in decline. To respond, ATHE recognized that it had to be more proactive. This involved two strands of activity: first, gaining a better understanding of the landscape of tourism higher education and, second, becoming more proactive in lobbying and influencing.

The Executive Committee commissioned the Tourism Intelligence Monitor (TIM) in 2006 (EC meeting 67) to draw together the disparate data on the subject. When published, the TIM pointed out that:

> Despite the growth in provision of tourism as a subject in UK higher education institutions (HEIs) 'hard data' on this phenomenon have been difficult to come by. Certainly, no single source existed which provided an overview of data available on course provision, academic institutions, student numbers and tourism qualifiers.
>
> (Walmsley, 2007: 5)

The TIM was a valuable first step in improving the knowledge base from which ATHE could argue for its subject. Once the importance of improved lobbying had been recognized, efforts were made to take it forward, in parallel with developing improved knowledge and data. In 2007, lobbying became a more explicit objective (EC meeting 69) and the Association took a table at a lunch arranged by the Academy of Social Sciences in the House of Lords so that it could invite guests from organizations with which it wanted to build relations – ESRC,

Department of Culture, Media and Sport (DCMS, the government ministry responsible for tourism), Tourism Alliance, VisitBritain (the national tourism marketing body), People First (the sector skills council that covers tourism), and the World Travel and Tourism Council (WTTC). This proactive work was a new departure for ATHE. The success of such initiatives is inevitably hard to measure, but soon after ATHE succeeded in gaining the ESRC's agreement to its nominating a number of grant reviewers – having successfully argued that tourism-related applications suffered since they were normally reviewed by scholars from other subject areas. The selection of subject reviewers was made in an exhaustive and transparent manner that was time-consuming, but a list of nominations was accepted by ESRC in late 2008. This consultative selection process illustrates an emerging concern to find ways of involving members more effectively in ATHE's work. Initiatives to overhaul the website, and commission a new corporate identity and branding during 2007 and 2008 can be seen as reflecting an awareness both of public image for a more proactive organization and the importance of marketing the work of the association to its own members (for example EC Meeting 70, February 2007).

By 2010, lobbying and research had begun to emerge as ATHE's key functions. For the first time, one of the Executive Committee meetings was expanded to an Awayday with substantial time away from day-to-day business for a prolonged discussion of the organization's objectives and priorities and how they would be achieved. The result was an action plan that sought to 'maintain the academic health and development of Tourism as a distinct subject area' through actions focused around making the case for tourism in higher education (principally by assembling data and evidence that could be used in lobbying); developing partnerships in the UK and internationally; and engaging the membership (Action Plan: Executive Committee meeting 87). At the AGM at the end of year the Chair summed up the approach:

> to make sure ATHE can be an effective voice for Tourism in HE, and can maintain and improve its relevance and viability in these turbulent times . . . we need to maximize our ability to influence the policy and pressures affecting tourism in HE, and to do that we must be sure we can speak authoritatively. Our efforts this year have centred on improving our research base so that ATHE can make the case for tourism in HE; increasing our membership and ensuring we can communicate with them better, so we are more representative; and improving the administration of ATHE so we make best use of members' subscriptions and the time committed by the Executive Committee.
>
> (Chair's Report, 2010)

These efforts continued, and included work carried out on the research landscape (for example, numbers of PhD completions); on student motivations to study tourism; and on commissioning of a new edition of TIM. The website was updated and redesigned (and achieved high ranking on Google for the search term 'tourism education'), the annual conference was reconfigured, and that boosted numbers and satisfaction; active responses were made on key matters such as the Research Excellence Framework (REF) – the system for assessing the quality of research in UK higher education institutions. That tourism has been named for the first time within one of the REF 2014 units of assessment (Unit 26: Sport and Exercise Sciences, Leisure and Tourism) can be seen as the successful outcome of years of lobbying by ATHE and its allies, and as evidence that it has been accepted as an insider organization whose views should be given some weight. Membership engagement was promoted with the construction of a database of individual tourism academics at member institutions, improving communication; new members were drawn in and the constitution was changed to allow universities overseas to become associate members;

prizes for undergraduate and postgraduate students at member institutions were offered, and paper prizes at the annual conference introduced. This represented considerable progress, but was insufficient to develop a more proactive lobbying role that could begin to shape policy development.

For some time, the Executive Committee had aimed to be able to make the case for tourism, and had focused on assembling an evidence base of (mainly) numerical data, and drawing on this to respond to and lobby policymakers. That had proved effective in extending ATHE's influence, but it was becoming clear that the limits of the approach were being reached and that further development would require ATHE to be able to tell a more coherent story about the importance of tourism in higher education, rather than simply cite data. The model of the Academy for Social Science's campaign 'Making the Case for Social Science' was influential. In order to make progress on this one of ATHE's Emeritus Fellows was commissioned to develop an approach, that after discussion with the Executive Committee was agreed at the 2012 conference in December. This involves focusing on three narrative lines as the basis for 'making the case' for tourism in higher education:

Narrative 1: Building leadership and management capacity in the tourism industries
Under this narrative the familiar case of the economic importance of tourism, employment, career development, organization and management studies knowledge, workplace experience.
Skills set: project planning, time management, communication skills.
(It is interesting to note that this narrative line is dominant in current course descriptors of ATHE members.)

Narrative 2: Understanding global complexity through tourism
The concepts under this narrative include mobility, transnationality, cosmopolitanism, globalization, communications, and risk.
Skills set includes: critical and analytic thinking, problem solving, political and historical sensitivity.

Narrative 3: Making a difference through action in tourism
The concepts under this narrative relate to 'Quality of Life' indicators and include: social development, social justice, inclusivity, ethics, community vulnerability and capacity building, community cohesion, environmental issues, performativity and embodiment.
Skills set includes: advocacy, emotional intelligence, interventions, evaluation toolkits, action learning.

The intention is to use the narrative lines to structure representations of messages about tourism higher education, illustrated by examples from research and from teaching. The examples will feature specific projects, tutors, and students and thus bring the narratives alive. The Executive Committee decided to encourage the membership to provide vivid examples by offering prizes under each category, to be sponsored by prestigious organizations such as VisitBritain – the Making the Case for Tourism in Higher Education Awards. These were launched at the annual conference in December 2013. This was ATHE's twentieth anniversary conference and Making the Case illustrates how far it has travelled over that time from a group liaising between industry and academics at a time of rapid growth in tourism to an association seeking to manage an established subject in turbulent times.

Looking to the future

Our review of 20 years of the ATHE's development provides us with some pointers to the challenges it is likely to continue to face in the future. We see no sign of a slackening off in the pace or intensity of turbulence surrounding tourism higher education. Ours is a partial list of challenges, but we begin with the issue of the quality of tourism higher education courses that are delivered in mixed economy, further education/higher education public sector colleges, and the incorporation of private sector 'alternative providers' into the UK higher education landscape. These trends will exacerbate competition without, perhaps, the collaborative, collective, and mediating influence of ATHE unless it can find a means to incorporate these providers into its network. The full impact of student fee increases, particularly in England, are still working their way through the institutional structure of UK higher education, the practices of individual institutions, and the fortunes of academic subjects. The ATHE EC will need to be vigilant on this matter. Off-campus, satellite campus, offshore and online delivery mechanisms are likely to proliferate in the next decade and ATHE's ability to engage with these players will challenge the UK-centric focus of ATHE's membership and its constitution. The globalization of tourism higher education is likely to further challenge the current anglophile dominance of tourism knowledge creation and dissemination. The ATHE's experimentation with a Mediterranean chapter may provide a forerunner of the future shape of the association but its own meagre resources may thereby be spread even more thinly and constrain its ability to mature as a lobbying force within the UK system.

As the first 20 years have shown, breaking into established policy networks with a new subject is possible but requires persistence, evidence, and energy in order to gain, and then hold, credibility. Inclusion in the policy landscape as a consultee is a first step, but real influence involves shaping ideas and agendas and requires stories that can have longer term effects. How far the ATHE has penetrated into elite established policy networks is unknown. The choice of some UK universities that offer tourism higher education to persistently eschew ATHE membership, particularly the research-led pre-1992 universities, is perhaps indicative of an assessment of the relative limits of ATHE's current influence.

Our final point relates to the necessary continuing health of ATHE. Writing this chapter has caused us to reflect upon how the journey of the association is very closely correlated with our own journeys in tourism higher education. The shifts in sophistication needed to function as a respected subject association were often achieved in parallel with the upward career trajectories of some of its EC members; thankfully the upward moves outnumbered the career stumbling of a few! As tourism academics increasingly attained broader university management experience so the activities of the ATHE and its subject association allies benefited from insider knowledge and pressure group strategy and tactics. The creation of the ATHE Emeritus Fellows provides a vehicle for retaining knowledge within the subject community but, at the same time, it is vital that the association leadership is vigilant about succession planning within the EC. New generations of tourism academics should be encouraged to contribute to ATHE as a part of their individual development as academic leaders because they are most likely the best equipped to find appropriate responses to the new challenges the organization will undoubtedly face in the next 20 years, thereby, protecting and enhancing the integrity of tourism as a higher education subject.

References

Airey, D., & Johnson, S. (1998). *The Profile of Tourism Studies Degree Courses in the UK: 1997/98*. London: NLG.

Airey, D., & Middleton, V. T. C. (1995). *Education and Training in Tourism in the UK: guidelines for those seeking further information about courses and careers in tourism*. London: NLG.

Beioley, S., Maitland, R. A., & Vaughan, R. (1990). *Tourism and the Inner City*. London: HMSO.

Botterill, D. (1996). *Making Connections between Industry and Higher Education in Tourism*. London: NLG.

Botterill, D., & Tribe, J. (2000). *Benchmarking and the Higher Education Curriculum*. London: NLG.

Council for National Academic Awards (CNAA). (1993). *Review of Tourism Studies Degree Courses*, London: CNAA Committee for Consumer and Leisure Studies.

Dearing, R. (1997). *National Committee of Inquiry into Higher Education*. Available: https://bei.leeds.ac.uk/Partners/NCIHE/ (Accessed 30 September 2013).

Fidgeon, P. R. (2010). 'Tourism Education and Curriculum Design: a time for consultation and review?'. *Tourism Management, 31*, 699–723.

Filippakou, O., Salter, A., & Tapper, T. (2012). 'The Changing Structure of British Higher Education: how diverse is it?'. *Tertiary Education and Management, 18*(4), 321–33.

Grant, W. (1999). *Pressure Groups and British Politics*. Basingstoke: Palgrave Macmillan.

Higher Education Funding Council for England (HEFCE). (2003). *Review of Research Assessment: A Report by Sir Gareth Roberts to the UK Funding Bodies*. Bristol: HEFCE.

Holloway, C. (1995). *Towards a Core Curriculum for Tourism*. London: NLG.

Martin, B. R. (2012). 'Are Universities and University Research Under Threat? Towards an evolutionary model of university speciation'. *Cambridge Journal of Economics, 36*, 543–65.

Middleton, V. T. C., & Ladkin, A. (1996). *The Profile of Tourism Studies Degree Courses in the UK: 1995/6: summary report of a survey undertaken by the NLG*. London: NLG.

Roberts, A. (1995). *Guidelines for Tourism Industry Practitioners Newly Appointed as External Examiners to Tourism Courses at Degree Level*. London: NLG.

Tourism Alliance. (2013). 'What is the Tourism Alliance?'. Available: http://www.tourismalliance.com/details.cfm?p=ab&s=w (Accessed 30 September 2013).

Tribe, J. (1997). 'The Indiscipline of Tourism'. *Annals of Tourism Research, 24*(3), 638–57.

Walmsley, A. (2007). *Tourism Intelligence Monitor*. Eastbourne: Association for Tourism in Higher Education.

Part V
Curriculum delivery

20

Teaching about tourism in a post-disciplinary planning context

Caryl Bosman
Griffith School of Environment, Griffith University, Australia

Dianne Dredge
Department of Culture and Global Studies, Aalborg University, Denmark; Urban Research Program, Griffith University, Australia

Introduction

Urban and environmental planning has a substantial impact on social, economic and environmental welfare, and getting it right is a complex challenge facing governments, the private sector and communities (Australian Government, 2011). Over time, the complexity of planning has grown and planners today are asked to address a wide range of pressing problems in a context of constantly changing interests and demands. Tourism destinations are locations that are characterized by a complex layering of social, economic, political, environmental and cultural forces operating over time and across different spatial scales. Tourism adds an additional layer of complexity, where tourism destinations are vulnerable to global–local shifts in market demand and product development cycles. This dynamic context presents particular challenges for urban planners and is something that planning education must address if future professionals are to address issues of rapid change and uncertainty. In Australia, for example, tourism is a major driver of social, economic and environmental change in coastal environments, where over 85 per cent of the population live (Hugo, 2011). Some of the issues confronting planners in coastal tourism regions include managing and responding to significant shifts in population growth, migration, an ageing population seeking retirement lifestyles, urban design for both tourists and residents, urban congestion, access and efficient functioning of transportation, ensuring adequate energy and water supplies, adapting to climate change, responding to disasters, preserving natural and cultural heritage and community consultation (Bosman & Dredge, 2011; Australian Government, 2011: XXI). In these locations, tourism management and environmental and urban planning are inextricably related, and yet our educational programmes often provide little opportunity for students to explore the real-life complexities of post-disciplinary *place* management.

In this chapter we argue that the education of future professionals who have responsibility for managing complex, dynamic landscapes must extend beyond narrow fields and disciplinary divides. Such professionals must be able to understand and appreciate how planning and management in different sectors, such as tourism, environmental planning, economic development and land-use planning intersect and influence each other. We explore an integrated and holistic approach to curriculum design and delivery – studio teaching – that puts the planning and management of touristed places within a broader post-disciplinary context. Here, 'touristed places' are taken to be those places that are consumed by tourists but are also part of a much larger pre-existing network of socio-cultural, economic, political and ecological activity. In other words, the term emphasizes that place is a far more complex compilation of forces including but not limited to tourism, and is not produced specifically for tourism as the term 'tourism destination' tends to emphasize (Cartier & Lew, 2005). In taking this approach, this chapter challenges the tourism-centric nature of tourism management curricula by presenting a case study of a planning studio wherein students' understandings of tourism and urban planning are framed within the broader context of social, economic, political and cultural change. In taking this approach, we challenge traditional approaches to higher education that package up degree programmes into discipline- or field-specific curricula that can inhibit post-disciplinary explorations of complex historic–spatial dynamics, wicked policy and management problems (Curaj et al., 2012). In such traditional approaches, tourism-related subject matter receives minimal attention in urban planning programmes, and tourism programmes struggle to take a broader place-based approach to tourism management, often favouring instead a narrow industry focus.

Studio pedagogy is a student-centred, collaborative, inquiry-based/problem-based pedagogy based on a 'real-world' project that provides a unique and valuable learning and teaching method used to educate planners. There is no one definitive description of what a 'studio' entails. The 'studio' as a pedagogical concept is as much about the place or physical environment in which learning and teaching takes place as it is about the modes of learning and teaching. The term 'studio' as it is used in this chapter is derived from the disciplinary association that planning has with architecture, and that studios have historically been an invaluable learning and teaching context, pedagogy and learning space in many creative discipline areas. This mode of teaching is widely used in architecture, urban and regional planning, fine arts, interior and industrial design, and has also been used in fields such as physics in an effort to assist students to engage in hands-on learning. The studio as a place is often characterized by creative disorder, a degree of messiness and a place that is appropriated by the students to suit their needs. Here, there is a clear link with the physical and social spaces in which problem-based learning takes place.

Studio pedagogy teaches students how to successfully work, in a collaborative way, to explore wicked complex issues and develop and evaluate plausible management solutions. In this context, wicked problems are those that are difficult to definitively describe, are resistant to solution, where no single stakeholder has control, and multiple actions are required by various actors (Rittel & Webber, 1973; Head, 2008). In the studio environment, the development of practical, problem-solving skills, professional communication and collaboration also enables students to become leaders in their field (Long, 2012; Balassiano, 2011; Spronken-Smith et al., 2011).

Planning studios are student-centred learning and teaching environments characterized by problem-based learning and learning by inquiry pedagogies which emphasize active independent student-focused learning (O'Neill & Woei, 2010). Planning studios require students to draw upon personal knowledges and experiences as well as their academic learning from all their courses. Students are required to work collaboratively with input from the profession and staff. The studio curriculum provides a balance of theory and professional practice, using multiple teaching and learning approaches, with the aim to equip students with the skills, knowledge and practices that underpin their academic and professional careers. Properly conceptualized, designed and delivered, planning studios and similar pedagogies can empower students by providing students with confidence, self-esteem, substantive knowledge about post-disciplinary planning and a range of generic skills including communications skills, creative problem solving and critical thinking (Bovill *et al.*, 2011). Studio learning and teaching practices can positively impact retention, the student experience and engagement with professional practice (Bosman *et al.*, 2012). The contribution of this chapter then is to explore how post-disciplinary studio pedagogy can effectively respond to a range of current institutional, sectorial and professional challenges.

Approach and methods

This chapter reviews the planning studio model delivered at an undergraduate Urban and Environmental Planning degree, at Griffith University, Queensland, Australia. The first author draws from her experience in teaching the studio subject to first-year students between 2006 and 2013, and the second author draws upon experience and observations made while teaching the same studio subject prior to the data collection period. Both authors/teachers consider themselves generalists although their original fields of study heavily influence them: for the first author, architecture and urban design, and for the second author, planning and policy studies. They also call from a wide range of knowledge accrued from periods in both public and private sector employment prior to taking up academic careers. In the studio environment, teachers can supplement their own knowledge with specialists (academics and practitioners) who cover specific content and skills.

A case study approach is adopted drawing upon both qualitative and quantitative data. Between 2010 and 2013 the same student experience surveys were administered to all student cohorts enrolled in the studio. Two types of surveys were administered. The first comprised in-class paper surveys distributed in weeks one, five and nine in a 13-week semester, and the second was an online, generic, university-administered evaluation in weeks 12–13. These evaluations were not compulsory. The response rate to the in-class paper surveys averaged 85 per cent and the online university survey response rate averaged 30 per cent. Both sets of data consistently indicated very similar responses. Both survey instruments also allowed students to write general comments about their experiences of the studio learning and teaching environment. Each year, at the end of the semester, a focus group was undertaken with sessional staff. The aim of the focus groups was to discuss teaching experiences and, in particular, to frame strategies to improve teaching and capitalize on what was working well in terms of the student experience. In total seven staff participated in four focus groups. In addition participant observation, reflective note taking and peer review of the curriculum added to the data collection. These strategies were implemented in response to institutional changes at University, Faculty and School levels. The abilities and capabilities of many first-year students have shifted, reflecting lower academic entry levels and larger class sizes. The studio format is an unfamiliar environment for many first-year students because of its flexible structure and learning and teaching methods, and most students need time to become accustomed to this environment. Despite this, the studio format has remained relatively consistent over the years and the data collected provide a rich landscape of information and feedback about studio teaching.

Defining the studio

Approach to delivery

The studio as a pedagogical concept is as much about the place or physical environment in which learning and teaching takes place as it is about curriculum and delivery. Studio content, delivery methods and assessment change from year to year because topics have to be timely and relevant in order for students to feel engaged and connected to real world problems. Further, the main value of studios comes from shifting the role of the student from passive receiver of information to an active and engaged learner (Bovill *et al.*, 2011). Studios provide the opportunity for teachers and students to explore problems and identify and reflect on potential solutions in a reiterative way. Students learn from their teachers' experience, from their peers, their application of theoretical concepts and frameworks, and they develop deep understanding of the complexity of real-world problems by 'doing' (see Dredge *et al.*, 2012). Likewise, teachers gain reflexive knowledge of students' learning processes and their challenges in conceptualizing problems and in engaging in the theory–practice interface.

Studios allow students and staff to cross disciplinary boundaries where students are led by inquiry into complex real-word problems typical of those they might find in their work after graduation. Staff can also roam more freely across the curriculum space in a more authentic pursuit of complex understandings because they are not bounded by a formal, preconceived, tightly structured curriculum (Garraway, 2010). The studio environment is therefore an ideal conduit for a post-disciplinary education in which intimate connections can be made between, for example, urban planning, regional development, geography, politics, business, tourism, sociology, community development and economics, which were previously locked into narrow disciplinary programmes and fields of study. To demonstrate the post-disciplinary nature of the studio, the topics included in the last six years include those outlined in Table 20.1.

Content

The studio environment may take on different formats depending on the place management problem being explored and a range of institutional, resourcing and staffing factors (see Zehner, 2008). As a result, it is often difficult to outline exactly what knowledge and skills might be delivered. In this case study, the studio was taught within the environmental planning programme and was characterized by more frequent, longer and more informal contact with peers and teaching staff in a dedicated classroom space. In this sense, the planning studio became a place of transition into academia for first-year students, an opportunity to accumulate a wide range of knowledge and skills, and a place where fourth-year students prepared for professional practice (Bosman *et al.*, 2012). This environment encouraged students to become less isolated learners and to form collegial bonds which served them throughout their student life and into professional life (Tinto, 2003).

In terms of content, Table 20.2 illustrates the range of knowledge themes that were covered in the studios. There were variations in the depth and breadth of these themes as a result of the problem being explored. Students were provided with a brief presentation about that area of content and were provided with resources to assist in their self-directed learning with respect to its relevance and application to the problem being interrogated.

Table 20.1 Studio topics

Year	Project	Intersections between tourism and management explored	Data collected
2007 and 2008	Examination of a proposed next-generation cruise ship terminal on the Gold Coast Spit	Infrastructure requirements for a cruise ship terminal, marine and terrestrial impacts on the environment, community consultation processes, politics of tourism development, tourist–resident conflicts	Student surveys, participant observation and reflective note taking
2009	Understanding cultural heritage: A case study of Burleigh Heads	Importance of local heritage, built and cultural, to both locals and tourism industries, community consultation processes, politics of tourism development, tourist–resident conflicts	Student surveys, participant observation and reflective note taking
2010	Examination of the possibilities for the Commonwealth Games sporting and accommodation infrastructure on a greenfield site in Nerang	Infrastructure requirements for the Commonwealth Games, environmental and social impacts on the local area, politics of tourism development, tourist–resident conflicts	Student surveys and focus groups, participant observation and reflective note taking
2012 and 2013	Urban design and character study of a local urban centre to recommend improvements to economic, social, built and environmental contexts	Analysis of existing contexts, understanding of processes of change, community consultation processes, politics of tourism development, tourist–resident conflicts	Student surveys and focus groups, participant observation and reflective note taking

Assessment

The high degree of interaction between staff and students that characterized the studios also went some way to provide students with a sense of belonging and purpose. This was because, through regular and sustained interaction, students felt that staff and their peers knew them. Staff–student interaction was largely structured around feedback on assignment tasks which began on day one and continued over the semester. For first-year students, continual feedback and summative assessment was a means of encouraging and supporting students' adjustment to university life, and surveys revealed that it heightened their engagement and satisfaction. Consistent with Tippett *et al.* (2011: 28), the challenges for studio teaching were: the high demand for quality staff–student contact time; the demands associated with a high level of summative and formative feedback on assignments; staff role-modelling interactive, reflective discussions

Table 20.2 Knowledge covered in the studios

Discipline/field of study	Knowledge
Anthropology	Visitor–guest relationships
Psychology	Tourist motivations Visitor behaviour Place identity, sense of place, branding
Geography	Spatial aspects of tourism development Evolution of destinations, path dependency
Sociology	Social change including migration, demographic trends
Economics	Drivers of economic development Regional development Globalization and development
Political science	Politics of tourism development Civil society, public interest, participatory democracy Public consultation processes and requirements Identification of stakeholders
Environmental Studies	Impacts on terrestrial and marine environments Impact assessment regulations and procedures
Urban Planning	Land-use planning, planning processes
Law	Environmental planning legislation Regulatory instruments Roles of the state
Business	Business of tourism Structure and function of the development industry Place branding and marketing
Transportation	Characteristics of different modes of transport Transport hubs and networks Challenges of intermodal transport

about the complex and messy problems being encountered by students; the need for staff to stay up to date with rapidly changing environmental, political and urban contexts; problem solving and skill development associated with group work in a collaborative environment; and the scarcity of institutional resources (e.g. time, money, staff, provision of student resources such as maps, technical reports, etc.).

Institutional, sectorial and professional challenges

Many universities, both nationally and internationally, are placing increasing importance on the student experience, achieved principally through student engagement strategies targeted primarily at student retention. Retention is frequently aligned with student-centred approaches (Tinto, 2002; Scott *et al.*, 2008; Griffith University, 2012). The most significant focus is on the first-year experience (FYE) arena (Wilson, 2009) which has the potential to be extended into the second and third year of study. One of the principles underpinning the retention strategy at Griffith University (Griffith University, 2012: 5) is to:

> reflect a student lifecycle approach, that recognizes and supports diversity and social inclusion. It places students at the centre of interventions from the point of initial contact with the University and the early stages of orientation and transition to university study, succeeding in their academic studies, through to the point of graduation.

Many universities are developing and implementing retention strategies that focus on providing resources to ensure students are 'study ready' and the studio approach and teaching environment fit well with this agenda. At the same time there is a growing body of literature around the First Year Experience (FYHE, 2011; Barefoot, 2000; Palmer *et al.*, 2009) and innovative curriculum designs that respond specifically to the learning patterns of many Gen Y students are recommended. As reflected in Griffith University's retention strategy these include, among other things: increasing student-to-student and faculty-to-student interaction, increasing student engagement and time on campus, providing a specific physical environment and curriculum design (Higgins *et al.*, 2009; Krause, 2006; Lizzio & Wilson, 2010; Braxton *et al.*, 2000; Griffith University, 2013, 2012, 2011; Cross, 1998). Lizzio & Wilson (2010: 1) find that student success in universities is inextricably linked to their 'sense of connection, capability, purpose, resourcefulness and academic culture'. As already suggested, the above-described studio environment responds to and embraces all of these retention strategies (Higgins *et al.*, 2009; Zehner *et al.*, 2009).

The Planning Institute of Australia (PIA), the professional planning body, implements a stringent education accreditation policy, which is another factor impacting upon curricula design and delivery. The objective of this policy (PIA, 2011: 4) is 'to encourage and support students . . . to become planning professionals, who can think creatively, analytically and critically, undertake independent research, communicate effectively, and act ethically'. In addition this accreditation policy (PIA, 2011: 11) demands that students graduate with the 'capacity to apply theoretical and technical planning skills to unfamiliar or emergent circumstances, even with incomplete information'. This aligns with calls for a hopeful tourism education to develop graduates with the responsibility to become global citizens (Pritchard *et al.*, 2011) and the aspirations associated with the philosophical practitioner education (Tribe, 2002). All of these skills are embedded in planning studios and the pedagogy provides essential benefits for the student experience, retention and professionalism.

What we have seen change over the years, however, is the ability of students to problem solve. The studio curriculum design and the assessment all point to the necessity of students taking responsibility for their own learning. The role of staff is to support students in their learning, and to guide and direct them in their problem solving. Over the years we have found that more and more students are not able to take the initiative in identifying creative solutions, instead they are demanding, and getting more and more scaffolding to achieve the stated studio learning aims. This is problematic because, as Balassiano (2011: 449) explains, 'the more manageable the studio experience becomes, the less similar it is to actual planning practice, and the less useful it becomes to the future planning practitioner'. Practitioners working in this space of place management must be able to work in situations where solutions are unknown and where the political, economic, social, physical and technological environment is constantly changing. Practitioners need to be flexible and adapt to new and unknown situations and this is part of inquiry by learning (Spronken-Smith *et al.*, 2011).

Putting theory into practice: a post-disciplinary studio case study

The studio project

In the studios (see Table 20.1), the focus was specifically on a planning issue, often involving conflict that emerged as a result of different meanings, values and attachments that residents, tourists, business interests, developers and local government actors attach to an issue. For example, in 2007 and 2008, the site of this conflict was the Southport Spit, one of the last significant undeveloped public green spaces on the Gold Coast, Queensland, Australia. Proponents for the proposed cruise ship terminal saw opportunities to create a new place of tourist consumption while many locals held oppositional viewpoints as a result of their personal, historical and emotional attachments to that place. An important contributing factor to the development conflict on the Southport Spit was derived from the evolution of The Spit as a historically significant public leisure and recreation opportunity, which the proposed development would privatize. Not only would the resource be irrevocably changed but public access to the area would also be restricted. Students interrogated these multiple meanings of place via guest speakers from the community, secondary data from historical and contemporary media sources, site visits and some even attended a public demonstration. It became very clear to the students that place is socially constructed via dynamic social processes, individual and collective co-constructed narratives and meanings across space and time (Urry, 1995).

Another challenge for students is to understand how competing objectives in a complex problem might be reconciled, e.g. how to balance fostering new development whilst also preserving the heritage and character of the existing urban setting. Dekker *et al.* (1992) recognize that conflict often arises due to the differing interests of the 'new', pro-development, growth-oriented players and the 'old' players who value the status quo and who seek to preserve this situation. Place management professionals often unwittingly and unconsciously play the role of mediator in such conflict, striving to realize the interests of the various groups, 'new' and 'old'. The challenge many professionals face is to go beyond the role of the mediator to ensure various voices are identified and heard, including the marginalized and under-represented. In that sense, students need to appreciate the importance of building wide-ranging knowledge and skill sets, including knowledge about tourism. As the studios progress, students become increasingly aware that their previous understandings of planning as a rational technical activity melt away and a new complexity unfolds.

In the studios, the subject of this chapter, students were able to better understand the complexity and vulnerability of the Gold Coast in general, and the Southport Spit in particular. Teaching staff facilitated discussions about the role and capacity of planners, urban designers, developers, tourism marketing agents and other place management professionals to take into account these local everyday meanings and values and balance stakeholder demands. In doing so, students developed awareness about the role of planning and planners, and reflected on their relationship with other allied professionals involved in place management (e.g. tourism officers, environmental scientists, community facilitators, etc.). Teaching staff also prompted students to consider the range of professionals working in a variety of place management roles, in order to build students' awareness of the range of professionals they may be required to work with after graduation.

The studio practice/delivery

The studio course was taught once a week, on the same day, in two three-hour sessions (total of six hours with a lunch hour separating the sessions) plus an additional three hours of timetabled self-directed learning, totalling 117 hours per studio course delivered over a 13-week semester. The aims of the studios were twofold: to underpin the degree programme by application of the students' knowledge and skills to practical planning projects, and to equip students with the skills required for professional practice. The learning objectives of the studio were to equip students with the skills and knowledge outlined in Table 20.3.

The studio project involved students working in groups to produce a professional report and accompanying oral and poster presentations proposing a solution or other measures to resolve the issue. The curriculum was semi-structured but incorporated the flexibility for students to undertake self-directed exploration and show initiative. This studio curriculum combined a variety of teaching and learning approaches including formal presentations, discussions, debates, quizzes, role plays, one-on-one support, group work and individual work. The studio project focused on a particular problem and students formed groups to tackle different issues related to that problem. For example, students investigated economic drivers of growth and within this explored the role of tourism, physical changes to the environment as a result of tourism, the community of stakeholders and their relative influence and interests in the proposed development. The outcomes of each group were then presented to the class as a whole for discussion and debate. The final outcome was a professional document that proposed potential solutions.

The staff to student ratio was 1:17 with the teaching team comprising one full-time academic supported by high-achieving senior undergraduate students. Lizzio and Wilson (2004) present convincing arguments for the benefits of senior peer tutoring where these more advanced students act as role models and their cultural proximity to new students promotes peer-to-peer guidance. The role of the teaching team was to foster student engagement, encourage innovation and generally assist students in their learning. As such they provided important scaffolding necessary for achieving the learning objectives of the studio.

Table 20.3 Learning outcomes and skills delivered in the studio environment

Learning outcome	Skills
Identify, read and interpret a range of information	Problem-based inquiry that extends beyond disciplinary boundaries; familiarity in finding and analysing a range of information sources including legal instruments, environmental impact assessments, professional reports and other sources of statistics
Prepare maps, plans and written reports	Analysis and interpretation of different types of maps; map and figure preparation; report writing
Identify and critically discuss a range of discipline-specific issues	Critical thinking, problem solving, dispute resolution, ethics
Identify and use various sources of data to elicit information and analyse the situation	Finding, analysing and interpreting statistical data, archival searches, content analysis of documents, interviews/interviewing
Undertake site analysis using skills and techniques taught in class	Fieldwork, participant and non-participant observation, photography
Work and learn independently and in teams to identify and solve problems, to generate ideas and synthesize a range of information	Self-directed learning, group work, collaboration, problem solving, dispute resolution

Targeted diagnostic and formative assessments were included in the grading scheme, with the first formative assessment completed in studio in week one and the first summative assessment due in week five. The second summative assessment item was due in week 13 and this assessment was a recapitulation of all materials covered in the studio in the preceding 12 weeks. Each week students were given a specific activity, relating to the summative assessment. This activity was submitted at the end of the studio as part of the formative assessment component, marked and returned to students in studio the following week. A selection of the submissions was scanned and formed the basis for a whole of class discussion and feedback session at the start of the studio the following week. This formative assessment comprised 20 per cent of the student's final grade. The reason for the formative component having a token value was to encourage students to submit these items, because in the past students had treated this component as optional. The two summative assessments were weighted equally and comprised professional written and graphic documents and an oral presentation.

Studio outcomes, skills and capabilities

To evaluate the success or otherwise of the studio, by way of diagnostic assessment, three in-studio (paper-based) student experience evaluations were conducted at the beginning, midway and end of the semester. The generic and online university student experience instruments captured the students' responses to the course as a whole. The evaluation response rate to the three in-studio paper-based student experience evaluations averaged 95 per cent and weekly attendance was over 98 per cent. The student evaluations demonstrated that the studio succeeded in motivating students to learn and in developing collegiality.

Most students indicated that the learning environment was 'a good learning environment'; 'challenging'; 'fun'; 'practical and engaging'; 'balanced theory and practice'; 'supportive'; and 'friendly and sociable'. Students expressed that they had experienced a sense of ownership over the studio space and that they had developed friendships and networks that supported them in their learning. Student comments about what they enjoyed most about the studio included:

'Learning the basic theory . . . then beginning to implement that.'
'This was an excellent course in respect to providing an environment + tasks similar to the workforce.'
'I had lots of really good quality friends, especially in the studio classes. I think they're probably the best relationship building classes of all.'
'The interaction, there was so much interaction. It was like before you did anything for an assignment you'd ask people for their advice . . . and you'd come to a session with no idea . . . but then after having conversations . . . you'd just have heaps of material.'
'How to compile ideas onto a page and understand the many key aspects and rules of planning then putting them into practice.'
'Studio has given me a greater reality and passion for the real-life activities of a planner.'

Challenges

The studios have produced a number of positive outcomes but it is also important to note the challenges and concerns that have emerged, and which have been consistently identified.

Tenured academic educators

The teaching period is concentrated (one day a week) and therefore it frees up time to pursue research and other academic engagements. However, preparation time is critical and is very time-consuming as each studio session and each task/exercise have to be mapped out. Further, year upon year the studio topics change so that they are timely and relevant, but this means that previous studio themes and tasks cannot be used. Once the model has been established, however, preparation time is less intensive and only project-specific details require amendment. In this way, preparation time does not necessarily reduce or streamline teaching time but enables better and more efficient face-to-face teaching and facilitated student discussions. Over time, like in many universities across the world, the neoliberal drive for cost efficiencies, the expansion of student markets and the industrialization of teaching processes have resulted in a reduction of contact hours and higher staff to student ratios. In turn this has heightened the importance of studio preparation so that the stated studio learning aims can be achieved. Teaching/contact hours have also reduced because the students' skill base is developed early in the semester which enables students to become independent learners more quickly. An increase in student enrolments has not affected the structure of the studio, but it has had a bearing on the staff to student ratio and the physical space requirements. Because studio learning and teaching transcend disciplines it is essential that the educator has some practitioner experience to be able to weave together and make relevant all the disciplinary terrain. This can also mean including guest presentations from professionals in different fields. In this case the academic benefits from professional development and the students see a direct relationship with their project and professional practice.

Sessional/casual staff

Many sessional staff are employed in some capacity outside the university as are the students themselves. They found it easier to commit to one full day rather than to a three-hour studio timetabled twice a week. An advantage of the studio curriculum is that it allows for specialist input; however, this input is increasingly difficult to fund as university budgets are being constrained. Alumni are sometimes more willing to casually participate in studio learning and teaching for less financial outlay.

Students

The student surveys demonstrate that the studio develops collegiality and that it frees up students' time to pursue other activities. In keeping with Gen Y characteristics discussed elsewhere in this book, the studio engages students in meaningful, practical and relevant learning. The studios increase students' commitment to learning by creating a sociable learning environment and they also respond to Gen Y's expectation for customized and scaffolded learning (Taylor, 2005; Gardner & Eng, 2005). A base of relevant theory/knowledge and skill development is woven into the learning experience, and disciplinary divisions and structures do not limit the exploration of the studio themes. Instead, disciplinary divisions are broken down and students learn where and how to access different knowledge and information, and to develop skill sets ranging from reading and interpreting planning legislation and regulations, to statistical analysis of tourism visitation and population data and the interpretation of environmental surveys. However, this can also represent challenges especially where the complexity of the studio theme gives rise to 'overload' for both the students and staff. Sometimes students comment that 'Staying engaged [was a challenge] because the days were long' or that the studio had 'been mentally draining but now it's over it was worth it'. In addressing this problem of 'overload', staff have to be very reflexive in their teaching, adjusting their pace in unpacking complexity or in the theoretical backgrounding of the studio theme.

Universities

There are resourcing implications for institutions that also need to be acknowledged. Teaching takes place in a dedicated studio space that incorporates group work tables, individual desks, drawing boards, computers, whiteboards, data projectors, map draws and so on. These spaces are not easily adapted for other uses such as lectures and they also become social spaces – students' 'home away from home' during the semester. University administrators can see this space as being used inefficiently, especially if the studio is technically timetabled over one day. Not surprisingly, there are instrumental pressures for this space to be converted to more traditional teaching spaces where space is in short supply.

Staff resourcing is also a potential issue. The staff student ratio of 1:17 is critical for the success of the studio, and this is clearly at the lower end of the spectrum in neoliberal universities where there is increased pressure for industrialized teaching of larger classes using fewer human resources (see Bosman et al., 2011). Studio learning and teaching can positively impact retention and the student experience, in part because of the staff to student ratio and also because of the dedicated teaching space which provides the context for developing community-oriented learning and student sociality. As a result, the positive learning outcomes, student satisfaction and learning communities that develop from studio teaching are very valuable features of a student-centred curriculum.

Conclusion

This chapter challenges the narrow focus of tourism planning and management curricula by presenting a case study of an urban and environmental planning studio wherein students' understandings of tourism are framed within the broader context of social, economic, political and cultural change. In this chapter we have explored a holistic post-disciplinary studio teaching approach which has self-directed problem-based learning about 'real' problems as its central feature.

Increasingly higher education institutions seek effective, efficient and relevant teaching methods and content to produce well-rounded, critical thinking, employable leaders in their profession. The studio approach, where a diverse range of skills and knowledge is delivered within a coherent problem-based framework, has been proven to transcend traditional disciplinary structures and methods. In this chapter we have argued for the importance of this post-disciplinary studio teaching and learning environment as students learn about tourism as a driver of social, economic, political change. Students also develop an awareness of the range of other professions that are involved in managing place change. In other words, the planning and management of tourist places does not exist in a vacuum but is inextricably interwoven into the way urban and rural landscapes are planned and function. Tourism affects the daily lives of the people who inhabit the places that tourists also want to visit, so it is also important to understand the broader and more complex dynamics and management challenges associated with tourist landscapes.

However, in delivering a learning experience that tries to transcend these (urban planning and tourism) disciplinary boundaries, we are also conscious of university structures and processes, and the implications for post-disciplinary teaching and learning. Whilst we have sought to establish a post-disciplinary learning environment through a complex problem-based approach, the studios discussed in this chapter are offered by the School of Environment and are not open to students from other programmes (and disciplines). Further, university cost structures and workload models still impede staff from other schools participating in a truly post-disciplinary learning environment. For this reason, the skills and professional background of staff who can transcend these boundaries, despite being located in a specific school or department, are very important.

References

Australian Government. (2011). Developing a Framework for Teaching and Learning Standards in Australian Higher Education and the Role of TEQSA. Available: http://www.deewr.gov.au/HigherEducation/Policy/teqsa/Pages/TeachingandLearningStandardsDiscussion.aspx (Accessed 11 August 2013).

Balassiano, K. (2011). 'Tackling "Wicked Problems" in Planning Studio Courses'. *Journal of Planning Education & Research,* 31(4), 449–60.

Barefoot, B. (2000). 'The First Year Experience: are we making it any better?' *About Campus,* 4(6), 12–18.

Bosman, C., & Dredge, D. (2011). 'Histories of Placemaking in the Gold Coast City: the neoliberal norm, the State story and the community narrative'. Brisbane: Urban Research Program.

Bosman, C., Coiacetto, E., & Dredge, D. (2011). 'The Shifting Ground of Australian Higher Education through the Lens of Reflexive Modernisation: compromising the quality of planning education?' *Australian Planner,* 48(2), 72–83.

Bosman, C., Dedekorkut, A., & Dredge, D. (2012). 'The First Year Experience in Higher Education and Planning Studio Pedagogies: an Australian case study'. *CEBE Transactions,* 9(1), 3–19.

Bovill, C., Bulley, C., & Morss, K. (2011). 'Engaging and Empowering First-Year Students through Curriculum Design: perspectives from the literature', *Teaching in Higher Education,* 16(2), 197–209.

Braxton, J., Milem J., & Sullivan A. S. (2000). 'The Influence of Active Learning on the College Student Departure Process'. *Journal of Higher Education,* 71(5), 569–90.

Cartier, C., & Lew, A. (2005). *Touristed Landscapes: geographical perspectives on globalisation and touristed landscapes.* Abingdon: Routledge.

Cross, K. P. (1998). 'Why Learning Communities? Why now?' *About Campus,* July/August, 4–11.

Curaj, A., Scott, P., Vlasceanu, L., & Wilson, L. (2012). *European Higher Education at the Cross-Roads: between Bologna Process and national reforms.* Dordrecht: Springer.

Dekker, A., Goverde, H., Makowski, T., & Ptaszynska-Woloczkowicz, M. (1992). *Conflict in Urban Development.* Aldershot: Ashgate.

Dredge, D., Benckendorff, P., Day, M., Gross, M. J., Walo, M., Weeks, P., & Whitelaw, P. (2012). 'The Philosophic Practitioner and the Curricula Space'. *Annals of Tourism Research,* 39(4), 2154–76.

First Year in Higher Education (FYHE). (2011). FYHE Centre. Retrieved 3 April 2013, from: http://fyhe.com.au

Gardner, S., & Eng, S. (2005). 'What Students Want: Generation Y and the changing function of the academic library'. *Libraries and the Academy,* 5(3), 405–20.

Garraway, J. (2010). 'Knowledge Boundaries and Boundary-Crossing in the Design Work-Responsive University Curricula'. *Teaching in Higher Education,* 15(2), 211–22.

Griffith University. (2011). *Academic Plan: implementing our vision 2011–2013.* Brisbane, Queensland.

Griffith University. (2012). *Operation Student Success: Griffith's student retention strategy 2012–2014.* Brisbane, Queensland.

Griffith University. (2013). *Strategic Plan 2013–2017.* Brisbane, Queensland.

Head, B. (2008). 'Wicked Problems in Public Policy', *Public Policy,* 3(2), 101–18.

Higgins, M., Aitken-Rose, E., &. Dixon, J. (2009). 'The Pedagogy of the Planning Studio: a view from down under'. *Journal for Education in the Built Environment,* 4(1), 8–30.

Hugo, G. (2011). 'Is Decentralisation the Answer? In *A 'Sustainable' Population? Key policy issues* (pp. 133–70). Canberra: Productivity Commission.

Krause, K. L. (2006). 'On Being Strategic about the First Year'. Paper presented at the First Year Forum, 5 October, Queensland University of Technology, Brisbane, Australia.

Lizzio, A., & Wilson, K. (2004). 'Action Learning in Higher Education: an investigation of its potential to develop professional capability'. *Studies in Higher Education*, 29(4), 469–88.

Lizzio, A., & Wilson, K. (2010). 'Strengthening Commencing Students' Sense of Purpose: integrating theory and practice'. Paper presented at the 13th Pacific Rim First Year in Higher Education Conference, 27–30 June, Adelaide, Australia.

Long, J. G. (2012). 'State of the Studio: revisiting the potential of studio pedagogy in US-based planning programs'. *Journal of Planning Education & Research*, 32(4), 431–48.

O'Neill, G., & Woei, H. (2010). 'Seeing the Landscape and the Forest Floor: changes made to improve the connectivity of concepts in a hybrid problem-based learning curriculum', *Teaching in Higher Education*, 15(1), 15–27.

Palmer, M., O'Kane, P., & Owens, M. (2009). 'Betwixt Spaces: student accounts of turning point experiences in the first-year transition'. *Studies in Higher Education*, 34(1), 37–54.

Planning Institute of Australia (PIA). (2011). *Accreditation Policy for the Recognition of Australian Planning Qualifications for the Urban and Regional Chapter.* Kingston, ACT.

Pritchard, A., Morgan, N., & Ateljevic, I. (2011). 'Hopeful Tourism: a new transformative perspective'. *Annals of Tourism Research*, 38(3), 941–63.

Rittel, H. W. J., & Webber, M. (1973). 'Dilemmas in a General Theory of Planning'. *Policy Sciences*, 4, 155–69.

Scott, G., Shah, M., Grebennikov, L., & Singh, H. (2008). 'Improving Student Retention: a University of Western Sydney case study'. *Journal of Institutional Research*, 14(1), 9–23.

Spronken-Smith, R., Walker, R., Batchelor, J., O'Steen, B., & Angelo, T. (2011). 'Enablers and Constraints to the Use of Inquiry-Based Learning in Undergraduate Education'. *Teaching in Higher Education*, 16(1), 15–28.

Taylor, M. (2005). 'Generation NeXt: today's postmodern student – meeting, teaching and serving'. In *A Collection of Papers on Self-Study and Institutional Improvement* (pp. 99–107). Chicago, IL: The Higher Learning Commission.

Tinto, V. (2002). 'Establishing Conditions for Student Success'. Paper presented at the 11th Annual Conference of the European Access Network, 19–22 June, Prato, Italy.

Tinto, V. (2003). 'Learning Better Together: the impact of learning communities on student success'. *Higher Education Monograph Series,* New York: Syracuse University.

Tippett, J., Connelly, A., & How, F. (2011). 'You Want Me to Do What? Teaching a studio class to seventy students'. *Journal for Education in the Built Environment*, 6(2), 26–53.

Tribe, J. (2002). 'The Philosophic Practitioner'. *Annals of Tourism Research*, 29(2), 238–57.

Urry, J. (1995). *Consuming Places.* New York: Routledge.

Wilson, K. (2009). 'The Impact of Institutional, Programmatic and Personal Interventions on an Effective and Sustainable First-Year Student Experience'. Paper presented at the 12th First Year in Higher Education Conference, 29 June–01 July, Townsville, Australia.

Zehner, R. (2008). 'Studio Teaching in Australia: from art and architecture to urban design and planning'. Paper prepared for presentation at the ACSP/AESOP Joint Congress, Chicago, Illinois. Available: http://www.studioteaching.org/?page=publications (Accessed 1 November 2013).

Zehner, R., Forsyth, G., Musgrave, E., Neale, D., Harpe, B. D. L., Peterson F., & Frankham, N. (2009). 'Curriculum Development in Studio Teaching: STP final report'. Strawberry Hills: Australian Learning and Teaching Council.

21

Promoting critical reflexivity in tourism and hospitality education through problem-based learning

José-Carlos García-Rosell

Multidimensional Tourism Institute, University of Lapland, Rovaniemi, Finland

Introduction

Within the field of tourism and hospitality education, there is a current discussion on promoting a curriculum that aims to promote a balance between satisfying the demands of business and those of wider society (e.g. Dredge *et al.*, 2012; Tribe, 2002). Accordingly, tourism students should develop knowledge and competencies that enable them to work in the tourism industry while at the same time acknowledging their role in constructing a better tourism world (Fidgeon, 2010; Tribe, 2002). The purpose of the curriculum is not only to train students for the labour market, but to equip them with qualities such as breadth of disciplinary knowledge; the ability to distinguish among contested ideologies; an appreciation of the dialogue between knowledge and values; and an ability to connect ideas and information (Dredge *et al.*, 2012: 2156). This means that curriculum development and delivery is not simply about including critical tourism topics such as social equality, justice, ethics and sustainability, but using these topics to rethink our notions of tourism and hospitality education, learning and our professional identities (cf. Cunliffe, 2002).

Critical pedagogy has been suggested as a suitable vehicle for creating a sound equilibrium between social justice and tourism policy and practice (e.g. Belhassen & Caton, 2011; Pritchard *et al.*, 2011). As some studies suggest (García-Rosell, 2013; Fullagar & Wilson, 2012; Wilson & von de Heidt, 2013), critical approaches to teaching tourism and hospitality, which promote reflexivity, can help students develop the capacity to question tourism management practice, critically evaluate how decisions are made within the tourism industry and foster ethical tourism practice. These studies have drawn particular attention to the subject of sustainability as an opportunity for promoting critical reflexivity within tourism and hospitality education, given that as a discourse, sustainability represents an alternative to the dominant managerial discourse shaping contemporary tourism and hospitality practice.

In this chapter, I explore how the use of problem-based learning (PBL) in sustainability teaching opens up opportunities for going beyond reflection to support critical reflexive practice that might enable students to question assumptions embodied in both theory and professional practice (see García-Rosell, 2012, 2013). Although PBL has been widely discussed in relation to tourism and hospitality education (e.g. Duncan & Al-Nakeeb, 2006; Huang, 2005; Kivela & Kivela, 2005; Zwaal & Otting, 2010), the socially mediated and discursive nature of PBL approaches to tourism and hospitality education has been either neglected or given only cursory coverage in the literature. Most tourism and hospitality educators view PBL as an instruction method used to support students in acquiring and applying vocational knowledge and skills for managing tourism organizations in a rapidly changing market economy. This view of PBL is in line with the idea of a tourism and hospitality curriculum directed towards servicing the tourism economy, rather than building a better tourism society (see Tribe, 2002).

Drawing upon the postmodern social–constructivist perspective on PBL (Alanko-Turunen, 2005; García-Rosell, 2013; Lindén & Alanko-Turunen, 2006) and a relational social–constructionist orientation to management learning (Cunliffe, 2002, 2008; Ramsey, 2005; Watson, 2001), I problematize PBL, arguing that it should also allow students to critically evaluate, analyse, and question the basic premises underlying contemporary tourism and hospitality practice. In doing so, PBL is illustrated as a pedagogical tool that can support philosophic and vocational ends by promoting critical reflexivity and the deconstruction and reconstruction of tourism and hospitality knowledge and related identities.

From reflection to reflexivity

Reflection has become a key concept in theories of learning that inform tourism and hospitality education. As educators we are supposed to create learning environments that encourage and support critical thinking and reflective learning (Moscardo, 1997; Tribe, 2002). Reflection refers thus to thinking more critically about the content learned, learning process and personal experiences with the aim of gaining deeper understanding – of the so-called realities – of a subject area (Eyler et al., 1996; Hall & Davison, 2007). The works of David Kolb (1984) and Donald Schön (1983) have not only been instrumental in drawing attention to the value of reflective practices in experiential learning but also in tourism and hospitality education and the use of PBL (Alanko-Turunen, 2005; Ruhanen, 2005).

Many studies indicate that tourism and hospitality education should rely upon authentic contexts, personal experiences, guided reflection and feedback (see Fidgeon, 2010). According to these studies, students must live and experience tourism and hospitality work rather than simply acquiring knowledge about it. This way of thinking has, however, been criticized for emphasizing the role of the individual as the site for experience and reflection and thus neglecting the social, political and cultural aspects and discursive nature of learning (Conceição & Skibba, 2007; García-Rosell, 2012). Reflection, as described above, fails to address the central question of how to help students rethink their worldviews and critically evaluate the tourism and hospitality industry and the ethical issues associated with it (see Tribe, 2002).

We need to consider that tourism and hospitality schools have been widely influenced by the managerial discourse which serves to produce not only knowledge but also a certain kind of person deemed to be suitable for managerial work and encultured into the values of managerialism (Ayikoru et al., 2009; Morgan, 2004; Tribe, 2006). As a discourse, managerialism privileges business management practice over other ways of thinking and highlights profitability as the key end for appropriate action (Tribe, 2008). Understood in this light, it becomes evident why teaching – as it takes place in tourism and hospitality schools – may lead to the learning outcome in which social, cultural, spiritual and environmental values are only seen as relevant when they meet the profit-maximizing premise. Research has shown how indigenous culture, traditional livelihoods, heritage sites and nature are colonialized by managerial and organizational procedures (e.g. Hakkarainen & Tuulentie, 2008; Jamal et al., 2003; Puhakka et al., 2009).

Managerial language places a central emphasis upon tourism and hospitality practices as a way to promote efficiency, profitability and the competitiveness of tourism organizations (see Tribe, 2009). By framing and representing tourism's world within the axioms of managerialism, educators may consciously or unconsciously obscure the multidisciplinary nature of tourism and its associated social, cultural and environmental impacts (Wilson & von der Heidt, 2013). Moreover, it may silence sensitive issues in the classrooms of most tourism and hospitality schools (e.g. continuous growth, power politics, gender issues, human rights, mobilities) that are seen as potential threats to the legitimacy of existing managerial systems (see Tribe, 2006). However, if tourism and hospitality education should also problematize and articulate a critique towards contemporary managerial practices, as critical scholars suggest (e.g. Belhassen & Caton, 2011; Pritchard et al., 2011; Tribe, 2002), then there is a need to do the opposite; namely to question, deconstruct and reconstruct the nature of the tourism and hospitality industry through multi-stakeholder perspectives, ideologies, realities and meanings (Everett & Jamal, 2004; García-Rosell, 2013; Pritchard et al., 2011).

As an alternative to reflection, several scholars have thus drawn attention to the notion of critical reflexivity in business education (e.g. Chia, 1996b; Cunliffe, 2002, 2004; Ramsey, 2005) and tourism and hospitality education in particular (Dredge et al., 2012; Fullagar & Wilson, 2012). Whereas reflection promotes understanding about the realities of a subject area, critical reflexivity encourage students to challenge those realities and the basic assumptions, discourses and practices shaping them (Catterall et al., 2002; Pollner, 1991). Rather than reflecting on either an event or a situation, reflexivity involves recognizing ourselves, our ethical positions, values and our actions in relation to others (see Cunliffe, 2008; Dredge et al., 2012). In line with Cunliffe (2004) critical reflexivity allows students to examine the assumption that there is one rational way of working in the tourism and hospitality industry in which decisions and actions are justified solely on the basis of efficiency and profit. And this is of vital importance if we consider, as suggested by critical tourism scholars, that tourism and hospitality urgently requires new modes of decision-making and action completely different from the status quo (e.g. Tribe, 2002).

Even if reflective learning would promote awareness of ecological degradation, social inequality and unethical behaviour within a tourism context, the hegemonic power of the managerial discourse will make sure that the status quo and the legitimacy of contemporary tourism and hospitality practices remain unchallenged (see cf. Ramsey, 2005). Hence, critical reflexivity and alternative social discourses such as the sustainability discourse represent opportunities to break through the walls of the managerial discourse and thus question premises (e.g. continuous economic growth, profit maximization, efficiency and competitiveness) that are usually considered paramount in the training offered by tourism and hospitality schools (see Fullagar & Wilson, 2012; Wilson & von der Heidt, 2013).

Problem-based learning

Since its initial introduction to medical education in the late 1960s PBL has, in its many variations, spread to other fields of education, such as nursing, social sciences, architecture, arts, engineering, business and even tourism (Boud & Feletti, 1997; Major & Palmer, 2001; Zwaal & Otting, 2010). PBL has been seen as a means for transforming education because of its strong focus on learning processes and its atypical approach of viewing educators as learning facilitators. Bridges (1992) defines PBL as:

> an instructional strategy that uses a problem as a starting point for learning. The problem is one that students are apt to face as future professionals. The knowledge students are

expected to gain during their training is organized around problems rather than the subject topic. Students work in project teams of five or eight members on these problems and assume a major responsibility for their own instruction and learning.

Indeed, the use of a problem as a starting point for learning is the main characteristic of PBL (Savery, 2006).

In PBL, the term 'problem' refers to the idea of a research problem: namely the description of a situation at a certain moment involving an option for development or improvement (Margetson, 1994). PBL processes are usually organized around a 'vignette' that describes the situation in an ill-defined form. The vignette, which can range from a paragraph to a case study report (García-Rosell, 2013), represents the learning trigger. Whether PBL is viewed as a teaching technique or educational philosophy depends on how it is employed within the educational context (Poikela & Poikela, 2006). While the most common approach has been to convert courses and even entire curricula to a purely PBL format (Wee *et al.*, 2003), some educators have used PBL in combination with more conventional methods, such as formal lectures, seminars and in-class exercises. Peter Kahn and Karen O'Rourke (2005: 4) refer to the latter PBL approaches as 'hybrid PBL'.

Even though the development of PBL was not inspired by any particular educational model, as Barrows (2000) argues, its understanding and further development demanded that PBL be positioned within theories of learning. In particular, Dewey's pragmatism, Kolb's learning cycle, Lewin's equation of behaviour and Piaget's model of intellectual development have dominated the theorization of PBL (Portimojärvi, 2006). PBL's attempts to encourage students to be autonomous learners in managing information, collaborating with others, and developing their own perception, meanings and ways of making sense of reality are thus grounded in cognitive psychology and experiential learning.

This epistemological premise has, however, been criticized for its strong emphasis on the individual as a knowledge acquirer and problem solver. In line with Reed and Anthony (1992), it can be argued that the overriding emphasis given to cognitive, functional and technical skills in PBL literature might have crowded out any concern with the social, economic, political and moral context of learners' lives and future working environments. This omission has probably led some scholars to turn their attention toward a more social–constructivist approach to PBL that focuses on studying both internal cognitive processes and the role of students' interactions in knowledge construction (Savery & Duffy, 1995). According to the epistemological stances taken in these studies, a distinction can be made between a modern and a postmodern social–constructivist orientation. While the modern view takes into consideration the role of social interactions in promoting learning, it continues to view learning as a rational process that only occurs in the mind. The postmodern view, on the other hand, rejects the idea of an individual-centred locus of knowledge by approaching learning as a social process in which an amalgam of interpersonal and intrapersonal means are used in conversation with one's self and in joint action with others (Holman, 2000).

The adoption of PBL in business education, which has been growing since the early 1990s, has tended to rely extensively on a modern social–constructivist orientation (Alanko-Turunen, 2005). Most business educators view PBL as an instruction method used to support students in acquiring and applying a rationality (knowledge and personal competencies) for managing organizations in a rapidly changing global economy (Hallinger & Lu, 2011; Wee *et al.*, 2003). This is also the case in the field of tourism and hospitality education where educators view PBL as a simple means to sensitize students to the realities of working life in the demanding tourism industry (Duncan & Al-Nakeeb, 2006; Huang, 2005; Kivela & Kivela, 2005; Zwaal & Otting,

2010). Furthermore, due to its role in promoting teamwork, creativity, problem solving and leadership, among other skills, PBL has been regarded as a practical way to respond to the criticism that new graduates lack flexibility and adaptability to respond to the socio-technological changes that are taking place in the tourism and hospitality industry (Kivela & Kivela, 2005). This view of PBL is in line with the idea of transforming educational processes into a matter of economic efficiency at the service of potential employers, rather than a matter of building societies (see Lindén & Alanko-Turunen, 2006; Skålén et al., 2008).

This way of thinking about PBL has been criticized by business educators who take a postmodern social–constructivist perspective (e.g. Alanko-Turunen, 2005; García-Rosell, 2012, 2013; Lindén & Alanko-Turunen, 2006). According to this view, PBL should go beyond the idea of producing human capital for the labour market to create spaces where students are encouraged to critically challenge the underlying assumptions of business practice and to think more reflexively about how these assumptions affect other people's lives (García-Rosell, 2012; Lindén & Alanko-Turunen, 2006). This view of PBL seems to be particularly relevant for promoting reflexive practice in tourism and hospitality education. A postmodern social–constructivist perspective on PBL allows students to explore the ethics of contemporary tourism practices by engaging in critical and dialogical processes with instructors and fellow students (see Cunliffe, 2008).

The study

I discuss here a case that draws from an action research (AR) study conducted at the Faculty of Tourism and Business[1] of the University of Lapland, Finland. The aim of the study was to look into how hybrid PBL can promote sustainability learning and enable students to think more critically about the role of business in society. To that end, I explored two Master's-level sustainability courses – one focusing on business ethics and one on environmental marketing – over a period of four years. Before the adoption of PBL, both courses were taught with a conventional pedagogy consisting of formal lectures and the use of case studies. The study did not require ethics approval from the University's Advisory Board on Research Ethics. It was enough that the Faculty of Tourism and Business gave consent for the study and that it was performed in accordance with general principles of research ethics and good scientific practice.

On average, 15 to 20 business and tourism students representing different nationalities (both European and non-European) attended each sustainability course. Both courses had a 'non-obligatory' or elective status in the curriculum. The ages of the students were between 23 and 35, and both genders were equally represented. I was the instructor for both courses and the tutor facilitating all of the PBL meetings. I began implementing PBL in these courses in 2007, and eight AR cycles took place from 2007 to 2010. My role as an action researcher in the study is worthy of special attention; after all, students were only involved as collaborators and not as co-researchers, as is typically done in most AR studies (see Coghlan & Brannick, 2009). However, due to the inherent power relationship between instructor and students, a more collaborative form of AR might have been difficult (Reason, 1988). Furthermore, the participation of students would have been limited to only one AR cycle (the duration of the course in which they were enrolled).

The main sources of data for this study included a fieldwork journal about my observations of the lectures; class assignments; PBL meetings (videotaped in 2010); presentations; and students' interactions in a virtual learning environment. In addition to records of speech and action, the fieldwork journal also included a description of the context, including actors, space, time, feelings and setting (Spradley, 1980). The visual material consisted of six videos with a length of about 120 minutes each. The visual data helped reconstruct the PBL meetings that took place during the last AR cycle (see Collier, 2001). The videos were particularly useful in bringing to my attention such attributes as embodied positions, body movements, gestures, emotions, eye contact and other non-verbal elements that I had possibly neglected when involved in the meetings as the tutor (see Probyn, 2004). Following Hammersley and Atkinson's (1996) advice, I also relied on my memory to fill in and re-contextualize recorded events and utterances.

The fieldwork journal was complemented with students' feedback. I asked students to fill out an evaluation form at the end of each course and to record their PBL experiences in their learning journals. Over 90 per cent of the students fulfilled both requests. Learning journals were a powerful tool not only for receiving feedback on PBL but also for exploring how students engage in their own learning and develop critically reflexive capabilities (see Bickford & Van Vleck, 1997). As suggested by Cunliffe (2004), learning journals may encourage students to think about themselves from a subjective perspective, requiring them to be attentive to their assumptions, ways of being and acting and ways of relating. Verbal and written guidelines were provided to the students on how to write the learning journal. Special emphasis was placed on encouraging students to link personal experiences to the topics covered in the course, to question their assumptions, to explore their learning and to identify possibilities for self-development (see Cunliffe, 2004).

Reflexivity was further promoted by giving each group the task to co-write a report in wiki format that described the PBL process and its results. The co-creation of such a narrative provides an opportunity to challenge hidden assumptions and thus influence the thinking of one's colleagues in a more interactive way (Gabriel & Connell, 2010). The use of multiple methods and sources of data in this study makes it possible to gain access to different types of knowledge and perspectives (Phillips & Jorgensen, 2002) as well as a variety of situations where students exercise critical reflexivity (see Moisander & Valtonen, 2006).

The fieldwork journal was an essential tool for starting the analytical reading of the data, reflecting on the significance of the data and its implications for further data collection (Hammersley & Atkinson, 1996; Rantala, 2011). As this study does not seek to explain individual learning experiences, the empirical material is analysed as social texts that are produced, shared and used in culturally specific and socially organized ways (see Moisander & Valtonen, 2006).

To interpret the social texts produced in the AR process and to understand the logic of their production, I draw upon discourse analysis (Fairclough, 2003; Phillips & Jorgensen, 2002; Phillips & Hardy, 2002). By analysing how students talk about business and its relation to society, what they take for granted, what sort of meanings they contest and what they do not think about (Moisander & Valtonen, 2006), discourse analysis helps to identify discursive patterns that reveal forms of critical reflexive practice. More specifically, this analytical framework highlights how the use of PBL in sustainability courses may help students question their assumptions about the role of business in society, giving them a chance to redefine their identity as business and tourism students.

The analysis involved the careful examination of fieldwork journals, transcripts from the hybrid PBL setting, questionnaires and student-learning journals. The use of different data sources as well as the comparison of data collected from different phases and temporal points of the fieldwork gives added depth to the critical reflexive practices involved in the study (Hammersley & Atkinson, 1996). To enhance the process of analysis, the observational data were organized around spatial dimensions (e.g. classroom, first meeting, blog, breaks) and episodic units (e.g. class exercises, watching movies, class discussions, presentations) (see Rantala, 2011). This helped me link my field notes with the data available in the learning journals, transcripts and other documents.

Reading and rereading the data made it possible to identify textual elements, such as recurrences, regularities, contrasts, paradoxes and irregularities that could be associated with the social, environmental, economic, ethical and political aspects of sustainability. In the analysis, particular attention was given to moments that students found puzzling or controversial or that generated emotions (see Tomlinson & Egan, 2002). By using numerous examples extracted from the data, in the next section PBL is illustrated as a discursive site that offers a fertile ground for critical reflexivity.

Developing critical reflexive practice within a PBL context

This section illustrates how PBL contributed to promoting critical reflexivity among the business and tourism students involved in this study. Figure 21.1 offers an illustration of the hybrid PBL approach used in both sustainability courses. After two introductory lectures, the classes were divided into three groups of five to eight students. Each group was invited to attend the first meeting under my facilitation. As a tutor, I dedicated most of my efforts to smoothing out the PBL process by asking thought-provoking questions dealing with substance and by encouraging students to be attentive to their own assumptions, their sayings and doings and their ways of relating.

The whole hybrid PBL process was organized around the so-called 'vignette', which describes a situation in an unstructured form. The vignette represented the trigger for

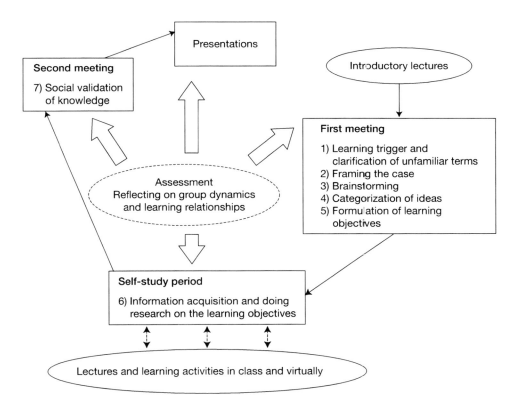

Figure 21.1 Hybrid problem-based learning

sustainability learning and critical reflexivity. In this case, the vignettes were memos describing a business situation in which values were in conflict. Students were asked to set the research strategy and learning objectives that were needed to deal with the situation. From the point of view of sustainability learning, improving the situation was not the goal; the goal was to trigger critically reflexive engagement by unsettling assumptions about business practices and their impact on society and the natural environment.

As Master's-level students, course participants were already familiar with the managerial jargon. However, in the 'learning trigger' step, there was a need to clarify terms such as vulnerable consumers, sweatshops, stakeholders, greenwash, whistle-blower and non-governmental organization (NGO). With a few exceptions, the students participating in both courses had not attended a sustainability course before. Theoretical concepts such as business ethics, sustainability and stakeholder theory were completely new to them. If, as Chia (1996a) argues, language plays a key role in representing and communicating our thoughts of reality, the students faced limitations in framing the situation in the vignette from a sustainability perspective. Furthermore, students' perceptions of responsible business and being a responsible manager could only be expressed and understood through the categories and meanings available to them inside the managerial discourse (cf. Katila & Meriläinen, 1999; Moisander, 2001). These factors had direct consequences on how students framed the situations in the vignettes.

Student 1: Well, I think that we need to think about the savings that we can obtain by switching to the new supplier [company implementing a sweatshop strategy].
Student 2: But it's not only about costs . . . products have to be of high quality.
Student 1: Yeah, changing suppliers is a tricky thing. It's like getting divorced and married again [smile]. I mean, we need to start working on the relationship, and we don't know whether it'll work.

(Excerpt 1, conversation first meeting)

As the excerpts above indicate, there was a tendency to examine the vignettes in terms of profit and efficiency. The students seemed to have assimilated a rational way of managing (Skålén *et al.*, 2008) that made them immune to the social and environmental implications of business practices. Human beings and nature were seen as problems to be solved and objects to be framed within a managerial language in terms of competitive advantages and sales figures (Jones *et al.*, 2005). However, after three weeks of attending lectures and conducting research on the learning objectives set in the first meeting, each group met with me again to discuss and reflect upon their findings in relation to the situations presented in the vignettes. As I encouraged students to assess their findings from the perspective of group dynamics and learning relations, they were able to break down the assumptions that led them to frame the cases in their first meeting.

I don't really understand how we were not able to see the bigger picture. It was in front of us. I remember that we were too focused on the reduction of costs, legal liability and whether our decision may fit our customer segment [referring to discussions in the first meeting]. How was it possible that we didn't think of human life at first? [The vignette was built upon the 'Ford Pinto' case (see Gioia, 1992)]. The problem was much broader and complex than we initially thought; it went beyond a simple business decision. I think that in our conversations [referring to group discussions] we were able to question our initial thoughts.

(Excerpt 2, conversation second meeting)

The role of discourse as a way of apprehending and reconstituting worldviews is central in Excerpt 2. As the example above indicates, discourse is not simply a matter of what is being said in the vignettes used in this study but also of how bits of information are ultimately interpreted and assembled into coherent stories or accounts (see Dryzek, 1997; Jonker & Marberg, 2007). The vignettes used in this study could thus be conceived differently depending on the discourse that is drawn upon. Extract 1 first illustrated how the managerial discourse influenced the way that business and tourism students framed and tackled the social and environmental challenges presented in the vignettes. In contrast, Excerpt 2 shows how the sustainability discourse offered students a new way of talking and understanding the PBL cases; thus, it enabled them not only to openly recognize critical issues that were not visible when relying only on the managerial discourse but also to question their initial way of thinking.

While lectures, in-class exercises and the self-study period offered an opportunity for students to become familiar with sustainability literature, they also served as the basis for students to question their own practices and assumptions as business and tourism students. In line with Fairclough (2003), as a discursive site PBL encouraged students to act, think, talk and see themselves in terms of the sustainability discourse. Furthermore, as employees, employers, consumers, activists, politicians and, above all, citizens, these students brought traces of wide discursive structures, ideologies and power relations into the PBL process (see Cunliffe, 2002). This wide array of voices offered a fertile ground for establishing dialogues that went beyond the realm of business and tourism management (see Fullagar & Wilson, 2012).

> When we [referring to her family] went a few times for a trip to Malaysia I was amazed for the difference that these countries have [referring to Singapore as the other country]. When we travelled to Malaysia by bus, I expected to see there green, beautiful jungle, but all I saw on whole five to six hour-time was palm oil trees What has happened? What kinds of responsibilities have the companies whose production the palm oil trees are grown up for? Foreign companies claim to be committed to efforts aimed at immediately halting the destruction of rainforest and developments that reduce biodiversity. I really couldn't see any biodiversity or protected rainforests in trip to Malaysia. I think that companies may consider responsibility in their action, but they don't necessarily behave in a manner of responsibility. As D. expresses in her article, I'm worried about the superficial side of sustainability.
>
> (Excerpt 3, journal)

The excerpt above illustrates how connecting the course reading material with personal experiences and social relations from the past and the present stimulates critical reflexivity. Indeed, the reading material seemed to trigger a multi-stakeholder dialogue, shaping her understanding of sustainability and her notion of being and acting as in a sustainable way (see Cunliffe, 2008). By including personal experiences and social relations into the learning process, PBL offers an opportunity to highlight and legitimize voices that are usually excluded or silenced within a managerial context.

> I learned a lot from the picture which illustrated the connection between law and ethics and the idea of a grey area [referring to Matten & Crane, 2007]. This is something that I have been thinking a lot about, but I haven't been successful in drawing such a clear picture in my mind. When I see this picture, I start to ask myself as a management student: How many students – future managers – are aware of the difference between acting legally and ethically? How many are willing to do more than what is required by the law? . . . The

more I get into this CSR [corporate social responsibility] topic, the more I start to analyze my own behaviour and thoughts, my previous actions and experiences.

(Excerpt 4, journal)

As Excerpt 4 shows, sustainability theory was used provocatively to encourage students to explore and evaluate ideas that could improve their professional practices (Ramsey, 2011). In particular, between the self-study period and the presentations (see Figure 21.1), students had the opportunity to experiment with those ideas and take actions that they had not previously considered. The excerpts illustrated how the introduction of the sustainability discourse within a PBL context created room for talking about and critically analysing issues that had been silenced or neglected during the tourism and business studies of the course participants.

Conclusion

By illustrating the implementation of PBL in two Master's-level sustainability courses, this study offers a concrete example of how critical reflexivity can be promoted in tourism and hospitality education. PBL represents one of many pedagogical methods that can be used to provide the tourism sector with critical thinkers who are able to find practical solutions to rising challenges and build sound relationships with tourism stakeholders. While this benefit may portray PBL as a response to the demands of a growing labour market for highly skilled tourism and hospitality professionals, PBL also represents an opportunity to transform contemporary tourism business and development practice.

Although PBL seems to be a useful vehicle for promoting critical reflexivity, there are some challenges that need to be considered. First, questioning contemporary tourism and hospitality practice can result in disruptive emotional consequences and students' resistance (see García-Rosell, 2012; Wilson & von der Heidt, 2013). The disconfirmation of assumptions about how tourism works as well as challenging of one's own identity as a management-oriented tourism student can lead to a sense of anger, frustration and powerlessness. The introduction of critical reflexivity in the curriculum thus requires instructors to be prepared to deal with students' feelings and emotions without silencing their voices or forcing them to give up their managerial identity.

Second, the strong emphasis of PBL on problem solving may undermine attempts to stimulate critical reflexivity. By representing critical tourism issues such as environmental degradation, social inequality and ethical dilemmas as problems PBL may reproduce the managerial approach to tourism and hospitality and even downplay its role as a discursive site for moral deliberation, negotiation, transformation and learning with regard to how to work towards a better tourism world. In this sense, the instructor plays a crucial role in leading students beyond the problem-solving spectrum and in using the discursive dynamics generated in the PBL process as a means for reflexive practice.

In respect to the implications of this study, these extend beyond the use of PBL in tourism and hospitality education. Through highlighting the importance of critical reflexivity and how it can be stimulated by redesigning existing pedagogical methods, this study has implications for delivering a curriculum that promotes both philosophic and vocational competencies.

Note

1   As a consequence of a structural development of higher education systems in Finland, the Faculty of Tourism and Business was merged with the Faculty of Social Sciences in 2010.

References

Alanko-Turunen, M. (2005). *Negotiating Interdiscursivity in a Problem-Based Learning Tutorial Site: A Case Study of an International Business Programme.* Tampere: University of Tampere.

Ayikoru, M., Tribe, J., & Airey, D. (2009). 'Reading Tourism Education: neoliberalism unveiled'. *Annals of Tourism Research,* 36(2), 191–221.

Barrows, H. (2000). 'Foreword'. In D. H. Evensen & C. E. Hmelo (Eds.), *Problem-Based Learning: a research perspective on learning interactions* (pp. vii–ix). Mahwah, NJ: Lawrence Erlbaum.

Belhassen, Y., & Caton, K. (2011). 'On the Need for Critical Pedagogy in Tourism Education'. *Tourism Management,* 32(6), 1389–96.

Bickford, D., & Van Vleck, J. (1997). 'Reflections on Artful Teaching'. *Journal of Management Education,* 21(4), 448–63.

Boud, D., & Feletti, G. I. (1997). 'Changing Problem-Based Learning: introduction to the second edition'. In D. Boud & G. I. Feletti (Eds.), *The Challenge of Problem-Based Learning* (pp.1–14). London: Kogan Page.

Bridges, E. M. (1992). *Problem Based Learning for Administrators.* Eugene: ERIC Clearinghouse on Educational Management.

Catterall, M., Maclaran, P., & Stevens, L. (2002). 'Critical Reflection in the Marketing Curriculum'. *Journal of Marketing Education,* 24(3), 184–92.

Chia, R. (1996a). 'Teaching Paradigm Shifting in Management Education: university business schools and the entrepreneurial imagination'. *Journal of Management Studies,* 33(4), 409–28.

Chia, R. (1996b). 'The Problem of Reflexivity in Organizational Research: towards a postmodern science of organization'. *Organization,* 3(1), 31–59.

Coghlan, D., & Brannick, T. (2009). *Doing Action Research in Your Own Organization.* London: SAGE.

Collier, M. (2001). 'Approaches to Analysis in Visual Anthropology'. In T. Van Leeuwen & C. Jewitt (Eds.), *Handbook of Visual Analysis* (pp. 35–60). London: SAGE.

Conceicão, S. C. O., & Skibba, K. A. (2007). 'Experiential Learning Activities for Leisure and Enrichment Travel Education: a situative perspective'. *Journal of Teaching in Travel & Tourism,* 7(4), 17–35.

Cunliffe, A. L. (2002). 'Reflexive Dialogical Practice in Management Learning'. *Management Learning,* 33(1), 35–61.

Cunliffe, A. L. (2004). 'On Becoming a Critically Reflexive Practitioner'. *Journal of Management Education,* 28(4), 407–26.

Cunliffe, A. L. (2008). 'Orientations to Social Constructionism: relationally responsive social constructionism and its implications for knowledge and learning'. *Management Learning,* 39(2), 123–39.

Dredge, D., Beckendorff, P., Day, M., Gross, M. J., Walo, M., Weeks, P., & Whitelaw, P. (2012). 'The Philosophic Practitioner and the Curriculum Space'. *Annals of Tourism Research,* 39(4), 2154–76.

Dryzek, J. (1997). *The Politics of the Earth: environmental discourses.* Oxford: Oxford University Press.

Duncan, M. J., & Al-Nakeeb, Y. (2006). 'Using Problem-Based Learning in Sports Related Courses: an overview of module development and student responses in an undergraduate sport studies module'. *Journal of Hospitality, Leisure, Sports and Tourism Education,* 5(1), 5–57.

Everett, J., & Jamal, T. B. (2004). 'Multistakeholder Collaboration as Symbolic Marketplace and Pedagogic Practice'. *Journal of Management Inquiry,* 13(1), 57–78.

Eyler, J., Giles, D. E. Jr., & Schmiede, A. (1996). *A Practitioner's Guide to Reflection in Service-Learning.* Nashville, TN: Vanderbilt University Press.

Fairclough, N. (2003). *Analysing Discourse: textual analysis for social research.* London: Routledge.

Fidgeon, P. R. (2010). 'Tourism Education and Curriculum Design: a time for consolidation and review'. *Tourism Management,* 31, 699–723.

Fullagar, S., & Wilson, E. (2012). 'Critical Pedagogies: a reflexive approach to knowledge creation in tourism and hospitality studies'. *Journal of Hospitality and Tourism Management,* 19, 1–6.

Gabriel, Y., & Connell, N. A. D. (2010). 'Co-Creating Stories: collaborative experiments in storytelling'. *Management Learning,* 41(5), 507–23.

García-Rosell, J. C. (2012). 'Struggles over Corporate Social Responsibility Meanings in Teaching Practices: the case of hybrid problem-based learning'. *Management Learning,* 5 July, 1–19.

García-Rosell, J. C. (2013). *A Multi-Stakeholder Perspective on Sustainable Marketing: promoting sustainability through action and research.* Rovaniemi: Lapland University Press.

Gioia, D. A. (1992). 'Pinto Fires and Personal Ethics: a script analysis of missed opportunities'. *Journal of Business Ethics,* 11(5/6), 379–89.

Hakkarainen, M., & Tuulentie, S. (2008). 'Tourism's Role in Rural Development of Finnish Lapland: interpreting national and regional strategy documents'. *Fennia*, 186(1), 3–13.

Hall, H., & Davison, B. (2007). 'Social Software as Support in Hybrid Learning Environments: the value of the blog as a tool for reflective learning and peer support'. *Library & Information Science Research*, 29, 163–87.

Hallinger, P., & Lu, J. (2011). 'Assessing the Instructional Effectiveness of Problem-Based Management Education in Thailand: a longitudinal evaluation'. *Management Learning*, 42(3), 279–99.

Hammersley, M., & Atkinson, P. (1996). *Ethnography: principles in practice*. London: Routledge.

Holman, D. (2000) 'Contemporary Models of Management Education in the UK'. *Management Learning*, 31(2), 197–217.

Huang, R. (2005). 'Chinese International Students' Perceptions of the Problem-Based Learning Experience'. *Journal of Hospitality, Leisure, Sports and Tourism Education*, 4(2), 36–44.

Jamal, T., Everett, J., & Dann, G. M. S. (2003). 'Ecological Rationalization and Performative Resistance in Natural Area Destinations'. *Tourist Studies*, 3(2), 143–69.

Jones, S., Ten Bos, R., & Parker, M. (2005). *For Business Ethics*. London: Routledge.

Jonker, J., & Marberg, A. (2007). 'Corporate Social Responsibility – Quo Vadis? A critical inquiry into a discursive struggle'. *Journal of Corporate Citizenship*, 27, 107–18.

Kahn, P., & O'Rourke, K. (2005). 'Understanding Enquiry-Based Learning'. In T. Barret, I. Labhrainn, & H. Fallon (Eds.), *Handbook of Inquiry and Problem Based Learning* (pp. 1–12). Galway: CELT.

Katila, S., & Meriläinen, S. (1999). 'A Serious Researcher or Just Another Nice Girl? Doing gender in a male dominated scientific community'. *Gender, Work and Organisation*, 6(3), 163–73.

Kivela, J., & Kivela, R. J. (2005). 'Student Perception of an Embedded Problem-Based Learning Instructional Approach in a Hospitality Undergraduate Programme'. *Hospitality Management* 24, 437–64.

Kolb, D. (1984). *Experiential Learning*. Englewood Cliffs, NJ: Prentice Hall.

Lindén, J., & Alanko-Turunen, M. (2006). 'Deconstructing Conceptions of Problem-Based Learning'. In E. Poikela & R. Nummenmaa (Eds.), *Understanding Problem-Based Learning* (pp. 51–64). Tampere: University of Tampere.

Major, C., & Palmer, B. (2001). 'Assessing the Effectiveness of Problem Based Learning in Higher Education: lessons from the literature'. *Academic Exchange*, 5(1), 1–2.

Margetson, D. (1994). 'Current Educational Reform and the Significance of Problem-Based Learning'. *Studies in Higher Education*, 19(1), 5–20.

Matten, D., & Crane, A. (2007). *Business Ethics: managing corporate citizenship and sustainability in the age of globalization*. New York: Oxford University Press.

Moisander, J. (2001). *Representations of Green Consumerism: a constructionist critique*. Helsinki: Helsinki School of Economics.

Moisander, J., & Valtonen, A. (2006). *Qualitative Marketing Research: a cultural approach*. London: SAGE.

Morgan, M. (2004). 'From Production Pine to Drama School Higher Education for the Future of Tourism'. *International Journal of Contemporary Hospitality Management*, 16(2), 91–9.

Moscardo, G. (1997). 'Making Mindful Managers'. *Journal of Tourism Studies*, 8(1), 16–24.

Phillips, L. J., & Jorgensen, M. W. (2002). *Discourse Analysis as Theory and Method*. London: SAGE.

Phillips, N., & Hardy, C. (2002). *Discourse Analysis: Investigating Processes of Social Construction*. Thousand Oaks, CA: SAGE.

Poikela, E., & Poikela, S. (2006). 'Problem-Based Curricula: theory, development and design'. In E. Poikela & R. Nummenmaa (Eds.), *Understanding Problem-Based Learning* (pp. 71–90). Tampere: University of Tampere.

Pollner, M. (1991). 'Left of Ethnomethodology: the rise and decline of radical reflexivity'. *American Sociological Review*, 56, 370–80.

Portimojärvi, T. (2006). 'Synchronous and Asynchronous Communication in Online Problem-Based Learning'. In E. Poikela & R. Nummenmaa (Eds.), *Understanding Problem-Based Learning* (pp. 91–104). Tampere: University of Tampere.

Pritchard, A., Morgan, N., & Ateljevic, I. (2011). 'Hopeful Tourism: a new transformative perspective'. *Annals of Tourism Research*, 38(3), 941–63.

Probyn, E. (2004). 'Teaching Bodies: affects in the classroom'. *Body & Society*, 10(4), 21–43.

Puhakka, R., Sarkki, S., Cottrell, S. P., & Siikamäki, P. (2009). 'Local Discourses and International Initiatives: sociocultural sustainability of tourism in Oulanka National Park, Finland'. *Journal of Sustainable Tourism*, 17(5), 529–49.

Ramsey, C. (2005) 'Narrative: from learning in reflection to learning in performance'. *Management Learning,* 36(2), 219–35.

Ramsey, C. (2011). 'Provocative Theory and a Scholarship of Practice'. *Management Learning,* 42(5), 469–83.

Rantala, O. (2011). 'An Ethnographic Approach to Nature-Based Tourism'. *Scandinavian Journal of Hospitality and Tourism,* 11(2), 150–65.

Reason, P. (1988). *Human Inquiry in Action.* London: SAGE.

Reed, M., & Anthony, P. (1992). 'Professionalizing Management and Managing Professionalization: British management in the 1980s'. *Journal of Management Studies,* 29(5), 591–613.Ruhanen, L. (2005). 'Bridging the Divide between Theory and Practice: experiential learning approaches for tourism and hospitality management education'. *Journal of Teaching in Travel & Tourism,* 5(4), 33–51.

Savery, J. R. (2006). 'Overview of Problem-Based Learning: definitions and distinctions'. *Interdisciplinary Journal of Problem-Based Learning,* 1(1), 9–20.

Savery, J. R., & Duffy, T. M. (1995). 'Problem-Based Learning: an instructional model and its constructivist framework'. *Educational Technology,* 35(5), 31–8.

Schön, D. (1983). *The Reflective Practitioner: how professionals think in action.* New York: Basic Books.

Skålén. P., Fougère, M., & Fellesson, M. (2008). *Marketing Discourse: a critical perspective.* London: Routledge.

Spradley, J. P. (1980). *Participant Observation.* New York: Holt, Rinehart and Winston.

Tomlinson, F., & Egan, S. (2002). 'Organizational Sensemaking in a Culturally Diverse Setting: limits to the valuing diversity discourse'. *Management Learning,* 33(1), 79–97.

Tribe, J. (2002). 'The Philosophic Practitioner'. *Annals of Tourism Research,* 29(2), 338–57.

Tribe, J. (2006). 'The Truth about Tourism'. *Annals of Tourism Research,* 33(2), 360–81.

Tribe, J. (2008). 'Tourism: a critical business'. *Journal of Travel Research,* 46(February), 245–55.

Tribe, J. (2009). 'Philosophical Issues in Tourism'. In J. Tribe (Ed.), *Philosophical Issues in Tourism* (pp. 3–35). Bristol: Channel View.

Watson, T. J. (2001). 'The Emergent Manager and Processes of Management Pre-Learning'. *Management Learning,* 32(2), 221–35.

Wee, L. K. N., Alexandria, M., Kek, Y. C., & Kelley C. A. (2003). 'Transforming the Marketing Curriculum Using Problem-Based Learning: a case study'. *Journal of Marketing Education,* 25(2), 150–62.

Wilson, E., & von der Heidt, T. (2013). 'Business as Usual? Barriers to education for sustainability in the tourism curriculum'. *Journal of Teaching in Travel & Tourism,* 13(2), 130–47.

Zwaal, W., & Otting, H. (2010). 'The Process of Problem-Based Hospitality Management Education'. *Journal of Hospitality, Leisure, Sport & Tourism Education,* 9(2), 17–30.

22

Transforming tourism education through Web 2.0 collaboration

The case of the global TEFI courses

Janne J. Liburd
University of Southern Denmark

Introduction

Currently enrolled tourism students are likely to be occupying jobs in the future that do not even exist today and even more can expect to leave university without any assurance that they will find a job in the field for which they should be qualified. Pointing to the global population increase, and related competition, less dependence on manual labour and the mass-university producing more graduates, Robinson and Aronica (2009: 232) assert that: 'The plain fact is that a college degree is not worth a fraction of what it once was. A degree was a passport to a good job. Now, at best, it's a visa. It only gives you provisional residence in the job market.'

This implies that tourism students will need fundamental understandings of change and unpredictability as part of complex adaptive systems, which can cause multifaceted and non-linear outcomes that are hard to foresee (Gunderson *et al.*, 2005; Miller & Twining-Ward, 2005; Liburd, 2010). Concerned that few undergraduate and graduate tourism programmes are preparing students to meet the challenges of the present and to be instrumental in forming a complex future (Tylor, 2009; Sheldon *et al.*, 2008; Liburd & Hjalager, 2010, 2011), let alone promoting a balance between satisfying the demands of business and those of the wider society and the world (Tribe, 2002; Inui *et al.*, 2006) these challenges set the context for the Tourism Education Futures Initiative (hereinafter TEFI).

Attempting to transform the quality of tourism education by use of values-based education, Web 2.0 technologies and collaboration, this chapter presents the case of the Global TEFI Courses. These courses were jointly developed and taught by innovative tourism educators based in Brazil, USA, Austria, Switzerland, Denmark and New Zealand in 2010 until the present time of writing. Here, tourism educators contribute with expert knowledge in various thematic fields. Each course lecture is streamed via *Adobe Connect* and uploaded onto a Web 2.0 platform entitled INNOTOUR (www.INNOTOUR.com). Lecturers are accompanied by related student exercises designed to be solved in groups across the involved campuses by students collaborating through the use of blogs, wikis and discussion forums.

The overall aim of this chapter is to investigate an innovative, collaborative phenomenon within contemporary practices in tourism higher education. It is based on the author's involvement in creating and implementing the Global TEFI Courses, and professorial dissertation, entitled 'Towards the Collaborative University. Lessons from Tourism Education and Research' (Liburd, 2013). First, the context for the creation of TEFI's five values-based principles that tourism students should imbibe upon graduation will be briefly outlined. Second, conditions for collaborative teaching will be discussed. Adopting a Web 2.0 philosophy, these include teacher training, didactic and pedagogical perspectives as the implementation of values-based learning, which calls for a new learning paradigm and methodologies that transcend traditional boundaries. Third, initial student and teacher evaluations of the Global TEFI Courses will be addressed. Evidence here suggests that successful integration of Web 2.0 in higher education requires students and educators to take on radically different roles from the traditional ones. Fourth, reflections are provided on the importance of alignment to ensure consistency between the formal course requirement, semester activities and the final evaluation (Biggs & Tang, 2007). Fifth, critical reflections are offered on how the initiative challenges and transforms tourism education through collaborative practice.

The TEFI values

Since TEFI's 2007 inauguration at Modul University Vienna, Austria, some 150 scholars and a handful of industry leaders have been engaged in a process of rebuilding the tourism education process. Whilst much effort has been expended on addressing the short-term needs of the tourism sector, it appears critical that longer-term perspectives are adopted so that the future will be shaped by people educated to commit to a sustainable world (Sheldon et al., 2008). Based on annual summits and a number of ongoing working groups, the key outcome of the TEFI process is a set of five relational values: 'Ethics, Knowledge, Professionalism, Mutuality and Stewardship'. The values are portrayed as interlocking value principles because of their interconnectedness and their permeability. It is envisaged that educators can infuse these values into courses where relevant, so that tourism graduates become responsible leaders and stewards for the destinations in which they work and/or live. Readers are encouraged to see the TEFI White Paper (TEFI, 2009) for further elaboration of the five values.

Teaching objectives always involve making student learning possible. This involves attempts to alter students' understanding of ideas and phenomena in ways conceptualized by researchers or other experts, through the selection of course materials, and the implicit and critical ways of understanding. While a critical pedagogical approach covers many, not always unequivocal, types of scholarship (McLaren & Giroux, 1995), the focus is that teaching and learning are much more about the potential of transformative power and complex understandings, rather than merely a technical transfer of cognitive skills (Blasco, 2009: 14). Addressing the quality of teaching, student learning, and future challenges, TEFI's programmatic outcome is summarized as following:

> Tourism educational programs need to fundamentally re-tool and redesign – not incrementally by adding new courses – or simply by putting courses on-line – but by changing the nature of what is taught and how it is taught.
>
> (Sheldon et al., 2008: 63)

The ambitious vision of TEFI is not only to reshape tourism education worldwide, but to help the leaders of the tourism industry follow practices that are rooted in these basic values:

'TEFI seeks to provide vision, knowledge and a framework for tourism education programmes to promote global citizenship and optimism for a better world' (TEFI, 2009: 3). It should be noted that the values-based platform calls for further research and in-depth understanding about the transformative potentials, cultural interpretations, and contextualized meanings of ethics, knowledge, stewardship, professionalism, and mutual respect. In due course a group of TEFI delegates set out to explore the possibilities for transforming tourism courses in and across their institutional contexts.

Conditions for collaborative teaching

The following section reports on the pedagogical and didactic reflections and practical conditions for setting up the Global TEFI Courses. In April 2010, an initial scoping exercise was undertaken by six tourism educators to explore the TEFI values in transnational and multicultural contexts. Agreeing on the feasibility, content, and extent of collaboration, attention was directed toward constraints in meeting institutional course requirements and the differences in time and place of participating institutions. In the light of discussion, the group of educators found e-learning to be a feasible solution that could be adopted into existing or complementing courses. E-learning is a common denomination for electronic learning characterized by learning mediated by digital media, i.e. the Internet, which makes participants independent of time and space. The asynchronous element of learning necessitates virtual learning and communication spaces, which in this case were facilitated via the Web 2.0 platform, INNOTOUR (www.INNTOUR.com). E-learning has a relatively long history but until recently, electronic learning resources and devices have mostly been considered auxiliary attributes to the 'real' classroom teaching (Salmon, 2002; Sigala, 2002; Dohn, 2009). Research in e-learning practices is comprehensive but there is a lack of understanding of the didactic potentials of, for instance, blogs and wikis in higher education, not least when applied in transnational, multicultural contexts. The experiences from the Global TEFI Courses can be seen as an attempt to fill this void.

Also acknowledging that the vocational element in tourism university education is challenged, reinterpretation of students' learning styles and preferred media is essential (Thomson, 2007; Asraf, 2009; Benckendorff et al., 2010; Lee & Wicks, 2010). Sigala (2002) argues that active student engagement for personalized learning may enhance relevance and authenticity for the learners through user-generated content. Attempting to meet students where they are, as well as adhering to institutional norms, including prerequisites on curriculum and in some cases physical presence in the classroom, five of the six educators opted for a blended learning approach to integrate online lectures with face-to-face education. Only one teacher had the privilege to redesign an existing curriculum to be entirely based on the Global TEFI Courses. Three of the teachers created an optional class for students. Next, each of the partners identified two or three preferred topics of course delivery and committed to online recording of their lectures.

Communication via blogs and a discussion forum in the 'Teachers and Tutors' area on INNOTOUR exposed a number of didactic, pedagogical, and epistemological challenges of adopting a Web 2.0 philosophy in teaching and learning. Theoretically underpinning these considerations were the socio-cultural learning theories of Piaget (1972), Vygotsky (1992 [1926]), Kolb (1984), Lave and Wenger (1991) and Perkins (1996), orienting focus towards students' different learning styles, the significance of the learning environment, and the concept of collaborative learning. Notable elements are interaction, co-construction, reflection, and collaboration between learners and educators. The practice perspective is backed by a view inspired by phenomenology (Merleu-Ponty, 1962) that sees learning practices, attitude, and technology in a dialectical relationship informing each other. Denoting certain types of *use* of web-mediated technology, Web 2.0 activities are characterized by 'bottom-up' participation, open access, interactive, multi-way communication, user-centred focus and content generation (Dohn, 2009).

Among the group of TEFI educators the available experience base of Internet-based teaching methods, tools, and learning was minimal. To address these shortcomings, two teacher training courses were designed by the University of Southern Denmark's E-learning Unit. Materials from the teacher training session can be freely accessed from INNOTOUR's Teacher & Tutor's area, where they are located under TEFI courses.

When designing Web 2.0 activities, it is important to orchestrate the students' online interaction and explicate appropriate academic standards. This is not a paradox. The open and equitable participation, which underlines the Web 2.0 philosophy, places significant and new demands on students. In the initial phase it is important to formulate instructions so that they clearly indicate to students what is expected of them. As the students become familiar with Web 2.0 learning, subsequent tasks can gradually be formulated more freely. A key challenge is to convert students' private use of Web 2.0, which is often characterized by fast and superficial information exchanges, into reflective academic contributions.

Importantly, addressing the didactic design of Web 2.0 activities, inspiration from Gilly Salmon's (2002) five-phase model and *e-tivities* concept sets the frame for student collaboration (Table 22.1). An e-tivity denotes 'a framework for *active and interactive online* learning' (Salmon 2002: 1). The e-tivity provides students with guidelines for solving a specific online task, in addition to elements of how to motivate and engage students in active participation online. Table 22.1 can be used as a template for preparation of e-tivities.

A task title and subject are written in the top row. At the same time, a motivating factor may be included to inform students why it is interesting to deal with this topic and how they benefit. Under the resources/tools heading attention is drawn to texts and other material to be studied and where the task should be carried out, e.g. e-learning platform, open source system, discussion forum, blog, etc. The aim describes the specific learning outcome that is fulfilled when the student completes the task. This provides a direct connection to the curriculum. Following this, specific instructions are given about the task the student should complete. Your task denotes what students should do, for example, make written contributions to a blog or start a wiki on a specific topic. Qualitative and quantitative requirements may be included to make the task more transparent. The response is that which creates online interaction and thereby supports the rewarding collaborative learning processes. The response may be that the student should read and comment on the blog posts of at least three fellow students. Deadlines are essential in order to initiate and drive online learning. Completion dates should preferably be early. This ensures that there is something to 'respond' to in the second part of the task. A second deadline that is a little later may be needed for this response. If preferable, a third deadline may be set,

Table 22.1 E-tivities template

Task title and subject/motivating input:
Resources/tools:
Aim:
Your task:
Response:
Deadlines:

Source: Adapted from Salmon (2002).

for students to return to their initial input, reflect upon the comments received from other students, and formulate new content taking these into account.

When facilitating online student collaboration, it is important not only to articulate the vocational goals, but also to formulate specific objectives for the use of the Web 2.0 tools involved. Emphasizing that all of the tools applied serve an educational purpose contributes to the students' perceptions of Web 2.0 activities as a meaningful element in their studies. This should also avoid seeing the use of the tools as an end in its own right. Table 22. 2 lists examples of goals when using Web 2.0 tools.

In the learning objectives of the Global TEFI Courses, the student should also be able to critically reflect upon the TEFI values where infused into course lectures, discussions, and joint assignments.

In short, the Global TEFI Courses inspired thinking not only about *what* to teach but also on *how* to teach. Examples from the 2010 Global TEFI Course portfolio will explicate the relations between didactical practice, tools, and technology. Using Salmon's (2002) e-tivities template (Table 22.1), Phase 1 and Phase 5 e-tivities designed by this author are illustrated in Tables 22.3 and 22.4.

Table 22.2 Learning objectives for inclusion of Web 2.0 tools

---

The student should be able to:

- Take part in individual and collaborative knowledge construction (produce texts themselves and in collaboration with others) via Web 2.0 tools provided on INNOTOUR as a virtual, open platform;
- Contribute to discussions on vocational topics from differing perspectives and values via Web 2.0 tools;
- Build up a virtual network of vocational contacts and make use of them in the educational activities;
- Act as a partner for others in virtual, professional networks;
- Transfer and make use of knowledge/material in a variety of contexts – use and reuse; and
- Apply a critical approach to used and reused material.

Source: Liburd and Hjalager (2010: 118–19). (Reproduced with permission from Elsevier.)

Table 22.3 Global TEFI Course E-tivity Phase 1

Introduction to Tourism & Leisure Management – PHASE 1

Resources: Please visit www.INNOTOUR.com. This is the main Internet site we will be using for the course. Click on the '01 Students' on the right on the screen and log into the platform after creating your username and password. Use the Student blog.

Purpose: To share your reasons for studying tourism and your expectations about the course, and to learn more about your fellow students.

Your task: Write a short blog post (10–15 lines) about why you chose to study tourism. You may include your course expectations. In addition suggestions and ideas for course activities are much appreciated.

Response: Read the blog posts of your fellow students and write comments to those you find particularly interesting. Write at least one comment.

Deadline: One week from now (Sept. 14, 2010).

Source: Liburd (2011).

Table 22.4 Global TEFI Course E-tivity Phase 5

Introduction to Tourism & Leisure Management – PHASE 5

Resources: www.INNOTOUR.com Student's area Wiki, discussion takes place in the Innovation Forum

Purpose: To prepare for your final exam and strengthen your reflective, collaborative and networking skills.

Your tasks:
1. You must contribute to the final improvement of the wiki content by inserting your suggestions and references, where relevant.
2. Then export relevant wiki content to your own notes.
3. Network with students enrolled in TEFI Courses at other universities.
   • Student group A will secure final wiki contributions from all
   • Student group B will provide new perspectives based on 'outside' links (e.g. useful websites)
   • Student group C will invite other TEFI students to comment on the TEFI courses
   • Student group D will gather feedback from other TEFI students. Ideas for future collaboration are welcome.

Deadlines: Nov. 30, 2010
• Student group A secures final contributions by November 22.
• Student group B provides new perspectives by November 25.
• Student group C invites other TEFI students to comment on the TEFI courses no later than November 29.
• Student group D will gather and summarize feedback from other TEFI students by November 22. Ideas for future collaboration are welcome.

Source: Liburd (2011).

The Phase 1 e-tivity (Table 22.3) was created to familiarize students with each other and identify course expectations by use of writing and commenting in a designated blog on INNOTOUR. TEFI students have been given similar assignments (with new deadlines if their semester started later) at partner universities. By way of commenting on some of the existing blog posts the group of students known to each other and available for future joint assignments was gradually expanded (Table 22.4).

Illustrating the orchestrated interaction and use of specific Web 2.0 tools, in the final Phase 5 e-tivity (Table 22.4) students are challenged to build and critically reflect upon shared knowledge construction including ethics, mutual respect, stewardship, and professionalism. In line with the increased frequency of multi-level interaction, different roles and tasks are accorded to students groups, while also involving individual pursuits aimed at strengthening the final assignment. The Web 2.0 tools used include wikis and a discussion forum where students engage across universities by means of written and oral exchanges.

Due to the difference in academic calendars only a window of five weeks was available with all classes in session. The gradual progression formed through the e-tivities model meant that courses were not entirely independent of time and space; a feature otherwise distinctive for e-learning. Consequently, the Global TEFI Course students were never at the same phase at the same time, which meant that a few assignments, such as joint delivery to a discussion forum, were not viable. The organization of trans-university and international courses has to be cognizant of different time zones, semesters, and timetabling issues. By enabling learning across international time zones, institutions, and cultures, the TEFI values of professionalism, mutual respect, and knowledge were thought to enhance students' abilities to meet deadlines in a global environment in which many will be seeking future employment. University schedules and contexts at large have to be considered when planning collaborative, transnational education, which will next be discussed in the frame of teacher and student evaluations and need for alignment.

Evaluating the Global TEFI Courses

Teacher feedback

Inquiring into how educators think about learning, what to learn, and the effect of activities on student learning is crucial to any improvement in higher education (Ramsden, 2003: 7). Acutely aware of the methodological challenges involved in evaluating and researching one's own teaching practices, the following explanation relies on the group of TEFI educators making explicit the often introspective thoughts, beliefs, and decision-making processes that shape planning of lectures, student assignments, and dialogue. For example, an inherent danger in reporting on only successes that glosses over the problems and contradictions at work is consciously avoided in the following evaluation.

Experience from the early trials with the Global TEFI Courses demonstrated that a number of considerations are necessary in order to prepare a thorough e-tivity. In hindsight, the initial investment of time appears to pay off as results can be reused by the teacher and ideally by others. Still, it continues to be very much against the grain for teachers, as well as for institutions, to allow for open posting of slides, tutorials, and streamed material on the Internet. These materials are often regarded as private, and may be intellectual property of the institution, which require a significant shift in thinking, administration, and everyday teaching practice. On top of this are speculations about whether the material is of sufficient quality for open distribution. Such reflections cannot simply be attributed to intellectual humility, but also to a genuine fear of colleagues' judgements. Also the technical aspects of working with Web 2.0 have been mentioned by the group of teachers. Given the novelty of these tools of instruction and moderation, including the recording of one's lectures, the sense of being 'less professional' and 'not as knowledgeable as one's students' were addressed upfront by the teachers, but not encountered in the process of course delivery.

The role of the teacher-as-expert is reconstructed as teachers increasingly become mentors or facilitators of knowledge given their topical expertise. The group of TEFI teachers unanimously appreciated the ability afforded by collaboration to provide new topical perspectives by means of the online lectures, from which they were also learning. This only proved vaguely frustrating when students continue to look for definite truths about a given problem, to which the teacher-as-expert ought to be able to provide a definitive answer.

Creating the foundation for collaborative teaching, the Global TEFI Courses led to transformation of didactic and pedagogical perspectives by adopting a Web 2.0 learning paradigm, activities, and methodologies. For example, blogging across the curriculum enables students and teachers to infuse academic writing into all activities and to facilitate connections between topics and across contexts by establishing relations in ways that plain paper cannot (Richardson, 2009). Moreover, by clearly expressing course objectives through tools and course methods, a culture of creativity and mutual respect is nurtured that is highly flexible and capable of learning from mistakes.

The engagement by the group of TEFI educators setting the framework for students in different educational environments also aimed at providing an exploration of culture that went beyond dominating perceptions of culture and cultural values as *difference* between people and places. Reduced to an ontological essence in which misunderstandings are accorded to national (cultural) differences (Hofstede, 2005), culture is subjected to managerial intervention either avoiding 'clashes of difference' or enabling 'differences for sale' (Liburd & Ren, 2009: 77). Rather than seeing culture as static and incommensurable 'Otherness' to be explored, or exploited, the Global TEFI Courses add an experiential, affective dimension. This has to do with self-awareness and critical reflexivity when collaborating with students in multicultural and transnational learning environments.

One of the Global TEFI Course lectures on 'Tourism and Stereotypes' addresses some of these issues, with corresponding e-tivities challenging students to blog about their own encounters with national stereotypes and how they are enacted. Insights can also be gleaned from anthropology where scholars more recently have debated how to heighten students' awareness of their own ethnocentrism, position in the field, and professional responsibility to deliver accurate and sensible portrayals of others' way of life (Pedelty, 2001; Higgins, 2001; Blasco, 2009: 28). Embedded in the TEFI value of mutuality, research on these aspects emphasizes that reflexivity about one's own culture is a prerequisite for cultural understanding (Lafayette, 2003: 65; Blasco, 2009: 24).

Student feedback

When accessing the Global TEFI Courses on the INNOTOUR platform, students encounter the message shown in Table 22.5.

Evidently, it is not new for students to collaborate on solving assignments but experience with the Global TEFI Courses and other forms of Web 2.0-based learning indicate that new behavioural norms are necessary (Sigala, 2002). In relation to blogs and wikis, it is necessary for students to be able to give and receive criticism in a constructive and a future-oriented spirit in order to raise the quality of the joint product. Many are simply too cordial whereas others appear uncomfortable with making their views known. Issues about how to interact and what is acceptable online behaviour, also referred to as 'netiquette', should be addressed at the beginning of a course and agreeable standards set by the group of users (Liburd & Christensen, 2012: 102). Students' insecurity about posting blogs in an open context raises concerns over safety and access. For assessment purposes obviously the name of each contributor must be known to the teacher. The use of a pseudonym for students recognizable only to the teacher and/or peer group was accepted as a viable option and made available when registering as a user on the INNOTOUR platform. The openness also caused concerns related to control, as expressed by one of the Global TEFI Course students: 'I liked the posting of blogs and wikis very much, but the thing with user-generated content is that everyone can change anything . . . and so you're losing control over who does what.'

Table 22.5 The global TEFI Courses on INNOTOUR

The Global TEFI courses are taught by an international group of educators delivering tourism courses online. Each course is infused by the TEFI values of Knowledge, Ethics, Mutual respect, Professionalism and Stewardship.
The delivery of courses will be highly flexible in order to adhere to different requirements at the respective universities. Students will be exposed to joint assignments, tutorial exercises and different roles (some of which will be in the form of e-tivities) to support the collaborative learning processes.

Source: http://www.innotour.com/student-area/tefi-courses

Student experiences demonstrate the need for a clear explanation of students' roles, expectations for online moderation, and agreement on the frequency and types of contribution at the beginning of a course to mitigate substantial variation in students' contributions. Evidence further suggests that successful integration of Web 2.0 in higher tourism education requires students and teachers to take on different roles from the traditional ones. Everyone is a contributor, helping one another to create a knowledge base, within a given subject area. Everyone helps to improve and update texts in the employed wikis. Everyone contributes with new angles and nuances on a topic in the related blogs.

Participation requires an outgoing personality and courage, which may take time for a student to develop. It is obvious that a certain professional modesty may exist in the first semester of a course. Feasibly, teachers can act as role models and coach their students through the first Web 2.0 learning activities. In a couple of the Global TEFI Course contexts, English was not the primary language of instruction. Some of these students felt inhibited when contributing to blogs and wikis, again calling for an explanation of course expectations in different contexts. These contexts can be educational, pedagogical, geographical, cultural, political, and/or technical, necessitating translation and localization. Translation and localization involves more than the translation of English-language course materials or swapping a photo to reflect a culture. It exemplifies mutuality, openness, and reusability of materials to suit different contexts. Localization is the process of taking educational resources developed in one context and reusing or adapting them for other contexts, which is at the heart of the Global TEFI Courses. Many students in anonymous course evaluations expressed an appreciation of the international perspectives and diverse contextualization enabled by online lecturers and student comments. One student stated:

> The TEFI course I am taking at Universidade Anhembi Morumbi is surprisingly interesting, quite different from other on line courses I've taken. The subject of each lesson is always an up-to-date content about the tourism sector, and involves study cases from all over the world. That helps me to understand tourism as a global phenomenon and at the same time try to use successful examples in my country. The debates in the classroom help me to open up my mind and see many aspects of the lesson's subject and the possibility of exchanging information with students from other countries are very interesting.

Another student commented: 'I have to say that it was a great opportunity to be part of this innovative framework, but for the future you could combine classroom reality with blog posts.'

Importantly, online activities should be clearly integrated into the overall course workload. Student contributions need to be weighed and moderated carefully so that they do not become an extra burden to students or educators, or cause students to 'feel lost in cyberspace' when the teacher's physical presence is limited. Thereby, participation and content-related criteria can be more effectively applied to evaluate the quality of student learning.

Alignment

Whereas a number of positive motivational factors are readily acknowledged, including student motivation, and personalized, collaborative knowledge formation (Sigala, 2002; Liburd & Christensen, 2012), the inherent epistemology of Web 2.0 practices and the formal educational system pose conceptual tensions.

In Web 2.0, knowledge is conceived of as a process, activity, in communities of practice, whereas the traditional, Cartesian view is that knowledge is something to be acquired through the formal education setting, where learning is an acquisition of this state within the formal educational system (Dohn, 2009). Web 2.0 activities are characterized by bottom-up production and negotiation of meaning by collective intelligence and by the continuous application, reuse, and transformation of material across contexts.

Inherent in such Web 2.0 activities is a view of communication as interaction, of knowledge as transitory and in flux, of competence as situated doing, and of learning as participation and co-creation (Lave & Wenger, 1991). This is to be contrasted with more traditional views of communication as transmission of meaning, of knowledge and competence as states, or dispositions possessed by the individual, and of learning as the acquisition of such states and skills (Sfard, 1998; Dohn, 2009).

Working with Web 2.0 in higher education, a key issue is to enable consistency between the semester activities and appraisal; also referred to as alignment (Biggs & Tang, 2007). Web 2.0 activities implicitly view learning as active participation and knowledge as a process/activity. This means that there is little correlation with traditional final test forms such as individual written assignments or oral examinations. Involvement of Web 2.0 necessitates new thinking in relation to course evaluation and assessment (Christensen, 2009). While it is important that assessment focuses on the process rather than solely valuing the end result, it is also essential that part of the evaluation procedure becomes the responsibility of the participants. The new forms of evaluation may be in the form of peer review based upon comments from fellow students, constructive criticism during the process, portfolio exams, etc. This places significant demands on the established educational system to renew and, not least, accept the idea that students assume a more active role in evaluating, learning, and assessment. Accepting students as co-creators of knowledge, cognitive growth lies not just in knowing more, but in restructuring and reusing what is already known in order to connect with new knowledge. Coupled with use of Web 2.0 technology and a new learning paradigm, such transformation is necessarily epistemological in its implications (Barnett, 2010).

For the Global TEFI Courses, this transformation also highlights the institutional–didactic dimension to the values-based axiology: the university contexts and conditions under which tourism teaching and learning take place; and their impact on student and teacher identities and motivation. Bringing to the forefront reflections about Web 2.0 approaches to learning, and how innovative learning may enhance university teaching and reputation, the implementation of the Global TEFI Courses faces a number of immediate challenges. At the forefront of these are the adaptation and alignment of courses, forms of assessment, but also intellectual property rights. Only gradually are new ways of handling copyright issues emerging, for example in the institutionalization of 'Creative Commons' and the 'copyleft' movement (Berry, 2008; Liburd & Hjalager, 2010; Liburd, 2012). Here, users can obtain license to modify, or remove, copyright restrictions based upon the requirement that this right be maintained in future versions, which also underpins materials on the INNOTOUR platform.

Concluding reflections

International experiences are often critical for future professionals wanting to engage in a global industry like tourism. However, not all tourism students have the opportunity to have exchange experiences or study at institutions in different countries. The Global TEFI Courses provide future tourism professionals with an international experience through which they get to interact with students and faculty in other countries, meet deadlines across multiple time zones, practise their English-language skills, increase cultural awareness and mutual respect though joint-learning experiences. Illustrated in the teacher training courses as well as in the student e-tivities, collaboration helped knowledge develop by challenging learners at their level. This implies that collaboration in the Global TEFI Courses is in its most generous sense 'reciprocal' and 'pedagogical' in character. Course materials are given and received; they can be reused and added to over the coming semesters thereby advancing the possibilities for new transformations from which students and teachers profess to have benefited.

Advanced learning through open sharing of knowledge and transnational collaboration in higher tourism education is still novel. Collaborative learning rests on the hypothesis that the sum of the work is larger than its individual parts, and that focus should be as much on the process as on the end result. The knowledge created is a joint product based on critical reflection, discussion, and collective understanding. The transformation from closed and controlled tourism education toward openness and transparency thus occurs through dialogical forms of reconstruction and collaboration. This does not imply that Web 2.0 technologies or the Global TEFI Courses should be seen as the only way to prepare tourism students for their future field of practice. TEFI was borne out of a concern that tourism higher education is not sufficiently addressing the challenges of the present and creating responsible worldmakers for the future, herein satisfying not only the demands of business but also those of wider society (Tribe, 2002). TEFI's approach to values-based education is in part a response to uncertainty and complexity, but it should not be seen as an end to uncertainty or complexity. The case of the Global TEFI Courses illustrates a transformational and embedded understanding of professionalism, reciprocal relationships, and sustainability that goes well beyond a traditional transfer of knowledge, proficiency, and skills from teachers to students.

Working with the Global TEFI Courses and INNOTOUR have also exposed just how well-established institutional structures are, and how much effort is required for even just incremental innovation in tourism higher education. The traditional university systems of teacher expertise, power, and evaluation are not easily transformed. Also sitting rather uneasily with current neoliberal notions in tourism higher education including standardization (Munar, 2007) and university management (Ayikoru et al., 2009), innovative education activities are generally neither rewarded nor encouraged (Liburd & Hjalager, 2010). So, even if 'man produces himself through labour' (Marx & Engels, 1999: 21), which may hold true for academics in particular, the engagement and aims of the Global TEFI Courses should be put into further critical perspective.

Barnett (1990: 22) emphasizes that 'higher education implies more than the mere acquisition of knowledge. It requires a sceptical and questioning attitude towards knowledge'. In the context of the Global TEFI Courses it is imperative that the five value-sets are not seen as dogma but topics of critical reflection, where relevant. Adopting a relational and holistic understanding towards learning, where the entities of teaching and analysis are constituted in and through constantly unfolding processes, different relations of power and cultural values are a priori at stake (Liburd, 2010). Learning by making connections in different domains of life, between new concepts, things, phenomena, and existing knowledge will enable students (and learners outside of formal educational systems) to see the relationships both within and between topics in different and overlapping contexts. Hereby, students may be liberated from a partial knowledge perspective, which continues to limit the knowledge production and education of 'philosophic practitioners' (Tribe, 2002). Tourism educators in particular may appreciate that the epistemological key lies in multidisciplinary or indeed pluralist knowledge (Boisot, 1998; Liburd, 2012). Given its transnational scope, dynamisms, and pluralist epistemology, tourism education should be in a prime position to experiment with and drive inquiry into a new collaborative agenda for universities (Liburd, 2013).

References

Asraf, B. (2009). 'Teaching the Google-eyed YouTube Generation'. *Education + Training,* 51(5/6), 343–52.

Ayikoru, M., Tribe, J., & Airey, D. (2009). 'Reading Tourism Education: neoliberalism unveiled'. *Annals of Tourism Research,* 36(2), 191–221.

Barnett, R. (1990). *The Idea of Higher Education.* Buckingham: Open University Press.

Barnett, R. (2010). 'Foreword'. In I. Walsh & P. Kahn, *Collaborative Working in Higher Education* (pp. xv–xviii). New York: Routledge.

Blasco, M. (2009). 'Teaching the Hard Stuff: appending culture to interdisciplinary studies'. In M. Blasco & M. Zølner (Eds.), *Teaching Cultural Skills: adding culture in higher education* (pp. 11–40). Copenhagen: Nyt fra Samfundsvidenskaberne.

Benckendorff, P., Moscado, G., & Pendergast, D. (Eds.). (2010). *Tourism and Generation Y.* Wallingford: CABI.

Berry, D. M. (2008). *Copy, Rip, Burn. The politics of copyleft and open source.* London: Pluto Press.

Biggs, J., & Tang, C. (2007). *Teaching for Quality Learning at University,* 3rd edn. Maidenhead: Open University Press.

Boisot, M. (1998). *Securing Competitive Advantage in the Information Economy.* Oxford: Oxford University Press.

Christensen, I. F. (2009). 'How Can Examination Practices Reflect the Use of Collaborative Web 2.0 Tools in Courses?' *Conference Proceedings from Online Educa Berlin 2009.*

Dohn, N. B. (2009). 'Web 2.0: inherent tensions and evident challenges for education'. *International Journal of Computer-Supported Collaborative Learning,* 4(3). Available: http://www.citeulike.org/journal/springerlink-120055 (Accessed 2 May 2009).

Gunderson, L. H., Holling, C. S., Pritchard, L., & Peterson, G. D. (2005). 'Resilience of Large-scale Resource Systems'. In L.H. Gunderson & L. Pritchard, Jr. (Eds.), *Resilience and the Behaviour of Large-Scale Systems* (pp. 3–18). Washington, DC: Scope 60. Island Press.

Higgins, P. (2001). 'Comment on Teaching Anthropology through Performance'. *Anthropology & Education Quarterly,* 32(2), 254–526.

Hofstede, G. (2005). *Cultures and Organisations – software of the mind.* New York: McGraw-Hill.

Inui, Y., Wheller, D., & Lankford, S. (2006). 'Rethinking Tourism Education: what should schools teach?' *Journal of Hospitality, Leisure, Sport & Tourism Education.* 5(2), 25–36.

Kolb, D. A. (1984). *Experiential Learning.* Englewood Cliffs, NJ: Prentice Hall.

Lafayette, R. C. (2003). 'Culture in Second Language Learning and Teaching'. In D. L. Lange & R. M. Paige (Eds.), *Culture as the Core* (pp. 53–70). Charlotte, NC: Information Age Publishing.

Lave, J. & Wenger (1991). *Situated Learning.* Cambridge: Cambridge University Press.

Lee, B. C. & Wicks, B. (2010). 'Podcasts for Tourism Marketing: university and DMO collaboration'. *Journal of Hospitality, Leisure, Sport & Tourism Education,* 9(2), 102–14.

Liburd, J. J. (2010). 'Sustainable Tourism Development'. In J. J. Liburd & D. Edwards (Eds.), *Understanding the Sustainable Development of Tourism* (pp. 1–18). Oxford: Goodfellow Publishers.

Liburd, J. J. (2011) Introduction to Tourism. www.INNOTOUR.com, Student Area, TEFI Courses 2011.

Liburd, J. J. (2012). 'Tourism Research 2.0'. *Annals of Tourism Research,* 39(2), 883–907.

Liburd, J. J. (2013). 'Towards the Collaborative University: lessons from tourism education and research'. Professorial Dissertation. University of Southern Denmark.

Liburd, J. J., & Ren, C. (2009). 'Selling Difference: conceptualising culture in tourism education and management'. In M. Blasco & M. Zølner (Eds.), *Teaching Cultural Skills. Adding culture in higher education* (pp. 71–89). Copenhagen: Nyt fra Samfundsvidenskaberne.

Liburd, J. J., & Hjalager, A-M. (2010). 'Changing Approaches to Education, Innovation and Research: student experiences'. *Tourism Journal of Hospitality and Tourism Management,* 17, 12–20.

Liburd, J. J., & Hjalager, M. (2011). 'From Copyright to *Copyleft*: towards tourism education 2.0'. In *The Critical Turn in Tourism Studies,* 2nd edn (pp. 96–109). Abingdon: Routledge.

Liburd, J. J., & Christensen, I-M. F. (2012). 'Using Web 2.0 in Higher Tourism Education'. *Journal of Hospitality, Leisure, Sport and Tourism Education,* 12, 99–108.

McLaren, P., & Giroux, H. (1995). 'Radical Pedagogy as Cultural Politics: beyond the discourse of critique and anti-utopianism'. In P. McLaren (Ed.), *Critical Pedagogy and Predatory Culture* (pp. 29–57). London: Routledge.

Marx, K., & Engels, F. (1999). *The Communist Manifesto.* Oxford: Oxford University Press.

Merleu-Ponty, M. (1962). *Phenomenology of Perception*. London: Routledge & Kegan Paul.

Miller, G., & Twining-Ward, L. (2005). *Monitoring for a Sustainable Tourism Transition: the challenge of developing and using indicators,* Wallingford: CABI Publishing.

Munar, A. M. (2007). 'Is the Bologna Process Globalizing Tourism Education?' *Journal of Hospitality, Leisure, Sport & Tourism Education,* 6(2), 68–82.

Pedelty, M. (2001). 'Teaching Anthropology through Performance'. *Anthropology & Education Quarterly,* 32(2), 244–53.

Perkins, D. N. (1996). 'Minds in the Hood' (preface). In B.G. Wilson (Ed.), *Constructivist Learning Environments.* Englewood Cliffs, NJ: Educational Technology Publications.

Piaget, J. (1972). *Epistémologie des sciences de l'homme.* Paris: Gallimard.

Ramsden, P. (2003). *Learning to Teach in Higher Education,* 2nd edn. Abingdon: Routledge Falmer.

Richardson, W. (2009). *Blogs, Wikis, Podcasts, and Other Powerful Web Tools for Classrooms,* 2nd edn. London: Corwin Press.

Robinson, K., & Aronica, L. (2009). *The Element. How finding your passion changes everything.* London: Penguin Group.

Salmon, G. (2002). *E-tivities – the key to active online learning.* Abingdon: Routledge Falmer.

Sfard, A. (1998). 'On Two Metaphors of Learning and the Dangers of Choosing Just One'. *Educational Researcher,* 27(2), 4–13.

Sheldon, P., Fesenmaier, D., Woeber, C., Cooper, C., & Antonioli, M. (2008). 'Tourism Education Futures 2010–2030: building the capacity to lead'. *Journal of Travel and Tourism Teaching,* 7(3), 61–8.

Sigala, M. (2002). 'The Evolution of Internet Pedagogy: benefits for tourism and hospitality education'. *Journal of Hospitality, Leisure, Sport & Tourism Education,* 1(2), 27–42.

Thomson, J. (2007). 'Is Education 1.0 Ready for Web 2.0 Students?' *Journal of Online Education,* 3, 4. Available: http://www.innovateonline.info/pdf/vol3_issue4/Is_Education_1.0_Ready_for_Web_2.0_Students_.pdf (Accessed 31 May 2010).

Tourism Education Futures Initiative (TEFI). (2009). *A Values-based Framework for Tourism Education: building the capacity to lead.* Available: http://www.tourismeducationfutures.org/ (Accessed 2 February 2011).

Tribe, J. (2002). 'The Philosophic Practitioner', *Annals of Tourism Research,* 29(2), 338–57.

Tylor, M. C. (2009). 'The End of the University as We Know It'. *New York Times,* 26 April. Available: http://www.nytimes.com/2009/04/27/opinion/27taylor.html?_r=1 (Accessed 1 May 2009).

Vygotsky, L. S. (1992). [1926] *Educational Psychology.* Winter Park, FL: St Lucie Press.

23

Approaches in the design and delivery of hotel/hospitality management undergraduate degree programmes within Australia

Noreen M. Breakey, Richard N. S. Robinson and Matthew L. Brenner

UQ Business School, The University of Queensland, Brisbane, Australia

Introduction

Hospitality education is a relatively new academic arena which has expanded and developed rapidly (Williams, 2005a, 2005b). This growth is evident in Australia where the number of hotel/hospitality undergraduate degree programmes has evolved from two educational choices in the 1970s, to more than 40 degree programmes offered by 30 institutions today (Breakey & Craig-Smith, 2011). This growth reflects similar patterns in other countries such as the UK (Airey & Tribe, 2000; Craig-Smith, 1998), the USA (Boger, 2000; Chathoth & Sharma, 2007) and, more recently, China (Gu & Hobson, 2008; Xiao & Liu, 1995) and Brazil (Knowles *et al.*, 2003). Institutions that offer hotel/hospitality undergraduate degree programmes include universities, hotel schools, and technical/polytechnic colleges. Approaches to curriculum and delivery vary from institution to institution and sector to sector.

Dramatic increases in hotel/hospitality programme numbers have been in response to labour market demands for qualified candidates in the rapidly growing industry (Williams, 2005a). This has led to increasing competition between the hotel/hospitality programmes at Australian universities (King *et al.*, 2003). Programmes at most universities are developed out of existing course offerings (Riegel & Dallas, 1999). Consequently, hotel/hospitality programmes 'differ widely and lack the standardization that characterizes many traditional fields of study' (Williams, 2005a: 71). For this reason, hospitality educators are faced with the challenge of ensuring that curricula are industry relevant (Gursoy & Swanger, 2005) and academically sound.

There is much discussion regarding the concept of hospitality and the appropriate content for the curriculum (Craig-Smith & French, 1990; Morrison, 2006). While some researchers argue that hospitality curricula should focus on operational skills, others advocate in favour of generic transferable skills (e.g. Lashley, 2009; Martin & McCabe, 2007; Nickson, 2007; Nield, 2006; Tesone & Ricci, 2009). Scholars have discussed the merging of theoretical and practical elements, which has been termed 'professional education' (Dredge *et al.*, 2012a; Lum, 2009). Such intellectual debates are not unique to hospitality and can be seen as a healthy challenge necessary for the development of hospitality as an academic field (Morrison & O'Gorman, 2006). Indeed, it could be argued that hospitality education has evolved organically. Many of the works that inform this study's framework drill down to matters of curriculum and practice (e.g. Riegel & Dallas, 1999), yet the philosophy of education is a substantial discipline in its own right. With this in mind, the chapter limits itself to the philosophy of hospitality education in a broad and applied sense. Nonetheless, it aims to invigorate the debate underpinning hospitality education philosophies. Although this chapter reports on the findings of a study conducted in Australia, there is clearly an international relevance. A multi-tier hospitality education system that competes for student enrolments, and which is greatly influenced by industry recruitment also exists in many other parts of the world. Furthermore there is increasing globalization of both the hospitality/hotel degree providers, and the student cohort.

In preparing tomorrow's managers for the hospitality industry, programme directors are perpetually reassessing and reinventing their offerings (Ashley *et al.*, 1995). As Baum (2002) noted, the level of skills in the sector are determined by the social, economic, political and technological context within which the industry operates. Therefore, one of the most powerful forces that drives these changes in hospitality education is the industry itself. The industry dictates the set of skills and competencies that hospitality managers require at a particular time (Rowe, 1993). Some scholars argue that hospitality educators should resist these demands and focus on providing a more holistic educational approach which prepares graduates for the requirements of the present and develops the skills needed to face the challenges of the future (Airey & Tribe, 2000; Pavesic, 1993).

From this concept of a more holistic education arose a germane dialogue regarding hospitality studies as informing hospitality management. Although liberal arts based educational models for hospitality programmes date from the 1980s (e.g. Nailon, 1982), they gained traction in the 2000s as the benefits of reflective education became clear (Lashley, 1999; Lashley & Morrison, 2000). The liberal arts approach embraces multidisciplinary content from cultural studies, anthropology, philosophy and sociology (Morrison & O'Mahony, 2003) and has matured to a point where hospitality studies and management now coexist in curricula (Lashley *et al.*, 2007). The aim of these critical developments in hospitality education is more about cultivating a hospitality disposition among students, rather than skills per se.

Tribe (2002) argues that the proper balance within a tourism programme educates graduates to be 'philosophic practitioners'. This balance would not only prepare graduates to successfully enter the present workforce, but also lay the academic foundation necessary for long-term career and personal growth. Many scholars have argued that a balance between vocational and reflective abilities is needed to prepare future industry leaders with the skills to critically examine the cultural, philosophical, sociological and environmental impacts of tourism and hospitality (Belhassen & Caton, 2011; Inui *et al.*, 2006; Ring *et al.*, 2009).

Hospitality education: approaches

Scholars are beginning to develop classifications of hospitality programmes in order to better understand the field. Riegel and Dallas (1999) proposed that there are five approaches to hospitality degree programmes: tourism, foods and home economics, craft and skill, business administration and, finally, a combined approach. Craig-Smith (1998) classified hospitality degree programmes based on their level of hospitality focus, ranging from degrees specifically focused on hospitality to general degrees with just a few hospitality courses. Recent trends have somewhat complicated these classifications. As a result, Breakey and Craig-Smith (2007) proposed a revised typology which includes hospitality-focused, non-hospitality-focused and hybrid programme types which combine hospitality with either business or tourism.

The increasing diversity of programmes has confronted hospitality educators with the following questions:

- Can there be an established and comprehensive framework or model for the design of hospitality programmes and their curriculum?
- Does such a framework or model have the ability to garner unanimous agreement from all stakeholders in the field of hospitality education?

To date, there is no single dominant or established framework which exists for the purposes of informing the design or delivery of hospitality education. Nonetheless, valuable information on underlying approaches to hospitality education can be gleaned from the extant literature. Based on earlier work (Breakey et al., 2011), we devise a series of spectrums describing known approaches to hospitality education comprising, first, programme orientation spectrums and, second, curriculum design, delivery and structure spectrums (see Figure 23.1). Each of these spectrums will be discussed briefly below.

Programme orientation approaches

Industry–academia

The first approach spectrum captures an industry-driven orientation versus an academic-driven orientation. Currently, the general academic consensus is to design hospitality education

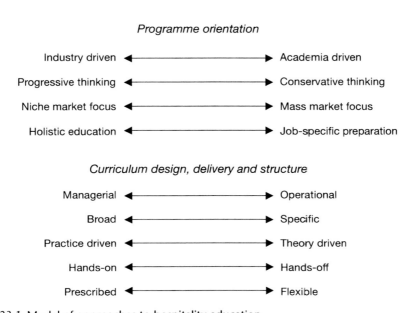

Figure 23.1 Model of approaches to hospitality education

curricula according to industry demands (Chung, 2000; Lefever & Withiam, 1998; Swanger & Gursoy, 2007). Some have advocated for a more pragmatic approach to higher education via direct collaborations with industry (Szambowski et al., 2002). A criticism of this approach is that an overly industry-driven orientation is focused too heavily on the past and the present and can often ignore the industry's future needs (Pavesic, 1991b, 1993). Proponents of a more academic approach maintain that critical, analytical and problem-solving skills are required for future industry leaders to meet future challenges in a rapidly globalizing field (Inui et al., 2006; Pavesic, 1991b, 1993).

Progressive thinking–conservative thinking

The second spectrum examines progressive versus conservative programme orientation. Advocates of the progressive approach maintain that hospitality curricula should be innovative, proactive, designed to anticipate future issues, and avoid a narrow focus on current industry needs (Pavesic, 1991b, 1993). A progressive approach is also supported by scholars who argue that reflective practice should be incorporated into hospitality education (Lashley, 1999). Conversely, supporters of a conservative approach argue that educators should not take risks with curricula design and hence it should be grounded in readily apparent realities and established protocol (Powers & Riegel, 1993).

Mass market–niche market

The third spectrum examines mass market versus niche market approaches. The mass market approach could be described as a standardized programme, which aims to replicate the curriculum of its competitors in the hospitality education marketplace. Proponents of a niche market approach, on the other hand, maintain that each programme must find its niche, and focus on serving that niche. Pavesic (1991a) and Powers and Riegel (1993) are proponents of the niche market approach, and argue that trying to be all things to all people will lead to mediocrity in hospitality education. Pavesic (1991a: 38) states that, 'there is no room in most programme core requirements to include courses representing all areas of the hospitality industry to the satisfaction of advocates in each industry segment'. Niche market supporters advise programmes to focus their design on the needs of the unique population they are trying to serve (Powers & Riegel, 1993). Interestingly, while there is academic discussion regarding the mass market approach, no support for this end of the spectrum was found anywhere in the literature to date.

Holistic–job specific

The fourth spectrum addresses holistic versus job-specific approaches. Proponents of a holistic approach suggest university education should prepare students for a full, rewarding and productive life. Education should have the potential to influence the total development of students, not just prepare them for a specific job (Lashley et al., 2007; Morrison & O'Mahony, 2003; Pavesic, 1991a; Riegel, 1990). Our literature review did not find any support for a job specific orientation in the design of bachelor-level hospitality education programmes.

Curriculum design, delivery and structure approaches

Managerial–operational

The first spectrum geared to curriculum design concerns managerial versus operational emphases. Advocates of a managerial approach maintain that in order to develop future industry leaders curricula need to develop an academic foundation which will foster lifelong learning. They maintain this approach can best meet the demands of an ever-changing marketplace, rather than just producing day-one technically efficient employees (Marshall, 1997; Powers & Riegel, 1993; Sheldon *et al.*, 2008; Umbreit, 1992). This, however, does not minimize the importance of day-one operational skills according to Pavesic (1991a), who maintains that certain operational skills training such as culinary arts, bartending and front office activities are very important, though are better acquired at an associate programme level where the curriculum is focused on instilling technical expertise. The majority of the literature advocates for a managerial approach, as per the citations above (see also Ingram, 1999; Tews & van Hoof, 2011), rather than an operational approach to bachelor-level hospitality programmes.

Broad–specific

The second spectrum concerns broad versus specific programme orientation. Proponents of a broadly designed curriculum maintain a more generalist approach and believe that hospitality education should teach concepts that have more universal applications. They maintain that an overly specific curricula design often produces graduates who cannot think analytically or transfer concepts from one discipline to another. To avoid this, Pavesic (1993) recommends that hospitality programmes broaden their curriculum and not limit themselves to a myopic, world-according-to-hospitality perspective. In contrast to this perspective, Tews and van Hoof (2011) maintain that a hospitality-based curriculum best prepares a graduate to enter the hospitality field. They argue that a general business emphasis ignores the unique hospitality-related concepts and theories expected of a graduate when entering the industry.

Practice–theory

The third spectrum addresses practice versus theory. Pavesic (1993) classifies academics as individuals who examine theory, while industry professionals focus on proven practices. Proponents of a theoretical approach suggest that teaching practice without a theoretical base does not provide a proper academic foundation to fully comprehend the nature of the practice, and will inhibit the ability to develop new theories in the future (Pavesic, 1993). For this reason many scholars argue for curricula grounded in theoretical perspectives drawn from the social sciences (e.g. Airey & Tribe, 2000; Morrison & O'Mahony, 2003). This is not to say that scholars dismiss the importance of practice. Many scholars maintain that theory is best comprehended when a student has the benefit of learning a concept, and then has the opportunity to apply the understanding to a real-world situation (Cooper *et al.*, 2010). Proponents of the integration of theory and practice maintain that learning occurs when students reflect on their engagement in work practice using theoretical concepts and models (Cooper *et al.*, 2010). Dredge *et al.* (2012a) term these programmes 'professional education'. Marshall (1997) proposed an educational model that blends both approaches by maintaining a faculty of non-doctorate industry professionals and academics with PhDs, incorporating expertise in theory and practice. No publications to date support a strictly practice-driven curricula approach.

Hands-on–hands-off

The fourth approach refers to how course content is delivered: hands-on versus hands-off. Riegel and Dallas (1999) describe several hotel and restaurant programmes in the USA that have production labs designed to assist in hands-on teaching through an interactive learning process. They praise these education systems for being able to provide work experience for students in addition to classroom teaching. No research to date explicitly praises completely hands-off learning experiences.

Prescribed–flexible

The fifth and final spectrum deals with the structure of the programme: prescribed versus flexible. This spectrum reflects the level of autonomy given to students in choosing the mix and timing of their own courses. Pavesic (1991a) argues that students should not be allowed to take courses on an à la carte basis or they will never see how the courses integrate into the larger body of knowledge or, in other words, see the big picture. Allowing students to take courses out of sequence often disregards the academic foundation needed for comprehension of more complex higher level theory. Students may also see courses as separate entities, and may be quick to discard any material found to be inapplicable to their current jobs or specific career interests. No publications so far advocate a flexible curriculum, although operationally a certain nimbleness is required by educators and management to account for circumstances such as staff and resourcing availability, unforeseen circumstances and the like. Clearly, flexible in this context refers to the degree to which students can customize or individualize their programme of study.

University, hotel school or college? – What is your orientation?

In this study the model of approaches of hospitality education (Figure 23.1) was utilized to examine the philosophical differences and similarities of three institutions in Australia: a university, The University of Queensland, School of Tourism (UQST); a hotel school, Blue Mountains International Hotel Management School (BMIHMS); and a technical/polytechnic college, the Northern Melbourne Institute of TAFE (NMIT). The material collected on each institution was that available publically in 2010 as this is the information that both industry and potential students could access when considering the offerings of the various providers. The analysis considered the similarities and differences across the provider, programme and course levels. Categorization into the model was undertaken collectively by members of the research team. In addition, the Programme Directors from the respective institutions were all involved in reviewing the initial categorization to ensure their institution and programme were represented appropriately. As Robinson, Breakey and Craig-Smith (2010) noted, a perennial problem confronting any researcher investigating cross-institutional education delivery is the varying use of nomenclature. For the purpose of this chapter, the building block of a degree programme is called a course.

Provider-level comparison

The University of Queensland, School of Tourism (UQST), a member of the Australian Group of Eight Universities, offers a Bachelor of International Hotel and Tourism. The Blue Mountains International Hotel Management School (BMIHMS) represents a traditional Swiss-style hotel school and offers a Bachelor of Business in International Hotel and Resort Management. The Northern Melbourne Institute of TAFE (NMIT) is a technical/polytechnic institution which offers a Bachelor of Hospitality Management. To undertake the provider-level comparison, the marketing material of each of the institutions was reviewed. This highlights the focus and priorities of each provider.

UQST offers a comprehensive range of hospitality undergraduate, postgraduate coursework and postgraduate higher degree research programmes, which at the bachelor level is the Bachelor of International Hotel and Tourism Management. 'These programmes and courses are professionally-oriented and academically rigorous and aimed at meeting the needs of students seeking rewarding careers in areas such as tourism, hotel, leisure and event management' (UQST, 2010).

BMIHMS is part of Laureate International Universities which has more than 50 accredited institutions within 21 countries offering career-focused, undergraduate, Master's, and doctoral degree programmes to more than 550,000 students. The mission of BMIHMS is 'to offer the best hand-on experience, academic curriculum, and professional internships to create the leaders of tomorrow' (BMIHMS, 2010). The institution offers the Bachelor of Business (International Hotel and Resort Management).

The mission of NMIT is to deliver 'vocational training and higher education for a global workforce' (NMIT, 2009: 2) and has the vision that 'the graduates will be recognized as practical and solution oriented, making meaningful contributions to their chosen field of endeavour' (NMIT, 2010: 3). NMIT also has six training centres where students develop practical skills through supervised work designed to mirror real-work environments. The offering of hospitality programmes begins with Certificate I and progresses up to their Bachelor of Hospitality Management.

These three institutions position themselves very differently. The University of Queensland positions itself as a research intensive institution and, by implication, its teaching and learning are informed by the latest research that its staff both generate and have access to. On the other hand, the BMIHMS positions itself as a dedicated provider of hospitality and hotel management education on the Swiss hotel school model and claims to have a refined fit-for-purpose educational product. Finally, NMIT offers hospitality education as one of a suite of vocational programmes, with the emphasis of all programmes being on skills-based learning outcomes for graduates. To consider how these three differing institutions articulate their educational philosophies in practice we drill down to the programme, and then course levels, for comparative purposes.

Programme-level comparison

UQST offers a Bachelor of International Hotel and Tourism Management programme which is a three-year degree and comprises a total of 24 courses, with 12 core courses and six additional courses required for a Major. Studies may be undertaken with a major or double major in Hotel Management, Tourism Management and/or Event Management. Students also complete a compulsory industry placement as part of a Professional Development course.

The BMIHMS has a Bachelor of Business (International Hotel and Resort Management) degree which is a three-year programme offered in an accelerated two-and-a-half-year full-time format. BMIHMS works closely with the industry, ensuring the programme offers industry relevant course content. The programme comprises 12 compulsory core courses, 12 compulsory hospitality specialization courses, plus two internships totalling 600 hours. Following the Swiss hospitality education model students also learn in a simulated operational hotel, which is part of the BMIHMS campus.

NMIT offers a three-year full-time Bachelor of Hospitality Management programme. The programme focuses on the knowledge and skills required to manage hotels, motels, restaurants, convention facilities and events in a range of business environments. The programme comprises 26 core courses which include two slots of industry work placement completed in the second and third years of the programme.

These degree programmes share a similar number of required courses, ranging from 24 to 26. Considering the courses within each of the programmes, it is clear that there are some common business courses, including accounting and marketing, and common hospitality-specific courses, such as food and beverage management (see Table 23.1). There are also some courses that appear consistent across two of the three providers (see Table 23.2). Finally, there

Table 23.1 Similar course offerings across all three programmes

UQST Hotel Management Major	BMIHMS	NMIT
Accounting For Decision Making	Accounting Fundamentals	Accounting for Decision Makers
Financial Mgmt.	Accounting Revenue Mgmt. (Specialized Subject)	Finance
Business Law	Business Law	Business Law
Introduction to Mgmt.	Mgmt. & Leadership	Mgmt. Principles
Hospitality Small Business Operations	Business Mgmt. & Entrepreneurship	Business Planning & Entrepreneurship
Foundations of Marketing	Marketing Fundamentals	Marketing Principles
Tourism & Travel Marketing (Elective)	Services Marketing (Specialized Subject)	Sales & Marketing Mgmt.
Introduction to Human Resource Mgmt.	Human Resource Mgmt.	Human Resource Mgmt.
Tourism, Leisure, Hospitality: Principles	Introduction to the International Hospitality Industry	Introduction to the Hospitality Industry
Food & Beverage Mgmt.	Food & Beverage Operations Mgmt. Food & Beverage Mgmt. & Control	Food & Beverage Mgmt. 1 Food & Beverage Mgmt. 2
Hotel Mgmt. Technology Applications	Business Communication & Technology	Hospitality Mgmt. Information Systems
Qualitative Business Research Methods (Elective)	Research Skills & Practices	Research & Analysis in the Hospitality Industry
Quantitative Business Research Methods (Elective)		
Global Cultures & Tourism	Cross-cultural Issues in Tourism & Hospitality	International Culinary Culture

are also noticeable differences between the courses covered and the focus of particular specializations within the three programmes (see Table 23.3). In addition, it is worth noting that the programmes offered by the BMIHMS and NMIT are prescribed, with all students taking the same courses. In contrast a student taking the Hotel Management Major within UQST's programme has three-quarters of the programme prescribed and the final six courses as electives. These electives may be selected from the other Majors within UQST, such as courses presented in Tables 23.1, 23.2 and 23.3; selected to further extend an existing business-based course, such as marketing; or selected from the broader university offerings, such as a language course.

Course-level comparison

For purposes of comparison, a Food and Beverage (F&B) and a Marketing course within each of the programmes were analysed. In selecting the courses for comparison, courses with similar names and structure were selected (see 23.4 for the courses selected).

Table 23.2 Similar course offerings across two of the three programmes

UQST Hotel Management Major	BMIHMS	NMIT
	Rooms Division Mgmt.	Accommodation Mgmt. 1
		Accommodation Mgmt. 2
	Economics	Economics
	Strategic Planning & Mgmt.	Strategic Business
	Hotel & Resort Facilities Mgmt. & Design	Facilities Mgmt. & Design
Professional Development		Industry Practicum 1
		Industry Practicum 2
Managing Service in Tourism International Services Mgmt.		Services Mgmt.
Event Operations Mgmt. (Elective)		Planning Event Mgmt. 1
Event Mgmt. Principles & Practices (Elective)		Event Mgmt. 2
International Hotel Mgmt. Operations	Operations & Environment Mgmt. (Specialized Subject)	

Aim and content of the courses

Food and beverage courses

The UQST F&B Management course aims to introduce students to the core principles and practices of food and beverage management systems which optimize the marginal and operational efficiency of food and beverage production and service facilities in the international hotel industry. The course is theory based and does not contain a hands-on practical component. Modules in the course include an overview of Food and Beverage Management; The Menu; Bar and Beverage; Systems Models; Financial Management for Food and Beverage; Marketing for Food and Beverage; Food and Beverage, Society and Culture; International Hotel Food and Beverage Management; and International Food and Beverage Management.

BMIHMS offers two F&B courses, though for the purposes of comparison Food and Beverage Management and Control was selected. The aim of the course is to introduce students to the theories, concepts and skills required for effective control and management of Food and Beverage Operations. The course is industry-specific and incorporates lectures and tutorials; it is delivered through hands-on food production and service sessions. The course builds upon the skills and knowledge introduced in F&B Operations Management and introduces the key factors of control together with operational aspects of a successful food and beverage outlet.

Similar to the BMIHMS, NMIT also offers two Food and Beverage courses. For purposes of comparison F&B Management 2 was selected. The aim of this course is to extend the knowledge, skills and understanding of the concepts, principles and theories of management in contemporary commercial food and beverage operations. In this course students observe, analyse and apply information and management systems in a range of food and beverage operations. This course is hands-on and industry specific.

Table 23.3 Unique course offerings within the three programmes

UQST Hotel Management Major	BMIHMS	NMIT
International Hotel Mgmt. & Operations	Organizational Development & Change Mgmt.	Project Mgmt.
International Gaming Mgmt.	Contemporary Issues in Tourism, Hospitality & Events Mgmt.	Hospitality Management Systems
Festivals & Special Events (Elective)	Tourism & Hospitality Business Ethics	
Event Sponsorship & Fundraising (Elective)	Specialist Resort Facilities Mgmt. [Golf/Spa]	
Event Mgmt. & the Arts (Elective)		
Meetings & Conventions Mgmt. (Elective)		
International Event Mgmt. (Elective)		
Commercial Recreation Entrepreneurship (Elective)		
Adventure Recreation & Tourism (Elective)		
Sport Management (Elective)		
Leisure Venues & Attractions (Elective)		
Tourism & Leisure Behaviour		
Principles of Sustainable Tourism		
Sustainability for Tourism Business (Elective)		
Sport Management (Elective)		
International Transport & Tour Operation (Elective)		
Travel Distribution Mgmt. (Elective)		
Travel & Tourism Planning (Elective)		
Tourism: Principles & Practices (Elective)		
Travel & Transport Systems (Elective)		

Table 23.4 Summary of selected courses

Course title	Duration	Contact hours per week
F & B Mgmt. (UQST)	1 semester	2 hours lecture + 1 hour tutorial
F & B Mgmt. & Control (BMIHMS)	1 semester	13 hours per week
F & B Mgmt. 2 (NMIT)	Not specified	Not specified
Foundations of Marketing (UQST)	1 semester	2 hours lecture + 1 hour tutorial
Marketing Fundamentals (BMIHMS)	1 semester	4 hours
Marketing Principles (NMIT)	Not specified	Not specified

Marketing courses

The aim of the Foundations of Marketing course offered by UQST is to provide students with an introduction to the role of marketing, its importance in contemporary organizations and the socially responsible role marketers have when influencing the attitudes and buying behaviour of the consumer. The course introduces students to the theories of markets, consumer behaviour, applications of behavioural science and basic marketing principles and is delivered by the UQ School of Business.

The aim of the Marketing Fundamentals course offered by the BMIHMS is to develop students' skills and knowledge of the operating environment, and to recognize the basic principles and practices of marketing in relation to the importance of the consumer and market trends. Similarly, the Marketing Principles course offered by NMIT provides students with an understanding of the concepts, philosophies and practices of marketing. In summary, the philosophical foundation of all three marketing courses offered is very similar in concept, philosophy and practice.

Course texts

Consistency in the content of these courses is maintained by the utilization of similar core textbooks. UQST and NMIT's food and beverage courses use the same text. All three institutions use the same textbook for their marketing courses.

Assessment methods of courses

An analysis of student assessment methods indicates both similarities and differences among the three institutions (see Table 23.5). All six courses have three assessment components and a written final exam. However, the F&B courses indicate vast differences within the assessment methods. For example, in addition to the final examination, the UQST's F&B course is assessed through a consultancy report and a reflective journal. On the other hand, BMIHMS's F&B course has a tutorial and practicum portfolio. While NMIT's F&B course comprises practical components, the assessment of the course is based solely on written assessments. Within the marketing courses both BMIHMS and UQST have a group assignment and a group presentation, whereas the NMIT course has individual assessments only.

Discussion

The provider, programme and course profiles of the three institutions can be placed on the model of approaches to hospitality education (see Figure 23.2). This figure shows the

Table 23.5 Assessment methods

Course title & (programme)	Method	Percentage
F&B Mgmt.	Individual reflective journal	20
(UQST)	F & B consultancy research project	40
	Final written examination	40
F & B Mgmt. & Control	Tutorial and practicum portfolio	40
(BMIHMS)	Analytical supervisor report	20
	Final written examination	40
F &B Mgmt. 2	Written test	30
(NMIT)	Written assignment	40
	Final written examination	30
Foundations of Marketing	Group assignment	25
(UQST)	Presentation (combined group and individual)	25
	Final written examination	50
Marketing Fundamentals	In-class multiple choice examination	30
(BMIHMS)	Group presentation	30
	Final written examination	40
Marketing Principles	Class test	20
(NMIT)	Written assignment	40
	Final written examination	40

Programme orientation

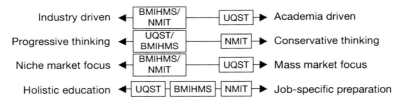

Curriculum design, delivery and structure

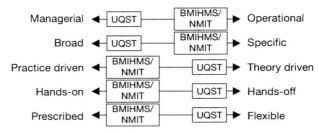

Figure 23.2 Model of approaches to hospitality education applied to the three Australian providers

approximate location of each institution on the four spectrums of programme orientation, and the five spectrums of the curriculum design, delivery and structure.

Analysis of the programme orientation spectrums

Due to the practical orientation of the programme content of both BMIHMS and NMIT, these higher education providers are placed on the 'Industry-driven' end of the continuum. This reflects the general academic consensus that the curricula must meet industry demands (Chung, 2000; Lefever & Withiam, 1998; Swanger & Gursoy, 2007). In contrast, UQST programme offerings lean more towards the 'Academia-driven' end of the continuum, an academic orientation supported by Pavesic (1991b, 1993).

Analysis of the programme orientation indicates that all three institutions appear to include a number of progressive elements, which are combined with some traditional elements, placing all three towards the centre of the 'Progressive–Conservative thinking' continuum. For example UQST offers courses such as Principles of Sustainability and BMIHMS covers Organizational Development and Change Management. However, without a review of the details of all of the courses it is not possible to determine the true location of each offering on the Progressive–Conservative spectrum.

As the BMIHMS and NMIT have small intakes and class numbers with a specific focus on hospitality/hotel/resort management, these institutions are towards the 'Niche market' end of the spectrum. Contrary to this, the UQST has large student cohorts, and students may be focused on a number of related areas, such as tourism, leisure, marketing, human resources, a language or psychology, and undertaking various electives in a self-directed pattern, placing this institution on the 'Mass market' end of the continuum.

In addition to a variety of broad-ranging courses, as well as the honours programme and with the four different major offerings, UQST is located on the 'Holistic education' end of the continuum. On the other hand, both BMIHMS and NMIT with the aim of imparting knowledge of food and beverage and rooms division operations are on the 'Job-specific preparation' end of the continuum. However, BMIHMS is located closer to the middle of this continuum as they also aim for broader development of the student, evidenced by their student-centred extra-curricular hospitality-based residential living experiential programmes. Job-specific preparation of students is supported by Riegel (1990), who notes that a college (university) education should include preparation for a full, rewarding and productive life – as opposed to a full, rewarding and productive career alone.

Programme curriculum design, delivery and structure spectrums

The curriculum design, delivery and structure offered by UQST lie more towards the 'Managerial' aspect of the model. The UQST programme has 17 courses with management in the title while BMIHMS and NMIT have 12 and 14 occurrences of management in course titles respectively. In contrast, the latter two institutions' programmes aim to combine the managerial aspects with the operational needs, placing them in the middle of this continuum.

The UQST programme is very broad, offering a range of elective courses as well as specialization courses. The degree offers majors in Hotel Management, Tourism Management, Event Management and Commercial Recreation and Sport. As such, this programme is on the 'Broad' end of the spectrum. BMIHMS and NMIT offer many specialization courses in their programmes. Hence, BMIHMS and NMIT appear at the 'Specific' end of the spectrum.

Therefore, it can be concluded that both BMIHMS and NMIT are geared towards industry's need for people with practical skills, an orientation advocated by Connolly and McGing (2006).

Both BMIHMS and NMIT's programmes have hands-on practical components. This reflects the course offerings in some of the hotel and restaurant programmes, such as in the USA (Riegel & Dallas, 1999). Conversely, UQST's programme has few practical elements. As such both BMIHMS and NMIT are located on the 'Hands-on', 'Practice-driven' ends of the model whereas UQST's programme is on the other end of the 'Hands-off' and 'Theory-driven' continuums.

Both BMIHMS and NMIT's programmes have prescribed courses. On the contrary, UQST's programme has some degree of student choice and so is categorized as 'Flexible', predominantly in the offering of elective courses. The course offerings at BMIHM are highly prescriptive, a programme design criticized by Pavesic (1993) who states that programmes with such a focus produce hospitality managers who cannot think analytically or transfer concepts from one discipline to another. Interestingly, the UQST programme offering is in contrast to Pavesic's (1991a) earlier view that students should not be allowed to take courses on an 'à la carte' basis. While there is a substantial core and major requirements, a prescribed order, or pathway mapping, is not enforced on students at UQST. Moreover, their freedom of choice regarding electives does provide some flexibility.

Conclusion and future research

This chapter has highlighted the similarities and differences across three Australian bachelor degree granting institutions through an examination of curriculum orientation, design and delivery. Our findings indicate that there are considerable differences from programme to programme. While BMIHMS and NMIT share similar industry-driven approaches, offer job-specific preparation and provide for a niche cohort of students, UQST's programme is more academically driven, progressive, aims to provide a holistic education and has a mass market approach. UQST's curriculum (i.e. design, delivery and structure) is based on a broad, managerial, theory-driven and hands-off approach which is offered in a more flexible manner. Conversely, BMIHMS and NMIT offer programmes that are more specific, practice-driven and hands-on, and balance managerial and operational aspects, within a more prescriptive structure.

From this comparative study some key insights to the different approaches to hotel/hospitality education across three educational sectors can be extrapolated. UQST's style of curriculum is more 'committed to higher order social science and humanities knowledge and teaching and learning practices, seeking to deliver graduate capabilities within this focus' (Dredge et al., 2012a: 2169–70). BMIHMS and NMIT are 'primarily committed to graduates' capabilities and will deliver social science and humanities knowledge to the extent that it supports graduates' capabilities' (Dredge et al., 2012a: 2170). Our findings indicate that despite some similar course offerings, two distinct approaches to hospitality and hotel education are discernible in Australia. Programme design which is mindful of these different approaches can assist administrators and educators to define programme orientation, develop curricula, and position their offerings in the marketplace. Emphasizing the strengths of each approach can assist industry partners and potential students in understanding the available options and making more informed choices.

These findings echo the rhetoric evident in much recent tourism education scholarship, which recognizes the complexity of contemporary education, particularly the tension between vocational versus liberal outcomes (Dredge et al., 2012a; Tribe, 2002). More specifically, the polarization of various indicators on the spectrum suggests UQST leans further towards a liberal orientation while BMIHMS and NMIT are inclined towards vocational ends. While this is revelatory of a philosophy of hospitality education to some degree, however, there is no evidence from the current study that any of the institutions subjected to analysis were adopting elements of hospitality studies, and broader social science perspectives, as advocated since Nailon (1982) and reiterated by Lashley et al. (2007). While it could be assumed that a university, with a liberal orientation, might be more naturally inclined to adopt broader social science perspectives, it is intriguing to consider the possibility that vocationally oriented providers, such as hotel schools and colleges, might also be seeking such outcomes. This is suggestive of the fact that the liberal/vocational and university/hotel school/college approaches might not be entirely mutually exclusive. Moreover, it has been observed that accreditation requirements across various educational jurisdictions have contributed to a convergence of programmes across sectors. For example hospitality management academics are invited as programme deliverers, designers, examiners, auditors and even agents in the formal accreditation (e.g. the Tertiary Education Quality Standards Agency, in Australia) for, and of, other institutions (see Dredge et al., 2012b).

Clearly, the current study has offered insights into a number of dimensions that reveal aspects of the philosophy of three distinctly different hospitality education providers. Agendas for future research investigating the underpinning philosophies could, however, drill down further into course content to consider disciplinary foundations and perspectives. Moreover, this study only compared three institutions at the provider, programme and course level. Future research could encompass more Australian bachelor programmes, as well as other institutions outside Australia to gain a global perspective. Further research might also examine the marketing of programmes, cost of enrolment, average class size, certification of instructors, graduate employment rate and career trajectories as well as student perspectives as to whether the idiosyncrasies of the programme typologies modelled in this chapter reflect in their perceived graduate outcomes. Analysis of these factors can further illuminate how different philosophical approaches influence the success of hotel/hospitality bachelor degree programmes and their graduates.

Acknowledgements

The authors wish to acknowledge the Blue Mountains International Hotel Management School for their initial funding of the project; the Programme Directors at the three institutions for their support of the project; and the research partners and assistants who worked with us on various stages of the project: Helen Batey, Dominic Szambowski, Bjorn Shen, Aishath Shakeela and Motaz Zaitouni.

References

Airey, D., & Tribe, J. (2000). 'Education for Hospitality'. In C. Lashley & A. Morrison (Eds.), In Search of Hospitality: theoretical perspectives and debates, (pp. 276–92). Oxford: Butterworth Heinemann.

Ashley, R. A., Bach, S. A., Chessar, J. W., Ellis, E. T., Ford, R. C., & LeBruto, S. M. (1995). 'A Customer-based Approach to Hospitality Education'. Hotel and Restaurant Administration Quarterly, 36(4), 74–9.

Baum, T. (2002). 'Skills and Training for the Hospitality Sector: a review of issues'. Journal of Vocational Education and Training, 54(3), 343–64.

Belhassen, Y., & Caton, K. (2011). 'On the Need for Critical Pedagogy in Tourism Education', Tourism Management, 32, 1389–96.

Blue Mountains International Hotel Management School (BMIHMS). (2010). 'About' Blue Mountains International Hotel Management School. Available: http://www.bluemountains.edu.au/about-us/ (Accessed10 April 2010).

Boger, C. A. (2000). 'The Future of the Hospitality Curriculum: a criteria for evaluating general or specific curriculum tracks'. Frontiers in Southeast CHRIE Hospitality and Tourism Research, 3(2), 63–5.

Breakey, N. M., & Craig-Smith, S. J. (2007). 'Hospitality Degree Programs in Australia: a continuing evolution'. *Journal of Hospitality and Tourism Management*, 14(2), 102–18.

Breakey, N. M., & Craig-Smith, S. J. (2011). 'One Vision? Or Many Visions? trends and developments in tourism, hospitality, events & leisure degree programs throughout Australia'. Paper presented at the 9th APacCHRIE Conference, 2–5 June, Hong Kong.

Breakey, N. M., Robinson, R. N. S., Szambowski, D., & Craig-Smith, S. (2011). 'Australian Hospitality Education: a "brilliant blend" of degree programs'. Paper presented at CAUTHE Conference, 9–11 February, Adelaide.

Chathoth, P. K., & Sharma, A. (2007). 'Core Curricular Issues in hospitality and Tourism Education: present structure and future directions'. *Journal of Hospitality & Tourism Education*, 19(1), 10–19.

Chung, K. (2000). 'Hotel Management Curriculum Reform Based on Required Competencies of Hotel Employees and Career Success in the Hotel Industry'. *Tourism Management*, 21(5), 473–87.

Connolly, P., & McGing, G. (2006). 'Graduate Education and Hospitality Management in Ireland'. *International Journal of Contemporary Hospitality Management*, 18(1), 50–9.

Cooper, L., Orrell, J., & Bowden, M. (2010). *Work Integrated Learning: a guide to effective practice.* New York: Routledge.

Craig-Smith, S. J. (1998). 'Degree Programs for the Tourism Industry in Australia: their development, evolution and future direction'. Unpublished Master's, University of Queensland, Brisbane.

Craig-Smith, S. J., & French, C. (1990). 'Australian Hospitality and Tourism Education: current issues and future directions'. *Hospitality Research Journal*, 14(2), 617–19.

Dredge, D., Benckendorff, P., Day, M., Gross, M. J., Walo, M., Weeks, P., & Whitelaw, P. (2012a). 'The Philosophic Practitioner and the Curriculum Space'. *Annals of Tourism Research*, 39(4), 2154–76.

Dredge, D., Benckendorff, P., Day, M., Gross, M. J., Walo, M., Weeks, P., & Whitelaw, P. A. (2012b). 'Building a Stronger Future: balancing professional and liberal education ideals in tourism and hospitality education'. Office of Teaching and Learning Report, Australian Government.

Gu, H., & Hobson, P. (2008). 'The Dragon is Roaring . . . the development of tourism, hospitality & event management education in China'. *Journal of Hospitality & Tourism Education*, 20(1), 20–9.

Gursoy, D., & Swanger, N. (2005). 'An Industry-Driven Model of Hospitality Curriculum for Programs Housed in Accredited Colleges of Business: part II'. *Journal of Hospitality & Tourism Education*, 17(2), 46–56.

Ingram, H. (1999). 'Hospitality: a framework for a millennial review'. *International Journal of Contemporary Hospitality Management*, 11(4), 140–8.

Inui, Y., Wheeler, D., & Lankford, S. (2006). 'Rethinking Tourism Education: what should schools teach?'. *Journal of Hospitality, Leisure, Sport & Tourism Education*, 5(2), 25–35.

King, B., McKercher, B., & Waryszak, R. (2003). 'A Comparative Study of Hospitality and Tourism Graduates in Australia and Hong Kong'. *International Journal of Tourism Research*, 5(6), 409–20.

Knowles, T., Teixeria, R. M., & Egan, D. (2003). 'Tourism and Hospitality Education in Brazil and the UK: a comparison'. *International Journal of Contemporary Hospitality Management*, 15(1), 45–51.

Lashley, C. (1999). 'On Making Silk Purses: developing reflective practitioners in hospitality management education'. *International Journal of Contemporary Hospitality Management*, 11(4), 180–5.

Lashley, C. (2009). 'The Right Answers to the Wrong Questions? Observations on skill development and training in the United Kingdom's hospitality sector'. *Tourism and Hospitality Research*, 9(4), 340–52.

Lashley, C. & Morrison, A. (Eds.). (2000). *In Search of Hospitality: Theoretical Perspectives and Debates.* Oxford: Butterworth Heinemann.

Lashley, C., Lynch, P., & Morrison, A. (Eds.). (2007). *Hospitality: A Social Lens.* Oxford: Elsevier.

Lefever, M. M., & Witham, G. (1998). 'Curriculum Review: how industry views hospitality education'. *Cornell Hotel and Restaurant Administration Quarterly*, 39(4), 70–8.

Lum, G. (2009). *Vocational and Professional Education.* London: Continuum International Publishing.

Marshall, A. G. (1997). 'Taking the Hospitality Industry to School'. *Hotel and Motel Management*, 212(13), 17.

Martin, E., & McCabe, S. (2007). 'Part-Time Work and Postgraduate Students: developing the skills for employment?'. *Journal of Hospitality, Leisure, Sport & Tourism Education*, 6(2), 29–40.

Morrison, A. (2006). 'New Curriculum: hospitality studies'. Paper presented at the CAUTHE Conference, 6–9 January, Melbourne, Australia.

Morrison, A., & O'Gorman, K. D. (2006). 'Hospitality Studies: liberating the power of the mind', Paper presented at the CAUTHE Conference, 6–9 February, Melbourne, Australia.

Morrison, A., & O'Mahony, G.B. (2003). 'The Liberation of Hospitality Management Education'. *International Journal of Contemporary Hospitality Management*, 15(1), 38–44.

Nailon, P. (1982). 'Theory in Hospitality Management'. *International Journal of Hospitality Management*, 1(3), 135–42.

Nickson, D. (2007). *Human Resource Management for the Hospitality and Tourism Industries*. Oxford: Butterworth-Heinemann.

Nield, K. (2006). 'Enhancing Hospitality-Graduate Employability'. *Hospitality Review*, 8(3), 52–7.

Northern Melbourne Institute of TAFE (NMIT). (2009). *Annual Report 2009*. Melbourne: NMIT.

Northern Melbourne Institute of TAFE (NMIT). (2010). *NMIT Strategic Plan – The Northern Journey*. Melbourne: NMIT.

Pavesic, D. V. (1991a). 'Another View of the Future of Hospitality Education' [Letter to the Editor]. *Cornell Hotel and Restaurant Administration Quarterly*, December, 8–9.

Pavesic, D. V. (1991b). 'Pragmatic Issues in Hospitality Education'. *Hospitality and Tourism Educator*, 3(3), 38–9.

Pavesic, D. V. (1993). 'Hospitality Education 2005: curricular and programmatic trends'. *Hospitality Research Journal*, 17(1), 285–94.

Powers, T. F., & Riegel, C. D. (1993). 'A Bright Future for Hospitality Education: providing value in the 21st century'. *Hospitality Research Journal*, 17(1), 295–308.

Riegel, C. D. (1990). 'Purpose, Perspective and Definition: toward an encompassing view of HRI Education'. *Hospitality & Tourism Educator*, 3(1), 18–32.

Riegel, C. D., & Dallas, M. (1999). 'Hospitality and Tourism: careers in the world's largest industry'. In *A Guide to College Programs in Culinary Arts, Hospitality, and Tourism*, 6th edn. New York: John Wiley.

Ring, A., Dickinger, A., & Wöber, K. (2009). 'Designing the Ideal Undergraduate Program in Tourism: expectations from industry and educators', *Journal of Travel Research*, 48, 106–21.

Robinson, R., Breakey, N., & Craig-Smith, S. (2010). 'Food for Thought: investigating food and beverage curricula in Australian hospitality programs'. *Journal of Hospitality & Tourism Education*, 22(1), 32–43.

Rowe, M. (1993). 'Hard Times in the Ivory Tower'. *Lodging Hospitality*, 49(11), 59.

Sheldon, P., Fesenmaier, D., Woeber, K., Cooper, C., & Antonioli, M. (2008) 'Tourism Education Futures, 2010–2030: building the capacity to lead'. *Journal of Teaching in Travel & Tourism*, 7, 61–8.

Swanger, N., & Gursoy, D. (2007). 'An Industry-driven Model of Hospitality Curriculum for Programs Housed in Accredited Colleges of Business: program learning outcomes – part III'. *Journal of Hospitality & Tourism Education*, 19(2), 14–22.

Szambowski, D. J., Szambowski, L. B., & Samenfink, W. H. (2002). 'The Reality Approach to Educating Hospitality Managers: an Australian model'. *Journal of Hospitality and Tourism Education*. 14(2), 53–8.

Tesone, D. V., & Ricci, P. (2009). 'Hotel and Restaurant Entry-Level Job Competencies: comparisons of management and worker perceptions'. *FIU Hospitality Review*, 27(1), 77–89.

Tews, M. J., & van Hoof, H. B. (2011). 'In Favor of Hospitality-Management Education', *FIU Hospitality Review*, 29, 121–9.

The University of Queensland, School of Tourism (UQST). (2010) 'Programs and Courses', *The University of Queensland School of Tourism*. Available: http://tourism.uq.edu.au/programs-courses (Accessed 9 April 2010).

Tribe, J. (2002). 'The Philosophic Practitioner'. *Annals of Tourism Research*, 29(2), 338–57.

Umbreit, W. T. (1992). 'In Search of Hospitality Curriculum Relevance for the 1990s'. *Hospitality & Tourism Educator*, 5(1), 71–4.

Williams, D. A. (2005a). 'Contemporary Approaches to Hospitality Curriculum Design'. *Consortium Journal of Hospitality & Tourism*, 9(2), 69–83.

Williams, D. A. (2005b). 'Hospitality Management Curriculum Design and Graduate Success in the Hospitality Industry'. *Consortium Journal of Hospitality & Tourism*, 9(1), 25–33.

Xiao, Q. H. & Liu, Z. J. (1995). 'Tourism and Hospitality Education in China'. In A. A. Lew & L. Yu (Eds.), *Tourism in China: geographic, political, and economic perspectives* (pp. 107–17). Boulder, CO: Westview Press.

24

Lifelong learning in tourism education

Yahui Su

Teacher Education Center, National Kaohsiung University
of Hospitality and Tourism, Taiwan

Introduction

Traditionally, tourism education and training focus on vocational knowledge and skills, which are necessary for competence and employability in the tourism industry. Vocationally oriented tourism education, which is targeted at 'preparation for specific occupations' (Young, 1998: 75), has been criticized by many scholars as too narrow (e.g. Airey, 1997; Higgins-Desbiolles, 2006; Tribe, 2002a). Vocationalism may result in a focus on short-term employment outcomes (Collins *et al.*, 1994) at the expense of sustainable employability and a dismissal of the active role of tourism students in influencing and changing tourism. With changes in the global market, technology and customer expectations, the requirements of tourism graduates have also changed. For instance, when employers recruit graduates, they seek individuals not only with specialized knowledge and skills but also with the capacity 'to be proactive and to see and respond to problems creatively and autonomously' (Zehrer & Mössenlechner, 2009: 267). Given the mobility and uncertainty of the tourism industry (Sheller & Urry, 2004), in addition to the need for specialized knowledge and skills, this chapter proposes that long-term learning abilities must be addressed if significant and lasting adaptability, flexibility and improvements are to occur.

Recognition of the changes in and complexity of postmodern tourism (Uriely, 1997) requires the development of lifelong tourism learning opportunities that equip students for future learning, employment and life. Instead of only focusing on developing specific, standardized knowledge and skills, truly developing the ability of tourism graduates to confront tourism's postmodern changes requires an understanding of lifelong learning within a framework that is focused on student affect, thought and action, which makes possible and takes into account the significance of a student's ability to connect with the dynamic tourism world.

This chapter introduces the lifelong learning perspective and proposes a model of four learning pillars, an idea from the Delors Report (Delors, 1996; International Commission on Education for the Twenty-first Century, 1996), for sustaining tourism employment in the face of the dynamic changes in the tourism world. This model is a conceptual framework for tourism curriculum that can ensure graduates' continuity of knowledge, competencies and other skills that change with the changing demands of the tourism industry and can improve and broaden tourism development.

Lifelong learning

Lifelong learning has been characterized as a lifelong and life-wide process (Falk *et al.*, 2012) that extends the time period of tourism education at all levels (Cuffy *et al.*, 2012). In addition, lifelong learning also refers to learning in a wide variety of settings, including formal (e.g. a university education programme), non-formal (e.g. in-service training, certification) and informal learning settings (e.g. travel, reading). To some, lifelong learning is a reflection of the increased accessibility of knowledge through technology. However, beyond the vertical extension and horizontal expansion of tourism education and training, the raison d'être of lifelong learning is to sustain tourism development in global change and to make tourism a sustainable and long-term career path for tourism graduates. With the long-term focus on the tourism environment and employment, tourism's 'liquidity' (Bauman, 2000) must be the primary focus in thinking about tourism reflexivity and change. The ideas of reflexivity and change in tourism are based on the assumption that the tourism industry is not a closed system. Rather, it is a system that is related to, and thus open to, the broader human environment. How the tourism industry endeavours to maintain its long-term development and the sustainability of the broader environment, which is inescapably related to industrial development, have been examined in the literature, particularly in studies on the role of tourism education (e.g. Airey, 1997; Tribe, 2005). In recognizing the challenges and the importance of tourism sustainability, this chapter proposes that to make graduates competitive and employable, tourism education must provide training not only in tourism knowledge and skills but also in *openness* toward movement and change in tourism. Tourism graduates no longer work at only one company throughout their careers, and tourism work can no longer be described as a set of specific and routine tasks. The focus of tourism education for the development of the sustainable competitiveness of graduates is not so much on the development of specific knowledge and skills as it is on the ability to change, develop and renew knowledge and skills throughout life (Crebbin, 1997). To keep up with, and contribute to, change in the tourism industry and broader society, tourism graduates are expected to think and act as contributors to both the tourism industry and society.

Therefore, a structure for tourism education that cultivates student capacity to address the dynamics of the tourism world is necessary. In such a structure, the word 'learning' has the primary function of connecting learners with the world on a lifelong, continuous basis. Because tourism is reflexive and changing, tourism education and training must relinquish the pursuit of permanent, fixed tourism knowledge and skills. It must develop students' capacity to learn continuously and to conceptualize knowledge and skills not as final goals but as gateways to change in the tourism industry and society on a lifelong, sustained basis.

Four learning pillars

Many scholars choose to use terms such as 'competency' (e.g. Lowry & Flohr, 2005) and 'key competencies' (e.g. Zehrer & Mössenlechner, 2009) rather than 'basic skills' and 'technical skills' to describe the ability of tourism graduates to address the indeterminacy and uncertainty of tourism practices. Competence is typically considered to be a holistic concept (Rychen, 2004: 22) that consists of 'a combination of knowledge, skills, attitudes and values' (Hoskins & Fredriksson, 2008: 11) and possesses cognitive and non-cognitive dimensions (Rychen & Salganik, 2003: 43). Zehrer & Mössenlechner (2009) enumerate four types of competences (professional competences, methodological competences, social competences and leadership competences), whereas López-Bonilla and López-Bonilla (2012) consider that the content of different competences may be developed depending on whether a person is 'learning to know', 'learning to do' or 'learning to develop attitudes'.

Developing the competencies of graduates to sustain personal strength and competitiveness is an important issue in any professional programme. Tang (1999: 59) considers that 'the workplace is now entering global competition, facing cultural diversity, challenged by technology invention and application, and using new management processes. These factors require workers not only with higher levels of professional competence but also the ability to think critically, solve problems, and skillfully communicate'. Candy (2000) argues that because disciplinary knowledge is transient, graduates must develop generic, long-term skills, such as communication, leadership, teamwork, and analytical and critical thinking, irrespective of their discipline. Lio *et al.* (2006) note that in a college graduate employability survey 'an employer said [to us] that if a person has an insufficient work attitude, communication skills, problem-solving skills, and adaptability, the person with great specialized skills and expertise is in fact inadequate enough [to meet industry demands]'. It seems that graduate requirements increasingly surpass the possession of specific knowledge and include the generic capacities of adaptability and knowledge transfer in addressing the unknown (Harvey *et al.*, 1997; Bowden & Marton, 1998; Barrie, 2004; Yorke & Harvey, 2005). Studies on human resources and employer expectations in the tourism industry (e.g. Baum *et al.*, 1997; Zehrer & Mössenlechner, 2009) similarly indicate the increasing demand for generic abilities (e.g. communication, problem solving, technology use and human relations) rather than the ability to complete specific technical tasks.

In terms of international education policies, a conceptual framework for lifelong learning was proposed by the International Commission on Education for the Twenty-First Century (1996), also known as the Delors Report (after Jacques Delors, former president of the European Commission). In this framework, lifelong learning is based on four pillars – learning to know, learning to do, learning to live together and learning to be – that are key for growth and development in today's knowledge-driven, twenty-first-century societies. The Organization for Economic Cooperation and Development (OECD) emphasized three categories of competencies that are necessary for individual success and the functioning of society: the 'use of tools', 'acting autonomously' and 'interacting in heterogeneous groups' (OECD, 2005). The European Union working group recommended eight key competences for lifelong learning (i.e. communication in the mother tongue, communication in foreign languages, mathematical competence and basic competences in science and technology, digital competence, learning to learn, social and civic competences, the sense of initiative and entrepreneurship, and cultural awareness and expression), which were adopted by the European Council and the European Parliament in December 2006 (European Council, 2006). These key competences are argued to be essential for each European citizen 'for personal fulfilment and development, active citizenship, social inclusion and employment' (Deakin, 2008: 312).

To understand and further measure the lifelong learning conditions across Europe, the European Lifelong Learning Indicators (ELLI) were developed based on the four pillars of learning (Hoskin *et al.*, 2010). Similarly, the Canadian Council on Learning used the four pillars of lifelong learning as a framework to develop the Composite Learning Index (CLI) and to measure Canada's progress in lifelong learning (Canadian Council on Learning, 2010). Under the four-pillar framework, lifelong learning is understood as a means not only to economic outcomes and employment but also to social development and personal empowerment.

Following the global trend in lifelong learning, tourism employers are increasingly more concerned with generic attributes that make graduates flexible and adaptable to change. Tourism employers value graduates' capabilities for communication, problem solving, working with others and self-management (López-Bonilla & López-Bonilla, 2012). We may need to think of tourism education as developing lifelong learning capacities in graduates, which help them not only to meet industry demands but also to live within a larger natural or social environment that is inevitably influenced by, and can influence, tourism. To this end, this chapter argues that the four learning pillars constitute a broader framework that encompasses more than the concerns of immediate, short-term employability and performance. These pillars, shown in Figure 24.1, emphasize the connection between the learner and society while synthesizing knowledge about commercial and non-commercial tourism as well as the vocational and the liberal education (Tribe, 1997, 2002a, 2005):

1   *Learning to know*: The ability to learn to construct, change and renew tourism knowledge in scope with the changing tourism industry. These abilities, presented in a non-exhaustive list (Figure 24.1), include learning to understand, to use computer technology, to search for and integrate information, to analyse, to reason and think critically, to learn in a broader, liberal context and beyond disciplines, and to create.
2   *Learning to do*: Not only the ability to apply knowledge and skills and to operate and practise them in occupational contexts but also to adapt and be flexible, to solve problems, and to participate in tourism renovation and change with broader social and environmental interests in mind.
3   *Learning to live together*: The ability to communicate orally and through writing, to work collaboratively and lead groups, to be sensitive to customers and individuals from different cultures, and to listen to, respect and express concern for larger social and environmental needs and benefits.
4   *Learning to be*: Development of the will to learn, to be curious and open-minded, to take initiative, to manage oneself, to find self-worth and meaning, and to be confident in being engaged with and making contributions to tourism and non-tourism contexts.

Agency-based

In thinking of tourism education as a lifelong practice of learning based on the four pillars above, the idea of tourism learning becomes imbued with active agency rather than knowledge and

Learning to know	Learning to do	Learning to live together	Learning to be
• learning to acquire a solid understanding of 'concrete' tourism knowlege • learning to use computers • learning to search for and integrate tourism information • learning to analyse • learning to reason and think critically • learning to know in a broader, liberal context and beyond disciplines • learning to create	• learning to apply knowledge • learning to operate and practise • learning to adapt and to be flexible • learning to solve problems in real contexts • learning to take part in tourism renovation and change to serve a larger social and environmental purpose	• learning to communicate orally and through writing • learning to work collaboratively and to lead groups • learning to be sensitive to customers and individuals from different cultures • learning to listen to, respect and express concern for larger social and environmental needs	• the will to learn • learning to be curious and open-minded • learning to show initiative • learning to manage oneself • learning to find self-worth and meaning • learning to be confident in being engaged with tourism and non-tourism contexts

Figure 24.1 Tourism learning within the four learning pillars

skills per se. This view suggests a focus on the ability of tourism graduates to be adaptable, to renew knowledge and to value learning as a lifelong enterprise. The focus on clear and specific knowledge and skills for particular occupations is 'something only feasible when occupations are at least relatively static' (Young, 1998: 145). Yet tourism is increasingly not a 'career for life' characterized by finite and fixed employment but a changing career (Johnston & Watson, 2006). When emphasizing the dynamic nature of the tourism industry and employment, the focus shifts to the mental, physical and emotional engagement of students and their ability to accumulate and manage the energy required to sustain their efforts.

In this sense, tourism education is no longer simply the delivery of 'solid' knowledge and skills but should be directed toward inquiry into the development of a student's tacit self-concept, attributes and motives (Spencer & Spencer, 1993). 'Learning to know' is not simply concerned with understanding 'solid' concepts but emphasizes student agency as an integral factor within the learning process. The object-centred approach, which focuses on static and solid content, cannot fully explain why lifelong learning for tourism can be activated. However, learner agency and motivation emphasize the dynamics of learner engagement and reflection, and account for why, not only how, tourism graduates are willing to commit themselves to learning and development. Furthermore, the four-pillar framework shown in Figure 24.1 is not simply a list of generic, desirable learning abilities, and is not intended to be exhaustive or prescriptive. The framework should be taken as a tool not only for identifying generic, desirable abilities but also for examining whether students develop these abilities and how these abilities enable students to be effective and find meaning in their role in the tourism industry.

Multiplicity

None of the four pillars alone can characterize student learning. That is, a single learning activity can be designed to involve knowing, doing, living and being. The four learning pillars are not four separate processes for learning. Each process (pillar) presupposes and mutually involves one another. 'Learning to do' is only one of the pillars required for learners to develop competency. While tourism students learn to operate, act and participate in solving problems or completing tasks, they also require 'learning to know' in the sense of reflecting on their own actions through 'critical knowing' (Tribe, 2002b), a practice also known as 'critical vocationalism' (Young, 1998). The inclusion of 'learning to know' is congruent with the view of tourism researchers such as Haywood (1989), who argues for a more reflective learning approach in hospitality and tourism education, and Tribe (2002a), who proposes the idea of a reflective vocational and a reflective liberal education. Without the development of 'learning to know', 'the critical and transformative possibilities of higher education are lost' (Tribe, 2005: 59). The inclusion of 'learning to know' prompts students to engage more critically and reflexively with ongoing tourism practices and the unknown future. 'Learning to know' includes not only reflection but also the links between reflection and action (Tribe, 2002a, 2002b, 2005), which are formed through the development of 'reflection-in-action' (during action) and 'reflection-on-action' (after action) (Schön, 1983).

While the development of 'learning to know' and 'learning to do' are necessary, they are not sufficient for navigating the complexities of a life in tourism. More than the mastery of tourism knowledge and action, the framework includes 'learning to live together', which reveals that tourism involves not only the understanding and the provision of service but also an understanding of people and ethical actions (Tribe, 2002b). In addition to knowing, doing and living together, students must also 'learn to be' (Figure 24.2), which conceptualizes tourism education as not only empowering graduates to be effective in the workforce but also as being concerned with personal career development and life fulfilment. This approach is supported by

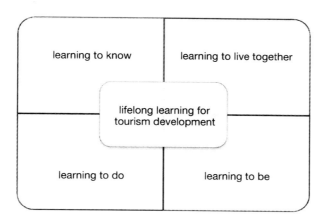

Figure 24.2 The four pillars of lifelong learning for tourism development

scholars who argue that students need to develop not only their abilities to know and act but also 'to be' (e.g. Barnett, 2004; Dall'Alba & Barnacle, 2007; Kreber, 2009; Su, 2011a, 2011b). The four learning pillars broaden the focus of tourism education from vocational competence to a learner commitment to life and work, and from pursuing performance to searching for the meaning of tourism in a broader context. The framework avoids reducing tourism education to 'technical' training in preparation for manual labour and low-status jobs and instead tries to identify tourism education as a process of sense-making and self-formation.

Connectedness

Based on the four learning pillars, the learner learns to be open to certain possibilities of connectedness between different areas of knowledge and therefore develops the ability to view the tourism industry within the broader environment. The four-pillar framework must account for an individual's entire tourism career as a part of the life and environmental cycles. The framework rejects dualistic ideas, such as the mind–body and self–world dichotomies, and avoids the development of tourism education that is simply tailored to the needs of the tourism industry as a means of supplying labour to feed economic and business growth. Instead, the four pillars direct tourism learners toward expanding their 'awareness of the human environment and how to cope with this environment rather than exclusively developing job-related information and skills' (Gunn, 1998). The focus is on the reciprocal relationship between the self and the world, the commercial and the non-commercial (Tribe, 1997), and the vocational and the liberal (Tribe, 2002a, 2005). Rather than distinguishing between mental and manual labour, the liberal and the vocational, or general learning and specific learning, the four learning pillars encourage students to view tourism as 'liberal vocationalism' (Silver & Brennan, 1988) and a reflection-in-action practice (Schön, 1983).

The openness and connectedness of tourism learning to broader society and the world reflect concern regarding the tourism industry's effects on the natural environment and human society and culture, and tourism education becomes responsible for developing social, liberal and ethical action in students. Thus, tourism education based on the four learning pillars enables the student to perceive the transformative potential of tourism. Far from epistemological dualism, the four learning pillars involve the unity of the learner's body–mind–spirit. which plays a role in creating the structure of reality or meaning. Thus, there is the possibility for tourism learning to influence tourism, i.e. the possibility for 'influencing and changing the phenomenon of tourism itself' (Tribe, 2005: 50). For instance, as Morgan (2004) predicts, future tourism may develop as part of an 'experience economy'. To succeed in this economy, tourism education must do more than reflect the functional needs of the tourism industry. In addition, tourism education must address the intellectual and liberal needs to develop the ethical and cultural awareness as well as the creativity and interpersonal sensitivity of students. Being conscious of short- and long-term tourism development creates a balance between social development and profit growth. Students are expected to simultaneously think, act and feel tourism in the vocational sense as well as in the liberal sense. Under the four learning pillars, students are evaluated not only in terms of personal performance and economic productivity but also in terms of their understanding of the social, cultural and environmental issues raised by tourism products and their ability to reflect and act on these issues.

Curriculum

The question thus arises of how the four pillars of lifelong learning should be taught in the tourism curriculum. The focus of a tourism curriculum for lifelong learning is on the whole learner (Figure 24.3), for whom, by whom and through whom interdisciplinary boundaries are transcended (Tribe, 1997) so that learners can create their own horizons for learning. By focusing on the ability to learn, students are expected to connect different disciplines and develop new insights or strategies to accommodate changes in tourism. This learner-centred, agency-based approach is congruent with a view that argues for establishing interdisciplinary, multidisciplinary or extra-disciplinary curricular content (e.g. Tribe, 2002a; Jamal & Jourdan, 2008), which centres on the unity of information content and the actual learning process. In attempting to develop a lifelong learning curriculum, it is necessary to elevate student agency to primacy by focusing on the development of their mental and physical abilities and their persistence in learning. Because it focuses on the whole person, the learner-centred approach surpasses the dichotomy between disciplines by concentrating on agentic thinking, acting and feeling holistically. What matters

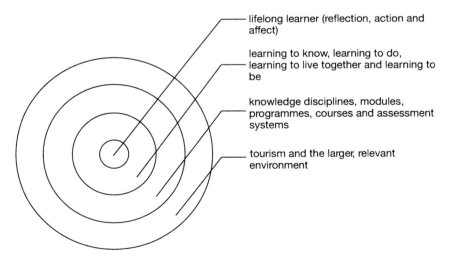

lifelong learner (reflection, action and affect)

learning to know, learning to do, learning to live together and learning to be

knowledge disciplines, modules, programmes, courses and assessment systems

tourism and the larger, relevant environment

Figure 24.3 Tourism curriculum for developing lifelong learners

in this approach is not which dimension in a pair (theory/practice, reflection/action, liberal/professional) is more crucial than the other, but whether one of the dimensions has been hindered by the overwhelming domination of the other. The content of a lifelong learning curriculum extends beyond business aspects by 'introducing wider issues not specifically related to the operation of the tourism industry' (Airey, 2005: 16) and helps develop the broader vision of the tourism learner by knowing and considering in building up creative and better solutions to tourism change, and makes students become aware of the culture, identity and conditions in which tourism lives. It is imperative to ensure 'a balanced curriculum which avoids the narrow confines of vocationalism and operationalism or academicism and idealism' (Tribe, 2005: 54).

The four pillars model of lifelong learning is generic and can be employed across a wide range of disciplines that, for instance, may include cultural, psychological and anthropological disciplines of knowledge, depending on the perceptions of curriculum designers regarding what is needed and involved in broader tourism. Figure 24.3, as a metaphor, lays out how the four pillars are employed and embedded in disciplines and courses. The generic lifelong learning attributes are not a set of additional outcomes requiring an additional discipline. They are rather outcomes by their being embedded, surrounded and learned within and across contexts of various disciplines, modules, programmes, courses and assessment systems. Certain scholars (e.g. Jones, 2009a; Litchfield et al., 2010; Yorke & Harvey, 2005) consider the development of generic attributes to be most effective when the attributes are embedded within the context in specific ways. A number of discipline-based studies have concerned themselves with what these attributes actually look like in various disciplines. While Jones's (2009a, 2009b) research concerns generic attributes such as critical thinking, problem solving, and communication in physics, history, economics, medicine and law, tourism education requires similar research in investigating and teaching the generic attributes in contexts of tourism disciplines. Only through the discipline base can the four pillars be learned and developed for the sake of quality and validity.

While tourism educators and institutions may be prepared to link and integrate the four pillars with the curriculum, integrating the four pillars with the curriculum can attain full effectiveness only to the extent that the curriculum reaches teachers and learners. In other words, a linear, top-down alignment strategy is insufficient. The beliefs and attitudes of both teachers and learners play important roles in initiatives to reshape the curriculum to include a focus on lifelong learning and to create 'a validated and living curriculum' (Bath et al., 2004).

The typology of curriculum development proposed by Goodlad et al. (1979), and adapted by van den Akker (1998; van den Akker et al., 2006), is helpful for ensuring the alignment of and translation between educational goals, pedagogy and the student's experience and learning. Broad distinctions in curriculum development can be made between the intended curriculum, the implemented curriculum and the attained curriculum. According to van den Akker et al. (2006: 69; original emphasis):

> The *intended* curriculum contains both the ideal curriculum (the vision or basic philosophy underlying a curriculum) and the formal/written curriculum (intentions as specified in curriculum documents and/or materials). The *implemented* curriculum contains both the perceived curriculum (interpretations by users, particularly teachers) and the operational curriculum (as enacted in the classroom). The *attained* curriculum is comprised of the experiential curriculum (learning experiences from pupil perspective) and the learned curriculum (resulting learner outcomes).

Table 24.1 sets out a typology of a tourism curriculum for lifelong learning. At the level of the intended curriculum, an ideal curriculum would ensure that the four pillars of lifelong learning

Table 24.1 Typology of a tourism curriculum for lifelong learning

Typology of the curriculum		Examples of embedding lifelong learning into the tourism curriculum
Intended curriculum	Ideal curriculum	Educational institutions and departments: • creating the vision of developing lifelong learners as the curricular goal • using the four pillars of lifelong learning as the framework for tourism curriculum development
	Formal curriculum	Educational institutions and departments: • developing policies, guidelines and systems to support the lifelong learning development of tourism graduates • specifying lifelong learning development as part of the tourism curricular objectives • developing modules, programmes, courses and assessment systems based on the four learning pillars • mapping the tourism curriculum to align with the four pillars of lifelong learning • identifying which lifelong learning attributes are included in the curriculum • specifying the significance of lifelong learning in teacher guides and student materials • initiating programmes and strategic initiatives to support the tourism curriculum for lifelong learning
Implemented curriculum	Perceived curriculum	Teachers: • being aware of the policies on and the value of embedding lifelong learning into the curriculum • perceiving what lifelong learning development means and how it appears within the taught discipline • articulating the lifelong learning outcomes that the teachers expect of the students • designing the instructional processes for tourism students' lifelong learning development • developing assessment tools
	Operational (enacted) curriculum	Teachers: • realizing the actual instructional process as planned or adapted according to the dynamics of instruction • identifying and assessing lifelong learning outcomes
Attained curriculum	Experiential curriculum	Students: • possessing beliefs, attitudes and motives for transforming themselves into lifelong learners • participating in and engaging with the curriculum
	Learned curriculum	Students: • developing personal plans to store and update their records of lifelong learning activities • recognizing their own achievement of lifelong learning goals through self-assessment • thinking of the mutual relationship between the self and the tourism world • learning to share insights into the realities of tourism from economic, environmental, social and cultural perspectives

constitute the framework for tourism education and would conceptualize developing lifelong learners as the curricular goal. In the formal curriculum, the lifelong learning vision is specified and made visible through developing, for example, concrete policies. guidelines, programmes, systems, curriculum maps and outlines, teacher guides and assessments that support and embed lifelong learning. At the level of the implemented curriculum, the teachers would be aware of the policies on and the values of lifelong learning development. They would perceive and interpret what lifelong learning means and how it appears within a course or across a tourism programme. Jones (2009b) notes that generic attributes 'such as critical thinking, analysis, problem solving and communication are conceptualized and taught in quite different ways in each of the disciplines'. The teacher would design the dynamics of the instructional processes according to his or her interpretation of lifelong learning (the perceived curriculum). Finally, the teacher would realize the actual instructional process as planned or would adapt the process according to the dynamics of instruction and identify the lifelong learning outcomes of the students (the operational curriculum).

The attained curriculum consists of what is actually experienced and learned by the tourism students. At the experiential level, the curriculum is viewed as the totality of the student learning experience. This level includes the participation and engagement of the student in, for example, learning to think critically, solve problems, listen and communicate, and have confidence. At the learned curriculum level, students do more than experience the curriculum. In addition, they reflect on and assess their learning processes to become aware of what they have achieved. Students at this level think about the mutual relationship between the self and the tourism world while reflecting on what they have experienced and done as well as expressing insights into the reality of tourism from economic, environmental, social and cultural perspectives.

The typology of a tourism curriculum for lifelong learning (Table 24.1) provides a sense of alignment between the curricular vision and the goal (the intended curriculum), the delivery of instruction (the implemented curriculum), and student learning experiences and outcomes (the attained curriculum). While the six levels of curriculum development are all necessary, what matters most is the attained curriculum. In reality, learners rarely develop competences completely as directed by the intended and implemented curriculum. The level of action and change is never simply the work of the top-down delivery system. Lifelong learning, when based on learner agency, is always individual and personal. Students do not develop the ability to learn from textbooks and materials offered by teachers. Instead, students learn through knowing, doing, feeling, living, experiencing and being with the curriculum. Moreover, the lifelong learning efforts and development of students can be extended beyond the delivery of the curriculum to include the development of learning initiated by the students themselves (e.g. participating in volunteer work, part-time work, leisure activities, extra-curricular activities and the local community). The inclusion of student autonomy in learning validates a wider range of lifelong learning experiences, including those not constructed by tourism academics.

Implications

This chapter has proposed tourism education and training based on the four pillars of lifelong learning, which is a framework that elevates learner agency to the level of a primary function. The focus on the ability to learn, which represents the ability to be dynamic and interactive, produces tourism learners who can be flexible in response to change. The four learning pillars encourage multiplicity and subjectivity, and avoid reducing the complexity of tourism practices to vocationalism and technicalism. While tourism education for immediate employment in the tourism industry is important, sustainable employability and learning how tourism can work in concert with the broader socio-cultural and natural environment are also emphasized in this lifelong learning perspective.

The lifelong learning perspective has important implications for tourism education research, practice and policy. First, while the idea of lifelong learning has been used and keenly discussed within adult and higher education, lifelong learning as a framework for developing tourism education practices remains a relatively under-researched field. It is hoped that the development of tourism learning from the lifelong learning perspective offered here will stimulate future research on this pedagogical method. Second, if lifelong learning development is to be authentic, the beliefs and attitudes of teachers and students are important. Teachers must comprehend the value of integrating lifelong learning into the curriculum, whereas students must become aware of their own agency and their power to think, act, feel and learn. Teachers who understand their role as producing teaching-specific, vocational material require continuous and systematic support to change their mindset (Gardner, 2006) so they can start to appreciate the value of including the lifelong learning development of their students in their teaching goals. Third, there is a need for higher education policy to address broader tourism education development beyond the current focus on instrumental performance standards and benchmarks. The government must balance effectiveness-driven concerns regarding performance with the awareness that for tourism to be sustainable, student abilities to know, do, live and be within and across disciplines must be seriously considered in curricula. Tourism education policy could benefit over time from research on the lifelong learning approach. The application of the four learning pillars proposed in this chapter requires further empirical study in different contexts. It is hoped that this chapter, which is aimed at the development of lifelong learning practice, will contribute to the establishment of broader and more positive tourism education programmes.

Acknowledgements

The author wishes to thank the National Science Council of Taiwan for its support of this research through the project entitled 'The Four Learning Pillars: A Framework for Employability Cultivation of Technical and Vocational University Students'.

References

Airey, D. (1997). 'After 25 Years of Development: a view of the state of tourism education in the UK'. In E. Laws (Ed.), *The ATTT Tourism Education Handbook* (pp. 9–12). London: Tourism Society.
Airey, D. (2005). 'Growth and Development'. In D. Airey & J. Tribe (Eds.), *An International Handbook of Tourism Education* (pp. 13–24). Oxford: Elsevier.
Barnett, R. (2004). 'Learning for an Unknown Future'. *Higher Education Research and Development,* 23(3), 247–60.
Barrie, S. C. (2004). 'A Research-Based Approach to Generic Graduate Attributes Policy'. *Higher Education Research and Development,* 23(3), 261–75
Bath, D., Smith, C., Stein, S., & Swann, R. (2004). 'Beyond Mapping and Embedding Graduate Attributes: bringing together quality assurance and action learning to create a validated and living curriculum'. *Higher Education Research and Development* , 23(3), 313–28.
Baum, T., Amoah, V., & Spivack, S. (1997). 'Policy Dimensions of Human Resource Management in the Tourism and Hospitality Industries'. *International Journal of Contemporary Hospitality Management,* 9(5/6), 221–9.
Bauman, Z. (2000). *Liquid Modernity.* Cambridge: Polity.
Bowden, J., & Marton, F. (1998). *University of Learning: beyond quality and competence in higher education.* London: Kogan Page.
Canadian Council on Learning (2010). *The 2010 Composite Learning Index: five years of measuring Canada's progress in lifelong learning.* Ottawa: Canadian Council on Learning). Available: http://www.ccl-cca.ca/pdfs/CLI/2010/2010CLI-Booklet_EN.pdf (accessed 20 January 2014).

Candy, P. C. (2000). 'Learning and Earning: graduate skills for an uncertain future'. Paper presented at the International Lifelong Learning Conference, July, Yeppoon, Australia.

Collins, S., Sweeney, A., & Geen, A. (1994). 'Training for the UK Tour Operating Industry: advancing current practice'. Tourism Management, 15(1), 5–8.

Crebbin, W. (1997). Teaching for Lifelong Learning. In R Ballantyne, J. Bain, & J. Packer (Eds.), Reflecting on University Teaching Academics' Stories (pp. 139–50). Canberra: CUTSD and Australian Government Publishing Service.

Cuffy, V., Tribe, J., & Airey, D. (2012). 'Lifelong Learning for Tourism'. Annals of Tourism Research, 39(3), 1402–24.

Dall'Alba, G., & Barnacle, R. (2007). 'An Ontological Turn for Higher Education'. Studies in Higher Education, 32(6), 679–91.

Deakin, R. C. (2008). 'Key Competencies for Education in a European Context: narratives of accountability or care'. European Educational Research Journal, 7(3), 311–18.

Delors, J. (1996). Education for the Twenty-First Century: issues and prospects. Paris: UNESCO.

European Council. (2006). Recommendation of the European Parliament and the Council of 18 December 2006 on key competences for lifelong learning. Official Journal of the European Union, L394. Available: http://eur-lex.europa.eu/LexUriServ/site/en/oj/2006/l_394/l_39420061230en00100018.pdf (Accessed 20 January 2014).

Falk, J. H., Ballantyne, R., Packer, J., & Benckendorff, P. (2012). 'Travel and Learning: a neglected tourism research area'. Annals of Tourism Research, 39(2), 908–27.

Gardner, H. (2006). Changing Minds: the art and science of changing our own and other people's minds. Boston, MA: Harvard Business School Press.

Goodlad, J. I., Frances Klein, M., & Tye, K. A. (1979). 'The Domains of Curriculum and their Study'. In J. I. Goodlad et al. (Eds.), Curriculum Inquiry. The study of curriculum practice (pp. 43–76). New York: McGraw-Hill.

Gunn, C. A. (1998). 'Issues in Tourism Curricula'. Journal of Travel Research, 36(4), 74–7.

Harvey, L., Moon, S., & Geall, V., with Bower, R. (1997). Graduates' Work: organisational change and student attributes. Birmingham: Centre for Research into Quality (CRQ) and Association of Graduate Recruiters (AGR).

Haywood, K. M. (1989). 'A Radical Proposal for Hospitality and Tourism Education'. International Journal of Hospitality Management, 8, 259–64.

Higgins-Desbiolles, F. (2006). 'More than An "Industry": the forgotten power of tourism as a social force'. Tourism Management, 27(6), 1192–208.

Hoskins, B., & Fredriksson, U. (2008). Learning to Learn: what is it and can it be measured? Brussels: European Commission.

Hoskins, B., Cartwright, F., & Schoof, U. (2010). The ELLI Index Europe 2010: ELLI European Lifelong Learning Indicators: making lifelong learning tangible! Gütersloh, Germany: Bertelsmann Stiftung. Retrieved from: http://www.icde.org/European+ELLI+Index+2010.b7C_wlDMWi.ips

International Commission on Education for the Twenty-first Century (The Delors Report). (1996). Learning: the treasure within. Paris: UNESCO.

Jamal, T., & Jourdan, D. (2008). 'Interdisciplinary Tourism Education'. In B. Chandramohan and S. J. Fallows (Eds.), Interdisciplinary Teaching and Learning in Higher Education: theory and practice (pp. 105–23). New York: Routledge.

Johnston, B., & Watson, A. (2006). 'Employability: approaches to developing student career awareness and reflective practice in undergraduate business studies'. In P. Tynjala, J. Valimaa, & G. Boulton-Lewis (Eds.), Higher Education and Working Life (pp. 231–45). Amsterdam: Elsevier.

Jones, A. (2009a). 'Generic Attributes as Espoused Theory: the importance of context'. Higher Education, 58(2), 175–91.

Jones, A. (2009b). 'Redisciplining Generic Attributes: the disciplinary context in focus'. Studies in Higher Education, 34(1), 85–100.

Kreber, C. (2009). 'Supporting Student Learning in the Context of Diversity, Complexity and Uncertainty'. In C. Kreber (Ed.), The University and Its Disciplines: teaching and learning within and beyond disciplinary boundaries (pp. 3–19). London: Routledge.

Lio, M. C., Chiou, J. R., & Hu, J. L. (2006). Enhancing Employability in the Formal Education: college graduate employability survey [in Chinese]. Taipei: National Youth Commission, Executive Yuan.

Litchfield, A. J., Frawley, J. E., & Nettleton, S. C. (2010). 'Contextualising and Integrating into the Curriculum the Learning and Teaching of Work-Ready Professional Graduate Attributes'. Higher Education Research and Development, 29(5), 519–34.

López-Bonilla, J. M., & López-Bonilla, L. M. (2012). 'Holistic Competence Approach in Tourism Higher Education: an exploratory study in Spain'. *Current Issues in Tourism*, iFirst Article, DOI:10.1080/13683500.2012.720248.

Lowry, L. L., & Flohr, J. K. (2005). 'No Student Left Behind: a longitudinal assessment of the competency-based framework used to facilitate learning in a capstone tourism course'. *Journal of Hospitality and Tourism Education*, 17(4), 28–35.

Morgan, M. (2004). 'From Production Line to Drama School: higher education for the future of tourism'. *International Journal of Contemporary Hospitality Management*, 16(2), 91–9.

Organization for Economic Cooperation and Development (OECD). (2005). 'The Definition and Selection of Key Competencies: executive summary'. Available: http://www.deseco.admin.ch/bfs/deseco/en/index/02.parsys.43469.downloadList.2296.DownloadFile.tmp/200five.dskcexecutivesummary.en.pdf (Accessed 13 January 2014).

Rychen, D. S. (2004). 'Key Competencies for All: an overarching conceptual frame of reference'. In D. S. Rychen & A. Tiana (Eds.), *Developing Key Competencies in Education* (pp. 5–34). Paris: UNESCO.

Rychen, D. S., & Salganik, L. H. (2003). 'A Holistic Model of Competence'. In D. S. Rychen & L. H. Salganik (Eds.), *Key Competencies for a Successful Life and a Well-functioning Society* (pp. 41–62). Göttingen: Hogrefe and Huber.

Sheller, M., & J. Urry (Eds.). (2004). *Tourism Mobilities: places to play, places in play*. London: Routledge.

Schön, D. A. (1983). *The Reflective Practitioner*. London: Maurice Temple Smith.

Silver, H., & Brennan, J. (1988). *Liberal Vocationalism*. London: Methuen.

Spencer, L., & Spencer, S. (1993). *Competence at Work: models for superior performance*. New York: John Wiley.

Su, Y. (2011a). 'The Constitution of Agency in Developing Lifelong Learning Ability: the "being" mode'. *Higher Education*, 62(4), 399–412.

Su, Y. (2011b). 'Lifelong Learning as Being: the Heideggerian perspective'. *Adult Education Quarterly*, 61(1), 57–72.

Tang, Y. (1999). 'The Roles of Technical and Vocational Education under the Comparative of Lifelong Education and Job Training'. *Modern Research Issue*, 20, 57–67.

Tribe, J. (1997). 'The Indiscipline of Tourism'. *Annals of Tourism Research*, 24(3), 638–57.

Tribe, J. (2002a). 'The Philosophic Practitioner'. *Annals of Tourism Research*, 9(2), 338–57

Tribe, J. (2002b). 'Education for Ethical Tourism Action'. *Journal of Sustainable Tourism*, 10(4), 309–24.

Tribe, J. (2005). 'Tourism, Knowledge and the Curriculum'. In D. Airey & J. Tribe (Eds.), *An International Handbook of Tourism Education* (pp. 47–60). Oxford: Elsevier.

Uriely, N. (1997). 'Theories of Modern and Postmodern Tourism'. *Annals of Tourism Research*, 24(4), 982–4.

Van den Akker, J. J. H. (1998). 'The Science Curriculum: between ideals and outcomes'. In B. J. Fraser & K. G. Tobin (Eds.), *International Handbook of Science Education* (pp. 421–47). Dordrecht: Kluwer Academic Publishers.

Van den Akker, J., Gravemeijer, K., McKenney, S., & Nieveen, N. (Eds.). (2006). *Educational Design Research*. London: Routledge.

Yorke, M., & Harvey, L. (2005). 'Graduate Attributes and their Development'. *New Directions for Institutional Research*, 128, 41–58.

Young, M. F. D. (1998). *The Curriculum of the Future: from the 'New Sociology of Education' to a critical theory of learning*. London: Falmer Press.

Zehrer, A., & Mössenlechner, C. (2009). 'Key Competencies of Tourism Graduates: the employers' point of view'. *Journal of Teaching in Travel and Tourism*, 9(3–4), 266–87.

25

Work-integrated and service learning at HAAGA-HELIA Porvoo Campus in Finland

Learning for life

Annica Isacsson and Jarmo Ritalahti

HAAGA-HELIA University of Applied Sciences, Finland

Introduction

HAAGA-HELIA (HH) University of Applied Sciences is a large business and tourism educator in the south of Finland with more than 10,000 students at six campuses aspiring to complete a bachelor or Master's degree. Tourism as well as business courses are taught in both English and Finnish at Porvoo Campus. Porvoo is a historic town 50 km east of Helsinki. In Finland the universities of applied sciences (polytechnics) are part of the higher education system and emphasize regional development, learning and applied research.

The new HH Porvoo Campus was opened in January 2011, having been designed from Living Lab and a constructive approach involving a vast amount of collaboration with stakeholders, such as the town of Porvoo, development organizations, advisory board, architects, companies, lecturers, staff and students. The Living Lab process gave birth to a vision for Porvoo Campus and the constructivist research and development process provided the tools to reach the vision (pedagogical approach and curricula). The working life integration began at the planning stage with the specific aim of enhancing the crossover or poly-contextual input, connectivity and collaboration between stakeholders. The aspiration was to open an innovative and exciting study place to enhance learning, to facilitate transparency and teamwork. The construction and planning of curriculum was undertaken in parallel with the Campus design process and lasted roughly three years (2007–10). Furthermore, 50 companies were interviewed as a part of the Campus concept development process.

HH Porvoo Campus can be described as an open, post-modern, transparent, innovative, well-equipped building filled with natural light, with spaces on three levels designed for learning, well-being and embedded technology. The materials used in its construction are of glass, steel and wood. Figure 25.1 illustrates these design features.

In the curriculum process the HH Campus inquiry learning pedagogy and concept was incrementally shaped in an effort to make sure that school and the outside world were not

Figure 25.1 HAAGA-HELIA Porvoo Campus (© 2014 HAAGA-HELIA University of Applied Sciences)

separated, but were integrated. The vision for the Campus was to create a Living Lab for Creativity, Learning and Innovations and the inquiry learning model was the foundation for the integrated architecture and design, formal and informal collaboration and teamwork facilities. The idea was that students should be made owners and contributors to their own learning processes. Values such as well-being and a strong sense of both individual and collaborative responsibility were considered in the design of the architecture and curricular processes. Well-being was considered to be found in the Campus library, restaurant, in collaborative learning opportunities in the curriculum and in the different learning spaces. According to conference proceedings at Grasping the Future (2008) transparency has a calming and positive effect on students' learning when the environments are made visible, transparent, open, stimulating and versatile.

Working life projects are implemented and executed on Campus in collaboration with the outside world, integrating learning with interaction and inquiry involving the outside world. Every semester has its own working life project. Students work primarily in teams. Campus teachers have taken the role of facilitators and coaches who support individual and collective learning processes instead of being theoretical knowledge providers. The inquiry learning model implies that learners integrate theory with practice, stimulate curiosity among themselves and build understanding and knowledge together (see e.g. Eteläpelto, 2007).

Both Sincero (2006) and Hakkarainen *et al.* (2004) present inquiry-based learning models that imply new theory and knowledge as the output of such learning. In contrast, the Porvoo Campus model focuses on learning and the development of applied knowledge, and less on theory building. The learner(s) with her (their) questions and curiosity is (are) at the centre. Inquiry and theory are related to semester projects, to project aims, phases, tasks, processes, outcomes, deliverables and structures in relation to aims related to competences as stated in the curriculum. The Porvoo Campus model involves discussions related to context and practices, applied theory and cooperation in addition to continuous reflection on practices and learning on an individual and team level. Sharing, learning, independency, responsibility and reflection are attributes emphasized in the model. Connectivity and poly-contextuality, knowing how to be and act in worklife and project contexts are the expected outcomes. The Campus pedagogical knowledge construction and learning is thus inquiry-based, building upon learning and practice in semester projects. It strives at a knowledge acquirement culture as advocated by Scardamalia & Bereitner (2006). Furthermore, it supports Bunting's (2004) ideas that learning spaces should not only be functional, but also friendly and agreeable.

This chapter contributes to the understanding of how tourism worklife-based projects, inquiry and service learning, as applied and defined at HAAGA-HELIA University of Applied Sciences, Porvoo Campus, enhance poly-contextual and connectivity skills as well as empower Tourism Education Future Initiatives (TEFI) values in general and individual, shared and social responsibility in particular.

Work-integrated learning: a process

One educational consideration that universities of applied sciences in Finland constantly face is how and why to embed authentic worklife needs and competences such as knowledge, attitude and skills, with theoretical research-based content. How can universities of applied sciences ensure that worklife and higher educational institutions are integrated not separated? This chapter suggests an intensified collaboration between educational institutions and society as implemented by HAAGA-HELIA University of Applied Sciences, Porvoo Campus, through pedagogical approach, curriculum, work experience and working life commissioned projects thus empowering connectivity, poly-contextuality, responsibility and learning for life.

It seems that the conceptualization and understanding of quality-based work-integrated learning (WIL) in Finland is developing rapidly in the field of higher education and VET (vocational education and training). It is, however, seen as important not only to launch the student into a work-integrated project, but to mediate and monitor the process, as connections between formal and informal learning, and between conceptual development and developing the capacity to work in different contexts, are important. The core competences that should be aimed at during work-integrated learning relate to meta-competences, connectivity, responsibility and social skills as well as to 'boundary-crossing' and 'poly-contextual' skills which give students the ability to work in changing and new contexts, to transfer skills and to connect knowledge. Poly-contextual and connective learning can be achieved during a training period, but also within worklife-based projects, e.g. community-based projects involving service learning that prepare students not only for the industry, the future and the prevailing job market, but for life.

In 1991 Jean Lave and Etienne Wenger introduced a new way of understanding learning through the concept of communities of practice. Originally it was used in the context of understanding situational learning processes in organizations, but has also become quite influential in participatory design as a way of understanding relations between different groups of users in a specific context (Wenger, 1998). The situational learning concept (Lave & Wenger, 1991) is not a pedagogical strategy, learning technique or a theory of learning – it is a way to understand learning. Learning is seen as a social process, integrating individual needs and cultural backgrounds, with specific aims, contexts and situations. Work-integrated learning on Porvoo Campus occurs in specific working life contexts such as ferries, natural parks, restaurants, museums, in relation to others.

Dewey (1938) was one of the first educational theorists who strongly believed that people learn by doing, and that all genuine education is achieved through experience. Dewey, however, did not only believe in learning by doing; his notion of 'vocation' as a calling to a deeply felt and ethically grounded identity within a chosen career encompasses the importance of critical and scholarly engagement with the key issues of public life that link professional and vocational competence. Subsequent theorists, such as Kolb (1984) have similarly pointed out that while 'experience' is a part of learning, it is not, on its own, a sufficient condition for learning.

Donald Schön (1983) points out the importance of reflection and reflective practice in the education of professionals. More recently the theoretical underpinnings of Kolb's experiential learning cycle and Schön's 'reflective practitioner' model have been challenged. Humans do not necessarily learn from experience, or from general reflection, particularly if they do not think critically about or take responsibility and ownership for the experience of learning. Hence, if work-integrated learning is seen only as a tool to gain information in a context (e.g. to complete an assignment) or to link technical knowledge with workplace applications (e.g. to complete a task encountered in the workplace), then its effectiveness is not fully developed. Work-integrated learners must be made part of their own learning and experimental processes through individual and shared inquiry- or task-oriented development-based reflection and analysis.

Work-integrated learning is accepted by both employers and the higher education sector with the following rationale:

- Academic benefits include general academic performance, enhancement of interdisciplinary thinking, and increased motivation to learn.
- Personal benefits include increased communication skills, teamwork, leadership and cooperation.
- Career benefits include career clarification, professional identity, increased employment opportunities and salaries, development of positive work values and ethics.
- Skills development includes increased competence and increased technical knowledge and skills.

Work-integrated learning is conceptualized in this chapter to be dealing with more than just work placement or as a mediator of functional skills, as it also deals with inquiry- and development-based reflection with the recognition and acknowledgement of the social/ situational, contextual, connective, collaborative, implicit and tacit aspects of knowledge, knowing and skills. WIL can thus be understood to enhance 'learning how to be', how to act, transfer knowledge and connect with one another between and within communities of practice. Learning can hence occur during a training period, but also in a worklife-based project.

The challenge is to identity the right balance between worklife and traditional educational approaches, the appropriate guidance and support for reflective practices, in order to ensure that skills, underlying norms and practices transfer and develop. Figure 25.2 illustrates the approach taken at Porvoo Campus to address these challenges. The teachers are seen as coaches who integrate the competence-based curriculum with inquiry-based pedagogy, support the acquirement of knowledge and integrative working methods and reflective practices to enhance learning in the context of an authentic working life assignment.

Learning on Campus is viewed as an interactive and iterative process of participating in various cultural practices and shared learning activities that structure and shape cognitive activity in many ways, rather than something that happens inside individuals' minds (see e.g. Brown *et al.*, 1989). Accordingly, learning is seen as a process of becoming a member of a community and acquiring the skills to communicate and act according to socially negotiated norms within a professional setting.

Another learning consideration is whether some studies can be community-based, i.e. if giving service to the community can increase students' sense of social responsibility and citizenship. In that respect, Porvoo Campus curriculum emphasizes meta-cognitive skills and a holistic competence-based approach that include service learning.

Coaches – Competence-based curriculum, inquiry-based model; acquiring knowledge for semester projects, adapting work methods and project aims with theory and substance, sharing and reflection

Students – reflective individual and shared processes

Inquiry learning: what kind of knowledge and analysis is needed for project, how to implement and adjust it to project aims and configure it with collaborative working methods involving individual and shared learning, reflection and development processes with connectivity, poly-contextuality and responsibility as the aspired outcome

Porvoo Campus concept: design, architecture, well-being – stimulate knowledge culture and teamwork

Community   Society   Working Life   Regions

Figure 25.2 Work-integrated learning at HAAGA-HELIA Porvoo Campus

Service learning in tourism, a holistic approach at Porvoo Campus

Curricula that base learning and knowledge according to working life skills and needs are competence-based. Education can be described through the behaviouristic, generic and holistic approaches. The behaviouristic approach cannot provide guidelines for an educational curriculum according to the likes of Barnett (1994), who advocates competence-based curriculum in making the transition from and collaboration between educational institutes and working life smooth. The generic approach has, on the other hand, been criticized for being too generic (Gonzi, 1994).

The Porvoo Campus competence-based curriculum is holistic in nature focusing on meta-competences, social, connective and poly-contextual skills, with responsibility and work-integrated learning as central features. Futhermore, it is also a friendly and agreeable place to be. The holistic approach is seen as being most appropriate for the competence-based education offered on Porvoo Campus as it has features of both the behaviouristic and generic approaches, i.e. it offers a holistic approach to knowledge, skills, capabilities and attitudes within a context (Hodkinson & Issit, 1995).

One way of enhancing education beyond the classroom is by applying a holistic approach through service learning. One definition of service learning proposed by Campus Compact (Gelman *et al.*, 2001) focuses on service learning as pedagogy: 'service learning is an educational methodology which combines community service with academic learning objectives, preparation for community work and deliberate reflection' (p. v.).

How service learning is included, embedded and implemented in the current Porvoo Campus tourism curriculum can be exemplified through the subjects Responsible Self-Management 1 and 2. Both subjects are worth three points in the European Credit Transfer System and are seen as a vital part of tourism students' core studies. In these units service learning is understood through personal reflection integrated with analysis, development and inquiry related to individual and shared responsibility. Student outcomes for these subjects are shown in Table 25.1.

A semester community-based project called Porvoo Works provides another example of how service, inquiry and work–integrated learning is delivered on Porvoo Campus involving a holistic approach enhancing responsibility, connectivity and poly-contextuality as well as skills advocating learning for life. The Porvoo Works project has stemmed from a concern involving work marginalization, unemployment, fear of work situations, false information on working life, etc. Local congregations, youth institutions and mental health institutions are participating in the annual Porvoo Campus based project. Porvoo Works integrates learning, entrepreneurship, youth,

Table 25.1 Responsible self-management

Responsible Self-Management 1
- Upon completion of the course (Responsible Self-Management 1), the student is able to:
  - acquire self-management skills
  - act in a responsible way in the learning environment
  - give and receive feedback in a constructive way
  - adapt to inquiry learning in the studies
  - practise self-assessment and peer assessment
  - develop professional identity and reflect on career plans
  - reflect on ethical considerations in business

Responsible Self-Management 2
- Upon completion of the course, the student is able to:
  - advance self-management and project management skills
  - act in and optimize in a responsible way the learning and working environment
  - organize feedback sessions in a constructive way
  - apply the principles of the inquiry learning in the studies
  - apply the results of self-assessment and peer assessment
  - demonstrate professional identity and focus on career planning
  - demonstrate socially responsible identity in work
  - possess reliable time-management skills

Source: HAAGA-HELIA University of Applied Sciences (2013).

well-being and worklife themes over a period of one week. HAAGA-HELIA Porvoo Campus tourism students take full responsibility for its planning and implementation in collaboration with lecturers and working life. Students manage the project in which they prepare and advise, inform and support students at secondary institutions, in both vocational and general studies, for job and worklife situations by the use of drama, play and orientation, introducing aspiring worklife possibilities including a variety of career fields and work descriptions with the help of professionals.

More than a thousand students have over a period of two years participated in Porvoo Works. Active and interactive participation, social, individual and shared responsibility as well as fun have been the keys to this successful concept.

Through Porvoo Works, stewardship, 'choosing service over self-interest' (Sheldon, 2010), social, individual and shared responsibility, the obligation to act to benefit society at large, and responsible citizenship, are learned and given.

On Porvoo Campus individual, shared and social learning as well as responsible behaviour and ethical behaviour are reflected upon through means of systematic consultations involving small group meetings with teachers and team members. In the weekly consultations, student questions related to a project, its theoretical context, assignments, aims and tasks at hand are raised and discussed. Discussions and learning related to collaboration in teams, the role and responsibilities of team leaders, team members and individual students are reflected upon and involve active inquiry, problem solving, acquiring both know-how and skills. Responsibilities related to knowledge sharing and learning, actions and implications, impact and well-being are emphasized, reflected upon, enacted and elaborated upon. The meetings enhance professional and personal development, students' ability to undertake analysis, teamwork skills and a sense of community (Heinonen, 2013).

According to TEFI values (Sheldon, 2010), tourism students should embody upon graduation five sets of values (see Figure 25.3) in order to become responsible leaders and stewards for the future of tourism. These values are delivered within the HAAGA-HELIA Porvoo tourism curriculum, Campus concept and spirit.

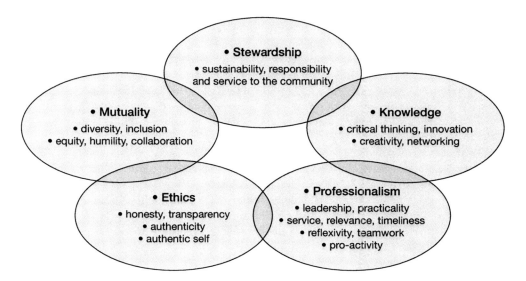

Figure 25.3 Tourism Education Futures Initiative (TEFI) values

Learning in practice on Campus – a student perspective

Six students were asked to write about their study experiences on Campus. All students were third-year tourism students, with two having recently returned from their exchange-year abroad. Three students replied to the request and their narratives can be found below.

Student story number 1

I began my studies in the HAAGA-HELIA University of Applied Sciences Tourism program in Porvoo in January 2010. It was the first time I had ever attended a college or a university so my expectations were based on what I had heard from other people and seen in the media. I had heard mostly positive things about HAAGA-HELIA Porvoo so my expectations were high.

Right from the beginning I noticed that HAAGA-HELIA Porvoo emphasizes independent work a lot in the course. Group work also plays a major role. This was a positive surprise coming from a vocational institute where I studied business, seeing as the studies were not very independent and the instructors were closely involved in all the projects from start to finish. I noticed that in HAAGA-HELIA Porvoo the instructors are there to help you but they try to make you find the solutions first by yourself before turning to them to help you make progress in the projects.

As my studies progressed, the emphasis on independent work grew even more. You were the one responsible on keeping up with the course work. There have been points when I have felt maybe a little more guidance in the studies would not have hurt, even though I understand it is a good thing to make students feel responsible for their own progress.

At times I have also been a little confused as to what courses I should be taking and what exactly is required in order for me to graduate in time. Staying on track has been especially difficult during the times when I have been away for a while, like in the Fall of 2011 when I was doing my exchange program and this Fall 2012 when I was doing my international work placement abroad. Coming back and getting into the right courses after the periods abroad has been quite challenging.

Learning methods at HAAGA-HELIA Porvoo differ a lot from the teaching methods I experienced while doing my exchange period abroad at San Diego State University in the USA. San Diego State University (and as far as I know most universities in the USA) focus a lot more on lectures and independent work at home, either by yourself or in groups. HAAGA-HELIA Porvoo has lectures as well but the emphasis is more on the actual work rather than in lectures. I see this as a positive thing, it is easier to learn things by doing them by yourself rather than hearing how someone else has done it. Lectures are a good thing in the beginning of courses to give you the essential information you need to know of what is to come and after that you can focus on the actual work. I believe HAAGA-HELIA Porvoo has found a good balance between lectures and actual work.

The studies have included a lot of reports as well and the students are required to reflect their own experiences every now and then in the form of personal reports. This has sometimes felt a little silly at first, but I do see the reasoning behind it. It is good to reflect on your own experiences and see how certain ways of doing things have worked personally for you and how certain things may have not. It is also good that the teachers in HAAGA-HELIA Porvoo are interested in what the students have to say and are willing to make improvements if something is seen as inconvenient.

Overall I have been quite satisfied in the teaching methods used in HAAGA-HELIA University of Applied Sciences. It has been quite like what I expected when I first started my studies, and though it has been very different from my previous study experiences, it has been a pleasant surprise. The balance between independent work, group work and the help you get from the instructors is what I see as the most important thing when it comes to making my studies feel useful and pleasant.

Student story number 2

Searching and developing as the ways to study are the idea of HAAGA-HELIA Porvoo Campus and that is why the studies include a lot of projects. The projects' mission is to create the bond between studying and worklife so there are different affiliates, for example small companies, who we, the students, work with. This is how we gain valuable knowledge how to work in projects, how to first search information and then use it and develop the issues and how to be innovative, for instance. All the skills gained are appreciated in the worklife. I have been part of three projects during my studies and all of them have taught me something. Mostly the projects have been creating and implementing some kind of event. Seriously, when we have a project, we plan and do *everything* by ourselves. I have had various tasks; cook, waitress, program planner . . . I try to get the tasks which are diverse from each other. This is how *I* learn.

Learning has always been easy for me. I actually do not have a specific learning style. I feel that this Campus' 'learning by doing' is my cup of tea. It has grown my work skills, encouraged self-esteem and the ability to adapt to different situations. I have always been pretty good at paper (you know, for example, to write fancy essays) but the ability to apply those skills to real life has been, and it still sometimes is, a challenge. Gladly, I learn quite fast.

Working as a group is one important way to work on Porvoo Campus and this method has, of course, both pros and cons. The positive side is that together there will be more ideas and ways to think, for example. There are different personalities in a group so diverse opinions can cause fights. Despite the possible differences of opinions, I see working as a group is fresh and stimulating.

In addition, the new Porvoo Campus is the centre of studying, working and cooperation. The learning spaces are open so there is not the traditional hierarchy between the students and teachers. The aim is that learning together and sharing the knowledge is easier. At first I felt that the Campus is too clinical and missed the old school. But after couple of months I noticed that the open and comfortable classes are actually quite inspiring.

HAAGA-HELIA also provides a laptop for all students. The purpose is to support sustainable development and offer a modern tool for learning. In my opinion the laptop has helped to create certain assignments. It has also improved my technical skills, such as how to use different programs, Microsoft Office, for instance. And because the internet is an endless source of information, it has been easier to filter information because I use the laptop and internet practically every day. In addition, I do not have papers and hand-outs all over. Of course, some of the students can have problems concentrating because of the laptop since the internet also offers entertainment. I personally believe that at The University of Applied Sciences, learning is everyone's own responsibility. If someone browses the internet during lessons, that is ok for me. But then there is no need to cry if they do not pass the course.

All the spaces have modern equipment, such as projectors. Some include also so called smart boards. I think that technological devices can be helpful and in the future, their part as a learning tool will grow. But still, at the same time, it is important to handle the basics, for example how to search information from books.

I will graduate in 3 years even if the duration of my degree programme is 3.5 years. I am motivated to graduate quickly since I want to study more in the future. Probably it will be something else, I am not sure yet.

All in all, for me the learning methods at the University of Applied Sciences and HAAGA-HELIA fit. I personally believe that learning by doing is suitable for me because I practically learn what and how to do things. Maybe someday I will try to apply to an academic university, but right now this is the right way for me.

Student story number 3

I have been studying Hospitality Management for 2.5 years now of which I have accomplished 1.5 years on Porvoo Campus. The one year I spent in England as an exchange student studying at the University of Lincoln. I was asked to do a task of telling my personal student experiences mirroring the methods of learning in Porvoo HAAGA-HELIA.

First of all, this whole Porvoo experience that I have received has been outstanding. I currently live in Porvoo again after living one year abroad. I am from Helsinki and many of my friends are driving to Porvoo from there for their studies almost every day, but I moved to Porvoo because of not wanting to spend time driving back and forth. The main reason, however, was that last time when I lived here the 1.5 years I liked very much living in Porvoo and spending time on Campus because of its atmosphere where I really liked to spend my leisure time as well. Nowadays, I am near to my graduation and I do not have many classes at University but naturally having a nice and warm lunch is a considerable reason itself for going to the University, but seeing my co-students and other students are also good motivation to visit the Campus.

The ways of learning and study methods have been excellent for me. Sitting in a lecture listening to the lecturer for 1.5 hours and writing an essay about it is not my cup of tea. Instead of listening, learning by doing something with own hands and knowing the goal to aim at is a much more pleasant method of learning and studying. The transparent glass walls and doors of the classrooms bring the light differently everywhere and give the feeling of having more open space around the Campus inside which is very nice. Having the tiny ski-resort, almost in the back yard, brings a marvelous and a unique asset to the Campus. IT labs are available at all times to the students and printing is free of charge which contributes to a sense of studying at home.

However everything has its negative sides. In my experience what I have observed this far is that teacher and/or professor are almost always occupied by some meeting, work/ business trip, having a class or another reason not to be available to help the student with his/her studies. Usually problems are solved by emails between the student and the teacher. Study advisors/ student counselors are always unavailable for assisting the students, if not agreed way in advance for a 15 minutes of assistance. Sometimes I wonder myself why there are not two study advisors because I am, for instance, still one of the people who really need personal assistance and guidance rather than sorting things virtually.

Learning in worklife-commissioned projects

Poly-contextual skills refer to the ability to work in changing and new contexts, and to transmit underlying patterns, norms and tacit knowledge from one context to the next. The work-integrated, inquiry- and competence-based learning and project-based implementations including service learning and a holistic approach enhance outcomes related to meta-competences involving poly-contextual, social and connectivity skills as well as individual and shared responsibility.

The projects' mission is to create the bond between studying and worklife so there are different affiliates, for example small companies, who we, the students, work with. This is how we gain valuable knowledge how to work in projects, how to first search information and then use it and develop the issues and how to be innovative, for instance. All the skills gained are appreciated in worklife.

I noticed that at HAAGA-HELIA Porvoo the instructors are there to help you but they try to make you find the solutions first by yourself before turning to them to help you make progress in the projects. Searching and developing as to the ways to study are the idea of HAAGA-HELIA Porvoo Campus and that is why the studies include a lot of projects. It is easier to learn things by doing them by yourself than hearing how someone else has done it.

Students talk about doing and how to work in projects and how to search, acquire and apply information as valuable meta-worklife competences and outcomes when referring to the inquiry-based model and way of learning.

I understand it is a good thing to make students feel responsible of their own progress.

Learning has always been easy for me. I actually do not have some specific learning styles. I feel that this Campus' 'learning by doing' is my cup of tea. It has grown my working skills, encouraged self-esteem and the ability to adapt to different situations. I have always been pretty good at paper (you know, for example, to write fancy essays) but the ability to apply those skills to real life has been, and it still sometime is, a challenge.

Projects and group work is a challenging working and learning method and the counsellor's role is crucial. The work–integrated model involves connectivity, self and group responsibilities, in addition to taking responsibility for your own actions and adapting knowledge in poly-contextual situations and finding solutions to authentic working life problems.

The design, agreeable and friendly atmosphere seem to matter and encourage as well as stimulate to at least the social aspects of learning.

The studies have included a lot of reports as well and the students are required to reflect their own experiences every now and then in the form of personal reports. This has sometimes felt a little silly at first, but I do see the reasoning behind it. It is good to reflect on your own experiences and see how certain ways of doing things have worked personally for you and how certain things may have not. It is also good that the teachers at HAAGA-HELIA Porvoo are interested in what the students have to say and are willing to make improvements if something is seen as inconvenient.

The idea of reflection is understood as a vital part of the Campus based learning process.

The Campus is only two and a half years old and the curriculum has been applied and tested only for two years. The inquiry learning pedagogical model as applied on Porvoo Campus through its project-based implementations and worklife integration as well as competence-based application and holistic approach can be said to be integrating service learning through emphasizing responsibility and reflexivity. Moreover, the Porvoo Campus model enhances worklife competences and meta-cognitive skills, poly-contextuality and connectivity in addition to competences and learning related to stewardship, mutuality, professionalism, knowledge and ethics.

One educational consideration that universities of applied sciences in Finland constantly face is how and why to embed authentic worklife needs and competences such as knowledge, attitude and skills, with theoretical research-based content. The Porvoo Campus concept and model is one example of how and why worklife competences and skills can be ensured, and theory adapted to project aims and applied in practice through project implementations. Another consideration is whether some studies can be community-based, i.e. if giving service to the community can increase students' sense of social responsibility and citizenship. There is some evidence of this, and the aspiration is there and the community-based projects and implementations on Campus are perceived and valued as much as any other projects.

Conclusions

Porvoo Campus is a new and creative concept for learning. During the development process, a traditional construction project changed into the creation of a modern learning environment. The results of the project – a new curriculum and pedagogical approach linked to the Campus design – have now been implemented for three years. The academic staff have changed from traditional teachers to coaches and mentors aiming at new competences with new tools to enhance learning. The new methods to work have been assessed by them and this self-assessment process is ongoing as well as a part of the normal tasks of teacher teams. Self-assessment is a part of an action research approach that aims to develop both organization and work.

After the first round of implementing the curriculum at Porvoo Campus there is a need to evaluate and to sum up the experiences. The challenges and shortcomings in the implementation process have to be identified and necessary actions taken in order to improve the way of implementing the curriculum. The curriculum as such is flexible and does not need to be updated at the current time.

However, what needs to be agreed upon better is the understanding and interpretation of inquiry learning among teachers at Porvoo Campus. This is a question of leadership. The programme directors at Porvoo Campus have a responsibility for this; however, the traditional roles are difficult to eradicate. Traditional teacher roles shouldn't exist anymore at Porvoo Campus as the working method is team-based. The new way to work at Porvoo Campus demands joint principles and guidelines, as well as reflective practices and spaces for teachers where joint understanding can be created. Service learning is part of our future at Porvoo Campus.

References

Barnett, R. (1994). *The Limits of Competence: knowledge, higher education and society.* Buckingham: Open University Press.

Brown, J. S., Collins, A., Duguid, P. (1989). 'Situated Cognition and the Culture of Learning', *Educational Researcher*, 18(1), 32–42.

Bunting, A. (2004). 'Secondary Schools Designed for a Purpose: but which one?' *Teacher*, 154, 10–13.

Dewey, J. (1938). *Experience and Education.* New York: Collier Books.

Eteläpelto, A. (2007). 'Työidentiteetti Ja Subjektius Rakenteiden Ja Toimijuuden Ristiaallokossa'. [Work Identity and Subjectivity in the Cross-Current of Structures and Agency]. (Eds.), A. Teoksessa, K. Collin Eteläpelto, & J. Saarinen, *Työ, identiteetti ja oppiminen. [Work, Identity and Learning]* (pp. 90–142). Helsinki/Porvoo: WSOY.

Gelman, S., Holland, B., *et. al.* (2001). *Assessing Service-Learning and Civic Engagement: principles and techniques.* Providence, RI: Campus Compact.

Gonzi, A. (1994). 'Competency Based Assessment in the Profession in Australia'. *Assessment in Education,* 1, 27–44.

Grasping the Future. (2008). 'A Challenge for Future Learning and Innovation'. Available: https://www.wanhasatama.com/eman/ShowFair.phx?eid=eman.inno08&templatename=showfairen.htx%lang=en (Accessed 5 November 2010).

HAAGA-HELIA University of Applied Sciences. (2013). Degree Program in Tourism Porvoo Campus. Available: http://www.haaga-helia.fi/en/education-and-application/bachelor-degree-programmes/tourism/dp-in-tourism-porvoo-campus (Accessed 12 October 2013).

Hakkarainen, K., Lonka, K., & Lipponen, L. (2004). *Tutkiva Oppiminen. Järki. Tunteet Jakulttuuri Oppimisen Sytyttäjinä.* [Inquiry learning. Rationale, emotions and culture as triggers for learning]. Helsinki/Porvoo: WSOY.

Heinonen, J. (2013). Personal interview with Porvoo Campus lecturer conducted on 02 May, at HAAGA-HELIA Pasila Campu.

Hodkinson, P., & Issitt, M. (1995). *The Challenge of Competence.* London: Cassell.

Kolb, D. A. (1984). *Experiential Learning*, Englewood Cliffs, NJ: Prentice Hall.

Lave, J., & Wenger, E. (1991). *Situated Learning: legitimate peripheral participation.* Cambridge: Cambridge University Press.

Scardamalia, M., & Bereitner, C. (2006). Knowledge Building: theory, pedagogy and technology. Available: http://www.slideshare.net/moskaliuk/wikis-in-der-schule-potentiale-fr-kooperatives-lernen-presentation-777310 (Accessed 25 October 2013).

Schön, D. (1983). *The Reflective Practitioner. how professionals think in action*, London: Temple Smith.

Sheldon, P. (2010). 'Issues in the Future of Tourism and Hospitality Education'. CAUTHE. Available: http://www.slideshare.net/DianneDredge/cauthe-2010-pauline-sheldon (Accessed 10 December 2013).

Sincero, P. (2006). 'What Is Inquiry Learning?' Available: http://www.inquirylearn.com/Inquirydef.htm (Accessed 25 October 2013).

Wenger, E. (1998). *Learning, Meaning, and Identity.* Cambridge: Cambridge University Press.

26

Embedded research

A pragmatic design for contextual learning – from fieldtrip to fieldwork to field research in Australasia

Ariane Portegies, Vincent Platenkamp and Theo de Haan

NHTV Breda University of Applied Sciences, The Netherlands

Introduction

Fieldwork components in a tourism curriculum hardly need justification. Recognizing the multiple attractive dimensions of such 'escapades', such as getting away from school and seeing other landscapes, the purely educational benefits remain in principle undisputed by most, if not all, tourism programmes. In both bachelor and Tourism Destination Management (TDM) Master's programmes at the NHTV Breda University of Applied Sciences, in the Netherlands, the fieldwork component has become both a pivot and a pillar, feeding the overall tourism curriculum, both in content and design.

This chapter explores this dynamic relation between fieldwork and educational philosophy. Fieldwork is a conceptual space where people who work in and around tourism meet those who think and learn about tourism. It is an open space, creating room for many situations where students can apply their talents for observation, exploration and making their own discoveries. In that same space, practitioners share their successes and their failures. More importantly, there is room to discuss and exchange uncertainties about current livelihood practices, potential market developments and the unknown. Professionals and entrepreneurs of all sorts and sizes play a central role in the fieldwork. These people – players in this chapter – pragmatically cooperate with students and lecturers as part of an experience of 'learning on the spot', constantly aware of the uncertainties and of the limits of knowledge.

This chapter explores why we find this approach challenging but enriching and why this approach is preferred above the one where key questions and frameworks are predefined. The approach needs a high tolerance for the uncertain and the unknown, it is risky and there are multiple pitfalls. Nevertheless, in the world of tourism education, where relations with industry need continuous rethinking, where people, ideas and culture flow in smooth and rugged scapes, this approach seems most fit. The pleasures and pains of our learning experiences follow, together with the latest challenges in this, namely a growing accent on post-disciplinary research, as well as a deepening of the study of de- and re-contextualization practices. Post-disciplinary research in this context refers to a collaborative effort of academics from various disciplines and practitioners from many sides who jointly and without pre-established hierarchy are working on how to deal in an innovative manner with complex and emergent practices by focusing on both context-dependent and context-independent characteristics.

We will start with a review of what we have come to define as contextual learning through fieldwork practices at the International Tourism Management and Consultancy (hereafter ITMC) bachelor course at the NHTV Breda. This has been discussed in two previous publications (Portegies et al., 2009; Portegies et al., 2011). The first treats the gradual shift in our teaching and fieldwork practices, from an 'instrumental' to a contextual approach to learning processes and knowledge production. The second article is situated in the specific fieldwork of bachelor students in Cambodia in 2009. This chapter will then proceed to expose the current 'pragmatic' design of the TDM Master's fieldwork, paying particular attention to the fieldwork of Master's students, who spend three months in three different locations in Australasia. The conclusion will formulate a number of current challenges of this approach and aims for the future, joining discussions on post-disciplinarity and mixed methodology (Hollinshead & Ivanova, 2013).

Contextual learning and the international classroom

Destinations are dynamic and ever-changing spaces continuously performed and shaped by its visitors and inhabitants. Clearly, a destination is more than a sum of empirical facts related to tourism. It also includes the way people live and work, currently and in the past. Understanding a destination can only be done in that context. In his various publications on tourism of Asian origin, Winter (2007, 2009) also draws attention to this and argues that in its current form the field of tourism studies is institutionally and intellectually ill-equipped to understand and interpret the new era we are now entering. He suggests that the core–periphery dynamics, which characterizes the field today, should give way to cultural and political pluralism (Winter, 2009).

In order to have students discover the changes and dynamics of tourism destinations, a contextual approach has been developed at NHTV (Platenkamp, 2006; Portegies et al., 2009). Contextual education starts from the complexity of our network-society (Appadurai, 1996; Castells, 2000; Hannerz, 1993). In a phenomenological mood students are encouraged to start by – as much as possible – leaving their frameworks behind. Simultaneously to having preconceptions and stereotypes about tourism development, these students are very open to new information and new situations. The contextual approach departs from the idea that many relevant insights in the study object – for example a tourism destination – may be found in unwritten or implicit types of information. A master plan or a regional development plan, a destination value chain report, a marketing plan for a hotel, figures about beds, overnight stays and arrivals provide students with the illusion that they have all relevant insights into a destination. A contextual approach makes this type of information more secondary, more subordinate, while paying attention to what is happening 'on the street' becomes more relevant: how people sell souvenirs and develop other forms of entrepreneurship, how people spend their time, learning, working, caring for their families, but also the variety of tourists walking around at different times of the day and in different areas of the destination.

This contextual approach has grown gradually within the limits of a tourism practice in higher education at NHTV Breda University of Applied Sciences. At its start it was instrumentalist in outline, and step by step in an 'incremental' way; gradually, an educational practice developed that can be characterized by a 'contextual practice' of higher education. Earlier work provides a history of this practice and a critical reflection on the added value of this approach (Portegies et al., 2009).

The practice of the International Classroom (IC) mixes with tourism practice in international destinations in an inspirational manner and with mutual respect of all participants. Students from a variety of backgrounds, and most of whom do not originate from the destination visited, bring within them their own contexts, their own learning resources, valuable for themselves and for their fellow students, but also for the teaching staff. The IC is composed of hybrids, footloose, sedentary, tourists, indigenous, strangers, migrants, friends and family; it is a cross-section of our network-society and in which networks interfere. The awareness of students of their own contexts increases significantly while living and researching in another context. This self-reflexive perspective is a necessary step in the opening up to new situations and for the development of new insights (Ricoeur, 1990). In addition to actively using this phenomenon of 'being overwhelmed', the contextual approach also encourages students to open up to it further. Students' observations, their encounters with the people they meet unexpectedly or without a study purpose, but also their diaries, emails and text messages they send home, these all become part of the field research. Applying the IC concept thus expresses the intention and practices in ITMC to recognize, bring to the fore and actively put to work the plurality that is reality in most classrooms – and tourism destinations – today. It is a space where discussions take place between perspectives. These discussions are impregnated with hidden moral and existential questions (Isaac *et al.*, 2009). These types of questions are dealt with inadequately in education, business and academic contexts. The identification and introduction of these questions in professional analyses is thought to enhance understanding and scientific reflection.

Pragmatic design for contextual learning

There is a recent development in approaches to fieldwork from a phenomenological design to a more pragmatic design. The phenomenological design came into being because we wanted to enable the experience of having the variety of practices emerge, instead of recognizing pre-existing frameworks. This approach is one of 'What does the situation have to say to us?' and leads to many discoveries, revealing worlds behind this, and making the situation more understandable. In Bali, Indonesia, under former President Suharto, the military were the basis of his power; they had economic power which extended to tourism for example through concessions given to beach-bars, etc. With the fall of Suharto, the opposition who gained power wanted to make the point: 'we now have power'. They made a road along the beach, with the idea to give access to the beach for all residents. With that road they destroyed the privileges of the businesses that had enjoyed the military concessions, and they destroyed prime beach locations suitable for hotels. Later, these hotels struck back by ensuring that no motorized traffic was allowed to use these roads. The idea here was that by focusing on a phenomenological approach the learner dives into an understanding of the political context that prevails in this example and the consequences it had, and still has, for hotels in this destination.

The current pragmatic approach to fieldwork is a result of the experience with this previous phenomenological phase. There was a tendency to 'drown' in a situation that was growing in complexity but without focus. Everything seemed equally important and too little selection of key factors was made from within fieldwork situations. Hereto, a pragmatic reorientation on practice taught us to look at the focused interests of relevant stakeholders. Looking in such a detailed way at the context, we tended to pay less attention to the vested interests of the relevant actors in the developments we were studying. This made us realize that we once again had to look more carefully at practices, but in a different and pragmatic manner. In Bali, as elsewhere, small business operates within a context of larger interests. In this climate, small, independent food outlets were tolerated or neglected as long as they didn't sell beer (alcohol) and they conformed with what the highly competitive syndicates dictated. This type of information evolves from the repeated conversations of students with the same players in the destinations. Through the recognition of clusters of interests in the destination, a focus emerges on hidden information that adds insights into what is happening in a more selective, pragmatic way. Instead of moving from one paradigm (phenomenology) to another (pragmatism), we try to broaden the scope 'to identify, explore and confront multiple paradigms and values that underpin education'. An interesting but crucial element in this process – that will be of later concern in this chapter – is the creation of the basic value of mutual trust between the students and local players.

A first phase

A first phase in the fieldwork is the learning of 'what matters'. Hearing the speakers, observing people at work, triangulating and discussing further, students see both conjuncture and disjuncture of interests in the destination's dynamics. From this chaotic context – sometimes fluid, sometimes rigid – key matters of concern can be defined, locsely and slowly.

In the process of learning 'what matters', the people who students meet deserve ample consideration. The challenge of understanding who they are, is of utmost importance, particularly the recognition of the almost impossibility thereof. An open, careful and self-reflexive approach is therefore introduced and practised in the taught part of the Master's prior to departure. The design of the 'organized' part of the programme on location reflects this open approach. A selection of players is made, and these people are introduced to students on site visits, during more formal presentations or panel discussions. In a mutual process, the fieldwork staff and key players engage with the destination, they develop long-term views and ideas, and recognize complexities. This results in a selection of players to introduce the students to the destination upon their arrival. Prior to their arrival, the fieldwork staff have usually made two or three preliminary visits. These scouting and inception missions are of crucial importance to the long-term relationship building and engagement with the destination. Here too, the relation with a pragmatic approach goes without saying: you need a shared interest in this specific educational practice between academics and destination players.

This first encounter is surely not exhaustive, many interesting people and actors are not part of it. This leads to the next reflection on the people students meet. The major part of their fieldwork is left for students to make their own encounters: partly planned and partly accidental. Master's students are encouraged to start with the latter. People 'on the streets', the vendor, the taxi driver, the surfboard rental operator, the laundry lady, and people they meet while settling in at the location. This gives them the time and the opportunity to let the situation speak for itself. In addition, this also gives more room for relations to develop in an indirect way. Finally, and perhaps most important, is the growing awareness that the people they meet are as complex, multifaceted, evolving and in transition as anywhere else. The concept of actor as introduced and developed by Bruno Latour (2005) is therefore useful because it demonstrates the struggle in 'learning on the spot'. Thinking of a person as an actor or a player, or a representative of a profession is static. Latour problematizes the concept of actor and draws attention to the agencies impacting upon, having effect, leading to actions, whether intentional or not. The implications of Latour's Actor–Network Theory in the study of destinations in NHTV's curriculum are yet to be studied in the context of the polyphony and multi-layeredness of people who are and remain at the core of the fieldwork approach.

Polyphony relates to the fact that so many interest groups are involved that need to be heard in a multi-vocal dialogue. To realize this, an appeal is also made to the self-reflexivity of the student researcher who plays a crucial role in this interpretive process. Self-reflexivity, therefore, is also an essential part of the fieldwork approach. Students are trained to explicate aspects of their selves as they learn and research in an international context. It is the interaction between self and other (Ricoeur, 1990) that teaches us who we are and can be. Without this awareness students, as all researchers, would jump to pre-established conclusions without realizing their own biases. Here, too, reflective openness is needed in order to avoid this.

An emphasis on 'encounters' enhances student researchers' self-reflexivity and promotes understanding. These encounters, e.g. formal, accidental, pleasant, confusing, etc., are central in the students' fieldwork. The relation between tourism education and tourism praxis is a priority and leads in the field to spaces of trust, a basic value as stipulated before. All parties involved in this education space – students, teaching staff and players – seek inspiration, understanding and reflection often not found in their daily competitive environment. In the space of trust, uncertainties can be exchanged, questions can be raised and engagement with the destination can be further enhanced. It is also clearly a learning situation. All parties become aware of the wealth and variety of knowledge and experiences present in the space; equally, they become aware that 'solutions' are difficult. People in top positions often feel alone: they like to share their thoughts, worries and uncertainties; there are not many opportunities for them to share their concerns in an 'interest-less' and trustworthy setting. This is a great opportunity for learners.

A second phase

The basic principle in the first phase was 'knowing what matters' as it emerges from the slow approach to learning. In this contextual approach, a development has been signalled whereby student learning has shifted from a phenomenological approach to a combination of phenomenology and a pragmatic and engaged approach that includes developing an understanding of the vested interests of diverse academics, educators and practitioners at the same time. From this combination a realistic view on what matters is supposed to have a bigger chance of emerging. In a methodological reflection on this type of knowledge production, a reference to the distinction between mode 1 and mode 2 types of knowledge production seems relevant (Gibbons et al., 1994; Tribe, 1997; Kunneman, 2005; Portegies et al., 2009).

In mode 1 knowledge production, theories are generated and tested in a context governed by the (inter-)disciplinary problems of the academic community. This mode of knowledge production aims at knowledge that is universally valid, independent of contexts. The research community is divided into sub-communities based on existing disciplines. Knowledge is generated in mono-disciplinary worlds and tied to the basic theoretical concepts and central assumptions of a specific discipline or domain. This type of knowledge is highly formalized and its existence in tourism studies is debatable (Tribe, 1997; Platenkamp & Botterill, 2012).

Mode 2 production of knowledge is much more complex, derived from exploiting social connections in the much debated network-society. The scientific status of knowledge is much less clear than in mode 1 knowledge production, because of the role contexts, know-how, tacit knowledge or vested interests play in the understanding and solution of problems. This constitutes the focal point of this pragmatic approach. Universally valid knowledge is questioned, with the best intervention to address a problem based on the set of possible solutions for practical problems and questions. Mode 2 knowledge production is carried out through trans-disciplinary (in our case even post-disciplinary) research in a context of application (i.e. fieldwork in the destination). The interests of different players play a role and are negotiated during a process in which consensus is conditioned by the demands of the context of application. Much more might be said about this type of knowledge production, but in this chapter this mode has been translated into the first basic principle of this contextual education, to study 'what really matters', such as in the case of Bali, the accessibility to the beach.

The second basic principle is to look at these matters of concern (that determine or shape tourism development) from different (embedded) angles. The implications of this second basic principle are also methodological, to say the least. A mixed methodology, in which quantitative and qualitative research are complementary instead of exclusive, is a self-evident assumption here. In order to identify and understand these matters of concern in a destination, facts and figures have a place. Tourist arrivals, market characteristics, trends and projections – just to mention a few quantitative aspects – are needed. But at the same time, a methodological challenge has appeared right from the start in this contextual approach. The emergent change from an instrumental to a contextual type of research approach underpinning student fieldwork generates some clear implications for innovative qualitative research in combination with the use and analysis of the existing quantitative data identified above (Portegies *et al.*, 2009; Portegies *et al.*, 2011). In this context, mode 2 knowledge production as a type of action research with a pragmatic accent, and including some critical and self-reflexive aspects as well, were included in the fieldwork approach.

Triangulation was an obvious way of drawing together qualitative and quantitative fieldwork findings along with other sources of knowledge including observations, tacit knowledge and self-reflexivity. When students drew conclusions based on the stories of some expatriates who spoke their languages, it was obvious to let them check this information by what we called 'changing perspectives'. Students were supposed to place themselves in the role and position of other players and confront the resulting perspective with the ones of the expats. Different interpretations are to be integrated if a pragmatic approach has to be successful. How to proceed with this challenge appeared to be a constant concern for all parties involved. How do you assemble interesting information from this interpretive angle and how do you translate that information into 'knowledge' that is relevant for different types of players? Through this question, the way has been opened to different new avenues of qualitative research such as case studies of parts of a destination, narrative inquiries into encounters between different interest groups, visual methodology into the interpretation of new, visual developments in the destination or self-reflexive analyses of relevant biographies.

Methodology does not develop without theoretical reflection. Here, too, some basic developments are taking place in the evolution of this international fieldtrip approach. Over the course of the fieldtrip's evolution year upon year, it became clear that the more instrumental types of theoretical support have been abandoned in this contextualized fieldtrip education. In its place, however, more challenges are appearing at the horizon of understanding the international tourism destination as embedded in different economic, political, social, cultural, technological and other contexts than those that the students are familiar with.

In this second phase of looking from different angles at matters of concern, methodological and theoretical implications have been made clear. They illustrate the growing entanglement of theory and practice in the fieldwork.

Conclusions and future orientations

The accent in this chapter is on the fieldwork learning and its theoretical and methodological considerations. Therefore it will be relevant to conclude this chapter with some reflections on the future of this fieldwork.

Our Master's students do research in three different locations in Australasia, one month in each location. In 2013 these three locations were Sunshine Coast Australia, Bangkok and Bali.

In 2014 they will be Melbourne, Fiji and Bali. The students are to be acquainted, like their professors and the players in the field, with post-disciplinary research. This post-disciplinary approach is crucial to the success of the educational concept: high value is attributed to a broad diversity of sources of knowledge including experiential knowledge, practitioners' knowledge, narratives, popular culture and the arts. Furthermore the concept is very much dependent on following interrelated elements: stimulating diversity of student cohorts, fieldwork staff experienced with the IC, opportunity to engage with the destination. Clearly, this international fieldwork learning experience has its risks and its challenges but is also very rewarding. In this post-disciplinary approach to fieldwork all participants, and particularly students, are able to develop a highly comprehensive understanding and experience that is similar to their future professional life. Post-disciplinarity also figures in this respect as an exemplary research practice. In the future, we consider this form of learning practice will evolve even more and case study research insights will also develop concomitantly. In particular, the ways in which practitioners and academics could learn from each other through joint research point to an open field that has had some research (Dredge & Jenkins, 2011) but more is required.

A post-disciplinary type of fieldwork instruction also implies the growing entanglement of theory and research. For the future, it will be interesting what the reflections of this whole process of learning will tell us, and how it will contribute to new cycles of research and education. In this chapter it became clear that there has been a development, first, from instrumental to contextual education and, second, from an exclusively phenomenological orientation to a combined phenomenological–pragmatic outlook. Apart from this, theoretical and method-ological debates constitute the core of this fieldwork approach to learning. Such reflections are characteristic for the international fieldwork approach. More of these discussions are to be expected as well as theoretical inspiration of all participants through self-reflection, narration and contextualization. One of the basic skills in this fieldwork is to be able to change perspectives. This requires not only open-mindedness of the participants, but also the critical intellectual skill of self-reflection.

Self-reflection implies that a person can look at him or herself and recognize their own subjectivities and those of others. In the context of this international fieldwork exercise, students gain self-knowledge and incorporate and share that in the learning processes and their outcomes. This will be useful to them in professional life. The whole experience inspires the Master's students, and in the future this inspiration, this sense of wonder, will remain an important life skill. It makes one think and reflect, also in a theoretical sense. Tourism tends to freeze places and essentialize people. The challenge of tourism education through embedded research and contextual learning is to deconstruct these obstacles to further understanding, and to inspire students to act and intervene in meaningful ways.

References

Appadurai, A. (1996). *Modernity at Large: cultural dimensions of globalisations.* Mineapolis: University of Minnesota Press.
Castells, M. (2000). *The Information Age: economy, society and culture* (Vols. I, II and III). Oxford: Blackwell.
Dredge, D., & Jenkins, J. (Eds.). (2011). *Stories of Practice: tourism policy and planning.* Farnham: Ashgate.
Gibbons, M., Limoges, C., Nowothy, H., Schwartzman, S., Scott, P., & Trow, M. (1994). *The New Production of Knowledge.* London: Sage.
Hannerz, U. (1993). *Cultural Complexity: studies in the social organization of meaning.* New York: Columbia University Press.
Hollinshead, K., & Ivanova, M. (2013). 'The Multilogical Imagination: tourism studies and the imperative of postdisciplinary knowing'. In G. Richards, & M. Smith (Eds.), *The Routledge Handbook of Cultural Tourism* (pp. 53–62). London: Routledge.

Isaac, R. K., Platenkamp, V., & Portegies, A. (2009). 'Introduction'. In: R. K. Isaac, V. Platenkamp, & A. Portegies (Eds.), *Voices in Tourism Development: creating spaces for tacit knowledge and innovation*. Breda: NHTV Expertise Series 8.

Kunneman, H. (2005). *Voorbij het Dikke-ik*. Amsterdam: B.V. uitgeverij SWP.

Latour, B. (2005). *Reassembling the Social – an introduction to actor-network-theory*. Oxford: Oxford University Press.

Platenkamp, V. (2006). *Contexts in Tourism and Leisure Studies: a cross-cultural contribution to the production of knowledge*. Wageningen: Wageningen University.

Platenkamp, V., & Botterill, T. (2012). 'Critical Realism, Rationality and Tourism Knowledge'. *Annals of Tourism Research*, 41, 110–29.

Portegies, A., de Haan, T., & Platenkamp, V. (2009). 'Knowledge Production in Tourism: the evaluation of contextual learning processes in destination studies'. *Tourism Analysis*, 14, 523–36.

Portegies, A., de Haan, T., Isaac, R., & Roovers, L. (2011). 'Understanding Cambodian Tourism Development'. *Tourism, Culture and Communication*, 11, 103–16.

Ricoeur, P. (1990). *Soi-meme comme un autre*, Paris: Seuil.

Tribe, J. (1997). 'The Indiscipline of Tourism'. *Annals of Tourism Research*, 24(3), 638–57.

Winter, T. (2007). *Post-Conflict Heritage, Postcolonial Tourism, Politics and Development at Angkor*. New York: Routledge.

Winter, T. (2009). 'Asian Tourism and the Retreat of Anglo-Western Centrism in Tourism Theory'. *Current Issues in Tourism*, 12(1), 21–31.

27

Teaching service quality, innovation management and other service considerations in the hospitality management discipline

Using digital technology to facilitate student learning outcomes

Robert J. Harrington

Dale Bumpers College of Agricultural, Food and Life Sciences,
University of Arkansas, USA

Michael C. Ottenbacher

School of International Business, Heilbronn University, Germany

F. Allen Powell

Dale Bumpers College of Agricultural, Food and Life Sciences,
University of Arkansas, USA

Introduction

The integration of technology into higher education has become pervasive over the past two decades with growing opportunities for distance education programmes, a greater availability of information and content through electronic sources, as well as the integration of technology as a method of communication through learning platforms (such as Blackboard), social media and mobile applications. While these uses of technology obviously provide greater access to education, more information and ease of communication, it remains a question as to how technology can be used to enhance the education process providing higher forms of learning to enable students to address complex challenges and issues not readily addressed based on memorization or having the ability to restate what has been presented to them in the classroom.

Hospitality education has long been viewed as being an area of study that is: (1) vocational in nature; or (2) primarily based on lecture directly applicable to the field (Barron & Anastasiadou, 2009; Johnson, 2009). Several studies have indicated a need to create a balance between liberal education and vocational approaches to the curriculum (Morrison & O'Mahony, 2003) or suggested there are numerous new learning arenas to investigate (Airey & Tribe, 2000). Studies assessing the needs of hospitality education by industry call for greater skills in problem solving, foreign language skills, communication, service quality, human resource management, leadership and innovation management in a field of growing complexity and diversity (Harrington et al., 2005; Müller et al., 2009). A second key challenge for hospitality education is greater diversity of the student body driven by cultural differences (home country differences, ethnic differences, age differences, etc.) with implications for effectiveness of teaching methods. Studies have indicated vast differences in preferred learning styles for student groups based on age, home country and ethnic differences (Sulkowski & Deakin, 2009).

The skills that are demanded for success in professional careers in the hospitality field require higher levels of learning. Bloom's taxonomy (1956) provides a framework for differing levels of learning. Many traditional teaching methods primarily tap into the lower levels of learning such as: (1) recalling information; (2) changing information into a different form; and (3) solving problems by using knowledge and appropriate generalizations. The question raised in this chapter is: how can the hospitality learning process move to analysis and synthesis levels of learning outcomes? Analysis is defined as when the student is able to separate information into its component parts and synthesis is when the student is able to solve a problem by putting information together that requires original and creative thinking.

More specifically, the research questions raised in this chapter include: can digital technology be used to facilitate these higher levels of student learning in hospitality education? and, can technology be used to facilitate learning in service quality, service management and gain a better understanding of customer satisfaction? The following sections provide an overview of technology uses in hospitality education in general, and two cases as examples of technology use as part of the student learning process are presented: crowdsourcing and audio/visual technology methods for learning in service quality and guest satisfaction.

Current uses of technology in hospitality education

Online learning and teaching includes conceptual learning, collaborative learning, research and analysis and presentations, such as PowerPoint (Lominé, 2002). Despite the growing importance of online education, a survey of international hospitality and tourism higher education administrators found that only 22.5 per cent of them had online education significantly implemented. However, more than 80 per cent anticipated that the majority of their students are going to take one or more courses online within five years but the majority of hospitality/tourism administrators still will have concerns regarding the quality of online education (Sciarini et al., 2012).

A vast majority of technology used in education refers to the use of Internet and computer-based technology. Cho et al. (2002), for example, support *just-in-time education* which practices critical thinking through Internet research, collaborative learning through interacting in chat-rooms and newsgroups and also enhances the ability to use and accept technology. Thus, just-in-time education encourages a more active and more time-flexible way of learning that is designed to prepare students for the kind of challenges they are going to face on the job (Dawson & Titz, 2002; Newman & Brownell, 2008). A study of Chinese hospitality students (Yan & Cheug, 2012) revealed that virtual learning on the Internet is for them more interesting, modern and individual in comparison to the standard frontal teaching. In addition, hospitality students who take part in computer-based courses, outperform students who learn in standard lectures, regardless of their attitude towards e-learning (Behnke, 2012). Still, the success of online learning and teaching depends on, among other things, the theme of the course.

Another way to make use of technology in learning and teaching is the use of online discussion boards or blogs to organize team members while undertaking a project. A study of hospitality management undergraduates indicated that the vast majority of students view online discussion boards as useful for the convenience and that they enjoyed posting and reading messages (Robinson, 2011). Furthermore, more than 60 per cent of the students who regularly participated on blogs thought this might lead to better grades and over 70 per cent would use this technology again for future projects. This was confirmed by Cobanoglu (2006), who suggests that online blogging can be used as a helpful learning tool.

Aside from Internet-based teaching methods, there also are other innovative ways to implement technology into hospitality teaching. The most used software in lectures still might be PowerPoint, and with an add-on called Microsoft Producer it is even simpler to insert rich text, videos or sound files to create multimedia presentations. An alternative to PowerPoint is Prezi, which is an online-based presentation software that can be used free of charge. A benefit of this software is its ability of zooming in and out of charts to give emphasis on different sections of the slides. PowerPoint, as well as Prezi, has its limitations in the fact that the lecturer has to break down sentences into key points (Harris, 2011) and nuanced explanations and deeper reflections often get lost or overlooked.

Though students use their mobile devices primarily for social networking, there also is a way to use these mobile devices for teaching and learning through a flash-based gaming application called StudyMate (Smith, 2012). This program allows lecturers and students to enter course concepts into 12 different games such as jeopardy, crosswords or hangman, in order to learn in a more interactive way. Students' perceive the advantages of such interactive learning tools to be the ability to learn anywhere and anytime, and the convenience of not having to carry books. Disadvantages included the small screen size or the lack of social interaction but 100 per cent of the students responded that they would do it again.

A further technology that can be brought to the classroom of hospitality and tourism education is the Classroom Response Systems (CRS) (or also called Audience Response Systems, or Personal Response Systems or simply clickers) (Miller et al., 2012). The Classroom Response System is a remote control that helps to assess the understanding of students of a concept presented in the course or to promote discussion. The instructor puts questions to which the students have to answer anonymously via the CRS. Multiple-choice questions are presented to the students and the responses are analysed giving the instructor immediate feedback. In Miller's study this technology was helpful in reinforcing course concepts and in encouraging students to participate in class (Miller et al., 2012). Overall, there has been a positive attitude of students towards the CRS through enhanced learning and understanding.

The concept of crowdsourcing is another technological concept that can be used for hospitality education which will be discussed in more detail in the following section.

Case study 1: Crowdsourcing techniques – lessons learned in innovation and service management innovation

In a study using integrated and experiential teaching methods, Harrington et al. (2010) indicated that classroom practices with experiential and collaborative elements are likely to be useful in enhancing student learning. Further, the authors suggested student learning can be maximized by integrating underutilized content with collaborative learning approaches to enhance and highlight key managerial behaviours. This case looks at the usefulness of this approach with the integration of technology to determine if it is useful to facilitate the innovation process and related learning outcomes.

Specifically, this case integrated the crowdsourcing concept into a class project, in part, to determine its effectiveness. Basically, crowdsourcing uses the Web to exploit the collective efforts of a group of people (the 'crowd') to assist an individual or firm to resolve a problem, create a new product, etc. Example websites featuring this approach include CrowdSPRING, Crowdtap, IdeaOffer, and GeniusCrowds. This basic process appears to provide interactive modes such as discussion-based learning, which have been shown to enhance curriculum delivery and communication using reflective teaching methods (Hellsten & Prescott, 2004). Based on a synthesis of the innovation literature, this case assessed the integration of a crowdsourcing approach to learning innovation management in the hospitality curriculum. Way *et al.* (2011) provided a theoretical model suggesting that the crowdsourcing concept is likely to improve and facilitate the innovation process in four main areas.

Crowdsourcing sites are likely to move a new idea or concept to idea optimization or concept refinement by increasing the number of ideas generated, the quality of ideas by engaging others, the amount of information available and making use of specific knowledge (Way *et al.*, 2011). This process is likely to increase learning outcomes from feedback and an external peer learning process.

This case integrated the crowdsourcing process into a class assignment to determine the potential for moving the learning process to higher levels. As part of the case design, the study considered several factors in the learning process related to idea creation and innovation that are likely to facilitate synergistic learning including a cross-functional team experience, peer learning, critical factor identification, concept/idea refinement, increased diversity of ideas and a general problem-solving process.

The crowdsourcing class project used a food and wine menu item development assignment as the decision vehicle. Specifically, students enrolled on a semester-long food and wine course were required to complete an individual project. Students developed an idea for a food item that represented the region where the university was located in some fashion. For the crowdsourcing project, students were instructed to post the food item idea on a specified website (www.gameofbeads.com). This site was used as a result of a local website developer's offer to students of a mid-south United States hospitality programme. This site was determined to be appropriate for crowdsourcing use as it facilitated crowdsourcing-type communication, feedback and the ability to allow changes to postings, as well as allowing students to post pictures, video, music and written descriptions. Students provided a description of the food/menu item (traditional recipe, preparation, any history, photographs, any proposed contemporary revisions and suggested wine pairings). Example student dishes included biscuits with chocolate gravy, venison loin with blueberry glaze and fried catfish fiddlers paired with chardonnay.

The website allowed external comments and changes that the 'crowdsourcers' could accept or not. Peers were required to comment and suggest changes to at least two posted items; posting of comments and changes from external users were also allowed. Participants solicited feedback for 30 days on:

- Feedback from others on the proposed food item
- Suggestions for modification or further improvement
- Thoughts on wine or other beverages selection that would create an ideal match

- Likelihood of 'willingness to purchase' by consumers
- Pricing suggestions and if the price point fitted with the cost of the food item.

After the 30-day period, student participants wrote a synopsis of the process, the impact on their food item/wine pairing ideas, and learning outcomes from the project. The crowdsourcing project and written synopsis represented 10 per cent of each student grade. This process resulted in 23 written records of the crowdsourcing and student learning process. The researchers coded and categorized the qualitative data based on a series of close readings. The descriptions were coded by process descriptions and learning outcomes. These key phenomena created a provisional list of code clusters associated with the use of crowdsourcing methods as part of the hospitality education process. This coding process provides an interpretive method to define and describe crowdsourcing as an innovative tool and student learning mechanism (Miles & Huberman, 1994).

Results using crowdsourcing in the student learning process

The qualitative data were coded into two main outcome categories: Innovation Project Outcomes from Crowdsourcing; and Learning Outcomes using Crowdsourcing. Two researchers coded the data (written documents) received from student participants. These data were put through an extensive content analysis, using a three-step process: open coding, axial coding and selective coding.

Data from students coded into innovation project outcomes and the interpretation from selective coding provide support for relationships of idea optimization or concept refinement by increasing the number of ideas generated, the quality of ideas by engaging others, the amount of information available and making use of specific knowledge. Based on the analysis, the findings indicate that crowdsourcing technology can enhance project outcomes and is an effective and productive tool. The process enhanced the number of ideas generated (60 for 23 participants) with most of the idea submissions being internal, a percentage were based on external idea submissions (11.7 per cent). All students felt that the crowdsourcing process and technology had increased the quality of ideas submitted, and 17 of 23 students indicated that crowdsourcing had produced more information based on individual recipe entries. Eight students indicated that use of specific knowledge had been augmented related to particular ingredients used in the recipes and cooking procedures. Different menu items received different levels of feedback and benefited from the process to a greater or lesser extent. Example student perceptions of the technology included:

> The thing that really impressed me about this tool was how you come up with a good idea and then you just have to put it on auto pilot. For example, the chocolate biscuits that Student 1 submitted took off like a rocket. She started off with a unique recipe, and all kinds of things branched off of that. Fellow students offered her advice of adding fruits, changing the biscuit to a croissant, and even wine pairings. Another great example of this was the roasted corn with lime submission. The submission was great on its own, but students and external participants went on to offer thoughts of wine pairings, how to serve it, and different events it would work best at.

In regards to learning outcomes using the crowdsourcing technology, the study results indicated six learning outcomes that were impacted: (1) cross-functional team experience; (2) general peer learning; (3) concept refinement process; (4) critical control factor identification; (5) cost-effectiveness; and (6) increased diversity learning experience . Eighteen students revealed that cross-functional team experiences were enhanced by crowdsourcing. All 23 students felt that the process increased general peer learning through creative and positive feedback and encouragement from peers. The concept refinement process was enhanced (17 responses of 23 participants) in most cases through expanding knowledge, open and honest interaction, and a channel for critical thinking. Five students stated areas of critical control factor identification (5 of 23 respondents) and five students identified areas of cost-effectiveness of crowdsourcing, such as in the industry meetings and chefs working in foodservice operations. All students stated an increase in diversity learning experiences through the crowdsourcing technology and process.

This case study explored the concept of crowdsourcing technology in hospitality education and its implications for advanced learning outcomes such as synergy. Based on data from this study, the crowdsourcing process applied using technology provided enhanced learning and outcomes that enable students to solve problems by putting information together in original and creative ways. This process enabled synthesis and synergy from peers and those external to the class. Additionally, based on the descriptions by participants, the results indicate that crowdsourcing and similar technologies offer the opportunity to enhance learning methods through interaction with other websites such as YouTube, posting tutorials, pictures and learning games such as quizzes or puzzles. From this process, it can be theorized that integrating crowdsourcing and similar practices via technology is a productive way of enhancing learning outcomes and knowledge retention while fostering critical thinking skills for a new technologically based learning generation.

Case study 2: Using digital video and audio technology to facilitate synthesis learning outcomes in service quality and customer satisfaction issues

Many university hospitality and tourism programmes integrate some sort of experiential restaurant operation experience for students. This experiential learning process can take many forms including special events, catered meals, student-run restaurants and other foodservice lab situations. For the case in this study, junior and senior level university students were enrolled in a course where they designed the menu, planned the service and executed a simulated restaurant operation. The simulated restaurant facility was a recently renovated space that included a culinary kitchen with commercial equipment, simulated restaurant space seating 36 guests and digital technology that can be used to record video and audio of the consumer restaurant/service setting. The digital technology includes seven cameras and wireless microphones in the dining/service area, three cameras in the culinary lab and a computer workstation for viewing, analysing and editing recorded video/audio.

The main research question in this case study was to assess: how can digital technology be used to enhance learning outcomes of students as part of the class process in the study of foodservice management? This raised the following questions: (1) how to analyse the recorded material? (2) how to integrate the technology into class discussions and final project reflections? and (3) is the technology useful for understanding consumer perceptions of food, service and atmosphere quality?

To test this process, the authors created a subgroup of students who enrolled in an upper-level special problems course. These students worked with students enrolled in the restaurant simulation class during two meal periods to test menu items developed over the course of the fall 2012 semester. As part of the learning process, four students enrolled in this special problems class developed, tested and evaluated local foods using traditional recipes, modernist cuisine techniques, and a structured innovation and evaluation process. Learning outcomes associated with technology in the development of menus for the video/audio assessment included testing and evaluating menu items for the simulated restaurant that integrated modernist techniques such as sous vide, PacoJet preparation, healthier cooking methods, injecting CO_2, and manipulating textures to create foams, airs and food dirt.

Assessment methods

To assess the customer satisfaction and perceptions of quality using the video/audio technology, the students used two methods: traditional customer comment card evaluations available for guests on each simulated restaurant table (five-point scale for assessing food quality, menu layout, service quality, atmosphere, cleanliness, favourite menu item and other comments), and student analysis of the recorded video and audio.

For the student analysis of the video/audio of the customers, faculty and students brainstormed to determine a method to provide both qualitative and quantitative feedback on the guest experience and how it differs based on demographic characteristics. This process resulted in a standardized assessment guide (see Figure 27.1) for all students assessing the guest experience to ensure consistency in coding across students but also to allow for meaningful observations by students on guest behaviours. Items included:

- Gender and age group
- When the food item arrived, was the facial expression – S = Mostly Smiling, N = Mostly Neutral, F = Mostly Frowning?
- Start = time that food item arrived
- Finish = time guest finished eating food item
- Time (food item consumption time) = Start minus Finish time
- Consumed per cent = What percentage of the food item was consumed by the guest (0 to 100 per cent)?
- Comments by guests
- Observations by student evaluations.

Descriptive statistics based on this coding process are provided in Table 27.1. Students also created a reflection paper regarding the learning experience from the class in general and the video/audio inquiry process in particular.

Results based on video and audio usage by students

The use of the video and audio technology by the students as part of the learning process resulted in several outcomes based on student reflections and feedback. First, it provided a closer connection and interaction with fellow students providing greater potential for peer learning. Second, for students, it was rewarding to see empty plates and satisfied customers as well as reinforcing the importance and value of the required course used in this case study. Third, the process improved student confidence and knowledge in culinary skills, service quality and other management aspects.

Consumer feedback derived from video and audio usage for customer satisfaction of individual menus and menu items was as follows. For the contemporary version of the traditional Arkansas souse, guests appeared divided on liking – some loved it and others did not (25 per cent consumed 0 per cent of this food item). Another observed consumer behaviour was that nearly all guests looked at the menu before tasting this food item and didn't know whether to use hands to pick

	Sex	Age	S/N/F	1st Start	1st Finish	1st Time	Consumed %	S/N/F	2nd Start	2nd Finish	2nd Time	Consumed %	S/N/F	3rd Start	3rd Finish	3rd Time	Consumed %
G1																	
G2																	
G3																	
G4																	
G5																	
G6																	
G7																	
G8																	

Date:

Table:

Rater:

Comments (rater observations or guest comments of note):

Sex = M or F

Age = Student (Y) or Parent/Staff/Faculty (O)

When the food item arrived, was the facial expression – S = Mostly Smiling, N = Mostly Neutral, F = Mostly Frowning?

Start = time that food item arrived

Finish = time guest finished eating food item

Time – Start minus Finish time

Consumed % = What percentage of the food item was consumed by the guest (0 to 100%)? 0% = nothing consumed, 50% about half consumed, 100% everything consumed

Figure 27.1 Assessment guide

Table 27.1 Results based on video/audio analysis

Categories	Mean (in minutes)	% Smiles	% Consumed
Overall total (n = 54)	7.68	63	93.93
First courses	5.6	58	87
Second courses	9.8	60	97
Third courses	7.65	71	97.50
Gender			
Male (n = 14)	8.05	64.10	94.68
Female (n = 40)	7.55	64.20	93.53
Age group			
Younger (n = 5)	9.47	88.90	94.72
Older (n = 49)	7.46	62.20	93.72
Menu item			
Arkansas souse	5.37	24	77.07
Fried catfish appetizer	5.88	73.30	99.58
Modernist fried chicken	8.67	41.67	96.17
Chicken & dumplings	11.21	87.50	97.50
Peach cobbler	5.93	44	97.10
Choc biscuits dessert	9.79	96.90	97.90

it up or use silverware. For the modernist fried chicken, feedback indicated that, while it was a success, some guests would prefer a less spicy version and the sous vide technique made it moist, tender and healthier. Sous vide is one of several techniques used in modern kitchens and part of what is often called 'molecular cuisine' or modernist cuisine (e.g. Myhrvold, 2011). Therefore, the final chicken recipe was described as modernist fried chicken in this exercise.

There were several overall learning outcomes from this process that were not readily apparent from standard observation or comment cards: (1) the importance of providing a brief explanation of each course when served; (2) most contemporary guests don't pay attention due to conversation and smart phones; (3) detailed menus provided a good resource for diners; (4) facial expressions provided non-verbal feedback on meal enjoyment; (5) the ability to assess the amount of food left on the plate provided feedback on level of liking and appropriateness of portion sizes; (6) the audio provided feedback on other dining elements such as menu design and folded napkins; and (7) video timing provided feedback on any problems related to slow or inconsistent service times and the impact on guests waiting to begin eating until others had received their food items – particularly at large tables of six or eight guests. This demonstrates important implications for the usefulness of video/audio technology for facilitating student learning in hospitality education, particularly in fast-paced experiential situations.

This teaching and learning process resulted in several outcomes for the faculty as well as the students. First, this technology has a number of potential uses in both research and teaching. The video/audio clips from the previous semester can be used to drive class discussions prior to menu design and reiterate service quality or customer satisfaction issues. For example it can be used as a training tool for service practice sessions with students reviewing mock service sessions and to fine-tune concepts of service and food quality. Second, in regards to research, the simulated restaurant setting provides an opportunity to assess the impact of numerous sensory elements in the dining experience: colour, sound, smell, taste, presentation, etc. It also provides an opportunity to engage students from all levels in participatory action research (Chevalier &

Buckles, 2013), facilitating higher levels of student learning such as synthesis as well as allowing students to create innovative solutions to service quality issues.

Summary and future implications

Using digital technology to facilitate student learning outcomes can be measured by the following two cases as examples of technology used as part of the student learning process. The first one is crowdsourcing and the second is the utilization of audio/visual technology methods for learning in service quality and guest satisfaction issues.

Crowdsourcing is the collective efforts of a group of people (the 'crowd') to assist an individual or firm to resolve a problem, create a new product, etc. while using the Web. A theoretical model was developed by Way et al. (2011) suggesting that the crowdsourcing concept is likely to improve and facilitate the innovation process in four main areas including: number of ideas generated, quality of ideas, more information and the use of specific knowledge. In regards to learning outcomes using the crowdsourcing technology, the student results indicated six learning outcomes were positively impacted including: cross-functional team experience, general peer learning, concept refinement process, critical control factor identification, cost-effectiveness and increased diversity learning experience.

The second case included using digital video and audio technology to facilitate synthesis learning outcomes in service quality and customer satisfaction issues. For this case, junior and senior level university students were enrolled in a course where they designed the menu, planned the service and executed a simulated restaurant operation. The simulated restaurant facility included guest service for 36 people along with digital technology that can be used to record video and audio of the consumer restaurant/service setting.

Learning outcomes associated with technology in the development of menus for the video/audio assessment included testing and evaluating menu items for the simulated restaurant that integrated modernist techniques such as sous vide, PacoJet preparation, healthier cooking methods, injecting CO_2, and manipulating textures to create foams, airs and food dirt.

The use of the video and audio technology by the students as part of the learning process resulted in several outcomes based on student reflections and feedback. First, it provided a closer connection and interaction with fellow students providing greater potential for peer learning. Second, for students it was rewarding to see empty plates and satisfied customers as well as reinforcing the importance and value of the required course used in this case study. Third, the process improved student confidence and knowledge in culinary skills, service quality and other management aspects. Also, the use of video and audio technology increased faculty learning outcomes including: the use of both teaching and research, video/audio clips may help drive classroom discussions on service quality, organizational behaviour, leadership qualities, team-building, foodservice safety and sanitation practices and real-world problem-solving tools.

In the future, digital technology use will facilitate student learning outcomes in several different ways. First, in the classroom, hospitality programmes are using Google Sketch-Up as a learning tool for designing a restaurant, hotel or convention centre. In the area of restaurant management, the use of point-of-sale computer software is being used in many student-run restaurants. However, it remains a question if this technology is used to its fullest extent to maximize student learning in the context of hospitality management reports, food inventories, menu engineering and food costing analysis.

Second, the use of digital technology may be complex and expensive for some hospitality programmes. Complex and ever-changing software programs may be daunting for hospitality educators to learn quickly and effectively, creating a continuing potential barrier to their adoption.

Third, the use of digital technology can also be used in several different research projects including organizational behaviour, team-building, implementing safety and sanitation practices, and quality service initiatives. The use of crowdsourcing and the use of audio/visual technology methods have the potential to enhance the way educators teach and the way student learners' excel when developing future hospitality leaders.

References

Airey, D., & Tribe, J. (2000). 'Education for Hospitality'. In C. Lashley & A. Morrison (Eds.), *In Search of Hospitality* (pp. 276–92). Oxford: Butterworth-Heinemann.

Barron, P., & Anastasiadou, C. (2009). 'Student Part-Time Employment: implications, challenges and opportunities for higher education'. *International Journal of Contemporary Hospitality Management*, 21(2), 140–53.

Behnke, C. (2012). 'Examining the Relationship between Emotional Intelligence and Hospitality Student Attitudes toward e-learning'. *Journal of Hospitality & Tourism Education*, 24(2–3), 12–20.

Bloom, B. S. (1956). *Taxonomy of Educational Objectives, Handbook I: the cognitive domain*. New York: David McKay.

Chevalier, J. M., & Buckles, D. J. (2013). *Participatory Action Research*. New York: Routledge.

Cho, W., Schmezler, C. D., & MacMahon, P. S. (2002). 'Preparing Hospitality Managers for the 21st Century: the merging of just-in-time education, critical thinking, and collaborative learning'. *Journal of Hospitality & Tourism Research*, 26, 23–36.

Cobanoglu, C. (2006). 'An Analysis of Blogs as a Teaching Tool as Perceived by Hospitality Management Students'. *Journal of Hospitality, Leisure, Sport & Tourism Education*, 5(2), 83–8.

Dawson, M., & Titz, K. (2012). 'Problem-Based Learning as a Strategy to Teach Service Quality: an assessment of on-line reviews'. *Journal of Hospitality & Tourism Education*, 24(2–3), 67–72.

Harrington, R. J., Mandabach, K., VanLeeuwen, D., & Thibodeaux, W. (2005). 'A Multi-Lens Framework Explaining Structural Differences across Foodservice and Culinary Education'. *International Journal of Hospitality Management*, 24(2), 195–218.

Harrington, R. J., Ogbeide, G. C., & Ottenbacher, M. C. (2010). 'Maximizing Hospitality Learning Outcomes: an integrated experiential in-class approach'. *FIU Review*, 28(1), 108–30.

Harris, D. (2011). 'Presentation Software: pedagogical constraints and potentials'. *Journal of Hospitality, Leisure, Sport & Tourism Education*, 10(1), 72–84.

Hellsten, M. & Prescott, A. (2004). 'Learning at University: the international student experience'. *International Education Journal*, 5(3), 344–51.

Johnson, K. (2009). 'Corporate Sperm Count and Boiled Frogs: seeds of ideas to kindle innovation in students'. *International Journal of Contemporary Hospitality Management*, 21(2), 179–90.

Lominé, L. L. (2002). 'Online Learning and Teaching in Hospitality, Leisure, Sport and Tourism: myths, opportunities and challenges'. *Journal of Hospitality, Leisure, Sport & Tourism Education*, (1) 1, 44–9.

Miles, M. B., & Huberman, A. M. (1994). *Qualitative Data Analysis*. Thousand Oaks, CA: Sage.

Miller, J. P., Milholland, E. S., & Martin Gould, S. (2012). 'Determining the Attitudes of Students toward the Use of a Classroom Response in Hospitality Courses'. *Journal of Hospitality & Tourism Education*, 24(2–3), 73–9.

Morrison, A., & O'Mahony, G. B. (2003). 'The Liberation of Hospitality Management Education'. *International Journal of Contemporary Hospitality Management*, 15(1), 38–44.

Müller, K. F., VanLeeuwen, D., Mandabach, K., & Harrington, R. J. (2009). 'The Effectiveness of Culinary Curricula: a case study'. *International Contemporary Journal of Hospitality Management*, 21(2), 167–78.

Myhrvold, N. (2011). *Modernist Cuisine: the art and science of cooking*. Bellevue, WA: The Cooking Lab.

Newman, A., & Brownell, J. (2008). 'Applying Communication Technology: introducing email and instant messaging in the hospitality curriculum'. *Journal of Hospitality, Leisure, Sport & Tourism Education*, 7(2), 71–6.

Robinson, J. (2011). 'Assessing the Value of Using an Online Discussion Board for Engaging Students'. *Journal of Hospitality, Leisure, Sport & Tourism Education*, 10 (1), 13–22.

Sciarini, M., Beck, J., & Seaman, J. (2012). 'Online Learning in Hospitality and Tourism Higher Education Worldwide: a descriptive report as of January 2012'. *Journal of Hospitality & Tourism Education*, 24(2–3), 41–4.

Smith, S. L., & Walters, A. (2012). 'Mobile Learning: engaging today's hospitality students'. *Journal of Hospitality & Tourism Education*, 24(2–3), 45–9.

Sulkowski, N. B., & Deakin, M. K. (2009). 'Does Understanding Culture Help Enhance Students' Learning Experience?'. *International Journal of Contemporary Hospitality Management*, 21(2), 154–66.

Way, K. A., Ottenbacher, M. C., & Harrington, R. J. (2011). 'Is Crowdsourcing Useful for Enhancing Innovation and Learning Outcomes in Culinary or Hospitality Education?'. *Journal of Culinary Science & Technology*, 9(4), 261–81.

Wikipedia. (n.d.) Bloom's Taxonomy. Available: http://en.wikipedia.org/wiki/Bloom's_Taxonomy (Accessed 13 October 2013).

Yan, H., & Cheung, C. (2012). 'What Types of Experiential Learning Activities Can Engage Hospitality Students in China?'. *Journal of Hospitality & Tourism Education*, 24(2–3), 21–7.

Part VI
Issues and challenges

28

Design in tourism education
A design anthropology perspective

Kurt Seemann
Swinburne University of Technology, Australia

Introduction

Tourism, hospitality, sport, leisure and events in the twenty-first century are increasingly reliant upon, and transformed by, sophisticated systems of technologies and designed environments throughout their operations. The choice and design of tourism[1] symbols, facilities, devices and spaces (both virtual and physical) offer a key area for graduates of tourism qualifications to both build knowledge about, as well as develop new skills to navigate through, the array of material, digital and spatial assets in their business. The dependencies on technically complex, yet increasingly intuitive and mobile information systems have become so embedded across the sector that understanding how to strategically manage and effectively exploit such systems has become a necessary leadership capability.

What is only recently becoming clear is that the understanding and choice factors involved in managing the natural and designed environments that define tourism experiences and locations is both a socio-technical as well as a socio-ecological form of knowledge (Seemann, 2009). In addition, how staff, client groups and observers engage in their 'technocology'[2] of built devices and sensory environments has a direct transformative effect on perception and so how they form judgements. From a tourism and hospitality education position, the teaching and learning of, and immersed engagement with, our designed world of objects, spaces and symbols, and the way these things interact to form the technocology of the traveller's and stayer's environment demands a much more sophisticated educational response than anything previously considered. To not develop this pedagogical depth in how we teach and learn about the designed environments that define tourism and hospitality experiences, and internal operations, would leave that aspect of the field's education exposed to graduating mis-educated managers whose judgements in these matters may be suboptimal.

The consequence of poor judgement in tourism design matters may be too substantial to alter where an insight could prevent collateral misadventure. Designed environments and work systems can significantly mitigate risk in a business including but not limited to risks associated with facility repair and maintenance, branding uptake, flow of work and people, personal work-place health and safety, new venture investment risk, ecological impact risk and, as a consequence, cash, data, energy and financial risk. Good design is informed by how design alters human perceptions and behaviour. Possessing strategic design knowledge offers tourism managers capabilities that are of global significance to their sector. It is also an area of leadership that ought not be naively surrendered to contract designers, as the manager needs to form informed judgement in context to their local business requirements. Similarly, management ought not to trivialize the strategic significance of design and innovation.

Our designed systems have historically been viewed as largely benign technical devices, systems and structures employed to facilitate the processing of tasks, sharing of information or locating of organizational functions, that is as tools we wield at our command in a largely one-way flow of influence: from us, via the 'made thing', to the task. The focus has been on the 'device or gadget' as an object or 'tool' that is independent from social behaviour, ecology or the market and so operational context of an organization. We have been largely ignoring the mutual return path of influence altering our perceptions and judgements. This chapter outlines new understanding about how people, technology and their eco-environment interact as dependent systems. The transformative nature that technologies and designs play in altering the experiences of clients, staff and observers is examined. This is of critical importance in educational terms, as tourism managers and leaders face the task of forming situational judgements based on their degree of coherent insight of the technocology of their sector and the way it engages with people at all levels of their immediate organization.

Understanding, using and teaching the link between people, technology choice, and design in tourism education can also offer a rich and effective strategy for fostering whole graduate development. This chapter will appeal to tourism educators interested in exploring what a more advanced perspective of tourism facility, service, 'gear' and user-experience (UX) design can offer the rounded development of their graduates with the goal of better assuring capacities for reasoned and contextualized business decisions.

Given much of tourism is naturally focused on the traveller, understanding human cultural diversity to accommodate in strategic design continues to be a rising concern. Where an educational interest lies in how to effectively embrace culture and design in tourism education, the broad fields of anthropology, ethno-technology and socio-technical systems offer the most authentic disciplines of choice. We will draw specific attention to the sub-discipline of design anthropology in this chapter due to its currency in profile transnational companies. From a hands-on perspective, design anthropologists have been instrumental in many contemporary product, service and system designs that exist around us today.[3] From an educational development perspective the ideas behind design anthropology provide solid foundations for guiding human development that is informed by the way people respond to, and embed their values within, their built, social and transformed tourism environments. The mutual value-add of combining the goals and frames of tourism education with those of relevant branches of design anthropology, offers fresh and exciting learning opportunities for tourism teachers and students alike.

Two ideas (represented by two sections in this chapter) have been selected from the broad fields of design and anthropology to help demonstrate how culture presents a critical educational experience in the strategic act of what I will refer to as designing and working technologically. In the first section I explore how understanding culture, as examined through an ethnographic lens, can scaffold the act of designing services, experiences, spaces and products in tourism. In the second section, I explore the formidable role that our engagement with the made world plays in human development itself. In this second part the chapter combines anthropological and related philosophy of technology propositions to present insights into how, as a species, we define what it means to be human through the making of the world around us and, in so doing, literally also producing ourselves as a product of our own making. From a tourism education perspective, this 'making-of-ourselves' is an extraordinary proposition that sits at the heart of how strategies in the tourism sector can thoughtfully develop and manage the design of their technical and spatial environments and systems, and the core curriculum role it can play in transforming the staff and people who engage in, and deploy, tourism services. It is arguably one of the most sophisticated ideas underpinning the potency of strategic technology and design in tourism education and as such ought to be nurtured carefully and deliberately by the subject's custodians: tourism business and government agencies, and education providers and teachers.

1 Using ethnography to inform the strategic choice and design of tourism technologies, services and spaces

Design anthropology offers ideas for how to enhance and creatively inform the teaching of design and technology where the goal is to design for and with people, and the social networks with which they feel they have a peer affinity. Ethnography positions the individual as a member, as well as a product, of a socio-cultural context. For the tourism management student and teacher alike, the social dimension of design raises rich educational as well as technical choice information that can guide both the learning experience for the student, as well as the material output objective of the tourism design and technology task in which they are engaged. It is asserted that tourism management students ought most definitely to have an immersive engagement experience in the transformative process of a strategic tourism design and development project. Such undergraduate experience offers authentic insight about the effect of the designed and technical world experienced by clients and staff, as well as validating a process of producing innovative tourism artifacts, spaces, systems or symbols – even if only to mock-up/prototype, or proof of concept levels during their undergraduate studies.

While exceptions remain, the conventional representation of teaching design and technology projects in many educational settings has favoured a focus on the technicality of designing and making an artifact, like a website or even a model structure. In some schools this technical focus can be portrayed in the form of a specific product to be made in accordance with a set (given) brief. These briefs typically assume an individual-archetype as the end-user of that product. One result of this convention is that the human factor can be very easily discounted, reducing the end-user to a benign, stereotypical and essentially passive client persona. One effect of taking a stereotypical view of clients and end-user contexts is that it can cause the designer (the tourism student) to focus most of their efforts on the 2D (sketching) or 3D (making) of their 'given' design brief. The product of their effort becomes the object rather than the living end-user, while the context within which the product is meant to succeed or be sustained can equally be discounted. If we now extend this line of thinking to the human end-user as a social member of a group, and the values and beliefs they are a part of, we then have a whole new range of 'market' impact to accommodate when designing and working technologically in the tourism sector. The historical fixation on the designed system, space or object (i.e. the artifact) as the end-point of evaluation in strategic management misses the whole reason why the artifact was created. The end-point of evaluation in strategic design, from a pedagogical and human valuing viewpoint, must be the transformation of the targeted end-user: the beneficiaries. The beneficiaries, of tourism design are typically the tourist, the staff, the suppliers and the partners. Put simply, strategic design education in tourism evaluates design success not in the form of the design itself, but in the form of the transformational change that design creates in the targeted beneficiaries. The strategic role of design is to transform the end-user: the artifact is the 'cause', and the end-user transformation is the evaluated 'effect'.

When designing for people who identify with larger human groups and communities, culture becomes the main game to factor and value for the designer. The person undertaking design, and the clients belonging to their groups, raise opportunities to embed not only new intellectual frames for guiding tourism practice in design, but also for revealing rich educational opportunities for the student who is given the task to reflect on the roles they play when designing and working technologically for, and with, other people.

The socio-cultural dependencies linking design in tourism with technology and ecology

If there is one pattern that many people may have noted over the last decade it is the rise of social technologies. Social technologies include Facebook, mobile communication devices, and products designed to target specific human group interactions and identity. The move to design for groups, rather than for individuals, demands a new range of conceptual frames for how we understand technology and the relationships groups form with their designed world. New group-based methods are required to check, challenge or redefine the given design briefs. The very processes of design can also require redress. These shifts in how design is approached when it is for small, moderate or large groups of people, such as workplace groups, communities of practice, or age segments in society, have given rise to new techniques. These new techniques in strategic design management and development include co-design/collaborative design and participatory design methods. They may also include design techniques for products targeting other human groups such as families, clans, tribal groups or even human settlement systems. The latter would be the case for international aid projects where cross-cultural technology transfer investments are designed and deployed (Button, 2000). Anthropological theories about how humans identify with tribal groups, for example, may be appropriate when designing phone apps or product ecosystems for growing and maintaining sporting club team membership numbers. All these techniques are founded on design-ethnography theory and methods, and target how groups form, maintain and evolve common values and beliefs that bond them to the cultural norms of the human groups to which they feel they belong. One obvious advantage for using such group-based design strategies is that groups generally sustain a bigger and longer lasting market. Individuals who perceive a belonging to a group, such as a club, or a sporting team membership group, have many social rewards and reminders to keep that social sense of belonging viable.

Products, services and systems that were co-designed and framed from the beginning of a process to work with groups of people offer strong opportunity for more socially sustainable commitment to new innovative designs as a direct result of using such participative design research techniques. The application of an anthropological or specific ethnographic frame to strategically guide design has been applied to contexts as diverse as housing standards in remote Aboriginal Australia (Fisher, 2002; Karanja et al., 2010; Seemann, 1986; Singh & Hiremath, 2010; Singh et al., 2009; Smillie, 1991; Tao & Wall, 2009), through to the way transnational companies design their websites to accommodate regional cultural preferences of targeted end-users. In his online article summarizing key business ideas Christian Arno (2012) noted,

> The anthropologist Edward T. Hall theorised that 'high-context cultures' (such as many African and Asian ones) tend to use symbols more, and expect people to interpret meaning from fewer words. . . . 'Low-context' cultures, such as America and Europe, tend to use more text, and spell out their messages explicitly. While these aren't hard and fast rules, they are often reflected in website preferences. . . . Chinese, Japanese and Korean users

often expect to see a greater use of images, videos and sidebars, compared to more text-heavy Scandinavian or German designs.

To include culture as a key factor for enriching design, it is desirable to develop an awareness of how thinking, feeling and acting on the social–material world around us contributes to the systems of values and perceptions we hold true of the world 'we perceive'. If we pay attention to the world as it is perceived by clients rather than as we guess it to be as tourism managers, we then can appreciate that designing and working technologically is a scholarship that demands we learn techniques to help us understand what drives human groups, their values and their cultural belief structures. Armed with such knowledge, strategic design management can more effectively develop solutions that fit naturally with a client's world view as framed by their culture. The difference in how strategic design managers, and their clients and end-users perceive the world, can be minimal; 'they' are like me, or substantial, 'they' are nothing like me. Designing for other groups thus requires the designer to appreciate how the social and material context in which their clients are reared, or enabled to be productive at work, defines, at least in part, the expectations they hold of the world designed about them.

2 Design anthropology as humanizing tourism education: a way to build graduate empathy for the needs of others

Tourism and anthropology share an interest in how people develop, socialize and seek experiences that help them express their identity or demonstrate their efficacy. These common interests in human experience already position the two areas of knowledge as offering a good fit for examining the mutual value of linking anthropological ideas with aspects of tourism education. When we refine this association to the common ground between design anthropology, and the design of tourism spaces, devices and environments, the mutual advantage compels the prospect of new tourism innovations. Design anthropology is forward looking, and seeks to significantly enhance the knowledge, skills and processes involved in designing and working technologically. The design of tourism experiences also seeks to foster and create such qualities in its clients as well as manager graduates.

In this second part of the chapter, I outline how novel approaches for including strategic tourism design and technology education can contribute to humanizing tourism education, and how this humanization effect is also of interest to the field of design anthropology. The common area of interest pertains to how humans socially and culturally 'make themselves' when they engage in deliberate, and contextually validating, social–material praxis – the context in which much of tourism experience and business processes operate. Through the social and technical processes of investigating, and practically integrating knowledge and environmental resources into artifacts that condition a traveller's experiences (an artifact in this context refers to the production of anything made by humans that transformed natural, digital or processed resources towards a tourism experience or tourism business operation), not only are resources transformed into the 'object', but also the traveller is transformed as the 'subject', being the agent of the transformation process. Human transformation is more overtly fostered when designing and working technologically requires the manager to learn, contextually validate that learning, and critically reflect on the new knowledge, skills and social insight acquired through the act of producing the said artifact. The manager comes out 'changed', alongside the change that has occurred to the consumed resources used to produce the product. The manager engaged in tourism design activity has changed in that they have emerged from a deliberate and reflective material activity with new knowledge, new social awareness and new motor practice as a result of seeking to validate their designs for a set context of application. Even if the application was familiar, the change is at least one of affirmation of prior knowledge, skills and social insight being tested.

If the educational experience of tourism managers engaged in designing and working technologically was based on deliberate co-transformation strategies of learning, and if the learner builds new knowledge, social and practical skills, then both a designed 'object or product' of tourism and a transformed learner are produced. The transformed products of a humanized education in tourism design and technology development may therefore be empirically observed as both the object produced and the subject that produced it. The transformed object or product for a tourism context gives evidence of the transformed subject (the learner) but, equally, the transformed subject must give evidence of the transformed object (they must defend the design choice). When these co-transformations are both given as evidence for meeting the researched requirements of the object to succeed in the applied social and material tourism context in which it was intended to operate, we can assert a basis for validating the humanization effect of the designs and spaces that define that aspect of a tourism business.[4] I will refer to this co-transformation thesis, and the need to validate the object against the applied context for best fit, as the unique epistemic foundations of strategic design and technology as a discipline.

Ideas and methods in design anthropology have facilitated both the processes and products of design. These methods provide educators with a unique and powerful insight to how designing and working technologically helps us understand what it means to be human. The transformative effect on the learner, if guided well, is a formidable educational outcome that design and technology offer the curriculum in ways no other subject can – without, of course, looking like they are conducting design and technology lessons. The humanizing value of being able to bring together in one learning objective the co-transformation of our physical, intellectual and social capabilities into the one contextually validating process of designing and working technologically is a very powerful quality to foster in the classroom. While all other areas of the curriculum certainly can synthesize the students' affective, cognitive and motor development, none offers the necessary range and depth of such content as the body of knowledge that design and technology demand of its students. This centrality of the humanizing value of praxis when it is derived from socially informed transformations of our natural and made world around was also of great interest to scholars such as Marx Wartofsky.

> The 'other'[5] in which human beings come to recognize themselves as human, is no longer simply the 'thou' of religious consciousness, but the natural world itself insofar as it becomes a world-for-us – a world either designed or made to meet the needs of human existence. It is this transformation of the world into a resource for human existence that makes of it a mirror of our needs, and thereby, the representation, in this form, of our species–nature or our essence. It is thus in this humanization of nature that human beings come to be human – the humanized world becomes the 'other' whereby humanity achieves itself.
>
> (Wartofsky, 1979: 361)

Humanization so far has been presented through the thesis of co-transformation, where contextual validation of 'best fit' is a necessary and so required condition to claiming that change in knowledge and resources have occurred. However, socially and culturally, people are also adapters and adopters of worlds designed by others. We usually move passively through, and accommodate, most of the ordinary spaces, tools and things designed and made by unknown others around us. Over time, we get so socially used to the technologies in our lives, and within our bodies, if not also as extensions to our bodies, that they become quite invisible to our ordinary consciousness. This is the second, and much more socializing, transformative effect of the designed world around us. This 'disappearance' and 'semi-transparent' nature of how humans socially relate to the worlds created for them and by them aligns with Don Ihde's (1979: 19) thesis for the developmental telos of tools and instruments. So normalizing is this relationship with the world we have made, that much of it blends invisibly to our consciousness, and yet forms the basis of a deal of our socially aligned or 'group think' expectations for how to navigate the worlds we have grown up with and passively accommodated (De Tezanos-Pinto et al., 2010; Fernandez, 2007; Hamre, 2003; Millar, 1985; Ochara et al., 2012; Reeve, 2006).

What I will call the domestication of the world we have made means we have come to share with others common beliefs, behaviours and perceptions around the digital and material worlds that we live in. This cultural a priori of consciousness with our made world in tourism sectors is starkly contrasted, however, when our designs and technologies are transferred into the worlds of other cultures: when technologies are transferred across the boundaries into new cultural and material contexts. We cannot assume the end-user will be like us: the designers and makers of the object. We need to validate our design knowledge contextually in the social and material setting of that end-user in order to build our body of knowledge. We tend to notice mostly the new, the novel and the failed when it comes to technologies in our lives. Subliminally, if not overtly, our concepts of what we value, what we expect in ordinary life, and how we view such ideas as safety and comfort have been conditioned since birth in a culturally normalized manner with the made world about us. Many of the ideas and social patterns humans hold as normal have already been conditioned, or primed, by both the designed and the natural worlds within which people live.

We initially design and make our technological worlds precisely because we seek to influence, or be influenced by, the world we make; if this was not so, the entire premise of designing and making anything, including service design, is moot. We design corridors in buildings and cities to influence how people move through our structures and how they interact. We design fashions to express a desired view of what is powerful, friendly, attractive or protective. In agreement with Feenberg (2010), we can design to influence our world, only because we are a part of it. Our membership in the world we transform brings into play our need to critically anticipate how we, as designers, are going to be affected by our creations, and as ordinary people who share in common with our identity groups, the creations of others placed in our world. The act of designing and working technologically asserts an ethic of reciprocity, the denial of which is at best an illusion, and at worse a global consequence.

> Every one of our acts returns to us in some form as feedback from the other. But this means that in acting we become the object of action. . . . In more formal philosophical language the paradox of action says that human beings can only act on a system to which they themselves belong. Because we belong to the system any change we make in it affects us too. This is the practical significance of our existence as embodied and social beings. Through our body and our social belonging we participate in a world of causal powers and meanings we do not fully control. We are exposed through our body to the laws of nature. And we are born into a cultural world we largely take as given. In short, we are finite beings. Our finitude shows up in the Newtonian reciprocity of action and reaction.
> (Feenberg, 2010: 31)

People are influenced in their thoughts and social actions by the behaviours that designs evoke among their social peers. As social creatures we are influenced by what smartphone our peers choose. We expect others to abide by the behaviour-regulating rules of machines we install in our 'technocology' like traffic lights (technocology is a relatively new term used to describe the linked-up interdependencies of other technologies that new technologies require in order for them to operate as designed. Examples include functioning electricity grids to power a wide network of mobile phone towers that in turn need to be in place so that mobile phones can operate as they were intended and so on). My point being, in time we learn to accommodate and automate how we ought to change our behaviours around new technologies so that, socially, we may live in sync with them. I call this stage of social accommodation as living with technologies that we have domesticated. In an affront to domesticated technologies in our lives, we are also exposed to new devices and systems for which we socially have yet to accommodate (I refer here to the social–psychology interpretation of accommodation, where people adjust, alter, even compensate their behaviours and reasoning as a cost–benefit decision in response to a social intrusion or novel encounter. The more people accommodate the more they have developed behavioural patterns that normalize and accept the intrusion). If a design innovation enters the social space of a human group its uptake (its trend to being socially accommodated and domesticated) is more likely if the designer had mastered the necessary ethnographic 'tools' in the development of their designs. While this proposition may seem obvious, the serious and accurate use of techniques and theory to guide the process of gathering, filtering and translating necessary ethnographic information into effective design processes and products remains a weak area in most design and technology education programmes.

Whether conscious of it or not, we are usually compliant to the made world around us: we normally choose to accommodate it. We learn to live in the context of our surrounding technocology and after a while of this find our technocology to be rather invisible and normal to us; that is until we move across into a new technocology context with many unfamiliar systems and expected behaviours. It is no surprise then how well-established high-density urban human groups (city dwellers), view time, fashion and communication often quite differently to long-established rural or remote groups (country dwellers). How cultures are different across contrasting social–material contexts is a branch of design anthropology that is rich with opportunity to grow knowledge and techniques for improving, at least the initial value of, new designs for such situations. For our increasingly connected and complex global societies, researching and designing with, and for, cultural and social groups, and forming good group personas, are design anthropology techniques that have become intensively interesting for designers (Bichard & Gheerawo, 2011).

These principles also help us better design ideas if our clients' products are to succeed in cross-cultural technology transfer processes such as from urban east coast Australia to remote desert and predominately Aboriginal communities in central Australia (Seemann, 2010, 2009). Similarly, workplace cultures and the technical systems with which they are meant to be productive, demand a critical method to ensure those technical choices are indeed designed to achieve the cultural productivity a workplace seeks. The transformative effect that designing and working technologically plays in 'self' and 'artifact making', is the basis to the view that design anthropology is concerned with 'how the processes and artifacts of design help define what it means to be human' (Tunstall, 2011). The worlds that different human groups make give clues to who they are, what they value and how they socially organize and innovate given the priming role played already in their own social–material histories.

Sustainability and culture as truth conditions for an education in and through design and technology

In the same way that anthropologists seek to learn how the wider resource context within which humans lived altered their social and material ways of life, design anthropology takes a deliberate interest in how the world we design and make, and our socialized relationship with it, is defined by the natural resource conditions upon which they are eternally dependent. This absolute constraint, that both humans and our designs must obey the ecological limitations that make our artifacts and us possible, establishes the truth condition that design and technology education is necessarily a study in sustainability. To diminish or exclude the systemic inter-dependencies between people, their 'making of worlds', and the ecological foundations that resource them would give rise to a concern as to whether an education in design and technology has occurred. Understanding how different groups of people socially respond to, and exploit, their created and natural resource environments offers powerful frames for designing and making sustainable futures.

The assertion that sees humans, their innovations, and their natural and designed context as combined into necessary, rather than optional, interrelated systems is a key idea evident in design anthropology. The field is concerned often with how these three systems engage in mutual transactions where people, their made things or spaces and their resource conditionality co-transform towards a co-dependent relationship with each other. In this systemic frame, design anthropology presents a rich new branch for educators and designers alike. It offers a way to both review the past, as well as design probable futures that inform the basis for sustainable choices in design and technology.

Conclusions

Design anthropology has been defined in this chapter as concerned with the interplay of social and material culture, and the role that the designed world plays in transforming human perceptions of the self, as well as of others. The feedback effect on cultural evolution caused by the very act of people socially engaging in the production and reproduction of their surrounding world offers a key point of interest to both tourism educationists as well as design anthropologists. In the tourism undergraduate degree that chooses to more coherently prepare graduates in tourism design and technology management, students don't just make *stuff*, they make *themselves* and, along the way, they validate their newfound situational knowledge in *material* as well as *social* frames. No other area in the curriculum is so well placed to provide such a rich and wholly humanizing process of both the student and the object of knowledge than a coherent education in tourism design. Design anthropology is ideally placed as a scholarly and well-respected field to accompany a new and rewarding dimension to designing, learning and working technologically in tourism education.

Designing, that purposeful effort to transform the perceived world, produces much more than an object or system. At the very least, the act of designing produces our private subjective world. To the extent that we often design for others, or where others encounter the world we have transformed, as designers we are also in the thick of altering the subjective world of others. These propositions of transformation, however, are incomplete, for the world we transform in the act of designing necessitates we have something to alter – a natural or made ecology. Indeed, we exist because of that ecology, and through drivers of survival, if not social norms, we are influenced by it in how we presuppose our next act of design.

From an ethnographic viewpoint then, the act of designing in human societies is a socio-cultural act, which bonds people to others as a process of empathy development. It is a process that influences the learner's sense of self as human, and necessitates a domestication and transformation of the natural world about them. In short, designing and working technologically in the operating context of tourism ventures offers a humanization process in tourism education that is heavily engaged in both creative as well as social production. This necessary social underpinning to the act of designing and working technologically as a capability for tourism graduates raises many important ethical as well as social and epistemological questions that educationists and learner alike can explore. It is an experiential mode of social–material learning that invites designers to examine the way they make meaning and validate applied contextual knowledge from the social and material world around them. However, the cultural embeddedness of designing and working technologically for self and others also invites a new chapter in tourism education research: how are our socio-technical actions in the design and management of tourism technologies, spaces and structures reciprocally tied to the truth of our ecological dependencies?

Tourism education has both a need and an opportunity to include strategic design management in the professional knowledge of its sector. Much of the motivations to engage in travelling and staying at locations and events includes subliminal and overt experiences with the made world with which the traveller and staff engage. A curriculum in the study and strategic management of design in tourism may be framed to both build knowledge about how humans are transformed by designed experiences, and how design success may be evaluated based on the quality of how a design transforms the groups targeted.

We may organize a curriculum in strategic tourism design management around a few core themes. These include:

- *Strategic design management of tourism assets*. This may include facilities and safety, spaces, work-flow systems, sensations and products. Products may include the design of clothing, food, services and accessories.
- *Strategic design management of tourism communications*. This may include social organization design, security design and risk, way-signage, data and information design.

In addition, there is a requirement to equip managers with a few key ideas that will assist them with conceptualising how the made-world in tourism engages with people and ecology. Such ideas assist with forming situational judgements by drawing upon principles that guide the task of managing the designed world of tourism in novel and varying circumstances. Key ideas to include in the epistemic framing of strategic design management in tourism are:

- The mutual transformation of people, ecology and technologies/made worlds (all three as a combined whole system) underpinning all effective design. Pedagogically, tourism undergraduate and professional development education ought to provide at least simulated, if not in context, strategic design projects so that a richer engaged transformation in design may manifest with the learner.
- The role of design for the individual and for the group, where culture and values play key transforming variables that strategic design must define and accommodate as criteria for success.
- The contextually reliant nature of technologies to their designed context of end-use: what is designed for one operational context is unlikely to succeed in a different operational context, unless both contexts share sufficient conditional similarity.
- The end-usership of strategic tourism design extends beyond the traveller, to include staff, partners and suppliers involved in the sector's value-chain.

In a world where we are interacting with other cultures more, both in the workplace and across political geographies, learning and sharing cross-cultural tourism design and technology knowledge can offer much-needed new ideas to help the sector address pressing new design challenges.

Notes

1   'Tourism', unless further qualified hereafter, will be used as the shorthand expression to cover all dimensions of the sector that affects travellers, stayers, engagers and observers of the sector. It is inclusive of Hospitality, Events Management, Sports and Leisure sectors of the industry.
2   Technocology in the context of the Tourism sector refers to the vast array of interconnected and contextual systems of devices and structures that partly or wholly depend on each other to operate, and as such provide a necessary 'made-ecology' context for new devices, facilities and systems in order for such things to work. Examples of technocologies include wifi networks systems, general power, water and waste flow systems, flow and design of corridors and transport systems, and the human and natural systems necessary to maintain and evolve such systems in response to stochastic and emergent demands.
3   Examples of transnational companies that have been drawing on the expertise of design anthropologists to help use culture as a way of improving their products and service designs include Xerox PARC(tm) (Suires & Van DeVenter, 2012: 289–310), Intel(tm) (Bell, 2013) and even Coca-Cola(tm) and Boeing(tm) (Kirah, 2013, 2012).
4   It is suggested that the co-transformation thesis of object and subject, and the process of epistemic validation having to occur in the context of the object's intended application, presents a key framework for exploring post/trans-human development via advances in biotechnology, genetic engineering and bio-engineering. In this case, the object transformed is validated *within* the bio context of the transformed subject. Trans-humanization and related texts include Dickenson, 2012; Hughes, 2004; Al-Rodhan, 2011; Graham, 2002; Haag *et al.*, 2013; McNamee, 2008; Petrina & Feng, 2006.
5   Marx Wartofsky's reference to 'other' and 'thou' is referring to the world outside our mind, and includes both the natural and made worlds that we consume, transform and interact with socially, virtually and materially that exist around us in our general environment.

References

Al-Rodhan, N. R. F. (2011). *The Politics of Emerging Strategic Technologies Implications for Geopolitics, Human Enhancement, and Human Destiny.* New York: Palgrave Macmillan.

Arno, C. (2012). *Web Designs that Communicate across Cultures.* Available: http //econsultancy.com/au/blog/10204-web-designs-that-communicate-across-cultures (Accessed 2 June 2013).

Bell, G. (2013). *Intel Innovator Genevieve Bell: intel anthropologist.* Available: http://www.intel.com/content/www/us/en/corporate-responsibility/better-future/intel-anthropologist-geneieve-bell.html (Accessed 17 June 2013).

Bichard, J., & Gheerawo, R. (2011). 'The Designer as Ethnographer'. In A. J. Clarke (Ed.), *Design Anthroplogy: object culture in the 21st century* (pp. 45–55). Vienna: Springer.

Button, G. (2000). 'The Ethnographic Tradition and Design'. *Design Studies*, 21, 319–32.

De Tezanos-Pinto, P., Bratt, C., & Brown, R. (2010). 'What Will the Others Think? In-group norms as a mediator of the effects of intergroup contact'. *British Journal of Social Psychology*, 49, 507–23.

Dickenson, D. (2012). *Bioethics: all that matters.* London: Hodder Education.

Feenberg, A. (2010). 'Ten Paradoxes of Technology'. In R. Hansen & S. Petrina (Eds.), *Technological Learning & Thinking: culture, design, sustainability, human ingenuity,* 17–19 June 2010 (26–38/716). University of British Columbia: University of British Columbia.

Fernandez, C. P. (2007). 'Creating Thought Diversity: the antidote to group think'. *Journal of Public Health Management and Practice*, 13, 670–1.

Fisher, S. (2002). *A Livelihood Less Ordinary: applying the sustainable livelihoods approach in the Australian indigenous context.* Alice Springs: Centre for Appropriate Technology.

Graham, E. L. (2002). *Representations of the Post/Human : monsters, aliens, and others in popular culture,* New Brunswick, NJ: Rutgers University Press.

Haag, J., Peterson, G., & Spezio, M. (2013). *The Routledge Companion to Religion and Science,* Abingdon: Routledge.

Hamre, J. J. (2003). 'Intel Plus "Group Think" Equaled Weapons of Mass Destruction in Iraq'. *Aviation Week & Space Technology*, 159, 66.

Hughes, J. (2004). *Citizen Cyborg : why democratic societies must respond to the redesigned human of the future,* Cambridge, MA: Westview Press.

Ihde, D. (1979). *Technics and Praxis,* Dordrecht: D. Reidel Publishing.

Karanja, N., Yeudall, F., & Mbugua, S. (2010). 'Strengthening Capacity for Sustainable Livelihoods and Food Security through Urban Agriculture among HIV and AIDS Affected Households in Nakuru, Kenya'. *International Journal of Agricultural Sustainability,* 8, 40–53.

Kirah, A. (2012). The Silent Heroes: Anna Kirah at TEDxOslo 2012. Available: http://www.youtube.com/watch?v=TmoJ0dl_edY (Accessed 17 June 2013).

Kirah, A. (2013). EDEN Conference Webinar with Anna Kirah Design Anthropologists, Innovation Anthropologist. Available: http://www.eden-online.org/node/818 (Accessed 16 June 2013).

McNamee, M. J. (2008). *Sports, Virtues and Vices : morality plays.* London: Routledge.

Millar, G. W. (1985). 'Think Group Technology – before System Integration'. *Manufacturing Engineering,* 95, 75–6.

Ochara, N. M., Asmelash, D., & Mlay, S. (2012). 'Group Think Decision Making Deficiency in the Requirements Engineering Process: towards a crowdsourcing model'. *Innovation Vision 2020: Sustainable Growth, Entrepreneurship, and Economic Development,* Vols. 1–4, 1654–1674.

Petrina, S., & Feng, F. (2006). 'On Techno-Theology and the Sacred: exploring technology and spirituality' (Keynote address). In H. Middleton (Ed.), *Fourth Biennial International Conference on Technology Education Research (7–9 December).* Gold Coast, Queensland, Australia (pp. 1–10). Technology Education Research Centre: Griffith University Press. Available: http://blogs.ubc.ca/technotheology/ (Accessed 14 January 2014).

Reeve, E. (2006). Group Think. *New Republic* 235, 38.

Seemann, K. (1986). 'Appropriate Technology in Iriri : a micro-hydroelectric project in the Solomon Islands'. University of New South Wales.

Seemann, K. (2009). Technacy Education: understanding cross-cultural technological practice'. In J. Fien, R. Maclean, & M-G. Park (Eds.), *Work, Learning and Sustainable Development: opportunities and challenges* (pp. 117–31). Bonn: Springer.

Seemann, K. (2010). 'Learning How Everything is Connected: research in holistic and cross-cultural indigenous technacy education'. In S. Patrina & R. Hansen (Eds.), *International Conference of Research in Technological Learning & Thinking (17–19 June 2010)* (pp. 554–62). University of British Columbia, Vancouver, Canada. Available: http://blogs.ubc.ca/tlandt/files/2013/03/TLTproceedings.pdf (Accessed 26 January 2014).

Singh, P. K., & Hiremath, B. N. (2010). 'Sustainable Livelihood Security Index in a Developing Country: a tool for development planning'. *Ecological Indicators,* 10, 442–51.

Singh, R. K., Singh, H. N., & Singh, V. N. (2009). 'Helping Farmers adapt to Climate Change: the NEFORD way'. *Indian Journal of Genetics and Plant Breeding,* 69, 319–24.

Smillie, I. (1991). *Mastering the Machine: poverty, aid and technology,* London: Intermediate Technology Publications.

Suires, S., & Van DeVenter, M. L. (2012). 'Communities of Practice'. In D. D. Caulkins & A. T. Jordan (Eds.), *A Companion to Organisational Anthropology* (pp. 289–310). Chichester: Wiley-Blackwell.

Tao, T. C. H., & Wall, G. (2009). 'Tourism as a Sustainable Livelihood Strategy'. *Tourism Management,* 30, 90–8.

Tunstall, E. (2011). 'What is Design Anthropology? An introduction'. In Swinburne Univeristy of Technology (Ed.). *Design Anthropology.* Faculty of Design: Swinburne University of Technology. Available: http://www.swinburne.edu.au/design/courses/design-anthropology-postgraduate-course.html (Accessed 10 December 2013).

Wartofsky, M. (1979). *Models,* London: D. Riedel Publishing.

29

The evolution of the employability skills agenda in tourism higher education

Petia Petrova

Centre for Learning and Academic Development, University of Birmingham, UK

Introduction: higher education – an era of change

The establishment and growth of tourism degrees has taken place in a context of growth, widening participation and increased societal interest in the employability outcomes of graduates. The first concerted government effort to grow the number of higher education (HE) graduates in the United Kingdom took place in the 1960s, following the Robins report (1963).[1] This report set the tone of seeing HE as a positive force able to benefit not only graduates, but also society at large (Barnett *et al.*, 1994), with a stronger emphasis being placed on the contribution of graduates to the labour market (Ward, 2006). The increasing influence of the labour market and the concerns of employers on HE was further evident in the 1980s (Bennett *et al.*, 2000). The 1987 White Paper 'Higher Education: Meeting the challenge' saw the lower HE participation rates as impacting negatively upon the productivity of the economy. The UK government estimated that the percentage of young people going to university was not sufficient to reflect the needs of the knowledge-based economy and undertook a policy of HE expansion by allowing polytechnics to assume university status (Jarvis *et al.*, 1998; Bennett *et al.*, 2000). This trend was not confined to the UK (Brew, 2006). For example, Australia saw the introduction of a widening participation agenda aimed at 40 per cent of the younger population having at least a bachelor-level qualification (Dredge *et al.*, 2012). The expansion of HE was also seen as a social project, enabling access by a wider proportion of young people to the opportunities offered by HE (HM Treasury, 2004). In the early 21st century HE continued to be seen as having a central role to play, with an emphasis on the *knowledge economy*, and ensuring competitiveness in the global market (Jarvis *et al.*, 1998; Bennett *et al.*, 2000; Blackstone, 2001). The British government in 2005 was of the view that HE delivers 'the advanced skills that a knowledge-intensive economy values' (HM Treasury, 2005:8).

Concurrent with the widening participation agenda and the transformation of former polytechnics into universities, were the changes in the funding regime of HE, namely the introduction of student fees in England and introduction of a new framework for allocating research funding (the focus of research excellence as a measure of research productivity and basis for allocation of government funds for research). Governments were choosing to commit extra funding to established research institutes (Brew, 2006). This has resulted in a separation between former polytechnics and older universities, and an emphasis on employability of graduates was adopted in newer universities (the focus being placed on a 'capability curricula'), while older universities continued to pursue prestige through their research activities (Brew, 2006). Focusing research funding on a few elite institutions has resulted in a strong research focus of 'old' universities as a key differentiator between 'old' and 'new' universities (Williams & Light, 1999). This, King (2004) argues, instead of opening up opportunities for a wider proportion of graduates, can lead to solidifying social hierarchies with students from non-traditional backgrounds joining post-92 institutions in increasing numbers.

Graduate employers have been seen to place higher value on the prestige and reputation of the university, for example when major employers recruit for the highly contested graduate training programmes they would often target graduates from the Russell Group universities (Pitcher & Purcell, 1998). Graduating from such institutions has been seen as an assurance by employers that their employees will perform well not only in their first jobs, but also further in their career (Cranmer, 2006).

This chapter reflects upon the impacts of these changes in HE policy. It outlines how the focus on graduate employability has resulted in a range of new policy agendas. This chapter reflects upon the impacts of these changes on tourism degrees, given the specific nature and origins of these degrees. The chapter then examines to what extent the focus on employability and employability skills is applicable to the specific context of tourism in HE and the tourism industry.

Tourism in HE: the era of change

The origins of tourism degrees have been often traced back to technological colleges and vocational training routes. Tourism degrees are run mostly in 'new' (post-1992) universities (Busby et al. 1997; Stuart-Hoyle, 2003; Morgan, 2004). Comparing the list of institutions that teach tourism courses, as identified by Walmsley (2012), against the Russell Group universities suggests that only the University of Exeter provides tourism courses.[2] Hence, the majority of tourism degrees are being taught outside the older and what are perceived to be 'elite' universities. It is within these older universities that the majority of research income is concentrated. Dale and Robinson (2001) note that the lack of academic credentials of tourism (in comparison to other subject areas such as the humanities) is evident in the lack of recognition of tourism as a discrete research area in the Research Assessment Exercise (RAE). This continues to be the case in 2013 where the imminent Research Excellence Framework (REF)[3] also does not include tourism as a discrete area for research funding. Similarly Tribe (2003: 228) notes that 'tourism research is not considered an important, significant or distinct cognate area by those in positions of power in the academic community in the UK'.

Thus, the struggle for legitimacy becomes twofold, on the one hand, governments need to concentrate research funding within an expanding HE sector to the detriment of newer degrees and universities. Therefore, striving for legitimacy in 'research' terms is a difficult proposition. On the other hand, the establishment and growth of tourism degrees has benefited from (or coincided with) government HE policy aimed at widening participation to meet perceived economic needs. Legitimacy for tourism degrees in this policy context is measured by graduate outcomes and employer satisfaction.

Tourism academics and their priorities: research, employability and legitimacy

The influence of government and employers over HE policy and increasingly over curriculum design is often criticized as limiting the academic freedom and growth of tourism as a subject in its own right. Yet, this issue may be of a rather more complex nature. Marion Stuart's early work (Stuart-Hoyle, 2003) demonstrated that individual academics' research interests were the primary influences on the establishment of tourism in HE (within the UK context). Despite these early influences on the nature and focus of tourism degrees, a strong discourse has been adopted by universities (and the UK government) reflecting the implicit vocational link of tourism and hospitality courses and aligning HE with the needs of the economy (Airey & Johnson, 1999; Ayikoru et al., 2009). Hence it can be argued that although the vocational link has been adopted in describing tourism courses and graduate outcomes, it may not feature as key in tourism academics' priorities when these courses were established, and that their academics' research interests and passions may continue to take precedence.

In a HE context, research often takes priority. Research is first important in legitimizing a new field of study. High-quality research reflects favourably on and establishes credibility of both academics and their respective institutions. A sizable amount of research on academic identities (Duke, 2003; Archer, 2008; Trede et al., 2012) and on the research–teaching divide (Brown, 2002; Gibbs, 2002; Brew, 2006, 2007; Boshier, 2009) suggests the increasing importance of research outputs where promotion opportunities are concerned. This may imply that tourism academics and their respective departments may prioritize research over enhancing the vocational relevance of their courses and employability of their graduates. This may be especially the case where the vocational relevance of courses is not seen by the academics as important.

In a strong economy and labour market, there was less of an imperative to focus academic effort to enhance the employability prospects of tourism graduates. When the economy is growing, there is a range of employment opportunities for graduates. However, most recently, with the slowing of economic growth and the introduction and increases of student fees, the ability of graduates to secure a job to pay off student fees and sizable student debt has become of increasing importance.

Despite the primacy of research in HE (in reputational terms), there is currently a trend where graduate employability is becoming more and more important in benchmarking exercises and for league table rankings of HE institutions (HEIs) in the UK. With the increasing importance of league tables and the introduction of increased student fees in 2012, there has arguably been some rebalancing between the perceived importance of HE metrics in relation to research, against that of teaching and employability. Some league tables such as that of the Guardian newspaper in the UK focus on teaching and employability, and exclude research output from their calculations. Students' employment outcomes have become important in prospective students' decision making (Dale & Robinson, 2001, Morgan, 2004). This has gone some way to refocus HEIs' efforts in this direction.

Tourism degrees – industry scepticism

Pursuing an explicit vocational link is a complex endeavour. Tourism studies are often cross-disciplinary, linking areas such as business studies, geography, sociology and many more. Tribe (2004) refers to the 'indiscipline' of tourism, whereby the range of tourism degrees provided by universities means that there is no common agreement about the nature of skills provided by tourism degrees. The resulting lack of consistency leads to confusion about what is on offer and what to expect (Petrova, 2008).

With the growth of tourism courses, after the expansion of HE in the 1990s, industry concerns about the vocational relevance of tourism and hospitality courses and graduates' preparedness for the labour market became more prominent. Research capturing employers' perspectives claimed that there was a mismatch between skills and knowledge required by industry and those provided by universities (Cooper, 1993; Evans, 1993; Dale & Robinson, 2001; Churchward & Riley, 2002; Airey, 2005). Original research by the author suggested that the tourism industry's scepticism is only partially based on perceived mismatch between what is required and what tourism and hospitality graduates offered (Petrova, 2008). Tourism employers' views and indeed predispositions to employ tourism graduates were also affected by the existing size and nature of employment opportunities, coloured by employers' own personal educational and career backgrounds, and exposure to tourism degrees and graduates (ibid.).

The industry is known to have a smaller proportion of managers who are educated to degree level, compared to other industries (Ritchie, 1993; Kusluvan & Kusluvan, 2000; Cooper, 2001; Litteljohn & Watson, 2004). The lack of management-level qualification continues to be prevalent in the industry, including lack of strategic management skills (State of the Nation Report, 2013). Entry points into the industry (first jobs upon graduation) would often not require degree-level qualifications, while graduates are faced with barriers to recruitment in the form of 'bottom-up' careers and the practice of not advertising jobs externally (Petrova, 2008). This would imply that graduate-level employment opportunities in tourism are low.

General views on government policy in HE, and specifically the widening participation agenda, can also colour some employers' perceptions of tourism graduates from post-92 institutions (Petrova, 2008). Wilton (2012) observed that graduates from generic business disciplines have stronger graduate outcomes than those of specialist degrees (such as tourism and marketing). This, he reflects, may be because such courses are mostly taught in post-92 universities and have a higher proportion of women taking these courses, and women have been found to fare consistently worse than their male counterparts in securing employment in the labour market.

An added complexity in discussing tourism graduates' employment prospects arises from the contested boundaries of both the tourism industry and tourism as a field of study, aptly captured by Youell in 1998:

> This is due, in most part, to two principal factors, namely the broad nature of the subject and the fact that the tourism industry comprises a multitude of diverse, yet interrelated, industry sectors. If we consider that the study of tourism impinges on such disciplines as geography, psychology, sociology, economics, anthropology, planning, business studies, politics and economics, to name but a few, it is easy to understand the difficulty in agreeing a workable definition. On the industry side, sectors as diverse as hotels, leisure centres, local government planning departments, airlines, conservation bodies, travel agencies, museums, transport providers and entertainment complexes all lay claim to inclusion in any definition of tourism.
>
> (Youell, 1998: 9)

As such it may be difficult to meet rather varied requirements of a range of small and large organizations, sectors and sub-sectors. Due to this complexity, there is no single professional body in tourism, and the range of types of employers, sectors and career routes varies considerably (Baum, 2007). This creates difficulties in identifying professions within tourism (Busby, 2005).

This in turn affects the ability of HEIs to design programmes that can clearly meet (directly) employers' needs and, importantly, are able to communicate this to employers.

These complexities suggest that the vocational link of tourism and hospitality courses, which is often featured in the way these courses are advertised, and is part of tourism students' considerations when embarking on their HE studies, is contested. This chapter now examines the definition, importance and applicability of employability skills in this context.

Defining employability skills

As noted above, within a UK context, the focus on responding to economic needs featured in the 1960s in the Robbins (1963) report, where transferable, intellectual and personal skills were emphasized as key to the economy (Bennett et al., 2000). With this in mind, in the 1990s the UK government commissioned the Dearing Report (1997), which investigated HE, and how changes in direction of HE could better respond to changes in society. The Dearing Report underlined the importance of capabilities and being equipped for work.

Transferrable skills and skills descriptors

In the 1990s, the UK government saw transferrable skills as key to ensuring that the labour force is flexible and able to adapt to the rapidly changing labour market (DfEE, 1998, as cited in Stewart & Knowles, 2000: 68). The HM Treasury (2004) thus saw employability as dependent upon meeting employers' skills needs. Later, Coopers & Lybrand in another government-commissioned report (1998) identified four aspects of skills concerned with promoting employability (moving beyond transferable/key skills):

- Traditional intellectual skills – critical evaluation of evidence and its interpretation, 'error-free' reasoning, the ability to sustain a logical argument and reach a conclusion that can be defended as reasonable.
- The 'new' core or key skills – communication skills, numeracy, the use of information technology, and knowing how to learn.
- Personal attributes deemed to have market value – self-reliance, adaptability, flexibility, drive, nous, creativity.
- Knowledge about how organizations work and how people in them do their jobs.

It was expected that universities would adapt their provision to develop these skills in graduates. Concurrently, many universities commenced concerted efforts to strengthen graduates' abilities to recognize and communicate their skills to employers. There can be therefore a twofold understanding of 'employability skills' – one which talks about possessing skills deemed important by employers, and another which is directly concerned with the job application process (i.e. interview skills).

Generic skills lists produced by governments and employers often exclude reference to the possession of specialist skills. Increasing focus on non-specialist skills is not limited to the UK. Jackson & Chapman (2012), similarly to Kuijpers and Meijers (2012), note the increasing importance of non-specialist competencies in the global economy (capturing perspectives from the Netherlands, UK, Australia and China). The UK and Australia also focused upon HE for the development of skills and 'employment related competencies', as did the USA (Bennett et al., 2000). Furthermore, Jackson and Chapman (2012) also observe consistency between

Australian and UK academics in the chosen importance of soft competencies. They argue that globalization may have contributed to harmonization of views across culturally similar environments (ibid.).

In both the UK and Australian literature, however, the theoretical and empirical base upon which employer wish lists have been generated to guide HE curriculum has been questioned (Bennett *et al.*, 2000). There has been ongoing confusion over terms and definitions (semantic confusion) (ibid.). Bennett *et al.* (2000) question the terms used and how they may be interpreted differently ('core skills', 'transferable skills'). In their research into graduate transitions into work, Bennett *et al.* showed that there is a wide interpretation given to skills definitions, and that in cases where the same vocabulary was used what was being practised was found to be quite different. They argued that:

> The discourse on generic skills and all its variants, is confused, confusing and under-conceptualized. Employers and policymakers alike have been seduced by the slogans, with scant consideration of their definition, characteristics, transferability or utility. . . . Allied to the above is evidence of a lack of a common language of skills between higher education and employers.
>
> (Bennett *et al.*, 2000: 175)

Bennett *et al.* (2000) adopt the term generic skills, and suggest that HE curricula should include four intertwined elements: disciplinary knowledge, disciplinary skills, workplace awareness and workplace experience. More recently, Jackson and Chapman (2012) use the term competence, adopting Grzeda's definition which encompasses skills, attributes, values and abilities. The use of their definition of non-technical competence is aligned to what other authors see as 'generic skills' and 'generic attributes'. Jackson and Chapman (2012) argue that the use of process–driven, active task behaviours will be easier to define; this is seen as 'reducing ambiguity and enabling easier assessment' (p. 543). They also move forward the development of profiles as opposed to listings of a range of competency requirements. This way, they argue, HEIs can move away from a passive stance towards skills wish lists imposed upon them by employers and governments. Instead, the development of profiles can provide a basis for 'devising recruitment tools which more precisely reflect organizational requirements' (Jackson & Chapman, 2012: 543–4). Thus Jackson and Chapman take a twofold approach – reducing the ambiguity of terms as well as taking a more proactive stance towards informing (and arguably educating) employers about better suited recruitment tools. This is important to them as they see their approach as not only resulting in a better match between graduate positions and recruits, but also easier translation into learning outcomes (ibid.).

Reducing the ambiguity of language is seen as important, as even when academics and industry perceptions of required non-technical competency are aligned, discrepancies may exist due to these competencies not being developed appropriately in the curriculum (Jackson & Chapman, 2012). Hence, reducing the ambiguity of terms, providing (and 'educating' employers about) appropriate selection techniques, while developing sound curriculum to support the development of these skills and enabling graduates to transfer competencies from one setting to another, are all seen as important steps to ensure graduate employability (ibid.).

What of the definition of the term employability? How is the term employability defined and how do we support the development of employability skills? Widely adopted definitions of employability (in the university sector) are discussed below as well as how these have been interpreted by universities and their work in this area.

Defining employability

A decade ago, employability was defined by the UK government as 'the relative chances of finding and maintaining different kinds of employment' (Brown et al., 2003: 9), whereas the Enhancing Student Employability Co-ordination Team (rather than emphasizing the chances of securing and maintaining employment) emphasized the individual's skills development:

> a set of achievements – skills, understandings and personal attributes – that make graduates more likely to gain employment and be successful in your chosen occupations, which benefits themselves, the workforce, the community and the economy.
>
> (Yorke & Knight, 2006: 3)

This emphasis by Yorke and Knight (ibid.) could be seen in the practice of HEIs adopting the language of skills and focusing on the development of transferable skills and personal attributes deemed desirable by employers and the government.

The Higher Education Academy's (HEA)[4] definition emphasized the ability of graduates to reflect upon their experiences. Based on this work, a number of projects, funded opportunities and resources were produced to help HEIs and academics support students, not only in skills development, but also in aiding the development of their ability to reflect upon their learning and development so as to be better able to communicate them to potential employers.

> employability goes well beyond the simplistic notion of key skills, and is evidenced in the application of a mix of personal qualities and beliefs, understandings, skilful practices and the ability to reflect productively on experience.
>
> (Yorke, 2006: 13)

The HEA subject centre for the sector – the Hospitality, Leisure, Sport and Tourism Network's[5] *Resource Guide in: Employability* (HLSTN, 2004: 1) emphasized the ability to secure a graduate-level job, maintain employment and adapt to changes in the labour market:

> At its most simplistic level, the term employability refers to the potential of a student to gain a graduate level job following graduation. However, employability is about much more than the acquisition of a first job. It relates to a broader set of achievements that enhance students' capabilities to operate self-sufficiently in the labour market, for example, in being able to maintain employment and have the flexibility to deal with change.

The guidance included in the HLSTN document included embedding employability skills in the curriculum, as well as reflecting upon and documenting student's achievements.

Importance of reflection

As a result of the above trends, there was initially a focus on transferable skills development, followed soon after by a focus on reflection. The importance of reflection was to aid skills development as well as awareness, and in turn a focus on academics being able to make skills development explicit (Bennett et al., 2000). Reflection is seen to ensure long-term development of individuals.

> While reflection underpins personal qualities within employment and the preparation for seeking employment, the ability to stand back and assess one's position in particular

circumstances (work, age, education achieved and needed, ambition and other lifespan issues), is a third role for reflection which we will sum up as contributing to 'lifelong learning'.

(Moon, 2004: 4)

Reflection and self-awareness were linked to students being able to communicate and demonstrate skills, and thus be successful in the labour market.

Employability and personal development planning (PDP)

The term 'PDP' was often used in discussion and policy implementation efforts in relation to employability (see Ward, 2006; Kumar, 2007). PDP became a banner under which a number of initiatives were created. The Quality Assurance Agency for Higher Education (QAA) for England defines PDP as: 'structured and supported processes to develop the capacity of individuals to reflect upon their learning and achievement and to plan for their own personal, educational, and career development' (QAA, 2001: 2).

A number of HEA projects, programmes and initiatives were funded and supported to enhance the employability prospects of graduates across disciplines. Recent work on employability skills in the Netherlands suggests that HEIs can foster a learning environment that enhances the career competencies of students and hence enhances their career prospects in a changing and uncertain labour market by:

> providing a learning environment that stimulates real-life work experiences, that gives the student opportunities to influence their own course of study by offering them the opportunity to make choices.

(Kuijpers & Meijers, 2012: 462)

Kuijpers and Meijers found that a positive relationship between career reflection, work experience, proactive career action and networking contribute to establishing a career-related learning environment and can compensate for personal factors that are normally associated with worst career outcomes (ibid.).

Recent trends – employability and the increased focus on higher order skills

A slight shift of focus was observed in the mid-2000s when developing and demonstrating *graduate*-level skills (as opposed to *transferable*, *key* or *core* skills), and securing *graduate*-level jobs became the focus. The focus moved upon learning through research, as research was seen as means of developing and demonstrating graduate-level skills (Brew, 2006; Jenkins & Healey, 2009). This was also manifested in national policy and funding initiatives (both in Australia and the UK, with a much more established focus in this area in USA universities). The Higher Education Funding Council for England has been offering funding for 'Research Informed Teaching' (RIT) initiatives since 2006, where funding was offered in inverse proportion to the research income of universities. The purpose of this policy was twofold: to balance the underfunding of staff research activity in post-92 institutions' research focus (considering the tensions discussed in the Introduction of this chapter), as well as emphasizing the importance of learning opportunities and skills development of students from engaging with original research (Jenkins & Healey, 2009). With the introduction of the new/higher funding regime in England in 2012, where students pay fees as much as £9,000 per year, the importance of securing a graduate-level job which enables students to start promptly repaying their student loan has become important. Research and associated skills are seen as providing evidence of 'graduateness' and competitive ability in the labour market (Healey, 2005; Johnes, 2006; Robertson & Blackler, 2006).

The squeeze on public finances, following the financial crisis of 2008, and the austerity regime that followed, have now taken funding and focus away from such initiatives. Many universities are currently focusing on providing job-centre style services, work placement and international opportunities to their students (Shiel, 2008; Walmsley et al., 2012). Reflecting macro-economic trends (such as high unemployment rates among young people), the more recent QAA guide in England is titled 'Enterprise and Entrepreneurship Education: Guidance for UK Higher Education Providers' (first draft was released in February 2012). Such initiatives attempt to prepare graduates not only for flexible career patterns and easy transition between jobs and careers, but also to enable graduates to create their own gainful employment in a market where job opportunities are limited.

Contesting employability skills

The employability definitions and policies explored above omit a number of external factors which may have an impact on one's employability outcomes. Employability is not solely person-centred (possessing and being able to successfully communicate their skills and attributes to a potential employer and meeting the requirements of a job). It also includes how one compares within the hierarchy of job seekers (Brown et al., 2003). The unique history of tourism in HE in the UK context has been shown to be linked to the way employers perceive tourism graduates and their ability to compete in the graduate labour market (Petrova, 2008). Employers' views such as that students from 'classier institutions' are likely to have a 'better academic track record' and be 'better and brighter' (ibid.) can impede tourism graduates' employment prospects. Tourism suffers from a lack of respect as an academic subject, as well as being perceived as a fun and frivolous subject by students, and hence attracting the less academically able (Stuart, 2002). Hence the perceived academic legitimacy of tourism-related courses may have an impact on the employability of tourism graduates, an issue which falls outside the employability definitions above.

Due to the increasing importance of league tables and measuring graduate employability, increasingly the term 'employability' has come to be seen as equivalent to employment six months after graduation, when the Destination and Leavers survey is conducted in the UK capturing the employment prospects of graduates and whether they have managed to secure a graduate-level job. As discussed earlier in this chapter, measuring employability can become another measure of legitimacy. However the vastness of the tourism industry and lack of defined professional routes may have an impact on short-term (six months) graduate careers. Due to external factors such as industry recruitment practices and career patterns, many tourism graduates are faced with lower level entry-level jobs early in their tourism carer. Hence there is a danger that due to external, industry-related factors, the results from such surveys can lead to further discrediting tourism degrees, regardless of the quality of the degrees and graduates.

Conclusion

This chapter provided an overview of HE policy developments and their impact on the increasing importance of graduate employability. The widening participation agenda, changes in HE funding regimes, a debilitating financial crisis and the rise in the unemployment of young people have focused attention on the employability of graduates. A range of policy initiatives to enhance the employability of graduates were examined in this chapter. It was argued that the implicit vocational focus of tourism degrees should not be assumed. That, although the development of tourism in HE coincided with growth in HE in general and the focus on HE as an instrument of economic growth, the tourism HE courses (in the UK) were largely established based on the research interests of tourism academics. Hence the assumed vocational link (for what are assumed to be vocationally relevant courses), may be less pronounced than anticipated. Furthermore, considerable importance is currently placed (by universities and academics) on research, as it is seen to secure the legitimacy of courses, universities and indeed individual academics. Furthermore, employers' views were shown to be affected by a number of subjective, preconceived ideas, not necessarily based on direct experiences and understanding of tourism degrees (and graduates), but rather are intertwined with their positions in relation to the government's HE policy and widening participation agenda. Overall, there is a dearth of systemized large-scale research focusing on recent graduates and their transition to employment (Bennett et al., 2000). This needs to be undertaken to provide much-needed evidence to inform the debate and practice around tourism graduates' employability.

Notes

1   The focus here is primarily on the UK, although parallels are drawn to other countries such as Australia and the USA.
2   It must be noted that the Russell Group is only one indicator of the profile of universities. Institutional rankings are now widely used, taking account of a range of measures (depending on the particular league table), including teaching, research and employability.
3   The Research Excellence Framework is a system for assessing the quality of research in UK HE institutions. The results of the latest REF are released in December 2014 (see http://www.ref.ac.uk/)
4   The Higher Education Academy is an independent organization funded by UK government HE bodies and HEIs (through subscriptions and grants). The purpose of the organization is supporting HE providers in enhancing the quality of their teaching and learning provision (for further information see: http://www.heacademy.ac.uk/about).
5   An HEA-supported subject centre.

References

Airey, D. (2005). 'Growth and Development'. In D. Airey & J. Tribe (Eds.), *An International Handbook of Tourism Education* (pp. 13–24). Oxford: Elsevier.

Airey, D., & Johnson, S. (1999). 'The Content of Tourism Degree Courses in the UK'. *Tourism Management*, 20, 229–35.

Archer, L. (2008). 'Younger Academics' Construction of "Authenticity", "Success" and Professional Identity'. *Studies in Higher Education*, 33(4), 385–403.

Ayikoru, M., Tribe J., & Airey, D. (2009). 'Reading Tourism Education: neoliberalism unveiled'. *Annals of Tourism Research,* 36(2), 191–221.

Barnett, R., Parry, G., Cox, R., Loder, C., & Williams, G. (1994). *Assessment of the Quality of Higher Education: a review and evaluation.* Institute of Education, University of London; available from the Higher Education Funding Council for England, Bristol

Baum, T. (2007). 'Human Resources in Tourism: still waiting for change'. *Tourism Management*, 28, 1383–99.

Bennett, N., Dunne, E., & Carré, C. (2000). *Skills Development in Higher Education and Employment.* Buckingham: SRHE/Open University.

Blackstone, T. (2001). 'Why Learn? Higher education in a learning society'. *Higher Education Quarterly*, 5(2), 175–84.

Boshier, R. (2009). 'Why Is the Scholarship of Teaching and Learning Such a Hard Sell?' *Higher Education Research & Development,* 28(1), 1–15.

Brew, A. (2006). *Research and Teaching: beyond the divide.* New York: Palgrave Macmillan.

Brew, A. (2007). *Research and Teaching from Students' Perspective. International policies and practices for academic enquiry.* An International Colloquium, 12–21 April, Marwell Conference Centre, Winchester, UK.

Brown, P., Hesketh, A., & Williams, S. (2003). 'Employability in Knowledge-driven Economy'. In P. Knight (Ed.), *Innovation in Education for Employability: Notes from the Skills Plus Conference.* Manchester Metropolitan University.

Brown, R. (2002). 'Research and Teaching – repairing the damage'. *Exchange: Ideals, Practices, News and Support for Decision Makers in Active Learning and Teaching,* (3), 29–31.

Busby, G. (2005). *Work Experience and Industrial Links.* In D. Airey & J. Tribe (Eds.), *An International Handbook of Tourism Education* (pp. 93–110). Oxford: Elsevier.

Busby, G., Brunt P., & Baber, S. (1997). 'Tourism Sandwich Placements: an appraisal'. *Tourism Management,* 18(2), 105–10.

Churchward, J., & Riley, M. (2002). 'Tourism Occupations and Education: an exploratory study'. *International Journal of Tourism Research,* 4, 77–86.

Cooper, C. (1993). 'An Analysis of the Relationship between Industry and Education in Travel and Tourism'. *Teros International,* 1(1).

Cooper, C. (2001). 'Tourism Industry and Education Symposium'. *International Journal of Tourism Research,* 3, 59–64.

Coopers & Lybrand. (1998) *Skills Development in Higher Education.* Report for CVCP/DfEE/HEQE, November, London: Committee of Vice-Chancellors and Principals of the Universities of the UK (CVCP).

Cranmer, S. (2006). 'Enhancing Graduate Employability: best intentions and mixed outcomes'. *Studies in Higher Education,* 31(2), 169–84.

Dale, C., & Robinson, N. (2001). 'The Theming of Tourism Education: a three-domain approach'. *International Journal of Contemporary Hospitality Management,* 13(1), 30–4.

Dearing, R. (1997). *Higher Education in the Learning Society* ('The Dearing Report'). London: National Committee of Inquiry in Higher Education.

Dredge, D., Benckendorff, P., Day, M., Gross, M. J., Walo, M., Weeks, P., & Whitelaw, P. (2012). 'The Philosophic Practitioner and the Curriculum Space'. *Annals of Tourism Research,* 39(4), 2154–76.

Duke, C. (2003). 'Changing Identity on an Ambiguous Environment: a work in progress report'. *Higher Education Management and Policy,* 15(3), 51–67.

Evans, J. (1993). 'Current Issues: the tourism graduates: a case of overproduction'. *Tourism Management,* 14(4), 243–6.

Gibbs, G. (2002). 'Institutional Strategies for Linking Research and Teaching'. *Exchange: Ideals, Practices, News and Support for Decision Makers in Active Learning and Teaching,* 3, 8–11.

Healey, M. (2005). 'Linking Research and Teaching to Benefit Student Learning'. *Journal of Geography in Higher Education,* 29(2), 183–201.

HM Treasury (2004). *Skills in the Global Economy.* HM Treasury, London: Stationery Office

HM Treasury (2005). *Skills: Getting on in Business, Getting on at Work.* HM Treasury, London: Stationery Office.

Hospitality, Leisure, Sport and Tourism Network (HLSTN). (2004). *Resource Guide in: Employability.* Retrieved 12 December 2006 from the Higher Education Academy: HLSTN: http://www.heacademy. ac.uk/hlst/resources

Jackson, D., & Chapman, E. (2012). 'Non-Technical Competencies in Undergraduate Business Degree Programmes: Australian and UK perspectives'. *Studies in Higher Education,* 37(5), 541–67.

Jarvis, P., Holford, J., & Griffin, C. (1998). *The Theory and Practice of Learning.* London: Kogan Page.

Jenkins, A., & Healey, M. (2009). *Institutional Strategies to Link Teaching and Research.* York: Higher Education Academy.

Johnes, M. (2006). 'Student Perceptions of Research in Teaching-led Higher Education'. *Journal of Hospitality, Leisure, Sport & Tourism Education,* 5(1), 28–40.

King, R. (2004). *The University in the Global Age.* Basingstoke: Palgrave Macmillan.

Kuijpers, M. & Meijers, F. (2012). 'Learning for Now or Later? Career competencies among students in higher vocational education in the Netherlands'. *Studies in Higher Education,* 37(4), 449–62.

Kumar, A. (2007). *Personal, Academic and Career Development in Higher Education: SOARing to success.* Abingdon: Routledge.

Kusluvan, S., & Kusluvan, Z. (2000). 'Perceptions and Attitudes of Undergraduate Tourism Students towards Working in the Tourism Industry in Turkey'. *Tourism Management,* 21, 251–69.

Litteljohn, D., & Watson, S. (2004). 'Developing Graduate Managers for Hospitality and Tourism'. *International Journal of Contemporary Hospitality Management*, 16(7), 408–14.

Moon, J. (2004). 'Reflection and Employability: learning and employability guides', 4. York: LTSN and ESECT.

Morgan, M. (2004). 'From Production Line to Drama School: higher education for the future tourism'. *International Journal of Contemporary Hospitality Management*, 16(2), 91–9.

Petrova, P. (2008). *The Value of Tourism Degrees: an investigation of the tourism industry's views on tourism degrees and tourism graduates.* PhD: 410. Tourism, Leisure and Sport Management, University of Bedfordshire, Luton.

Pitcher, J., & Purcell, K. (1998). 'Diverse Expectations and Access to Opportunities: is there a graduate labour market?' *Higher Education Quarterly*, 52(2), 179–203.

Quality Assurance Agency for Higher Education (QAA). (2001) *Guidelines for HE Progress Files.* Gloucester: QAA.

Ritchie, J. R. B. (1993). 'Educating the Tourism Educators: guidelines for policy and programme development'. *Teros International*, 1(1).

Robbins, L. [Chairman] (1963). Higher Education Report of the Committee Appointed by the Prime Minister under the Chairmanship of Lord Robbins, 1961–63. London: Her Majesty's Stationery Office.

Robertson, J., & Blackler, G. (2006). 'Students' Experience of Learning in a Research Environment'. *Higher Education Research and Development*, 25(3), 215–29.

Shiel, C. (2008). 'Introduction'. In R. Atfield & P. Kemp (Eds.), *Enhancing the International Learning Experience in Business and Management, Hospitality, Leisure, Sport, Tourism* (pp. v–xv). Newbury: Threshold Press.

State of the Nation Report. (2013). *An Analysis of Labour Market Trends, Skills, Education and Training within the UK Hospitality and Tourism Industries.* London: People 1st.

Stewart, J., & Knowles, V. (2000). 'Graduate Recruitment and Selection: implications for HE, graduates and small business recruiters'. *Career Development International*, 5(2), 65–80.

Stuart, M. (2002). 'Critical Influences on Tourism as a Subject in UK Higher Education: lecturer perspectives'. *Journal of Hospitality, Leisure, Sport & Tourism Education*, 1(1), 5–18.

Stuart-Hoyle, M. (2003). 'The Purpose of Undergraduate Tourism Courses in the United Kingdom'. *Journal of Hospitality, Leisure, Sport & Tourism Education*, 2(1), 49–64.

Trede, F., Macklin, R., & Bridges, D. (2012). 'Professional Identity Development: a review of the higher education literature'. *Studies in Higher Education*, 37(3), 365–84.

Tribe, J. (2003). 'Delivering Higher Quality: a comparative study of lecturers' perceptions and QAA subject review in tourism'. *Journal of Hospitality, Leisure, Sport & Tourism Education*, 2(1), 27–47.

Tribe, J. (2004). 'Knowing about Tourism: Epistemological Issues'. In J. Phillimore & L. Goodson (Eds.), *Qualitative Research in Tourism: ontologies, epistemologies and methodologies* (pp. 46–64). London: Routledge.

Walmsley, A. (2012). *Tourism Intelligence Monitor: ATHE Report on Tourism Higher Education in the UK 2012.* Brighton: Association for Tourism in Higher Education.

Walmsley, A., Thomas, R., & Jameson, S. (2012). 'Internships in SMEs and Career Intentions'. *Journal of Education and Work*, 25(2), 185–204.

Ward, R. (2006). 'Introduction: employability in context'. In N. Becket. & P. Kemp (Eds.), *Enhancing Graduate Employability on Business, Management, Hospitality, Leisure, Sport, Tourism* (pp. vi–xi). Newbury: Threshold Press.

Williams, G., & Light, G. (1999). 'Student Income and Costs of Study in the United Kingdom'. *European Journal of Education*, 34(1), 23–42.

Wilton, N. (2012). 'The Impact of Work Placements on Skills Development and Labour Market Outcomes for Business and Management Graduates'. *Studies in Higher Education*, 37(5), 603–20.

Yorke, M. (2006). *Employability in Higher Education: what it is – what it is not.* York: Higher Education Academy.

Yorke, M., & Knight, P. (2006). *Embedding Employability into the Curriculum.* York: Higher Education Academy.

Youell, R. (1998). *Tourism: an introduction.* Harlow: Longman.

30

Employment and career development in tourism and hospitality education

Adele Ladkin
Bournemouth University, UK

Introduction

The growth and development of tourism, hospitality and events education over the last 40 years has been outlined in Chapter 1. Set against this background of growth and change, it is clear that the demand for qualified people to fill academic positions in these diverse fields is increasing, providing opportunities for employment (Metcalf *et al.*, 2005). This is particularly the case in regions where the expansion of courses is prevalent, for example in the cases of India and China. In China, growth has been considerable (Xiao, 2000). In 1990, 55 institutions offered programmes to 8,263 students, rising to 494 programmes for 199,682 students in 2004 (Zhang & Fan, 2006) and 967 institutions offering degrees to 596,100 in 2010 (Yang & Song, 2011). In this chapter, the focus is on those who are responsible for the delivery of this ever-increasing and diverse number of programmes: the tourism, hospitality and event educators. It is these academics who take the lead in the design, delivery, monitoring and review of the curriculum to meet the needs of a range of stakeholders, whilst at the same time contributing towards research and professional practice in these fields. Academia as a career choice offers many positive and worthwhile experiences, and also a number of challenges and increasing pressures (Ladkin & Weber, 2009). The purpose of this chapter is to explore issues of employment and career development in academia in the tourism, hospitality and event fields. Although the three subjects have developed independently and at different times, the employment and career development issues for academics in all three areas are broadly similar. Events education, however, is the most recent and rapidly developing area of the three. Questions have been raised as to whether there are jobs available for all of the people with an education in these areas, and whether in certain areas demand for programmes may be beginning to decline (Fidgeon, 2010). The wider trends of student choice and institutional challenges will in turn affect the need for academic jobs.

In pursuit of its purpose the chapter is organized in the following way. After this introduction, the next section sets the wider scene and explores the characteristics of academic labour markets and examines the nature of academic jobs. This is followed by an exploration of academic career development and academic careers. Then academic career development in tourism and hospitality is explored, using evidence from previously published research. This is followed by a focus on the issues and challenges that tourism, hospitality and event educators are currently facing. Finally, some conclusions are drawn.

Academic labour markets and the nature of academic jobs

Fundamentally, labour markets represent the supply and demand for labour, and comprise the individuals in any given population who are considered to be of working age. Labour markets can be defined in a number of ways, including their size, skill level, the cost of labour, mobility patterns and geographical location. At any given time, people will be seeking employment or trying to change their jobs, and employers will be seeking new employees (Riley, 1991). Labour markets are fluid, and at one level the labour market supply and demand are driven by the price of labour. However, only focusing on the economic characteristics of a labour market masks the independent decisions of individuals, who may not necessarily be driven by wage rates. Whilst economic factors clearly influence labour market behaviour, individual choice, opportunity, freedom, barriers and constraints and decision-making processes are also important. Typically, the characteristics (adapted from Riley, 1991) of a labour market are:

- Size (large/small – the numbers of people they contain)
- Geographical boundaries (local, national and international)
- Dual labour markets (Doeringer & Piore, 1972) split the market into primary and secondary jobs
- Skill base (the variety of skills required for the jobs, and the skills of the workforce)
- Pay level (high/low)
- Response to supply and demand changes (fast/slow).

Academic labour markets

Academic labour markets can be viewed in these and other descriptive terms. For example, Musselin (2005) identifies that comparative studies on academic careers (Altbach, 2000; Enders, 2001) commonly describe academic labour markets in a formal description and include procedures to access, grade structures, status, career development stages and salaries. Alternatively, economists have been interested in academic careers with a focus on supply and demand and its effect on wage rates and mobility (Ehrenberg, 2002).

One of the challenges in exploring academic labour markets is that differences exist at a national level. Certainly at the most basic level terminology is not unified, for example in the case of job titles and institutional structures. Musselin (2004) points out that salaries, status, recruitment procedures, career patterns, work loads and promotion rules vary between different countries, which is a challenge for international mobility. In response to this difficulty, Musselin (2005) argues that academic labour markets can be characterized by specific interplay among four factors. These are: selection processes and devices; the length and role of the tenure period; the balance between internal and external labour markets; and the determination of the price of academics. This is a useful framework to understand the labour market processes and also how they might affect career development. Selection processes and devices affect the way in which people are hired from both the internal and external labour market and comparative competition. Tenure directly affects job security and gives rise to and defines the parameters for career progression or contracted employment. The balance between the internal and external labour market presents the options for career development, and the price of labour for academics is often set bureaucratically or by negotiation according to supply and demand (Musselin, 2005). Certainly for those academics who are seeking international experience, there are variations in processes and structures to consider. In Europe, the Bologna Process has been seeking to create a European Higher Education Area which, amongst other things, intends to facilitate mobility within the region (Bologna Process, 2009).

In practical terms, for those seeking an academic career, employment opportunities can be considered using the following classifications: type of institution, level of education, type of contract, job levels and location of programme, as shown in Table 30.1.

The types of institution to a certain extent reflect the historical development of educational structure after schooling and what educational level is offered at each type of institution. The level of education reflects the many opportunities available, with tourism, hospitality and event education now being offered from certificates up to doctoral level. Contract types and job levels refer to career structures. These are not standardized globally, but have national variations. The job levels assume a hierarchical career progression, although this is not necessarily reflected in individual careers that may appear more of the boundaryless type as defined by Arthur (1994). The location of the programme reflects individual institutional structures and trends. These characteristics define the broad structures of employment in academia, giving rise to the variety

Table 30.1 Classification of academic employment structures

Classification	
Type of institution	University
	Higher education institutions
	Technical colleges
	Further education colleges
Level of education	Doctoral
	Master's (Postgraduate)
	Degree (Undergraduate)
	Diploma
	Certificate
Contract type	Permanent or fixed contract
	Tenured/non-tenured
	Full-time/fractional
	Part-time hourly paid
	Research-only contracts
	Teaching-only contracts
Job levels	Chair Professor
	Professor
	Reader/Associate Professor
	Principle Lecturer
	Senior Lecture
	Lecturer/Assistant Professor
	Tutor
	Instructor
Location of programme	Department
	School
	Faculty

of opportunities in the field. A further point to note is that considerable variation exists between countries in terms of emerging educational courses or those that are fully developed. For example it may be tourism courses are prevalent at undergraduate level in a country, but postgraduate education is only emerging.

The nature of academic jobs

Structurally, although the academic labour markets may have national variations, the nature of academic jobs is surprisingly similar on a global scale. Hsu (2005) and Barrows and Bosselman (1999) provide a detailed consideration of the different roles and duties undertaken by hospitality academics. Although terminology may differ slightly, the role of an academic typically combines research, teaching, administration and leadership responsibilities. These different aspects will vary across different stages of a career, and according to the type of institution and the nature of the post. The roles may be described by grouping them into the four categories of research, teaching, administration, and leadership.

Research typically includes the supervision of doctoral students, submitting grant applications for both publically funded research and contract/consultancy research, publication of journal articles, books, book chapters and conference papers, knowledge transfer activities and building research collaborations. Research is important as a benchmark of institutional quality, theoretical and practical development in the field, and to inform teaching. As identified in Chapter 1, measures of research output and quality are becoming increasingly important for institutions and, consequently, individual career development.

Teaching is all aspects associated with curriculum planning, design, implementation and review, assessment and the student experience. Essential elements in teaching include keeping up to date with the subject and responding to the changing nature of student and other stakeholder demands. Engagement with industry advisory bodies and consideration of stakeholder needs is important here.

Administration is at department, faculty and institutional level and includes all elements of institutional service and academic citizenship. This may include attending meetings and committees, and all student and research-related administration.

Leadership contains administrative responsibilities but is also concerned with strategic decision making and leadership of staff. Leadership opportunities are one element of career development.

Clearly, within an academic environment there is a wide range of opportunities and scope for specialization over a career. These different aspects present different opportunities for career development and also serve to illustrate the demands of an academic life. It is generally expected that an academic will be involved in each of these areas at some point over their careers, and certain experiences and competencies are an essential part of career development.

These four roles require a variety of skills and characteristics (prospects.ac.uk, 2013) for an academic career, including:

- Passion for your research
- Organizational and time management skills
- People and networking skills
- Communication skills
- Willingness to work long and flexible hours
- Administrative skills
- Self-motivation
- Teamworking.

This list provides an illustration of the varied nature of academic employment, and is far removed from the traditional view of academics as people who spend all their time on research and scholarly activity, suggesting the changing nature of academic careers. Academics' careers ultimately are shaped by the changing needs of the institutions they exist within, which explains much of the shifts in emphasis or requirements.

Career development and academic careers

Career development is an umbrella term for organizational or personal career planning. Careers are the outcome of structural opportunities made available to an individual, for example the size of the industry, organizational structure and knowledge requirement, and human ability and ambition (Weber & Ladkin, 2009). The structural opportunities in an industry provide the framework for any occupation, and individual ability and ambition determine how people make choices within the structural opportunities (Ladkin & Weber, 2009). Closely related to career planning, career development is seen as the outcome for the individual from both personal and organizational career planning (Simonsen, 1986). Chartrand and Camp (1991) identify two common themes across definitions for career development: (1) career development viewed as a sequence of positions over time, and (2) emphasis placed on the process rather than the content of the career (Ladkin & Weber, 2009). In career development literature there is a consensus that the responsibility for career development rests neither solely with the individual nor the organization, but is shared by both (Pazy, 1988). More recently, traditional concepts of a career based on organizational structures and hierarchies have been in decline (Eaton & Bailyn, 2000; Sullivan, 1999), being replaced by a career with fewer boundaries and extension to the boundaryless career (Arthur, 1994). This is the concept of a multidimensional career that develops beyond the constraints of a single organization or occupational setting (Collin & Young, 2000).

Academia has long been regarded as a setting where the individual takes responsibility for career self-management (Weber & Ladkin, 2008). Aspects of multidimensional careers in academia are evident in that networks with other academics both inside and outside host organizations are important for career development (Nixon, 1996; Fries-Britt, 2000), and mobility is a feature of academic jobs (Altbach, 1996; Blaxter et al., 1998; Welch, 1997). Harley et al. (2004), in the context of the UK and Germany, explore the implications for academic careers as a consequence of the global trend towards marketization and managerialism in higher education (Weber & Ladkin, 2009).

Other issues that have received attention in the literature have been reviewed previously by Weber and Ladkin (2009). These include the changing nature of academic labour markets (Musselin, 2005), gender issues, for example the characteristics of high-flyer female academics (Maimunah et al., 2005), and the gendered nature of careers of university professors at a country level (Ozbilgin & Healy, 2004), or a specific field (Cochran et al., 2013), and specific elements of the job. For example, Janasz and Sullivan (2004) explore the role of mentoring in the development of academic careers. Research into career paths has shown that traditional career progression is evident in academic careers, as they commence from junior positions to follow a reasonably well-structured path of upward mobility (Fulton, 1996; Halsey, 1992). Within institutions, traditional career structures dominate the way in which academic careers are understood and evaluated (Forster, 2001) with many academic careers evolving in a structured hierarchy (Weiner, 1996). However, subsequently, Harley et al. (2004) discussed the global trend of moving away from academic communities towards managed organizations, with academic careers becoming boundaryless and taking more entrepreneurial forms. In these situations, individual career strategies become an important way to advance careers. Career strategies are central in career development and refer to an individual's activities aimed at achieving his or her career goals (Gould & Penley, 1984). Adopting suitable career strategies can have a positive effect on that individual's rate of progression and pay levels in an organization.

Academic career development in tourism and hospitality

Given the role of academics in educating future graduates and preparing them for entry into the industry or education, it is interesting that little is known about the people who comprise the tourism and hospitality educators' workforce. Arguably, due to the infancy of the development of the subject area, even less is known about event educators. Despite many studies that have explored tourism as a career choice (Richardson, 2009), the careers of tourism and hospitality graduates (O'Leary & Deegan, 2005), academics and researchers (Zhao & Ritchie, 2007) and student evaluation of hospitality teachers (Leung et al., 2013; Gursoy & Umbriet, 2005; Sullcowski & Dean, 2010), surprisingly few studies have been undertaken on the careers of tourism and hospitality academics. In some ways this is not surprising, as within the wider field of career research academic careers have often been ignored. However, there are some exceptions.

A review of research into the careers of tourism academics is provided by Pearce (2005) in his consideration of what it means to be a tourism academic. Pearce identifies the early work of McIntosh (1992) as an important description of a feature of early academic life, the need to pioneer the curriculum and texts for students. Reflections on the development of research by academics are also considered (for example Gunn, 2004; Cohen, 2004; Hall, 2004). In his study, Pearce (2005) reflects on the key issues confronting the tourism academics' role. Concerns with disciplinary status and methods, the perceived relevance of tourism education and research and the management of tourism academic careers are cross-generational and cross-national areas that are considered.

O'Leary (2005) reflects on building academic staff careers, and suggests that career planning and development of tourism faculty cannot be done without understanding the direction of the department and the institution. In this way, the structure, funding autonomy and other issues all impact on career development.

Detailed studies into the career development and advancement of academic careers in tourism and hospitality have been provided by Weber and Ladkin (2008) and Ladkin and Weber (2009). Taken from the same study (Ladkin & Weber, 2009), the authors examined perceptions of tourism and hospitality academics on the importance of select career strategies in general and for their personal career advancement, and also barriers to career development. Undertaken in 2008, the research resulted in a sample of 342 academics located in varied locations across the globe who provided information on reasons for entering academia, their industry experience, career histories, importance and use of career strategies, and job career barriers. In terms of developing a career in tourism and hospitality, the results of this research show what is deemed important from the perspective of those who are working in the sector.

Table 30.2 shows the importance of career advancement tools in the respondents' current work environment at aggregate level and by gender.

Table 30.2 illustrates the perceived importance of career strategies in general, according to mean values, and the resulting ranking. The strategies academics perceived as the three most important ones for career advancement in general were: the publication of research articles; the maintenance of a network of influential contacts; and continuous study. Attainment of teaching excellence awards and engagement in cross-university activities were perceived as less important. The ranking of these career strategies did not differ between male and female academics. However differences in perceptions of importance relating to other career strategies are evident. For example

Table 30.2 Importance of career advancement tools in current work environment at aggregate level and by gender

Career advancement tools	Mean	SD	Rank Male	Female
Getting research articles published	6.36	1.19	1	1
Keeping a network of influential contacts	6.07	1.15	2	2
Undertaking further study	5.67	1.49	3	3
Having long-term career plans and goals	5.52	1.45	4	7
Having short-term career plans and goals	5.37	1.49	5	8
Attending conferences	5.37	1.37	7	6
Being a member of professional associations	5.34	1.40	8	4
Being prepared to relocate	5.30	1.57	6	10
Always undertaking training opportunities	5.22	1.58	9	9
Developing courses	5.10	1.43	10	12
Playing internal politics	5.09	1.69	12	5
Engagement in cross-university activities	5.05	1.46	11	11
Gaining teaching excellence awards	4.85	1.45	13	13

Sources: Weber and Ladkin (2008); Ladkin and Weber (2009).

Notes

All variables were measured on a seven-point scale with a value of 1 indicating not important at all and a value of 7 indicating very important. Significant differences in ranking between males and females are highlighted in bold. (N = 342)

playing internal politics exhibited the most significant difference in rankings with males assigning it rank 12 versus females placing it at rank 5. Differences in rankings, though less significant, were also observed for two other career strategies, namely membership in a professional association and relocation. The former was ranked higher by female academics while the latter was ranked higher by male academics.

Locational differences in career strategies of academics in hospitality/tourism were also evident based on respondents' current place of employment (North America, Europe, Australia/New Zealand). For example academics from North America placed a higher importance on short-term career goals than academics from Europe. Differences were also observed relating to the importance of relocation with Europeans and Australians/New Zealanders placing greater importance on relocation than North American academics (Weber & Ladkin, 2008).

In addition, the research discovered that in addition to ranking pre-identified career strategies, respondents also identified several additional strategies that they perceived as important in advancing their career. In order of frequency of mention, these strategies were: obtaining external research grants (11); gaining an international reputation/having an international focus (6); and hard work (4) (Weber & Ladkin, 2008).

In considering careers over time, Table 30.3 contrasts the perceptions of senior academics with those of junior academics on the importance of career strategies in general. There are no differences in ranking between senior and junior academics for the top three career strategies, confirming the strength of these factors. There also appeared to be agreement on 'gaining teaching excellence awards' being least important to career advancement. In particular, senior academics attributed greater importance than junior academics to relocation for career advancement. While the willingness to relocate did not specifically differentiate between relocation nationally or internationally, an assessment of senior academics' career paths indicated that international

Table 30.3 Ranking of career advancement tools by senior academics versus junior academics

Ranking of career advancement tools by senior academics	Ranking by junior academics
1 Getting research articles published	1
2 Keeping a network of influential contacts	2
3 Undertaking further study	3
4 **Attending conferences**	8
5 Having long-term career plans and goals	4
6 **Being prepared to relocate**	12
7 Having short-term career plans and goals	5
8 Being a member of professional associations	6
9 Always undertaking training opportunities	11
10 Playing internal politics	9
11 Developing courses	10
12 **Engagement in cross-university activities**	7
13 Gaining teaching excellence awards	13

Source: Weber and Ladkin (2008).

Note
Career advancement tools in bold denote significant differences in rankings between senior and junior academics. (N = 342)

relocation featured prominently. Furthermore, senior academics ranked attending conferences, presumably to establish and maintain influential contacts, much higher than junior academics. Finally, an aspect that was ranked much higher by junior academics, compared to senior ones, was the engagement in cross-university activities. This difference in ranking may be indicative of senior academics placing more importance on external/international exposure rather than exposure within the university (Weber & Ladkin, 2008).

The difficulties of being a tourism academic have been explored by Pearce (2005). In this research, the views of 54 academics (12 through in-depth interviews, and 42 through a survey) were sought. Major difficulties identified include the status of tourism in the university, maintaining or starting research, balancing teaching and research, and career planning. These research findings will be returned to in the final section of this chapter, the issues and challenges that tourism, hospitality and event educators are currently facing. Before doing so, a point to note is that, at the time of writing, there has not been any recent research into this topic area. There is a clear need for more recent research that could perhaps reflect more recent changes.

Issues and challenges

The development of academic careers and employment in the tourism, hospitality and events sector face a number of issues and challenges. The ones identified here are not exhaustive, but have been selected due to their global commonality, their relevance to the development and delivery of the academic curriculum and the future of tourism, hospitality and events education. In this way they are linked to some of the themes introduced in Chapter 1.

Balancing a vocational and academic curriculum

There is continuing debate surrounding the extent to which the tourism, hospitality and events curriculum should be influenced by industry in terms of vocational orientation, and academics in terms of academic pursuit (Dredge *et al.*, 2012; Lynch *et al.*, 2011; Tribe, 2002). Certainly when looking at career development, both sides are valued and have merit.

The research by Weber and Ladkin (2008) demonstrates that around 80 per cent of the sample of academics had work experience in the tourism and hospitality industry. Of those, 48 per cent had work experience in the tourism sector and 74 per cent in the hospitality sector. However, the length of work experience and seniority of the position varied considerably, depending on the time of entry into academia. For example with work experience now being part of many tourism and hospitality degree programmes, more recent entrants into academia with a tourism and hospitality educational background had some work experience, yet it was typically short in duration (about one year) and low in seniority. This is in contrast to more senior academics who had previous industry experience prior to an academic career. The vocational nature of many of the programmes values industry experience and in terms of curriculum delivery is beneficial if not essential. On the other hand, recent years have seen increasing importance placed on a doctoral qualification as a requirement for an academic career. A doctorate is generally an entry requirement for a research career (Pearce, 2004). In many countries, institutions are no longer prepared to hire new entrants who do not have a doctoral qualification. Again, evidence from research by Weber and Ladkin (2008) shows that from their 342 respondents, 69 per cent had attained a doctoral degree, and a further 25 per cent had a Master's degree as their highest level of education. Of these 25 per cent, half were currently enrolled in a doctoral programme, indicating that a PhD qualification was essential to maintain a career in academia and for promotional criteria. Whilst industry experience and having a doctoral qualification are not diametrically opposed, the doctoral qualification as a requirement narrows down the potential labour market. The challenge is how to maintain both of these requirements. If vocational experience is valued, then this is likely to become more problematic if new recruits are expected to have a doctoral qualification.

The volume and value of research outputs

Increasing competition and a shifting funding pattern for many universities have resulted in an increase in the volume and value of research outputs as a measure of institutional quality. The focus on quality research publications has already been stressed in numerous studies in other disciplines (Marginson, 2000; Ramsden, 1999) but is particularly interesting given that historically at least tourism, hospitality and event education tends to reside in the newer and more vocationally oriented institutions that historically have placed less emphasis on research outputs and more on vocational relevance.

The perceived importance of research outputs by academics is evident. In the research by Weber and Ladkin (2008), and Pearce (2005), the publication of research articles emerged as the single most important career advancement factor. Conversely, being unable to publish in top-tier journals was considered by those academics dissatisfied with their career progression as a critical barrier to further advancement.

In the past, there has been an ongoing debate about the value of quality teaching versus quality research in universities, with calls for assigning more prominence to teaching as a factor for staff promotion. However, funding allocations in universities are often based on the research output of faculty. For example studies on the ranking of hospitality and tourism programmes are based entirely on the publication output of the faculty, excluding any measures of teaching quality and/or service to the greater community (Jogaratnam *et al*., 2005). This is in contrast to the reasons why many chose academia as a career path, which is a commitment to quality teaching. This can result in career dissatisfaction and frustration given the lack of recognition in this area. Teaching and research are not at opposite ends of a scale, and in fact are complementary. However, both have distinct demands and the tensions in how academics can best use their time are clear. A related issue is the development of journals in the field that provide opportunities for publication.

Maintaining networks

A number of studies into academic careers point to the importance of networks (Horrigan et al., 1996; Musselin, 2004). Networks can be critical for a number of career-related issues such as an awareness of and consideration for job opportunities. In this context, conference attendance and membership in professional associations can become important as meeting places for such contacts. The issue in times of tighter funding environments and increasing workload pressures is for academics to select conference attendance and professional association membership as likely to be of most value in their career advancement. In the research by Weber and Ladkin (2008) conference attendance was considered important by senior academics. However, as pointed out by Oppermann (1997), presenting one's paper is only a minor part of conference attendance, with networking, exploring job opportunities and marketing oneself being much more strategic and ultimately more important benefits of attending conferences. Given the multitude of tourism and hospitality conferences organized each year, the selection of the conference most suitable to a person's objectives is critical (Weber & Ladkin, 2008). There is also the related issue of the value of conference papers to an individual's research profile. If they are seen as of lesser value than journal articles, paper submissions may begin to decline.

Career mobility

Research by Weber and Ladkin (2008) highlighted the importance of being mobile and relocation for career advancement. This is in agreement with previous studies that have examined international relocation in general (Harvey, 1997; Riusala & Suutari, 2000) and in academia in particular (Richardson & McKenna, 2003; Schermerhorn, 1999). However, the ability to be mobile may not be easy as relocation is also accompanied by numerous challenges, for example family considerations, the cost of moving and wage rates set against the cost of living. The willingness of those entering the academic labour market to be mobile will affect future career structures. Certainly mobility as an important part of career development is clearly evident, mirroring trends towards new work structures and boundaryless careers evident in other labour markets (Baruch & Hall, 2004; Cheramie et al., 2007; Hess et al., 2012). The challenge is to find ways to enable academics to become more easily mobile.

Conclusion

The value and volume of tourism, hospitality and events employment is widely recognized. This combined with the popularity of the courses and the expansion of higher education in general terms has resulted in the burgeoning of educational programmes, providing increasing academic employment opportunities in these fields. From this perspective, the situation is a positive one for those seeking employment in academia in this field. Those entering academic employment are more likely than before to have been educated in these fields, and increasingly a doctoral qualification is a minimum educational requirement. Vocational industry experience is also seen as important, either gained through part of an educational programme or a period of time spent in industry prior to an academic career. New academics are joining an environment whereby their subjects are becoming more mature with established curriculum and research areas. The work environment for an academic is likely to be increasingly pressured in terms of competing time demands to engage with and produce tangible outputs for research and teaching. Alternatively, specialization in the early stages of a career may be common, with faculty on teaching-only or research-only contracts. Ultimately, employment in tourism, hospitality and event education will be influenced by general global trends in higher education. For example reduced public sector funding, student mobility and the internationalization of programmes, increased competition, mixed and flexible modes of programme delivery, greater scrutiny of teaching and research and their associated quality measures will all affect the characteristics of academic employment and career development opportunities. Furthermore, survival of the courses will depend on their attractiveness to students, along with the value given to them by their institutions as universities are faced with increasing financial pressures. From this perspective, the continued growth of tourism, hospitality and event programmes is by no means guaranteed. Certainly an academic career in these subjects is likely to require a wide variety of research, teaching and personal skills, with the ability to be flexible and responsive to changing demands.

References

Altbach, P. G. (Ed.). (1996). *The International Academic Profession: portraits of fourteen countries*. Princeton, NJ: Carnegie Foundation for the Advancement of Teaching.

Altbach, P. (Ed.). (2000). *The Changing Academic Workplace. Comparative perspectives*. Boston, MA: Boston College Center for International Higher Education.

Arthur, M. B. (1994). 'The Boundaryless Career: a new perspective for organizational Inquiry'. *Journal of Organizational Behaviour*, 15, 295–306.

Barrows, C. W., & Bosselman, R. H. (Eds.). (1999). *Hospitality Management Education*. Binghamton, NY: Haworth Hospitality Press.

Baruch, Y., & Hall, D. T. (2004). 'The Academic Career: a model for future careers in other sectors'. *Journal of Vocational Behavior*, 64(2), 241–62.

Blaxter, L., Hughes, C., & Tight, M. (1998). *The Academic Career Handbook*. Buckingham: Open University Press.

Bologna Process (2009). 'Bologna beyond 2012. Report on the development of the European Higher Education Area'. Available at: http://www.ehea.info/Uploads/Irina/Bologna%20beyond%202010.pdf

Chartrand, J. M., & Camp, C. C. (1991). 'Advances in the Measurement of Career Development Constructs: a twenty year review'. *Journal of Vocational Behavior*, 39(2), 1–39.

Cheramie, R. A., Sturman, M. C., & Walsh, K. (2007). 'Executive Career Management: switching organizations and the boundaryless career'. *Journal of Vocational Behavior*, 71(3), 359–74.

Cochran, A., Hauschild, T., Elder, W. B., Neumayer, L. A. Brasel, K. J., & Crandall, M. L. (2013). 'Perceived Gender-Based Barriers to Careers in AcademicSurgery'. *American Journal of Surgery*, 206, 263–8.

Cohen, E. (2004). *Contemporary Tourism: diversity and change*. Oxford: Elsevier.

Collin, A., & Young, R. A. (2000). 'Framing the Future of Career'. In A. Collin & R. A. Young (Eds.), *The Future Career*. Cambridge: Cambridge University Press.

Doeringer, P., & Piore, M. J. (1972). *Internal Labor Markets and Manpower Analysis*. Lexington, MA: Heath.

Dredge, D., Benckendorff, P., Day, M., Gross, M. J., Walo, M., Weeks, P., & Whitelaw, P. (2012). 'The Philosophic Practitioner and the Curriculum Space'. *Annals of Tourism Research*, 39(4), 2154–76.

Eaton, S. C., & Bailyn, L. (2000). 'Career as Life Path: tracing work and life strategies of biotech professionals'. In T. Morris (Ed.), *Career Frontiers: new concepts of working lives* (pp. 177–98). Oxford: Oxford University Press.

Ehrenberg, R. G. (2002). 'Studying Ourselves: the academic labor market'. National Bureau of Economic Research Working Paper 8965. Available at: http://www.nber.org/papers/w8965

Enders, J. (2001). *Academic Staff in Europe: changing contexts and conditions*. Westport, CT: Greenwood Press.

Fidgeon, P. (2010). 'Tourism Education and Curriculum Design: a time for consolidation and review?' *Tourism Management*, 31(6), 699–722.

Forster, N. (2001). 'A Case Study of Women Academics' Views on Equal Opportunities, Career Prospects and Work–Family Conflicts in a UK University'. *Career Development International,* 6(1), 28–38.

Fries-Britt, S. (2000). 'Developing Support Networks and Seeking Answers to Questions'. In M. Garcia (Ed.), *Succeeding in an Academic Career* (pp. 39–56). Westport, CT: Greenwood Press.

Fulton, O. (1996). 'Which Academic Profession Are You In?' In R. Cuthbert (Ed.), *Working in Higher Education* (pp. 157–69). Buckingham: Society for Research into Higher Education and Open University Press.

Gould, S., & Penley, L. E. (1984). 'Career Strategies and Salary Progression: a study of their relationships in municipal bureaucracy'. *Organizational Behaviour and Human Performance,* 34, 244–65.

Gunn, C. (2004). *Western Tourism: Can paradise be reclaimed?* New York. Cognizant.

Gursoy, D., & Umbreit, T. (2005). 'Exploring Students' Evaluations of Teaching Effectiveness: what factors are important?'. *Journal of Hospitality and Tourism Research,* 29(1), 91–109.

Hall, C. M. (2004). 'Reflexivity and Tourism Research; situating myself and/with others'. In J. Phillimore and L. Goodson (Eds.), *Qualitative Research in Tourism: ontologies, epistemologies and methodologies* (pp.137–55). London: Routledge.

Halsey, A. H. (1992). *The Decline of Donnish Donation.* Oxford: Clarendon Press.

Harley, S., Muller-Camen, M., & Collin, A. (2004). 'From Academic Communities to Managed Organisations: the implications for academic careers in UK and German universities'. *Journal of Vocational Behaviour,* 64(2), 329–45.

Harvey, M. (1997). 'Dual-career Expatriates: expectations, adjustment and satisfaction with international relocation'. *Journal of International Business Studies,* 28(3), 626–58.

Hess, N., Jepsen D. M., & Dries, N. (2012). 'Career and Employer Change in the Age of the Boundaryless Career'. *Journal of Vocational Behavior,* 81(2), 280–8.

Horrigan, L., Poole, M., & Nielsen, S. (1996). 'Gender Differences in Support Networks'. *Australian Journal of Career Development,* 5(3), 37–40.

Hsu, C. H. C. (Ed.). (2005). *Global Tourism Higher Education: past, present and future.* Binghamton, NY: Haworth Hospitality Press.

Janasz, S. C., & Sullivan, S. E. (2004). 'Multiple Mentoring in Academe: developing the professional network'. *Journal of Vocational Behaviour,* 64(2), 263–83.

Jogaratnam, G., McCleary, K. W., Mena, M. M., & Yoo, J. (2005). 'An Analysis of Hospitality and Tourism Research: institutional contributions'. *Journal of Hospitality & Tourism Research,* 29(3), 356–71.

Ladkin, A., & Weber, K. (2009). 'Tourism and Hospitality Academics: career profiles and strategies'. *Journal of Teaching in Travel & Tourism,* 8(4), 373–93.

Leung, X. Y., Jiang, L., & Busser, J. (2013). 'Online Student Evaluations of Hospitality Professors: a cross cultural comparison'. *Journal of Hospitality, Leisure, Sport & Tourism Education,* 21(1), 3–46.

Lynch, P., Molz, J. G., McIntosh, A., Lugosi, P., & Lashley, C. (2011). 'Theorising Hospitality'. *Hospitality and Society,* 1(1), 3–24.

McIntosh, R. W. (1992). 'Early Tourism Education in the United States'. *Journal of Tourism Studies,* 3(1), 2–8.

Maimunah, M., Mohd Rasid, R., & Abdul Wahat, N. W. (2005). 'High-Flyer Women Academicians: factors contributing to success'. *Women in Management Review,* 2092, 117–32.

Marginson, S. (2000). 'Rethinking Academic Work in the Global Era'. *Journal of Higher Education Policy & Management,* 22(1), 23–35.

Metcalf, H., Rolfe, H., Stevens, P., & Weale, M. (2005). 'Recruitment and Retention of Academic Staff in Higher Education'. Brief No. RB658. London: National Institute of Economic and Social Research.

Musselin, C. (2004). 'Towards a European Academic Labour Market? Some lessons drawn from empirical studies on academic mobility'. *Higher Education,* 48, 55–78.

Musselin, C. (2005). 'European Academic Labor Markets in Transition'. *Higher Education,* 49, 135–54.

Nixon, J. (1996). 'Professional Identity and the Restructuring of Higher Education'. *Studies in Higher Education,* 21(1), 5–16.

O'Leary, J. T. (2005). 'Thoughts on Building Academic Staff Careers and a Successful Department.' *Journal of Tourism Studies,* 16(2), 10–16.

O'Leary, S. & Deegan, J. (2005). 'Career Progression of Irish Tourism and Hospitality Management Graduates'. *International Journal of Contemporary Hospitality Management,* 17(5), 421–32.

Oppermann, M. (1997). 'Tourism Conferences: academic titillation, social interactions or job market?'. *Tourism Management,* 18(5), 255–7.

Ozbilgin, M., & Healy, G. (2004). 'The Gendered Nature of Career Development of University Professors; the case of Turkey'. *Journal of Vocational Behaviour*, 64(2), 358–71.

Pazy, A. (1988). 'Joint Responsibility: the relationship between organizational and individual career management and the effectiveness of careers'. *Group and Organizational Studies*, 13(3), 311–31.

Pearce, P. L. (2004). 'History, Practices and Prospects for the PhD in Tourism'. *Journal of Teaching in Travel and Tourism*, 4(3), 31–49.

Pearce, P. L. (2005). 'Professing Tourism: tourism academics as educators, researchers and change leaders'. *Journal of Tourism Studies*, 16(2), 21–33.

Prospects.ac.uk (2013). Your PhD, What's Next? Academic jobs. Available at : http://www.prospects.ac.uk/your_phd_what_next_academic_jobs.htm

Ramsden, P. (1999). 'Predicting Institutional Research Performance from Published Indicators: a test of a classification of Australian university types'. *Higher Education*, 37(4), 341–58.

Richardson, J., & McKenna. S. (2003). 'International Experience and Academic Careers: what do academics have to say?'. *Personnel Review*, 32(6), 774–95.

Richardson, S. (2009). 'Undergraduate Perceptions of Tourism and Hospitality as a Career Choice'. *International Journal of Hospitality Management*, 28(3), 382–8.

Riley, M. (1991). *Human Resource Management*. Oxford: Butterworth-Heinemann.

Riusala, K., & Suutari, V. (2000). 'Expatriation and Careers: perspectives of expatriates and spouses'. *Career Development International*, 5(2), 81–90.

Schermerhorn, J. R. (1999). 'Learning by Going? The management educator as expatriate'. *Journal of Management Inquiry*, 8(3), 246–56.

Simonsen, P. (1986). 'Concepts of Career Development'. *Training and Development Journal*, 40(1), 70–4.

Sullcowski, N., & Dean, M. K. (2010). 'Implications of Internationalisation on Learning and Teaching: listening to the winds of change'. *Journal of Hospitality, Leisure, Sport & Tourism Education*, 9(1), 110–16.

Sullivan, S. E. (1999). 'The Changing Nature of Careers: a review and research agenda'. *Journal of Management*, 25(3), 457–84.

Tribe, J. (2002). 'The Philosophic Practitioner'. *Annals of Tourism Research*, 29(2), 338–57.

Weber, K., & Ladkin, A. (2008). 'Career Advancement for Tourism and Hospitality Academics: publish, network, study and plan'. *Journal of Hospitality and Tourism Research*, 32(4), 448–66.

Weber, K., & Ladkin, A. (2009). 'Career Anchors of Convention and Exhibition Industry Professionals in Asia'. *Journal of Convention and Event Tourism*, 10(4), 243–55.

Weiner, G. (1996). 'Which of Us Has a Brilliant Career?' In R. Cuthbert (Ed.), *Working in Higher Education* (pp. 58–68). Buckingham: Society for Research into Higher Education and Open University Press.

Welch, A. (1997). 'The Peripatetic Professor: the internationalisation of the academic profession'. *Higher Education*, 34(6): 323–45.

Xiao, H. (2000). 'China's Tourism Education in the 21st Century'. *Annals of Tourism Research*, 27(4), 1052–5.

Yang, J., & Song, H. (2011). 'Tourism Education Programmes in Mainland China'. *AngloHigher, The Magazine of Global English Speaking Higher Education*, 2, 8–9.

Zhang, W., & Fan, X. (2006). 'Tourism and Hospitality Education in China: past and present, opportunities and challenges'. *Journal of Teaching in Travel & Tourism*, 5(1–2), 117–35.

Zhao, W., & Ritchie, J. R. B. (2007). 'An Investigation of Academic Leadership in Tourism Research 1985–2004'. *Tourism Management*, 28(2), 476–90.

31

Industry engagement with tourism and hospitality education

An examination of the students' perspective

Rong Huang

School of Tourism and Hospitality, Plymouth University, UK

Introduction

Solnet *et al.* (2007) argue that tourism-related fields can be thought of as applied subject areas. This means that academics, students and curricula develop and benefit from close links with industry (Cooper & Westlake, 1998). Some authors (e.g. Cooper & Westlake, 1998; Busby, 2003, 2005; Solnet *et al.*, 2007) criticize tourism linkage strategies in many education institutions; this is because they are often haphazard, lack vision, focus, commitment and resources. Due to the traditional importance of universities as research centres and sources of innovation, a review of relevant literature sources indicates that most studies of industry engagement have revolved around knowledge transfer and tourism innovation (e.g. Shaw & Williams, 2009; Baggio & Cooper, 2010; Weidenfeld *et al.*, 2010). Few literature sources have considered the impacts of industry engagement on the enhancement of the teaching experience. Moreover, many papers have been written from a university or industry perspective. As the key stakeholder of such engagement, the students' voice is missing in the research (Chapleo & Simms, 2010). Higher education institutions (HEIs) in the UK face challenges from many different directions, and the institutions' value to students and also wider society is regularly questioned (Department for Business Innovation and Skills, 2009, 2011; Gannon & Maher, 2012). A lack of a clear understanding of the students' expectations and experiences in such relevant engagements generates serious problems when trying to integrate the tourism industry with tourism and hospitality education.

The aim of this chapter is to analyse industry engagement with tourism and hospitality education from students' perspective. More specifically, three objectives are sought to (1) discuss different engagements between the tourism and hospitality industry, and the universities which run tourism and hospitality programmes; (2) summarize the benefits that students gain from those engagements; and (3) examine problems and challenges faced by the students. The views of students on different types of university engagement with the tourism and hospitality industry at a tourism and hospitality school in Britain are discussed. The initial findings from class surveys with undergraduate students are presented.

Industry engagement

Industry engagement in higher education

The term university as observed by Georges Haddad (cited in Neave 2000: 29) finds its origin both in legal Latin *universitas*, meaning 'community', and in classical Latin *universus*, meaning 'totality'. These days, the university's communities may indeed be said to encompass a great number of constituencies. Jongbloed *et al.* (2008) argue that internally they include students and staff (the community of scholars), administration and management, while externally they include research communities, alumni, businesses, social movements, consumer organizations, governments and professional associations.

Frasquet *et al.* (2012) summarize that universities operate in an environment characterized by fast technological progress, changes in funding systems, increased competition and more demanding stakeholders. Several authors (e.g. Plewa *et al.*, 2005; Plewa and Quester, 2008; Department for Business Innovation and Skills, 2009, 2011) argue that these changes force universities to address the basis of their competitiveness. Ensuring that programmes of study are relevant to industry and society is a prevalent part of the UK government agenda for university education.

Jongbloed *et al.* (2008) discuss that there are many forms of higher education–business interaction of both a formal and informal nature. The dominant interaction channels are research publications, public meetings and conferences, research contracts, research staff acting as consultants, sharing of equipment, and students doing internships or on-the-job training. Due to the traditional importance of universities as research centres and sources of innovation, most studies have revolved around those issues, with examination of aspects such as the university's impact on local development (Baggio & Cooper, 2010; Gunasekara, 2006), knowledge transfer (Crespo & Dridi, 2007; Weidenfeld *et al.*, 2010) and the contribution to innovation (Abramo *et al.*, 2011; Hjalager, 2002, 2010). A review of relevant literature indicates that few extant publications consider universities and industry relationships from the teaching and learning perspective although exceptions do exist such as a growing number of studies published in relation to work-based learning (e.g. Bailey *et al.*, 2003; Boud & Solomon, 2001; Cornford & Gunn, 1998; Litteljohn & Watson, 2004; Nixon *et al.*, 2006) . Furthermore, limited consideration is given to the views of the students about such collaborations, even though many authors (Chapleo & Simms, 2010; Gannon & Maher, 2012; Jongbloed *et al.*, 2008; Solnet *et al.*, 2007) agree that in higher education the students are the core stakeholders. Without knowledge of the students' interests and experiences regarding their engagement with the tourism industry during their studies, efforts at improving this aspect of the experience for students may be unnecessarily disjointed.

Industry engagement in tourism and hospitality education

Solnet *et al.* (2007: 66) argue that 'tourism-related fields such as hospitality, leisure, sport and events, are applied subject areas, demanding that academics, students and curricula develop, and benefit from, close links with industry'. Airey and Johnson (1999) and Busby and Fiedel (2001) examine British tourism degrees, and highlight that a key feature of these degrees is the vocational nature of the programme. In reality, as Busby and Huang (2012: 108) state, 'most undergraduate tourism degrees, in Britain, comprise at least one module which examines the nature of the tourism industry'.

Thomas (2012) points out that successive British governments have introduced schemes designed to strengthen the articulation between universities and businesses. Yusuf (2008) argues that the anticipation is that universities will, via such schemes, play a growing role in supporting future business development and innovation. Jauhari and Thomas (2013) argue that synergy between universities and industry can lead to enormous economic growth, and the vision of universities should encompass usable research and partnerships that help them to build competencies that matter to industry and to other professionals. There is consensus in the literature on the value of knowledge to successful innovation (Cooper 2006; Hjalager 2002). However Xiao (2006) and Xiao and Smith (2007) suggest that in tourism, knowledge transfer has been less marked than in other sectors of the economy. Furthermore, such schemes emphasize the traditional role of universities as research centres, and pay less attention to their role as centres for producing the industry's future workforce.

Industry is a primary stakeholder group for tourism and hospitality education institutions (Chapleo & Simms, 2010; Lewis, 2006; Rawlinson & Dewhurst, 2013; Solnet et al., 2007). As a result, tourism and hospitality education could be enhanced significantly if employers themselves were able to play a key role in the design and delivery of the tourism curricula (Dale & Robinson, 2001). Tribe (1999) delineates a number of groups that have an interest in, and may seek to exert their influence over, the tourism curriculum. He argues that stakeholders have different interests that can influence the framing of the tourism curriculum (Tribe, 1999). Dale and Robinson (2001) go further and emphasize that to meet the evolving needs of stakeholders, tourism education should become more specialist in nature.

Researchers (e.g. Gannon & Maher, 2012; Gursoy & Swanger, 2004, 2005; Kneale, 2009; Lewis, 2006; Solnet et al., 2007) emphasize the importance of students having better representation in the tourism and hospitality industry for which they are being prepared, and, through their educational experience, the students need to develop impressions and contacts in the industry. Dale and Robinson (2001) argue that educators, often the conduit between industry and students, should focus on providing quality education that prepares students for their working life, and furnishes them with employment opportunities appropriate to their qualifications.

Many authors (e.g. Hay, 2011; Polonsky & Waller, 1999; Raelin 1994; Thomas & Busby, 2003; Vince, 2004) observe that over the years business education has changed from a traditional classroom approach, to a more innovative, practical approach involving an element of 'action' that addresses the needs of their key stakeholders, in particular academics, employers and students. Reg Revans pioneered one such approach, 'action learning', in the UK in 1945 (Keys, 1994). The premise behind action learning is that students and managers will learn more effectively with, and from, other managers and teachers, when they are all engaged in the solution of actual problems in real work settings (Revans, 1971). A range of action-oriented techniques (e.g. live cases/projects, business consultancy projects, industry collaborative projects) are reported by different academics (Hay, 2011; Polonsky & Waller, 1999; Thomas & Busby, 2003). Keys (1994) reports that action learning, and related approaches are now being used by many companies, consultants and universities in the UK, United States, Sri Lanka, and Sweden.

Industry placements have long been a part of tourism and hospitality education (e.g. Aggett & Busby, 2011; Busby, 2005; Busby & Gibson 2010), with the majority of tourism-related programmes requiring a period of practical experience, which is normally essential for graduation. On those programmes where an internship occurs, there is clearly a link with industry (Tribe, 1997; Cooper & Westlake, 1998; Airey & Johnson, 1999; Evans, 2001; Busby, 2003, 2005).

Indeed, Aggett and Busby (2011: 107) argue that internships could 'be the single most important link with industry'; and internships are an activity emphasized by Dearing (1997), Harvey *et al.* (1998) and Harvey *et al.* (2002) in their extensive reviews. Busby (2001: 35) explains that an internship plus a degree equates to the 'necessary base' for employment.

While these programmes come in different forms and guises (such as industrial experience, industrial placement, supervised work experience and internships), Solnet *et al.* (2007) recognize that such industrial placements tend to follow a similar pattern: the lengths of the programmes vary between institutions and programmes, but generally the format includes a compulsory section where students are exposed to working life in an industry segment and, essentially, the educator develops links with industry, communicates these to students, becomes involved (to varying degrees) in the selection process, perhaps visits the student while on placement and assesses the experience upon their return to study (Barron, 1996).

The contribution of alumni to the success of higher education institutions is a key feature in some countries, and Greenaway (2010) points out that UK institutions are encouraged to pursue these network ties as long-term benefactors and supporters of their work. The value of 'real-world' insights into the practicalities of managers' roles, their organizations and industries and the impact on society is widely discussed in business and management areas, as well as in the hospitality and tourism higher education sectors (Robertson, 2008). For instance, Gannon and Maher (2012) report upon a specific Alumni Mentoring programme developed in Oxford Brookes University (UK) and explore the contribution of the programme to students, faculty and industrialists in developing future hospitality and tourism industry professionals.

The use of educational field trips has long been a major part of the education programmes of schools, colleges and universities. Lisowski and Disinger (1987) call this 'learning in the environment', and they trace, in relevant literature dating back to the 1930s, significant increases in the effective learning of techniques and subject knowledge. Novelli and Burns (2010) point out that field-based experiences gained specifically through field trips have a long tradition in disciplines such as geography, biology, anthropology, archaeology and literature, as well as more multidisciplinary fields of study, including tourism. Huang (2012) assesses the effectiveness of the use of experiential learning to integrate classroom lessons and field trips organized for postgraduate students studying tourism and hospitality management in Plymouth University (UK). The students were satisfied with their field trip experience, but, unless the lecturers provided a clear induction, the students were less clear about the links between field trips and classroom teaching (Huang, 2012).

Benefits and challenges perceived by students

Different authors (e.g. Ball *et al.*, 2006; Bullock *et al.*, 2009; Busby, 2003, 2005; Easterly & Myers, 2009; Gannon & Maher, 2012; Little & Harvey, 2006; Myers & Jones, 2004; Rawlinson & Dewhurst, 2013; Thomas & Busby, 2003) identify a range of benefits for using different types of industry engagement in tourism and hospitality education. Such benefits are addressed from different perspectives (e.g. for employers, for wider business community, for states, for universities, for students). The following section summarizes those benefits, as reported by relevant authors, from the students' perspective.

Live projects

The action-oriented approach has several advantages. Thomas and Busby (2003) report that the benefits of developing live projects, as implemented at Birmingham College of Food, Tourism

411

and Creative Studies in the UK, include the development and improvement of a range of skills (e.g. teamwork, communication skills, research skills and time management) which students need for working in industry as well as boosting the students' confidence. Such an approach also enhances the opportunities to use a range of skills (e.g. research, IT, communication and teamwork skills) and enriches the understanding of an organization (Hay, 2011; Thomas & Busby, 2003; Vince, 2004).

Industrial placement

Based on interviews with 82 students from several HEIs, Little and Harvey (2006) report that students are keen to participate in industrial placement because of benefits such as gaining an insight into a particular industry or type of work, seeing how theory applies in the workplace, supplementing learning with practical experience, and the belief that placement experience is more 'saleable' than other types of work experience in the graduate job market. An internship not only increases the ability of students to critically reflect on the tourism business (Tribe, 2001), it also provides an opportunity to observe others in a workplace setting, and may enhance the students' common sense (Gerber, 2001). According to Bullock *et al.* (2009: 482), placements benefit students as they 'have enhanced their understanding of their own life choices, enabled the acquisition of transferable skills and provided a tangible link between theory and application'. Ball *et al.* (2006) list nine different types of benefits that work placements can bring to students such as working in a setting in which to put theory into practice; developing an awareness of workplace culture; an appreciation of the fluidity of a rapidly changing world of work; plus an opportunity to develop a range of personal attributes such as time management, self-confidence and adaptability.

Employer mentoring scheme

The benefits of an employer mentoring scheme are strongly allied to many of the recent initiatives in teaching and learning in business and management subjects. Several studies (e.g. D'Abate & Eddy, 2008; Gannon & Maher, 2012; Robertson, 2008) argue that such schemes, by providing connections to the practical world of business, as well as a glimpse behind the mystique of what managers actually do, can further extend and enhance the students' educational experience above and beyond the areas covered in their study programmes. Gannon and Maher (2012) argue that, from the evidence on mentoring and the briefly identified needs of industry and education, a mentoring programme for hospitality and tourism undergraduates has resonance.

Field trips

Numerous research studies have documented significant increases in the participants' factual knowledge and conceptual understanding after participation in well-planned field trips (Myers & Jones, 2004). Field trips allow students to experience something that would not be possible inside the four walls of a classroom. They allow students to have the direct experience that can be the beginning of the experiential learning cycle (Kolb, 1984). Well-planned field trips and experiential learning are useful on their own, but together they provide an opportunity for students to experience class content firsthand, learn from their experience in the field, and apply what they have learned (Easterly & Myers, 2009). Based on data collected as part of an innovative field-based education project on international tourism development and management with field-based work activities that was conducted in the Gambia, Novelli and Burns (2010) argue that such activities facilitate mutually beneficial exchanges between hosts and guests.

Although there are pertinent benefits to be gained from the adoption of the stakeholder approach, and the development of close relationships with industry, such an approach raises a number of concerns with the practical application of the method. Based on analysing the findings from a stakeholder enquiry conducted in three Caribbean islands, Lewis (2006: 23) raises three concerns in curriculum decision-making in the Caribbean that need to be considered as (1) 'stakeholder inclusion in decision-making is a lengthy, time-consuming, expensive exercise that can dissuade educators from embarking on the process'; (2) conflict would arise in addressing the 'common' interests from the various stakeholders in the tourism curriculum because of a limited tourism curriculum space; and (3) selecting individuals from within a complex and diverse group presents a particular challenge for a stakeholder inclusive approach to tourism curriculum development.

Industrial engagement

Solnet *et al.* (2007: 67) summarize the problems in managing industry engagement as the:

> generation of a plethora of surface-level industry contacts; contact with industry personnel at relatively low levels of the organization, such as at the human resource administration or operational level; staff responsible for these programmes are often not academics and lack the industry background to develop these relationships fully. For an academic there is no career advantage in a heavy time commitment to the management of this type of industry engagement; the quality of the student experience is often poor, with low-level tasks and little attempt to structure the experience on the part of industry.

Many factors affect students who participate in industrial engagement (Morgan, 2006; Solnet *et al.*, 2007; Busby & Gibson, 2010; Aggett & Busby, 2011). Morgan's (2006) research concludes that while students recognized the value of work experience, a number of factors influence their decision as to whether or not to undertake it, for example concerns relating to financial and personal costs, the level of support from the university, finding the right employer, uncertainty over career aspirations and the employer having high entry requirements. Ball *et al.* (2006) report that while many respondents were willing to pursue a placement, they alluded to a number of difficulties and barriers. These include the burden of finding a placement themselves, difficulties in 'cold-calling' employers (a lack of response or rejection dampened their resolve), a lack of awareness, unenthusiastic departmental tutors and self-reported idealistic expectations. After investigating the reasons that Tourism, Hospitality and Events students at one British university opt out of the placement year, Aggett and Busby (2011) emphasize that two key obstacles – a failure to understand the value of work experience and a lack of drive and determination – must be overcome in order to increase the numbers of students opting to undertake a work placement. The research done by Gannon and Maher (2012) discusses a range of challenges that affect students' participation in an employer-mentoring scheme; these include knowing what to say to the mentor, pressure of academic work, difficulties in making contact, time management, a mismatch between mentor and mentee.

An analysis of relevant literature sources shows that it is clear that students' views in relation to different industry engagements have attracted attention from different researchers when they discuss different practice in their own institution or region. However, most of those studies only consider one type of industry engagement in their research. Furthermore, very limited studies report to what extent students were involved in different engagements. As different stakeholders are normally involved in a range of industry engagement opportunities, the views of the students are needed in all relevant engagement opportunities, so as to generate a balanced understanding of provision and facilitation of industry engagement in the universities.

The students' perspectives of different opportunities for industry engagement

In order to develop a picture of the students' views in relation to different types of industry engagement in tourism and hospitality education, a research project was undertaken with permission from the head of the School of Tourism and Hospitality at Plymouth University (UK). Given its exploratory nature, a questionnaire survey of undergraduate students in the School of Tourism and Hospitality was developed. The questionnaire was composed of three sections to collect information in relation to (1) demographic profile of the respondents, (2) their interest and experience in industry engagement provided in the school, and also (3) the perceived benefits that were gained from their experiences of different engagement and challenges which affected their participation of industry engagement opportunities. The questions were developed based on a review of relevant literature sources (Aggett & Busby, 2011; Busby, 2003, 2005; Busby & Gibson, 2010; Gannon & Maher, 2012; Gursoy and Swanger, 2004; Little & Harvey, 2004; Morgan, 2006; Solnet et al., 2007; Thomas, 2012). The questionnaire survey was carried out between 1 March and 30 May 2013. In total 273 questionnaires were returned but only 255 questionnaires were usable. Therefore more than half of the total undergraduate population (528 students) in the school participated in the survey.

Students' interests in industry engagement opportunities

When the students were asked to what extent they are interested in taking part in the different industry engagement opportunities provided by the school, the results summarized in Table 31.1 make it clear that the most popular industry engagement opportunities are: 'Field trips', 'Internships' and 'External visits to relevant businesses'. The industry engagement opportunities

Table 31.1 Students' interests in industry engagement opportunities

	Mean	Std. deviation
Field trips	4.29	.948
Internships (short-term work opportunities)	3.84	1.249
External visits to relevant businesses	3.83	1.053
Industrial placement (48 working weeks)	3.72	1.452
Honours projects associated with relevant businesses	3.66	1.107
Attending relevant industrial exhibitions/shows	3.44	1.106
Guest lecture from industry practitioners	3.29	1.039
Employer-mentoring programmes	3.28	1.090
Through work-based modules	3.27	1.191
Volunteering in businesses	3.17	1.164
Business games/competitions	3.16	1.258
Consultancy projects for businesses	2.99	1.131

Notes
1 means least interested and 5 means most interested.
(n = 255)

that received the least interest from undergraduate students are: 'Consultancy projects for businesses', 'Business games/competitions' and 'Volunteering in businesses'.

The high agreement in 'Field trips' is consistent with findings reported by a range of research related to field trips/work (e.g. Kaya et al., 2010; Novelli & Burns, 2010; Smith, 2007). This finding also confirms Huang's (2012) research on field trip experience of students at Plymouth University, namely that the students were very keen to participate in field trips so as to understand the tourism and hospitality industry in relation to future careers. The students' positive personal experiences of different field trips organized by Plymouth University (e.g. visits to Roscoff, Bratislava, Vienna, Prague and Barcelona) and also strong financial support (the school funded most of the field trips) might be possible reasons for students' strong enthusiasm for field trips. Strong interests in 'Internships (short-term work opportunities)' might explain the decline in the numbers of students at HEIs in the UK that are opting to undertake a work placement (Bullock et al., 2009; Walker & Ferguson, 2009). A preference for internships, as opposed to industrial placement (48 working weeks), might be due to the difficulties/challenges that students face in securing a long-term paid placement, as well as a lack of drive and determination (Aggett & Busby, 2011). Support by students for 'External visits to relevant businesses' might be due to well-organized external visits to relevant tourism and hospitality businesses such as Pennywell Farm, National Marine Aquarium and also Kitley House Hotel. This finding is consistent with the students' positive evaluation of such activities which is shown in the relevant module evaluation implemented by the school.

From an analysis of results in Table 31.1, it is apparent that the students show strong interests in most opportunities for industry engagement except 'Consultancy projects for businesses'. The relatively low mean score for 'Consultancy projects for businesses' (m = 2.99) agrees with findings from Thomas and Busby (2003) that although the students gain positive experience from such activities, the challenges of working with peer groups, the sheer quantity of work involved and their time management to achieve deadlines, mean the students are not very keen to participate. In the context of Plymouth University, this type of engagement opportunity is a key element of a final year module, and is set as a group assessment. A keenness to perform well in the final year, and also frustration and difficulties in dealing with group dynamics, mean the students show less enthusiasm in such engagement.

Student involvement in engagement with the tourism and hospitality industry

Table 31.2 summarizes the extent of the students' involvement in different stages of various industrial engagement opportunities when they were asked to indicate to what extent they have been involved in the following industry engagement opportunities provided by the School of Tourism and Hospitality and tick all the relevant stages for each opportunity.

Following an analysis of their positive answers for each opportunity the following two conclusions can be made. First, as far as the different stages of each opportunity are concerned, it is apparent that the students show the highest involvement in participation in many types of industrial engagement, less involvement in the initial setting up, and even less involvement in the evaluation of those industrial engagement opportunities. Such findings support Frasquet et al.'s (2012) argument that students tend to be passively involved in the different industrial engagement opportunities organized by their universities, and their voices are missing in the planning of different engagements. The finding is also consistent with Jongbloed et al.'s (2008) discussion that students are not extensively involved in the evaluation of different industrial engagements. However exceptions do exist. The students seem to indicate more involvement

Rong Huang

Table 31.2 Student involvement in engaging with the tourism and hospitality industry

	Setting up	Participation	Evaluation
Industrial placement (48 working weeks)	86	53	26
Internships (short-term work opportunities)	69	62	20
Through work-based learning modules	35	111	26
Consultancy projects for businesses	45	61	28
Volunteering in businesses	48	89	20
Employer-mentoring programmes	45	49	19
Guest lectures from industry practitioners	28	160	31
Attending relevant industrial exhibitions/shows	39	102	18
External visits to relevant businesses	32	120	29
Field trips	22	175	49
Business games/competitions (e.g. Flux)	37	77	15
Honours projects associated with relevant businesses	47	52	16

(n = 255)

in setting up of industrial placements or internships than the other two stages. Second, the students show the highest involvement in taking part in field trips, guest lectures from industry practitioners and external visits to relevant businesses, but the lowest involvement in employer-mentoring programmes, honours projects associated with relevant businesses and industrial placement. To some extent such findings reflect the availability, to the school, of different industrial engagement opportunities. But low involvement in industrial placement might be due to two key obstacles identified by Aggett and Busby (2011), i.e. practical constraints such as peer group pressure, and being forced by accommodation agencies to make early decisions about living arrangements.

Perceived benefits and challenges of industry engagements

Table 31.3 reports the answers that students gave when they were asked to identify the different types of benefits which they gained from the experience of different industry engagement opportunities provided by the school.

It is clear that the most recognized benefits are 'More industry knowledge', 'Better understanding of industry opportunities', and 'Greater self-awareness of own skills'. The highest agreements in benefits 'More industry knowledge' and 'Better understanding of industry opportunities' are consistent with Gannon and Maher's (2012) findings about the main benefits which the students gained from employer-mentoring programmes organized by Oxford Brookes University. The emphasis of self-awareness of own skills is in agreement with many authors (e.g. Busby, 2005; Busby & Gibson, 2011; Little & Harvey, 2004; Rawlinson & Dewhurst, 2013; Solnet et al., 2007; Thomas & Busby, 2003), i.e. industrial engagement opportunities provide a good chance for students to assess their own skills. However students indicate a relatively low agreement in benefits such as 'Opportunity to see managers at work', 'Gaining tailored training certificates' and 'External support for my career'. The low scores in these benefits support the arguments of several authors (e.g. Busby & Gibson, 2011; Rawlinson & Dewhurst, 2013; Solnet et al., 2007; Thomas & Busby, 2003) that problems in industry engagement, for example conflicts of interests between different parties involved in such universities and industry engagement, and contact with industry personnel at relatively low levels of the organization, mean that students could not fully realize the benefits of industry engagement.

416

Table 31.3 Perceived benefits from the experience of different industry engagements

Benefits	Mean	Std. deviation
More industry knowledge	3.84	1.058
Better understanding of industry opportunities	3.78	1.045
Greater self-awareness of own skills	3.55	1.186
More confidence about my career	3.54	1.132
Increased reflection on goals	3.33	1.129
Enhance my professional network	3.21	1.134
Confirmation of career path	3.20	1.207
External support for my career	3.18	1.149
Gaining tailored training certificates	3.08	1.303
Opportunity to see managers at work	3.06	1.167

Notes

1 means least beneficial and 5 means most beneficial.

(n = 255)

Table 31.4 Challenges influencing participation in industry engagement opportunities

Challenges	Mean	Std. deviation
Pressure of academic work	3.51	1.242
Time management	3.35	1.129
Financial difficulties	3.06	1.263
Mismatch between opportunities and personal interests	3.06	1.054
Limited information available in relation to different opportunities	2.87	1.226
Own previous industrial experience	2.87	1.311
Pressure of peer group	2.70	1.143
Domestic and care duty	2.44	1.151
Immigration control	1.91	1.193

Notes

1 means least influential and 5 means most influential.

(n = 255)

The students were asked to what extent different challenges affected their participation in the industrial engagement opportunities that were provided by the school. Table 31.4 summarizes their responses. The most influential challenge perceived by the students is 'Pressure of academic work'; this seems consistent with other authors (e.g. Aggett & Busby, 2011; Chapleo & Simms, 2010; Frasquet *et al.*, 2012; Gannon & Maher, 2013) that pressure from other academic assessments is perceived as the biggest barrier to students participating in industry engagement. However, as the mean scores of each challenge range from 1.91 to 3.51 shown in Table 31.4, this seems to indicate those challenges are not perceived to seriously impact upon the students' participation in the industry engagement opportunities. Governments are increasingly pressurizing universities to provide opportunities for higher education students to acquire and develop the skills and attributes required by industry (Thomas & Busby, 2003). Therefore the results of this research could mean that initiatives that emphasize the value of different industry engagements, and continuous encouragement of the students to make a more determined approach to their career development (Aggett & Busby, 2011), could improve the students' enthusiasm and abilities to overcome perceived challenges.

Conclusion

The range of collaborations between universities and the tourism and hospitality industry is both diverse and variable. This chapter has explored the contributions and challenges from different types of collaboration, and argues that such collaborations should not only be considered from the point of view of the benefits to industry of the universities' research abilities, but also from the point of view of the development of the industry's future workforce. Previous studies from different academics share their experience of different industry engagement opportunities in their institution or region. However, given growing demand from our students, the role of students in each engagement needs to be more active.

The results of the primary research undertaken in the School of Tourism and Hospitality shed light on a wide range of opportunities available to our tourism and hospitality students. When academics are designing the tourism and hospitality curriculum, the involvement of the students' interests and enthusiasms in different types of engagement will provide a sound basis for superior curriculum development. The students' relatively low involvement in setting up each engagement, and even less involvement in evaluating each engagement, call for academics to become more reflective practitioners, and thus create a more engaging approach so as to further empower students. The students' responses indicate that they are in agreement with previous studies regarding a wide range of benefits they can gain from different industry engagement opportunities. However, although different researchers may perceive various challenges that affect student participation, the results of this research seem to suggest that the students themselves showed less concern about these matters.

Future research in this subject area could be explored by comparing results from different academic years at Plymouth University, or with other British universities which offer similar programmes. The perspectives of different stakeholders (e.g. industry, universities and students) involved in collaboration could be investigated, in order to get a more balanced view of industry–universities relationships.

References

Abramo, G., D'Angelo, C. A., & Di Costa, F. (2011). 'University–Industry Research Collaboration: a model to assess university'. *Higher Education*, 62(2), 163–81.

Aggett, M., & Busby, G. (2011). 'Opting Out of Internship: perceptions of hospitality, tourism and events management undergraduates at a British university'. *Journal of Hospitality, Leisure, Sport & Tourism Education*, 10(1), 106–13.

Airey, D., & Johnson, S. (1999). 'The Content of Tourism Degree Courses in the UK'. *Tourism Management*, 20, 229–35.

Baggio, R., & Cooper, C. (2010). 'Knowledge Transfer in a Tourism Destination: the effect of a network structure'. *Service Industries Journal*, 30(10), 1–15.

Bailey, T. R., Hughes, K. L., & Moore, D. T. (2003). *Working Knowledge: work-based learning and education reform*. New York: Routledge.

Ball, C., Collier, H., Mok, P., & Wilson, J. (Eds.). (2006). *Research into Barriers to Work Placements in the Retail Sector in the South East*. Available: http://www.work-experience.org/assets/assets/documents/Barriers_Final_Report.pdf (Accessed 14 May 2010).

Barron, P. E. (1996). 'The Theory and Practice of Industrial Placement: an analysis of hospitality students' experiences'. *Australian Journal of Hospitality Management*, 4(1), 15–26.

Boud, D. E., & Solomon, N. E. (2001). *Work-Based Learning: a new higher education?* Florence: Taylor & Francis.

Bullock, K., Gould, V., Hejmadi, M., & Lock, G. (2009). 'Work Placement Experience: should I stay or should I go?' *Higher Education Research & Development*, 28, 481–94.

Busby, G. (2001). 'Vocationalism in Higher Level Tourism Courses: the British perspective'. *Journal of Further and Higher Education*, 25, 29–43.

Busby, G. (2003). 'Tourism Degree Internships: a longitudinal study'. *Journal of Vocational Education and Training*, 55(3), 319–34.

Busby, G. (2005). 'Work Experience and Industrial Links'. In D. Airey & J. Tribe (Eds.), *An International Handbook of Tourism Education* (pp. 93–107). Oxford: Elsevier.

Busby, G. & Fiedel, D. (2001). 'A Contemporary Review of Tourism Degrees in the United Kingdom'. *Journal of Vocational Education & Training*, 53(4), 501–22.

Busby, G., & Gibson, P. (2010). 'Tourism and Hospitality Internship Experiences Overseas: a British perspective'. *Journal of Hospitality, Leisure, Sport & Tourism Education,* 9(1), 4–12.

Busby, G., & Huang, R. (2012). 'Integration, Intermediation and Tourism Higher Education: conceptual understanding in the curriculum'. *Tourism Management*, 33, 108–15.

Chapleo, C., & Simms, C. (2010). 'Stakeholder Analysis in Higher Education'. *Perspectives: Policy and Practice in Higher Education*, 14(1), 12–20.

Cooper, C. (2006). 'Knowledge Management and Tourism'. *Annals of Tourism Research*, 33(1), 47–64.

Cooper, C., & Westlake, J. (1998). 'Stakeholders and Tourism Education: curriculum planning using a quality management framework'. *Industry and Higher Education*, 12(2), 93–100.

Cornford, I., & Gunn, D. (1998). 'Work-Based Learning of Commercial Cookery Apprentices in the New South Wales Hospitalities Industry', *Journal of Vocational Education & Training,* 50(4), 549–67.

Crespo, M., & Dridi, H. (2007). 'Intensification of University–Industry Relationships and its Impact on Academic Research'. *Higher Education*, 54, 61–84.

D'Abate, C. P., & Eddy, E. R. (2008). 'Mentoring as a Learning Tool: enhancing the effectiveness of an undergraduate business mentoring program'. *Mentoring & Tutoring: Partnership in Learning*, 16(4), 363–78.

Dale, C., & Robinson, N. (2001). 'The Theming of Tourism Education: a three-domain approach'. *International Journal of Contemporary Hospitality Management*, 13(1), 30–4.

Dearing, R. (1997). *Higher Education in the Learning Society: The Dearing Report.* London: National Committee of Inquiry into Higher Education.

Department for Business Innovation and Skills. (2009). 'Higher Ambitions: the future of universities in a knowledge economy'. Available: www.bis.gov.uk/wp-content/uploads/publications/Higher-Ambitions.pdf (Accessed 25 November 2012).

Department for Business Innovation and Skills. (2011). 'Higher Education: students at the heart of the system'. Available: www.bis.gov.uk/news/topstories/2011/Jun/he-white-paperstudents-at-the-heart-of-the-system (Accessed 9 July 2012).

Easterly, T., & Myers, B. (2009). 'Using Experiential Learning to Integrate Field Trips and Laboratory Experiences'. *American Association for Agricultural Education.* Available: http://www.aaaeonline.org/files/national_09/posters/Using_Experimental_Learning.pdf (Accessed 10 December 2010).

Evans, N. (2001). 'The Development and Positioning of Business Related University Tourism Education: a UK perspective'. *Journal of Teaching in Travel & Tourism*, 1(1), 17–36.

Frasquet, M., Calderon, H., & Cervera, A. (2012). 'University–Industry Collaboration from a Relationship Marketing Perspective: an empirical analysis in a Spanish university'. *Higher Education*, 64, 85–98.

Gannon, J. M., & Maher, A. (2012). 'Developing Tomorrow's Talent: the case of an undergraduate mentoring programme'. *Education + Training*, 54(6), 440–55.

Gerber, R. (2001). 'The Concept of Common Sense in Workplace Learning and Experience'. *Education + Training,* 43, 72–81.

Greenaway, D. (2010). 'We Did It Before'. *Times Higher Education.* Available: http://www.timeshigher education.co.uk/410163.article (Accessed 11 June 2011).

Gunasekara, C. (2006). 'Leading the Horses to Water: the dilemmas of academics and university managers in regional engagement'. *Journal of Sociology*, 42(2), 145–63.

Gursoy, D., & Swanger, N. (2004). 'An Industry-Driven Model of Hospitality Curriculum for Programs Housed in Accredited Colleges of Business'. *Journal of Hospitality & Tourism Education,* 16(4), 13–20.

Gursoy, D., & Swanger, N. (2005). 'An Industry-Driven Model of Hospitality Curriculum for Programs Housed in Accredited Colleges of Business: Part II'. *Journal of Hospitality & Tourism Education*, 17(2), 46–56.

Harvey, L., Geall, V., & Moon, S. (1998). *Work Experience: expanding opportunities for undergraduates.* Birmingham: Centre for Research into Quality, University of Central England.

Harvey, L., Locke, W., & Morey, A. (2002). *Enhancing Employability, Recognising Diversity: making links between higher education and the world of work.* London: Universities UK.

Hay, A. (2011). 'Action Learning in International Settings: possibilities for developing organising insight'. *International Journal of Management Education*, 9(3), 23–36.

Hjalager, A. (2002). 'Repairing Innovation Defectiveness in Tourism'. *Tourism Management*, 23(5), 465–74.

Hjalager, A. (2010). 'A Review of Innovation Research in Tourism'. *Tourism Management*, 31, 1–10.

Huang, R. (2012). 'An Effective use of Experiential Learning to Integrate Field Trips and Classroom Teaching'. Paper presented at the 2nd Advances in Hospitality and Tourism Marketing and Management Conference, 31 May–3 June, Corfu: Alexander Technological Institute of Thessaloniki, Democritus University of Thrace, Washington State University, and Research Institute of the Hellenic Chamber of Hoteliers.

Jauhari, V., & Thomas, R. (2013). 'Developing Effective University–Industry Partnerships: an introduction'. *Worldwide Hospitality and Tourism Themes*, 5(3), 238–43.

Jongbloed, B., Enders, J., & Salerno, C. (2008). 'Higher Education and its Communities: interconnections, interdependencies and a research agenda'. *Higher Education*, 56, 303–24.

Kaya, H., Demirkaya, H. & Aydn, F. (2010). 'Undergraduate Students' Experiences in a Geography Fieldwork'. *Middle-East Journal of Scientific Research*, 6(6), 637–41.

Keys, L. (1994). 'Action Learning: executive development of choice for the 1990s'. *Journal of Management Development*, 13(8), 50–6.

Kneale, P. (2009). 'Raising Student Awareness of Enterprise Skills: accredited and non-accredited routes'. *Planet*, 21, 39–42.

Kolb, D. A. (1984). *Experiential Learning: experience as the source of learning and development*. Englewood Cliffs, NJ: Prentice Hall.

Lewis, A. (2006). 'Stakeholder Informed Tourism Education: voices from Caribbean'. *Journal of Hospitality, Leisure, Sport & Tourism Education*, 5(2), 14–24.

Lisowski, M., & Disiner, J, (1987). 'Cognitive Learning in the Environment: secondary students'. *Environment Education Digest* No. 1. Available: www.ericdigest.org/pre-927/secondary.htm (Accessed 1 November 2009).

Little, B., & Harvey, L. (2006). 'Learning Through Work Placements and Beyond'. *A report for the Higher Education Careers Service Unit and the Higher Education Academy's Work Placements Organisation Forum*. Sheffield: Centre for Research and Evaluation, Sheffield Hallam University, UK.

Litteljohn, D., & Watson, S. (2004). 'Developing Graduate Managers for Hospitality and Tourism'. *International Journal of Contemporary Hospitality Management*, 16(7), 408–14.

Morgan, H. (2006). 'Why Students Avoid Sandwich Placements'. *Education in a Changing Environment, Conference Proceedings*, University of Salford, UK. Available: http://www.ece.salford.ac.uk/proceedings/papers/hm_06.rtf (Accessed 10 April 2012).

Myers, B., & Jones, L. (2004). *Effective Use of Field Trips in Educational Programming: a three stage approach*. Florida Cooperative Extension Electronic Data Information Source, Document AEC 373. Available: http://edis.ifas.ufl.edu/WC054 (Accessed 10 October 2011).

Neave, G. (2000). *The Universities' Responsibilities to Society*. Oxford: Pergamon.

Nixon, I., Smith, K., Stafford, R., & Camm, S. (2006). *Work-Based Learning: illuminating the higher education landscape*. Available: http://www-new1.heacademy.ac.uk/assets/Documents/tla/web0597_work_based_learning_illuminating_the_higher_education_landscape.pdf (Accessed 10 June 2013).

Novelli, M., & Burns, P. (2010). 'Peer-to Peer Capacity-Building in Tourism: values and experiences of field-based education'. *Development Southern Africa*, 27(5), 741–56.

Plewa, C., & Quester, P. (2008). 'A Dyadic Study of "Champions" in University–Industry Relationships'. *Asia Pacific Journal of Marketing and Logistics*, 20(2), 211–26.

Plewa, C., Quester, P., & Baaken, T. (2005). 'Relationship Marketing and University–Industry Linkages: a conceptual framework'. *Marketing Theory*, 5(4), 431–54.

Polonsky, M. J., & Waller, D. S. (1999). 'Using Student Projects to Link Academics, Business and Students', *Journal of Teaching in International Business*, 10(2), 55–78.

Raelin, J. A. (1994). 'Whither Management Education? Professional education, action learning and beyond'. *Management Learning*, 25, 301–17.

Rawlinson, S., & Dewhurst, P. (2013). 'How can Effective University–Industry Partnerships be Developed?'. *Worldwide Hospitality and Tourism Themes*, 5(3), 255–67.

Revans, R. (1971). *Developing Effective Managers*. New York: Praeger.

Robertson, C. (2008). 'Employer Engagement'. *LINK 22*, Higher Education Academy Network for Hospitality, Leisure, Sport and Tourism, Oxford. Available: www.heacademy.ac.uk/assets/hlst/documents/LINK_Newsletter/link22_employer_engagement.pdf (Accessed 11 June 2011).

Shaw, G., & Williams, A. (2009). 'Knowledge Transfer and Management in Tourism Organisations: an emerging research agenda'. *Tourism Management*, 30(3), 245–69.

Smith, M. G. (2007). 'Case Studies on Location: taking to the field in economics'. *Journal of Economic Education*, 38(3), 308–17.

Solnet, D., Robinson, R., & Cooper, C. (2007). 'An Industry Partnerships Approach to Tourism Education'. *Journal of Hospitality, Leisure, Sport & Tourism Education*, 6(1). 66–70.

Thomas, R. (2012). 'Business Elites, Universities and Knowledge Transfer in Tourism'. *Tourism Management*, 33, 553–61.

Thomas, S., & Busby, S. (2003). 'Do Industry Collaborative Projects Enhance Students' Learning?'. *Education + Training*, 45(4), 226–35.

Tribe, J. (1997). 'The Indiscipline of Tourism'. *Annals of Tourism Research,* 24, 638–57.

Tribe, J. (1999). 'The Developing Curriculum'. Paper presented at the NLG Annual Conference, 1 December, University of Luton.

Tribe, J. (2001). 'Research Paradigms and the Tourism Curriculum'. *Journal of Travel Research*, 39, 442–8.

Vince, R. (2004). 'Action Learning and Organizational Learning: power, politics and emotion in organisations'. *Action Learning: Research and Practice,* 1, 63–78.

Walker, F. & Ferguson, M. (2009) Approaching Placement Extinction? Exploring the reasons why placement students are becoming a rare breed at the University of Central Lancashire: Work in progress. Available: http://www.work-experience.org/ncwe.rd/products_136.jsp (Accessed 1 April 2010).

Weidenfeld, A., Williams, A. M., & Butler, R. W (2010). 'Knowledge Transfer and Innovation among Attractions'. *Annals of Tourism Research*, 37(3), 604–62.

Xiao, H. (2006). 'Towards a Research Agenda for Knowledge Management in Tourism'. *Tourism and Hospitality Planning and Development*, 3(2), 143–57.

Xiao, H., & Smith, S. L. J. (2007). 'The Use of Tourism Knowledge: research propositions'. *Annals of Tourism Research*, 34(2), 310–31.

Yusuf, S. (2008). 'Intermediating Knowledge Exchange between Universities and Businesses'. *Research Policy*, 37(8), 1167–74.

32

Generation Y and the curriculum space

Pierre Benckendorff
UQ Business School, The University of Queensland, Brisbane, Australia

Gianna Moscardo
School of Business, James Cook University, Australia

Introduction

Generations or generational cohorts can be defined as 'groups of individuals who are born during the same time period and who experienced similar external events during their formative or coming-of-age years (i.e., late adolescent and early adulthood years)' (Noble & Schewe, 2003: 979). Formative events include the attitudes and behaviours of parents, education, memorable incidents and shared experiences. It is argued that these shared formative experiences influence the world view, behaviours and values of an entire age cohort throughout their lifespan (Lyons et al., 2005; Mannheim, 1952). These formative experiences are significant because they help to shape specific preferences, beliefs and psychographic tendencies. They influence the attitudes of individuals from a particular cohort and how they might behave in order to satisfy their values and desires (Gursoy et al., 2008).

Generational cohorts have been studied for quite some time in sociology (Pendergast, 2010) and the concept is accepted in sociology and psychology as a variable that influences individual and group behaviour in a similar fashion to culture, birth order and educational background (Moscardo et al., 2011). Despite this academic history, the idea has only relatively recently been given serious attention in the spheres of business, government and public debate. Much of this recent attention has focused on the Baby Boomers, Generation X and Generation Y. Table 32.1 provides a summary of some of the distinctions between these three generations.

Within this more public discussion of the generations considerable attention has been given to the youngest of these, Generation Y. The majority of definitions of Generation Y include individuals born between 1977 and 1996, although some have argued that the generation extends until 2000 (Donnison, 2007). This focus reflects the fact that Generation Y is a large cohort and also the first generation to have their formative years in a mobile, globalized connected market system. The size of the cohort, their relative affluence and their exposure to a wider world of products, cultures and experiences, has made them a prime target for marketers

Table 32.1 Characteristics of selected living generations

Factors	Baby Boomer	Generation X	Generation Y
Traits	Idealistic, materialistic, ambitious, self-absorbed	Sceptical, disloyal, independent, informal, pragmatic, adaptable	Social, confident, competitive, narcissistic, multi-taskers, tolerant
Beliefs & values	Strong work ethic, security, loyalty, personal fulfilment, equality	Variety, work–life balance, self-reliance	Lifestyle, fun, optimism, innovation, civic responsibility
Motivations	Advancement, responsibility	Individuality	Self-discovery, escape, novelty, relationships
Change	Avoid change	Accept change	Expect change
Earning & spending	Conservative, pay up front	Credit savvy, confident investors	Short-term wants, credit dependent
Learning styles	Auditory, content driven monologue	Auditory, visual dialogue	Visual, kinaesthetic, multi-sensory stimulus junkies
Marketing & communication	Mass	Descriptive, direct	Participative, viral, word of mouth

Source: Benckendorff and Moscardo (2013).

(Noble *et al.*, 2009). They have also been a focus for the attention of tertiary education institutions. Generation Y became college and university students towards the end of a period of major growth, expansion and internationalization in the higher education sector, making them the main target market for educational institutions that had to be much more competitive and commercial in their approach to recruiting and engaging students (Nimon, 2007). Not surprisingly, researchers have mostly focused on Generation Y as students, newly recruited employees and young consumers.

A number of untested and often contradictory claims have been made both about the characteristics of this generation and the specific mechanisms and early life experiences that have shaped these characteristics (Moscardo & Benckendorff, 2010; Moscardo *et al.*, 2011). According to DiLullo *et al.* (2011), the majority of published papers on Generation Y are based on authors' opinions and perceptions rather than on evidence-based research methodologies. In addition the majority of the discussion has been about Generation Y's current attitudes, values and behaviours with most attention paid to the antecedents of these attitudes, values and behaviours. This discussion ignores both changes connected to their movement through the life cycle and Generation Y futures.

Until recently Generation Y have been a very young group of people still in their adolescence and early years of adulthood. Many of their attitudes and behaviours could be linked to their life-cycle or developmental phase, as much as to their generational cohort (Goodwin & O'Connor, 2009). Only now as they move beyond their teens and early twenties can we begin to map out the features that are more likely to be associated with their cohort in the longer term. It is also possible that Generation Y's current attitudes and behaviours reflect their aspirations, concerns and expectations as much as their upbringing and formative experiences. An examination of Generation Y futures, especially as they move out of early adulthood, could generate some unique insights into this particular cohort. Of particular interest to this chapter are claims made about their preferences and attitudes toward education. This chapter will examine these claims using the literature on the curriculum space and on Generation Y as well as the results of two studies of Generation Y. The purpose of this chapter is to consider how the curriculum space needs to evolve in order to accommodate the values and future aspirations of Generation Y students studying tourism, hospitality and event management.

The curriculum space

The meaning of the term 'curriculum' is elusive. The Latin origins of the term correspond with a track or race course but the concept has evolved to represent the content and skills that make up a course of study or syllabus (Prideaux, 2003). The term 'curriculum space' denotes the expanse or area that contains the range of possible contents of a curriculum (Tribe, 2005). A more expansive view is that the curriculum is more than content and extends to the entire learning experience including content, delivery, assessment, values, standards and outcomes (Kerr, 1968).

Prideaux (2003) offers a useful curriculum design and delivery framework that places students at the centre of the curriculum space and highlights the important role of several components:

- Situation: the background, abilities and experience of students
- Intents: the aims, goals and outcomes
- Content: scope, sequence, related to aims, related to practice
- Teaching learning: variety of methods, opportunity for self-direction, learning in real life settings
- Assessment: formative and summative
- Organization: blocks, units and timetables
- Evaluation: questionnaires, focus groups, participation.

The curriculum space is influenced by a range of factors which may result in the planned curriculum not always being the same as the curriculum that is delivered or experienced by learners. There are many decisions to make when designing the curriculum and these decisions are often informed by the competing expectations of various stakeholders including the students themselves, academic staff, industry representatives, university administrators and the community more generally (Tribe, 2005). As a result, curriculum design has traditionally occurred in an ad hoc way with individual educators having a great deal of autonomy and flexibility in determining the focus of content and assessment. However, changing student expectations coupled with the emergence of new technologies and an increasingly competitive marketplace and quality assurance standards mean that more formal and systematic planning and design are now needed.

Within the tourism and hospitality literature, a number of authors have commented on the curriculum. Jafari and Ritchie (1981) and Umbreit (1992) provide some early advice on curriculum design in tourism and hospitality, while Airey and Middleton (1984), Pavesic (1993), Wells (1996) and Airey and Johnson (1999) review programme trends in these areas. These early contributions focused mainly on content and knowledge. More recent commentaries have adopted a more expansive view of the curriculum and have discussed the need for action and reflection as well as a balance between liberal and vocational aspects to produce graduates who are 'philosophic practitioners' (Tribe, 2002; Morrison & O'Mahony, 2003).

Building on this work, Dredge et al. (2012) present a curriculum space framework. The Greek philosopher Aristotle argues that learning is associated with three kinds of competencies: episteme, techne and phronesis. Episteme (theoretical knowledge) is concerned with knowledge

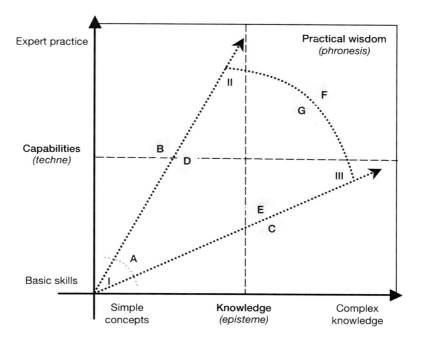

Figure 32.1 The curriculum space

Source: Dredge *et al.* (2012). (Reproduced with permission from Elsevier.)

that is systematic and universal across particular contexts. Techne (practical skill) refers to the skills, routines and techniques associated with making, creating and doing. Phronesis (practical wisdom) is about the development and application of experiential knowledge to specific contexts. These three competencies correspond with what Barnett and Coate (2005) describe as knowing, acting and being. The framework proposed by Dredge *et al.* (2012) and presented in Figure 32.1 incorporates these aspects to present a grid composed of knowledge on the horizontal axis and capabilities on the vertical axis.

Knowledge can be arranged on a continuum from simple concepts to complex knowledge, while capabilities are organized along a continuum ranging from basic skills to expert practice. Dredge *et al.* (2012) argue that when expert practice interacts with complex knowledge there are opportunities for the development of practical wisdom. It is further suggested that different institutions can occupy different parts of the curriculum space, and that a number of forces influence the shape of the curriculum in this space. These forces are represented by the letters B–F in the figure and represent various internal and external pressures and opportunities. Such a framework can help us to understand the dynamic nature of the tourism curriculum space and how an external force, such as generational change, may create pressures and opportunities to rethink the tourism and hospitality curriculum.

Generation Y and learning

As noted earlier a great deal has been written about Generation Y both as consumers and as learners. A full review of the characteristics of Generation Y and the formative events that have shaped them is beyond the scope of this chapter. However, the following points are evident in the literature on Generation Y and their learning preferences:

- Primarily visual learners (Weiler, 2005; Black, 2010).
- Seek interaction and respond well to questions, discussion and hands-on activities (Weiler, 2005; Gardner & Eng, 2005; Oblinger & Oblinger, 2005).
- Expect integration of technology into learning (Gardner & Eng, 2005; Black, 2010; Oblinger & Oblinger, 2005).
- Crave stimulation and variety and have a lower tolerance for boredom (Black, 2010).
- Adept at multi-tasking (Black, 2010).
- Desire relevance and learning in realistic contexts and simulated environments (Black, 2010; Oblinger & Oblinger, 2005).

While these characteristics have intuitive appeal and are underpinned by important events or trends in the formative years of Generation Y, some authors have cautioned that they are not an entirely homogenous cohort and that differences are evident in learning styles and preferences (DiLullo *et al.*, 2011). In this context, an appropriate analogy is to consider generations in the same way as cultures. Just like cultures, generational cohorts share some common traits but not every individual will conform to these stereotypes. Likewise, while individuals within a culture may share common traits there are also likely to be differences. The analysis in this chapter focuses on the similarities between individuals in the same generational cohort but this cautionary note highlights that while the study of generational cohorts is useful for identifying broad trends and changes in behaviours and preferences, there are some limitations. As a result, the emphasis in this chapter is on reporting themes and observations that appear to be consistent across the Generation Y cohort.

Methods

This chapter draws on selected data from two separate studies of Generation Y respondents. The first study was a nationwide questionnaire administered to 632 students studying undergraduate degrees in tourism, hospitality and event management in Australia. This study will be referred to as the Student Survey. The second study was more qualitative and was based on two future scenario activities conducted with a range of Generation Y participants in Australia and Europe. This second study will be called the Generation Y Futures Study.

The Student Survey: sample and data collection

The questionnaire used in this first study was developed following a critical review of the education literature and extensive consultation with an international reference group of tourism, hospitality and event management educators. Students were surveyed in 2011 using both online and paper-based surveys. Twenty-two Australian institutions were represented, ranging from Group of Eight universities (a coalition of leading Australian universities) to private, externally accredited degree-granting institutions in the vocational education and training sector. Table 32.2 provides a profile of respondents from this survey study.

The Generation Y Futures Study: sample and data collection

The second study focused on Generation Y perspectives on their personal futures and involved two future scenario activities conducted with students enrolled in an undergraduate business

Table 32.2 Profile of respondents in the Student Survey

Characteristics	No.	Percentage	Characteristics	No.	Percentage
Gender (n = 627)			*Birthplace (n = 632)*		
Female	452	71.5	Australia	352	55.7
Male	175	27.7	International	280	44.3
Age groups (n = 632) (mean = 22.5)			Studying part-time	46	8.1
18 to 20	121	19.2	Scholarship recipient	47	8.3
21 to 22	242	38.3	Working while studying	360	60.0
23 to 25	200	31.6	Have more than one job	75	13.3
Over 25	69	10.9	First in family at university	164	29.0

research methods class at a regional Australian university and students enrolled in an MBA class at a European university. In the first activity students were invited to participate in an online discussion about Generation Y futures in which they were asked to think ahead 10 years and describe what they might be like and what they might be doing. They were also invited to comment on the things about this future that were exciting and to describe any concerns or worries that they had about their future. The same questions were used to guide the second activity although the method of delivery and the sample were different. In the second activity the MBA students did not provide information for themselves, rather they were asked to put the questions to five acquaintances, family members or colleagues who were born between 1977 and 1996. They were asked not to include students from the same university where they were based. These students used a mixture of face-to-face interviews, online discussions, emails and phone conversations to generate the future scenarios.

These two activities resulted in 80 future scenarios from a wide range of Generation Y individuals including university students and graduates in a variety of disciplines, respondents with no higher education experience, full-time and part-time employees across several sectors and at different levels of seniority, some still living at home with parents, others living independently and others living with their spouses/partners and young children, as well as respondents from a variety of countries across Europe, Asia and the Middle East. At the time of describing their futures the sample ranged in age from 14 to 30 years, thus spanning the entire cohort range, although the majority (58 per cent) were aged between 20 and 27 years. The sample was made up of 47 females and 33 males. The futures were described in multiple languages and those not in English were translated and transcribed in English before being analysed using a grounded theory approach and following the guidelines for thematic coding suggested by Maxwell (2005) and DeCrop (2004).

Results and discussion

The Student Survey

Examining the activity patterns of contemporary students offers a useful starting point for considering Generation Y and the curriculum space. A number of authors have argued that the curriculum extends beyond core content to include a broad range of co-curricular and extra-curricular activities (Prideaux, 2003). In this context James *et al.* (2010) have conducted one of the largest longitudinal studies of undergraduate students and have noted that Australian students are engaging in an increasing number of activities beyond their university studies. Of particular note is an increasing reliance on the Web for personal use and study, the growing prevalence of paid part-time work while studying, and a decrease in the amount of time spent on campus. The data collected from tourism, hospitality and event management students in the first survey study reinforces the importance of paid work as well as other activities such as volunteer work (see Table 32.3).

Students were asked to estimate how many hours per week they actually spent on each activity and to indicate how many hours per week they would ideally like to spend on each activity. The results also indicate that students wished they could spend more time on most activities, suggesting that many Generation Y's are increasingly time poor.

When the type of work students were doing was explored in more detail, the responses revealed that a majority of students are working part-time, usually in the hospitality and travel industries (see Table 32.4). The results confirm that most sampled Australian Generation Y students are working between 10 and 19 hours per week, but, perhaps more interestingly, a majority of students have had two or more previous employers. This scenario is markedly different to the study experience of previous generations in Australia (James et al., 2010).

Students were asked to rate the importance and performance of a range of curriculum space attributes. The attributes were adapted from the curriculum space framework developed by Dredge et al. (2012). The results presented in Table 32.5 indicate that the performance ratings for all items were below the importance ratings, resulting in statistically significant differences for all items. This may suggest that the curriculum is not meeting the needs of the Generation Y cohort. Students rated the importance of basic skills and simple concepts most highly, with a particularly strong emphasis on practical and technical skills and the application of knowledge. However, there was a significant difference between the student-rated importance and performance of these attributes. An importance–performance analysis (IPA) of these items also indicates that they represent areas that Australian institutions need to improve (see Figure 32.2).

The results also indicate less support from students for the importance of complex knowledge, including 'the need to widely read and understand relevant theories in tourism and related disciplines'. Other items that mentioned reading and reflection were also deemed to be less important, including the view that students should be equipped with the skills necessary for reflection and lifelong learning (1, 9, 10). These items were located in the 'low priority' quadrant of the IPA grid.

Table 32.3 Actual and ideal time spent by students on different activities (hours/week)

Activity	Actual		Ideal		t score	p
	n	Mean	n	Mean		
Paid work	377	11.0	352	12.9	−5.351	.000
Course contact	387	10.4	365	11.9	−6.301	.000
Using the Web for study/research	388	8.0	358	9.0	−4.658	.000
Private study	384	7.7	363	11.0	−11.780	.000
Volunteer work	342	7.6	336	10.0	−6.564	.000
Family commitments	355	6.1	336	9.3	−5.000	.000
Social & extra–curricular activities	360	4.8	342	10.5	−1.998	.047
Using the library	366	4.3	348	6.2	−9.033	.000
Course readings	374	3.6	360	8.1	−12.116	.000
Group work	367	2.7	348	3.7	−7.125	.000

Table 32.4 Employment characteristics of tourism, hospitality and events students

Work characteristics	Frequency	Percent
Employment status (n = 600)		
Working full-time in a position related to my degree	14	2.3
Working full-time in a position not related to my degree	13	2.2
Working part-time in a position related to my degree	163	27.2
Working part-time in a position not related to my degree	170	28.3
Further study	24	4.0
Looking for my first job	34	5.7
Unemployed but have previously been employed	112	18.7
Neither employed nor looking for employment	48	8.0
Other	22	3.7
Sector (n = 388)		
Tourism/hospitality/events	236	60.8
Retail	94	24.2
Other	58	14.9
Work hours (per week) (n = 449)		
Under 10 hours	108	24.1
10 to 19 hours	205	45.7
20 to 29 hours	88	19.6
30 hours or more	48	10.7
Number of previous employers (n = 615)		
None	59	9.6
One	98	15.9
Two	140	22.8
Three	127	20.7
More than three	191	31.1

Students were also asked to rate the importance and performance of a range of graduate attributes. These attributes were based on the work of Ring *et al.* (2009). The analysis of these attributes indicates a focus on employability and management, leadership and entrepreneurial skills (see Table 32. 6 and Figure 32.3).

The understanding of tourism, hospitality and events from a multidisciplinary perspective was regarded as a 'low priority'. The items that deal with lifelong learning, the future and technology (3, 4, 8) were all located close to the centre of the grid, while there was a feeling that Australian institutions may be over-servicing in the areas of sustainability, impacts and ethics (1, 5).

To supplement the quantitative analysis, respondents to the questionnaire in the Student Survey were also asked to provide further comments about tourism, hospitality and events education in Australia. Figure 32.4 provides a word cloud of the open-ended comments provided by 159 students. The emphasis of words such as work experience, practical, industry and skills reinforce the findings that students are increasingly concerned about developing practical skills. This may be motivated by the need to develop a portfolio of experiences that makes them more competitive in an increasingly challenging labour market.

The following quotes from the tourism students surveyed in this first study illustrate these key themes:

Table 32.5 Students' attitudes toward the curriculum space

Curriculum space attributes	Importance	Performance	t score	p
■ **Basic Skills – Simple Concepts**				
2 Students should be encouraged to develop technical competency in applying methods and processes to manage tourism, hospitality and events	4.8	4.0	15.440	.000
4 Students should be given the technical skills and learn how to apply them in different situations and contexts	5.0	4.1	15.995	.000
8 Students should receive practical skills and training in communication, problem solving and interpersonal skills	5.1	4.1	16.093	.000
△ **Basic Skills – Complex Knowledge**				
3 Students should be encouraged to be widely read and understand relevant theories in tourism and related disciplines	4.4	4.3	2.105	.036
7 Students should be provided with a critical knowledge about the impacts of tourism, hospitality and events	4.8	4.4	10.348	.000
12 Students should understand tourism, hospitality and events from multiple disciplinary perspectives	4.8	4.2	12.696	.000
◈ **Expert Practice – Simple Knowledge**				
5 Students should develop and apply important values such as ethics, stewardship, knowledge, professionalism and mutuality	4.8	4.2	12.432	.000
9 Students should be equipped with the skills necessary for reflection and lifelong learning	4.7	4.0	14.278	.000
11 Students should be encouraged to think outside the square to solve practical problems creatively	4.9	4.1	16.042	.000
● **Expert Practice – Complex Knowledge**				
1 Students should be encouraged to read, reflect and critically develop their own theories about tourism, hospitality and events and apply these in practical situations	4.6	4.1	10.655	.000
6 Students should be encouraged to apply theory to real tourism, hospitality and events settings	4.9	4.3	10.205	.000
10 Students should read, reflect and develop creative solutions to applied problems	4.6	4.1	11.311	.000

Notes
Means based on 1 = Not very important/poor performance to 6 = Very important/strong performance.
(n = 570)

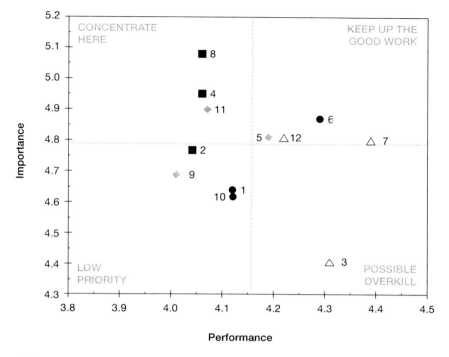

Figure 32.2 Importance–performance analysis of curriculum space attributes

'Emphasis needs to be on preparing students for the *practical* demands that arise when starting a new job through providing workplace *experiences* within the curriculum.'

'I think that undergraduate tourism, hospitality and events should definitely include more *practical learning* because after we graduate we do not have as much *experience* . . . we learn a lot of theories but without practical learning, it is hard to apply these theories appropriately to real life.'

'Students should have more chance to *practice* the knowledge they have learned in the real workplace. This *industry* is more about *experiences*, theory is good but it will be more beneficial with the real experiences.'

'Students should *practice skills* and training in the *industry* related with their course, not only study all the theories in the class. Students need to learn from the real world.'

Having explored the student experience and attitudes toward the curriculum space, the analysis now moves to the future aspirations and concerns of Generation Y students. In the Student Survey, respondents were asked to describe their ideal job after graduating. This question was intended to explore the aspirations of Generation Y graduates. Figure 32.5 provides a word cloud of the phrases used by respondents.

The emphasis on management acknowledges the fact that that most of the respondents were studying bachelor degrees with a management or business core and envisaged themselves in a professional role. Most of these programmes focus on tourism, hotel and event management. To better understand the underlying themes these common words were removed from the word cloud, allowing the themes presented in Figure 32.6 to emerge more clearly.

Pierre Benckendorff and Gianna Moscardo

Table 32.6 Students' attitudes toward graduate attributes

		Importance	Performance	t score	p
1	Understanding of the wider world and society, including understanding the industry as well as impacts of tourism, hospitality and events and the environments in which these industries are embedded	4.9	4.4	11.351	.000
2	Understanding tourism, hospitality and events from a multidisciplinary perspective (including sociology, philosophy, psychology, anthropology, economics natural sciences, etc.)	4.4	3.9	11.319	.000
3	Developing transferable skills such as lifelong learning, creativity, critical and flexible thinking, and social skills	4.9	4.2	13.098	.000
4	Thinking critically and creatively about the future of tourism, hospitality and events, including stewardship and personal responsibility to take part in the creation and shaping of the future of these industries	4.8	4.3	12.603	.000
5	Understanding sustainability and ethical responsibilities	4.9	4.6	6.625	.000
6	Preparing students for future employment	5.3	4.3	15.741	.000
7	Developing management, leadership and entrepreneurial skills	5.1	4.3	15.287	.000
8	Understanding how to use information technologies for tourism, hospitality and events	4.9	4.2	13.732	.000

Notes
Means based on 1 = Not very important/poor performance to 6 = Very important/strong performance.
(n = 556)

The figure highlights that the aspirations of Generation Y include well-paid jobs, international work and interacting with people or providing service. However, many respondents also described their ideal job as interesting, dynamic, flexible and fun and a number of respondents wanted work that was challenging and provided opportunities for learning and creativity. Examples of comments reflecting these themes include:

'Leadership initiatives, ambition, fast paced, *dynamic* environment, good conditions, *well paid*',
'Ability to express myself, *flexible* hours, ability to *interact people*',
'*Flexible*, exciting, productive, rewarding, social',
'*Flexible, well paid*, chance to *challenge* and *broaden my knowledge*, allows travel and cultural exchange',
'Great career *development* and employment benefits',
'Good environment, *good pay*, more *incentives*, more *vacation*',
'*Learn* more skills, related to my major, *well paid*' and
'My ideal job is where I am constantly learning and being challenged'.

432

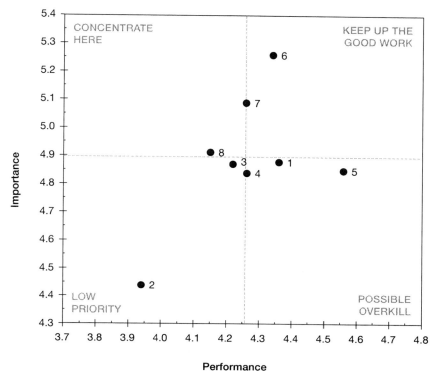

Figure 32.3 Importance–performance analysis of graduate attributes

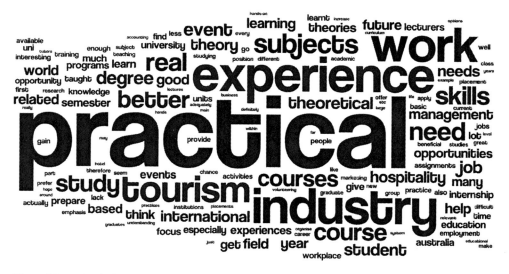

Figure 32.4 Word cloud of comments about tourism, hospitality and events education in Australia (n = 159)

Figure 32.5 Word cloud of ideal jobs identified by Generation Y respondents (n = 561)

Figure 32.6 Word cloud of key themes for ideal jobs identified by Generation Y respondents
(n = 561)

The Generation Y Futures Study

The second study was more qualitative in approach and extends the findings from the Student Survey, especially in the area of futures, aspirations and concerns. Six key related themes emerged from the grounded theory approach taken in this second study to the content analysis of participants' discussions of their personal futures – the centrality of *family*, a consistent picture of *work values* and expectations, ambivalence about *technology*, a focus on *sustainability*, expectations of a highly *mobile* lifestyle and intentions related to *lifelong learning*.

The first and most dominant and consistent theme was the importance of family. All the futures were centred on family with the majority describing a future in which they had a partner and/or children and many also highlighting their desire to be close to their parents and other immediate family members:

'I hope to be married with children on the horizon',
'I'm excited about the idea of seeing my son growing up' and

'I would be able to support my *parents* and supply them with everything they need to live comfortably'.

Arguably a future based on family is unlikely to be peculiar to any one generation, but the centrality of family contradicts claims about Generation Y's focus on themselves as individuals (Spinney, 2012).

The second key theme that emerged was related to work and ambition and reinforces the findings from the larger questionnaire. Many of the people described themselves in the future as being in a professional role, senior management position or successful entrepreneurs or business owners. Again this is not a surprising option, but these discussions of work had three noteworthy features. The first was a strong emphasis on being productive, challenging, and of value beyond simply salary and status. For example:

'I would like to contribute to society',
'In a company I feel makes a difference in society',
'Perhaps work in the public sector at a local level to build . . . a nice community'.

The second noteworthy feature was the description of working enough, or making enough money, to meet a set of moderate ambitions. The following was a very common sentiment: 'I'd like enough funds to buy a car and my own apartment. Also I would like to be able to take care of my parents.'

This concern with earning enough to support a family was linked to the third feature – a strong concern about work–life balance. For some not being able to achieve such a balance was a major concern: 'I worry that I will not have time to spend with people that I love', while for others it was stated as a goal: 'I will not work too much – time with friends and family is also important.'

Generation Y are often characterized as immersed in a variety of technologies (Eisner, 2011). This was consistent with the most common theme for the answers to a prompt about what was exciting about the future: 'I am also excited that technological advances may enable us to find cures for life threatening diseases.'

While technology was often described as solving many of the world's current problems, it was also a common source of worry with many comments suggesting that managing the negative effectives of technology and controlling excessive technology use could be a serious future challenge: 'with the rise of technology I'm getting the creeps about the ever expanding surveillance society'.

This ambivalence about technology in the future was the second of two key themes about future concerns with the other being sustainability: 'worry that people do not value nature's resources and have no respect towards living creatures, animal and/or humans, wars and diseases, and that too much technology will make us dependent'.

The fifth key theme was mobility with many of the Generation Y respondents describing a lifestyle consistent with that proposed by Urry (2002) as a major element of modern society in the new mobilities paradigm. These respondents described moving on multiple dimensions – from short holidays to longer term stays for work and education, and regular travel required to maintain social networks. Statements such as:

'I plan to travel and see the world. I'm sure my work will be connected with travel and of course I will travel since I have friends in many parts of the world' and

'I have already travelled a lot and don't plan to stop. It's part of my profession and a part of my worldview. I'm a person of the world, I have to travel.'

These themes were also evident amongst some of the questionnaire respondents.

Consistent with the Student Survey responses, self-development, learning and education represented the sixth key theme in the futures described by Generation Y. Many Generation Y futures included an expectation that they would continue to learn skills through both formal and informal opportunities. Typical comments were:

'I would like to attend professional courses and seminars all over the world',
'I am excited about opportunities to develop my qualifications',
'The future is exciting because of the possibility to make myself a better person, to obtain more education and live a good life',
'I want to do my MBA somewhere abroad' and
'I want to learn new things'.

Implications for higher education curriculum and approaches

The results presented in the previous sections have a number of implications for the future curriculum space in tourism and hospitality education. It appears that students while largely satisfied with the development of knowledge in the curriculum, do have a desire for more practical learning experiences that support skills development. Students are less enthusiastic about the importance of theory and the reading commonly associated with communicating these theories in a traditional higher education context. This theme emerges against the backdrop of the democratization of knowledge brought about by convenient access to digital content. Google, Wikipedia, YouTube and other resources provide access to courses, online tutorials, learning communities, social media tools and Massive Open Online Courses (MOOCs). These technology-enhanced learning tools liberate learners from the need to memorize facts and to perform mundane learning tasks.

What is the role of the tourism and hospitality curriculum under these circumstances? It is argued that within this context, the tourism and hospitality curriculum should complement existing and emerging technology-enhanced learning resources by focusing on Barnett and Coate's (2005) acting (capabilities) and being (practical wisdom) dimensions rather than attempting to cover the entire tourism and hospitality knowledge domain. This suggests a need to rebalance the curriculum to dedicate more space to the development of skills, professional values and expert practice which are otherwise difficult to develop through technology-enhanced learning. This includes a consideration of how theory could be applied to both liberal and vocational ends.

In the Australian context, the findings also indicate that many students are volunteering or working while studying and that a majority are working within the tourism and hospitality sectors. This raises some questions about the tacit knowledge and skills Generation Y students are developing while they study and the capacity of the curriculum to acknowledge and accommodate these as part of a more holistic learning experience. While the curriculum space framework presented earlier in this chapter advocates a balance between knowledge and practice it implies that this balance should be evident in the formal curriculum. However, the prevalence of part-time employment creates opportunities to design learning experiences which provide flexibility for co-curricular and extra-curricular activities and which assimilate part-time work and volunteering into the formal curriculum. While this may suggest a focus on vocational aspects, there is also scope to integrate work experiences into the curriculum to deconstruct tourism and hospitality through liberal reflection. As Tribe (2005) suggests, this can then be taken a step further by translating a wider understanding of tourism and hospitality into action.

The key themes related to students' responses about their ideal job indicate a desire to be challenged and to access opportunities for growth and development. This suggests a need for lifelong and life-wide learning and a curriculum that is more permeable and responsive to students moving in and out of the formal education sector. The overall pattern of connection between personal development, work, travel and educational aspirations described in the Generation Y futures raises two challenging and closely related issues about what is meant by lifelong learning and who is higher education for? Many higher education institutions include statements related to lifelong learning as either an important goal or a desired graduate attribute (Jarvis, 2009). Arguably, this is often stated but rarely defined in any detail nor linked to specific strategies to achieve this or measure it (Watson, 2009). The results from both studies make it clear, however, that this is a group interested in, and actively seeking, opportunities to continue their learning and education beyond the traditional formal educational qualifications.

For Generation Y, lifelong learning is about regularly seeking skills and qualifications that will support their changing careers and personal interests. Several made it clear that they were seeking flexible, shorter educational opportunities, often linked to travel, rather than structured, formal degree qualifications. With such a strong interest in continued learning, Generation Y offers an opportunity for educational organizations to achieve their aims of supporting lifelong and life-wide learning, but they may need to rethink the way they structure and offer educational experiences. In particular, the perspectives of Generation Y students suggest the need to focus on short courses, flexible modules, technology-enhanced learning and subjects and skills related to personal development as well as the requirements of professions and industry sectors.

Conclusions

In recent decades the attention of higher education institutions has been directed towards professional societies, industry associations and business representatives in discussions around what should be taught to students and how these should be organized into recognized qualifications. But there is a growing debate about the purpose of higher education with discussion about who and what universities are for (Collini, 2012). The Generation Y perspectives summarized in this chapter suggest a need to rethink the tourism and hospitality curriculum space to offer:

- Less emphasis on knowledge presented without context or application and a greater focus on skills, expert practice and the application of knowledge;
- Assimilation of extra-curricular and co-curricular activities; and
- Opportunities for lifelong and life-wide learning through short courses, flexible modules and technology-enhanced learning.

The findings point to a more fluid education experience where students move in and out of the higher education space over an entire lifetime. In the aspirations of Generation Y, for both themselves and the world more generally, education is about personal development and practical skills to support work that contributes in a positive way to their families and communities and provides a pathway to tackle a range of sustainability issues.

References

Airey, D., & Middleton, V. (1984). 'Course Syllabi in the UK: a review'. *Tourism Management*, 5(1), 57–62.

Airey, D., & Johnson, S. (1999). 'The Content of Tourism Degree Courses in the UK'. *Tourism Management*, 20(2), 229–35.

Barnett, R., & Coate, K. (2005). *Engaging the Curriculum in Higher Education*. New York: Open University Press.

Benckendorff, P., & Moscardo, G. (2013). 'Generational Cohorts and Ecotourism'. In R. Ballantyne & J. Packer (Eds.), *International Handbook of Ecotourism* (pp. 135–53). Cheltenham, UK: Edward Elgar Publishing.

Black, A. (2010). 'Gen Y: who they are and how they learn'. *Educational Horizons*, 88(2), 92–101.

Collini, S. (2012). *What are Universities For?* London: Penguin.

DeCrop, A. (2004). 'Trustworthiness in Qualitative Tourism Research'. In J. Phillimore & L. Goodson (Eds.), *Qualitative Research in Tourism: ontologies, epistemologies and methodologies* (pp. 156–69). London: Routledge.

DiLullo, C., McGee, P., & Kriebel, R. M. (2011). 'Demystifying the Millennial Student: a reassessment in measures of character and engagement in professional education'. *Anatomical Sciences Education*, 4(4), 214–26.

Donnison, S. (2007). 'Unpacking the Millennials: a cautionary tale for teacher education'. *Australian Journal of Teacher Education*, 32(3), 1–13.

Dredge, D., Benckendorff, P., Day, M., Gross, M. J., Walo, M., Weeks, P., & Whitelaw, P. (2012). 'The Philosophic Practitioner and the Curriculum Space'. *Annals of Tourism Research*, 39(4), 2154–76.

Eisner, S. P. (2011). 'Teaching Generation Y College Students: three initiatives'. *Journal of College Teaching and Learning*, 1 (9), 69–84.

Gardner, S., & Eng, S. (2005). 'What Students Want: generation Y and the changing function of the academic library'. *Portal: Libraries and the Academy*, 5(3), 405–20.

Goodwin, J., & O'Connor, H. (2009). 'Youth and Generation: in the midst of an adult world'. In A. Furlong (Ed.), *Handbook of Youth and Young Adulthood: new perspectives and agendas* (pp. 22–30). Abingdon: Routledge.

Gursoy, D., Maier, T. A., & Chi, C. G. (2008). 'Generational Differences: an examination of work values and generational gaps in the hospitality workforce'. *International Journal of Hospitality Management*, 27(3), 448–58.

Jafari, J., & Ritchie, B. J. R. (1981). 'Toward a Framework for Tourism Education: problems and prospects'. *Annals of Tourism Research*, 8(1), 13–34.

James, R., Krause, K. L., & Jennings, C. (2010). *The First Year Experience in Australian Universities: findings from 1994 to 2009*. Melbourne: Centre for the Study of Higher Education, University of Melbourne.

Jarvis, P. (2009). 'Lifelong Learning: a social ambiguity'. In P. Jarvis (Ed.), *The Routledge International Handbook of Lifelong Learning* (pp. 9–18). Abingdon: Routledge.

Kerr, L. (Ed.). (1968). *Changing the Curriculum*. London: University of London Press.

Lyons, S., Duxbury, L., & Higgins, C. (2005). 'An Empirical Assessment of Generational Difference in Work-Related Values'. *Human Resources Management*, 26, 62–71.

Mannheim, K. (1952). 'The Problem of Generations'. In K. Mannheim & P. Kecskemeti (Eds.), *Essays on the Sociology of Knowledge* (pp. 276–322). London: Routledge & Kegan Paul.

Maxwell, J. (2005). *Qualitative Research Design: an interactive approach*. Thousand Oaks, CA: Sage.

Morrison, A., & O'Mahony, G. B. (2003). 'The Liberation of Hospitality Management Education'. *International Journal of Contemporary Hospitality Management*, 15(1), 38–44.

Moscardo, G., & Benckendorff, P. (2010). 'Mythbusting: Generation Y and Travel'. In P. Benckendorff, G. Moscardo, & D. Pendergast (Eds.), *Tourism and Generation Y* (pp. 16–26). Wallingford: CAB International.

Moscardo, G., Murphy, L., & Benckendorff, P. (2011). 'Generation Y and Travel Futures'. In I. Yeoman, C. H. C. Hsu, K. A. Smith, & S. Watson (Eds.), *Tourism and Demography* (pp. 87–99). Oxford: Goodfellow Publishers.

Nimon, S. (2007). 'Generation Y and Higher Education: the other Y2K'. *Journal of Institutional Research*, 13(1), 24–41.

Noble, S., & Schewe, C. (2003). 'Cohort Segmentation: an exploration of its validity'. *Journal of Business Research*, 56(12), 979–87.

Noble, S. M., Haytko, D. L., & Philips, J. (2009). 'What Drives College-Age Generation Y Consumers?'. *Journal of Business Research*, 62(6), 617–28.

Oblinger, D., & Oblinger, J. L. (2005). *Educating the Net Generation*. Boulder, CO: EDUCAUSE.

Pavesic, D. V. (1993). 'Hospitality Education 2005: curricular and programmatic trends'. *Journal of Hospitality & Tourism Research*, 17(1), 285–94.

Pendergast, D. (2010). 'Getting to Know the Y Generation'. In P. Benckendorff, G. Moscardo, & D. Pendergast (Eds.), *Tourism and Generation Y* (pp. 1–15). Wallingford: CABI.

Prideaux, D. (2003). 'ABC of Learning and Teaching in Medicine: curriculum design'. *British Medical Journal*, 326(7383), 268–70.

Ring, A., Dickinger, A., & Wober, K. (2009). 'Designing the Ideal Undergraduate Program in Tourism: expectations from industry and educators'. *Journal of Travel Research*, 48, 106–21.

Spinney, L. (2012). 'The Curse of Generation Y'. *New Scientist*, 214(2862), 44–7.

Tribe, J. (2002). 'The Philosophic Practitioner'. *Annals of Tourism Research*, 29(2), 338–57.

Tribe, J. (2005). 'Tourism, Knowledge and the Curriculum'. In D. W. Airey, & J. Tribe (Eds.), *An International Handbook of Tourism Education* (pp. 47–60). Amsterdam: Elsevier.

Umbreit, W. T. (1992). 'In Search of Hospitality Curriculum Relevance for the 1990s'. *Hospitality & Tourism Educator*, 5(1), 71–4.

Urry, J. (2002). *Sociology beyond Societies: mobilities for the twenty-first century*. Abingdon: Routledge.

Watson, D. (2009). 'Universities and Lifelong Learning'. In P. Jarvis (Ed.), *The Routledge International Handbook of Lifelong Learning* (pp. 102–13). Abingdon: Routledge.

Weiler, A. (2005). 'Information-seeking Behavior in Generation Y Students: motivation, critical thinking, and learning theory'. *Journal of Academic Librarianship*, 31(1), 46–53.

Wells, J. (1996). 'The Tourism Curriculum in Higher Education in Australia: 1989–1995'. *Journal of Tourism Studies*, 7(1), 20–30.

33

Groundswell

A co-creation approach for exploiting social media and redesigning (e-)learning in tourism and hospitality education

Marianna Sigala

Department of Business Administration, University of the Aegean, Chios, Greece

Introduction: educational challenges and transformational needs

The environment, the conditions and the context in which educational institutions operate are not only different from in the past, but they are also under a continuous and dynamic change. The same is true for the knowledge, skills and competencies that industry requires from graduates as well as the expectations, the needs and the learning styles of learners. Table 33.1 provides an overview of these educational transformation challenges by comparing past and current beliefs about the major issues in terms of knowledge, learners' profiles and skills, and learning processes.

Social media have changed the way people find, read, share, disseminate and (co-)create knowledge, and this has affected the way people learn, acquire and create knowledge. For example, social media enable learners (Deng & Yuen, 2011; Sigala, 2007) to: aggregate, share, store and synthesize knowledge from various sources to create new meta-knowledge; manage their own meaning-making processes; and identify and join social networks for staying informed and participating in collective knowledge generation for sharing and criticizing experiences and theories. As the technology performs many of the cognitive operations previously performed by learners (information storage, retrieval and interconnections) (Huang *et al.*, 2011; Sim & Hew, 2010), it also frees up cognitive resources that people can in turn use for becoming more knowledge productive and creative (Sigala, 2013).

Moreover, social media enable individuals to engage in learning activities that transcend and blur the spheres of work, formal education, personal and social life (King *et al.*, 2009). Consequently, social media afford numerous opportunities to scale up and blend informal and formal learning at an international and cross-industry level. Since informal learning is highly important (e.g. it accounts for 80 per cent of an employees' knowledge about his/her job (Attwell, 2007)), it becomes evident that educators should also exploit social media for actively involving industry stakeholders in learning processes in order to connect formal and informal learning processes, and so to optimize the learning and knowledge acquisition benefits (Hall, 2009). Indeed,

Table 33.1 Educational challenges and transformational needs

	Traditionally	Now
Knowledge	• slow creation and the evolution of knowledge • knowledge is held and transmitted by selective institutions and experts	• short life of knowledge and rapid knowledge growth due to the implications of the interconnections between knowledge fields • technology expands the people's information ecology (i.e. the sources and interconnections of knowledge) • social networks are major co-creators, distributors and owners of knowledge • none possesses the necessary knowledge and expertise of any subject • knowledge ownership is less important than the ability to access and co-create the knowledge ad hoc when needed
Learners' profiles, roles and learning styles	• learners are passive receivers of information	• learners are active creators of knowledge • learners are highly connected, collective and creative • learners should develop the capacity to engage and form connections with various sources of information
Learning processes	• formal learning dominates: learning mainly occurs in highly structured learning contexts in classrooms and/or course • learning happens in a linear formal way	• learning occurs continuously in blended formal and informal ways (e.g. observation, trial and error, asking for help, conversing and listening to others, self-reflections, personal networks) • learning is highly self-motivated, open, networked, autonomous, informal and always happening
Learners' required skills	• qualifications ensure getting a job • heavily required competencies: technical, administrative, interpersonal and leadership competencies	• companies are increasingly looking for staff who can identify the nature, the sources and the techniques for accessing and acquiring the required knowledge on a continuous basis • new competencies are more important: information literacy, connectiveness, social presence and online self-identity construction/management, self-regulation, network building and management

Sources: Arguments synthesized from Farkas (2012), Sigala (2013), Ravenscroft (2011) and Tess (2013).

the expansion of learning ecosystems to include the participation of external stakeholders is also supported by arguments in open education and co-creation, as the former can contribute and enrich the learning process with their numerous resources (e.g. knowledge, experience, access to networks).

To address the current challenges and exploit the learning affordances of the mass participatory and collaborative tools, numerous educational institutions and educators are increasingly using the social media (Conole & Alevizou, 2010; Sigala, 2012; Dabbagh & Kitsantas, 2012). The literature in the educational use of social media is also mushrooming and a plethora of new concepts has emerged demarcating these transformations (Tess, 2013): e-learning 2.0, pedagogy 2.0, student 2.0, faculty 2.0, and classroom 2.0, with the suffix 2.0 characterizing themes such as openness, personalization, collaboration, social networking, user/student-generated content, collective wisdom and user/learner-driven and centred education. The tourism and hospitality discipline is not an exception from such trends. Market changes and technology advances have transformed the tourism industry and education (Sigala, 2013; Sigala *et al.*, 2012) by affecting: the tourists' behaviour and needs; the operations and the human resource needs of tourism firms; the curricula design and the content of higher education; the teaching and learning practices of tourism and hospitality schools.

However, the shift in the way people learn is challenging the ability of traditional pedagogies to engage and educate the current generation of learners as well as to develop the newly required competencies. Indeed, the three broad learning theories (namely behaviourism, cognitivism and constructivism) that have been frequently utilized in the creation of instructional environments were developed in a time when learning was not impacted through technology (Ravenscroft, 2011). As technology has changed the way people live, work, communicate and learn, there is an urgent need to update and enhance these traditional theories of learning. Hence, there is a need to connect the use of social media to a learning theory and appropriate pedagogical practices in order to ensure that learning exploits social media and not the opposite. A new learning theory is also required to guide the development of effective pedagogical practices that can make effective use of social media and ensure that learners can acquire, excel and enrich the new competencies and knowledge capabilities that are required in the new networked and collaborative world (Testa & Sipe, 2011). Pedagogical practices should also exploit the social media affordances enabling the connection of formal and informal learning processes and the enrichment of learning by opening up learning ecosystems to external stakeholders.

The aims of this chapter are twofold: (a) to investigate new learning theories that can be used for designing pedagogical practices that make effective use of social media; and (b) to demonstrate the applicability and benefits of these new learning theories in exploiting the social media for designing learning activities that can significantly enhance the learning processes and benefits. The redesign of the learning processes of a tourism course is used as a case study in order to better demonstrate the value of these aims in practice. Redesigning learning processes in tourism is of a high importance and need, since knowledge development, business operations and people's behaviour and learning were critically affected in the tourism industry during the last decades due to the technological advances and the socio-cultural changes that followed. To that end, the chapter first critically reviews and assesses traditional learning theories in relation to the current needs, challenges and transformations of educational and work contexts. Connectivism and conversational learning are proposed as 'new' learning theories that can address the limitations of the existing learning theories and can be used for exploiting social media in order to support the development of newly required competencies. The chapter continues by developing a framework showing how these new theories can be used in practice for developing learning activities that effectively integrate social media in educational contexts and adopt co-creation approaches for redesigning and enriching learning ecosystems and processes. The applicability of the framework is shown by discussing the redesign of the learning processes of a tourism course related to revenue management. Finally, the chapter concludes by advocating how these pedagogical activities can support and empower learners to develop and excel at new capabilities such as soft skills and information literacy competencies that are currently highly demanded in the tourism industry (Kalargyrou & Woods, 2011).

A critical review of learning theories and pedagogies: contribution and limitations

Traditional theories

There are three major theories explaining how people learn and so how (e-)learning pedagogies and practices are built: behaviourism, cognitivism and (social) constructivism (Ravenscroft, 2011; Siemens, 2005). Table 33. 2 summarizes the major tenets and influences of these theories on knowledge and learning processes. Each of these theories holds a different tenet in terms of what is knowledge and how it is created, and so it focuses on different learning processes and aspects that have to be designed in order to create and acquire knowledge (Sigala, 2004). In this vein, each theory has resulted in a different use of technologies and their affordances for supporting their acclaimed learning processes (Laurillard, 2009).

However, these three learning theories are based on the assumption that knowledge is an objective or a state that is attainable through either reasoning or experiences. Moreover, another central tenet of these learning theories is that learning occurs inside a person. Even social constructivism promotes the principality of the individual in internalizing and interpreting knowledge and learning. Hence, these theories do not address learning that occurs outside people (i.e. learning that is stored and manipulated by technology tools) and learning that is conducted with the support of and within social networks. For example, recent studies have shown that the Internet has become a primary form of external transactive memory (Sparrow et al., 2011) and an external repository of collective memory (Sigala, 2013) whereby people collectively store interpreted/annotated information outside themselves. Searching and accessing this external memory significantly changes the way people remember, access, make meaning out of information and so learn. Actually, Sparrow et al.'s (2011) argument that people have become symbiotic with computer tools and are growing into interconnected systems with social communities substantially highlights that learning cannot anymore be considered as an exclusively internal cognitive process.

Thus, the ignorance of these previous issues significantly limits the power of the three traditional theories to explain how social technologies have transformed the way in which learning processes are currently taking place. These learning theories and practices may have been sufficient in the past, whereby knowledge was scarce, instructors had to transmit it to learners and the latter had to demonstrate that they had achieved learning through assessments. However, in the continuously evolving knowledge ecology, the context is different (Table 33.1). As the knowledge is non-ending, interconnected, dynamic as well as stored, shared and co-created ad hoc within social networks and through participatory technology tools, new learning theories are required to explain how learning processes are taking place, which in turn will inform how to design teaching and learning practices that can effectively exploit the new technologies.

New theories

Siemens (2005) proposed connectivism as a new pedagogical theory to address the new context and educational affordances of social media. Connectivism builds upon social constructivism and the principles of chaos, network, complexity and self-organization theories. Table 33.3 summarizes the major principles of connectivism, and the following discussion reviews connectivism based on the dimensions that were also used to evaluate the traditional theories (Table 33.2). Analytically, connectivism makes the assumption that no one isolated individual can know enough to make good decisions. This is based on the tenet that knowledge is continually

Table 33.2 Learning theories: tenets and influences on (e-)learning pedagogies (learning processes and methods)

Tenets about knowledge	Tenets about learning processes	Aspect of learning process that is important	Learning/teaching methods and use of technology to support them
Behaviourism			
• objectivism: reality is external to people and is objective • knowledge as an object external to the people • thus, knowledge is gained by memorizing content	• since knowledge is objective and external to the learner, the learning process is the act of transmitting information and internalizing knowledge • learners are empty vessels that need to be filled with knowledge	the organization and the presentation of the content of instruction (i.e. knowledge as object to be delivered)	*Instructionism learning/teaching methods* • instructor fully responsible for transferring knowledge and learning processes • teaching and learning processes aim to encourage the desired behaviour (i.e. the acquisition of specified learning outcomes) by rewarding or reinforcing it. • learners receive known information from the instructor in a lecture format *Use of technology* • the use of presentational and testing capabilities of technology for presenting/visualizing knowledge and for testing the acquisition of knowledge • technology is used for testing predictable learning, e.g. through multiple-choice questions, give right/wrong feedback
Cognitivism			
• pragmatism: reality is interpreted • knowledge is negotiated through experience and thinking, but knowledge still external to the learner • knowledge is gained through experiences	• the learning process is an act of internalizing knowledge through simulated experiences (learning by doing) • learning is viewed as a process of inputs, managed in short-term memory, and coded for long-term recall (i.e. a computer information processing model by processing inputs to produce outputs)	construction of a model or object as an aspect of learning	*Constructionism (Piaget, 1977) teaching methods* • instructors create environments or scenarios demonstrating the application of knowledge, that enable learners to try and understand knowledge in order to facilitate their knowledge understanding and internalization (i.e. only internal cognitive processes of reflection) *Use of technology* • making use of the programmable, simulation and modelling properties of technologies

Constructivism

- interpretivism: reality is internal and subjective
- knowledge is constructed
- knowledge is created when learners actively participate in meaning making
- reality is also influenced by contextual and situational factors
- knowledge is socially determined
- knowledge is co-created in collaborative meaning-making processes whereby people negotiate and debate knowledge/concepts

- the learning process is an act of knowledge creation when learners attempt to understand their experiences, and then assimilate and/or accommodate this knowledge into their already existing worldview
- learning is very personal and each learner does not respond to stimulus in the same way (as the behaviourists suggest)
- learning processes as an act of social constructivism (combination of Piaget and Vygotsky approaches) whereby individuals not only learn from their experiences, but also construct knowledge collaboratively with others
- active learning, 'learning is in the doing': learners construct their own knowledge, individually but also in a social context

Groupwork and group discussions

- use of technologies' simulated capabilities (e.g. simulations, educational games, trial-and-error exercises) to internalize and assimilate knowledge

Socio-cultural learning (Vygotsky, 1978) and collaborative learning or social constructionism (Piaget and Vygotsky approaches for combining the social and construction elements of the learning process)

- learners are active participants in learning processes who construct knowledge based on their existing understanding as well as on their interactions with peers and the instructor
- learners have to share and discuss the actions they take and the knowledge they gain in the practice environment. Then learners have to share their reflections and interpretations of what happened within their practice
- the instructor is not wholly responsible for student learning
- the instructor should act as a facilitator, creating a positive environment that encourages collaborative learning and construction/creation of knowledge

Use of technology

- making use of the communication, networking and collaborative aspects of technologies for enabling and fostering collaborative learning processes and discussions/communication amongst learners and the instructors

Sources: Arguments compiled from Laurillard (2009), Ravenscroft (2011), Driscoll (2000) and Siemens (2005).

Table 33.3 The principles of connectivism

• Learning and knowledge rests in diversity of opinions.
• Learning is a process of connecting specialized nodes or information sources.
• Learning may reside in non-human appliances.
• Capacity to know more is more critical than what is currently known.
• Nurturing and maintaining connections is needed to facilitate continual learning.
• Ability to see connections between fields, ideas and concepts is a core skill.
• Currency (accurate, up-to-date knowledge) is the intent of all connectivist learning activities.
• Decision-making is itself a learning process. Choosing what to learn and the meaning of incoming information is seen through the lens of a shifting reality. While there is a right answer now, it may be wrong tomorrow due to alterations in the information climate affecting the decision.

Source: Siemens (2005).

evolving and growing, and so knowledge is acquired by continually trying to acquire new information by being able to distinguish between important and unimportant information. Moreover, as decisions are based on rapidly altering foundations, the ability to recognize when new information alters the landscape based on decisions made yesterday is also critical. Thus, according to connectivism, being able to rapidly find and evaluate the abundant knowledge that is found outside is more important than what one currently knows. Individuals learn from the diverse knowledge contained within other individuals and their networks, and they also contribute their own knowledge to a collective understanding. In this vein, learning is defined as actionable knowledge, and the learning processes occur within nebulous environments of shifting core elements – not entirely under the control of the individual. In other words, connectivism recognizes that: learning can reside outside ourselves (within an organization, a social community or a database); and learning processes are focused on connecting specialized information sets, and the connections that enable us to learn are more important than our current state of knowing. Thus, based on connectivism, the most important aspects of the learning processes are: the networks and their building as well as the critical thinking about the information learners get from their network.

As a learning theory, connectivism addresses many of the previously analysed challenges in education related to knowledge, learning processes, social networks and informal learning, knowledge management activities and literacy competencies currently required for getting a job. Knowledge that resides in a database needs to be connected with the right people in the right context in order to be classified as learning. Behaviourism, cognitivism and constructivism do not attempt to address the challenges of knowledge management and sharing as a critical part of learning processes. However, in a knowledge economy, the use of social media for managing and utilizing information flows is a key learning activity enabling learners to co-construct knowledge and to learn (Sigala & Chalkiti, 2014). According to connectivism, personal knowledge comprises a network, which feeds back into the network, and then continues to provide learning to individuals. This cycle of knowledge development (with iterative information flows between people and networks) allows learners to continually update their knowledge through the connections they have formed. In this vein, the network (pipe/infrastructure) is more important than the content within the network (oil). As the aim of any learning theory is to actuate knowledge at the point of application, connectivism aims to build the learners' capabilities that would enable them to plug into information sources to meet their ad hoc requirements. As knowledge continues to grow and evolve, access to what is needed is more important than what the learner currently possesses. Hence, the current knowledge of graduates is less important than their ability to exploit the social networks to support their learning. Consequently, connectivism provides a learning model that considers the transformations in the society and it recognizes that learning is not only an internal, individualistic activity.

Laurillard (2009) has provided another learning theory called conversational learning that builds upon social–constructivism and connectivism and further expands the latter, as it provides a learning model explaining how people learn and co-create knowledge when interacting within social networks. Thus, conversational learning shifts the focus in terms of the important aspect of influencing the learning processes from building and accessing networks to the exploitation of networks through the development of dialogues and interactions. In other words, interactions are perceived as the most important component of learning experiences, and so conversational learning is a more qualitative approach explaining how learning occurs within networks.

Analytically, conversational theory builds on the work of Pask (1976) and perceives learning as a form of conversation; i.e. learning is described as a process of coming to know through conversations across multiple contexts, amongst people and personal interactive technologies (Laurillard, 2009). Thus, according to conversational learning, learning processes are built and occur by developing continual iterations of two dimensions: (1) between teachers and learners; and (2) between the two categories of information flows and exchanges, namely: (a) the discursive, articulating and discussing theory, ideas, concepts and forms of representation; and (b) the experiential, acting on the world, experimenting and practising on goal-oriented tasks. Both categories of information flows and exchanges are essential and there is a need of iterative interaction on both levels. This is because by connecting the two forms of interactions, it is possible to support adaptive and reflecting processes in learning: adaptive actions in the light of understanding and reflective on practice to inform theory or concept development.

For example, learners have to adapt their understanding of theories to develop their practices (e.g. projects, simulated exercises, decisions at work), but then, they should also reflect on the feedback and the result of their actions in order to adapt their understanding and application of theories. Similarly, instructors develop their learning processes according to their understanding of theories, but they also have to reflect on the results of their learning processes in order to learn how to better teach, articulate theories and/or amend and expand their understanding of theory and application. These represent two-way information flows in both categories of interactions taking place at the dimension of an individual (learner or instructor), and so represent internal cognitive processes. But interactions can also take place at the level of inter–individual exchanges as external learning processes. For example learners can read the understanding and/or the experience/practice of other learners, reflect on this content by commenting on it or by discussing it with others, and then use this feedback for adapting their understanding of theory. Thus, external learning processes occur via interactions taking place amongst the teacher, the learner and the learners' peers.

Cress & Kimmerle (2008) provided a better explanation of the conversational theory's arguments that learning is a conversational process occurring through internal and external adaptive and reflective interactions. By using wiki as an example, they described how collaborative technologies help knowledge creation and learning through an iterative process of both social/external and individual/internal cognitive processes. Wikis enable conversational learning through four forms of knowledge building (Cress & Kimmerle, 2008): internal assimilation, internal accommodation, external assimilation, external accommodation. Assimilation refers to understanding new information on the basis of existing knowledge and then integrates this information into existing knowledge (a quantitative approach to knowledge building). Accommodation refers to people's interactions with new information in a way that changes their knowledge to better understand the environment and its information (a qualitative approach to knowledge building).

Thus, based on conversational learning, learning is an active process of how an individual integrates encountered information with pre-existing knowledge and develops one's knowledge through social interactions in different dimensions. Conversational learning also suggests that the learning relies on the development of meaningful interactions between the learner and the theory/content, the practice and the other peers. Hence, conversational learning also addresses current transformational challenges, as it highlights that learning is not a simple reproduction of knowledge and skills, but it is rather a meaning-making process facilitated by social communications and discussions of theory and practice.

Extensions to the new theories

Conversational and connectivism learning theories can offer a better solution to current educational challenges, as they propose a paradigm shift from content learning to greater understanding of learning processes and knowledge creation, such as reflection and critical thinking. However, there are also some other approaches that can further enrich the arguments, implementation and benefits of these new learning theories.

Cooperative education is an old instructional method combining formal education with practical work experience (John et al., 1998). Cooperative education is being promoted again as an effective method for addressing the current challenges of the new economy (e.g. fluid and demanding workplaces, new technologies, the fast redundancy of knowledge and the need for continuous learning). However, the effectiveness of cooperative education had been undermined, as it is basically treated as a tool to provide work experience and to link theoretical knowledge with workplace application. However, as learning from experience is not automatic, cooperative education needs to strengthen its reflective component and to use a sound learning theory for informing the design of its effective learning processes (Wilson et al., 1996). Conversational learning can be an appropriate theory to design effective cooperative learning processes, as it does focus on the development of reflective and adaptive interactions between theory and practice for supporting learning. To ensure that cooperative education also supports the continuous improvement and update of curricula (Cates & Cedercreutz, 2008), conversational learning also suggests that interactions should be developed amongst learners, instructors and professionals. Connectivism theory highlights the importance of building networks for getting access to and co-creating knowledge, but it has not specifically stressed the need to build networks with industry professionals. Thus, cooperative education expands connectivism theory by showing how to provide learning opportunities beyond the classroom walls and by stressing the need for universities to establish formal partnerships with professionals. Moreover, the mutuality, conversations and interactions that can be developed amongst learners, instructor and professionals, can lead to the mutual development (called co-evolution) of each entity, which then constitutes the foundation of collaborative understanding and co-creation of knowledge (Luhmann, 1995). In other words, conversational, connectivism and cooperative education can significantly enrich the benefits of their implementation when they are integrated together.

In addition, the notions of developing interactions and exchanges amongst a network of actors in order to co-create knowledge and support mutual development are also compatible with the tenets of service-dominant logic (SDL) and value co-creation. According to SDL, instead of customers being viewed as consumers of value, they interact with firms, other customers and other stakeholders within an ecosystem for exchanging and integrating resources and creating value-in-use that aims for the mutual betterment of each entity of the system. SDL also highlights the need for actors to interact in order to create value-in-context, as value-in-use gets different meanings in different situations. Similarly, as learning is also perceived as an exchange and interactive knowledge-building process that occurs in various socio-contextual environments, the context can provide more opportunities for making connections to what is being learned (Lin & Tsai, 2012). Thus, interactions between learner and context can significantly influence the meaning-making processes and the co-creation of knowledge. In this vein, effective learning processes should aim to support interactions that do not only enable the co-creation of knowledge-in-use (i.e. cooperative learning) but also of knowledge-in-context. Consequently, conversational theory should be expanded to include interactions between learners, instructors, professionals but also context as well. For example, learners can develop better meaning-making processes when they explore and reflect not only on how a theory is applied in practice, but also why a theory may have different implications when applied in different contexts.

Social media and new learning theories

Affordances of social media for implementing the new learning theories

Social media afford many capabilities to support and enhance the implementation of new learning theories. Specifically, the participatory and communication capabilities of social media enable educators to develop learning activities that demand learners engage in rich discussions and reflective interactions. The networking capabilities of social media can maximize the full potential of connectivism learning, as it enables learners to identify and join various networks for expanding their learning opportunities and knowledge co-creation activities. Indeed, by using social networks for collecting, sharing, representing and discussing theories, experiences, ideas and opinions with others, the use of social media supports a conversational and connectivism pedagogy, which encourages learners to construct personal understandings in socially interactive and contextual environments (Lin & Tsai, 2012; Sigala, 2012). For example, discussion forums, wikis and weblogs, are conversational technologies enabling knowledge creation and sharing through (Sigala & Chalkiti, 2014): discussions; 'questions and answers' processes (discussion forums); collaborative editing (wikis); and/or storytelling (weblogs). Hence, social media expand the cognitive and knowledge creation abilities of an individual by enabling him/her to process knowledge beyond his/her own inner cognitive processes and to consider the contextual and social aspects of this knowledge. Research also shows that using social media enhances not only the functional (information processing), but also the socio-affective contextual aspects of learning processes (Sigala & Chalkiti, 2014). For example, wikis and blogs allow collaboration and relationship building amongst individuals, while tagging (i.e. the assignment of 'labels' to content for interpreting and categorizing information) enables the formation of social networks.

The affordances and the use of social media as pedagogical tools are widely argued: learning is made conversational through dialogues and shared activities (Sigala, 2013; Tess, 2013; Lin & Kelsey, 2009); social networks become the impetus for inquiry-based approaches, collaboration and the development of a 'research culture' (Kerawalla et al., 2009; Deed & Edwards, 2011; Top, 2012). Thus, as social media applications can promote active participation, dialogues, reflection, networking learning and personal meaning and knowledge co-construction, social media can critically support the design of learning processes and activities according to the tenets of connectivism and conversational learning theories (Ravenscroft, 2011; Lampe et al., 2011; Sigala, 2013; Dabbagh & Kitsantas, 2012).

An example of social media use for designing connectivism and conversational learning activities

To unlock the learning benefits of social media, the tenets of connectivism and conversational theories were followed in order to redesign the learning process and activities of a tourism course, so that the learners would be able to network and interact with others in order to: collect, share and discuss learning material; contribute to and negotiate a collective understanding of the topic, so that 'the community is the curriculum' (Lili, 2010); the learning process becomes a reflective, socio-contextual, experiential and network-building process that supports conversational learning; and the networks continually reinforce and challenge what students are learning (Wang et al., 2011).

Design of e-learning processes and activities

The e-learning activities were developed for enriching the teaching and learning processes of a course on 'Revenue Management in Hospitality' that is taught in a traditional classroom. The course is a compulsory module of the curriculum of an 'MBA in Tourism & Hospitality' provided by a university in Greece. The learning aims of the course included: the understanding of the principles and implementation of revenue management in the hospitality sector; the impact of information and communication technologies on revenue management; the impact of revenue management on firm performance, customer satisfaction and quality; identification of the future trends and challenges in revenue management theory and practice. The class consisted of 12 students, who have all completed a first degree in management and several of them also had professional experience (not all of them in the tourism industry).

According to connectivism, learning should lead to the creation of actionable knowledge that can assist students in decision-making. Hence, the learning processes of the course were designed to support the stages of the decision-making process that learners/staff have to go through for solving a real business problem, namely how to implement revenue management in a hotel and how to update the revenue management system and processes given the challenges occurring in the continuous changing internal and external environment of the hotel. A local hotel easily accessible from the university campus was identified for setting the context of the learning activity, and cooperation was established for allowing students to interview and interact with the hotel staff as well as to collect internal information through observations and field trips. Since knowledge changes very frequently, connectivism highlights the importance of using networks for distinguishing important and unimportant information and developing critical thinking. In this vein, the learning processes required students to network with professionals from the hotel and from other online practice communities that the students could find and with which they could liaise.

Conversational learning highlights the importance of developing dialogues amongst the entities of the learning systems and the development of adaptive and reflective interactions amongst practice and theory for developing understanding and new knowledge. To that end, the learning processes required students to always reflect between theory/concepts and practice/experience at all stages of their decision-making process. Students were also asked to join online communities and participate in dialogues with others in order to get access to others' experiences and understandings, which in turn can assist them with their own critical and analytical skills as well as knowledge development competencies (enable the interplay between internal and external cognitive processes, i.e. conversational learning). Thus, the focus of the learning processes was always to motivate and request students to participate in dialogues with others. To enable students to develop and support their dialogues, a wiki platform with online forum capability was developed for supporting the learning processes of the course. The wiki platform was based on the software provided by www.pbworks.com (2013, see details of the platform below). To enrich the dialogues and allow the students to get access to others' resources (i.e. experiences, knowledge, understandings, etc.) so that the dialogues could support adaptive and reflective interactions between theoretical concepts and industry experiences, students were advised and allowed to register any appropriate person identified from other professional networks to the wiki platform (by using the add user functionality and community of the wiki), so that they could also join the online community and contribute to the online dialogues.

Table 33.4 provides more details about the use of conversational and connectivism learning theories in informing the design of the learning processes and activities of the course. Table 33.4 also shows how social media were used for supporting and enriching these learning activities. The social media tools that were purposefully developed for this case included: a wiki (www.pbworks.com was used as it provides free wiki software services for educational purposes); and a channel created in www.vimeo.com (2013, a free tool for privately uploading, sharing and discussing videos amongst a network; privacy was required for proprietary reasons related to the hotel participating in the learning activity). Figures 33.1, 33.2 and 33.3 describe how the functionality of the selected wiki platform supports the development of conversational and connectivism learning processes. Table 33.4 also demonstrates how these social media were integrated within the learning activities for supporting conversational and collaborative knowledge management processes (i.e. information collection, discussion, negotiations and synthesis) and so enabling learners to enhance their understanding, learning and knowledge (co)-creation abilities (Sigala & Chalkiti, 2014). To reduce the students' cognitive load and stress related to the use of the social media and allow them more time and cognitive efforts to concentrate on the learning processes (Sigala, 2013), a lecture was organized at the beginning of the semester (week 2) for explaining to them the functionality and the user interface of these tools.

Design of the assessment strategy

The success of any collaborative type of learning depends on the learners' level of participation with the learning activities and their type of technologies use (Sigala, 2004, 2013). Thus, to ensure and instil student participation and effective use of technologies, the course assessment was linked to the design of the learning processes (Sigala, 2005). The design of the course evaluation included two elements: (a) four collaborative reports (20 per cent of the individual course mark) that were co-written in the four wikipages as a result of the activities occurring during the four stages of the decision-making process; and (b) a reflective report submitted by each student (30 per cent of the individual course mark) that had to include various examples of the student's contributions in the online learning environment. The assessment of the four collaborative reports and their contribution to the final individual mark aimed to nurture a culture of team spirit and collaboration as well as motivate students to participate in the collaborative editing of the reports (i.e. to ensure that students develop their knowledge co-creation skills). The reflective report required from each student had two aims: (a) to encourage students to reflect on their own learning processes (i.e. better show them how-to-learn); and (b) to demonstrate to students how to effectively engage in the e-learning activities in order to support their learning. In other words, the reflective report also acted as a scaffolding tool for explaining to students what was expected from them and how to effectively contribute to the collaborative learning process. To that end, the reflective report required students to provide five examples

Table 33.4 Implementing conversational and connectivism learning: the design of learning processes for teaching the course 'Revenue Management in Hospitality'

Decision-making process	Learning process	Teaching/learning activity supported by social media
Problem definition	Aim: the development of conversations and interactions amongst learners, hotel staff and the educator for developing a common understanding of the problem	• Co-agree on the identification of hotel staff involved in revenue management and the establishment of liaisons with them • Organization of a hotel visit for interviewing and talking with key staff. Organization of front and back of the house tours for observations (information collection) • Interviews are recorded and uploaded on vimeo.com for sharing them amongst learners and hotel staff (information sharing) • A wikipage is created for sharing the link to the online interviews videos, so everyone can watch at their convenience • Online recorded videos are discussed and commented online by using the forum functionality of the wikipage (information discussion, debates) • The discussions and the conclusions of the interviews and discussions around them had to be summarized in a final co-agreed report by co-writing content in a wikipage. Everyone was able to contribute and edit content on the wikipage (creation of new knowledge by synthesizing information and discussions)
Identification formulation of solutions	Aim: the development of conversations and interactions amongst learners, hotel staff and the educator for brainstorming, generating and formulating appropriate solutions	• Another wikipage was created for supporting this learning activity • Users had to use the forum function for discussing and sharing ideas for possible solutions (information collection and discussion) • The wikipage was used for collaboratively developing a document that included and presented each idea, as the latter was formulated and agreed after the deliberation of the discussions (co-creation of knowledge by synthesizing debated knowledge)
Evaluation and selection of solution	Aim: the development of conversations and interactions amongst learners, hotel staff and the educator for identifying criteria for evaluating the alternative solutions and selecting the most appropriate	• A wikipage was created for enabling users to discuss and develop ideas about this third activity • Users had to use the forum function for discussing and sharing ideas about the criteria that had to be used for evaluating potential problem solutions (information collection and discussion) • The wikipage was used for collaboratively developing a document that included the methodology and rational for identifying the most appropriate idea (i.e. criteria used, evaluation and ranking of ideas) (co-creation of knowledge by synthesizing debated knowledge)

Implemen-tation of the solution	Aim: the development of conversations and interactions amongst learners, hotel staff and the educator for developing a business plan to implement the solution	• Another wikipage was created and dedicated to support the discussions and the content development for completing this learning activity • Users had to use the forum function of this wikipage for discussing and sharing ideas about the required actions and success factors of this business plan (information collection and discussion) • The wikipage was used for collaboratively developing a document that presented the commonly agreed business plan for implementing the solution (co-creation of knowledge by synthesizing debated knowledge)

Students were given three weeks to complete each stage of the decision-making process (i.e. the discussions and the co-writing of the report in the wikipage). So, the learning activity covered the whole period of the semester (13 weeks)

The following guidelines were given to the students in order to guide and help them in conducting the online activities:

For searching and collecting information:
− use the electronic sources of the university library for identifying appropriate information
− use content networks (e.g. YouTube, LinkedIn and Flickr) in order to identify information related to the problem and/or your information needs
− use social networks to identify and discuss with subject experts about the concepts that need to be analysed
− use social networks to remain updated and alerted about new information, e.g. follow experts, subscribe to blogs and professional networks
− before 'following' a person or a 'community/association' profile in a social network or blog, try to understand who this person/profile is, what are his/her aims, interests, context, etc. by using information provided on the profile, user-generated content, etc.

For reflecting, discussing and negotiating information in the forum:
− share identified and useful information (and the sources of this information) with your colleagues
− when contributing information:
− share your understanding of it
− explain how this information compares with existing knowledge and discussions and what extra value it adds to the discussions
− consider whether this information needs revising and/or updating
− explain how this information can be useful/applicable or related to the task problem
− alert others of this new post/contribution and invite them to post their comments and suggestions about it
− if necessary and appropriate invite subject experts identified in other networks to join and contribute to your wiki discussions
− when commenting on posts by others you should consider whether the argument is valid or not and/or if it should be revised and how by citing and directing to other useful and additional resources

For contributing to the co-writing of the report at the wikipage:
− look at forum discussions for any contribution showing agreement and/or summary of online debates
− identify the major issues discussed in every thread in order to synthesize and consolidate discussions
− compare discussions across threads to see if there are any overlapping or related discussions
− look at and investigate (compare–contrast) the different versions of the wiki (i.e. who and what contributed when) in order to understand how others learn and learn from them.

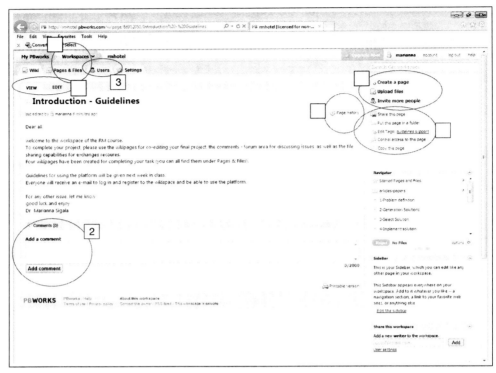

1 *Co-creation of content functionality:* students are able to create wikipages, edit/view wikipages, review the page history (who contributed/edited when and what)
2 *Communication – discussions:* a forum section for each wikipage where users can contribute comments for discussing the content of the wikipage; send alerts to users for changes/edit to specific wikipages/files and invite them to contribute/respond
3 *Networking:* user community; user profile information; users can invite others to join and access the wiki platform; restrict or permit access to wikipages to users
4 *Content sharing, categorization and storing:* sharing of files; creation of folders; tags for defining shared files and wikipages.

Figure 33.1 Functionality of the wiki

of their own online contributions for each of the three categories of interactions that they had developed with networks and the social media. Table 33.5 gives more details about the theoretical justification and types of these interactions.

New competencies and skills supported by the learning processes

The learning processes and the use of social media resulted in the development of a learner-centred education system, as they enabled the creation of personal and social learning spaces. The process enabled the learners to take charge of their own learning, while the community became the curriculum. Indeed, learners, industry professionals, subject experts and the educator were enabled to negotiate and define the problem as well as to determine the types of resources and the sources from where they could be acquired for discussing and co-developing an appropriate business solution. In this vein, the learning process enabled students to develop and enhance the following competencies and skills:

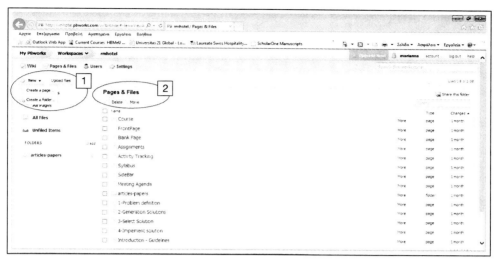

1 Creation of wiki-pages or folders in which files can be stored
2 List of wikipages and files: users can delete or move files and folders.

Figure 33.2 Functionality of wiki for sharing files and creating wikipages

- Self-regulation (Dabbagh & Kitsantas, 2012): ability to set goals and regulate own learning
- Meta-cognitive skills (Salovaara, 2005): obtaining more knowledge of your own cognition (i.e. what a person knows or does not know and his/her understanding of concepts) and regulation of own cognition (planning, monitoring and evaluating the acquisition/ development of knowledge, i.e. the achievement of learning outcomes)
- Online communication and social skills (Sigala, 2007, 2013)
- Social cognitive skills (Schmidt, 2007): such as self-presentation skills, relatedness (sense of being a part of the activity) and acceptance (social approval)
- Transferable and new information literacy skills (Johnson, 2007; Bobish, 2010; Piranec & Zorica, 2010) such as:
  - ability to decide when and why one might want to access information from specific types of sources
  - ability to investigate and understand the context in which information sources are produced and discussed
  - ability to form networks for accessing information
  - ability to evaluate information by critically understanding and assessing the social origins of information and the context in which it was produced
  - ability to define and articulate the type of information needs depending on the problem/context
  - ability to present and communicate own knowledge/arguments
  - ability to evaluate information and its sources critically, compare it with pre-existing knowledge, identify value-added knowledge and incorporate the selected information into the person's own or collaborative knowledge system
  - ability to understand and interpret the information through discourse with other individuals, subject-area experts and/or professionals
  - ability to apply knowledge to practice or to amend theory based on practical experience

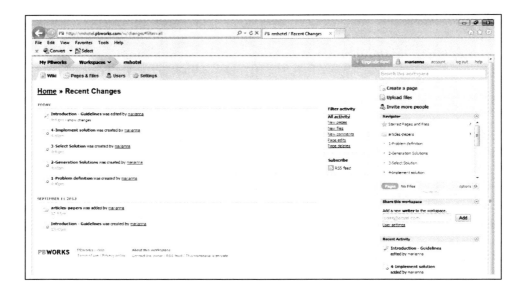

The platform tracks and publishes changes conducted on the online content. Each time a user logs in, he/she can view recent changes and/or search for changes conducted by user and for different types of content, e.g. comment, wikipage, file, etc. An RSS* (Real Simple Syndication) functionality is also available, so users can register to receive automated RSS feeds. Alerts and search facilities for keeping users updated to changes of content are important, as they support users to participate in communication and dialogues.

Note
*RSS enables users to be automatically alerted to any new content published on a website. The RSS software automatically sends news feeds to the users. Consequently, the user does not have to log into the website all the time to check for updates; when updates occur, the user is automatically informed and then he/she can visit the website to check updates.

Figure 33.3 Activity tracking capability

- ability to continually assess the information needs and adjust the information acquisition strategy
- Increased creativity and memory skills: Sparrow *et al.* (2011) found that people spend more cognitive efforts and memory resources for remembering where the information is stored than for remembering the substance of the information itself; as technology and networks enable people to easily find, externally store and locate information, then the use of technology frees up cognitive resources which empower people to increase their creativity and knowledge creation capabilities (Sparrow *et al.*, 2011).

However, as the above mentioned claims are based on previous studies and theoretical/ conceptual justifications, future research should be directed at testing, validating and refining the impacts of social media enabled learning processes on students' skills and capabilities.

Conclusions

Numerous changes and challenges are taking place in our current educational and workplace environment. The way people learn, the lifetime and nature of knowledge as well as the

Table 33.5 Design of the reflective report as a scaffolding tool

Knowledge management processes supported by social media for enabling learning and knowledge creation (e.g. Sigala & Chalkiti, 2014)	Interactions enabled by the social media in e-learning environments (Dabbagh & Reo, 2011; Dabbagh & Kitsantas, 2012)	Student guidelines for writing the reflective report: please provide 5 examples of your own contributions in the wiki that demonstrate (developed by the author/lecturer for the purposes of the course based on previous theory):
Information collection	Personal information management for information collection and understanding	• search strategies and methods used for information collection (including the sources of information) • contribution of new value-added information to the existing collective knowledge • your interpretation/understanding/use of this information • your use of this information for reflecting and adapting your understanding
Information sharing and discussions	Social interaction and collaboration	Your response/comment to information/opinion expressed by others that also explains the reasons/arguments of your agreement/disagreement/revising and/or appropriateness of the others' opinion
Knowledge (co)-creation	Information aggregation and management	Your own contributions to the wikipages reflecting: • entries of new content contributed by you • editing of text that was contributed by others

competencies required by graduates in order to survive in the new fluid environment have been totally transformed. After critically reviewing the tenets of the traditional learning theories, the chapter has argued their limitations to deal with these new challenges. To address this problem, the chapter analysed the principles and expanded the practice of two new theories – namely connectivism and conversational learning – whose adoption can enable learners to develop new information literacy and soft collaboration and communication skills. The implementation and the learning benefits of these two new theories are fully developed and enriched nowadays by the use of social media, since the social media afford numerous possibilities for mass communication, networking and collaboration.

To better demonstrate the affordances of social media to redesign learning that can enrich learning processes and outcomes, the chapter has also analysed the design of the learning activities and the assessment strategy of a tourism course that has adopted the tenets of the conversational and connectivism theories in order to enable learners to achieve better learning and cognitive abilities and competencies. Preliminary findings from other related studies confirm that such conversational and networking learning processes can significantly improve learners' abilities and competencies. Hence, the case study highlights the need for tourism and hospitality education to transform its learning pedagogies by opening up its learning ecosystems to include professionals and social networks who possess important resources (i.e. experiences, knowledge) that can enrich and facilitate the co-creation of knowledge.

References

Attwell, G. (2007). 'The Personal Learning Environments: the future of eLearning?'. *eLearning Papers*, 2(1), 1–8.

Bobish, G. (2010). 'Participation and Pedagogy: connecting the social web to ACRL learning outcomes'. *Journal of Academic Librarianship*, 37(1), 54–63.

Cates, C., & Cedercreutz, K. (2008). *Leveraging Cooperative Education to Guide Curricular Innovation. The development of a corporate feedback system for continuous improvement*. Cincinnati, OH: Center for Cooperative Education Research and Innovation.

Conole, G., & Alevizou, P. (2010). *A Literature Review of the Use of Web 2.0 Tools in Higher Education*. Technical report commissioned by the Higher Education Academy. Milton Keynes: Open University.

Cress, U., & Kimmerle, J. (2008). 'A Systemic and Cognitive View on Collaborative Knowledge Building with Wikis'. *Computer-Supported Collaborative Learning*, 3, 105–22.

Dabbagh, N., & Reo, R. (2011). 'Impact of Web 2.0 on Higher Education'. In D. Surry, R. Gray Jr., & J. Stefurak (Eds.), *Technology Integration in Higher Education: social and organizational aspects* (pp. 174–87). Hershey, PA: Information Science Reference.

Dabbagh, N., & Kitsantas, A. (2012). 'Personal Learning Environments, Social Media, and Self-Regulated Learning: a natural formula for connecting formal and informal learning', *The Internet and Higher Education*, 15(1), 3–8.

Deed, C., & Edwards, A. (2011). 'Unrestricted Student Blogging: implications for active learning in a virtual text-based environment'. *Active Learning in Higher Education*, 12(1), 11–21.

Deng, L., & Yuen, A. H. K. (2011). 'Towards a Framework for Educational Affordances of Blogs'. *Computers & Education*, 56(2), 441–51.

Driscoll, M. (2000). *Psychology of Learning for Instruction*. Needham Heights, MA: Allyn & Bacon.

Farkas, M. (2012). 'Participatory Technologies, Pedagogy 2.0 and Information Literacy'. *Library Hi Tech*, 30(1). 82–94.

Hall, R. (2009). 'Towards a Fusion of Formal and Informal Learning Environments: the impact of the read/write web'. *Electronic Journal of e-Learning*, 7(1), 29–40.

Huang, T. C., Huang, Y. M., & Yu, F. Y. (2011). 'Cooperative Weblog Learning in Higher Education: its facilitating effects on social interaction, time lag, and cognitive load'. *Educational Technology & Society*, 14(1), 95–106.

John, J. E. A., Doherty, D. J., & Nichols, R. M. (1998). 'Challenges and Opportunities for Cooperative Education'. *Journal of Cooperative Education*, 33(2), 10–16.

Johnson, W. (2007). 'The Application of Learning Theory to Information Literacy'. *College & Undergraduate Libraries*, 14(4), 103–20.

Kalargyrou, V., & Woods, R. H. (2011). 'Wanted: training competencies for the twenty-first century'. *International Journal of Contemporary Hospitality Management*, 23(3), 361–76.

Kerawalla, L., Minocha, S., Kirkup, G., & Conole, G. (2009). 'An Empirically Grounded Framework to Guide Blogging in Higher Education'. *Journal of Computer Assisted Learning*, 25(1), 31–42.

King, S., Greidanus, E., Carbonaro, M., Drummond, J., & Patterson, S. (2009). 'Merging Social Networking Environments and Formal Learning Environments to Support and Facilitate Interprofessional Instruction'. *Medical Education Online*, 14(1), 5–12.

Lampe, C., Wohn, D. Y., Vitak, J., Ellison, N., & Wash, R. (2011). 'Student Use of Facebook for Organising Collaborative Classroom Activities'. *Computer-Supported Collaborative Learning*, 6, 329–47.

Laurillard, D. (2009). 'The Pedagogical Challenges to Collaborative Technologies'. *Computer-Supported Collaborative Learning*, 4, 5–20.

Lili, L. (2010). 'Web 2.0 Integration in Information Literacy Instruction: an overview'. *Journal of Academic Librarianship*, 36(1), 37.

Lin, C. C., & Tsai, C. C. (2012). 'Participatory Learning through Behavioural and Cognitive Engagements in an Online Collective Information Searching Activity'. *Computer-Supported Collaborative Learning*, 7, 543–66.

Lin, H., & Kelsey, K. D. (2009). 'Building a Networked Environment in Wikis: the evolving phases of collaborative learning in a wikibook project'. *Journal of Educational Computing Research*, 40(2), 145–69.

Luhmann, N., (1995). *Social Systems*. Stanford, CA: Stanford University Press.

Pask, G. (1976). *Conversation Theory: applications in education and epistemology* Amsterdam: Elsevier.

Pbworks.com (Accessed 10 August, 2013).

Piaget, J. (1977). *The Development of Thought: equilibration of cognitive structures*. New York: Viking.

Piranec, S., & Zorica, M. B. (2010). 'Information Literacy 2.0: hype or discourse refinement?'. *Journal of Documentation*, 66(1), 140–53.

Ravenscroft, A. (2011). 'Dialogue and Connectivism: a new approach to understanding and promoting dialogue-rich networked learning'. *International Review of Research in Open and Distance Learning*, 12(3), 139–60.

Salovaara, H. (2005). 'An Exploration of Students' Strategy Use in Inquiry-Based Computer-Supported Collaborative Learning'. *Journal of Computer Assisted Learning*, 21, 39–52.

Schmidt, J. (2007). 'Social Software: facilitating information-, identity- and relationship management'. In T. N. Burg & J. Schmidt (Eds.), *BlogTalks reloaded: Social software research & cases* (pp. 31–49). Norderstedt, Germany: Books on Demand.

Siemens, G. (2005). 'Connectivism: a learning theory for the digital age'. *International Journal of Instructional Technology and Distance Learning*, 2(1), 3–10.

Sigala, M. (2004). 'Investigating the Factors Determining e-Learning Effectiveness in Tourism and Hospitality Education'. *Journal of Hospitality & Tourism Education*, 16(2), 11–21.

Sigala, M. (2005). 'e-Learning and e-Assessment Pedagogy'. In D. Airey & J. Tribe (Eds.), *An International Handbook of Tourism Education* (pp. 367–81). Oxford: Elsevier Science.

Sigala, M. (2007). 'Integrating Web 2.0 in e-Learning Environments: a socio-technical approach'. *International Journal of Knowledge and Learning*, 3(6), 628–48.

Sigala, M. (2012). 'Investigating the Role and Impact of Geovisualisation and Geocollaborative Portals on Collaborative e-Learning in Tourism Education'. *Journal of Hospitality, Leisure, Sports & Tourism Education*, 11, 50–66.

Sigala, M. (2013). 'Using and Measuring the Impacts of Geovisualisation on Tourism Education: the case of teaching a service management course'. *Journal of Hospitality, Leisure, Sports & Tourism Education*, 12, 85–98.

Sigala, M., & Chalkiti, K. (2014). 'Investigating the Exploitation of Web 2.0 for Knowledge Management in the Greek Tourism Industry: an utilisation–importance analysis'. *Computers in Human Behavior*, 30, 800–12.

Sigala, M., Christou, E., & Gretzel, U. (2012). *Web 2.0 in Travel, Tourism and Hospitality: theory, practice and cases*. Aldershot: Ashgate Publishers.

Sim, J. W. S., & Hew, K. F. (2010). 'The Use of Weblogs in Higher Education Settings: a review of empirical research'. *Educational Research Review*, 5(2), 151–63.

Sparrow, B, Liu, J., & Wegner, D. (2011). 'Google Effects on Memory: cognitive consequences of having information at our fingertips'. *Science*, 333(6043), 776–8.

Tess, P. (2013). 'The Role of Social Media in Higher Education Classes (real and virtual) – a literature review'. *Computers in Human Behavior*, 29(5), 60–8.

Testa, M. R., & Sipe, L. (2011). 'Service-Leadership Competencies for Hospitality and Tourism Management'. *International Journal of Hospitality Management*, 31(3), 648–58.

Top, E. (2012). 'Blogging as a Social Medium in Undergraduate Courses: sense of community best predictor of perceived learning'. *The Internet and Higher Education*, 15(1), 24–8.

Vimeo.com (Accessed 10 August 2013).

Vygotsky, L. S. (1978). *Mind in Society: the development of higher psychological processes*. Cambridge, MA: Harvard University Press.

Wang, Q., Woo, H. L., Quek, C. L., Yang, Y., & Liu, M. (2011). 'Using the Facebook Group as a Learning Management System: an exploratory study'. *British Journal of Educational Technology*, 43(3), 428–38.

Wilson, J. M., Stull, W. A., & Vinsonhaler, J. (1996). 'Rethinking Cooperative Education'. *Journal of Cooperative Education*, 31(2–3), 154–65.

34

Engaging students

Student-led planning of tourism and hospitality education – the use of wikis to enhance student learning

Mandy Talbot and Carl Cater

School of Management and Business, Aberystwyth University, Wales, UK

Introduction: learning context

In order to develop students that can succeed as effective planners and managers in the area of tourism, Tribe (2002) advocates the need to develop 'Philosophic Practitioners'. This requires that the tourism curriculum should develop both the transferable skills of students to prepare them to enter the tourism sector as well as their skills in critical thinking and reflective practice in order that they may effectively deal with the challenges presented by the industry. Students need to be provided with meaningful learning opportunities that draw on real-world examples if they are to develop these skills. Student-led learning activities can provide such opportunities. This chapter examines how using wikis as a coursework platform in a tourism management module has provided such learning opportunities for students.

Constructivist theory highlights that meaning is gained through active learning where students are given the opportunity to apply cognitive structures learnt in the classroom to real-world scenarios and construct their own knowledge (Bruner, 1990). Constructivist theory also highlights that active learning is dependent on creating a relevant context for learning activities. As such, the role of the instructor is not to provide the learning itself but to provide a context in which such learning can occur (West & West, 2009). This means that the instructor acts as a facilitator for the learning activity by setting the task goals, creating a supportive learning environment and ensuring that students have the adequate cognitive and practical skills to complete the task successfully. Such a setting can facilitate student-led learning.

The real-world workplace often requires that tourism practitioners work collaboratively to achieve their goals. Collaborative learning experiences not only provide students with the opportunity to develop their group work skills but can also improve their learning. Johnson *et al.* (2008) highlight that small groups of students working collectively on a task maximize both their own and each other's learning.

Learning environments have changed dramatically with the evolution of online technologies. Web 2.0 tools such as blogs, wikis, social networking software, media sharing and others have provided many new opportunities for online interaction, collaboration and learning (West & West, 2009). These tools provide a new age of participation enabling participants to create and collaborate rather than passively read (West & West, 2009). As such, the tools are highly suited to student-led, group learning activities in higher education. However, selecting the right tool should be based on the educational goal in mind rather than the desire to use the technology.

The tool examined in this case study is the wiki. The term means a collection of web pages that are immediate and live (West & West, 2009). A wiki is an online collaborative writing tool to which anyone, with access to the site, can add and edit content. They were designed to help groups collaborate, share and build online content together (Richardson, 2006). Wikis can also provide opportunities for interaction with people from outside the immediate group creating the wiki site. For example some wiki formats (e.g. Campus Pack) provide comment boxes for visitors to the wiki, enabling online discussion.

The use of wikis in higher education

While the use of wikis is relatively new to academia they are increasingly being used in a variety of teaching and learning scenarios, including: group work projects, collaborative writing activities and distance learning. Comprehensive ideas for the use of wikis can be found in West and West (2009) and Gokcearslan and Ozcan (2011).

Parker and Chao (2007) highlight that the use of wikis in the classroom brings together two key learning paradigms: the collaborative learning paradigm and the constructivist paradigm. They highlight that the creation of wikis develops the students' ability to collaborate and collectively create knowledge rather than just absorb it. Benckendorff's (2009) study found that a sense of audience played an important role for students in constructing meaningful content on the wiki site and it found that students relied on each other for feedback rather than relying on the teacher. Benckendorff's (2009) study also found that students enjoyed looking at each other's sites.

Various authors have highlighted that students may not be familiar with the use of Web 2.0 for educational purposes and need support developing both their IT skills and online group work skills. Benckendorff's (2009) study found that while wiki packages are designed to be 'easy to use' enabling students to focus on the task of collaboratively creating content (rather than learning about new IT technology), that a small group of students still struggled with the technological aspects of the task. Kennedy *et al.* (2008) found that while students were familiar with social media for personal use, 81.6 per cent of students had not used a wiki prior to entering higher education.

It is the instructor's role to facilitate effective online student learning (West & West, 2009). Salmon (2000) highlights how instructors can effectively facilitate student online learning in her 'Five Step Model for E-learning Activities', which shows the different stages of progression and intensity of interaction between online students as their work develops. In summary these stages include: familiarizing students with the wiki technology; developing trust between students through short interactive e-activities; providing opportunities for students to share information; providing opportunities for students to collaboratively create knowledge; and encouraging students to take ownership of their own learning and provide support to others.

If wiki learning projects are well designed they can allows students to develop a wide range of skills. For example Bruns and Humphreys (2005) found these skills to include: technical literacy, creative collaboration, consensus building, web page content creation and communication.

The case study

This chapter provides a case study of a student-led, collaborative learning project using wikis on the second-year, bachelor degree module: International Tourism Development. The module was taught on campus. The module coursework required students to work in small groups to identify and evaluate the tourism development strategies that were being followed in given tourist destinations and to compare these with approaches being taken elsewhere. Due to the collaborative and interactive nature of the assignment the most suitable web tool was the wiki.

The overall aim of the wiki intervention detailed in this chapter was to provide a student-led learning experience that would provide more opportunity for student collaboration and interaction, encourage the use of critical/higher order thinking skills (Bloom, 1956) and improve the quality of students' work.

This chapter aims to add to wiki literature in three main ways:

- By highlighting factors that need to be considered when setting up a wiki project in order to enable students to successfully complete the task.
- By specifically examining how students collaborate in the creation of their wikis and how they interact between sites.
- By examining the impact that the wiki project has on student learning.

These aims are explored by examining the use of wikis in the International Tourism Development module.

Module introduction

This section outlines the course format and coursework prior to the introduction of the wiki project. The module addressed both the conceptual and practical nature of tourism development and aimed to enable students to identify and evaluate tourism development strategies in a range of countries. The module also aimed to develop students' vocational skills in the areas of: making presentations, PowerPoint and group work. The coursework required students to work in small groups to address the following aims:

- Identify and evaluate the tourism development strategies that were being followed in a given tourist destination.
- Draw conclusions about the possible future direction of the destination.
- Compare and contrast the tourism development approaches of their destination with those in other countries.

Students undertook the exercise by creating and delivering a group PowerPoint presentation of 15 minutes to the class, with a further 10 minutes for questions. A wide range of countries were used to expose students to different development issues and strategies.

The format for the course was that students were taught key concepts around tourism development in the first part of the course. They then worked in small groups to apply these concepts to real-world scenarios and create a presentation in the second part of the course. The coursework provides an example of student-led, active learning. During the presentations students had the opportunity to learn about the development strategies being taken in other countries and question presenters on the approach being taken. The course was assessed 50 per cent on the coursework assignment (the presentation) and 50 per cent on the end of course written exam.

The use of wikis to improve the existing learning format

While the coursework format described provided a student-led learning activity that fulfilled the module's aims, there were opportunities to improve the format. The main issues with the old format included: a lack of cohesion in student presentations (some of these seemed rather segmented); and a lack of interaction and discussion from the students on each other's presentations. One of the main reasons for the lack of interaction was that the existing format only provided a short period of opportunity for this: the presentation followed by the 10-minute question and answer session. The presentations were content-rich and there was a lot of information for students to process in a short time.

Student groups often put a lot of effort into their presentations and these provided a bank of valuable examples of tourism development cases. However, once the presentations had been made, the opportunity for students to interact with, and learn from, each other's materials had passed. As a result students were not gaining the full benefits from the exercise. The wiki was deemed to be the best tool to address the issues raised in this scenario. The aims of using the wiki format were:

- *To improve the cohesiveness of student group work.* The wiki format provides a collaborative work space for students to develop their work.
- *To provide students with more opportunity to interact with the work of other groups.* The wiki format enables students to visit each other's presentations over an extended time period. Wiki pages also have comment boxes which enable students to pose questions and engage in discussion on the other sites.
- *To develop student IT skills.* Students will learn how to create and structure web pages.

The overall aim was that increased student collaboration and interaction would lead to an improvement in the quality of students' work. In this scenario the wikis were used in addition to the class presentations as it was felt that the two activities would complement each other.

Wiki project implementation

The implementation stage of the wiki project aimed to provide students with the context for the assignment and the skills to successfully complete it. In planning and implementing the wiki activity, the instructor needs to factor in the aims of the wiki project, the needs and experience of the particular group that they are planning the activity for and the time available. It is important that the instructor provides the appropriate level of training and support to students, as this will enable them to engage effectively in student-led learning and successfully complete the wiki project. Table 34.1 highlights the stages that were followed in planning and implementing the wiki project for the International Tourism Development module. The table highlights the role of the instructor and student at each stage. The implementation stages are discussed below.

Stage 1: Project planning and wiki familiarization

While a new format for the student coursework was introduced, the assignment goal remained the same. Under the new format students would be creating a wiki and then delivering a presentation based on this. Prior to the course the two instructors co-teaching the module undertook the planning activity for the course. This included: developing the materials required for the student induction, familiarizing themselves with the wiki software (Campus Pack) and

Table 34.1 Wiki project implementation stages

	Implementation stage	Instructors' role	Students' role	Time frame
1	Project planning	• Identify purpose of wiki: *'improve cohesiveness and interaction'* • Plan activity and prepare content for student induction • Understand wiki software and create example wiki		
2	Student induction	• Example wikis • Wiki software training • Wiki goals and template • Wiki guidelines and ground rules	• Attend induction	1 week
3	Wiki development: student collaboration within the group	• Encourage site development through comments, suggestions and questions • Monitor progress	• Assign group roles and plan project • Wiki development	4 weeks
4	Student interaction between groups	• Moderate wiki sites and class presentations and discussions	• Student interaction • *Students visit each other's wiki sites* • *Students make presentations* • Further wiki site development based on interaction	7 weeks
5	Wiki site closure	• Coursework assessment: 25% wiki and 25% presentation	• Exam revision: wikis provide a resource for this	

creating example wikis. Creating the wikis provided an opportunity for instructors to become familiar with the wiki software and its functions so that they could set students appropriate tasks and understand any challenges that they might face using it.

The class consisted of 24 second-year students. Students were familiar with each other and had prior experience of working together in class and undertaking group work exercises. While they were all IT literate Internet users who were familiar with Web 2.0 tools, the majority of them had not engaged in interactive e-learning activities nor had they constructed a wiki site before.

Stage 2: Student induction to the wiki project: factors to consider

The induction session set the context for the assignment and provided students with the skills needed to complete the exercise. It included:

Providing wiki examples. Example wikis were provided so that students would understand the output and activity required of them. Instructors showed students their example wikis so that they could see the structure of the web page, the type of content and level of analysis that was required. Ideas for student interaction between sites were role modelled by the instructors: mainly asking questions that would encourage the students to provide deeper explanations for any facts or figures presented and encourage them to develop their wiki further.

Wiki software training. The university's e-learning department provided a training session to equip students with the skills to use the wiki software. The session highlighted how to create the site, enter and edit text, upload pictures and diagrams and how to visit other sites and use the comment boxes. The training was given as a presentation in the lecture theatre.

Assignment template. Students were provided with a template to structure their wiki (see Table 34.2). The template provided a form of instructional scaffolding and provided a starting point for the learner from which they are able to self-organize, construct and modify their own knowledge (West & West, 2009). The level of detail provided on the template will depend on the level of the student with more advanced students being capable of more self-directed learning and needing less guidance. Having a clear structure and similar content on each wiki site enabled students to compare and contrast their countries more easily.

Establishing ground rules. Ground rules and social norms for online behaviour need to be established before the project commences (West & West, 2009). Ideas on how students should behave online were discussed as a class and focused specifically around the collaborative and interactive nature of the task. Key points included the need to be respectful,

Table 34.2 The wiki template

Contents page: Country name

Page 1: An overview of the history of international tourism development in your country
This should include at least one graph, e.g. tourist arrivals, tourism receipts.
It should discuss the political importance of tourism in the destination.

Page 2: An overview of the current pattern of tourism in the destination country
This should include at least one graph, e.g. where the tourists are from.

Page 3: Discussion of the economic significance of tourism
This should include various statistics, e.g. tourism's contribution to GDP and export earnings.

Page 4: The governance of tourism
Outline the current institutional frameworks within which tourism development in the destination country takes place, e.g. governmental organizations and tourism development policies.

Page 5: Problems associated with tourism
Analyse THREE specific problems that are currently faced by the destination's tourism industry (e.g. seasonality, political unrest, environmental impacts, etc.). Show in detail how the destination country's government and/or tourism industry are addressing each of these.

Page 6: Future prospects for tourism
Give your assessment of the future prospects for the development of tourism in the destination country.

Page 7: Reference list
Plagiarism: The wiki must be written in YOUR own academic language. The wiki should NOT contain large chunks of pasted material. This will be treated as plagiarism.

---

being open to other people's comments and suggestions, being sure to respond to other people's questions and seeking permission before making any major changes to people's work. It is a good idea for students to formulate and agree these rules as it gives them ownership of the process.

Plagiarism. Students need to be clear what is considered as plagiarism. This needs to be in writing so they can refer to it. This was both discussed in class and highlighted on the wiki template (see Table 34.2).

Group work considerations. Collaborative projects provide students with the opportunity to develop their group work skills. Johnson and Johnson (2006) highlight that effective group members need to be able to communicate clearly, share leadership, make decisions, engage constructively in arguments and negotiate conflict. Working towards a common goal in a group can be a challenging process. Tuckman (1965) highlights that all groups go through the process of: *forming, storming, norming* and *performing*, before they are able to work effectively together. The instructor needs to be aware of this process so that they can provide the support required at different stages. At the beginning of the wiki project students discussed the question: 'What makes a good team?' so that they were aware of the qualities required for working together effectively.

Wiki project commencement. With all the project training in place students were put in groups of three, assigned a country and provided a timeline. Having conducted group work projects on prior modules and being familiar with working in such a manner, students were tasked with organizing their workload together around the project goals and encouraged to create a project plan outlining roles and responsibilities.

The induction stage highlights that there are multiple considerations to address when setting up a student-led, collaborative wiki project. This is an important stage as failure to provide students with adequate support would hinder their ability to effectively engage in the activity.

Phase 3: Student collaboration: development of wiki sites and teacher monitoring of progress

Student group work. Students worked together within their assigned groups to construct their wiki and create their presentations. At this stage the only people able to access the wiki site was the group developing it and the instructor in a monitoring role. Students were given four weeks to populate their site with adequate information before it went *'live'* for interaction with other groups. At this early stage of the project group members built trust and started to put the foundations of productivity in place. The key activity here focused on sharing information and constructing knowledge as students developed their wikis together. There was a lot of communication within the group at this stage as students worked together to develop and improve their sites. The examples in Table 34.3 highlight that in the early stages of developing the wiki students worked together to share information sources, provide IT support to other group members and make decisions about how to organize their work. Table 34.3 also highlights examples from the later stages of the project where students were monitoring the quality of the work and questioning site content to encourage deeper thinking and improvements. These examples show that the wiki provides a format that can assist student collaboration and enable them to create a more cohesive piece of group work. They also show that students were working together to solve problems aiming for a high level of performance.

Table 34.3 Examples of student collaboration (pseudonyms used)

---

a) *Sharing content and ideas*

Economic information: Made by Claire at 3:38 PM,

Hey Neil, I found a good PDF for this category for you! Try and pull out some of the ideas for the site! I will send it to you on Skype when you come online!

b) *IT skills support*

Pictures: Made by Laura at 1:53 PM

I have a graph I would like to put in, I have tried inserting it the way we have been told though no success.

Re: Pictures: Made by Lisa at 3:10 PM

Hey save the picture to your own documents on your computer. Then on the wiki toolbar, there is an icon saying edit image, click on that to download the picture!

c) *Making suggestions & decisions/organising content*

National Park: Made by Hannah at 9:39 PM

Hey Helena – Should we make the National Park one special subject as there is so much to it?

Re: National Park: Made by Helena at 8:42 PM

We could do that, but do we need that much information about the National Park when the focus is supposed to be on tourism?

d) *Improving the quality of the site*

Electronic sources: Made by Neil at 8:02 PM

Hey Nora: Try to tidy up your sources. The right way to do them is by finding the source which is actually "SETE" and finding the date from the webpage. So for instance, it should be like this (SETE, 2010).

Re: Electronic sources: Made by Nora at 8:50 PM

Is this better?

e) *Encouraging further wiki site development*

Economic contribution: Made by Joanna at 9:57 PM

I'm surprised at the low contribution that oil and natural gas contributes to Dubai's economy. Are there any older figures to compare this to in order to determine if there is a shift to other money generating sectors such as tourism? Also, are there any more recent statistics we can add?

Teacher e-moderator role. The wiki format also enables instructors to provide tailored support for each group. While students were developing their wiki sites, course instructors monitored and encouraged site progress and set questions and tasks encouraging students to improve their site content. The example in Table 34.4 shows the instructor giving feedback and getting students to provide an explanation about the use and effectiveness of visitor taxes on the Galapagos Islands.

Phase 4: Interaction between student groups and teacher moderation

Interaction took place both on the wiki pages and in classroom discussions post-presentation.

Student wiki sites go live for interaction. After an initial period to construct the wiki sites within their groups, students' sites went live for interaction. This stage focused on information exchange between groups. Table 34.5 shows two examples of how students interacted between sites using the comment boxes. They provide examples ranging from a more basic interaction to a more sophisticated one. Both questions and answers were suitable for the task but highlight different levels of research and analysis. In the first question regarding

Table 34.4 Example of e-moderating

A good start: Galapagos: Made by one of the instructors at 12:44 PM

You have made a good start! I have a query:

Re: 'Between 2010 and 2011 over U.S. $ 21 million was collected through visitor taxes': What is this income used for? Is it used effectively? I am asking this, as I see there are visitor management problems in the national park!

Re: A good start: Galapagos: Made by Jane at 5:53 PM

Yes, while over $21 Million was collected between 2010 and 2011, only 8 Million $ were used for the National Park and the Marine Reserve. The National Park income goes to the State: which is Ecuador that then redistributes it. You will find a diagram of this shortly in the economics section. Also tourism has exploded recently and the National Park is struggling to manage the growing numbers of visitors. The park does not have enough management resources to cope and as such there are many problems: for example littering.

Table 34.5 Examples of student interaction between sites

---

a) *Visitor numbers: New Zealand*

In the graph showing annual visitor arrivals, there was a significant increase in numbers from 2001–2004 and then slowed down between 2007–2009. Why do you think this is? And do you think it had an impact on the country's tourism businesses?

Re: Visitor numbers: Made by Katherine at 10:48 PM

Increased number in visitor arrivals in 2001–2004 might have been caused by the improving transport links to NZ, such as more air-links and easier access to the island. The slow-down noted between 2007–2009 was caused by the world's economic break down. This difficult and uncertain financial situation discouraged tourists from expensive and long-haul travel.

Re: Visitor numbers: Made by Laura at 5:49 PM

Increased numbers may also have been due to the Rugby World Cup (which I have explained more on in the economic section). Holding the event would have increased visitor numbers significantly and boosted tourism business incomes such as accommodation.

b) *Comparing tourism strategies: Bhutan and Nepal*

How do you think tourism development in Bhutan compares to Nepal? Although similar in size and product they have developed very differently?

Re: Comparing tourism strategies: Made by Hayley at 9:20 PM

The uncontrolled, environmentally and culturally damaging tourism the Royal Governing body of Bhutan (RGOB) saw occurring in Nepal in the 1970s has meant that Bhutan has chosen to take a different approach to tourism in order to preserve their 'rich heritage and vibrant culture' which is essential as this is a key reason for visits to Bhutan (Brunet *et al*, 2001). In Nepal environmental degradation from large numbers of tourists is well-documented (Gurung & Scholz, 2008) and in the Annapurna Conservation Area 14 tons of fuel wood/day is used during peak season, consequently increasing deforestation and soil erosion (Nepal, 2008). As forestry is a key sector of the economy in Bhutan, they ensure their usage from tourism does not cause such severe impacts. Social problems are also evident in Nepal such as prostitution and drug abuse. Bhutan's economy has been growing slowly and the country prides itself in the 'restrictive tourism policy of the RGOB' (Seeland, 2000) which enables growth and development at a steady manageable rate.

---

changing visitor numbers to New Zealand two site authors provide short but differing explanations on the reason for the change in numbers. In the second question the site author provides a long, in-depth, referenced answer contrasting the different development approaches of two geographically similar countries.

Students interacted with wikis on countries that had both similar and different development contexts to their own in order to compare and contrast approaches to tourism development and draw wider conclusions. This encouraged the use of higher order thinking skills. The wiki provided students with the opportunity for increased and better quality interaction than undertaking the presentation alone. Their interaction provided students with a greater understanding of tourism development generally. Student feedback and wiki site observations highlighted that students interacted both passively by reading other wikis and actively by asking and answering questions using the comment boxes.

Not all students responded to questions in the format shown in Table 34.5. Others inserted their answers into the text on their wiki pages. While this approach may have improved the content of their wiki page, students did not always indicate what they had done to the person posing the question.

Class presentations. After the sites went live for interaction, students made class presentations. Exposure to issues in each other's countries on the wiki sites had better prepared students for the ensuing questions and discussion. Class discussions and presentations provided further ideas for students to update their sites. Students had the opportunity after class to ask questions through the wiki site. In this case study the wikis and the presentations complemented each other. The outcome for this stage was that students applied higher order thinking skills as they interacted with each other's presentations. Again the instructors' role in this process was to moderate the comment boxes and post-presentation discussion.

Phase 5: Wikis close for assessment

Towards the end of the semester the wiki sites were closed for assessment by the instructors. While the students could not update their sites any further the wikis remained accessible as a resource for exam revision. The new format for the coursework assessment was 25 per cent for the wiki site, 25 per cent for presentations. This consisted of a group work score with a small adjustment for individual effort assessed on interaction in class discussions and on wiki discussion boards.

An assessment of the wiki exercise

The assessment of the effectiveness of the wiki exercise was completed through: student feedback, an assessment of students' wikis, wiki monitoring tools and student coursework results. This multiple approach provided a comprehensive assessment and identified learning from the project.

Student feedback

Student feedback was gathered through a survey consisting of open and closed questions. Open questions were used to capture students' perspectives on the learning experience and provide students with the opportunity to reflect on their own learning experience: how they felt they had benefited from the wiki project, and how they felt their learning experience could be improved. The findings provided a valuable insight for the instructors on how to improve the wiki project. A summary of the open text responses is shown in Table 34.6. These have been categorized into themes. The frequency with which such comments were made is also shown.

Student responses highlight that they felt the main benefits of the wiki project to be: developing IT and research skills, being able to interact with other people's work and having a new, easy-to-use format to manage group work (Table 34.3 highlighted how groups were able to work together more effectively using the wiki format).

In terms of challenges several students reported 'using the software' to be the main difficulty with the activity. They reported finding it difficult to upload content and time-consuming to use. Most of the students' suggested improvements related to the software. These included more user-friendly software, IT support and instructions on how to use it, as well as induction sessions in the IT lab so that students could practise using the different functions. Despite the current generation of students being highly IT literate, feedback suggests that some of the students struggled with the technology. An inability to use the software can pose a barrier to participation.

While student feedback highlights the improvements that the instructors can make to the project, it also highlighted how the students could improve their own performance. Student responses included: spending more time on the project, doing more research, better teamwork and more interaction with other sites. Student-led learning requires that students take more

Table 34.6 Student feedback: open text responses

What was useful?
- The ability to interact with other groups' work: x 5 *'commenting on other people's work' 'seeing what others had done'*
- The wikis provided an easy way to manage the groups' work: x 6 *'It's easy to check and update our group's work'*
- IT skills development: x 6 *'Learnt how to structure a web page'*
- Doing research about new countries: x 4
- Useful for the exam x 1
- Other positive: x 2 *'a fun way to do work'*

What was not useful?
- The software was difficult to use: x 3 *'it was difficult to upload text and pictures'*
- The software was time-consuming: x 3
- Group members not doing their share of work: x 1
- Not necessary: x 2 *'presentation enough'*

How could the instructors improve the project?
- A more user-friendly wiki software package: x 2
- Inductions in the IT lab so students can practise the wiki functions: x 2
- IT support available for problems encountered with wikis: x 1
- Instructions on blackboard explaining how to upload data: x 1
- More time to complete the project: x 1

What could you (the student) have done better?
- Spend more time on the project: x 3
- Start the project earlier: x 1
- Do more research: x 2
- Better teamwork: x 2
- More interaction with other sites: x 3

responsibility for their own learning and identify ways to improve their own performance as well as identify any further support that they might need.

Interaction

The assessment identified how students interacted with other groups' work. The results are shown in Table 34.7.

The results show that 90 per cent of students visited other groups' wikis and that they had found the exercise useful both in terms of gaining ideas on structure and content of wikis to help them develop their own site as well as in drawing wider conclusions about tourism development in general. Students' responses show that while they were visiting each other's sites only 50 per cent of them were using the comment boxes for further discussion. The students who actively engaged in other sites (using the comment boxes) reported doing so to seek further understanding and suggest improvements. Those who reported finding the comments and questions that they received useful said that this had encouraged them to improve and extend their work.

Some students felt they didn't need to ask questions as the answers were already provided on the site. Others, however, stated that they had not asked questions for other reasons: 'I didn't like to', 'I had no time to', 'I forgot'. This group of students needs to be provided with more of an incentive to interact. Overall, the results suggest that although some students did not actively comment on the sites that they visited, they still found the activity useful. It is possible that this group may have interacted by drawing conclusions quietly themselves from the materials presented and have still benefited from the exercise. However, their contribution is missing from the discussion. Depending on the activity goal, it might be more beneficial to devise activities to capture their active engagement to share with the group.

Overall impact

Table 34.8 shows that overall student feedback on the exercise was positive. Some 72 per cent of students felt that looking at other wikis had improved the standard of their work. Despite

Table 34.7 Student interaction with each other's wikis

Activity	%	Why/Why not?
Percentage of students visiting other sites	90	
Percentage of students finding other sites useful	90	To get ideas on structure and content (for our own site)
		To compare countries
		To draw conclusions
Percentage of students commenting on other sites	50	To seek clarification and understanding
		To suggest improvements
Percentage of students not commenting on sites	50	The answer was already there, so it was not necessary
		I did not like to, I didn't have time, I forgot
Percentage of students finding comments useful	50	Useful: Encouraged improvement and extension of work
		Not useful: Some questions/comments were not useful and some answers were in the text already

Table 34.8 Overall impact

Statement	Agree %	Neutral %	Disagree %
Looking at other wikis improved the standard of MY work	72	12	6
The wiki exercise improved my group work skills	65	29	6
The wiki exercise improved my technology skills	72	12	12

the software challenges reported, 72 per cent of students felt that the exercise had improved their technology skills. However, 12 per cent disagreed, highlighting the need for further IT support here. Some 65 per cent of students felt that the exercise had improved their group work skills. Group work is a more difficult area to measure as any challenges working within the group can influence people's perceptions on the development of their skills in this area.

Student coursework scores

The results show that students' average coursework scores for the module had increased 5 per cent from the previous academic year from 55 per cent to 60 per cent, with students receiving an average score of 60 per cent for both their presentations and their wikis (see Table 34.9). This finding reflects students' perception of improved quality of work. It is probable that the greater collaboration and interaction that students had with each other's materials through the wikis improved the quality of their work both on the wiki sites and in class presentations.

The wiki monitoring tools

The wiki monitoring tools highlighted the number of visits per page. These were between 40 and 180 hits showing quite high levels of interaction. The groups that developed their wiki pages earlier on attracted the most visits and had higher levels of interaction in the comment boxes. The activity of individual students by hours and content upload could also be tracked. However, this is a less reliable way to assess students' contributions as it was not known how the group had agreed to work.

Conclusion

The wiki projects' aims were to improve the cohesiveness of students' group work and to increase the quality and quantity of student interaction with each other's wiki sites. The study also aimed to encourage critical thinking skills and improve the quality of student work. The study shows that the use of wikis has contributed towards these aims.

Table 34.9 Student coursework scores

Date	Average individual score	Course work breakdown
2011	55%	50% presentation
2012	Average: 60%: Presentation: 59.8% Wiki: 60.3%	25% presentation 25% wiki

Results span 50%–76%.

In order for student-centred learning activities to be effective they need to be well planned. Based on past findings highlighting students' lack of familiarity with the use of wikis for educational purposes a well-structured induction programme was developed for this project. This provided students with the skills (wiki software training and group working skills), support (wiki examples, wiki templates and online moderation) and operating environment (guidelines on plagiarism and online etiquette) that they needed to complete the project successfully.

The study found that the use of wikis as a coursework platform resulted in a more collaborative approach to group work. This confirms past findings (Parker & Chao, 2007; Gokcearslan & Ozcan, 2011). The study found that students collaborated more intensely as the task of creating their wiki progressed over time. It shows (Table 34.3) that students have moved up the different stages of Salmon's (2000) e-learning ladder in terms of: sharing information with each other (ideas and documents); collaboratively creating knowledge (making suggestions and decisions and co-creating site content); and in taking ownership of the group's learning (encouraging further development of site content and wiki site quality control). Overall the use of the wiki as a coursework platform led to higher standards and more cohesive group work.

While the use of wikis as a tool to enable a more collaborative approach to group work is well researched, inter-group wiki interaction is less well documented. This study found that the wiki format can provide students with the opportunity for increased and higher quality interaction. The study highlighted why and how students interacted between groups. It found that the vast majority (90 per cent) of students visited other groups' wiki sites and found it a useful activity both to support the development of their own wiki site as well as to draw wider conclusions about tourism development more generally. While not all students were actively involved in online discussion in the comment boxes they were still actively engaging with content across the wiki sites. However, the findings suggested that the inter-site discussion encouraged students to undertake a greater level of analysis and site development. Such discussion should therefore be encouraged so that students can gain the maximum benefit from the interaction part of the exercise. The study found that the collaborative and interactive nature of the task encouraged students to rely more on each other for feedback and take greater responsibility for their own learning. This is a finding also highlighted by Benckendorff (2009).

While most students reported engaging in online interaction and developing new IT skills there was a small number who did not. Student feedback highlighted that one of the main reasons for this was that some students found using the wiki software a challenge. This is a similar finding to that found in Benckendorff's (2009) study. Despite the relative ease of use of wiki software, this finding reiterates the need for a high level of IT support for students, so that they can focus on creating wiki site content rather than struggling with the software.

This chapter began by highlighting the need to develop tourism management students as 'Philosophic Practitioners' (Tribe, 2002) in order that they can effectively deal with the challenges presented by today's tourism industry. The case study has demonstrated that using wikis as a coursework tool and providing students with a meaningful coursework task can provide learning opportunities that can achieve this goal. Such coursework can develop students' vocational skills, critical thinking skills and reflective practice. The wiki project also provided students with the opportunity to have more of an input into their own learning and to take more responsibility for it. Such student-led learning activity can lay the foundations for students to further develop this approach to learning in subsequent activities.

Recommendations for improving the wiki project

While the wiki project met its overall goals, the instructors felt that there was scope for improvement. The main feedback from the students highlighted that further support was needed with the wiki technology. This included: more user-friendly wiki software, wiki induction sessions in an IT lab and improved IT support.

Ideas to improve the project were also identified by the instructors. Some of these are exercise-specific while others relate to wiki use more generally. Key points include:

- Agreeing on the amount of content to upload before the sites go live. Not all groups uploaded adequate content to enable other groups to effectively interact with their sites.
- Providing guidance on the number and type of wiki sites that students should interact with: for example there were 10 destination sites in the class and it wasn't possible for students to engage effectively with all of these. However, engagement will be difficult if other sites have not uploaded adequate content, which had been the case with a few sites in this project. Feedback suggests this may have been due to IT challenges and students' prioritization of time.
- Encouraging greater interaction between sites. This can be achieved by giving students a purpose to do so. This will be dependent on the activity goal. Some ideas include:
  - Setting some wider questions or tasks for students to encourage 'active' interaction between wiki sites
  - Using participatory assessment methods: assign students the task of assessing each other's sites.
- The number of assessment methods. While the wiki exercise complemented the presentation in this activity, a wiki or a presentation may be more suitable on its own, depending on the assessment goal.

Facilitating wiki exercises

This case study has provided an example of a student-led, collaborative learning exercise using wikis. The study has shown that such projects are multifaceted and that the instructor should consider many different factors when developing and implementing such an activity in order to enable students to perform successfully. In summary these include:

- Providing students with a meaningful project task that addresses relevant contemporary issues in tourism and hospitality management.
- Selecting an appropriate method to achieve the assessment goal. The project should determine the format used, not vice versa.
- Pitching the learning experience at the right level and for the right course format. The instructor will need to take into consideration the level, needs and experience of their particular group and the format of the course (campus-based or distance learning) when planning the activity.
- Ensuring that students are equipped with the appropriate cognitive structures to undertake the academic aspects of the task.
- Ensuring that students have the technical skills required to undertake the activity and that they are familiar with the particular software package they will be using.
- Providing the right level of instructional scaffolding to enable students to complete the project.
- Engaging students in establishing an operating environment. The collaborative and interactive nature of such group tasks requires that ground rules are set for the project. For the wiki project described these included: identifying acceptable ways to work within groups

and interact with each other on the Web. The instructor should engage students in creating any ground rules so that they have ownership of them.

- Providing a monitoring and supporting role. Once the project is under way the instructor will need to monitor project progress, support students in addressing any barriers to learning that they encounter along the way and facilitating further learning.
- Encouraging student reflection on their learning so that they can assess their progress and identify how their learning can be improved. This will also provide valuable feedback to the instructor both on the effectiveness of the task and enable them to identify how improvements can be made.

References

Benckendorff, P. (2009). 'Evaluating Wikis as an Assessment Tool for Developing Collaboration and Knowledge Management Skills'. *Journal of Hospitality and Tourism Management*, 16 (1), 102–12.

Bloom, B. (1956). *Taxonomy of Educational Objectives: the classification of educational goals.* New York: Longmans, Green

Bruner, J. (1990). *Acts of Meaning.* Cambridge, MA: Harvard University Press.

Bruns, A., & Humphreys, S. (2005). 'Wikis in Teaching and Assessment: the M/Cyclopedia project'. http://dl.acm.org/citation.cfm?id=1104976 (Accessed 30 October 2013).

Gokcearslan, S. & Ozcan, S. (2011). 'The Place of Wikis in Learning and Teaching Process'. *Social and Behavioural Sciences*, 28, 481–5.

Johnson, D. W., & Johnson, R. T. (2006). *Joining Together: group theory and group skills,* 9th Edn. Boston, MA: Pearson Education.

Johnson, D. W., Johnson, R. T., & Holubec, E. (2008). *Cooperation in the Classroom.* Edina, MN: Interaction Book Company.

Kennedy, G., Judd, T., Churchward, A., Gray, K., & Krause, K. (2008). 'First-Year Students' Experiences with Technology: are they really digital natives?'. *Australasian Journal of Educational Technology*, 24(1), 108–22.

Parker, K., & Chao, J. (2007). 'Wiki as a Teaching Tool'. *Interdisciplinary Journal of Knowledge and Learning Objects*, 3, 57–72.

Richardson, W. (2006). *Blogs, Wikis, Podcasts and Other Powerful Web-Tools for the Classroom.* Thousand Oaks, CA: Corwin Press.

Salmon, G. (2000). *E-Moderating: the key to teaching and learning online.* London: Kogan Page.

Tribe, J. (2002). '*The Philosophic Practitioner*'. Annals of Tourism Research, 29(2), 338–57.

Tuckman, B. (1965). 'Developmental Sequence in Small Groups'. *Psychological Bulletin*, 63(6), 384–99.

West, J., & West, M. (2009). *Using Wikis for Online Collaboration.* San Francisco, CA: Wiley.

35

Events higher education
Management, tourism and studies

Donald Getz

UQ School of Business, The University of Queensland, Brisbane, Australia

Introduction

Unheard of in the 1980s, the awarding of degrees in Event Management, and the teaching of event-specific courses within tourism, leisure, sports, hospitality and other fields, have rapidly become a global phenomenon. Barron and Leask (2012) called the growth 'unprecedented' but cautioned that in some countries it is resulting in an over-supply of programmes and graduates, a situation that will surely be followed by rationalization.

In part, this growth reflects the triumph of the so-called 'experience economy' which has made anything to do with experience design, media and entertainment very popular, and it can certainly be attributable to the widespread legitimation of planned events as instruments of government policy, corporate and industry strategy. This growth also stems from the insatiable need of many educational institutions to find new, fashionable subjects to offer students and the concomitant belief among students that an events-related career is desirable.

Like all applied fields, there is a certain faddishness about it, and an eventual decline in numbers of students and programmes is inevitable, as seems to be the case already in Leisure and Tourism studies in some countries. However, there is absolutely no logical reason why any area of studies, including Event Studies, should completely disappear. They might get merged or subsumed, and that happens first because of competition, then waning student demand. But once established, there will always be some level of academic interest. Institutions that excel in research and bring in money will likely retain their applied programmes as well.

Superficially, Event Management can be viewed as little more than the application of business and management principles to a range of planned events. That view certainly does a great injustice to what is being taught, and the knowledge needed to become a professional event manager, designer or successful owner/producer. Underpinning any credible Event Management degree or advanced curriculum with theory and problem-solving skills is essential. Furthermore, there is a huge and expanding body of factual knowledge and advice to master, found in numerous journal and magazine articles, professional association and government publications (including online toolkits), and books aimed at both students and practitioners that are packed with examples, case studies, expert opinion and additional sources.

Little has been written about curriculum development, pedagogy or the theoretical underpinnings of degree programmes in Event Management. The same can be said for Event Tourism, which is only being taught as a specific course, but will likely evolve into a specialization or area of concentration. Barron and Leask (2012) have provided an overview of the origins and evolution of event management education, observing that the industry has been instrumental in identifying skills needed by graduates (e.g. Jackson *et al.*, 2008). A number of authors have examined event management curriculum and particularly the value and methods of internships and other forms of experiential learning (e.g. McDonald & McDonald, 2000; Digance *et al.*, 2001; Moscardo & Norris, 2004; Berridge, 2007; Lee *et al.*, 2008; Lockstone *et al.*, 2008; Robinson *et al.*, 2008; Zeng & Yang, 2011). A broad overview of available knowledge is contained within the many generic and introductory textbooks that are available on event management (e.g. Getz, 2005 (2nd edn.); Goldblatt, 2011 (6th edn); Bowdin *et al.*, 2011 (3rd edn.); Allen *et al*, 2011 (5th edn.); Fenich, 2011 (3rd edn.)) and sub-topics which are too numerous to mention here.

But, if this applied field is to survive and prosper in academia, it must reflect upon its interdisciplinarity, strive to create new theory and methods, and remain connected to the various foundation disciplines. This is what I have called Event Studies. Without the 'studies' there is little academic justification for a university degree.

There are a number of generic ways to develop curriculum, and each of these is explored in the following section, beginning with the very pragmatic approach of emulation, or taking what's available and adapting it to a new situation. Although the primary focus is placed on stand-alone event-specific curriculum, some attention is given to how event studies fits into several closely related professional (or applied) fields.

A philosophical or ideological approach is also possible, but unlikely to find favour in academic institutions. My preferred approach is theoretical, that is based on a systematic approach to event studies combined with a pedagogical foundation. To that end, I apply my earlier thoughts on the three discourses found in the literature (Event Management, Event Studies and Event Tourism) to the matter of curriculum design and its underlying knowledge base.

This is quite a different approach from EMBOK – the Event Management Body of Knowledge; and MBECS – the Meeting and Business Event Competency Standards (MPI, 2012), or any other industry/professional approach to knowledge, because EMBOK (Silvers *et al.*, 2006) and MBECS (MPI, 2012) focus on factual knowledge and problem-solving skills, much of which have to be obtained through real-world experience.

Approaches to curriculum design

A number of distinct approaches to curriculum design can be taken, the first being a simple, *pragmatic design* derived from a review of what is being taught elsewhere and/or the teaching resources available. In the case of the UK this includes 2008 guidelines from the Quality Assurance Agency for Higher Education (QAA). The second approach *Keeping it close* starts with existing fields of study such as leisure and sport, then adds event-specific material as desired. In these contexts events are ancillary to the core of the field, being a specialization or simply one of many topics covered. A third approach is *philosophical* in nature, rooted in the belief that events are a service to the community and that they should fulfil important roles in society and the economy. A modification is a purely political approach in which events are expected to serve narrow political objectives such as social control, fostering national identity and pride, or manipulating opinion. Finally, there is a *theoretical approach* to curriculum design, which is given detailed examination. The theory is both pedagogical and event-specific in nature, involving the systematic framework for understanding and creating knowledge about planned events. Each of these is now discussed.

Pragmatic design

Pragmatic design is likely to be how most degree and diploma programmes begin, based on emulation, the dissemination of programme ideas, and the gradual legitimation of event studies. Mostly the title that has been adopted has been Event Management but, similar to leisure and recreation, there is a strong probability that Event Studies will emerge as a preferred name for those degree programmes that stress research and theory. Typically, changes are made to suit the institution's strengths, to gain competitive advantages, and of course reflecting available resources. Over time there will be shifts in emphasis and content as the field matures.

The available textbooks are a good starting point, as is the *Routledge Handbook of Events* (Page & Connell, 2012), plus material available from professional associations, followed by various standards and toolkits that have been developed. EMBOK and MBECS can be utilized here, at least as starting points. Benchmarking, or finding out which programmes are considered to be leaders and emulating their success, is recommended.

In addition to the generic event management degrees offered at so many universities (and also in diploma-granting schools) the following can be considered as specializations and elaborations (all found at university sites through an online search):

- event management and marketing
- international event management
- sport event; sports and event management
- cultural and major events
- festivals
- exhibition management
- meetings/conferences and conventions
- convention and event
- events, sports and entertainment
- event planning
- event tourism.

Events-related award titles (i.e. degree names) were provided by the Quality Assurance Agency for Higher Education 2008 in the UK, but these were not meant to be an exhaustive list:

> Art and event management; conference and exhibitions management; creative events; design and production; entertainment and events management; event and venue management; event fundraising and sponsorship; event management (sport); event management (tourism); event management; events management; events and entertainment management; festival and event management; international event management; international event market-ing; leisure, events and cultural management; live event technology; management in events; managing cultural and major events; resort and event management; special event management; and sports event management.

Countries and states/provinces typically do not standardize curriculum, and it is only in the UK that event management has been institutionalized to the degree that guidelines have been developed centrally. The following are selected excerpts from the UK Hospitality, Leisure, Sport and Tourism (QAA, 2008) standards applying to event management. The first quotation provides a succinct description of the field of study and broad areas of knowledge required by graduates:

> the nature of events as planned, temporary, short-term, unique activities designed to meet cultural, economic, social, political, leisure, life-cycle, marketing or business needs. A number of sectors have developed from this as recognized by People 1st, the Sector Skills Council for the Hospitality, Leisure, Travel and Tourism industries. Second, the temporary nature of events means that specific expertise is required to manage 'pulsating' organisations that rely upon supplying, coordinating and delivering safe, sustainable, rewarding and, often, creative experiences. Third, as event sectors have themselves matured, a fundamentally greater strategic perspective is required in terms of both policy and practice. Graduates need to be able to independently question why events are provided as well as the best methods to do so. Events programmes therefore need to explore a range of conceptual and theoretical areas, alongside vocational subjects, in order to meet the academic and employability needs of graduates, the events industry and the events subject area.

The following sections of the same document relate to the content of undergraduate programmes in event management, generally covering EMBOK/MBECS but broader issues as well:

3.5 Events programmes often involve the study of:
   - the nature of events and the structure, composition and management of the events industry, the sectors and their global environment
   - the administration, design, risk management, marketing and technical operations involved in planning events
   - the event consumer and client, and the event experience
   - the policy, strategy and impact of events.
3.6 In addition, the opportunity to participate in a period of industrial placement or work-related learning is a feature of most events programmes, which enables students to gain structured and relevant events industry experience.
3.7 Curriculum content may include the events industry, organisational behaviour, event environment, event operations, event planning process, applied technology, management support systems, event design, theming, hospitality, event risk management, production, conferencing, support services, event resource management, operations and project management, volunteer management, human resource management, event marketing, consumer behaviour, sponsorship, venue and facilities management, place/destination, safety and security, strategic management, entrepreneurship, creativity, financial management, fundraising, economics, public relations, small business management, event law and licensing, administration, event policy, cultural studies, globalisation, mega-events and spectacle, evaluation, event studies, research methods and market research.

Lastly, the standards provide additional insights into what is expected from an honours degree, over and above the previously mentioned content:

6.2 An honours graduate in events will be able to analyse and evaluate the concepts and defining characteristics of events as an area of academic and applied study, including being able to:

- explain, interpret and challenge theories and concepts which are used to understand the origin, purpose, meanings and development of events from a range of critical perspectives
- display an insight into the structure of event providers and their sectors, and analyse the political, technological, social, environmental and economic factors which affect, or impact upon, the supply of, and demand for, events
- analyse and reflect on the different cultural and business concepts, intercultural and international dimensions of events
- demonstrate a critical awareness and understanding of how core values, for example, ethics, integration, sustainability, creativity, strategy, and continuous improvement, relate to, and are reflected in, events.

6.4 An honours graduate will be able to recognise and value the centrality of the attendee and/or client and meet and respond to their needs and expectations, including being able to:

- analyse the nature, characteristics, needs and expectations of different consumers through applying consumer behaviour theories and concepts
- generate creative ideas/concepts, proposals, pitches and solutions to meet differing needs
- analyse and evaluate the quality of the event experience and its impact on the event consumer and/or client and the wider organisation
- evaluate the importance of cultural and other diversities in developing access to, and participation in, events by specific target groups
- demonstrate an understanding of the ways in which attendees behave at events and within the venue and surrounding destination.

6.5 An honours graduate will be able to utilise, and understand the impact of, rationales, sources and assumptions embedded in policy, planning and delivery mechanisms in an events context, including being able to:

- evaluate the contribution and impacts of events in social, economic, environmental, political, cultural, technological and other terms
- appreciate the ethical and sustainability issues associated with the operation and development of events
- write and critique event plans, event strategies and to recognise and meet the needs of specific stakeholders
- critically reflect upon the role of those organisations and structures charged with a responsibility for the promotion of, or the training of practitioners in events
- demonstrate a critical awareness and appreciation of existing and emerging standards, policies, initiatives, frameworks and contemporary issues.

The tendency to specialize by type of event or event setting is strong, in part because there are career paths associated with each, but in higher education it makes more sense to provide generic event management first. A useful typology of planned events groups them into four broad categories, each closely associated with specific venues: business events (or MICE) and convention/exhibition centres; sports and sport arenas and stadia; festivals and other cultural celebrations, utilizing parks, streets and art/cultural centres; and the mostly private entertainment events and functions which can utilize any of the venues as well as being frequent clients of hotels and resorts. For each of these sectors there are pertinent professional associations, specialized academic programmes and textbooks. The convention and exhibition sector is particularly well covered by texts, and there are books related to sports events, parties, weddings, retreats, festivals, corporate and entertainment events.

Keeping it close

Event-specific courses (or subjects or papers) are popular within a number of closely related fields including recreation, hospitality, arts administration, and sport management. Within these applied fields the emphasis will be on event management. Many universities have combined sport, leisure and events with tourism or hospitality.

Hospitality. All hospitality programmes cover meetings, conventions and private functions. The emphasis will be on design of settings, food/beverages, quality of service, and other technical components of event production for profit. Overlapping with tourism studies, hospitality programmes might include resort management and larger-scale events. Event managers frequently need these hospitality skills, and event studies can also benefit from the more theoretical and philosophical approach to hospitality based on social and cultural theory. In the *Sage Handbook of Hospitality Management* (Brotherton & Wood, 2008), for example, can be found chapters on the MICE industry (by Schlentrich) and 'Event Design and Management' (by Getz). The Fenich text (2011) combines meetings, expositions, events and conventions.

Recreation and Leisure. All recreation facilities are in the event business, if only at the level of informal social and recreational events. Traditional recreation settings include event programming, such as camps, while parks host numerous festivals and public facilities host sport competitions. Event Tourism is also relevant to recreation degree programmes that incorporate commercial recreation or recreation travel. The contributions of leisure studies to event studies are many, the most important of which are a theoretical basis (social psychological) for understanding leisure experiences and benefits. Recreation programming methods are useful in event design and have been discussed by Rossman and Schlatter (2011), while Torkildsen (2005) devoted a chapter to events in *Leisure and Recreation Management*.

Sport. A major element in sport management is the production and management of competitive athletic events, while the management of sport facilities automatically requires event management skills. The emphasis on sport performance and outcomes is not central to event studies, but the focus on athletes does provide valuable insights to personal motivations and outcomes. Sport events have tremendous value economically and therefore sport managers require an understanding of event impact assessment. The literature on sport events has become substantial, as reflected in these sample book titles: *Event Management for Tourism, Cultural, Business and Sporting Events* (Van Der Wagen, 2007); *Strategic Sports Event Management: Olympic Edition* (Masterman, 2012); *International Sports Events: Impacts, Experiences and Identities* (Shipway & Fyall, 2012); *Managing Major Sports Events: Theory and Practice* (Parent and Smith-Swan, 2013).

Arts and Culture. Many practitioners have begun in theatre or the arts and there is no doubt that theatre studies are important for many aspects of event design and production. Beyond that link, arts administration students will need a basic knowledge of the whole range of events because each form, including business events and sports, can offer artistic experiences and benefit from an arts perspective. The place of events in society is an important theme, including contrasting 'high and low culture', the entertainment industry, the influence of media (mass and social), and how events reflect or shape culture and subcultures. Cross-cultural studies are a neglected theme and much research is needed here. *Arts and Cultural Programming: A Leisure Perspective* (Carpenter & Blandy, 2008) deals specifically with programming festivals and events within a leisure context. Books taking a cultural studies or cultural anthropological view on festivals and events include Picard and Robinson's (2006) on *Festivals, Tourism and Social Change*.

Urban Studies. Increasingly events and related venues are taking prominence in urban design, animation, renewal and repositioning. How do various events generate or reflect distinctive urban lifestyles? The book *Eventful Cities* (Richards & Palmer, 2010) covers the importance of events in the modern city from many perspectives, while *Tourism, Culture and Regeneration* by Smith (2007) examines the roles of events in urban renewal.

Rural (and Regional) Studies. Events have become important to small towns and rural areas both for social/cultural and tourism purposes. Gibson and Connell in *Festival Places: Revitalising Rural Australia* (2011) draw on extensive research concerning festivals in rural and small town Australia.

Philosophically speaking

If we accept that events are services provided within a variety of economic, environmental, social and cultural policy fields, then the curriculum can be designed to reflect this orientation. Just as public administration differs from business management, so must event service administration differ from event tourism and private event management. The curriculum would start with instrumentation, that is the various roles events can play in various policy fields, and discussion of the legitimation process – or how events become policy instruments and even institutions in their own right. Social marketing must be an important part of this approach, with the ultimate aim being not merely satisfied and loyal customers, but fulfilment of the event's mission. Evaluation of outcomes becomes an enormous challenge in this scenario, as traditional measures of return on investment (ROI) and impact do not necessarily apply. In addition to traditional outcome and impact measures, attention must be focused on proof of goal attainment (i.e. effectiveness measures) and on efficiency (measures of how well resources are utilized).

This approach is inherently political, so discussion is necessary of political economy, ideology, party politics and power. Foucault will therefore find a sacred place alongside Maslow (i.e. basic human needs) in this curriculum. Other key topics will include public–private partnerships, how need is distinguished from demand, and why the not-for-profit sector in event production is crucial and how it can be supported.

It seems unlikely that this model will gain much support from universities as the basis for an entire curriculum, but it does suggest important additions to the curriculum and ones that could provide competitive advantages. In countries and regions where festivals and events are already viewed as social and cultural services, service-oriented elements of the event management curriculum should find ready support among public agencies.

In theory

Here we start with a generic, pedagogic construct and work through a model of event studies. This will yield a more comprehensive and balanced curriculum, one that is suitable for universities that insist that all programmes show academic rigour, and for all academics doing research.

An overview of tourism, hospitality and event degree programmes in Australia (Dredge *et al.*, 2012) provides the starting point. From this extensive documentation comes the following quote:

> Hicks (2007) laments that in Australia there has been little philosophical and intellectual engagement in curriculum design and that further engagement, particularly with respect to the wider implications of curriculum to societal goals, is warranted. Drawing from Barnett

and Coate (2005), Hicks argues for a schema of curriculum design that incorporates 'knowing', 'acting' and 'being' with different weightings being applied to each domain depending on disciplinary values and emphasis.

This framework (see Figure 35.1) is extremely useful, and corresponds to my own thinking on the interrelationships among event studies, management and tourism.

The 'acting' dimension

This is the realm of knowledge and skill-development that purports to prepare students for careers in event management and/or event tourism. In practice, tourism and management are seldom combined in events programmes, but it is very logical to do so and might prepare many students for broader, more flexible career paths. Within the 'acting' dimension are three main categories of professional or business action that students must be taught:

1   basic facts about the subject of interest (e.g. events and their management; events and tourism; events in the arts, or related to urban development)
2   problem-solving skills (such as how to conduct market intelligence for the purpose of preparing marketing plans, or how to analyse an event's competitive position)
3   learning skills (to facilitate self, and lifelong learning).

Theory will be taught where it is useful to understanding how to solve problems, and the range of pertinent problems includes event design, marketing to tourists, and evaluating outcomes. The models I prepared for *Event Studies* (Getz, 2012) and *Event Tourism* (Getz, 2013) called 'frameworks for understanding and creating knowledge' provide a suitable basis (see Figure 35.2).

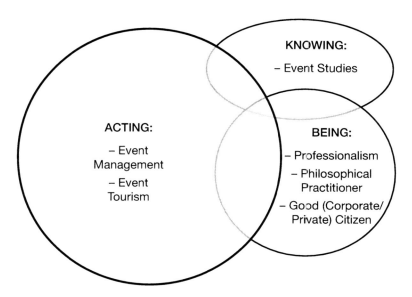

Figure 35.1 The curriculum space for professional event studies

Source: Adapted from Hicks (2007).

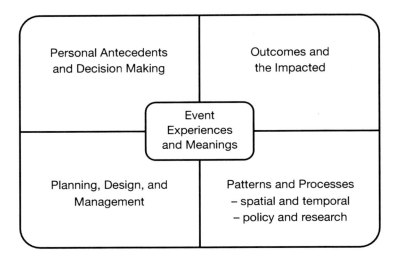

Figure 35.2 A framework for understanding and creating knowledge about planned events
Source: Adapted from Getz (2012).

Event experience and meanings. For event studies this is the core phenomenon, applied to all planned events. For event tourism the core consists of event and travel experiences combined, which in one sense is more restricted (because not all events are necessarily included), but it is also a broader core in the sense that we must combine what we know of all event experiences and meanings with all travel experiences and meanings.

Personal antecedents and decision making. While superficially this can be considered the demand-side of the economic equation, it in fact requires a much more fundamental understanding of the social and cultural significance of events in all societies, why they meet basic human needs for economic, social and symbolic exchanges, and the influences that lead to personal and group decisions. Appropriate theory comes particularly from the foundation disciplines of sociology, cultural anthropology, economics and psychology. Consumer behaviour theory is also necessary, but it is important to stress that events are not like simple consumer products. Planned events are needed, not individually but as sectors of society and the economy, and the reasons for attendance and event tourism are often complex, being rooted in lifestyle, high levels of ego-involvement and subcultural identification.

Outcomes and the impacted. All outcomes are to be considered, not just the purported benefits of events and event tourism that proponents often claim without providing much evidence. Those who feel impacted must be given their voices, and that includes those who gain and those who suffer from event-related policies, expenditures and activities. Economic impact assessment is very well developed, but we have little or no evidence of causes and effects when it comes to the social, cultural and personal effects of event attendance and engagement, nor of their secondary and indirect effects.

Planning, design and management. Event tourism, and closely related economic and urban development policy, is firmly anchored in a number of propositions or beliefs for which much evidence exists: events can attract tourists and distribute them temporally and geographically; events can act as catalysts for other forms of development and marketing advances; events animate resorts, facilities and places; events can generate positive images and contribute to branding, place marketing and re-positioning. Ontologically, these are the core concepts and related facts (including terminology) which define a field of study.

In contrast, the planning, design and management of events does not have a similar set of propositions, unless one takes a philosophical position much like that put forward by the advocates of leisure and recreation services. In this approach, planned events are either an element in the necessary leisure services offered to citizens, or could be considered a separate realm of essential services offered by government and the not-for-profit sector. This service orientation is not well developed, but is evident within the discourses on events and social/cultural capital, or regarding the value of events in fostering social integration or healthy lifestyles. I believe these are important justifications, as events create public goods in ways that are different from, and often more economical than building venues like arenas and stadia. Leisure and events professionals have to get together on this aspect of service provision.

In this knowledge domain are generic facts and skills, much as listed by EMBOK and MBECS, plus those with special significance for the full range of planned events. The diversity of knowledge and skills linked to event types and settings explains the current range of competing professional associations, and the tendency for academic institutions to specialize on sports, festivals, exhibitions or the meetings and conventions sectors. However, there is definitely a core that can be called generic event management and design that applies – at least as the starting point for careers – to every conceivable event and event setting.

Patterns and processes: The whole system is dynamic in terms of how society and events evolve together, the spatial and temporal distribution of events, and how all of these are affected by policy and corporate strategies. Researchers and teachers also seek to change the system through knowledge creation and its dissemination.

While event management has EMBOK and MBECS, as well as many specialized and general textbooks, event tourism is less-well developed academically. In *Event Tourism* (Getz, 2013) there are several very practical ways of looking at event tourism:

- in systematic terms, focusing on supply and demand interactions
- how to market events to tourists (a demand-side approach involving market intelligence on who travels for events and why)
- destination development and marketing with events as instruments of strategy (i.e. developing events as tourist attractions, place marketers and image makers; specific considerations including hallmark, iconic events and destination events)
- fitting event tourism into other policy fields including urban development and renewal.

Most recently distinct careers in Event Tourism have emerged, ranging from bidding on events and hosting them to strategy and policy-making. Perhaps the biggest challenge is to achieve fuller integration of all the agencies and venues that are stakeholders in developing and marketing Event Tourism.

The 'knowing' dimension

This dimension is what I call Event Studies, being the study of planned events for the sake of gaining understanding and contributing to theory development in foundation disciplines such as sociology, anthropology or economics. When applied to events there is a need to develop interdisciplinary theory that adds something unique to this body of knowledge.

This is not to say that Event Studies lacks value for career preparation, as that would be equivalent to saying that a broad, liberal arts education is useless for getting a good job. Academic programmes taking this traditional path will be interdisciplinary in terms of their research, and eclectic in their teaching. They might be able to teach general interest and more focused events-specific courses to students both within and outside event management and event tourism.

How knowledge is created and what constitutes knowledge (i.e. epistemology and ontology) are integral parts of event studies. Students need to understand how to do research (methodologies and methods) and what knowledge means for theory development as well as practical applications. In this regard, the event-specific research journals must be consulted and students have to acquire skills in searching, comprehending and making use of research. These journals include:

- *Event Management* (formerly *Festival Management and Event Tourism*)
- *Convention and Event Tourism* (formerly *Convention and Exhibition Management*)
- *International Journal of Festival and Event Management*
- *International Journal of Event Management Research* (online)
- *Journal of Policy Research in Tourism, Leisure and Events.*

In the book *Event Studies* (Getz, 2012) is a discussion of how knowledge is created and research is done, related to events. Most of our pertinent theory comes from the foundation disciplines, and very little interdisciplinary theory has emerged. Event studies does draw on theory filtered through closely related fields of study, such as leisure studies, which draws heavily on social psychology. In this way, emergent theory such as the 'event-tourist career trajectory' (Getz & Andersson, 2010; Getz & McConnell, 2011; Lamont *et al.*, 2012) combines sociology, serious leisure, ego-involvement and motivation theory to help understand a phenomenon specific to events. Knowledge is being generated on an ongoing basis with professional practice in order to understand and solve problems, and within various policy domains, but this is often not reported in any of the literature. One of the main limitations is the unwillingness, or inability, of practitioners and policy advisers to document their knowledge or even to make it available. Finally, we can anticipate the formation of think tanks devoted to creating knowledge for planned events, but the closest thing existing is that of informal networks of event scholars and clusters of researchers at a number of schools.

Increasingly, event studies will be an integral part of applied management and tourism degrees, mainly because professionals should be well versed in such matters as why planned events have always been fundamental aspects of every society, how events fulfil various goals and contribute to a number of policy fields, and the meaning of event outcomes and benefits.

The 'being' dimension

Students should be prepared to be good citizens (including their potential roles as public-sector, non-profit and corporate leaders), and to act as professionals. Professionalism requires the study of ethics, and that should clearly be related to the big issues of our time, including ecological sustainability and social equity. There is a need for a philosophy of planned events, in ways similar to the emergence (and ongoing debate) of leisure, arts and sport philosophy.

In Event Studies (Getz, 2012) I suggested the parameters of a philosophy of event service through a series of questions that should be addressed by 'event philosophers'. The following questions must be addressed in developing any philosophical position about 'event service':

- are all planned events fundamentally good?
- under what conditions is public support justified?

- must all events be environmentally sustainable in every possible way?
- should all events contribute positively to individual and community health?
- what obligations to society and the environment do event professionals hold? (consider morality and ethics)
- what is the value of art events? what events are in bad taste? how should we judge beauty? (this is aesthetics)
- what can we learn about the event experience and the multiple meanings attached to events? (such as through hermeneutic phenomenology).

The emerging paradigm shift in curriculum space

In Figure 35.1 the theoretical curriculum space is illustrated, featuring the three dimensions of knowing, acting and being. While a perfectly balanced merging of these three dimensions might be considered ideal from a purely academic perspective, on the assumption that it provides the most flexibility and soundest foundation for students, it is unlikely to find favour in very many settings. That is because the driving force for university programmes has been, and will probably continue to be, student demand for career-oriented programmes. Hence, Figure 35.1 illustrates more of a professional model (stand-alone, or tied to business, tourism or hospitality) in which the 'acting' dimension predominates.

The starting point for most existing degree and diploma programmes is management. Students will want to learn how to design and produce events, and this is often subdivided by type of event (festivals, meetings, sports, and exhibitions). Other options include teaching about events in specific settings (e.g. events for cities or resorts, events for amusement parks or convention centres), or events for specific target markets (such as youth, seniors, runners). In my opinion all such specializations should follow from teaching of the fundamentals, which we can call generic event management. Logically, these could be contained within a business/ management school in which those fundamentals (including theory) come first.

I believe more and more programmes will emerge with tourism as the starting point, or tourism plus hospitality. In this scenario less is needed about how to design and produce events (although that is highly useful knowledge to everyone in the tourism and hospitality industries) and more is required about how events act to enhance economic and tourism development, along with other roles pertaining to urban renewal and place marketing. Event tourism is entirely instrumentalist, meaning that events are exploited for their value in attaining externally generated goals.

It is only when elements of Event Studies are added to the curriculum that event management goes beyond application and event tourism goes beyond instrumentalism. These elements include considerations of multiple stakeholder perspectives on events and their consequences, broad issues such as sustainability, and discourse on social, cultural and environmental perspectives. And it is only when ethics, philosophy and citizenship are also introduced (the 'being' dimension) that a truly professional course of study emerges.

Distance and ongoing education

In a wireless, socially interconnected world, the traditional delivery models cannot survive unaltered. There will be a sharper need in the future for distance and particularly ongoing education within the professions, both to keep current with laws, knowledge and theory, and to stay networked with educators and institutions.

But there is only so much that can be taught at a distance, and that mainly consists of the 'acting' dimension. The most technical of coursework, in which students proceed at their own pace with immediate self-testing and feedback, works best at a distance. This is the realm of facts and technical competence that can be easily acquired and results measured, such as 'how do you solve this problem?', or 'what does the law say about this issue?'

The 'being' dimension can be facilitated by live and remote discussions, but when it comes to ethical issues, or developing a sense of reflection, there is no substitute for live interaction over a period of time. And the 'knowing' dimension basically requires that students get training and supervision in doing research. Consequently, we can expect more and more of the 'acting' dimension to go online, be taught at a distance, and involve lifelong learning and testing.

This emerging paradigm in new curriculum space will require considerable adjustment for educational institutions and will ideally involve a range of partnerships including:

- professional and educational associations working together (otherwise the associations will do the job completely on their terms)
- institutions, associations and the workplace (part of every work week can be devoted to online learning)
- individual professionals and mentors (for lifelong learning)
- event organizations and researchers (to facilitate research and knowledge creation that meets both academic standards and assists events to solve problems and improve).

What is left for the university or college in this new paradigm? Programmes will have to be restructured and made more flexible, then take a leadership role – which will be difficult given the inherent conservatism of institutions. I foresee a quite different set of models in the future of education for planned events (and other applied management fields). Assuming the partnerships mentioned above can be formed and sustained, the future degree programmes in event studies/management/tourism might look like this:

- Entry at any point in one's career, based on demonstrable factual knowledge and technical competence (i.e. the 'acting' dimension does not require a college or university programme, but it could be optional for those entering directly from secondary schools, in which case it could be delivered completely online through the partnerships).
- Ongoing, but self-testing of technical competence and factual knowledge, so that most classroom exams disappear (many of which simplistically test only memory recall).
- Flexible learning options through lectures, seminars, internships, action research, study tours and mentorship, all of which must count academically towards fulfilment of standards in the 'knowing' and 'being' dimensions.
- Since there is no single, or culturally appropriate ethical position to imbue (especially if learning is online and international), the testing has to be confined to candidates being able to articulate ethical issues and formulate defensible positions, which can be done as part of the continuous and online 'acting' testing; it might be useful, however, to require candidates to participate in seminars and debates in order to gain appreciation of others' opinions and positions.
- A research component should be required, as this is where the university must display its unique selling proposition! The research required for tourism and management-oriented students can be applied to problems, whereas higher-degree research needs to embody theory development; traditional examination methods of theses and dissertations might very well

give way to more flexible methods, so that candidates can learn through reiteration, rather than pass/fail situations.

- Graduation: institutions now bestow *compliance certificates* called diplomas and degrees which usually signify little more than graduates met the minimum exam standards, whereas what is really needed will have to be based on consideration of multiple and more flexible qualifications: the candidate's self-testing, a research project or thesis, mentors' reports, work experience, attendance and participation in seminars, etc. Probably the most destructive part of the current system is lengthy, multiple-choice exams that test mostly memory.

Where do event studies belong?

As mentioned earlier, there are very good reasons for incorporating event management, event tourism, and all other applied management fields, within a school or faculty of business or management studies. If the emphasis is to be more on event studies then a social science or humanities home makes more sense. But there is another possibility that should be considered.

Many of the applied fields discussed in this chapter have one thing in common – experiences and experience design, of which events are one major component. It can be argued that greater interdisciplinarity will occur, and theoretical developments advanced, through closer cooperation among tourism, hospitality, events, leisure, and sports. If institutions are looking for new programme ideas, and reduced overlap, the creation of 'experience design' makes sense. This will also require input from theatre and the arts, architecture and other existing design disciplines or areas of application.

Conclusions

In this chapter various approaches to curriculum design for events have been discussed, with emphasis placed on the theoretical approach that combines established pedagogy and a systematic framework of understanding and creating knowledge about planned events. In this context three discourses on events have been presented, namely event studies, event management and event tourism. These have been analysed within the pedagogic framework of 'knowing, acting and being' in which event studies constitutes the 'knowing' dimension and epistemological and ontological concerns are paramount. 'Acting', or professional practice, dominates the event management and event tourism dimensions, and professionalism with ethical considerations relates to the 'being' dimension. A complete and balanced curriculum would feature all three in harmony, although realistically it is concluded that under the current emphasis on work-ready graduates, most degree and diploma programmes will emphasize the 'acting' or doing, with the other two dimensions providing context and support.

Higher education in most countries still emphasizes a path to graduation that focuses on the classroom and obtaining adequate grades obtained through examinations. This institutionalization of 'discipline' is counterproductive and will have to change. More flexible, lifelong learning systems are needed in which various partnerships will provide the foundations and support for career development. This new paradigm requires much more than a rational approach to curriculum design employing the three discourses discussed in this chapter, it requires a complete rethinking of professionalism and education delivery.

Page and Connell (2012), wrapping up the *Handbook of Events*, concluded that event education today is much like tourism studies in the 1980s. Its rapid expansion must now be matched by a vast curriculum development effort and the research to support advances in the field. They particularly discussed the need for research on the visitor experience and technological advances, risk management, and sustainability.

The framework for understanding and creating knowledge about planned events also provides a research frame for the field. As well, Weed (2012) developed an interdisciplinary events research agenda across the interrelated fields of sport, tourism, leisure and health studies. His model (p. 67) depicts 'potential outcomes sought from events' as the starting point, and a matrix which crosses three perspectives on outcomes (host city priorities, audiences, and other regions' priorities) with five outcome dimensions (culture, sport and recreation; social and community; environmental; economic; and media and promotion). This framework has implications far beyond outcome or impact evaluation, as it focuses our collective attention on the need for systematic knowledge creation, interdisciplinary research, and theory development to support event management and event tourism – they cannot be taught or practised professionally without this firm foundation.

References

Allen, J., O'Toole, W., Harris, R., & McDonnell, I. (2011). *Festival and Special Event Management,* 5th edn. Milton, Qld: Wiley.

Barnett, R., & Coate, K. (2005). *Engaging the Curriculum in Higher Education.* New York: Open University Press.

Barron, P., & Leask, A. (2012). 'Events Management Education'. In, S. Page & J. Connell (Eds.), *The Routledge Handbook of Events* (pp. 473–88). London: Routledge.

Berridge, G. (2007). *Events Design and Experience.* Oxford: Butterworth-Heinemann.

Bowdin, G., Allen, J., O'Toole, W., Harris, R., & McDonnell, I. (2011). *Events Management,* 3rd edn. Oxford: Butterworth-Heinemann.

Brotherton, B., & Wood, R. (Eds.). (2008). *The Sage Handbook of Hospitality Management.* London: Sage.

Carpenter, G., & Blandy, D. (2008). *Arts and Cultural Programming: a leisure perspective.* Champaign, IL: Human Kinetics.

Digance, J., Davidson, M., & Gleeson, B. (2001). 'Taking the Classroom into the Real World'. *Journal of Convention & Exhibition Management,* 3(1), 31–43.

Dredge, D., Benckendorff, P., Day, M., Gross, M. J., Walo, M., Weeks, P., & Whitelaw, P. (2012). 'Key Issues in Tourism, Hospitality and Events Curriculum Design and Development'. Issues Paper No. 1, prepared for the project: Building a Stronger Future: Balancing Professional and Liberal Education Ideals in Undergraduate Tourism and Hospitality Education. Available: http://tourismhospitality education.info (Accessed 9 October 2013).

Fenich, G. (2011). *Meetings, Expositions, Events, and Conventions: an introduction to the industry,* 3rd edn. Upper Saddle River, NJ: Pearson.

Getz, D. (2005). *Event Management and Event Tourism,* 2nd edn. New York: Cognizant.

Getz, D. (2008). 'Event Design and Management'. In B. Brotherton & R. Wood (Eds.), *The Sage Handbook of Hospitality Management* (pp. 518–40). London: Sage.

Getz, D. (2012). *Event Studies,* 2nd edn. London: Routledge.

Getz, D. (2013). *Event Tourism.* New York: Cognizant.

Getz, D., & Andersson, T. (2010). 'The Event-Tourist Career Trajectory: a study of high-involvement amateur distance runners'. *Scandinavian Journal of Tourism and Hospitality,* 19(4), 468–91.

Getz, D., & McConnell, A. (2011). 'Serious Sport Tourism and Event Travel Careers'. *Journal of Sport Management,* 25(4), 326–38.

Gibson, C., & Connell, J. (2011). *Festival Places: revitalising rural Australia.* Bristol: Channel View.

Goldblatt, J. (2011). *Special Events,* 6th edn. New York: Wiley.

Hicks, O. (2007). 'Curriculum in Higher Education in Australia – Hello?'. Paper presented at the Enhancing Higher Education: Theory and Scholarship Proceedings of the 30th HERDSA Annual Conference, 8–11 July, Adelaide, Australia. Available: http://www.herdsa.org.au/wp-content/uploads/conference/2007/PDF/.../p227.pdf (Accessed 14 April 2013).

Jackson, C., Beeston, S., & Alice, D. (2008). 'Event Management Skills'. *LINK 20. The Hospitality, Leisure, Sport and Tourism Network:* 5–7.

Lamont, M., Kennelly, M., & Wilson, E. (2012). 'Competing Priorities as Constraints in Event Travel Careers'. *Tourism Management*, 33(5), 1068–79.

Lee, K. M., Lee, M. J., & Kim, H. J. (2008). 'Comparing Perceptions of Event Management Curriculum: a factor–correspondence analysis'. *Event Management*, 12, 67–7.

Lockstone, L., Junel, O., & Mair, J. (2008). 'Experiential Learning in Event Management Education: do industry placements in degree courses complement jobs available in the events industry?'. In S. Richardson, L. Fredline, A. Patiar, & M. Ternel *CAUTHE 2008 Conference: Tourism and Hospitality Research, Training and Practice, 'Where the "Bloody Hell" Are We?'*. Gold Coast, Griffith University.

McDonald, D., & McDonald, T. (2000). 'Festival and Event Management: an experiential approach to curriculum design'. *Event Management*, 6(1), 5–13.

Masterman, G. (2012). *Strategic Sport Event Management: Olympic edition*. London: Butterworth-Heinemann.

Meeting Professionals International (MPI). (2012). Meeting and Business Event Competency Standards Curriculum Guide (MBECS). Available: www.mpiweb.org/MBECS (Accessed 20 August 2013).

Moscardo, G., & Norris, A. (2004). 'Bridging the Academic Practitioners Gap in Conference and Events Management: running events with students'. *Journal of Convention and Event Tourism*, 6(3), 47–62.

Page, S., & Connell, J. (2012). *The Routledge Handbook of Events*. London: Routledge.

Parent, M., & Smith-Swan, S. (2013). *Managing Major Sports Events: theory and practice*. Oxford: Routledge.

Picard, D., & Robinson, M. (Eds.). (2006). *Festivals, Tourism and Social Change: remaking worlds*. Clevedon: Chanel View.

Quality Assurance Agency for Higher Education (QAA) (UK). (2008). 'Hospitality, Leisure, Sport and Tourism'. Mansfield, England. Available: http://www.qaa.ac.uk/Publications/InformationAnd Guidance/Pages/Subject-benchmark-statement-Hospitality-leisure-sport-tourism-2008.aspx (Accessed 20 August 2013).

Richards, G., & Palmer, R. (2010). *Eventful Cities: cultural management and urban revitalisation*. Oxford: Butterworth-Heinemann.

Robinson, R., Barron, P., & Solnet, D. (2008). 'Innovative Approaches to Event Management Education in Career Development: a study of student experiences'. *Journal of Hospitality, Leisure, Sport & Tourism Education*, 7(1), 4–17.

Rossman, J., & Schlatter, B. (2011). *Recreation Programming: designing and staging leisure experiences*, 6th edn. Urbana, IL: Sagamore.

Schlentrich, U. (2008). 'The MICE Industry: meetings, incentives, conventions, and exhibitions'. In B. Brotherton & R. Wood (Eds.), *The Sage Handbook of Hospitality Management* (pp. 400–20). London: Sage.

Shipway, R., & Fyall, A. (2012). *International Sports Events: impacts, experiences and identities*. Oxford: Routledge.

Silvers, J., Bowdin, G., O'Toole, W., & Nelson, K. (2006). 'Towards an International Event Management Body of Knowledge (EMBOK)'. *Event Management*, 9(4), 185–98.

Smith, M. (Ed.). (2007). *Tourism, Culture and Regeneration*. Wallingford: CABI.

Torkildsen, G. (2005). *Leisure and Recreation Management*. Oxford: Routledge.

Van der Wagen, L. (2007). *Event Management for Tourism, Cultural, Business and Sporting Events*. Upper Saddle River, NJ: Pearson.

Weed, M. (2012). 'Towards an Interdisciplinary Events Research Agenda across Sport, Tourism, Leisure and Health'. In S. Page & J. Connell (Eds.), *The Routledge Handbook of Events* (pp. 57–71). London: Routledge.

Zeng, X., & Yang, J. (2011). 'Industry Perceptions of the Event Management Curriculum in Shanghai'. *Journal of Convention & Event Tourism*, 12(3), 232–9.

36

Legend to launchpad

Le Cordon Bleu, gastronomy and the future of education

Roger Haden
Le Cordon Bleu Australia

Introduction: genesis of gastronomy as a discipline

The perception that both Hospitality and Tourism Management rightly belonged to vocational education arose because, in terms of education, training in both areas was carried out in direct association with industry. Aligning Hospitality and Tourism Management with vocational education thereby foregrounded the practical skills requirements of management rather than academic scholarship and research (Scarpato, 2002; Lashley, 2004). Given this context, this perception was understandable, as hospitality training had been routinely provided by hotels and developed into management programmes run in-house by industry. But a more academic perspective on Hospitality (and Tourism) began to emerge in the early 1980s, underlining the conceptual and not merely skills-based knowledge implied by the term 'hospitality' (Airey & Tribe, 2000: 282). Individual schools of hospitality and tourism continued to emerge, scholarship and research were supported and bachelors and master degree programmes served to establish Tourism and Hospitality Management as bona fide disciplinary approaches.

The genesis of gastronomy as a scholarly, academic field follows a slightly different track, although it is important to recognize that it was foregrounded as being a key complementary aspect of 'hospitality' in the related academic literature that emerged in the 2000s (Scarpato, 2002; Lynch *et al.*, 2007). The emergent theory associated with hospitality and tourism drew on gastronomy, defined in terms of its first modern conceptualization by Brillat-Savarin as 'the reasoned comprehension of everything connected with the nourishment of man' (cited in Scarpato, 2002). This alignment of gastronomy with the 'new hospitality' recognized how both sought to contextualize the world of food and eating within social and cultural settings (Brillat-Savarin, cited in Scarpato, 2002: 1).

It is important to situate the history, discourse and core principles of gastronomic culture in terms of emergent contemporary interdisciplinary approaches like Gastronomy, Food Studies, and Hospitality and Tourism, particularly because, during the nineteenth and twentieth centuries gastronomy came to be narrowly defined as 'the art and science of delicate eating' (Oxford

English Dictionary, 2010a), thereby losing the sense in which the term was given to encompass a wider understanding of eating and drinking from the social and cultural standpoint. Moreover, the perception also developed that gastronomy was an elitist, hedonistic pursuit, whereas as it was conceived of in early nineteenth-century France, it was linked to a philosophy of living (Ferguson, 1998; Spang, 2000; Gigante, 2005). Gastronomy implied questioning, observation and the development of values and ethics related to all aspects of food and drink (Ory, 1997). It is in this context that the literal meaning of gastronomy as 'the rules of the stomach' (taken from the Greek *gastro*, meaning stomach, and *nomos*, meaning order or rules) expresses a complement of conceptual and practical aspects related to food and eating; that is, extending well beyond a narrow definition of gastronomy as fine dining.

The earliest public arbiter of gastronomic taste who intended to educate and achieved fame as a writer was Alexandre Balthazar Laurent Grimod de la Reynière (1758–1837). According to historian Jennifer J. Davis, Grimod defined a 'gourmande' as distinct from a glutton in that they possessed 'a nobility of the senses and a discriminating taste that subordinates the appetite to a higher purpose' (Davis, 2013: 122). Grimod's self-styled role as the West's first modern food critic evolved in the wake of the dissolution of the French guild system (1792), which had until then maintained standards of quality, hygiene and education in the trades related to restaurants, cookery and food and drink provision. From that time on, however, quality assurance would be governed by individuals and by connoisseurs who could pass judgement with some authority on questions of quality and artistry and, via the new print media, communicate their views to the dining public.

Also, crucially, a philosophy of gastronomy developed according to which the ideal of pleasure was conceived of as a social and moral good, as advocated by the philosopher Charles Fourier (1772–1837). The so-called pleasures of the table were not in Fourier's estimation elitist or excessive by nature, and therefore not sinful either according to Christian teaching, but were at the very heart of civilized culture and its cultivation. Grimod de la Reynière's contemporary, Jean Anthelme Brillat-Savarin (1755–1826), the brother-in-law of Fourier, and from whom Brillat-Savarin no doubt derived some of his ideas, emerged as the first modern gastronomer, linking food, dining and culture as a moral duty to eat well (Haden, 2011).

These men set the stage for food, cookery, eating and dining to be taken seriously; that is to be considered in the public sphere alongside history, art, science and language as subjects worthy of serious scholarship. Gastronomic culture at that time implied specific spaces (restaurants, cafés, bars and hotels), literary and artistic culture (the chef-as-artist is a product of this time), discussion of professional practice (popular press) and education (of the public: diners and the workforce); in general, a whole 'cultural field' (Ferguson, 1998).

All of these conditions were met in Paris in the first quarter of the nineteenth century. Yet, over the course of the rest of that century, gastronomic culture developed in France and in other Western countries, including the United States, mainly as a more narrowly defined professional practice on one hand and as a practice of social elites on the other. Despite Grimod suggesting that gastronomy would one day be recognized as an academic discipline in its own right, a point echoed later by Brillat-Savarin, when he asserted that taste would inspire an 'academy of gastronomers' that 'before too many years' will have its own 'academicians, its professors, its yearly courses and its contests for scholarships', no such development took place (Brillat-Savarin, 2011: 64). Rather than expanding in scope to become a governing set of principles for life and for living, gastronomy became much more narrowly associated with fine dining and the middle-class elites that initially, in France, but also elsewhere (such as the United States during the late nineteenth century), asserted their social and cultural distinction through eating (Haley, 2011).

Against this historical backdrop of the rise of the restaurant, the chef-artist and of the elites that supported them in their desire for social distinction, Brillat-Savarin's definition of gastronomy as a broad cultural approach to food and eating faded into the background and was associated at best with a minor literature of connoisseurship and aesthetic appreciation. Social distinction developed as an intrinsic feature of the modern 'fine dining' restaurant, with an emphasis on both service, from a whole collection of staff, and ostentatious display on the part of diners, who in keeping with their role as taste-makers assumed the role of connoisseurs (Haden, 2011). Over the course of the nineteenth century and into the twentieth the public perception that fine dining restaurants and haute cuisine ('high' cooking) were socially and technically inaccessible was firmly entrenched. Fine dining restaurants evolved as showcases for technical skills deemed way beyond the powers of everyday cooks and for a clientele of diners whose bid for social distinction fully incorporated the notion of an elite cuisine, and corresponding knowledge of it, as much as ostentatious displays of wealth. Professional cookery texts were particularly influential in terms of aligning gastronomy with cookery and included trade journals, like *L'Art culinaire*, which was published between 1883 and 1939, with contributions from many leading chefs of the day (Mennell, 1985). The concentration of effort on 'a profound desire for progress and improvement', expressed in the *L'Art culinaire*'s statement of purpose, also suggests how gastronomy aligned with elite middle-class consumers, who almost by definition sought 'progress and improvement' (Mennell, 1985: 170).

In terms of academic scholarship, the perception that anything other than the scientific study of food, or a utilitarian understanding of cooking and dining, denoted a form of hedonism and self-indulgence, but also, conversely, that food denoted something too absolutely mundane to be a proper subject of academic inquiry, steered scholars away from gastronomy. As French social theorist Roland Barthes remarked in 1961: 'to the scholar, the subject of food connotes triviality or guilt' (Barthes, 2008: 28). Adding to this prejudice was the fact that the modernist approach to academic scholarship was itself mono-disciplinary, as Scarpato points out in his defence of gastronomy as a bona fide approach to the study of food and food culture. Scarpato quotes Brillat-Savarin importantly providing a clear sense of the everyday, rather than elite, aspects of the human–food relationship: 'Gastronomy, in fact, is the motive force behind farmers, winegrowers, fishermen, and huntsmen, not to mention the great family of cooks, under whatever title they may disguise their employment as preparers of food' (Scarpato, 2002: 5).

Defining gastronomy with too narrow a perspective was also recognized from within the domain of 'professional gastronomy'. Texts typically showed due deference to Brillat-Savarin adding a sense of intellectual rigour, hence legitimacy, to the 'profession' of chef. Cracknell and Nobis's widely used 1985 text, *Practical Professional Gastronomy* invokes Brillat-Savarin's name and quotes from his work numerous times as well as observing that: 'The subject of gastronomy as a body of knowledge is one that gives rise to much controversy, the main difficulty being to confine its scope within clearly defined parameters of conventional disciplines as associated with culinary practices' (Cracknell & Nobis, 1985: xi). Notwithstanding their wish to limit the scope of their book to providing guidance to culinary practitioners, the text expands on a wide range of gastronomic themes and subjects now standard in undergraduate and postgraduate gastronomy programmes: the development of eating habits; cultural and religious influences on food culture; the senses; and the history of dining. Even at the end of the twentieth century, such core values as expressed by Cracknell and Nobis, among others, did seemingly little to mitigate the widely entrenched popular sentiment that 'gastronomy' was an elitist and self-indulgent pastime. Professional texts highlighted gastronomy, but with more emphasis on culinary arts (production) than on consumption (see Bode, 1994; Gillespie 2001).

When the idea was expressed, at about the same time, that Hospitality and Tourism might be viewed as 'interdisciplinary in that they can serve as a focal point in which disciplines can come together to present new insights or new knowledge', the new perspective echoed Brillat-Savarin's definition of gastronomy as 'the reasoned comprehension of everything connected with the nourishment of man', which also appeared eminently compatible with the contemporary concept of multidisciplinarity (Airey & Tribe, 2000; Brillat-Savarin, cited in Scarpato, 2002: 4).

The broader academic context for this convergence of academically focused studies, which recognized hospitality and gastronomy to be social and cultural practices, was the intellectual outpouring of the late 1960s. The movement known as post-structuralism, influenced by continental philosophy and various offshoots of what was essentially a radical reappraisal of the very conditions of knowledge production and its social construction, led to a deep questioning of disciplinarity as such, as well as traditional academic values, methods, assumptions and paradigms. Discourse analysis (including Jacques Derrida's deconstruction), environmentalism, feminism (gender studies), postcolonial studies and, notably, cultural studies (premised on the redefinition of culture itself as 'a whole way of life') developed through the 1970s and 1980s, setting a new agenda for changes in scholarship and teaching methods that prepared the way for multidisciplinary and interdisciplinary studies (Williams, 1966; During, 2005). Crucially, Cultural Studies developed as a critical method or range of methods, rather than a discipline as such, and questioned the epistemological grounds and supposed disciplinary parameters of knowledge on which academic authority was based. The ground was thus prepared for the emergence of gastronomy as a bona fide critical field of inquiry.

Another galvanizing force in the development of gastronomy was the growth of consumerism, which as a result also became a focus of academic attention. The paradigmatic shift from a dominant economic paradigm of production (Fordism) to one based on consumption as a driver of economic activity, increased emphasis on human actors and on what motivated them as consumers (Featherstone, 1991). As Western consumerist culture blossomed in the 1950s, coinciding with a baby boom, more attention was directed to the desires of a broadening demographic of individual consumers, and to the products, services and, crucially, experiences that might attract them (Pine & Gilmore, 1998). Because hospitality, tourism and gastronomy were aiming as 'disciplines' to be holistic, reflective approaches that utilized combined sociological, anthropological and philosophical perspectives, the consumerist era provided the right climate. Today, the relevance of tourism, hospitality and gastronomy in terms of disciplinary expertise is implied by theorists: 'hedonic or experiential consumption is central to a comprehensive understanding of consumer behaviour in the hospitality and tourism context' (Titz, 2008: 325).

Historically, gastronomy had formed around the (social) activities of elites and the (technical) culinary arts that supported them, so it is not without irony that growing interest in food-related knowledge from an affluent middle class also contributed to the rebirth of gastronomy as an academic multidiscipline. Only this time, social ostentation or prestige were not goals in themselves: education and involvement in understanding food production and the sources of our food (provenance) were, as indeed was a deeper engagement in the moral and ethical landscape of 'food'. Gastronomes morphed into 'foodies' who while still aware of their social status via active expression of a lifestyle, increasingly, expressed this using sustainable, socially responsible means. The active pursuit of knowledge, pleasure and alternative ways of living became a statement about how to live – ethically. Key here is the notion of 'knowledge-based leisure', linking ethical decision-making about food purchase to, for example, sustainability, animal welfare, environmental protection, and health and well-being (De Solier, 2013: 33). In this manner, gastronomy focused attention on a broad spectrum of legitimate academic inquiry and also social spaces for the application of knowledge, such as is demonstrated by the increasing output of food-related academic texts published over the last decade and a half, with a combined ethical and academic purpose (see, for example, Pollan, 2006, 2008; Nestle, 2007; Petrini, 2006). Rising levels of consumer involvement during the 1990s and 2000s in 'gastronomic tourism' (also called culinary tourism or food and wine tourism), also contributed to the revitalization of rural communities through the rediscovery of local identity through (food) heritage and traditions and regional foodways long 'outmoded' by the economics of industrial food production. Consequently, a new space of academic inquiry in gastronomic tourism and related fields is also thriving today (Hjalager & Richards, 2002; Long, 2004; Hall & Gossling, 2012).

Gastronomy and education

The incorporation of gastronomy into higher degree curricula in various countries around the world began with the delivery of the Master of Liberal Arts in Gastronomy at the Metropolitan University of Boston (beginning as a part-time program in the late 1980s), the Graduate Program in Gastronomy at the University of Adelaide (2001–2009) and the Master's degree in Food Culture and Communication at the University of Gastronomic Services (Italy), which also appeared post-2000 and continues today. Gastronomy's relevance coincides with growing concerns about global warming and environmental degradation, rising population, social injustice for producers in third world countries, diet-related epidemics of obesity and diabetes, food allergies, food waste, water pollution, and overuse of fertilizer and pesticides. Gastronomy appeals to those who share such concerns because it offers a holistic understanding of the forces at play in creating such complex problems and a palpable sense of what can be done to improve the quality of life for humans, all living things and the environment. This approach is in the tradition of John Dewey, whose emphasis on *experience* (including practices like cooking) was integral to his philosophy of education (Dewey, 1938). Dewey's belief that 'engaging students in growing, preparing and eating food would provide the best learning opportunities', also suggests that the appeal of gastronomy today is partly because it links doing and thinking in a way that is empowering (Dewey, cited in Wessell, 2007: 141). Exercising responsible food choices can have direct social, economic, political and health benefits, as well as providing the immediate pleasure of consumption. Gastronomy therefore inspires re-engagement with practical activities like gardening and cooking, which link purposeful work and social and environmental benefits.

Cultural and economic factors also contributed to the interest in gastronomy including rising affluence linked to consumerism and the 'aestheticization of everyday life', which infers an interest, or even hyper-interest, in food and sensory experience (Howes, 2005). Interest in aesthetic pleasures also gives rise to concerns for environmental well-being, in raising awareness of the inherent beauty in natural processes (like fermentation) and the pleasures they bring (Katz, 2012).

Gastronomy programmes at undergraduate and graduate levels continue to come on stream (in Australia, Italy, France, New Zealand, Peru, Singapore, Spain, Sweden, Turkey, the UK and USA, for example) and interest in food-related scholarship from within and outside the university sector shows no sign of abating. When Brillat-Savarin suggested gastronomy's expression was as a 'culture which produces, the commerce which exchanges, the industry which prepares and the experience which invents . . . to dispose of everything to the best advantage' he described the kind of integrated food and drink-focused culture we see developing now, particularly in new world, regional areas where small producers are re-energizing rural foodways that for a century or more were turned over to industrialized farming and means of production (Brillat Savarin, 2011: 61–2). Still very much on the margins of a mainstream food culture given over to low cost and convenience, and barely aware of 'gastronomy', the new discipline is taking shape in an educational context that has come full circle from its incipient stage in nineteenth-century Paris. The complex interweaving of food culture in everyday life that Brillat-Savarin recognized is well represented in works highly critical of contemporary 'big food' (see Pollan, 2006). Scholarly publications like *Gastronomica: the Journal of Food and Culture* (University of California Press) and *Food, Culture and Society: An International Journal of Multidisciplinary Research* (Bloomsbury), *The British Food Journal* (Emerald) convey a powerful sense of how the study of food culture has come of age.

Le Cordon Bleu

Le Cordon Bleu is presented here as a case study in the contemporary marketing of gastronomy as a discipline, which also serves to foreground the challenge represented by showing leadership in socially responsible education at the community level. In a world increasingly shaped by communication technologies and the digital revolution, the notion that gastronomy provides an ethical guideline for students and for the wider community is arguably a key advantage for educators in pulling together educational and non-educational groups at a time when institutionalized education is coming under pressure to maintain relevance.

Le Cordon Bleu will mark its 120th year in business in 2015 and has for many years been a brand associated in many countries with culinary arts. Its iconic brand image, the 'blue ribbon' (*cordon bleu*) and medal-like badge, fuse mythologizing elements representing excellence, superiority, gastronomy and French culinary arts traditions. Graphic representations of the ribbon and medal feature strongly in marketing brochures and prospectuses, the medal deriving from the historic *Ordre du Saint Esprit*, created in 1578 by King Henri III to honour the achievements of particular knights (Brune, 1892). Included in the knights' livery was a blue sash upon which hung the Cross of the Holy Spirit. The gastronomically inclined knights were well known for holding sumptuous banquets, which became famous for their quality and, by degrees, the association between '*cordon bleu*', excellent cookery and gastronomic experience grew.

Paying homage to this tradition, Le Cordon Bleu's royal blue-coloured '*cordon*' and Le Cordon Bleu cross appear frequently in advertising copy and posters. Miniature versions of the cross are reproduced as bronze-, silver- and gold-coloured jacket pins and awarded to Le Cordon Bleu students who complete the diploma's basic, intermediate and superior stages (the 'classic cycle') in cuisine and patisserie.

While the story of 'Le Cordon Bleu', the cooking school, only begins centuries later with the opening of its Paris-based school in 1896, the nominal link back to the knights order, meant that the expression '*le Cordon Bleu*' had entered the French vernacular some time earlier as a general expression for culinary excellence. The widening readership of cookbooks in the nineteenth century further established '*cordon bleu*' to mean excellence in cookery. Horace-Napoléon Raisson (1798–1854) used the term explicitly to denote quality in cookery when he wrote *Le cordon bleu, ou Nouvelle cuisinière bourgeoise* in 1827. In 1842 the term was also used to describe a cook of quality in, *La Cuisinière des petits ménages, ou la Bonne ménagère en exercice, contenant, etc; par un petit cordon-bleu de Paris*, by Louise-Augustine Friedel. In 1833, Jourdan Lecointe produced his *Le Cuisiniers des Cuisiniers: 1000 recettes de cordon-bleu usuelles, faciles et économiques de cuisine et d'office d'après les praticiens les plus renommés, français, provencaux, anglais, allemands et italiens*, a book that clearly had some success in the marketplace. The eighteenth edition of the book was published in 1868 (Lecointe, 1868).

Notwithstanding that these examples suggest how the term '*le cordon bleu*' represented quality in cookery, it was arguably a magazine, *La Cuisinière Cordon-bleu*, first produced by French journalist Marthe Distel in 1895, that appeared to galvanize enough interest in learning how to cook to prompt the launch of a '*le cordon bleu*' school. Interestingly, the use of the feminine form of 'cook' – *cuisinière*– in the school's nomenclature, identified the key readership to be predominantly women, and the magazine, recently described as 'a nineteenth century version of *Gourmet*', focused on classic recipes and tips for entertaining (Flynn, 2007: 28). The magazine's immediate success prompted Distel to offer free cooking classes to subscribers and in November 1895, the first class was held in the kitchens of the Palais Royale, where, a century or so before, the first grand restaurants had opened and flourished in the aftermath of the French Revolution, at the dawn of the modern age of gastronomy (see Spang, 2000). The intertwining of history, gastronomy and Le Cordon Bleu was under way.

Having proved popular, by 1896, the cookery lessons were held for the first time at the duly named L'Ecole de Cuisine du Cordon-Bleu, which opened on Rue St Honoré (the patron saint of patissiers), still in the neighbourhood of the Palais, with a programme based on the formula foregrounded in the *La Cuisinière Cordon-bleu*: hands-on teaching, highly informative demonstrations by professional chefs currently working in the industry and the use of good quality produce (Villegas & Randell, 2005). Essentially, this mode of delivery is still adopted by Le Cordon Bleu cookery schools today. By providing innovative and up-to-date instruction that the public (mostly women) found attractive, the school was able to tap a new market and soon attracted paying students, often from outside France. It seems as if 'French cuisine' had an international following from the start (Trubek, 2000).

The school's kitchens were first managed by Henri-Paul Pellaprat (1869–1954), who would spend 32 years at Le Cordon Bleu. Pelleprat produced one of the most highly respected books on culinary arts from the first half of the twentieth century, *L'Art culinaire moderne* (1966), reflecting the knowledge gained in a career teaching cooking, the book was completed in the year he left the school. By the mid-1960s it had been translated into five languages and sold over a million copies. The gastronomic spirit of that text is expressed in the preface to the 1966 American edition, by Michael Field, who writes that it 'reaffirms lucidly, persuasively and precisely the dignity of man's relation to the food he eats'. Field also cites Maurice-Edmund Saillant (1872–1956; known as 'Curnonsky'), another pupil of Pellaprat's, one of France's most famous modern gastronomes and a prolific writer on, and recorder of, France's gastronomic legacy. Saillant describes *L'Art culinaire moderne* as 'a veritable encyclopaedia of the table and a text book of good living' (Pellaprat, 1966: xiii). Raymond Oliver (1909–1990), a modern-day chef-owner of Le Grand Véfour, one of France's first great restaurants that opened its doors in 1784 in the Palais Royale, also trained with Pellaprat and authored his own book on the history of French gastronomy (Oliver, 1967).

The magazine, *La Cuisinière Cordon-bleu*, which Pellaprat also edited, continued being published more or less continuously from 1895 to 1962, totalling over 1,000 issues and including instruction and commentary from leading chefs of the day. It arguably contributed much to the codification of French culinary methods and techniques, outlasting *L'Art culinaire*, the most influential culinary trade publication contributed to by leading chefs and published from 1883–1939 (Mennell, 1985).

This history suggests how closely Le Cordon Bleu's story is woven into the history and development of French culinary arts and the legacy of gastronomy that contributed to a culture based on knowledge of food, cooking and dining which encompassed, at its core, the utmost respect for the 'chef-artists' who traditionally had sacrificed much in following their vocation (see Tschumi, 1974: 193–202; Shaw, 1994: 65–95; Pratten, 2003: 454–9; Pépin 2003: 50–7, 79–84, 88–103). Except for relatively brief periods of difficulty, in particular during the twentieth century's Great Depression and world wars, Le Cordon Bleu continued in its first

90 years to acquire cultural capital on the strength of its attested quality culinary teaching, its model of instruction, the popular cultural association of 'le cordon bleu' with quality, the increased internationalization of French culinary art and the emergence of a culture based on food production and consumption but also supported by shared values, beliefs and goals. The school's growing public recognition attracted some who would go on to be famous advocates of French gastronomy, and of its underpinning core belief in the importance of good food. Dione Lucas, America's first television cookery show personality, and Rosemary Hume (both Le Cordon Bleu graduates) combined their skills and opened L'Ecole du Petit Cordon Bleu in London in 1933. It later became The Cordon Bleu Cookery School (London) Ltd. Culinary educator, Julia Child, also completed the Paris programme, in 1949, going on to co-author *Mastering the Art of French Cookery* in 1962, and hosting a television cookery programme that made her America's principal advocate of French cookery in the 1960s.

Under the direction of Madame Elizabeth Brassart, from 1945 to 1984, Le Cordon Bleu continued to deliver its internationally renowned cookery courses, but it took the acquisition of Le Cordon Bleu, in 1984, by André J. Cointreau, a member of the Cointreau and Rémy-Martin families and a long-time family friend of Brassart, to begin the transformation that would launch Le Cordon Bleu as an international educator in not only cookery and patisserie but also in hotel management hospitality and gastronomy.

International expansion and gastronomy in Australia

Cointreau expanded Le Cordon Bleu culinary schools internationally and entered the higher education market with programmes in hospitality management. In 1988 a culinary school opened in Ottawa (Canada) and in 1990 the School of Cordon Bleu Cookery in London was purchased. A school was opened in Tokyo in 1991, and in 1993 Cointreau partnered with the International College of Hotel Management (ICHM) in Adelaide, South Australia, offering two Le Cordon Bleu cuisine subjects in ICHM's diploma programme. This was followed in 1999 with the launch of Le Cordon Bleu's first bachelor degree in Restaurant Business Operations. Not itself accredited as a higher education provider, partnering with accredited higher education institutions was a vital component of Le Cordon Bleu's business model. Both the University of South Australia and the government-owned TAFE (Technical and Further Education) college became partners in Le Cordon Bleu's first degree programme.

Expansion continued into 2000 when the Career Education Corporation (CEC) in the USA partnered with Le Cordon Bleu, leading to 17 cooking schools across North America using the French brand. But, in the same year, a crucial development reflected the groundswell of interest in gastronomy described earlier. The University of Adelaide partnered with Le Cordon Bleu in the joint-badged Graduate Program in Gastronomy, the first full-time on-campus higher education gastronomy programme in the world. The case is instructive because it illustrates the contemporary relevance of gastronomy as a discipline but also raises questions about how to develop gastronomy further in the future.

Australia, a progressive Western democracy, but without a strong gastronomic history of its own, paradoxically embodied the type of culture where interest in and enthusiasm for gastronomy was likely to emerge strongly. English food and cookery has not traditionally been identified with fine dining, for example, yet London brims with fine dining restaurants and a global representation of cuisines. In Australia, a concentration of interest among a few led the way in the form of the first 'Symposium of Australian Gastronomy', held over two days in Adelaide, in 1984 (Santich, 1984). The symposium (inspired by the Oxford Symposium on Food and Cookery, which began in 1981) brought together a mix of intellectuals, practitioners and members of the public interested in food culture – in valuing it for its own sake, but also for the sake of improving people's lives; in short, to revaluate the importance of food culture in the life of the whole community. Bon vivant and cookery book author Don Dunstan, who later, as the premier of South Australia, would become a vocal advocate of the importance of food and wine culture, attended the symposium (Dunstan, 1998). Its convenor Graham Pont was an academic who in 1983 had created an undergraduate subject based on the writings of Brillat-Savarin, delivered at the University of New South Wales. Restaurateur and, later, award-winning food writer Gay Bilson was also among the organizers, as was journalist Michael Symons, author of a cultural critique of Australian foodways called *One Continuous Picnic*, first published in 1982, who in 1992 was awarded a doctorate from Flinders University (South Australia) for a thesis on 'Epicurean philosophy' (Symons, 2007 [1982]; Bilson, 2004) and Barbara Santich, a freelance food writer who later completed her PhD, a comparative study of French, Italian and Spanish cuisine. Santich, Symons and Bilson would all make significant contributions to subsequent symposia (Santich 1987).

The 'Symposium of Australian Gastronomy' was a success to the extent that it provided a forum for wide-ranging discussion on all matters related to food: history, production, consumption, social values, food and the arts (film, painting, performance, mixed media) while at the same time providing the context for experimentation in cookery and dining, exploration of cultural and ethnic difference and historical recreations. The provision of excellent eating and drinking experiences itself created a sense of *convivium* (a feast), a Greek word that, like *gastronomia* ('rules of the stomach') and *symposium* ('drinking party'), collectively express the special social and cultural value accorded food and drink's role in life. To date there have been 19 Australian symposia, the most recent held in 2013. Most published proceedings (collected papers), some of which are available online (see, for example, Mead & Bryan, 2007). Although the symposia remain fringe events, barely noticed by mainstream media, importantly, they embody the practice of thinking gastronomically as a form of personal and moral education, one that invites investigation and critical reflection on one's relationship with food and by association with others and with communities. These values are precisely those which align with the disciplinary scope of gastronomy, including ethical concern for environment and animal welfare, desire for knowledge about where our food comes from and what 'processing' entails, the desire to educate children about agriculture and cookery (school kitchen-garden projects), so that food is conceived of as central to community and indeed global well-being.

The advent of the first symposium had a serendipitous playing out in the development of the Le Cordon Bleu Graduate Program in Gastronomy, because, by 2000, Graham Latham, then a former director of Regency Park Institute of TAFE, had created a local entity 'Le Cordon Bleu Australia', with Cointreau's backing, and had approached the University of Adelaide with an initiative to partner in a hospitality management degree. But Latham had also conceived and designed the structure of a gastronomy programme at Master's level, which turned out to be exactly what the university wanted. The programme was fleshed out with input coming from independent food writer and historian Barbara Santich, who had remained an advocate of gastronomy and supporter of the symposium. Santich would also manage and teach in the programme. Latham's original vision, which included an emphasis on technical aspects of wine and food production, was altered to focus more on gastronomic history and culture, contemporary food culture, and communication (food media, television, film, literature and arts), developing under Santich's influence a clear academic focus (with no practical component), a major concentration on French gastronomic history and culture with emphasis given to de la Reynière and Brillat-Savarin, the history of the modern restaurant, professional culinary arts, wine and beer, and other drinks in history, with elective subjects in gastronomic tourism and food and wine technology. The programme experienced steady increases in student numbers, especially online enrolments, from 2001 to 2009.

Shortly following that period, due to a breakdown in talks over contractual arrangements, Le Cordon Bleu terminated its contract with the University of Adelaide. Intent on continuing to deliver its programme, however, and retaining its rights to the intellectual property, a new focus on gastronomic tourism was agreed to, one that would potentially increase the relevance of the qualification for graduates and industry professionals seeking employment. Burgeoning activity in culinary and wine tourism seemed more than ever before to be a space where gastronomy was advancing as a real-world practice, engaging local and regional small and artisan producers, restaurateurs and, increasingly, tourism operators newly aware of the value of 'place' (and its connection to food and drink). Working together in the common cause of sustainable quality food and wine production began to put regions and localities on the gastronomic tourism map (see Hjalager & Richards, 2002).

The Le Cordon Bleu Master of Gastronomic Tourism was launched as a fully online degree in partnership with Southern Cross University (Lismore, New South Wales), in May 2012. At the time of writing the programme has approximately 110 students enrolled, many of whom are industry professionals with varied backgrounds, but predominantly well-educated women seeking more engagement with the world of food, community and social change. A recent study of food tourists confirms a similar demographic (Robinson & Getz, 2014). The integration of study and career path is also a noticeable feature of current student profiles, with some enrolled in order to advance a personal range of already impressive entrepreneurial skills.

Profiles of current students in the new programme suggest that gastronomy today meets the needs of those who understand education to be a fully integrated aspect of living, fusing work and learning within a broader conceptualization of life as an ethical activity in support of broader goals of community and environmental well-being. Current students are applying what they learn with the knowledge they already have, demonstrating a core principle of contemporary constructivist theories of learning. Gastronomy has broken free of its restrictive definition within professional culinary arts, and has arguably moved beyond what Brillat-Savarin and his contemporaries envisaged. Today, gastronomy can be construed as a network of practices (which anthropologists call foodways), framed by values and generated in the field by small producers, artisan practitioners, chefs, cooks, farmers' markets, tourism operators, wineries, cellar doors, restaurants and, of course, the consumers. Crucially, gastronomy works best as a social movement, a collective, connective exercise that mobilizes communities to work together. The goals are simultaneously education, enjoyment, better eating, a cleaner environment and sustainable practice. Gastronomy now extends beyond the institutional, disciplinary and occupational contexts because it is connected with an organic cultural momentum of its own. The educational dynamic for change is now in the schools, the homes, the streets, the markets, the restaurants, as well as in the university.

Challenges: transnational and micro-cultural

The relatively rapid growth of Le Cordon Bleu in the international higher education context is not without its challenges. Transnational education brings with it increasing pressures to comply with differing governance structures, policies and processes. But from the gastronomic perspective the challenges are clear as well. The current grass-roots cultural groundswell of interest in gastronomy and food studies more generally seems likely to continue, with collaborative learning now extending between faculties such as horticulture, entrepreneurship, nutrition, agriculture and culinary arts (Ashford, 2013). Even the recognition of gastronomy and hospitality as holistic practices in the early 2000s, arguably did not anticipate the significant academic interest that would be generated by scholars and lay persons studying food culture from disciplinary perspectives as diverse as environmental science, philosophy, architecture, agriculture, climatology, health and well-being, social enterprise, and ethical business. Yet, all these areas converge in the study of food and its complex role in our lives. Gastronomy sends up a challenge not only to Le Cordon Bleu and its partners, but to the education system in general. With an eye on the future, gastronomic perspectives provide opportunities to engage young and old in community building, in ethical practice, in social interaction and in pleasurable activities that include, but are not limited to, eating and drinking. This is the micro-cultural level of education, where 'the culture or development of personal knowledge or understanding, growth of character, moral and social qualities, etc.', arguably needs to be focused today on the best possible integration of work and leisure, study and play; by the integration of learning into the practical context of living (Oxford English Dictionary, 2010b). Gastronomy's broad-ranging profile as a multidiscipline challenges educators to embrace such holistic learning opportunities at a time when the de-institutionalizing of learning is becoming a reality. Gastronomy thereby moves from being an elite to an everyday knowledge, shaped by the needs and shared values of communities everywhere and in step with the demand for more meaningful, satisfying forms of education.

References

Airey, D., & Tribe, J. (2000). 'Education for Hospitality'. In C. Lashley & A. Morrison (Eds.), *In Search of Hospitality: theoretical perspectives and debates* (pp. 276–92). Oxford: Butterworth-Heinemann.

Ashford, E. (2013). 'Interest Growing in Food Sustainability'. *Community College Daily*. Available: http://www.ccdaily.com/Pages/Sustainability/Interest-growing-in-food-sustainability-.aspx (Accessed 12 December 2013).

Barthes, R. (2008). [1961]. 'Toward a Psychosociology of Contemporary Food Consumption'. In C. Counihan & P. Van Esterik (Eds.), *Food and Culture* (pp. 28–35). New York: Routledge.

Bilson, G. (2004). *Plenty: digressions on food*. Camberwell: Penguin.

Bode, W. (1994). *European Gastronomy: the story of man's food and eating customs*. London: Grub Street.

Brillat-Savarin, J-A. (2011). [orig.1825]. *The Physiology of Taste*. M. F. K. Fisher (Ed. and trans.) New York: Everyman's Library.

Brune, P. (1892). *Histoire de l'Ordre Hospitalier du Saint-Esprit*. Paris: C. Martin.

Cracknell, H. L., & Nobis, G. (1985). *Practical Professional Gastronomy*. Basingstoke: Macmillan.

Davis, J. (2013). *Defining Culinary Authority: the transformation of cooking in France, 1650–1830*. Baton Rouge: Louisiana State University Press.

De Solier, I. (2013). *Food and the Self: consumption, production and material culture*. London: Bloomsbury.

Dewey, J. (1938). *Experience and Education*. New York: Macmillan.

Dunstan, D. (1998). *Don Dunstan's Cookbook*. Revised with additional recipes by the author; illus. Janet Bridgland. Unley, South Australia: Calypso.

During, S. (2005). *Cultural Studies: a critical introduction*. London: Routledge.

Featherstone, M. (1991). *Consumer Culture and Postmodernism*. London: Sage Publications.

Ferguson, S. (1998). 'A Cultural Field in the Making: gastronomy in nineteenth-century France'. *American Journal of Sociology, 104*(3), 597–641.

Flynn, K. (2007). *The Sharper Your Knife, the Less You Cry: love, laughter, and tears in Paris at the world's most famous cooking school*. New York: Viking.

Gigante, D. (Ed.). (2005). *Gusto: essential writings in nineteenth-century gastronomy*. New York: Routledge.

Gillespie, C. (2001). *European Gastronomy into the 21st Century*. Oxford: Butterworth-Heinemann.

Haden, R. (2011). 'Lionizing Taste: towards an ecology of contemporary connoisseurship'. In J. Strong (Ed.), *Educated Taste: food drink and connoisseur culture* (pp. 237–90). Lincoln: University of Nebraska Press.

Haley, A. (2011). *Turning the Tables: restaurants and the rise of the American middle class, 1880–1920*. Chapel Hill: University of North Carolina Press.

Hall, C., & Gossling, S. (Eds.). (2012). *Sustainable Culinary Systems: local foods, innovation, tourism and hospitality*. London: Routledge.

Hjalager, A-M., & Richards, G. (Eds.). (2002). *Tourism and Gastronomy*. London: Routledge.

Howes, D. (2005). 'Hyperesthesia, or, The Sensual Logic of Late Capitalism'. In D. Howes (Ed.), *Empire of the Senses: the sensual culture reader* (pp. 281–303). New York: Berg Press.

Katz, S. E. (2012). *The Art of Fermentation: an in-depth exploration of essential concepts and processes from around the world*. White River Junction, VT: Chelsea Green Publishing.

Lashley, C. (2004). 'Escaping the Tyranny of Relevance: some reflections on hospitality management education'. In J. Tribe & E. Wickens (Eds.), *Critical Issues in Tourism Education: Proceedings of the 2004 Conference of the Association for Tourism in Higher Education* (pp. 58–69). Missenden Abbey, Bucks., UK, 1–3 December. ATHE Publication no. 14.

Lecointe, Jourdan (1868). *Le Cuisinier des Cuisiniers: 1000 recettes de cordon-bleu usuelles, faciles et économiques de cuisine et d'office d'après les praticiens les plus renommés, français, provencaux, anglais, allemands et italien*, 18th Edn. Paris: A. Laplace.

Long, L. (Ed.). (2004). *Culinary Tourism*. Lexington: University Press of Kentucky.

Lynch, P., Morrison, A., & Lashley, C. (Eds.). (2007). *Hospitality: a social lens*. Hoboken, NJ: Taylor and Francis.

Mead, P., & Bryan, S. (Eds.). (2007). 'Beyond the Supermarket: learning to overcome gastronomic poverty'. Proceedings of the Fifteenth Symposium of Australian Gastronomy. 29 April–2 May, Dover, Tasmania.

Mennell, S. (1985). *All Manners of Food: eating and taste in England and France from the Middle Ages to the present*. Oxford: B. Blackwell.

Nestle, M. (2007). *Food Politics: how the food industry influences nutrition and health*. Berkeley: University of California Press.

Oliver, R. (1967). *Gastronomy of France*. London: Wine and Food Society.

Ory, P. (1997). 'Gastronomy'. In P. Nora & L. Kritzman (Eds.), *Realms of Memory: the construction of the French past*. Vol. 2. (pp. 443–67). New York: Columbia University Press.

Oxford English Dictionary online (2010a). 'Gastronomy' [current listing, 1898] Available: http://www.oed.com (Accessed 18 October 2013).

Oxford English Dictionary online (2010b). 'Education' [3rd listed meaning] Available: http://www.oed.com (Accessed 4 December 2013).

Pellaprat, H-P. (1966). *Modern French Culinary Art*. New York: World Publishing Company. (English language edition, based on the original 1936 French edition, *L'Art culinaire moderne: la bonne table française et étrangère comprenant plus de 3.000 recettes*. Paris: SADAG.)

Pépin, J. (2003). *The Apprentice: my life in the kitchen*. Boston, MA: Houghton Mifflin.

Petrini, C. (2006). *Slow Food Revolution: a new culture for eating and living*. Carlo Petrini in conversation with Gigi Padovani, translated by Francesca Santovetti. New York: Rizzoli.

Pine, B. J., & Gilmore, J. H. (1998). 'Welcome to the Experience Economy'. *Harvard Business Review*, 76(4), 97–105.

Pollan, M. (2006). *The Omnivore's Dilemma: a natural history of four meals*. New York: Penguin Press.

Pollan, M. (2008). *In Defense of Food: an eater's manifesto*. New York: Penguin Press.

Pratten, J. (2003). 'What Makes a Great Chef?' *British Food Journal*, 105(7), 454–9.

Robinson, R., & Getz, D. (2014). 'Profiling Potential Food Tourists: an Australian study'. *British Food Journal*, 116(4): 690–706.

Santich, B. (1984). 'The Upstart Cuisine: proceedings of the first Symposium of Australian Gastronomy'. 12–13 March, Carclew, Adelaide.

Santich, B. (1987). 'Two Languages, Two Cultures, Two Cuisines: a comparative study of the culinary cultures of northern and southern France, Italy and Catalonia in the fourteenth and fifteenth centuries'. PhD manuscript. Flinders University Library, South Australia.

Scarpato, R. (2002). 'Gastronomy Studies in Search of Hospitality'. *Journal of Hospitality and Tourism Management*, 9(2), 152.

Shaw, T. (1994). *The World of Escoffier*. London: Vendome Press.

Spang, R. (2000). *The Invention of the Restaurant: Paris and modern gastronomic culture*. Cambridge, MA: Harvard University Press.

Symons, M. (2007). [1982]. *One Continuous Picnic: a gastronomic history of Australia*. Carlton, Vic.: Melbourne University Press.

Titz, K. (2008). 'Experiential Consumption: affect – emotions – hedonism'. In H. Oh & A. Pizam (Eds.), *Handbook of Hospitality Marketing Management* (pp. 324–52). Amsterdam: Butterworth-Heinemann.

Trubek, A. B. (2000). *Haute Cuisine: how the French invented the culinary profession.* Philadelphia: University of Pennsylvania Press.

Tschumi, G. (1974). 'Chef'. In J. Burnett (Ed.), *Useful Toil: autobiographies of working people from the 1820s to the 1920s* (pp. 193–202). London: Allen Lane.

Villegas, M., & Randell, S. (2005). *The Food of France: a journey for food lovers.* Sydney: Murdoch Books.

Wessell, A. (2007). 'The Pleasures of Slow Learning: cultivating communities through food education'. In B. Van Ernst (Ed.), *Proceedings of the 2007 AUCEA Inc. National Conference Proceedings: the scholarship of community engagement: Australia's way forward* (pp. 140–4). Alice Springs, NT, 2–4 July, Australian Universities Community Engagement Alliance Inc.

Williams, R. (1966). *Culture and Society, 1780–1950.* New York: Harper & Row.

37

What makes Hotel ICON a teaching hotel?

Tony S. M. Tse

School of Hotel and Tourism Management, The Hong Kong Polytechnic University

Introduction

Many industry-based university degree programmes such as hospitality management face a dilemma in attempting to balance theory with the practical skills required by the industry that will ultimately employ their graduates (Ruhanen, 2005). Morrison and O'Mahony (2003) point out that knowledge about hospitality has largely been drawn from the industry itself, and, due to the immaturity of hospitality as an academic discipline, distinctive delivery methods and course designs have been developed to involve educators in the tourism industry (Cooper & Shepherd, 1997). Therefore, many hospitality management programmes include some elements of 'laboratory' time in kitchens, bars, restaurants, hotel reception and accommodation suites (Lashley, 2004).

Despite these widespread efforts to incorporate industry practices into the curriculum, recent research in Australia found considerable variance between the respective views of industry professionals and tourism educators concerning the value of tertiary education and the merits of various subjects taught at the university level (Wang et al., 2010). This research suggests a gap between the current tourism curriculum and the needs of the tourism industry, indicating that those involved in curriculum design should continue to work closely with the industry to ensure a stronger connection between theory and practice.

This chapter explains how a university-owned teaching hotel at The Hong Kong Polytechnic University (PolyU) is fulfilling the aims of hospitality management education by delivering balanced emphases on theory and practical skills. The hotel constitutes the first time that a university-level hospitality management programme has been redesigned to incorporate a dedicated teaching hotel into students' learning experience to develop liberal thinking and professionalism.

Literature review

Three perennial issues in hospitality management education are particularly relevant to this chapter. The first is the thorny issue of work experience. Whilst it is generally accepted that such education is industry-oriented and that some kind of experiential learning is beneficial to students, internships as an integral part of the curriculum often have negative effects on students. Leslie and Richardson (2000), in their investigation of the cooperative-education components of tourism undergraduate courses in the UK, identified substantial discrepancies between student perceptions and actual experience and found that work experience can negatively influence career choices after graduation. Jenkins (2001), in an Anglo-Dutch study, also found that students' perceptions of the international hospitality industry deteriorated as they progressed through their degree programme, noting that students who engaged in work experience in the industry become considerably less interested in making hospitality their first career choice. In a study of hospitality management students in Korea, Cho (2006) too established that there is a significant discrepancy between student satisfaction with and expectations of their placements, indicating that these expectations are not fully met. Similarly, Lam and Ching's (2007) study of hospitality students in Hong Kong showed student perception scores for internships to be lower than expectation scores. Research in Australia reported similar findings. Richardson (2008) found that more than 40 per cent of those with work experience in the industry claimed that they would not work in it after graduation, citing their work experience as the main reason for that decision. Lee and Dickson (2010) confirmed that students who have participated in experiential learning programmes are less motivated to persist to graduation than those who have not participated in such programmes. Acknowledging students' misgivings about internships, Tse (2010) set out to investigate what hospitality students value and consider important in internships, with the aim of better preparing academic institutions, receiving organizations and students in future. Interestingly, the student interns in his study cited a good working relationship with colleagues as by far the most important attribute of internships. Students most likely attach such great importance to their working relationships with colleagues because those relationships are perceived as the work experience itself. In fact, student interns' learning depends heavily on their colleagues' coaching and support, the way they are treated and the manner in which they are taught.

The second issue in hospitality management education is that, in balancing theory and practice, there appears to be a tendency amongst universities to make the curriculum overly pragmatic, thus reinforcing students' inclination towards avoiding reflection and theorizing. This tipping towards practice is referred to by Airey and Tribe (2000) as 'tyranny of relevance'. Peters (1966) believes that the value of a liberal education rests on opening up students' minds to alternative streams of consciousness and forcing them to delve deeper into a discipline to grasp from the inside what it entails. Scholars have questioned whether hospitality management education is too vocational in nature and how a more liberal base could be introduced into the curriculum to ensure that students are expected to evaluate conceptual frameworks in addition to reflecting upon and synthesizing materials (Morrison & O'Mahony, 2003). When the emphasis of the hospitality management curriculum is on practical industry-oriented content, higher education institutions have no choice but to meet the needs of industry and potential employers if they are to gain industry support (Lashley, 2004). The concern is that such managerialism is becoming the dominant mode of institutional decision-making, yielding to the control and influence of external constituencies such as the government and business community. The result has been a shift in the primary objectives of universities from the creation, preservation and dissemination of social knowledge to the production and distribution of market knowledge (Newton, 1994: 152, cited in Ayikoru et al., 2009).

The third issue in hospitality management education is related to innovation or the lack of it. Lewis (1993) carried out a critical review of hospitality education in the United States in the 1990s, on the basis of which he accused hospitality programmes of undertaking curriculum reviews largely based on perceived academic needs and then suddenly realizing that they were not meeting industry needs. Hospitality programmes need to be re-evaluated in the light of changing managerial and social needs, as well as industry needs that are not yet realized. Hospitality educators who prepare students for senior positions must anticipate the future needs of the industry and provide research and leadership to chart the path. Looking into the future of hotel education in the United States, Nelson and Dopson (2001) advocated for curriculum revision that meets the constantly changing needs of the industry. They also noted that curriculum revision must be a faculty-driven process that not only responds to industry needs but also drives innovation. In this light, Dredge *et al.* (2013) identified a number of challenges and opportunities for tourism, hospitality and event management education, in developing innovative curricula that enhance student outcomes.

Purpose and methodology

The purpose of this chapter is to illustrate how PolyU is making use of its new teaching hotel, Hotel ICON, to enhance the delivery of its hotel and tourism management programme. The chapter discusses how PolyU has used the hotel to overcome the three aforementioned issues in hospitality education and incubate a positive learning experience that strikes a balance between theory and practice.

PolyU's use of its teaching hotel to deliver its hotel and tourism management programme is presented as a case study. The methodology involves analysing relevant documents pertaining to the hotel's development, curriculum revisions and internship and media reports, and interviews with administrators, faculty members, students and hotel managers. The case study explores how students learn in a real commercial setting, how they solve problems, how they work and how they feel about themselves. Through systematically piecing together detailed evidence, this qualitative/inductive approach helps to reveal the possibilities and innovations in teaching and learning in the context of a teaching hotel.

It must be acknowledged that the author is the participant observer in this case study and a faculty member of the institution being studied. Given the author's involvement with the teaching hotel, the relationship has afforded privileged access to relevant information and a dimension beyond what is readily available from survey data. The researcher uses knowledge gained through personal involvement with the teaching hotel to interact with and gain further access to the stakeholders. The advantage of this kind of participant observation is the depth of knowledge that it allows the researcher to obtain. The author is aware of the fact that the study requires him to be an objective observer and record relevant findings that he comes across, not letting feelings and emotions influence his observations.

Like all case studies, the results of this study are not generalizable. Nevertheless, this type of participant observation and case study can provide rich details and insights into the issues at hand.

PolyU and Hotel ICON

PolyU is one of eight government-funded universities in Hong Kong, and with 32,000 students has the largest enrolment. The School of Hotel and Tourism Management (SHTM) is one of eight faculties and schools at PolyU, with 2,200 students enrolled in its doctoral (PhD and D.HTM), Master's (MPhil and MSc) and undergraduate (BSc, BA and HD) programmes. Since its establishment as the Department of Institutional Management and Catering Studies in 1979, the SHTM has evolved into an independent school within the university structure. It has positioned itself as a global centre of excellence in hospitality and tourism education and research, with a mission to serve the industry and academic communities through the advancement of education and dissemination of knowledge (SHTM, 2013a).

PolyU first contemplated the idea of a teaching hotel in 2005, and Hotel ICON opened for business in April 2011. One hundred per cent owned by PolyU, the hotel's stated purpose is to support the hospitality management programmes of the SHTM. So what exactly makes Hotel ICON a teaching hotel? The question will be answered in detail under the topics of hotel design, hotel management, subject integration, managers as teachers, internships, elite management programme, research, and the Food and Wine Academy. In short, Hotel ICON was developed with its educational purpose in mind, and the architecture of the hotel complex was thus designed to balance educational needs with commercial interests. Further, the hotel management model places student interests front and centre, and all subjects in the hotel management curriculum were reviewed, and revamped if needed, to identify possibilities for integration with hotel operations. The engagement of some of the hotel managers as subject lecturers is an innovation that has had to be managed carefully to meet both pedagogical needs and business requirements. The internship and elite management programmes were also designed in conjunction with the teaching hotel to ensure maximum benefit to students and integration with hotel human resources. Finally, the university and teaching hotel continue to work together to foster industry-relevant research projects.

Hotel design

The idea of incorporating a teaching hotel in hospitality education is not new (Tse, 2012). The innovation in PolyU's case lies in the concept of having the teaching hotel and school under one roof to facilitate hands-on experience, conduct research, and test innovative concepts and technology in hotel management (SCMP, 2012). The hotel and school have separate entrances, with a number of connecting passageways for students and faculty members. Hotel ICON was designed with its educational purpose in mind, and can thus accommodate daily student flows and observations and large-scale student internships, up to 150 per year. Such facilities as a 500-seat ballroom, three fine- and all-day dining restaurants, an executive lounge, a health club and spa, a heated outdoor swimming pool and 262 guestrooms provide students with hands-on practice in the full range of hotel operations.

While teaching hotels such as Statler Hotels, Hilton University of Houston and Courtyard Newark by Marriott are good solid business hotels largely catering for visitors to their respective campuses, Hotel ICON chooses to target an upscale clientele of independent travellers looking for deluxe accommodation and a high standard of service. To support those efforts, PolyU engaged iconic designers in various facets of the hotel: Rocco Yim masterminded the architecture; Terence Conran created the executive club floor and Chinese restaurant; Patrick Blanc crafted a green wall of 8,000 plants; Vivienne Tam fashioned the honeymoon suite; and William Lim shaped the guestrooms. The teaching hotel was carefully designed and equipped not just to accommodate guests but also to provide education and training to future and current hotel professionals and set high standards of performance to lead the profession. In the two years between September 2011 and August 2013, the hotel won 31 awards, including the Best Business Hotels 2011 award by Wallpaper* (Hotel ICON, 2013), and ranked consistently among the top three positions among 548 hotels in Hong Kong (TripAdvisor, 2013). These accolades are testimony of the hotel setting high standards of design and appointment.

Hotel management

PolyU has contemplated three options of managing its teaching hotel: (1) engaging a hotel management company, (2) franchising, and (3) creating its own management team. Whilst Hotel ICON is 100 per cent owned by PolyU with the purpose of supporting the SHTM's hospitality management programmes, the university decided to manage the hotel on a commercial basis by a wholly owned subsidiary. As an independent single-property hotel, Hotel ICON has had to build up its brand awareness from scratch without corporate office providing any kind of system support such as a reservations system or a global sales network (Tse, 2013). Such independence, while presenting commercial challenges, also gives the university neutrality among stakeholders in the hotel industry. This turns out to be an advantage for students and graduates because they are not identified or associated with any particular hotel group or brand.

All Hotel ICON staff members are recruited from the market, and they are fully aware of their dual role in hotel operation and education. Despite being a commercial hotel, the profits generated from the hotel operation are used to pay back the capital investment and ploughed back into the university for educational purposes. These ownership and management arrangements ensure academic freedom because the hotel is not dependent on the industry for funding and there is no commercial interest involved with any outside party. In addition, SHTM faculty members, in making use of the hotel for teaching and research purposes, are not expected to demonstrate any form of engagement beyond academia. They are assured of total academic freedom and the absence of control or influence by such external constituencies as the government and business community.

To date, the ownership and management model appears to be working. Hotel ICON achieved a positive cash flow in its second month of operation and generated gross operating profit in its third. Occupancy was above 70 per cent in the first four months and exceeded 90 per cent in the sixth. While good operational performance does not make Hotel ICON a teaching hotel, as the General Manager Richard Hatter has said, 'We can't very well teach people about hotels without running a successful one' (*Wall Street Journal*, 2011).

Subject integration

It was with the anticipation that various aspects of hotel operation could be used as teaching and learning resources that the syllabi of some 30 hotel-related subjects were revamped to tie in with the hotel (SCMP, 2011). The SHTM started the process of subject integration well before Hotel ICON opened for business. The syllabi of various courses were revised to incorporate guest speakers from hotel management, hotel operation-related student projects, observations of back office operations and knowledge extracted from hotel management.

It should be pointed out that in all cases of integrating a subject with hotel operation, the subject lecturer is responsible for student assessment, and students are not accountable to the hotel manager. The key challenge for hotel managers being involved in teaching is finding time for various classes, which will be addressed later in this chapter. The integration of Hotel ICON into the following five subjects illustrates the hotel's central role in teaching and learning.

Front Office Operations

The scheme of work for Front Office Operations (HTM2107) has been revised to include a group project involving role plays, which accounts for 20 per cent of the total assessment. Students are required to role-play various Hotel ICON front office operational activities such as handling guest reservations, checking in guests with and without reservations, checking out guests and handling guest complaints, with the hotel's managers invited to observe and make comments. Students are assessed on the basis of how well they present hotel information in an organized, integrated, interesting, creative and convincing manner, and the managers' comments are taken into consideration in the assessment.

Hospitality Facilities Planning and Maintenance

The scheme of work for Hospitality Facilities Planning and Maintenance (HTM3107) has been revised to include a group project involving Hotel ICON in the form of a presentation and written report that together account for 30 per cent of the total assessment. Students can choose from amongst such hotel facilities as lodging planning and design, environmental and sustainability management, water and wastewater systems, and safety and security, and then evaluate the facility's effectiveness on the basis of a hotel visit, interview with the relevant hotel manager and textbook information. In this subject, Hotel ICON serves as a real organization for students to study, analyse and critique the hotel's facilities and maintenance.

Human Resources Management in the Tourism and Hotel Industry

The scheme of work for Human Resources Management in the Tourism and Hotel Industry (HTM4115) has been revised to include a problem-based group project that accounts for 40 per cent of the total assessment. Students act as consultants to Hotel ICON, and prepare a proposal on one of eight human resources topics following careful study: staff recognition programme, staff grooming, staff retention, internship training programme, staff social activities, corporate social responsibility activities, annual staff party and staff birthday party. The hotel's Manager of Human Capital sits in on all student presentations and gives her comments to each group, which renders the learning more spontaneous and relevant.

Managing Marketing in the Hotel & Tourism Industry

The scheme of work for Managing Marketing in the Hotel & Tourism Industry (HTM534) has been revised to include a group project that accounts for 40 per cent of the total assessment. Students are tasked with devising specific proposals for five different sales and marketing-related functions at Hotel ICON: event, corporate sales, public relations, customer relations and branding. The hotel provides students with historical data such as prices and indicative volume of business, and information such as target customers and menu, for them to work on the projects. While the proposals may not be adopted by the hotel, students benefit from deliberating on some real-life issues and learn from the hotel managers who sit in and comment on the resulting presentations.

Leadership in Hotel & Tourism Management

Finally, the scheme of work for Leadership in Hotel & Tourism Management (HTM4123) has been revised to make use of primary research findings on leadership style. The subject lecturer undertook research on the leadership at Hotel ICON and identified the leadership styles in various departments such as demonstrative, autocratic and laissez-faire leadership. In class, the subject lecturer then related these various leadership styles to the functions of the respective departments. The hotel serves as a laboratory for concept demonstration, with students benefiting from seeing and feeling a real hotel environment in which abstract concepts such as leadership are put into practice.

Managers as teachers

Ultimately, it is the hotel colleagues who make Hotel ICON a teaching hotel. The hotel employs nearly 70 experienced associates at the manager level or above, and they come from companies such as Shangri-La, Mandarin Oriental, InterContinental, Four Seasons, The Ritz Carlton, Regal and Harbour Plaza. During the 2011/2012 academic year, four of these managers each taught one subject in a 14-week semester: the general manager taught 'Introduction to Hotel Operations', the Food & Beverages (F&B) manager 'Introduction to Food Service Operations', the executive housekeeper 'Housekeeping Operations' and the finance director 'Financial Management in Hospitality & Tourism'. These four managers were effectively subject lecturers, responsible for coming up with the scheme of work, teaching on a weekly basis and student assessments, while also playing their full-time roles in the hotel. Interestingly, each manager adopted different emphases on theory and practice in their teaching. It was 20/80 (theory/practice) in 'Introduction to Hotel Operations', 40/60 (theory/practice) in 'Introduction to Food Service Operations', 1/99 (theory/practice) in Housekeeping Operations and 80/20 (theory/practice) in 'Financial Management in Hospitality & Tourism'. The managers were clearly given the academic freedom to determine the appropriate emphases on theory and practice in accordance with the nature of the subject.

The hotel managers' respective industry experiences were obviously instrumental in their teaching. The general manager, for example, gave students a holistic view of his hotel management philosophy, including culture, people, revenue management, public relations, and the vital professional traits for working and being successful in the hotel business, whilst the F&B Manager related his personal knowledge of menu planning, menu selection and the service sequence in Hotel ICON. The executive housekeeper taught hotel practices, demonstrated with actual housekeeping items used in the hotel, and illustrated the role of executive housekeeper with real examples from the hotel. The finance director used Hotel ICON figures to explain the difference between profit and cash flow, the importance of deposits for major events, and different ways of allocating expenses.

To encourage students to reflect upon the practices taught in the classroom, the general manager shared anecdotes of events that had actually occurred at Hotel ICON, using the hotel as an example of thinking and acting fast, experimenting and seeking innovation rather than perfection. The executive housekeeper asked students to deliberate on the choice of guestroom amenities from both the guest's and hotel's points of view. The finance director used unresolved cases from the hotel to stimulate creativity and outside-the-box thinking. The F&B manager inspired students by asking them to criticize current practices and come up with alternatives. Although the four managers relied heavily on their own experiences and resources at Hotel ICON for teaching and learning, they all agreed that the course textbooks were essential. What was most important was their ability to supplement the textbooks where the information was obsolete or not applicable or simply to provide illustrative examples.

There are three important considerations in engaging hotel managers as subject lecturers. First, it is very demanding for a hotel manager to teach a subject over a semester and at the same time maintain a full-time role in hotel operation. This has been made possible in Hotel ICON because of a higher-than-average staff-to-room ratio. This higher-than-average staff-to-room ratio is also needed to support a large population of student interns, which will be explained later in the chapter. Second, the hotel managers who undertake to teach a subject have to be either academically qualified or sufficiently experienced in the topic he or she teaches. In Hotel ICON's case, the managers are trained in teaching and student assessment by the School's Learning and Teaching Committee before undertaking the role of a subject lecturer. Third, there is the remuneration question, which ought to be resolved beforehand. The question is whether the hotel manager should be remunerated for the teaching which he or she undertakes in addition to the regular hotel salary. There is no standard answer to this question, and in considering the issue, one should be prepared for the reciprocity that one day a regular teacher may also work part-time as a manager in the teaching hotel.

Internships

In addition to the sense of pride Hotel ICON has instilled, one of the most important benefits to students of Hotel IOCN has been the structured internship programme it has facilitated (So, 2011). Up to 150 student interns have the opportunity to participate in 10-, 24- or 48-week internship programmes each academic year. Accommodating 150 student interns in a medium-sized hotel is in itself a substantial commitment to education and training, given that the hotel assigns one trainer to three trainees, creates tailor-made training programmes and provides a stay-in experience to each intern. However, the most significant internship factor that makes Hotel ICON a teaching hotel lies in the working relationship between the student interns and their supervisors. These supervisors are no ordinary hotel associates because, in addition to their regular hotel duties, they embrace their teaching role wholeheartedly in recognition that students are the most important stakeholders of a teaching hotel.

The internship reports made by students after they have completed their internships are reviewed carefully, and those submitted to date clearly reveal one important theme: the interns' perceived relationship with their supervisors/trainers is most conducive to their sense of satisfaction and the perceived success of the internship experience. This theme echoes earlier findings suggesting that student interns' working relationship with their colleagues is by far the most important internship attribute, being perceived as the work experience itself (Tse, 2010). Student interns rely heavily on their supervisors' coaching and support, and the manner in which they are taught affects their perception of the experience. The following extracts from students' internship reports illustrate the importance and power of the supervisor–intern relationships.

Such supportive workplace relationships as this one go a long way towards creating a fruitful learning experience:

> My colleagues are nice and patient, and they are willing to teach me the things that I need to learn and give me advice on my work. Besides teaching me relevant knowledge and skills, they are concerned with my attitude and personal development. I also share my difficulties with them.

Once a supportive relationship has been established, student interns become more receptive to criticism:

> I feel much better after I have had a self-evaluation with my mentor. She suggests a lot of methods to solve problems, such as having a schedule listing all the tasks I need to do each day, so that I can monitor how much I have done and how much I haven't. She taught me that asking for clarification is extremely important because others have to know how much you really understand so that they can give you a helping hand in time.

Hotels today deal with many employees of Generation Y, to which Hotel ICON's student interns belong. Supervisors should be aware of the fact that this generation values self-expression, friendship and life outside work, as reflected in this comment:

> I talk to my colleagues to express my opinions and seek their feedback in order to know more about each other and for mutual respect; a good relationship helps create a happy working environment, which makes the operation smooth and enjoyable.

Hotel ICON supervisors are well aware that they must play the role of coaching in addition to their regular operation role. In fact, many of them were attracted to the hotel by their knowledge that their job would not be simply to make a profit for the organization but also to coach student interns. Can students tell the difference between a supportive coach and a supervisor who just wants to get things done? Of course they can, as the following comments make clear.

> They are mentors and not just trainers because they provide personal guidance to different aspects for the interns, including future career path, personal development and attitude towards study and work.

> Even though I sometimes make mistakes, they are willing to teach me and give me a second chance to do things right.

> Trainers view training as a part of their daily routine, and they assign a certain amount of time to teach interns new skills or concepts. Trainees in Hotel ICON feel [they are] treasured and respected, and that they are here to learn but not [to be] treated as cheap labour.

Such strong rapport between trainer and trainee, which is vital to the success of an internship programme, does not happen automatically. It must be actively cultivated by the hotel. The trainers at Hotel ICON are provided with the following pointers reminding them of their commitment to training students. (1) As a first step, become familiar with the trainee attached to you. Learn about his or her character and background. (2) Try to understand the trainee's learning style and potential obstacles to learning, i.e. whether he or she is a fast or slow learner and whether he or she can adapt well to the working environment. (3) Create a warm welcome for and caring social circle amongst the trainees and your team. Do not leave a trainee alone. If you need to take time off, please assign a colleague to take care of him or her. (4) Work according to the training programme. Stick to the schedule and make sure that every topic in the programme is covered and completed. (5) Remember that you are a mentor and that the trainee's success depends on your commitment. (6) Release trainees on time if possible because they may need to complete assignments or study. (7) Review the trainee's performance on a monthly basis. Sit down with them and give suggestions for improvement.

Nevertheless, there is room for improvement for internship in Hotel ICON. Some students find it difficult working with supervisors in the food and beverage area as the supervisors are extremely busy. They might not be always available to students for consultation and advice whenever they are needed. Some students find the training period too short, and there might not be enough time to cover everything during the training. Induction could be further enhanced as some of the students feel lost at the very beginning of their internship when they find the people and the environment unfamiliar. There are a small number of cases where students find their hotel colleagues a little remote, stern and sometimes unfriendly.

Elite management programme

Whilst most of the internships available at Hotel ICON are 10 or 24 weeks in duration, the hotel also works with the SHTM to offer the Elite Management Programme, a special 48-week full-time internship with a strong management focus. This programme is offered to a few select students, who undergo training in two phases. They acquire operational experience in all major divisions of the hotel in the first phase and managerial experience in the second. More specifically, during the 16 weeks of Phase One, students gain experience in six major divisions: engineering and environmental, finance and administration, rooms, food & beverage, human capital, and sales & marketing. In Phase Two, they choose one or two of these divisions and then work alongside the respective managers for the remaining 32 weeks of the programme. Customized training programmes and schedules are designed by the respective division heads. Acting as a management trainee, each student 'shadows' a department manager, sits in on all related meetings and shares the manager's workload. Students are also assigned special hotel projects to accomplish on their own, and their findings form part of their performance evaluation (PATA, 2012). Past projects have included an evaluation of guest comments on the top 10 hotels on TripAdvisor and identification of the key influential factors therein; identifying the differences between good and excellent service; comparing the loyalty programmes in competing hotels; and recommending menu engineering and a pricing strategy for the hotel's fine-dining restaurant.

The student trainees' findings may have significant implications for hotel operations, as the following examples show. One student trainee challenged the practice of treating VIPs as more equal than others by remembering their names and searching in advance for information about them in Tatler and LinkedIn. She questioned why she, as a young perhaps slightly innocent-looking person, would receive less attention than other guests in the hotel. She advocated for serving all guests with the same degree of passion and sincerity, based on her belief that passionate service should come from the heart naturally and without discrimination.

Another trainee was such a fast learner that, after the induction period, he was able to mentor three other student interns in the hotel's spa operation to provide the same high standard of warm and caring service. His passion for that operation drove him to study the spa and health club services of hotels in the competitive set and come up with such ideas as a tea + spa package targeting the young female market segment, reaching out to Internet bloggers and creating a weekend spa market segment.

A third student trainee developed a service attitude during her Hotel ICON experience that she refers to as 'moment of truth in reality'. She realized that although pleasing every guest and achieving a high level of guest satisfaction are usually the goals of customer service, in reality many practical issues get in the way of delivering that ideal customer service. Demanding and sometimes unreasonable guests are not uncommon, and thus fulfilling the expectations of each and every guest is not always possible. Based on textbook theories and her own experience, this trainee came to the conclusion that it is far more important to be fair to all guests and to show that the hotel values them, but that a line should be drawn when it comes to unreasonable demands.

These are the kind of soft skills and mentality that the Elite Management Programme has inculcated in trainees in addition to technical skills in hotel operations.

Research

PolyU ranked second (after Cornell University) in terms of scholarly contributions to 11 refereed hospitality and tourism journals from 1992 to 2006 (Severt et al., 2009). It is based on research that Hotel ICON has introduced innovative services like Timeless Lounge and free mini-bar. Timeless Lounge is a place for guests to take a rest and refresh in case they arrive before the regular check-in time and the rooms are not yet ready. Free mini-bar is offered as a service and nice gesture from the hotel, which also alleviates the workload of checking and charging for the consumption, and saves unnecessary argument over the consumption of a soft drink. The two innovative services have proven to be very welcomed by guests, and they are often mentioned and praised in guests' feedback.

Hotel ICON not only uses research to come up with innovative services, it has also enabled SHTM to expand the breadth and depth of its research in such areas as customer service, hospitality technology, marketing, human resources, forecasting and revenue management. The hotel provides a real-life research setting with 300 associates and nearly 1,000 guests each day, and in its first two years of operation worked with faculty members undertaking more than 10 research projects. They include research on whether hotel guests would pay more for luxury room amenities, the marketing role of the Internet in launching a new hotel, identifying competitor sets in the hotel industry, and the impact of weather on tourist behaviour. All of these projects have been facilitated by access to hotel practices and feedback from staff and guests.

In addition to serving as a setting for case studies, Hotel ICON has created three dedicated Tomorrow's Guestrooms (TGRs) for more in-depth research into the application of advanced concepts in the field of hotel management. The three TGRs can be considered a living and breathing laboratory. They allow students to experience and learn about new hotel technologies, designs and concepts, and faculty members to conduct research on new service concepts and hotel technologies in addition to learning about guest perceptions. The SHTM launched an online global competition in January 2013 inviting hospitality industry suppliers to enter products/services/solutions that represent the TGR concept. The competition committee included SHTM faculty members and students, members of Hotel ICON's executive team and an independent consultant. Winners were granted the unique opportunity for their products and services to be tested and researched in the three TGRs for six months. The list of winners included Bartech, Brintons Carpets, DNet Solution, Fingi, Salto Systems, Spicy Innovations, and VDA Asia Pacific (SHTM, 2013b). The TGR innovations support the SHTM's (2013c) supposition that the best way to predict the future is to create it.

Food and Wine Academy

The Food and Wine Academy is an SHTM–Hotel ICON endeavour that synthesizes food and beverage expertise, food production laboratories and a vinoteca (wine lab), and facilitates educational workshops in various related areas. In 2012, the Academy hosted 45 workshops in such areas as butchering, national cuisines, pastries and desserts, and beverages, including sake, whisky, tea and wines from different regions. Company sponsors for these workshops have included Fonterra, Absolut Vodka, Illy Coffee and Miele. A number of consulates, including the Spanish, Swedish and Mexican, have also supported the Food and Wine Academy in showcasing their national cuisines. Chefs, sommeliers and food & beverage suppliers also regularly meet with SHTM and Hotel ICON staff to share their knowledge and practices. In 2012, 1,174 people participated in the Academy's workshops, including students, industry practitioners and members of the public. Although the workshops are held independently of the SHTM's higher education programme, they serve the purpose of arousing awareness of and interest in very specialized and yet authentic food & beverage production. They also connect faculty members with the industry to help ensure that the information they teach is up to date.

Discussion and conclusion

This case study has explained how Hotel ICON functions as a teaching and research hotel. The hotel design, hotel management, subject integration, managers as teachers, internship, elite management programme, research, and the Food and Wine Academy are identified to be the elements which have helped address the three perennial issues identified in hotel and tourism management education: negative feedback in internship, 'tyranny of relevance' and lack of innovation.

As the research cited at the beginning of this chapter made clear, students' feelings towards their colleagues constitute a large part of their recollection of the internship experience. The key to making an internship meaningful and successful lies in the intricate working relationship between interns and colleagues. Hotel ICON was established in part to address the documented negative effects of internships on students, and to completely redesign the internship programme at one institution. The experiences of students who have undertaken internship in different departments in Hotel ICON shows that there is a new model of internship in the making. If academic institutions and the industry are indeed concerned with the quality of internships, they should revamp current internship practice by addressing student perceptions of their internship and work experiences. It is hoped that Hotel ICON's internship programme and Elite Management Programme will assist in setting the industry standard in future (Chon, cited in So, 2011).

In addressing the 'tyranny of relevance', the SHTM offers many hospitality and tourism subjects with strong underpinnings in the social sciences, amongst them 'Tourism and Society', 'Hospitality and Culture', 'Tourism Economics', 'International Tourism Studies', 'Cultural Tourism', 'Tourism Business', 'Ethics & Law' and 'Research Methods'. The teaching and learning of these subjects are reflective and liberal in nature and are not skills-based. The reflective and liberal approach is important because it forges a deeper model of scholarship, defines the boundaries of a discipline and gives it a leveraged position independent of industry (Flinders, 2013). It is believed that a liberal education can enhance hospitality management education by training students to be sufficiently cognizant of other ways of looking at the world. The SHTM also offers other subjects whose aim is to transmit expertise and proficiency in hotel management, and these subjects are now being taught with the support of Hotel ICON. Sheldon et al. (2011) advocated a fundamental shift in tourism education in order to respond to global challenges impacting tourism and defined a set of foundational values for tourism education programmes worldwide. Professionalism is one of those values, and it is defined as skills, competencies and standards, and an attitude and behaviour that reflect these. Professionalism, in the context of tourism education, is also defined as incorporating leadership, a practical approach, attention to services, concern for relevance and timeliness of evidence, reflexivity, teamwork and partnership building skills and proactivity. It can be argued that integrating relevant subjects with hotel operations and involving Hotel ICON managers as subject lecturers is a step towards answering the call for activating change in tourism education and imparting professionalism in hotel management education. The hotel has allowed the SHTM to liberate a predominantly specialist curriculum without jeopardizing its professional stance, producing graduates who are analytical, critical and able to think 'outside the box'. The hotel's ownership and management structure, abundant opportunities for active learning, and positive internship experiences suggest that it is possible to maintain the cogency of a hospitality management curriculum while embracing the pertinence of being relevant.

It has been explained that Hotel ICON not only embraces innovation in its operation but also provides fertile ground for research. With the research findings, the SHTM is able to teach students with originality and novelty. In addition, the Food and Wine Academy serves as a platform for engaging with the hospitality industry and facilitating exchange of innovative ideas between the industry and education. This way the curriculum could be modified or enriched to better meet the constantly changing needs of the industry. The PolyU–Hotel ICON model favours academic freedom and autonomy, facilitates a more sophisticated grasp of key concepts and ensures that the discipline engages with the industry in multiple ways. The university believes that the balance of a liberal and practical approach to hospitality education made possible by Hotel ICON prepares its students intellectually for a wide range of jobs, some of which may not even be available today.

Along with the initiative of Hotel ICON as a teaching hotel, there are some lessons learnt from managing a teaching hotel from the university's perspective. First of all, not all students would like to undertake their internship in the university-owned teaching hotel. Some students prefer to gain work experience in an established hotel with a well-known brand. They believe that a renowned international hotel brand may add more weight to their curriculum vitae. Some students also feel that a university-owned teaching hotel offers them too much protection and the work experience there is not real. The second lesson is the importance of managing industry expectation. Some hotels might think that Hotel ICON is privileged to have as many student interns as it likes and their access to student interns is reduced. Some hotels might think that there is no need to allocate internship to PolyU now that it has its own teaching hotel, and all available internship positions are allocated to other institutions. The university has to manage industry expectations and continue to work closely with them to ensure internships and other learning opportunities will be made available to PolyU. Third, there is the risk of excessive exposure of Hotel ICON in a semester. Faculty members might be so enthusiastic in integrating their subject with Hotel ICON operations that students have projects in all subjects in a semester related to Hotel ICON. It is therefore necessary to coordinate such projects among different subjects to avoid an overload situation.

Acknowledgements

The author would like to acknowledge the support of SHTM faculty members, Hotel ICON colleagues and the students practising at the hotel. He is grateful to them for generously sharing their teaching and learning experiences, without which this chapter would not have been possible.

References

Airey, D., & Tribe, J. (2000). 'Education for Hospitality'. In C. Lashley & A. Morrison (Eds.), *In Search of Hospitality: theoretical perspectives and debates* (pp. 192–276). Oxford: Butterworth-Heinemann.

Ayikoru, M., Tribe, J., & Airey, D. (2009). 'Reading Tourism Education neoliberalism unveiled'. *Annals of Tourism Research*, 36(2), 191–221.

Cho, M. (2006). 'Student Perspectives on the Quality of Hotel Management Internships'. *Journal of Teaching in Travel & Tourism,* 6(1), 61–76.

Cooper, C., & Shepherd, R. (1997). 'The Relationship between Tourism Education and the Tourism Industry: implications for tourism education'. *Tourism Recreation Research*, 22(1), 34–47.

Dredge, D., Benckendorff, P., Day, M., Gross, M. J., Walo, M., Weeks, P., & Whitelaw, P. A. (2013). 'Drivers of Change in Tourism, Hospitality, and Event Management Education: an Australian perspective'. *Journal of Hospitality & Tourism Education*, 25(2), 89–102.

Flinders, M. (2013). 'The Tyranny of Relevance and the Art of Translation'. *Political Studies Review*, 11(2), 149–67.

Hotel ICON. (2013). About the hotel. Available: http://www.hotel-icon.com/about-the-hotel.aspx#/unlike-any-other (Accessed 20 November 2013).

Jenkins, A. K. (2001). 'Making a Career of It? Hospitality students' future perspectives: an Anglo-Dutch study'. *International Journal of Contemporary Hospitality Management*, 13(1), 13–20.

Lam, T., & Ching, L. (2007). 'An Exploratory Study of an Internship Program: the case of Hong Kong students'. *International Journal of Hospitality Management*, 26, 336–51.

Lashley, C. (2004). 'Escaping the Tyranny of Relevance. Some reflections on hospitality management education'. In C. Cooper, C. Arcodia, D. Solnet, & M. Whitford (Eds.), *Creating Tourism Knowledge: a selection of papers from CAUTHE 2004*. Altona, Australia: Common Ground Publishing.

Lee, S., & Dickson, D. (2010). 'Increasing Student Learning in the Classroom through Experiential Learning Programs Outside the Classroom'. *Journal of Hospitality & Tourism Education*, 22(3), 27–34.

Leslie, D., & Richardson, A. (2000). 'Tourism and Cooperative Education in UK Undergraduate Courses: are the benefits being realized?'. *Tourism Management*, 21, 489–98.

Lewis, R. C. (1993). 'Hospitality Management Education: here today, gone tomorrow?'. *Journal of Hospitality & Tourism Research*, 17(1), 273–83.

Morrison, A., & O'Mahony, G. B. (2003). 'The Liberation of Hospitality Management Education'. *International Journal of Contemporary Hospitality Management*, 15(1), 38–44.

Nelson, A. A., & Dopson, L. (2001). 'Future of Hotel Education: required program content areas for graduates of U.S. hospitality programs beyond the year 2000 – Part one'. *Journal of Hospitality & Tourism Education*, 13(5), 58–67.

Pacific Asia Travel Association (PATA). (2012). 'Hotel ICON Launches Elite Management Programme'. http://www.pata.org/news/hotel-icon-launches-elite-management-programme (Retrieved 20 December 2012).

Peters, R. (1966). *Ethics and Education*. London: George Allen & Unwin.

Richardson, S. (2008). 'Undergraduate Tourism and Hospitality Students' Attitudes Toward a Career in the Industry: a preliminary investigation'. *Journal of Teaching in Travel and Tourism*, 8(1), 23–46.

Ruhanen, L. (2005). 'Bridging the Divide between Theory and Practice: experiential learning approaches for tourism and hospitality management education'. *Journal of Teaching in Travel & Tourism*, 5(4), 33–51.

School of Hotel and Tourism Management (SHTM). (2013a). 'Message from Dean of School'. Available: http://hotelschool.shtm.polyu.edu.hk/eng/school/director.html (Accessed 12 May 2013).

School of Hotel and Tourism Management (SHTM). (2013b). 'PolyU Launches Tomorrow's Guestrooms at Hotel ICON'. Available: http://hotelschool.shtm.polyu.edu.hk/wcms-common/temp/201307081815480651/news_08072013_TGR.pdf (Accessed 21 October 2013).

School of Hotel and Tourism Management (SHTM). (2013c). 'Tomorrow's Guestrooms Competition 2013'. Available: http://hotelschool.shtm.polyu.edu.hk/eng/school/tgr_competition.html (Accessed 1 May 2013).

Severt, D., Tesone, D., Bottorff, T., & Carpenter, M. (2009). 'A World Ranking of the Top 100 Hospitality and Tourism Programs'. *Journal of Hospitality & Tourism Research*, 33(4), 451–70.

Sheldon, P., Fesenmaier, D., & Tribe, J. (2011). 'The Tourism Education Futures Initiative (TEFI): activating change in tourism education'. *Journal of Teaching in Travel & Tourism*, 11, 2–23.

So, W. (2011). 'Back to School at Hong Kong's New Learning Hotel'. Available: http://www.huffingtonpost.com/winnie-so/its-backtoschool-at-hotel_b_949979.html#s350082&title=Would_You_Like (Accessed 1 May 2013).

South China Morning Post (SCMP). (2011). 'PolyU Further Advances Hospitality Education with Upgraded Facilities and Launch of Hotel ICON', 21 September.

South China Morning Post (SCMP). (2012). 'Creative Project Sways Judges', 14 May.

TripAdvisor. (2013). Hotel ICON. Available: http://www.tripadvisor.com/Hotel_Review-g294217-d2031570-Reviews-Hotel_ICON-Hong_Kong.html (Accessed 20 November 2013).

Tse, T. (2010). 'What do Hospitality Students find Important about Internships?'. *Journal of Teaching in Travel & Tourism*, 10(3), 251–64.

Tse, T. (2012). 'The Experience of Creating a Teaching Hotel: a case study of Hotel ICON in Hong Kong'. *Journal of Hospitality & Tourism Education*, 24(1), 17–25.

Tse, T. (2013). 'The Marketing Role of the Internet in Launching a Hotel: the case of Hotel ICON'. *Journal of Hospitality Marketing & Management*, 22, 895–908.

Wall Street Journal. (2011). 'A Hands-on Hotel Internship', 25 May. Available: http://blogs.wsj.com/scene/2011/05/25/a-hands-on-hotel-internship (Accessed 21 October 2013).

Wang, J., Ayres, H., & Huyton, J. (2010). 'Is Tourism Education Meeting the Needs of the Tourism Industry? An Australian case study'. *Journal of Hospitality & Tourism Education*, 22(1), 8–14.

38

Space for sustainability?

Sustainable education in the tourism curriculum space

Andrea Boyle, Erica Wilson and Kay Dimmock

School of Tourism and Hospitality Management,
Southern Cross University, Lismore, Australia

Introduction and background

There is little doubt that education is crucial in addressing the environmental, social and economic challenges facing humankind (Wright, 2004; UNESCO, 2006). The period 2005–14 marked the United Nations Decade of Education for Sustainable Development (UNDESD) which built on prior educational focused declarations, including the Rio Earth Summit (Agenda 21), the Millennium Development Goals (MDG) 2000 and the Education for All Dakar Framework 2000. The UNDESD goals were couched in the discourse of environmental education, with the intention of integrating the principles, values and practices of sustainable development into education across the globe, and at all levels of learning. The 2006 Framework for the UNDESD International Implementation Scheme set out a broad agenda considered essential in order to facilitate education for sustainable development (UNESCO, 2006). The framework identified three pillars of social, economic and environmental sustainability, which in turn 'give shape and content to sustainable learning' (UNESCO, 2006: 9).

While these goals were to apply across all levels of education, action within the arena of higher education was initially slow to take hold (Fisher & Bonn, 2011; Pigozzi, 2010; Shephard, 2010). However, sustainability initiatives are now evident on many university campuses, through various 'campus greening practices' such as dedicated sustainability offices, solar panel installations, recycling programmes and carbon footprint mapping (Leihy & Salazar, 2011; Shriberg, 2003). As of 2012, 440 education institutions across the globe (24 in Australia) have pledged their formal commitment to sustainability and signed the Talloires Declaration (ULSF, 2008).

While such steps are crucial in the move towards sustainability, there appears to be a lag in terms of how this translates into the 'classroom'. Indeed, it has been argued that a paradigm shift towards sustainability within higher education curricula remains constrained by a variety of logistical, pedagogical and political issues (Leihy & Salazar, 2011; Savelyeva & McKenna, 2011). According to Wals (2011), the planet can no longer afford a 'wait and see' attitude but requires action now and in a way that brings about a new kind of thinking. The response to this call requires a paradigm shift where principles of sustainability are embedded across the whole higher education institution (Sterling, 2010b).

As the UNDESD 2005–14 draws to a close, it is now timely to reflect on how universities have engaged with sustainability, particularly within the curriculum space. While it may be argued that awareness of sustainability has increased, there is still uncertainty about how higher education institutions can most effectively engage with sustainability (Fuller, 2010; Shephard, 2008; Wilson & von der Heidt, 2013). In the field of tourism, sustainability has been present on the research agenda for almost four decades, as scholars have increasingly voiced their concern over tourism's social, cultural and environmental impacts (Connell & Rugendyke, 2008). Yet, surprisingly, there is scant evidence of sustainability being clearly embedded throughout tourism, hospitality and events (TH&E) education (Deale & Barber, 2012; Sanders & Le Clus, 2011; Wilson & von der Heidt, 2013).

This chapter will evaluate the emergence and presence of sustainability education within tourism, hospitality and events higher education. It will do so by conducting a meta-level website content analysis of 'sustainability' within tourism curriculum at 25 universities across Australia. The chapter seeks to stimulate discussion on the contemporary curriculum space for sustainability in tourism and hospitality higher education and identify competing issues. We now draw attention to the central idea of sustainable education, which is Education for Sustainability ('EfS').

What is Education for Sustainability?

The foundations of Education for Sustainability emerged from the Western modern environmental movement of the 1960s and 1970s (Palmer, 1998). Over the following decades, philosophical debates and thinking around sustainability have resulted in a collection of terms and interpretations. Within environmental education there is lively discourse about appropriate terminology, as interpretations of 'sustainability' depend greatly on ideological viewpoint. These views range from a 'strong' (biocentric, deep green) to a 'weak' (anthropocentric, pale green) viewpoint on the sustainability ideological spectrum (Hunter, 1997). Further complicating the matter is that 'sustainability' is seen to be an amorphous concept, often appropriated for commercial rhetoric, green-washing and political hijacking (Mundt, 2011).

Within this contested landscape, Education for Sustainability (EfS) has emerged as a term based on the global concept of Education for Sustainable Development (ESD), although it is used more widely in the Australian and British contexts (Leihy & Salazar, 2011). Both EfS and ESD are focused on an agenda of action, with a clear mandate that education institutions, communities and individuals act in more sustainable ways (Shallcross & Robinson, 2007). EfS represents a move beyond education that is in and about the environment to one that is for the environment; an approach promoting critical reflection with an overt agenda for proactive and systemic social change (Tilbury & Cooke, 2005). In other words, EfS involves the use of education as a platform for action towards sustainable development, rather than students only learning 'about' the environment (Landorf et al., 2008).

Central to EfS is the development of capacity-building skills such as critical thinking, reflection, innovation and problem solving to acquire action-oriented skills for change (Huckle, 1993). Students need to learn alternative value systems and become reflexive to enable a resilient society capable of creative thinking and ethically responsible action (Sterling, 2010a, 2010b; Wals, 2011). Values education refers to the importance of the 'affective' domain of learning (Littledyke, 2008; Shephard, 2008; Sipos et al., 2008) allowing students to reflect on their values, beliefs and attitudes to generate learning about sustainability (Lewis et al., 2008; Nowak et al., 2008; Sterling, 1996).

To achieve the EfS capacity-building skills of critical thinking, reflection, innovation and problem solving advocated by Tilbury *et al.* (2005), opportunities for deep-learning and education that is transformative are recommended (O'Sullivan, 2004; Tilbury & Cooke, 2005; Warburton, 2003). The importance of 'real life' experience to explicitly engage with values in real life environmental contexts, rather than vague and abstract concepts, is discussed in the literature (Lewis *et al.*, 2008). It is recommended that the curriculum should include experiences that lead to a greater awareness of social and moral responsibilities (Jamal *et al.*, 2011; Sibbel, 2009), and which can be achieved through, for example, service learning (Jamal *et al.*, 2011).

EfS in tourism higher education

A growing body of knowledge on sustainable tourism demonstrates that tourism can no longer afford to focus solely on economic benefits at the expense of social–cultural, environmental and political impacts (Connell & Rugendyke, 2008; Mowforth & Munt, 2009; Telfer & Sharpley, 2008; Weaver, 2006). The emergence of scholarly thinking on sustainable tourism can be viewed through the prism of Jafari's 'platforms' (Jafari, 1990, 2001), namely the 'advocacy', 'cautionary', 'adaptancy' and 'knowledge-based' platforms. The advocacy platform heralded tourism as an economic driver or 'booster' for host communities, but then came under intense scrutiny in the 1960s and 1970s, in the form of the cautionary platform. From around this point onwards, there followed an 'is it or isn't it sustainable tourism?' debate, centred largely on the negative impacts of tourism (Clarke, 1997: 224). Through the adaptancy platform, alternative forms of tourism appeared such as ecotourism, nature-based tourism and cultural tourism, as apparent panaceas for the negative impacts of mass tourism (Fennell, 2008).

The notion of what constitutes sustainable tourism development has since been the subject of discourse and debate, and examined within Jafari's fourth 'knowledge-based platform'. As tourism discourse progressed into the twenty-first century, Macbeth (2005) suggested extending Jafari's ideal model and introduced a fifth platform of tourism thought: the 'ethical' platform. Macbeth has also called for a sixth platform of tourism thought, intended to oppose the positivistic–scientific paradigm which views knowledge as objective and all-knowable (Macbeth, 2005). As ethics is not value-free, Macbeth argues, the sixth platform aims 'to develop scholars' and practitioners' self-awareness with regard to their ethical positions and the implications of those positions for sustainable development and tourism' (Macbeth, 2005: 972). Others agree there is need for a new educational platform for tourism based on ethical consideration as ethical responsibility is often missing (Jamal, 2004; Nowaczek *et al.*, 2007).

At the same time, a wider discourse is evident about what 'tourism education' should represent and incorporate (Dredge *et al.*, 2012b; Fidgeon, 2010; Sheldon *et al.*, 2011; Tribe, 2005). Some have voiced concern about tourism education's overly vocational or industry-focused perspective (Ayikoru *et al.*, 2009; Higgins-Desbiolles, 2006; Lashley, 2013). A move towards a more balanced liberal and vocational style of education was recommended through Tribe's (2002b) philosophic practitioner, and later extended by Dredge *et al.* (2012b). Such an approach requires fundamental – if not radical – changes in tourism education (Sheldon *et al.*, 2011).

In all of this, limited discussion exists on how to specifically and practically integrate sustainability within tourism programmes. Indeed, Deale *et al.* (2009) report that while educators may think sustainability is important, few actually incorporate it within their learning and teaching practices, and in curriculum development. According to Boley (2011), sustainable tourism education is relatively piecemeal, with little evidence of a holistic or integrated approach. The results from a study by von der Heidt *et al.* (2012) concur with this, showing that although tourism and business academics agree sustainability is an important issue, this does not necessarily translate into sustainable curriculum. Many continue to argue for the need to integrate sustainability throughout the tourism programme (Boley, 2011; Jurowski & Liburd, 2001) and for further scholarly attention. Against this backdrop as Australian scholars and teachers interested in sustainable tourism, the aim of this study was to address the overarching research question: where is sustainability in the Australian tourism curriculum space?

Methodology

This chapter reports on a scoping study (undertaken as part of a larger study into EfS within tourism higher education) of sustainability education in Australian tourism programmes. A desk-top content analysis was conducted of publicly available information on Australian university websites. Curriculum content analyses have been found useful in previous studies of tourism and business programmes; through this method, key themes and messages can be counted, elucidated and discussed, using the curriculum as 'text' (see Dredge *et al.*, 2012a; Rundle-Thiele & Wymer, 2010; von der Heidt *et al.*, 2012).

The population for the web-based content analysis was all Australian universities offering tourism, hospitality and event (TH&E, for simplicity's sake) undergraduate programmes. In line with the recent comprehensive mapping of Australian TH&E curriculum (Dredge *et al.*, 2012a; Day *et al.*, 2012), this meant a full sample of the 25 public universities from all Australian states and territories. The focus was on universities only; Technical and Further Education (TAFE) colleges, hotel schools and other providers in the Australian vocational education and training sector were not included. A search for the terms tourism, event, hospitality, hotel, leisure, or any combination of these in the degree title name, identified 68 TH&E degree programmes. Across the 25 universities, the number of TH&E degrees offered ranged from one degree at four universities, up to a possible choice of six degrees at the university offering the highest number of degree options.

As outlined previously, this study's research design involved conducting a broad, meta-level content analysis of sustainability presence in the TH&E curriculum. We fully recognize that the 'curriculum space' is much broader and more complex than this, in that it is 'socially constructed; it will have multiple meanings, be dynamic and will always be a matter of debate and refinement' (Dredge *et al.*, 2012a: 11). For the purposes of this study, we have taken a fairly structured view of 'curriculum'; that is it is literally the content offered in a degree programme and the component parts that make up that degree (the subjects or 'units'). As such, we again drew a boundary around what was and was not to be included in the curriculum analysis. Text which formed the 'data' for curriculum analysis was thus limited to undergraduate degree name and description, followed by the subject name and description. We deliberately did not drill down into degree syllabus, assessment or full subject guides. While we realize the limitations in this approach, many websites do not provide such information publicly. Further, it was outside the scope of this present meta-analysis to delve further into substance of the curriculum.

To draw a discrete yet arbitrary chronological boundary for data capture, the content analysed was limited to information available in the first teaching semester of 2013. In total, 682 individual subjects were identified in the 68 degree programmes. The content analysis involved a number of steps. First, we were interested in counting the explicit use of the words 'sustainable' and 'sustainability', across the tourism degree and units on offer. Second, we were aware that 'sustainability' as a word is not the only way of capturing the full suite of EfS principles and skills; it is much broader than this, and should have a decidedly social and environmental platform. We needed a way to broaden, yet operationalize sustainability in the curriculum space. This was achieved using the three common pillars of sustainability described earlier in this chapter, namely the triple bottom line of socio-cultural, environmental and economic aspects, and adapted from the UNDESD International Implementation Scheme of 2006 (UNESCO 2006). The UNDESD's list of key characteristics of education for sustainable development, outlined as 'strategic perspectives' that 'must inform education and learning for sustainable development' (UNESCO, 2006: 17–21), formed part of the coding scheme when examining the curriculum documents for evidence of wider sustainability-related perspectives. Table 38.1 shows UNESCO's 15 educational strategic perspectives for sustainable development.

The TH&E degree titles and descriptions were entered into an Excel workbook. The same process was undertaken for every subject within each degree programme. To aid analysis the coded data were entered into SPSS (Statistical Package for the Social Sciences). The study combined a deductive and inductive or hybrid coding approach (Fereday & Muir-Cochrane, 2006) allowing different codes to be added as the data were read and new themes emerged. The sustainable education literature provided insight and meaning of topics and additional themes were included in the coding scheme. The inductive approach used words associated with the three pillars (socio-cultural, environmental, economic). Ethical learning is also an essential component of sustainable education (Schlottmann, 2008), which would extend to tourism and TH&E higher education (UNWTO, 2001; Kazimierczak, 2006; Tribe, 2002a). This ethical pillar was included along with evidence of political content which is important when thinking about sustainability (Gough & Scott, 2006).

Findings

By way of an overview, it should be noted that the majority of TH&E degrees were situated within a Business faculty or school. The exceptions were four degrees within Social Science/Arts faculties and two in the Environmental Sciences. We also found a recent fluctuation in the number of TH&E degrees on offer. Since the 2010 review by Dredge *et al.* (2012a), five

Table 38.1 UNESCO's educational strategic perspectives

Key areas	15 strategic perspectives
Socio-cultural:	Human rights Peace and human security Gender equality Cultural diversity and intercultural understanding Health HIV/AIDS Governance
Environmental:	Natural resources (water, energy, agriculture, biodiversity) Climate change Rural development Sustainable urbanization Disaster prevention and mitigation
Economic:	Poverty reduction Corporate responsibility Market economy and innovative technology

Source: Adapted from UNESCO (2006).

universities have completely withdrawn or reduced their TH&E degree offerings. Conversely, four universities released new TH&E degree programmes for the start of 2013. Other TH&E degrees are currently under review.

The most common degree type was tourism, accounting for 23 (34 per cent) of the 68 degree programmes available. This was closely followed by 22 degrees (32 per cent) with tourism and/or events and/or hospitality in the degree title. The majority of degrees included a combination of TH&E as a major in the title as opposed to a separately named TH&E title. Ten programmes (15 per cent) incorporated or gave credit for a TAFE or equivalent TH&E Advanced Diploma or Diploma towards their bachelor degree.

Across the 68 degree programmes, 682 subjects formed the TH&E curriculum. Some 531 subjects (78 per cent) were located or offered within a Business faculty. There were two separate Schools of Tourism and Hospitality Management (within a Business faculty), one at Southern Cross University and the other at the University of Queensland, contributing between them 71 subjects (10 per cent). The remaining 80 subjects (12 per cent) were offered either in a Social Science, Arts or Environmental Science faculty.

'Sustainability' in the TH&E curriculum space

Of the 68 TH&E degrees, only two included the word 'sustainable' or 'sustainability' within the full degree title. These were the 'Bachelor of Sustainable Tourism Management' at Deakin University (which included a TAFE Diploma of Sustainability) and the 'Bachelor of Business (Sustainable Tourism Management') at Griffith University. However, looking further at the actual degree descriptions that are promoted on university websites, just over one-third of the 68 degree descriptions (37 per cent) included the terms 'sustainability' or 'sustainable'. This suggests that while sustainability might not be explicitly present per se in the names of degrees, it is a term used more liberally when degrees are described.

As a further example of this, the B.Arts (Tourism & Events Management) offered at Murdoch University does not have anything about sustainability in its title, yet the degree description has an explicit focus on sustainability:

> In this unique course, you'll gain a deep understanding and appreciation of the tourism industry, with a special focus on sustainable events and festivals. You'll explore the wider tourism system, policy issues, and how cultural, environmental and economic factors impact the tourism industry and events.
>
> (Murdoch University, 2013)

For the University of Queensland's Bachelor of International Hotel & Tourism Management (Tourism Management), the degree description stated: 'You will learn about sustainability, ecotourism, visitor behaviour, and the physical, social and economic impacts of tourism' (The University of Queensland, 2011).

Moving from the degree to the subject level, of the total 682 TH&E subjects analysed, only 23 (3 per cent) had the words 'sustainable' or 'sustainability' in their titles. Interestingly, 'Sustainable Tourism' as a unit title was counted six times. Table 38.2 shows these subject names in full.

Looking at the descriptions of all 682 subjects in the sample shows that 88 per cent did *not* refer to sustainability within their subject descriptions.

When comparing the presence of sustainability by faculty/school location, 11 per cent of TH&E subjects held within a school of tourism/business faculty contained sustainability in their

Table 38.2 Subjects with sustainability/sustainable in title

Subject name
Creating Sustainable Futures
Economics for Sustainable Business
Environment, Technology and Sustainability
Ethics, Sustainability and Culture
Managing Sustainable Destinations
Marketing for Sustainability
Planning for Sustainable Destinations
Sustainable Community Events
Sustainable Event Development
Sustainable Operations
Sustainable Practice in Tourism Project
Sustainable Tourism (x 6)
Sustainable Tourism Development
Sustainable Tourism Management
Sustainable Tourism, Leisure and Event Management
Sustainable Tourism Practices
The Sustainable Hotel Environment
Tourism and Sustainability

descriptions. This was much higher when compared with subjects within an Arts (23 per cent), Social Science (19 per cent) or Environmental Science faculty (17 per cent) of their TH&E subjects. This provides some evidence that Business faculties/schools incorporated the term sustainable/sustainability much less in their subject descriptions when compared with the Social Sciences/Arts.

Other sustainability-related perspectives in the TH&E curriculum space

Recognizing the broader relevance beyond the words 'sustainable/sustainability', the study also explored the presence of other sustainability-related perspectives within the TH&E curriculum. Thus the analysis also looked for terms related to the UNDESD triple-bottom line pillars (social, cultural and environmental) and used UNESCO's (2006) educational strategic perspectives, as listed in Table 38.1, as a guide when searching for sustainability-related words in the degree names, subject titles and descriptions. Since the EfS literature considers 'political' perspectives (Levy & Zint, 2012; Gough & Scott, 2006) and 'ethical' perspectives (Kronlid & Öhman, 2012; Tribe, 2002a) to be relevant in a sustainability education discourse, the analysis looked for the presence of these additional pillars as well.

The majority of TH&E degree names (84 per cent) included the words 'business', 'management', 'commerce', 'international' or a combination of these. Five degrees used terms such as 'heritage', 'nature-based', 'cultural' or 'ecotourism' and two degrees were simply called Bachelor of Tourism. Within the degree descriptions, 11 degree programmes (16 per cent) were found to include references to these other sustainability-related pillars/perspectives. For example, the Bachelor of Business (Tourism Management and Marketing) at La Trobe University stated in its degree description that 'a triple-bottom line approach is adopted where economic, social and environmental impacts of tourism are examined'.

Extending the above analysis, we looked for evidence of these sustainability-related pillars in subject titles. In total, a fairly small number of 99 subjects (or 15 per cent) used the terms 'socio-cultural', 'environmental', 'economic', 'political' or 'ethical', or broader associated terms. Some examples of such titles were 'Ecotourism', 'Coastal and Marine Tourism', 'Responsible Tourism and Ethics', 'Global Cultures and Tourism', 'Indigenous Cultures and Tourism' and 'Global Politics of Tourism'. However, at the subject description level, just over half of the total subject descriptions (n = 385, or 56 per cent) referred broadly to at least one of the socio-cultural, environmental, economic, political or ethical pillars. Of the subject descriptions that did feature such sustainability-related concepts, most related to some aspect of the socio-cultural pillar (n = 136, or 36 per cent). The environmental and economic pillars were next most commonly shown, featuring in 91 (23 per cent) and 86 (22 per cent) subject descriptions, respectively. Less frequently referred to were the ethical (n = 47, or 12 per cent) and political (n = 25, or 7 per cent) pillars.

Discussion: where is EfS in the tourism curriculum space?

Returning to our original research question, the content analysis presented here reveals a wide spectrum of inclusion of the terms 'sustainable' and 'sustainability' in the course and subject descriptions of the TH&E curriculum under examination. Studies examining the presence of the term 'sustainability' or indeed an in-depth investigation of engagement with EfS within the TH&E curriculum space are missing. In line with findings from a British case study examining the concept of sustainable tourism within the higher education curriculum (Busby, 2003), the presence of 'sustainable' and 'sustainability' in this study can be located within a spectrum of engagement. One end of the continuum represents an incidental approach (absence of serious study about sustainability), moving to an incremental or ad hoc approach (overt issues of sustainability are covered in one or two subjects only) to evidence of sustainability finally holistically embedded throughout the curriculum. Most degrees examined in this study were located within an incidental or incremental spectrum as evidenced by either no subject or only one or two subjects explicitly referring to 'sustainable' or 'sustainability' in the subject title or description. Very few TH&E degrees had sustainable/sustainability concepts permeating throughout the entire degree. Similar to Busby (2003), the degrees which adopted more of a holistic approach to sustainability tended to be those with an overt ecotourism focus in the degree title. From the evidence provided, sustainability was not apparent as an underlying element or philosophy for the majority of TH&E degrees and subjects (although it was more prominent in tourism-focused programmes and subjects when compared with hospitality). It should be noted that this finding is not unique to TH&E programmes, as engagement with EfS in other disciplines also reveals a mixed response (Leihy & Salazar, 2011).

So, why is there such little room for explicit sustainability in the tourism curriculum space? One factor may be the primary location of a majority of degrees within Business faculties/schools. Indeed, it has been argued that progress with EfS in the curriculum has been the slowest in the neoliberal environments promoted in the business and management disciplines (Bates et al., 2009; von der Heidt et al., 2012). Indeed, our analysis showed that the small number of TH&E programmes located in a Social Science/Arts faculty had a greater propensity to holistically embed sustainability and a socio-cultural perspective throughout the TH&E curriculum.

Some studies have also discussed the impact of institutional technocratic pressures and other political forces which result in a compacted and squeezed curriculum. A study by Wilson and von der Heidt (2012) found TH&E teachers and curriculum decision-makers felt the current pressured teaching environment made it difficult to innovate and 'do something different'. Unless there are systemic changes to this current state of affairs, the paradigm changes considered necessary for EfS may remain evasive. This resonates with similar findings from a programmatic content analysis of sustainability within Irish accredited tourism and hospitality courses (Fáilte Ireland, 2008). That research found evidence to suggest that sustainability is a 'poorly understood and inconsistently applied concept' with 'little or no systematic treatment of sustainability issues' and 'incorporation of sustainability content largely discretionary and driven by an interest in such issues on the part of individual lecturers' (Fáilte Ireland, 2008).

In our Australian case, some degree programmes claimed sustainability to be present in degree descriptions, but on further investigation at the subject level, sustainability or sustainability-related concepts were not well incorporated. Conversely, some degrees did not mention sustainability at all in degree information, but then showed a high presence of sustainability across many of its subjects. Similarly, there was not always a strong connection between the presence of sustainability or sustainable-related concepts in the subject title and the term actually being included within the subject description.

Such inconsistencies suggest some confusion about and ambivalence towards sustainability, as well as a reluctance to make it explicit in the curriculum. Further analysis of syllabus/learning outcomes/topics and assessment was beyond the scope of this study, but may more deeply reveal a subject's 'true' aims and values. However, one may argue that this explicitness – on the most public form of communication, which is the university website – is crucial in conveying upfront the programmes' mission, pedagogy and values. Subject names and their constituent subject descriptions are important marketing tools, and indeed they are what make up the TH&E curriculum. In sum, our content analysis would suggest that across Australia, tourism, hospitality and events education is on the 'weaker' end of the ideological sustainability spectrum (Hunter, 1997). Our findings point to the tendency for engagement with sustainability to be located within an anthropocentric discourse (focus on profit and people) as opposed to a biocentric approach where an explicit environmental perspective is included. Few studies have critically examined the presence of sustainability and sustainable-related content in the TH&E curriculum. However, findings from Deale et al. (2009), Deale and Barber (2012) and Boley (2011) concur that more needs to be done generally to incorporate sustainability education into the TH&E curriculum. So far, there seems to be a disconnect between sustainability being broadly important to the tourism industry, and the actual teaching of sustainability in hospitality and tourism programmes (Boley, 2011). Similarly, Deale et al. (2009) report that while many educators think sustainability is important, very few actually address it within their learning and teaching practices, and in curriculum development.

We recognize that embedding EfS means more than just including the word 'sustainable' in the degree or subject name. Other sustainability perspectives are also important, reflected in the terminology around 'responsible', 'impacts', 'ethical' and 'futures thinking', which address the wide range of sustainable principles and practices too. Indeed, a report from the research group Fáilte Ireland (2008) suggests that avoiding the term 'sustainable' would help to remove the temptation to adopt a tokenistic approach. By engaging with other terminology and descriptions, we are forced to explicitly articulate our values instead of assuming sustainability is present merely because the word 'sustainable' is used.

The tendency to rely on a stand-alone 'sustainable' subject to cover the issues of sustainability was apparent within most TH&E degree programmes. These subjects must then 'carry the weight' throughout the entire programme. Fundamentally it seems to indicate an ad hoc and tokenistic approach to sustainability and its wider related concepts. In line with findings following the review of T&H programmes in Ireland (Fáilte Ireland, 2008), the Australian TH&E curriculum has treated sustainability as a self-contained curriculum module, rather than a philosophy underpinning all aspects of learning. It also suggests a reliance on individual teachers to champion EfS; research has shown a correlation between lecturer values, beliefs and attitudes and teaching sustainability (Cross, 1998).

Coverage of socio-cultural, environmental, economic pillars within the curriculum (most notably in the generic subject descriptions) reflects some engagement with sustainability issues without explicitly using the terms 'sustainable' or 'sustainability'. Nevertheless, it is apparent that the curriculum space is dominated by generic business content: management, marketing, accounting and so on. Overall, there was limited inclusion of the environmental perspective generally across all programmes. Despite tourism having a significant impact on the physical environment, it would appear many TH&E students graduate with sparse, if any, knowledge about the connection tourism business has with the natural environment. Of all the sustainability-related perspectives, the socio-cultural pillar was most represented in the TH&E curriculum space.

Conclusion

Environmental educators have been calling for a re-visioning of education, one which requires a paradigm change and new way of thinking about – and doing – education (Huckle, 2012; Sterling, 2001, 2010b). The results of the present study's analysis suggest that coverage of sustainability and other key sustainability themes is most successful when they are holistically distributed throughout the whole programme and equally across all (socio-cultural, environmental, economic and political) pillars. For many TH&E degree programmes, this involves an overhaul and reallocation of priority and space for content to include sustainability and wider sustainability-related concepts. Most pressing are the significant gaps in the hospitality and event degree programmes.

Ideally, sustainability issues should be incorporated throughout all modules, at all levels, with linkages between modules. As Barth and Rieckmann (2012: 34) contend, sustainability is not another topic that just needs adding to the curriculum space (or what might be termed the 'add sustainability and stir' approach). Rather, such issues represent a holistic and critically oriented approach which challenges traditional approaches in higher education. The success of embedding sustainability holistically into TH&E higher education will depend on the explicit support by institutional leaders as well as the motivation and confidence of teachers to follow through (Barth & Rieckmann, 2012). If these elements are lacking, it will be difficult for the tourism curriculum to make the sustainability paradigm shift, and ensure it is the 'golden thread' (Lozano et al., 2013: 1) throughout the entire university system.

References

Ayikoru, M., Tribe, J., & Airey, D. (2009). 'Reading Tourism Education: neoliberalism unveiled'. *Annals of Tourism Research*, 36(2), 191–221.

Barth, M., & Rieckmann, M. (2012). 'Academic Staff Development as a Catalyst for Curriculum Change towards Education for Sustainable Development: an output perspective', *Journal of Cleaner Production*, 26, 28–36.

Bates, C., Silverblatt, R., & Kleban, J. (2009). 'Creating a New Green Management Course'. *Business Review, Cambridge*, 12(1), 60–6.

Boley, B. (2011). 'Sustainability in Hospitality and Tourism Education: towards an integrated curriculum'. *Journal of Hospitality and Tourism Education*, 23(4), 22–31.

Busby, G. (2003). 'The Concept of Sustainable Tourism within the Higher Education Curriculum: a British case study'. *Journal of Hospitality, Leisure, Sport & Tourism Education*, 2 (2),48–58.

Clarke, J. (1997). 'A Framework of Approaches to Sustainable Tourism'. *Journal of Sustainable Tourism*, 5(3), 224–33.

Connell, J., & Rugendyke, B. (Eds.). (2008). *Tourism at the Grassroots: villages and visitors in the Asia-Pacific*. Abingdon: Routledge.

Cross, R. T. (1998). 'Teachers' Views about What to Do about Sustainable Development'. *Environmental Education Research*, 4(1), 41.

Day, M., Walo, M., Weeks, P., Dredge, D., Benckendorff, P., Gross, M., & Whitelaw, P. (2012). 'Building a Stronger Future: balancing professional and liberal education ideals in undergraduate tourism and hospitality education' (Issues paper 4: Analysis of Australian Tourism, Hospitality and Events Undergraduate Education Programs). Canberra: Australian Learning and Teaching Council.

Deale, C., & Barber, N. (2012). 'How Important is Sustainability Education to Hospitality Programs?'. *Journal of Teaching in Travel and Tourism*, 12(2), 165–87.

Deale, C., Nichols, J., & Jacques, P. (2009). 'A Descriptive Study of Sustainability Education in the Hospitality Curriculum'. *Journal of Hospitality and Tourism Education*, 21(4), 34–42.

Dredge, D., Benckendorff, P., Day, M., Gross, M. J., Walo, M., Weeks, P., & Whitelaw, P. A. (2012a). 'Building a Stronger Future: balancing professional and liberal education ideals in undergraduate tourism and hospitality education (Issues paper 1: Key Issues in Tourism, Hospitality and Events Curriculum and Design). Canberra: Australian Learning and Teaching Council.

Dredge, D., Benckendorff, P., Day, M., Gross, M. J., Walo, M., Weeks, P., & Whitelaw, P. A. (2012b). 'The Philosophic Practitioner and the Curriculum Space'. *Annals of Tourism Research*, 39(4), 2154–76.

Fáilte Ireland (2008). 'Educating for Sustainability: creating a comprehensive, coherent and compelling approach – Guidelines for sustainability standards and resource materials'. Ireland: Tourism Research Centre at Dublin Institute of Technology, National Tourism Development Authority.

Fennell, D. (2008). *Ecotourism*, London: Routledge.

Fereday, J., & Muir-Cochrane, E. (2006). 'Demonstrating Rigor using Thematic Analysis: a hybrid approach of inductive and deductive coding and theme development'. *International Journal of Qualitative Methods*, 5(1), 80–92.

Fidgeon, P. (2010). 'Tourism Education and Curriculum Design: a time for consolidation and review?'. *Tourism Management*, 31(6): 699–723.

Fisher, J., & Bonn, I. (2011). 'Business Sustainability and Undergraduate Management Education: an Australian study'. *Higher Education*, 62(5), 563–71.

Fuller, R. (2010). 'Beyond Cliche: reclaiming the concept of sustainability'. *Australian Journal of Environmental Education*, 26, 7–18.

Gough, S., & Scott, W. (2006). 'Education and Sustainable Development: a political analysis'. *Educational Review*, 58(3), 273–90.

Higgins-Desbiolles, F. (2006). 'More than an Industry: the forgotten power of tourism as a social force'. *Tourism Management*, 27(6), 1192–208.

Huckle, J. (1993). 'Environmental Education and Sustainability: view from critical theory'. In J. Fien (Ed.), *Environmental Education: a pathway to sustainability*. Geelong, Victoria: Deakin University.

Huckle, J. (2012). 'Sustainable Development'. In J. Arthur & A. Peterson (Eds.), *The Routledge Companion to Education* (pp. 362–71). Abingdon: Routledge.

Hunter, C. (1997). 'Sustainable Tourism as an Adaptive Paradigm'. *Annals of Tourism Research*, 24, 850–67.

Jafari, J. (1990). 'Research and Scholarship: the basis of tourism education' *Journal of Tourism Studies*, 1(1), 33–41.

Jafari, J. (2001). 'The Scientification of Tourism'. In V. Smith, & M. Brent (Eds.), *Hosts and Guests Revisited: tourism issues of the 21st century* (pp. 28–41). New York: Cognizant Communication.

Jamal, T. (2004). 'Virtue Ethics and Sustainable Tourism Pedagogy: phronesis, principles and practice'. *Journal of Sustainable Tourism*, 12(6), 530–45.

Jamal, T., Taillon, J., & Dredge, D. (2011). 'Sustainable Tourism Pedagogy and Academic–Community Collaboration: a progressive service-learning approach'. *Tourism and Hospitality Research*, 11(2), 133–47.

Jurowski, C., & Liburd, J. J. (2001). 'A Multi-Cultural and Multi-Disciplinary Approach to Integrating the Principles of Sustainable Development into Human Resource Management Curriculums in Hospitality and Tourism'. *Journal of Hospitality and Tourism Education*, 13(5), 36–51.

Kazimierczak, M. (2006). 'Code of Ethics for Tourism'. *Studies in Physical Culture and Tourism*, 13(1), 93–7.

Kronlid, D. O., & Öhman, J. (2012). 'An Environmental Ethical Conceptual Framework for Research on Sustainability and Environmental Education'. *Environmental Education Research*, 19(1), 21–44.

Landorf, H., Dorscher, S., & Rocco, T. (2008). 'Education for Sustainable Human Development: towards a definition'. *Theory and Research in Education*, 6(2), 221–36.

Lashley, C. (2013). 'Managing the Tyranny of Relevance: linking with industry – but not too much'. *Worldwide Hospitality and Tourism Themes*, 5(3), 283–95.

Leihy, P., & Salazar, J. (2011). *Education for Sustainability in University Curricula: policies and practice in Victoria.* Melbourne: University of Melbourne.

Levy, B. L., & Zint, M. T. (2012). 'Toward Fostering Environmental Political Participation: framing an agenda for environmental education research'. *Environmental Education Research*, 19(5), 553–76.

Lewis, E., Mansfield, C., & Baudains, C. (2008). 'Getting Down and Dirty: values in education for sustainability'. *Issues in Educational Research*, 18(2), 138–55.

Littledyke, M. (2008). 'Science Education for Environmental Awareness: approaches to integrating cognitive and affective domains'. *Environmental Education Research*, 14(1), 1–17.

Lozano, R., Lukman, R., Lozano, F. J., Huisingh, D., & Lambrechts, W. (2013). 'Declarations for Sustainability in Higher Education: becoming better leaders, through addressing the university system'. *Journal of Cleaner Production*, 48(1), 1–10.

Macbeth, J. (2005). 'Towards an Ethics Platform for Tourism'. *Annals of Tourism Research*, 32(4), 962–84.

Mowforth, M., & Munt, I. (2009). *Tourism and Sustainability: development, globalisation and new tourism in the Third World.* London: Routledge.

Mundt, J. (2011). *Tourism and Sustainable Development: reconsidering a concept of vague policies.* Berlin: Erich Schmidt Verlag.

Murdoch University. (2013). *Tourism and Events Course Information.* Online. Available: http://www.murdoch.edu.au/Courses/Tourism-and-Events-Management (Accessed 27 August 2013).

Nowaczek, A., Moran-Cahusac, C., & Fennell, D. (2007). 'Against the Current: striving for ethical tourism'. In J. Higham (Ed.), *Critical Issues in Ecotourism: understanding a complex tourism phenomenon* (pp. 136–57). Burlington, MA: Elsevier.

Nowak, M., Rowe, A., Thomas, G., & Klass, D. (2008). 'Weaving Sustainability into Business Education'. *Journal of the Asia-Pacific Centre for Environmental Accountability*, 14(2), 19–34.

O'Sullivan, E. (2004). 'Sustainability and Transformative Educational Vision'. In P. B. Corcoran & A. E. J. Wals (Eds.), *Higher Education and the Challenge of Sustainability: problematics, promise, and practice* (pp. 163–80). Dordrecht: Kluwer Academic.

Palmer, J. (1998). *Environmental Education in the 21st Century: theory, practice, progress and promise.* London: Routledge.

Pigozzi, M. (2010). 'Implementing the UN Decade of Education for Sustainable Development (DESD): achievements, open questions and strategies for the way forward'. *International Review of Education/Internationale Zeitschrift für Erziehungswissenschaft*, 56(2/3), 255–69.

Rundle-Thiele, S. R., & Wymer, W. (2010). 'Stand-Alone Ethics, Social Responsibility, and Sustainability Course Requirements: a snapshot from Australia and New Zealand'. *Journal of Marketing Education*, 32(1), 5–12.

Sanders, D., & Le Clus, M. (2011). 'Sustainability in the University Tourism Curriculum'. Paper presented at the Tourism and Hospitality Research, Training and Practice: 'Tourism: Celebrating a Brilliant Blend' 21st Annual Council for Australian University Tourism and Hospitality Education (CAUTHE) Conference, 8–11 February, Adelaide: University of South Australia.

Savelyeva, T., & McKenna, J. R. (2011). 'Campus Sustainability: emerging curricula models in higher education'. *International Journal of Sustainability in Higher Education*, 12(1), 55–66.

Schlottmann, C. (2008). 'Educational Ethics and the DESD: considering trade-offs'. *Theory and Research in Education*, 6(2), 207–19.

Shallcross, T., & Robinson, J. (2007). 'Is a Decade of Teacher Education for Sustainable Development Essential for Survival?'. *Journal of Education for Teaching*, 33(2), 137–47.

Sheldon, P., Fesenmaier, D. R., & Tribe, J. (2011). 'The Tourism Education Futures Initiative (TEFI): activating change in tourism education'. *Journal of Teaching in Travel & Tourism*, 11(1), 2–23.

Shephard, K. (2008). 'Higher Education for Sustainability: seeking affective learning outcomes'. *International Journal of Sustainability in Higher Education*, 9(1), 87–98.

Shephard, K. (2010). 'Higher Education's Role in Education for Sustainability'. *Australian Universities' Review*, 52(1), 13–22.

Shriberg, M. (2003). 'Is the "Maize-and-Blue" Turning Green? Sustainability at the University of Michigan'. *International Journal of Sustainability in Higher Education*, 4(3), 263–76.

Sibbel, A. (2009). 'Pathways towards Sustainability through Higher Education'. *International Journal of Sustainability in Higher Education,* 10(1), 68–82.

Sipos, Y., Battisti, B., & Grimm, K. (2008). 'Achieving Transformative Sustainability Learning: engaging head, hands and heart'. *International Journal of Sustainability in Higher Education,* 9(1), 68–86.

Sterling, S. (1996). 'Education in Change'. In J. Huckle & S. Sterling (Eds.), *Education for Sustainability* (pp. 18–39). London: Earthscan.

Sterling, S. (2001). *Sustainable Education: re-visioning learning and change.* Totnes, Devon, UK: Green Books.

Sterling, S. (2010a). 'Learning for Resilience, or the resilient learner? Towards a necessary reconciliation in a paradigm of sustainable education'. *Environmental Education Research,* 16, 511–28.

Sterling, S. (2010b). 'Living "in" the Earth: towards an education for our times'. *Journal of Education for Sustainable Development,* 4(2), 213–18.

Telfer, D. J., & Sharpley, R. (2008). *Tourism and Development in the Developing World.* Abingdon: Routledge.

The University of Queensland. (2011). Courses and Programs: Tourism Management Single Major. Online. Available: http://www.uq.edu.au/study/plan.html?acad_plan=TOURIX2194 (Accessed 27 August 2013).

Tilbury, D., & Cooke, K. (2005). *A National Review of Environmental Education and its Contribution to Sustainability in Australia: frameworks for sustainability.* Canberra: Australian Government Department of the Environment and Heritage and Australian Research Institute in Education for Sustainability (ARIES).

Tilbury, D., Keogh, A., Leighton, A., & Kent, J. (2005). *A National Review of Environmental Education and its Contribution to Sustainability in Australia: further and higher education.* Canberra: Australian Government Department of the Environment and Heritage and Australian Research Institute in Education for Sustainability (ARIES).

Tribe, J. (2002a). 'Education for Ethical Tourism Action'. *Journal of Sustainable Tourism,* 10(4), 309–24.

Tribe, J. (2002b). 'The Philosophic Practitioner'. *Annals of Tourism Research,* 29(2), 338–57.

Tribe, J. (2005). 'Tourism, Knowledge and the Curriculum'. In D. Airey & J. Tribe, (Eds.), *An International Handbook of Tourism Education* (pp. 47–60). London: Elsevier.

United Nations Educational, Scientific and Cultural Organization (UNESCO). (2006). *Framework for the UN DESD International Implementation Scheme.* (Section for Education for Sustainable Development (ED/PEQ/ESD) Division for the Promotion of Quality Education, Trans.): Paris: UNESCO. Available: www.unesco.org/education/desd (Accessed 10 December 2012).

United Nations World Tourism Organization (UNWTO). (2001). *Global Code of Ethics for Tourism.* General Assembly of the World Tourism Organization. Available: http://ethics.unwto.org/en/content/full-text-global-code-ethics-tourism (Accessed 15 October 2013].

University Leaders for a Sustainable Future (ULSF). (2008). *Talloires Declaration* [Online]. University Leaders for a Sustainable Future. Available: http://www.ulsf.org/programs_talloires_signatories.html (Accessed 5 September 2012).

von der Heidt, T., Lamberton, G., Wilson, E., & Morrison, D. (2012). 'To What Extent Does the Bachelor of Business Curriculum Reflect the Sustainability Paradigm? An audit and evaluation of current sustainability embeddedness in curriculum and assessment in the first-year Bachelor of Business in Southern Cross Business School and School of Tourism and Hospitality Management Lismore'. Unpublished Final Report. Southern Cross University, Lismore.

Wals, A. E. J. (2011). 'Learning Our Way to Sustainability'. *Journal of Education for Sustainable Development,* 5(2),177–86.

Warburton, K. (2003). 'Deep Learning and Education for Sustainability'. *International Journal of Sustainability in Higher Education,* 4(1), 44–56.

Weaver, D. (2006). *Sustainable Tourism.* Amsterdam: Elsevier.

Wilson, E., & von der Heidt, T. (2012). 'Is Transformational Change Possible through Education for Sustainability?'. Paper presented at the 6th Annual Conference Tourism Education Futures Initiative (TEFI), Transformational Leadership for Tourism Education, 28–30 June, University of Bocconi, Milan.

Wilson, E., & von der Heidt, T. (2013). 'Business as Usual? Barriers to education for sustainability in the tourism curriculum'. *Journal of Teaching in Travel and Tourism,* 13(2), 130–47.

Wright, T. (2004). Definitions and Frameworks for Environmental Sustainability in Higher Education'. In P. B. Corcoran & A. E. J. Wals (Eds.), *Higher Education and the Challenge of Sustainability* (pp. 7–19). Dordrecht: Kluwer Academic.

Part VII

Conclusions and future directions

39

Creating the future

Tourism, hospitality and events education in a post-industrial, post-disciplinary world

Dianne Dredge

Department of Culture and Global Studies, Aalborg University, Denmark

David Airey

School of Hospitality and Tourism Management, University of Surrey, UK

Michael J. Gross

School of Management, University of South Australia, Australia

Introduction

The transcendental changes taking place in higher education over the last decades have created a level of volatility previously unknown in the sector and have, as a consequence, focused attention on anticipating the future. This attention is not directed at trying to predict the future – which would be near impossible – but rather to consider the magnitude and direction of change and to answer questions about how we might plan for it (Universities UK, 2012; Ernst & Young, 2012; CHEPS, 2004; OECD, 2008, 2009a). Studies that contemplate the future of higher education involve a range of techniques and tools including interviews, environmental scanning, Delphi methods, simulation, scenario planning and trend analysis (Dator, 2001). While methodologies adopted in these studies are diverse, there is a significantly similar set of observations emerging. Futures research and foresight studies indicate that higher education in 5, 10 or 20 years' time will look very different: the organization of the modern university and its business models will be transformed; the infrastructure and facilities of higher institutions will also take varying forms as technology shapes new ways of learning; academic work will be recast; and the way students study and engage with their institutions will also change (Association of American Colleges & Universities, 2002; Barber *et al.*, 2013; Universiti Sains Malaysia, 2007; Munck & McConnell, 2010). In order to consider what the future might look like, an understanding of the complexity of this current context is required, as well as insights into how our current assumptions and perspectives influence how we perceive the future (Gidely, 2012).

Futurists argue that imagining the future also requires that we let go of our current frames of understanding (Tuomi, 2005, 2013). Innovation is not linear and incremental. It is unpredictable and radical and is borne out of a complex mixture of inheritance and imagination (Hospers, 2003). Our aim in this chapter then is to draw together a narrative around these higher education futures studies and to reflect upon how tourism, hospitality and events (TH&E) education may be impacted by such change. We start by summarizing the drivers of change, which have been woven into the warp and weft of the chapters of this *Handbook*, sometimes explicitly, but at other times, implicitly.

Higher education, policy and society

Governments in both developed and developing countries have, to varying extents, been aiming at building stronger links between macro-economic and education policy (Marginson, 2011). Supra-national agencies such as the World Bank and the Organization for Economic Cooperation and Development (OECD) have had a powerful influence in developing countries, actively engaging in setting these policy agendas (van der Wende, 2011; OECD, 2007; World Bank, 2012). Expanding employment and increasing productivity are top of their agendas and the role of higher education in building skills and, by corollary, innovation and productivity, is central to their interest in expanding access to and participation in higher education (World Bank, 2012).

But this interest in higher education sits within a set of complex global challenges. The extent and speed of change taking place in modern societies is causing transcendental changes in social, economic, ecological and political systems. 'Big societal issues', among them climate change, political unrest, poverty, food security, depletion of natural resources and a wide range of health issues, are causing great concern. The impact of these changes, the complexity of roles and responsibilities in addressing the causes, and a crisis in leadership are contributing to the possibility of a 'tragedy of the commons' where humanity could fail to take ownership and address these big societal issues. Higher education is implicated in these changes in profound ways:

> There is little question that higher education must be among the most important intellectual and creative resources assembled to address an array of critical challenges confronting society – including the sustainability of natural resources; the provision of health care for all in a growing, aging population; and the renewal of economic vitality across a wide demographic range, which entails helping more working adults acquire higher-level skills and knowledge, instilling core human values, and strengthening social structures to ensure that future generations experience lives of justice, equity, and fulfilment.
>
> (National Center for Public Policy and Higher Education, 2008: 1)

Gross and Lashley (Chapter 6) writing about hospitality education and Sharpley (Chapter 13) writing about tourism education argue that tourism and hospitality are multi-disciplinary areas of study that are deeply embedded in contemporary social and economic life. TH&E education provides a lens on our social world, a lens through which processes of change can be identified, understood and critically analysed. Moreover, where TH&E education provides a balance between liberal education and vocational aspects the mindful, world-making practitioners that emerge can assist in addressing broader societal issues (Hollinshead, 2009; Morgan, 2012; Sheldon et al., 2014). Within these arguments, the basis of the philosophic tourism and hospitality practitioner takes hold, a practitioner who not only demonstrates professional competence but also takes responsibility for stewardship and the ethical and aesthetic development of the wider world (see Tribe, Chapter 2; Caton, Chapter 4; Dredge *et al.*, Chapter 5). TH&E education can therefore contribute to broader societal challenges, but unlocking its potential requires not only an understanding of the broad social, economic, environmental and political changes taking place, but also a vision of the future.

The meta-processes of change described in the chapters of the *Handbook* and summarized below are of particular significance to TH&E education. Our narrative is provided not as an attempt to extrapolate the past into the future, but rather to assist in understanding our own limitations in the way that we consider the future, and as a means of trying to identify a wider array of potential changes. In this spirit, the following drivers of change are highlighted.

Globalization

Globalization processes have had far-reaching effects on both the education and tourism sectors (OECD, 2009b; Gomes *et al.*, 2012). Globalization is characterized by the increased mobility of capital, people and ideas, and has resulted in the expansion and diversification of markets and increased competition in almost all aspects of economic life (Harvey, 2005; Neubauer, 2010). Rightly or wrongly, proponents of globalization have identified higher education as an important tool for growth because it facilitates flows of knowledge and, by corollary, assists in economic innovation, employment generation and, ultimately, improvements in quality of life. Drawing from this logic, an idealistic and romantic line of reasoning has emerged that, by increasing access to education, all people including those in the poorest of countries will be able to improve their employment prospects, earn a living and contribute to economic growth which will in turn bring positive social, political and environmental benefits (UNDP, 2011). These arguments are well discussed in the literature where tourism has been identified as a tool to alleviate poverty, and to address a range of social and economic issues to improve the self-determination and self-sufficiency of marginalized groups and individuals (UNWTO, 2010). Yet, despite these arguments, the ideas that they represent remain idealistic and romantic because there is still little conclusive evidence that TH&E education has made wholesale advances in improving socio-economic conditions of many local populations (Hall, 2007). Furthermore, Sogayar and Rejowski (Chapter 16), Harrison (Chapter 17), Mayaka and Akama (Chapter 18) all point to the many challenges of delivering TH&E education when local industry and community needs and aspirations are quite different to global discourses about what and how such an education should be delivered.

Globalization has also contributed to a breaking down of the barriers to participation in higher education, an expansion in the global student market, expansion in the transnational operation of many universities and increased competition (OECD, 2009; CHEPS, 2004). At first, this competition was characterized by developed countries' competition for the international, globally mobile student, and the growth markets were made up of the expanding middle classes predominantly from Asia and Latin America. However this competition has now brought about a second phase of development where, in a relatively short time, investment in the higher education sector in countries like China, Singapore, Malaysia and Brazil has stimulated the growth and development of globally competitive educational products which have had a profound effect on global student flows. Hsu (Chapter 15) and Sogayar and Rejowski (Chapter 16) have provided insightful accounts of the Asian and Brazilian contexts respectively, and point to the important role and significant growth that higher education in these regions will have in the future. Such trends as described by these authors are likely to bring about significant changes in the dynamics of higher education supply and demand. Historically, the predominant flow of students has been from developing countries to developed countries in pursuit of a so-called 'western' education experience. As developing countries grow their own local capabilities of education design and delivery, we may expect to see a diminishing of the perception of premium value and the competitive advantage that western education destinations have enjoyed for decades (Globalization of Management Education Task Force, 2011).

Post-industrial society

Over the latter part of the twentieth century there was a profound restructuring of economic production and a move towards what is known as a post-industrial society (Bell, 1976). Post-industrialized societies are characterized by a decline in the industrial manufacturing-style growth witnessed in the early part of the twentieth century and an increase in the flexible production of goods and growth in the service sectors (Williams, 2008; Mullins, 2000). In this context, the higher education sector plays an important role in facilitating competition: it assists in addressing the increased demand for professional services, and it imparts higher-order lifelong learning skills that are thought to contribute to the creation of new job opportunities and work profiles that could not have even been imagined 20 years ago (Abeles, 2006; Snyder, 2006). The creative economy, which promotes artistic, cultural and social economy of place, has flourished under these post-industrialization processes and growth in professional programmes in areas such as tourism, hospitality and events reflect these shifts (Landry & Bianchini, 1995). Furthermore, the continued resonance of this change is illustrated in the development of new and growing areas of programme delivery in, for example, events (Getz, Chapter 35), and, more recently, gastronomy (see Sogayar & Rejowski, Chapter 16; Haden, Chapter 36).

Neoliberal management

The uptake of neoliberal economic management in both developed and developing countries has also had profound impacts on the higher education sector (Davis, 2008; Marginson, 2008; Ayikoru et al., 2009). As an ideology, neoliberalism emphasizes growth through deregulation and the breaking down of barriers to the operation of the 'free market'. It argues that governments do not have sufficient information about markets to make good decisions and that the private sector is best placed to deliver a range of goods and services, including higher education, that were once considered the domain of the public sector. In practice, neoliberalism has been performed in, for example, passing responsibility for funding from the state to the students and their families, opening higher education to competition, repeated cycles of funding cuts, restructuring of programmes to extract increased efficiencies, improving the efficiencies of programme delivery through standardized curricula and teaching approaches, and the implementation of higher education workforce productivity measures. The university machinery has also intensified its branding and marketing efforts to expand and diversify student markets, and to increase connectivity and mobility of students, educators and institutions to produce a globally competitive education product (Temple, 2011; Joseph et al., 2012).

Neoliberal policies have also opened up opportunities for the private sector to become more involved in higher education. In the case of Brazil, the agility and flexibility of private providers to meet market demands have already resulted in diversification of offerings and rapid growth in student numbers (see Sogayar & Rejowski, Chapter 16). By virtue of their perceived proximity to industry, private providers are able to bridge the gap between higher and vocational education, making their offerings very competitive. Moreover, the mobility of educators between 'public' universities and private providers means that there is often little difference in the content and quality of the programmes on offer (Day et al., 2012). As a result, public–private partnerships are increasingly common, and it is likely that in the future there will be many pathways to and within higher education that involve both traditional university and private providers.

The private sector is also responding to outsourcing opportunities where universities themselves cannot provide the service in a cost effective manner. In tourism and hospitality, the need for graduates to possess both mindful liberal education and vocational skills suggests that private providers able to offer vocational skills training where universities cannot are likely to consolidate their role and importance in the sector (Davis, 2008). In the future then, it is probable that TH&E education that combines both liberal education and vocational skills development might be delivered by various consortia of education providers specializing in aspects of a balanced programme.

In addition to the growing competition from the private providers, the tightening of public funding under neoliberal management is pushing universities to become more efficient and competitive. Not surprisingly, students are increasingly conceived as consumers, leading to a paradoxical situation where standards of education must be upheld whilst at the same time ensuring consumer satisfaction. As the number of providers has increased, the sector has become more complex, students become increasingly mobile and the barriers for transnational mobility disappear, the importance of articulating and maintaining standards and ensuring quality has becoming increasingly important (Brink, 2010).

Brink (2010) points out that 'quality' and 'standards' are important neoliberal management tools that are often confused, hotly debated and are open to being subverted by the marketing machinery of universities, especially where they are equated with 'excellence'. Quality assurance generally concerns the processes in place to ensure quality learning experiences, and responds to the question 'Is [the institution, the learning experience, etc.] good?' It reflects the management of the institution and its processes in supporting teaching and research. But measures of quality assurance do not answer the question 'Is it good enough?' In response there has been a growing emphasis on the development of standards that draws attention to outcomes (not processes) and levels of achievement in learning and research. This emphasis has produced a moving feast of academic standards, provider standards, qualification standards and teaching and learning standards in many countries. As Brennan (1997) notes, quality assurance and standards are mechanisms for protecting the higher education provider's reputation, a country's branding as a destination for education, and the consumer rights of students. With that, it becomes all too easy to assume that quality processes and meeting standards equates to excellence, and here the debate becomes controversial:

> The controversy about quality in higher education is partly about *language*, many of the terms used embracing values which some people find inappropriate and potentially threatening to higher education's traditions. The controversy is also partly about *power*, about the relative autonomy of higher education from other institutions of society . . . and about the relative autonomy of individual academic staff within the institutions in which they work. The controversy is also about *change*, about the many external social and economic changes which are requiring change in higher education, and about the managerial and other mechanisms with which higher education institutions seek to steer this change.
>
> (Brennan, 1997: 1)

In TH&E education, these neoliberal management tools and approaches have unleashed considerable competition between nations, and between and within universities, and have even put up barriers to collaboration across higher education systems (Fennell, 2013). As Peck (2010) remind us, neoliberalism is not a blueprint for reform, it is a rolling project, socially constructed and performed, and it does not have an end. In this perspective, the quality and standards work will continue, and questions of language, power, autonomy and managerialism will be progressively addressed. Institutions will develop better understandings of their potential roles and the education marketplace, which will be balanced with quality assurance and standards, and it will become possible that differentiation and niche programmes will start to emerge that respond to particular localized conditions and employment demands.

Markets, consumer protection, performance and obligation

Notwithstanding that the speed of change differs dramatically from country to country, the transition to a market-driven higher education system is bringing with it a range of funding and budgetary challenges (Marginson, 2001). In most countries, the expansion of the higher education sector to meet macro-economic policy objectives has not been accompanied by any significant increase in core government funding. To the contrary, in most contexts government funding has become tighter and subject to increased levels of contestability as pressure is placed on higher education institutions to become more efficient and accountable (Hicks, 2010). As a result, universities have started to aggressively seek out alternative funding streams and to find ways of expanding markets and reducing costs of programme delivery (Marginson, 2006). Paradoxically, governments have also stepped up their micro-management of the sector as a means of upholding standards, protecting the student-consumer, and aligning education policies and practices with other political, economic and social aspects of their national agenda.

These drivers have resulted in governments implementing performance measures with two main uses emerging: first, performance measures can help governments determine the distribution of competitive funding. Second, these frameworks help student-consumers in their decision-making processes and are thus seen as a tool to facilitate a competitive market. However, criticisms have emerged that these neoliberal tools are poorly conceptualized and introduce considerable bias because some institutions are better resourced to be able to 'play the game' (Hazelkorn, 2011; Harvey, 2008).

Nevertheless, these rankings, performance measures and other indicators have become quite powerful marketing tools because they allow universities to lay claims of excellence. At the time of writing, three league tables dominate the international arena: the Times Higher Education rankings, the Shanghai Jiao Tong ratings and the Quacquarelli Symonds (QS) rankings. All of these rankings have major weaknesses: for example the Times Higher Education rankings combine in one indicator measures of teaching quality and research and the Jiao Tong ranking includes only research. Furthermore, the methodologies themselves and the value of reducing university performance to one number in a ranked output have been much questioned because they take individual institutions and the challenges they face (e.g. regional context, resource availability, access to student markets, characteristics of the student population, etc.) out of context (Harvey, 2008; Davis, 2008). Yet despite their limitations, and in the absence of alternative measures, such league tables have become tools for distributing public funding to universities, and they are used to leverage marketing advantages in the student marketplace (Davis, 2008). This use of these simplistic proxies as a measure of quality should raise alarm bells where student-consumers rely on this information when making choices about their programme of study instead of assessing curricula content and delivery against their learning needs and aspirations (Drummond, 2004; Wood, 2011). It is an issue that will almost certainly increase in importance in the future as the social and moral obligations between higher education providers and their student-consumers come under greater scrutiny.

The seriousness of this narrow vision for subject areas like TH&E is made more acute at a time when senior managers are seeking to secure the competitive position of their institutions in national and global contexts. As Airey *et al.* (2014) have noted, while these subject areas have generally been successful in attracting students and hence finance, their limited contribution to institutional reputation, whether in student entry qualifications, research income, output and impact makes them unattractive to those making decisions about which subject areas to support in the universities of the twenty-first century.

In the meantime universities' obligations to students are already being tested. For example, in the marketplace, if a purchased product does not meet expectations, and it does not deliver on its promises, then the consumer is usually protected under law and a number of remedies are available such as lodging a complaint with an independent adjudicator or even being entitled to their money back. Experience has shown that where there is rapid growth in demand, and entry of a large number of private providers into the marketplace, international students in particular are vulnerable to unscrupulous practices. While there may be very few of these providers, and most offenders tend to be new private providers, poor consumer feedback can have enormous negative consequences not only for individual institutions, but also for a country's higher education export market. As a result, many governments have responded by setting up student consumer protection laws, codes of ethics and specialized units to deal with complaints (e.g. Australian Government, 2008; Cuomo, 2014; Mause, 2010) and student-consumer protection lobby groups are also emerging.

These issues are likely to become increasingly important as rising tuition fees magnify attention on the social and moral obligations that higher education providers have towards their student-consumers. Student debt in Australia is around $26.3 billion AUD and it is estimated that about $6.2 billion will not be paid back (in part because graduates will not reach the salary threshold required to start paying back their student loans and also partly because graduates are finding work overseas) (Universities Australia, 2013). In the UK, 40 per cent of students can find a graduate-appropriate job two years after graduating and according to the US Department of Education, student debt is now over $1 trillion, and an estimated 53.6 per cent of degree-holders in the USA are jobless or underemployed (Walker, 2013). Official complaints being registered against universities in the UK and Wales increased 20 per cent in 2010–11 with 16 per cent of these claims deemed to be justified or partially justified (BBC News, 2012). There have also been a small but increasing number of cases in both the USA and UK where students have sued their education provider, sometimes successfully, because they have been unable to find employment. Class actions are also looming from students who feel they have been misled about job prospects (Dolan, 2013). These employment and career implications are addressed by Petrova (Chapter 29), Ladkin (Chapter 30) and Huang (Chapter 31).

Flexible production, curriculum and pedagogy

Explored in a number of chapters in this *Handbook* (see Parts 5 and 6), the pressures on universities in recent decades have contributed to increasing calls for a creative and innovative rethink of traditional teaching models, pedagogies and approaches. The move towards flexible production of goods and services in post-industrial societies, the diversity of student markets and learning styles, increasing competition and mobility are already playing out in higher education in ways that require traditional 'sage on the stage' teaching practices to change (Biggs & Tang, 2007). In particular, the structure and delivery of programmes, infrastructure and resources, the role of physical and virtual learning spaces and the pathways that students take from entry to completion will vary significantly (Liburd & Hjalager, 2010; Cho & Kang, 2005). In the neoliberal higher education model, the student-consumer will decide when and how they study and, in order to stay competitive, universities will have to oblige with flexible production and choice in educational products.

In this context digital technologies are a disruptive force which bring both the possibility of heightening the learning experience, promoting mobility of ideas and understanding, but they can also present challenges to participation, to pedagogy and teaching practice (see Liburd, Chapter 22). O'Mahony and Salmon (Chapter 10) discuss Massive Open Online Courses (MOOCs) as one of the most visible signs of disruption and argue that whilst they have enormous potential to improve access to and participation in higher education, and to combine vocational and liberal studies, there are also concerns that have to be taken seriously. Munar and Bødker (Chapter 8) highlight that the sub-field of IT in tourism curricula is dominated by scientific-positivistic and technopian perspectives and that an expansion beyond these narrow boundaries is necessary in order to unlock deeper understandings about the evolution of tourism, technology and knowledge. The works of Sigala (Chapter 33) and Talbot and Cater (Chapter 34) contribute to this line of thought through their case analyses of social media and wikis. They highlight the utility of this emerging technology to facilitate students' roles in shaping their own education experience through sharing of ideas and creation of knowledge. Into the future, technology will not only transform the act of teaching and learning in instrumental ways, but a deeper appreciation of the socio-cultural–technological–tourism nexus is likely to transform curricula and break down disciplinary and knowledge divides.

However, technology is not the only driver of change. The infrastructure needs of higher education including campus and classroom design, libraries and learning resources, are also being rethought. An increasing emphasis on the employability of students and on 'real-world' experience (see Petrova, Chapter 29, and Ladkin, Chapter 30), in part driven by the discourses about higher education's contribution to economic policy objectives discussed earlier, are driving experimentation in critical reflexive pedagogies (see García-Rosell, Chapter 21), problem-based, work-integrated and service learning (see Isacsson & Ritalahti, Chapter 25; Portegies et al., Chapter 26). The student experience beyond graduation is also being reconsidered as learning is reconceptualized as a lifelong process (see Su, Chapter 24).

The implications for educators in this context of flexible production are also significant. As teaching and learning technologies expand and diversify, students already have access to a variety of delivery formats and are choosing their learning styles according to their situation, needs and aspirations. Taking this idea of consumer-led education forward, some have argued that students should take responsibility for their learning and that the role of educators is to empower students to take charge of their own learning and to drive what, when and how they learn. The 'flip class' concept returns the responsibility for learning back to the student. This implies that students have the inherent power and skills to be able to know what and how to learn. Educators are relegated a minor role to facilitate this learning by providing a range of resources. This position diverges from the historical Socratic position that students are on a learning journey, guided and challenged by their teachers to push boundaries and extend their thresholds of understanding (Boghossian, 2006). While these debates rage, it is evident that there is room for a range of different learning styles and pedagogic approaches just as there is room for a range of institutions offering different programmes and pathways. Low-cost models of self-learning higher education delivered using technology are likely to sit alongside Socratic models (and a range of models in between), but the impact on academic work is an important consideration.

Academic work: zombiedom and hope

Those of a more radical orientation argue that the industrial model of teaching is obsolete, that the aristocratic and elitist model of the teacher in the classroom is redundant, and that the 'end of the teacher' is near (Rosen, 2013). While these arguments are getting increased airplay in some quarters – especially those supporting increased cost-cutting, commercialization and globalization of education – others have pointed to the importance of social interaction and cognitive processes in learning and regard the 'teacherless' perspective as ill-informed:

> There are many uncomfortable realities of education that are generally avoided today; among them is that good education takes time and effort, personalised guidance, trust and work. An educated mind is built with imagination and work, and comfort is rarely associated with significant results. In this complex endeavour, technology will help the student to explore knowledge and ideas in collaboration with peers and guidance from a wise teacher.
>
> (Popenici, 2013)

The challenge for TH&E educators is how to achieve this agenda of quality learning so that students can take their place as mindful graduates able to address the big issues facing society (Sheldon *et al.*, 2014). It is a challenge that needs to be addressed in the face of increasing competition, uncertainty and mobility within a diminishing and highly contested pool of resources. The move towards neoliberalism and its consumer focus has served to shift priorities away from the traditional public purpose of education towards a new purpose crafted from rankings, evaluations, indicators and benchmarks and massive shifts in academic work have been observed (Poon, 2006; Coaldrake & Stedman, 1999; Henkel, 2005; Calvert *et al.*, 2011). Tongue in cheek, but some argue that 'universities are increasingly populated by the undead: a listless population of academics, managers, administrators and students, all shuffling to the beat of the corporatist drum' (Gora & Wheelan, 2010). Zombiedom is a coping strategy that goes beyond survival to protect and nourish the kernel of desire that the future can be different to the present (Ryan, 2012).

Our own position is that turning inward is not an option. We maintain that educators still have an important role in coordinating and crafting the public purpose of education, and we have a responsibility to question and not simply perform neoliberalism without thinking through its consequences and its impacts on TH&E education. Understanding and engaging in higher education policy from macro to micro levels is an important step in this regard. We have a responsibility to both understand and use our agency in ways that will enhance a hopeful TH&E education that meets institutional, student and personal objectives.

Tourism and hospitality higher education in the future

Having built the above narrative around the changes and trends observed in higher education in general, and in TH&E education in particular, has assisted in developing a picture of the complexity of the higher education sector as it currently exists. However, the future of higher education cannot be an extrapolation of the past. In the above narrative it has become increasingly clear that the current higher education systems in most countries are built around an old model of industrialization, where strategies such as market massification, the commodification of teaching and one-size-fits-all curricula have led to claims that many institutions are little more than 'degree factories' (Atkins & Herfel, 2006). If we are, as discussed above, moving from an industrial to a post-industrial world, then surely the future of higher education, and within this TH&E education, will also undergo seismic, non-linear change. This future cannot simply be contoured on the present system.

Moreover, the future of TH&E higher education cannot be considered independently from tourism, hospitality and events as broader social and economic phenomena. In economic terms, tourism is the largest services sector generating US$1.3 trillion in 2012 (UNWTO, 2013). However, as the early chapters in this *Handbook* attest, tourism is much more than an economic sector, it is also a social, cultural, political and environmental force that drives significant change. Understanding, responding to and managing this change will inevitably require knowledge workers who are able to address a range of problems associated with tourism, travel, hospitality and the increasingly complex operating environment within which they exist. Some of these problems are already known, such as the effects of travel demand on climate change, but many more problems are not yet known. Herein lies the challenge of TH&E education, to provide an education that facilitates critical understandings and creative, innovative thinking about complex problems, and to work collaboratively towards addressing them. It requires learners to actively constitute their understandings of problems, drawing from different types of knowledge that exist in different places. People who do not have the knowledge, do not have the skills to learn, or who are unable to move beyond fixed perspectives and their own boundaries of knowledge, will stumble.

In *The Avalanche is Coming*, the authors argue that a further phase of competition will shortly unfold, and the traditional university will come under pressure as its functions are unbundled and supplied by those providers that can do so more effectively and efficiently (Barber *et al.*, 2013; Anderson & McGreal, 2012). While currently universities are producing students targeted to specific jobs, they suggest that the mismatch between graduate employability and job opportunities will intensify. These authors argue that we need citizens who can apply knowledge to existing and future problems in creative ways, and current approaches only lock students into certain ways of thinking and expectations about future careers. The entire learning ecosystem needs to be reworked to provide learning experiences that transcend the boundaries of disciplines and professional programmes. Learning will be lifelong and life-wide, and divisions between 'town and gown' will disappear as the relationship between knowledge, its creation and location, are rethought. In this view, the traditional inclusive 'ivory tower' university model has a limited shelf life in many cases; alternative networked models of higher education institutions will emerge and programme structures will change dramatically. Scenarios of higher education help to envision this future.

Scenarios

Emerging from the myriad of futures studies about higher education that identify and evaluate trends and disruptive forces, there are a number of scenarios that have been developed that outline the potential future of higher education institutions. Table 39.1 summarizes four scenarios emerging from OECD futures research (OECD, 2009a). These scenarios are not intended to define higher education in the future, but have been developed to illustrate a set of 'alternative hypothetical futures that reflect different perspectives on past, present and future developments' (p. 1).

In a similar vein, Barber *et al.* (2013) have argued that as the traditional university is unbundled, some will specialize in teaching, others in research and yet others in serving the needs of their local communities. Purpose, local context, human and physical assets and expertise will become points of differentiation giving rise to:

Table 39.1 OECD scenarios for higher education futures

Open networking	In this scenario, the higher education system is heavily internationalized and strong collaborative networks exist amongst institutions, students and academics. Harmonization processes facilitate mobility and new technologies enable standardized courses to be delivered online. New technologies have changed teaching approaches and delivery methods. Classroom time is used for small seminars and interactive discussions and more time is spent with students on individual projects. Research has intensified around dense networking within and among institutions.
Serving local communities	In this scenario, higher education institutions focus on national and local engagement. Teaching and research are centred on addressing local economic and community needs. Institutions receive support from local funding sources and support local business and community interests. Universities also play a role in recreational learning and lifelong learning. The scope of research is diminished with strategic research (e.g. engineering, physics, etc.) being relocated to the government sector while university research focuses on humanities and the social sciences. A key driver in this scenario could be backlash against and scepticism of globalization and a reassertion of community values.
New public responsibility	In this scenario, there is increased focus on the efficiency and accountability of higher education institutions that are wholly or partly funded by the public purse. Under this scenario, higher education institutions continue to diversify their funding sources, but become increasingly accountable to the state and other funding sources. They become more attentive to learning needs of students and are increasingly driven by performance measures such as student satisfaction, employability and demand. Institutions become more differentiated, specializing in different teaching and research missions and staff also become more specialized and differentiated. There is increased national competition for research funding among a smaller number of institutions.
Higher education Inc.	In this scenario, global competition to provide teaching and research services using a commercial model is a key driver. Research and teaching are increasingly disconnected with institutions specializing on their core commercial strengths. Research and teaching are commercially driven. There is fierce competition for students with institutions opening up satellite and offshore campuses and they are specializing according to their competitive advantage. Rankings play an important role in differentiating institutions. Developing countries have established competitive advantage in certain areas and institutions in developed countries are outsourcing to these institutions. There is fierce competition for 'superstar' academic researchers and the research sector is rapidly becoming concentrated.

Source: Adapted from OECD (2009a).

- The elite university
- The mass university
- The niche university
- The local university
- The lifelong learning mechanism.

Other research investigating the future of higher education has identified likely lines of evolution. For example, in Australia, consultants Ernst and Young (2012: 4–5) identified the following 'broad lines of evolution' for higher education institutions in that country:

- 'Streamlined status quo' – Some universities will operate as broad-based teaching and research institutions, but will progressively transform the way they deliver their services and administer their organizations – with major implications for the way they engage with stakeholders.
- 'Niche dominators' – Some universities and new entrants will fundamentally reshape and refine the range of services and markets they operate in, targeting particular 'customer' segments with tailored education, research and related services.
- 'Transformers' – Private providers and new entrants will carve out new positions in the 'traditional' sector and also create new market spaces that merge parts of the higher education sector with other sectors, such as media, technology, innovation, venture capital and the like. This will create new markets, new segments and new sources of economic value. Incumbent universities that partner with the right new entrants will create new lines of business that deliver much needed incremental revenue to invest in the core business.

These above scenarios are meant to stimulate thought and reflection on what might be desired future directions and actions. However, the capacity of higher education institutions to shape these futures is influenced by global trends and shifts in values, national higher education policy and internal and localized influences. It is our premise that these influences and challenges, not only on higher education in general but TH&E education in particular, need to be understood and managed, and as educators we need to identify priorities and appropriate actions to shape the world we want to see. What actions are taken depends on leadership and the agency of academics involved in a variety of tasks spread more widely than the remit of senior leadership positions. A distributed leadership approach is required (Dredge & Schott, 2014).

Final thoughts

Tourism and hospitality are deeply embedded in contemporary social and economic life and the challenge of understanding and managing these phenomena are bound up in much bigger and broader challenges facing society. TH&E education therefore provides a lens on our social world, a lens through which processes of change can be identified, understood and critically analysed. The first tourism and hospitality programmes were built on dreams of hope and empowerment at a time when students, educators and institutions across the world were awakening to the transcendental change that tourism brings and the need to understand and manage that change. Over the last decades, our knowledge and understandings of these phenomena, and our roles in teaching, researching, knowledge (co-)creation and dissemination have evolved to the point that we are able to understand issues and problems from different perspectives and employ different problem-solving techniques. But, most of all, critical thinking and reflexivity have enabled us to consider the limitations of our knowledge and the boundedness of our thinking (Moore, 2011). This awareness is helping to propel the field forward. However, there is much still that we do not know, and much we can learn from breaking down disciplinary boundaries, professional programme structures, and the artificial divides between theory and practice, classroom and fieldwork, student and teacher, town and gown. For these reasons we are optimistic about the future of TH&E education, despite the inevitable metamorphosis that will take place in the broader realms of higher education.

Others disagree. Some say the university is bankrupt. This insolvency is not just financial but it is also political and economic. Others say it's an ideological crisis, brought on by the marketization of higher education, the industrialization of teaching and the neoliberal zeal for performance measures, audits and rankings. Others argue that many universities' current organizational and financial models will be obsolete in a matter of years (Ernst & Young, 2012). To be sure, the challenges facing the higher education sector today are much larger than any of our national systems can deal with in isolation, and beyond the scope of any single institution or professional group to address.

So, if there is a vision of the future, it cannot be from a rear-view mirror. We must collaborate internally and extend our reach externally to look beyond the outdated industrial models of higher education to new innovative and differentiated models to facilitate a hopeful TH&E education. We must allow ourselves to dream of new possibilities in a post-industrial age, where there is high student and educator mobility, the education experience can be bundled in different ways, and artificial boundaries imposed on learning are dissolved. In this future, curriculum content will still matter, but the experience of learning, the deep, intimate connections between knowledge and daily life, and the capacity to develop critical, mindful and reflexive practice must be foregrounded if TH&E education is to make a difference. The path that TH&E education has taken so far, in emerging from a strictly vocational starting point and becoming a post-industrial area of study where reflexivity, critical thinking and multi-disciplinarity are now common practice, leads us to the view that we remain well positioned to meet future challenges, but as educators we must also embrace the stewardship of our field in critical and creative ways.

References

Abeles, T. P. (2006). 'Do we Know the Future of the University?'. *On the Horizon*, 14(2), 35–42.

Airey, D., Tribe, J., Benckendorff, P., & Xiao, H. (2014). 'The Managerial Gaze: the long tail of tourism education and research'. *Journal of Travel Research*, 13 Feburary.

Anderson, T., & McGreal, R. (2012). 'Disruptive Pedagogies and Technologies in Universities'. *Journal of Educational Technology & Society*, 15(4), 380.

Association of American Colleges & Universities. (2002). 'Greater Expectations: a new vision of learning as a nation goes to college'. Available: http://www.greaterexpectations.org (Accessed 6 February 2014).

Atkins, J., & Herfel, W. (2006). 'Counting Beans in the Degree Factory'. *International Journal for Educational Integrity*, 2(1), 2–12.

Australian Government. (2008). *The National Code of Practice for Registration Authorities and Providers of Education and Training to Overseas Students 2007*. Available: https://aei.gov.au/Regulatory-Information/Education-Services-for-Overseas-Students-ESOS-Legislative-Framework/National-Code/Pages/default.aspx (Accessed 14 January 2014).

Ayikoru, M., Tribe, J., & Airey, D. (2009). 'Reading Tourism Education: neoliberalism unveiled'. *Annals of Tourism Research*, 36(2), 191–221.

Barber, M., Donnelly, K., & Rizvi, S. (2013). *An Avalache is Coming: higher education and the revolution ahead*. London: Institute for Public Policy Research.

BBC News. (2012). 'University Complaints rise by 20%'. Available: http://www.bbc.co.uk/news/education-18425282 (Accessed 14 January 2014).

Bell, D. (1976). *The Coming of Post-Industrial Society: a venture in social forecasting*. New York: Basic Books.

Biggs, J., & Tang, C. (2007). 'Teaching/Learning Activities for Functioning Knowledge'. In *Teaching for Quality Learning at University*, 3rd edn. (pp. 135–62). Maidenhead: Open University Press.

Boghossian, P. (2006). 'Behaviorism, Constructivism, and Socratic Pedagogy'. *Educational Philosophy & Theory*, 38(6), 713–22.

Brennan, J. (1997). 'Introduction'. In J. Brennan, P. de Vries, & R. Williams (Eds.), *Standards and Quality in Higher Education* (pp. 1–10). London: Jessica Kingsley Publishers.

Brink, C. (2010). 'Quality and Standards: clarity, comparability and responsibility'. *Quality in Higher Education*, 16(2), 139–52.

Calvert, M., Lewis, T., & Spindler, J. (2011). 'Negotiating Professional Identities in Higher Education: dilemmas and priorities of academic staff'. *Research in Education*, 86, 25–38.

Center for Higher Education Policy Studies (CHEPS). (2004). *The 20th Anniversary CHEPS Scenarios: European higher education and research landscape 2020*. Netherlands: CHEPS.

Cho, M. H., & Kang, S. K. (2005). 'Past, Present, and Future of Tourism Education: the South Korean case'. *Journal of Teaching in Travel & Tourism*, 5(3), 225–50.

Coaldrake, P., & Stedman, L. (1999). *Academic Work in the Twenty-First Century: changing roles and policies*. Canberra: Higher Education Division Department of Education, Training and Youth Affairs.

Cuomo, A. (2014). 'Governor Cuomo Announces New Student Protection Unit and Launch of Investigation into Student "Debt Relief" Industry'. Available: http://www.governor.ny.gov/press/01222014-student-debt-relief (Accessed 14 January 2014).

Dator, J. (2001). *Advancing Futures: futures studies in higher education*. Westport, CT: Praeger.

Davis, G. (2008). 'The Future of Australian Higher Education'. Available: http://www.futureleaders.com.au/book_chapters/Issues_Time/Glyn_Davis.ph (Accessed 19 January 2014).

Day, M., Walo, M., Weeks, P., Dredge, D., Benckendorff, P., Gross, M. J., & Whitelaw, P. A. (2012). *Analysis of Australian Tourism, Hospitality and Events Undergraduate Education Programs*. Sydney: Australian Government Office of Teaching and Learning. Available: https://www.academia.edu/2848602/Analysis_of_Australian_tourism_hospitality_and_events_undergraduate_education_programs (Accessed 20 January 2014).

Dolan, M. (2013). 'Class Action: law school grads claim misleading reports of success'. Available: http://articles.latimes.com/2013/apr/02/local/la-me-ln-class-action-law-school-grads-claim-misleading-reports-of-success-20130402 (Accessed 14 January 2014).

Dredge, D., & Schott, C. (2014). 'Academic Agency and Leadership in Tourism Higher Education'. In D. Prebežac, C. Schott, & P. Sheldon (Eds.). *The Tourism Education Futures Initiative: activating change in tourism education.* (pp. 36–60). Abingdon: Routledge.

Drummond, G. (2004). 'Consumer Confusion: reduction strategies in higher education'. *International Journal of Education Management*, 18(5), 317–23.

Ernst & Young. (2012). *University of the Future: a thousand year old industry on the cusp of change*. Melbourne: Ernst & Young.

Fennell, D. (2013). 'The Ethics of Excellence in Tourism Research'. *Journal of Travel Research*, 52, 417–25.

Gidely, J. M. (2012). 'Re-imagining the Role and Function of Higher Education for Alternative Futures through Embracing Global Knowledge Futures'. In A. Curaj, A. Scott, L. Vlasceanu, & L. Wilson (Eds.), *European Higher Education at the Crossroads: between the Bologna Process and national reforms* (pp. 1019–37). Dordrecht: Springer.

Globalization of Management Education Task Force. (2011). *Globalization of Management Education: changing international structures, adaptive strategies, and impact on institutions; Report of the Association to Advance Collegiate Schools of Business (AACSB) International Globalization of Management Education Task Force.* Bingley, UK: Emerald Group Publishing.

Gomes, A., Robertson, S., & Dale, R. (2012). 'The Social Condition of Higher Education: globalisation and (beyond) regionalisation in Latin America'. *Globalisation, Societies and Education*, 10(2), 221–46.

Gora, J. & Whelan, A. (2010). 'Invasion of the Aca-zombies', *Australian Higher Education Supplement*, 3 November. Available: http://www.theaustralian.com.au/higher-education/opinion/invasion-of-aca-zombies/story-e6frgcko-1225946869706 (Accessed 6 February 2014).

Hall, C. M. (Ed.). (2007). *Pro-Poor Tourism: who benefits? Perspectives on tourism and poverty reduction*. Clevedon: Channel View Publications.

Harvey, D. (2005). *A Brief History of Neoliberalism*. Oxford: Oxford University Press.

Harvey, L. (2008). 'Rankings of Higher Education Institutions: a critical review'. *Quality in Higher Education*, 14(3), 187–207.

Hazelkorn, E. (2011). *Ranking and the Reshaping of Higher Education: the battle for worldwide excellence*. Dublin: Centre for Social and Educational Research, Dublin Institute of Technology.

Henkel, M. (2005). 'Academic Identity and Autonomy in a Changing Policy Environment'. *Higher Education*, 49(1/2), 155–76.

Hicks, D. (2010). 'Overview of Models of Performance Based Research Funding Systems'. In OECD (Ed.), *Performance-based Funding of Public Research in Tertiary Education Institutions*: OECD. Available: http://www.oecd.org/science/sci-tech/performance-basedfundingforpublicresearchintertiaryeducation institutionsworkshopproceedings.htm (Accessed 14 January 2014).

Hollinshead, K. (2009). 'The "Worldmaking" Prodigy of Tourism: the reach and power of tourism in the dynamics of change and transformation'. *Tourism Analysis*, 14(1), 139–52.

Hospers, G. J. (2003). 'Fourastié's Foresight after 50 Years'. *Foresight*, 5(2), 11–14.

Joseph, M., Mullen, E. W., & Spake, D. (2012). 'University Branding: understanding students' choice of an educational institution'. *Journal of Brand Management*, 20(1), 1–12,

Landry, C., & Bianchini, F. (1995). *The Creative City*. London: Demos.

Liburd, J., & Hjalager, A.-M. (2010). 'Changing Approaches towards Open Education, Innovation and Research in Tourism'. *Journal of Hospitality and Tourism Management*, 17(1), 12–20.

Marginson, S. (2001). 'Trends in the Funding of Australian Higher Education'. *Australian Economic Review*, 34(2), 205–15.

Marginson, S. (2006). 'Dynamics of National and Global Competition in Higher Education'. *Higher Education*, 52(1), 1–39.

Marginson, S. (2008). *Higher Education and Globalization: issues for research Part II: cross-border mobility, flows and the globalization of the academic profession*. Berlin: EAIE Forum.

Marginson, S. (2011). 'Imagining the Global'. In R. King, S. Marginson, & R. Naidoo (Eds.), *Handbook on Globalization and Higher Education* (pp. 10–39). Cheltenham: Edward Elgar.

Mause, K. (2010). 'Considering Market-based Instruments for Consumer Protection in Higher Education'. *Journal of Consumer Policy*, 33(1), 29–53.

Moore, T. (2011). 'Critical Thinking: seven definitions in search of a concept'. *Studies in Higher Education*, 38(4): 506–22.

Morgan, N. (2012). 'Time for "Mindful" Destination Management and Marketing'. *Journal of Destination Marketing & Management*, 1, 8–9.

Mullins, P. (2000). 'Cities of Post-Industrialism, Cities of Post-Modernity. In J. M. Najman, & J. S. Western (Eds.), *A Sociology of Australian Society* (pp. 385–405). Melbourne: Macmillan.

Munck, R., & McConnell, G. (2010). 'University Strategic Planning and the Foresight/Futures Approach: an Irish case study'. Available: http://horizon.unc.edu/projects/seminars/KL/MunckandMcConnell.pdf (Accessed 14 January 2014).

National Center for Public Policy and Higher Education (2008). 'Engaging Higher Education in Societal Challenges of the 21st Century'. National Center for Public Policy and Higher Education special report. Available at: http://www.highereducation.org/reports/wegner/wegner.pdf

Neubauer, D. (2010). 'Ten Globalization Challenges to Higher Education Quality and Quality Assurance'. Available: http://www.eastwestcenter.org/education/international-forum-for-education-2020/education-leadership-institute/current-institute (Accessed 20 January 2014).

Organization for Economic Cooperation and Development (OECD). (2007). *On the Edge: securing a sustainable future for higher education*. (OECD Working Papers No. 7). Paris: OECD Publishing.

Organization for Economic Cooperation and Development (OECD). (2008). *Higher Education to 2030: what futures for quality access in the era of globalisation?*. Centre for Education Research and Innovation.

Organization for Economic Cooperation and Development (OECD). (2009a). *Four Future Scenarios for Higher Education*. OECD/Centre for Educational Research and Innovation.

Organization for Economic Cooperation and Development (OECD). (2009b). *High Education to 2030: globalization*. Centre for Educational Research and Innovation.

Peck, J. (2010). *Constructions of Neoliberalism*. Oxford: Oxford University Press.

Poon, T. S. (2006). 'The Commodification of Higher Education: implications for academic work and employment'. *International Journal of Employment Studies*, 14(1), 81–104.

Popenici, S. (2013). 'Devaluation of Teaching and Learning'. Popenici – a space for critical analysis and discussion on the future of education. Available at: http://popenici.com/ (Accessed 28 January 2014).

Rosen, D. (2013). 'It's Time to Get Rid of Teaching and Learning'. Available at: http://www.huffingtonpost.com/david-rosen/its-time-to-get-rid-of-te_b_3963695.html (Accessed 11 August 2013).

Ryan, S. (2012). 'Academic Zombies: a failure of resistence or a means of survival?' *Australian Universities' Review*, 54(2): 1–11.

Sheldon, P., Fesenmaier, D., & Tribe, J. (2014). 'The Tourism Education Futures Initiative(TEFI): activating change in tourism education'. In D. Prebežac, C. Schott, & P. Sheldon (Eds.), *The Tourism Education Futures Initiative(TEFI): activating change in tourism education* (pp. 14–35). Abingdon: Routledge.

Snyder, D. P. (2006). 'From Higher Education to Longer, Fuller, Further Education: the coming metamorphosis of the university'. *On the Horizon*, 14(2), 43–61.

Temple, P. (2011). 'University Branding'. *Perspectives: Policy and Practice in Higher Education*, 15(4), 113–16.

Tuomi, I. (2005). 'The Future of Learning in the Knowledge Society: disruptive changes for Europe by 2020'. Available: http://www.meaningprocessing.com/personalPages/tuomi/articles/TheFutureOfThe EuropeanKnowledgeSociety.pdf (Accessed 5 January 2014).

Tuomi, I. (2013). 'Losing the Future'. Available: http://samiconsulting.wordpress.com/2013/10/04/losing-the-future/ (Accessed 20 January 2014).

United Nations Development Programme (UNDP). (2011). *Discussion Paper: tourism and poverty reduction strategies in the integrated framework for least developed countries*. Switzerland: UN Steering Committee on Tourism for Development.

United Nations World Tourism Organization (UNWTO). (2010). *Tourism and the Millenium Development Goals*. Madrid: World Tourism Organization.

United Nations World Tourism Organization (UNWTO). (2013). *UNWTO Tourism Highlights*. Madrid: United Nations World Tourism Organization.

Universiti Sains Malaysia (2007). *Constructing Future Higher Education Scenarios: insights from Universiti Sains Malaysia*. Palau Pinang: Universiti Sains Malaysia.

Universities Australia. (2013). *University Student Finances in 2012: a study of the financial circumstances of domestic and international students in Australia's universities*. Canberra: Universities Australia.Universities UK (2012). *Futures for Higher Education: analysing trends*. London: Universities UK.

van der Wende, M. (2011). 'Global Institutions: the Organization for Economic Cooperation and Development'. In R. King, S. Marginson, & R. Naidoo (Eds.), *Handbook on Globalization and Higher Education* (pp. 95–113). Cheltenham: Edward Elgar.

Walker, S. J. (2013). 'UK Higher Education: let's not follow the leader but develop our own vision'. Available: http://www.theguardian.com/higher-education-network/blog/2013/may/21/uk-higher-education-own-vision (Accessed 14 January 2014).

Williams, C. (2008). 'Visions of the Future of Employment: a critical overview'. *Foresight*, 10(5), 24–33.

Wood, P. (2011). 'Higher Education's Precarious Hold on Consumer Confidence'. *Academic Questions*, 24(3), 262–81.

World Bank (2012). *Putting Higher Education to Work: skills and research for growth in East Asia*. Washington: International Bank for Reconstruction and Development/World Bank.

Index